PETER CALVOCORESSI, GUY WINT AND
JOHN PRITCHARD

Total War

The Causes and Courses of the Second World War

VOLUME II

THE GREATER EAST ASIA AND PACIFIC CONFLICT

SECOND EDITION

Penguin Books

PENGUIN BOOKS

Published by the Penguin Group
27 Wrights Lane, London W8 5TZ, England
Viking Penguin Inc., 40 West 23rd Street, New York, New York 10010, USA
Penguin Books Australia Ltd, Ringwood, Victoria, Australia
Penguin Books Canada Ltd, 2801 John Street, Markham, Ontario, Canada L3R 1B4
Penguin Books (NZ) Ltd, 182–190 Wairau Road, Auckland 10, New Zealand

Penguin Books Ltd, Harmondsworth, Middlesex, England

First published in Great Britain by Allen Lane The Penguin Press 1972
First published in the USA by Pantheon Books 1972
This revised edition published in one volume by Viking 1989
Volume II: The Greater East Asia and Pacific Conflict
published by Penguin Books 1989
1 3 5 7 9 10 8 6 4 2

Filmset in Monophoto Times

Made and printed in Great Britain by
Richard Clay Ltd, Bungay, Suffolk

If you say which ruler possesses moral influence, which commander is the more able, which army obtains the advantages of nature and the terrain, in which regulations and instructions are better carried out, which troops are the stronger, which has the better trained officers and men, and which administers rewards and punishments in a more enlightened manner – I will be able to forecast which side will be victorious and which defeated.

Sun Tzu, *The Art of War*, fourth century BC

Contents

The Greater East Asia and Pacific Conflict

Part I
ASIAN CONFLICT

Part II
OCEAN CLASH

List of Illustrations

List of Maps

Acknowledgements

The maps on pages 209 and 442 have been adapted from *History of the Sino-Japanese War (1937–1945)* by Hsu Long-hsuen and Chang Ming-kai, copyright © Chung Wu Publishing Co., 1971. The publishers are grateful to Mrs George R. Lipe for permission to reproduce the map on pp. 610–11. Cartography by Reginald Piggott except for the maps on pp. 670–71 and 672–3, which were drawn by Arthur Banks.

Introduction to Volume II

Originally published in a single volume as *Total War* in 1972, this history of the causes and courses of the Second World War has stood the tests of time and criticism. This new edition has been revised and extended and is now divided into two companion volumes. Volume I, revised by its original author, Peter Calvocoressi, contains the new Foreword to both volumes of the book and covers the war in the West; while Volume II, revised by John Pritchard in place of the late Guy Wint, covers the Greater East Asia and Pacific conflict.

This edition takes account of the flood of official archives and personal memoirs that have been made public over the past fifteen years. These have necessitated a review – to some extent a reassessment – of the policies of appeasement in Europe in the thirties and of the direction and motives of Japanese policies in the same feverish decade. Using his detailed knowledge of the pre-war problems and policies of the powers in East Asia and the proceedings of the Japanese war crimes trials, John Pritchard contributes a new description and explanation of the disintegration of the Japanese war on land and sea.

The Greater East Asia and Pacific Conflict

Part I
ASIAN CONFLICT

CHAPTER 1
China and Japan

THERE are two principal countries of the Far East with an ancient civilization, China and Japan: and the war in the Far East had its origin in the quarrel between them. This developed gradually out of events which began about a century earlier and set afoot historical processes which were seemingly uncheckable. With apparent fatalism inflammable materials were stacked.

Ultimately, the fire started and flames enfolded the two countries in a most bitter war of survival. This in turn caused a wider blaze in the Pacific; and the fire in the East coincided with Hitler's fire in Europe. The conflagrations merged, and the wars became one. Almost all the peoples of East Asia and South Asia were engaged.

The start of this great drama came with the different ways that China and Japan responded to the unfamiliar intrusion of the West into Asian affairs.

In East Asia China, even in its decadence, has always been a most absorbing topic. It has lain across the map of Asia, establishing standards and precedents, rather as the Roman Empire dominated the ancient western world. Traditionally, East Asia had no system of international relations in which independent countries coexist with one another, such as was known from the earliest times in Europe, but was a system in which all the lesser countries revolved like satellites around the great central structure, which was regarded by all men as central, necessary and almost unchanging. In the middle of the nineteenth century, this was still true, even though China was standing on the verge of one of the most calamitous periods of its history that was to cause its very name to be a reproach. It still dominated the political imagination, both of its inhabitants, and of visitors to East Asia. So much history had gone into its making, and so revered was Chinese civilization in Asia, that traces of mortal disease did not at first cause extreme alarm. Nevertheless China belonged to the ancient world, which, in 1850, was passing rapidly away.

What was threatening China was the impact of the western world. China was known as the Middle Kingdom for it seemed the centre round which all things revolved and it had flourished through so many ages because it was unique. Now, for the first time in its history, it was coming

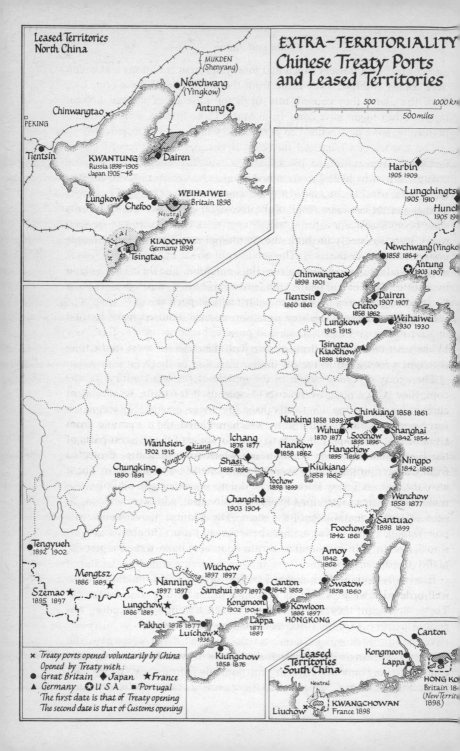

Leased Territories North China

MUKDEN (Shenyang)

PEKING

Chinwangtao ×

Tientsin

Newchwang (Yingkow)

Antung

KWANTUNG
Russia 1898–1905
Japan 1905–45

Dairen

Lungkow

Chefoo

WEIHAIWEI
Britain 1898

Neutral

KIAOCHOW
Germany 1898

Tsingtao

EXTRA-TERRITORIALITY
Chinese Treaty Ports and Leased Territories

0 ——— 500 ——— 1000 km
0 ——— 500 miles

Harbin
1905 1909

Lungchingts
1905 1910

Hunch
1905 19

Newchwang (Yingko
1858 1864

Antung
1903 1907

Chinwangtao
1898 1901

Tientsin
1860 1861

Chefoo
1858 1862

Dairen
1907 1907

Lungkow
1915 1915

Weihaiwei
1930 1930

Tsingtao
(Kiaochow)
1898 1899

Nanking 1858 1899

Chinkiang 1858 1861

Wuhu
1870 1877

Soochow
1895 1896

Shanghai
1842 1854

Ichang
1876 1877

Hankow
1858 1862

Hangchow
1895 1896

Ningpo
1842 1861

Wanhsien
1902 1915

kiang

Shasi
1895 1896

Kiukiang
1858 1862

Chungking
1890 1891

Yangtze

Yochow
1898 1899

Wenchow
1858 1877

Changsha
1903 1904

Santuao
1898 1899

Foochow
1842 1861

Tengyueh
1892 1902

Amoy
1842 1862

Mengtsz
1886 1889

Wuchow
1897 1897

Si-kiang

Nanning
1897 1897

Samshui 1897 1897

Canton
1842 1859

Swatow
1858 1860

Szemao
1895 1897

Lungchow
1886 1889

Kongmoon
1902 1904

Kowloon
1886 1897

HONGKONG

Pakhoi 1876 1877

Lappa
1871 1887

Luichow ×
1936

Kiungchow
1858 1876

Leased Territories South China

Canton

Kongmoon

Lappa

HONG KO

Neutral

KWANGCHOWAN
France 1898

Liuchow ×

Britain 18–
(New Territ
1898)

× Treaty ports opened voluntarily by China
Opened by Treaty with:
● Great Britain ◆ Japan ★ France
▲ Germany ✪ U S A ■ Portugal
The first date is that of Treaty opening
The second date is that of Customs opening

into contact with Powers which had totally different traditions and which were totally ruthless. They came from the other side of the world, but, from the alarm they caused, and from the absence of normal human rapport, they might have come from Mars. These Powers, well organized politically, were not inclined to concede to China a moral superiority.

The history of China and the West is chequered. The record of the foreign Powers is not so black as it is painted, whether by Chinese communists or by liberal western historians, who are overwhelmed, often quite unreasonably, by guilt. In some ways China's suffering was inevitable. It was the necessary result of the unavoidable process of a withdrawn state being thrust upon the world. Many of its experiences can be seen today to have been renascent; they conferred new and valuable matter upon an ancient civilization. The version put about by the communists is exaggerated, perverted and untrue. But something like their view is held by most of the Chinese people. The myth has been agreed upon. It must be attended to in any account of what really happened.

China, according to this view, was, for nearly a hundred years, harried by several foreign Powers which had projected themselves into East Asia by their navies and their fleets of merchantmen; and for most of the time it fought a losing battle against them.

The agony of China began in the middle of the last century. It was compelled by foreign governments to open itself for trade, which meant consenting to having its tariffs fixed by these agents; to accord to foreigners extra-territorial rights, which rendered them immune from Chinese law; and to permit them to set up in some of the choicest parts of the Empire small foreign communities which were thereafter protected from Chinese jurisdiction by warships and small bodies of troops. These were the famous Treaty Ports, now of dolorous memory. In addition, the same rights were exacted for Christian missionaries, who were let loose to subvert the ancient Confucian system. The Chinese Government was powerless to resist. It had neither the technical means (in arms and warships), nor the political stamina, nor the control of its own people, nor the ability to organize them.

Externally nothing had changed except for the establishment of neat, well-ordered townships side by side with the sprawling cities of China. They were clean; they appeared innocent. In this innocuous guise, imperialism came to China and soon began its work without anybody recognizing that it was initiating a new age. The first trade treaty, the Treaty of Nanking of 1842, which opened the five ports to British trade and residence, contained crippling restraints on China's sovereignty, but at the time was regarded as relatively innocuous. The Treaty provided that foreigners should administer their own justice to aliens and so appeared to be relieving the Chinese of a vexatious duty and to be keeping the foreigner at arm's length, which was very much the Chinese desire.

Moreover, by specifying areas where foreigners could live, it appeared to have spared the Chinese demands for the sale of land elsewhere. The foreigner was generally prohibited from acquiring real estate in China – a kind of apartheid set-up. But the foreigner had been given the means to enforce his will, and used it ruthlessly. He partly got round the rule that he should not own land by inducing the Christian missionaries, specifically exempt from the prohibition which applied to foreign businessmen, to hold the land in their name.

At first the Chinese did not understand what was being done to them, or how serious was the damage done to them in the Treaty Ports. But the misdeeds of the imperialists slowly became clear to everyone, and gradually produced a mood of terrible baffled rage.

China had not only to fear imperialism when it was seaborne. Before the coming of the foreign ships, it had been conscious of the land threat from its neighbour, Russia. This threat endured without interruption and in varying degrees of intensity. By land or sea China was surrounded by adversaries. It was still the Middle Kingdom, but no longer the axis round which the world turned; rather it could boast the name because it was the centre against which the spoliative instincts of the world were directed.

China was, it is true, saved from conquest and annexation. This was because the foreign Powers arrived not alone, but in multiplicity, because each was jealous of the other, because each realized that its trading rights depended on none achieving full political control of China. The Chinese Empire was thus permitted to continue.

It is important not to overstate the case. There were many personalities among the foreigners in China who bore nothing but goodwill to the country. There were institutions which were actively philanthropic. Foreign influence often brought about great changes, almost by accident. The Treaty Ports were often impressive for their neatness of construction and they disseminated new standards of public administration over a limited area. But the Chinese argued that this kind of imperialism did the maximum harm to China while ensuring that the imperialist Powers conferred no countervailing benefits.

Thus, groups of foreigners – nearly all businessmen – lived in China, organized entirely according to the customs and conventions of their homeland and subject to their own laws, in juxtaposition to the Chinese who were still subject to their ancient form of government. Most of the foreigners had only one interest: to make money through trade. Inevitably, even if the foreign communities had had no intention to influence Chinese society, the free action of the foreign groups deeply modified the Chinese society all around them, especially because the Chinese Government was unable to place limits on their activities. The operations of buying and selling, the freedom to conduct almost all forms of enterprise which private initiative could suggest, the freedom of money and its free use – all tended to erode the old Chinese civilization, which the Chinese, bound by treaty, were unable to safeguard.

The Chinese were in the position of a man bound hand and foot, watching the activities of an assailant who was openly plotting his ruin. As a result of the unwelcome guests, Chinese society was changing; but China could do nothing about it. Chinese anger mounted against the foreign communities, but China was impotent.

The Chinese feeling raged more strongly against the Chinese who collaborated with foreigners than against the foreigners themselves. The Chinese who showed himself unduly obliging to the foreigner, who set himself to make money by taking advantage of the conditions of foreign business, who was willing to act as the agent of the foreign business community and performed the indispensable role of interpreter and middleman, roused angry resentment. This class was called the compradors, from the Portuguese word meaning 'to provide': they were China's universal agents, at the disposal of the foreigner. Without the compradors, the pattern of the new type of imperialism would never have come into being.

The comprador class became extremely rich and prosperous. Eventually many of the Chinese Nationalists came from this class. So did many people who contributed in various ways to the new China: in arts, in science, in medicine. For many decades the Chinese creative energies seemed to be located in this class. The fact that it was hated was never sufficiently appreciated by foreigners, whose needs had called it into being.

The principal state in the hostile group ringing China was Great Britain, but there was one foreign country which behaved in a way unlike the others, the United States of America, which had a different history and different traditions from those of the European nation-states like Great Britain.

The United States, which came into being as the result of rebellion against Britain, did not form a new national state of its own, but was, rather, a repository of the elements of the western world which showed, by emigrating to America, that they desired to have a new political civilization. The United States did not altogether escape the nineteenth-century trend of western countries to be aggressive and self-assertive, but was distinctly less predatory, less remorseless, than others.

Thus in its relations with China the United States pursued a milder course than its western peers. True, it was drawn into the harrying. When the other states took the extra-territorial privileges, for the protection of their nationals, the United States joined in; and it took its share among the other powers in setting up the International Settlement at Shanghai. But its pursuit of China was not relentless, and it did not demand exclusive concessions of its own, which were the aim of other governments and which came to be dotted all over China like so many colonies. The United States' interest was in international trade – in contrast to Britain whose special concern was with the investment of capital in China – and in promoting it the United States was no more scrupulous than other states in forcing its activities upon China, which, officially, did not welcome them. But in this international trade the American concern was more with the attitude of other Western Powers than with that of China. The United States had always the fear that these would end in a policy of splitting up China into various spheres of interest, from which American interests would be excluded or discriminated against.

Hence the United States' aim of preserving the open door into China. On this principle American official policy turned. It sought to establish a system by which all the Powers voluntarily restricted the use of political influence to secure for themselves an economic privilege such as was not enjoyed equally by other Powers. The American activity on these lines culminated in securing in 1900 the assent of Powers interested in the China trade to this 'Open Door doctrine' and in guaranteeing American support for China's territorial integrity. The United States regarded this as a pro-Chinese policy, anti-imperialist, and in fact it was more so than suited the habits and interests of the other Powers. But it is understandable that later generations of Chinese should have pointed to the solid gains which it was the United States' intention to gain from it. They were not impressed by the advantages that this non-cooperation of the United States with the other Powers undoubtedly brought to China, and regarded these as incidental and not philanthropic.

Nevertheless, the United States was philanthropic. From the 1870s a section of the American public became aware of China as a great Asiatic people which might with justice call upon the United States for aid. This was the United States' first public response to the needs of a section of the world community; a response which afterwards became progressively wider, and embraced successively Japan, the states in Europe assisted by the Marshall Plan, and states of Latin America. They had no legal or other claim on the United States; the United States had no obligation to them. It responded in their cases to the simple fact that they had needs which the United States could fill, and the United States did not pass them by on the other side. Often, of course, there was, mixed with the practical philanthropy, a great deal of hypocrisy, of unscrupulous dealing, of serving a concealed interest, of power hunger only a little better than Europe's because it was veiled; but, though these existed, it was a remarkable fact that there was a genuinely philanthropic policy in which these found a place.

The initiators of the wave of goodwill were the American missionaries. Thousands of these were active in China and, through them, links were forged between innumerable small towns in the United States and similar units in China. To a remarkable extent the American people actually took the Chinese people by the hand, and led them over the first stages of their modernization. Politically, the organs of government in the United States impressed the Chinese people, many of whom recognized the remarkable behaviour of the US, even though their vast pride suffered from the American patronage. It was natural for the descendants of two thousand years of mandarins to feel disgust at becoming pupils of such a commercial people, lacking a long history, as the Americans. Relations were therefore not easy. But Chinese, in a more judicious mood, had to admit that this relationship was the most satisfactory that China had experienced in modern history.

This adventure in philanthropy was a part of the history of the American people, not the American Government. It was not officially inspired. The thousands of American missionaries, the vast expenditure, the use of skill and manpower, were all of them privately directed. So also American businessmen for the most part took their own risks and reaped their return, and largely did not employ American organized public force. The interplay of the missionary and the businessman, the clash between disinterest and the long-term interest which American activity promoted, was of course one of the principal themes for the historian of the time to savour. And in the United States the widespread goodwill to China set up currents which, in a society as democratic as that of the United States, were bound to influence the state and produce subtle changes in its policy towards China. So intertwined were most of the impulses of the United States.

Confronted with such acute danger, China made sporadic efforts to modernize itself and to generate a counteractive power; this should have been possible by reason of its size, its population and the reasonableness of its people. But for a long while its governing class was so set in conservative ways – as an essential part of their Confucian civilization – that the efforts failed. To reform and reorganize, China had to go through a shattering revolution, leave its ancient political civilization and venture out on ways new and untested. It had to experience a slow rebirth.

For a time the Chinese mandarins, the higher civil servants of the Confucian bureaucracy, had supposed that the secret of the terribly formidable strength of the West lay in some technical devices which had been added to the instruments of government. If they could discover what these were, the Government of the ancient Empire would be rejuvenated, and able to stand up for itself. Steam power, explosives, modern weapons were all of them the candidates for the shattering secret of western power. But the Empire's attempt to purchase these devices from the West left it no better off. It was clear that the Chinese Government lacked the talent to reorganize its society so that it might adapt itself to make proper use of these. It could not mobilize China. It remained inert, and a powerless victim to those who chose to victimize it.

Under constant strain, the old system of government was ceasing to act. The old régime had been based on the principle that a harmony had to be imposed on the disharmonious elements of which society consists. The policy was largely based on government by exhortation, and by displaying the example (at least in theory) of universal benevolence; and this proved workable because of the Confucian ideas which prevailed in all areas under Chinese rule. Confucianism, as much as the secular institutions of the old China, held the state together. But the old Confucian philosophy was being undermined as Chinese society, for the first time in two thousand years, began to change fundamentally. In the rough world which had developed, China had to discover new principles on which to base its government.

Some Chinese looked abroad at the new system of parliamentary democracy which was becoming so fashionable. Could this be the secret which made the West so strong, and could its institutions not be taken over by China? For a time there was enthusiasm and hope about these ideas. But it should have been clear that they were not likely to be a helpful model to China, which had its own powerful political traditions, built by more than two thousand years of history, and not readily set aside. Nor could a system of government be easily imported and acclimatized, which had been built up so painfully in Europe, which was the product of so many attitudes of action and habit, themselves born of wars, revolution, and the slow work of many centuries. China was too unlike Europe, and China was made a dangerous gift by its friends who intemperately supported this nostrum.

The course which China took was therefore quite unpredictable; it was empirical and, even today, with hindsight, it is hard to trace out what experiments it made, and how much China suffered.

One of the reforms which it made apparently without realizing the profound consequences which it had, was to abolish the Civil Service. This it did in 1905; the examinations by which it was recruited were suspended. Earlier, the existence of this college of administrators, chosen to serve the Empire by competitive public examinations, had been regarded, with some justification, as one of the strong points of Chinese civilization. But in the first decade of this century, the Chinese Civil Service was held to be old-fashioned and conservative. It was selected from among the classes which were steeped in Confucianism, and this made it the enemy of reform. The classes in favour of modernization all combined their resentment against it as constricting the development of the country. It was supposed that by striking it away, China would release forces which would transform it. That the mandarinate preserved standards of government and maintained the unity of the country was totally ignored. A great blow was struck at public order by its abolition, but the country thought that it was a blow in the cause of progress and liberation.

The Manchu Empire survived the sacrifice of the mandarins by only six years. The Empire and its outworn apparatus were discarded in 1911: it had stood in the way of reform; probably a revolution was the necessary prelude to recovery. But the first results of the fall were catastrophic. The power of the Empire was divided between war-lords, who commanded their own provinces. This was the worst and most helpless period of Chinese history up to that time. Chinese politics seemed to be without rhyme or reason. Power drifted from one war-lord to another with no meaningful result. The rise or fall of one provincial satrap or another brought no lightening of the gloom. There was no change, no regeneration, no significance.

The dawn for which men hoped first became visible with the rule at Canton, a city in the south of China, of the group called the *Kuomintang*, which had emerged from a revolutionary party of the last days of the Manchus. This group proclaimed itself the Nationalist Party of China and held its first National Congress in 1924. It was at first primitive, overlaid with the colour of circumambient war-lord governments, incompetent, corrupt, and very weak. But it was in certain aspects new, and had, at least in form, a modern party organization which was in part borrowed from western countries, though the methods of its operations were mainly drawn from China itself. It functioned in an authoritarian way, owing its power to its Army and police, but it claimed that this method of government was a transitory one. After a period during which it held the nation in tutelage, it would transfer the basis of government, and would become liberal and democratic. In after years, the length of this period of tutelage, the holding of the Kuomintang to its promise of democratization, became one of the principal questions of Chinese politics.

The Kuomintang slowly widened its authority; and came to be looked on as the party of national regeneration. It was a focus which attracted the support of all Chinese everywhere, who longed for a sign that China was at last reasserting its national strength.

It was the turning of the tide. Nationalism, with all the social and political reorganization which that connoted, began to do its work upon the Chinese people. The leader of the Kuomintang, Dr Sun Yat-sen (1866–1925), had described the great weakness of China, in its enforced competition with the Western Powers, as the absence of any cohesive power which could hold the people together. China, he said, was like a tray of sand: shake it and it fell apart. But, in China as in other parts of the world, the power of nationalism was to introduce a new faculty of maintaining social unity. How and why is one of the *arcana imperii* of the time. But it was abundantly clear that, as the movement proceeded and gathered strength, China was behaving quite differently from the recent past. The tray of sand was shaken; and the grains now tended to cohere in patterns which promised well for the future.

A fact which should have recommended the Kuomintang of the 1920s to serious attention by the outside observer was that in its organization and spirit it was not a copy of the western parliamentary parties. It was something devised for China, produced by Chinese thought to meet specific Chinese needs. It owed something to Soviet practice – many of the features in the organization of the party being borrowed from Russia at a time when Sun Yat-sen was enthusiastic, but had little understanding of Communism – and, with a rosy eye-wash, it professed to look forward to a time of universal democratic rights. But the Kuomintang – as it was to function in the 1930s – was a party of nationalist authoritarianism.

Cutting across the political vicissitudes of the times was a social crisis. In a sense China was doomed to experience disorders in any case. China has a long history, and has endured a time of acute crisis once in every three or four hundred years which is marked by troubles, the fall of a dynasty, civil commotion of a prolonged and hopeless kind. Various causes have been suggested for this clearly marked cyclical course of

Chinese history, but the most probable is that it is caused by pressure of population.

In the time of prosperity – when a dynasty is at the peak of its fortunes – the population is within manageable limits. The prosperity continues; the population grows; it becomes too large; there is intense pressure on the land; there are rising rents, and a diminishing food surplus for the towns; there are social distress, outbreaks of civil war and banditry, reverses in the struggle to maintain the frontier; there are corruption and extraordinary administrative decadence. After a time there comes the near or total collapse of government. China enters on a nadir of its history, from which there comes eventual recovery as the population regulates itself. Malthusian checks come into play, the extreme pressures are relaxed, the natural Chinese civilization reasserts itself.

There can be no doubt that China had entered on one of those adverse phases in the latter part of the eighteenth century. The Manchu dynasty ended its golden age in the unnaturally long reign of the Emperor Chien Lung (who reigned from 1736–96), and the population increased ominously. In the nineteenth century it would have been due for its time of troubles, regardless of the troubles brought on it by its new problems of foreign relations. The middle years of the century saw the Taiping rebellion and the revolt of the Chinese Muslims against the Government, both classic cases of a population explosion, both resulting in a very great slaughter. The two political maladies came together – the troubles from the cyclical character of Chinese history and the troubles from the totally new and exceptional strain of encountering its rivals in the world. Each set of troubles complicated the other; each intensified the other; recovery became ever more difficult.

The Kuomintang, and Chinese nationalism, promised to bring relief to the political problems of China in the 1930s. At the same time there were signs that the social causes which had brought political collapse were about to be ameliorated by process of time, and it seemed likely that the efforts of the Kuomintang at social and economic improvement would not continue to be dogged with adversity. These signs, however, were hard to read correctly, and may have been misconstrued.

For the relative slowness of China's regeneration there are a number of reasons. The rebirth of a nation – it was nothing less – takes time, which cannot be cut short beyond a certain measure. It is a natural process, not entirely controllable by political or human means. But China's peculiar and horrifying experience of the last century remains to some extent a mystery. China's progress in our day has been so rapid, so revolutionary, that it is hard to understand why in the fairly recent past it took so long to get off the ground. In the last resort one is left with the bare statement – that a crisis of population coincided with a crisis of foreign relations, that the results of both became merged, and that it took more than a century to work out the consequences.

The other country, Japan, had an altogether different experience and its past must also be studied if Japan's place in the world cataclysm is to be understood. Japan was a lesser country than China. Generally its population was only about one sixth of China's. But it was inhabited by a people, which, by vigour, by a genius for imitation and adaptation, and by artistic and warlike qualities, had made itself unique in the history of Asia. Japan had built up a civilization in many respects peculiar and outstanding. It responded to the stimulus of the coming of the westerners in a way which transformed the history of the region.

Since the beginning of the seventeenth century Japan had been exercised by the problem of relations with the West. It read the writing on the wall in the shadow cast by the Portuguese and Spanish galleons which at this time used to visit Japanese ports. Should Japan encourage them or should it deter them? After a brief period of cultivating their friendship it withdrew itself into seclusion. It persecuted mercilessly, as possible enemies of Japanese security, the missionaries about whom at first it had been enthusiastic. It cut all ties with the external world, diplomatic, cultural and, as far as this was possible, economic. It was the classic case of a hermit kingdom. This policy of exclusiveness preserved Japan intact until the United States, in the year 1853 and again in 1854, dispatched a naval squadron under the command of Commodore Perry and compelled it to resume normal intercourse and foreign trade.

Thereupon Japan was in danger of being reduced to a colony by the imperialist Powers. For its escape it had to thank the diplomatic adroitness, the skilful reasonableness of a few leading Japanese statesmen during the first years of the 1870s while Japan was renewing its contacts with the world. Once they had lost their first instinctive anti-foreignness they exposed themselves with zeal to all western influences. Japan's survival beyond this critical interval is owed to the remarkable changes which were brought about in Japanese society as a result of contact with western countries. From a militarily weak country, with a contemptible technology, Japan in a few years became like a hedgehog, which the imperial Powers, even at the height of their aggressiveness, thought twice about mauling.

Japan's history, which made this national strength possible, has been one of social change – a marked contrast to the sluggish conservatism of

China's official social history. Japan was able to accept change because the Japanese were born relatively free of an overpowering tradition. Its governing circles were able, in contrast to the Chinese, to produce men who were imaginative, forceful, and free of the deadening desire that life should be preserved exactly as it had been known in previous centuries. They were daring and iconoclastic. They were not bound by a thwarting public opinion, as was the mandarinate in China.

In China, the society, the civilization, took precedence over the Government. It was a civilization not disposed for change. But in Japan the Government was not held in invisible fetters by public opinion and by the past.

Furthermore a Japanese Government which desired to make changes was more likely to be able to implement them. Society was more responsive to governmental direction: it was more at its mercy. For this the main reason was geography. Japan consisted of a chain of islands, all of them comparatively small, all of them accessible by sea. Thus a fairly good system of communication could be established. This alone made it very different from China: in China there were, by the standards of that day, majestic roads, but, even so, the population in the outer provinces was at three months distance from the seat of central government. In consequence the ability of the centre to regulate the affairs of a large part of China was much reduced. But in Japan, no such inhibition palsied the national administration. Its efforts did not peter out in vast distances which separated it from its subjects.

The progress of Japan was rapid and, to the Western Powers spreading their influence through the world, unprecedented. In 1868 occurred the so-called Meiji Restoration. This was a revolution, not a restoration, although this great political change in Japan was dressed up as a revival of things past. An old, vestigial system of an Emperor, long confined to a kind of museum existence, and preserved partly for religious reasons, was called into employment; the existing system of government, a highly traditional one presided over by hereditary prime ministers or *Shōguns*, was suppressed. The new system was organized by the *Samurai*, the ex-feudatories of Japan's feudal past which it was abandoning. Exercising their remarkable talent for mimesis, they copied from what their intelligence judged to be the essentials of the formidable western system.

The Japanese surprised themselves by the ease with which they were able to reproduce in Japan most of what went into the making of western civilization. From Britain they copied the organization of the navy; from France the army structure, the nucleus of an educational system and hybrid neo-Napoleonic codes of criminal and civil law; from Germany the

Army General Staff organization, certain legal principles and commercial practices, modern medical training and some political institutions. Subsequently, the influence of the American educational system supplanted that of the French. Western-style agriculture, forestry and mining, the rapid expansion and efficient use of new railways, and phenomenal growth in the textile industry transformed the life of most Japanese, helping to provide sustenance for the engineering, shipbuilding and manufacturing industries which took somewhat longer to enter the modern era. The degree of Japan's modernization was often even greater in its appearance than in reality, for the old, and essentially Japanese, institutions and modes continued behind a façade of reform. Nevertheless, reform there was, and a purposeful – if eccentric – resolve to modernize. Soon Japan began to operate with a revolutionary change in efficiency.

For the European onlooker, the spectacle of Japan at this time was of remarkable fascination. For him it was a new experience to kick an ancient civilization, and to find that it did not crumble. It was bracing and fascinating. Enough of the old, graceful, picturesque, fragile civilization of old Japan still survived to make the process of the metamorphosis of Japan of almost incredible interest; and, in addition, of poignant pathos. American, British and French men of letters grasped the occasion of describing what was happening before their eyes, and the result was a series of books describing the topography, anthropology, ethics and aesthetics of Japan in transition. Among them Redesdale's *Tales of Ancient Japan* is especially valuable for the picture which it gives of the national ethos, and of the reaction to it of a civilized and imaginative westerner.

This was the elegiac tribute of the West to a country which showed spirit in resistance. It was quite different from the contemptuous tone and temper of the writings about India and China at the time. And for the foreigners who were blind to the more subtle qualities of a nation's progress, the rapid expansion of trade and of the whole economy were impressive and sobering.

By 1890 it was plain that the once real threat that Japan would fall a victim to straightforward western imperialism was ebbing. Instead, Japan shocked the Western Powers by joining with them in harrying and nibbling at China, whose disorders invited pressure.

The Japanese designs upon China cannot be explained by greed alone. British, and afterwards French, commercial penetration of China had been accompanied by the effective exercise of military power. United States interests in the area had grown, although more fitfully in response to the vagaries of American politics. Russian exploits, however, provided the immediate catalyst for Japanese expansion onto the Asian mainland.

When Tsar Alexander III's engineers began construction of the Trans-Siberian Railway in 1891, their picks and rails foretold the doom of an enfeebled China – and fatefully strengthened the influence of Japanese visionaries who sought a foothold on the Asiatic continent in the interests of self-defence but who also dreamt of Japan's development into a first-rate Imperial Power. Thus Count Yamagata Aritomo, principal architect of the modern Japanese Army and perhaps the most important Japanese oligarch of his era, advised the Emperor Meiji in October 1893 that the Russian railway 'poses an immediate threat to the Far East', predicting that within a decade the Tsar would snatch Mongolia, gain control of Manchuria and advance against Peking: 'the completion of the Trans-Siberian will sharply alter the situation in the Orient and exert a strong influence on our nation. It is not only for this reason that we must prepare adequate military power within the next eight or nine years; we must also be prepared to grasp any opportunity which may present advantages. This is a truly critical juncture in the fortunes of our nation.'*

Japanese concern over Russia's advance into the Great Power stakes of East Asia did not blind the Japanese to developments in other quarters, and Japanese eyes also fastened onto Korea, Japan's hereditary enemy. It was conventional military wisdom – in which the teachings of the ancients harmonized with advice tendered by a forceful imperial German general staff officer assigned to help educate the Japanese officer corps – that Korea, a 'dagger at the heart of Japan', must not fall under the sway of any third power. The Japanese had engaged in Korean political intrigues for almost a generation, and when the vassal Korean King turned to his suzerain, China, for military support to help subdue local uprisings fomented by the anti-western Tonghak Tong (Eastern Learning Society), the Dowager Empress of China quickly sent in a small armed force. This violated the spirit of the Kanghwa Treaty of 1876, signed by Japan and Korea, and the Sino-Japanese Treaty of Tientsin of 1885, which taken together bound China and Japan to refrain from (open) interference in Korean domestic and external affairs. The Japanese feared that this would lead to replacement of Korean independence or autonomy by the re-imposition of Chinese hegemony over the peninsula and the extinction of Japanese influence in Korea. Resorting to their rights under the Chemulpo Treaty of 1882, the Japanese responded by dispatching a mixed brigade of

* R. F. Hackett, *Yamagata Aritomo in the Rise of Modern Japan, 1838–1922*, Harvard University Press, Cambridge, Massachusetts, 1971, p. 157.

their own, deploying some seven thousand men ostensibly for the protection of Japanese diplomats, residents and property interests. The Tonghak Rebellion was short-lived, but in the aftermath of French and British encroachment during the past half-century into Chinese tributary states (which China had been powerless to prevent in Indo-China, Tibet and Burma), the Chinese were determined to suffer no such humiliation at the hands of the Japanese. The Japanese demands were treated with ill-concealed contempt. Western offers of mediation were rejected. Fighting soon developed. Japanese troops seized the Korean royal palace on 23 July, and two days later, following a brief naval engagement off P'ung Island (in which the Japanese routed a squadron of Chinese warships), a Japanese cruiser intercepted and sank a solitary British-registered steamship, the *Kowshing*, which was ferrying 1,100 Chinese troops, a German military adviser and a large quantity of weaponry to Korea. Following these developments, China and Japan formally exchanged declarations of war on 1 August 1894. Within six weeks, the Japanese Army won control of most of Korea through a succession of uninterrupted victories. The Japanese Navy proved equally adept in a sea battle off the mouth of the Yalu River which left it in command of the Yellow Sea. In October, two Japanese divisions crossed into South Manchuria and three more advanced upon Liaotung. Port Arthur fell to the Japanese on 21 November, and Wei-hai-wei on the Shantung Peninsula surrendered on 12 February 1895. As seven Japanese divisions prepared to march against Peking, the Chinese sued for peace.

After difficult negotiations, the Treaty of Shimonoseki was signed on 7 April 1895. The jubilant Japanese equated its harshness with the requirements of moral justice. Others viewed the outcome with alarm. By its provisions, China recognized the complete independence of Korea; ceded to Japan the Liaotung Peninsula (including Port Arthur), Formosa (Taiwan) and the Pescadore Islands; agreed to pay Japan a punitive indemnity that recovered two thirds of the military expenses incurred by Japan during the war; opened up portions of the Yangtze River to Japanese commerce; gave Japan trade concessions at Shasi, Chungking, Soochow and Hangchow; granted the Japanese highly prized most-favoured-nation privileges, and, to guarantee compliance with these provisions, sanctioned a temporary Japanese military occupation of Wei-hai-wei to be paid for out of the Chinese exchequer.

Japan had won a spectacular victory over China, but Japanese exhilaration was short-lived. The Shimonoseki Treaty proved to produce a Pyrrhic peace, as hard-hearted settlements are wont to do. Within China, demands for reform and a national re-awakening became irresistible.

Abroad, not for the last time, Chinese diplomats combined with western geopolitical schemers to deprive Japan of the fruits of conquest. Kaiser Wilhelm II of Germany, seeking better relations with Russia and hoping to stimulate even greater Russian attention to East Asia at the expense of the Franco-Russian Alliance in Europe, persuaded the impressionable Tsar Nicholas II, who had just succeeded to the Russian imperial throne, that Japan should be induced to retrocede the Liaotung Peninsula to China in consideration of a relative pittance. In any case, the Russians had a palpable fear that *any* Japanese presence on the Asiatic continent would spread, in the memorable phrase of Prince Lobanov, like 'a drop of oil on a sheet of blotting paper'.* Unwilling to see the European balance of power undermined by bilateral Russo-German collaboration, the French joined the Russians and Germans in this famous 'Triple Intervention', which their respective Ministers in Tokyo put to the Japanese Government on 23 April 1895. The Japanese were aghast: their Government hesitated, canvassing for support from the other Great Powers. The British Foreign Secretary expressed 'some doubts as to whether it would be prudent in the interests of Japan's future for her to acquire a toe-hold on the mainland. Not only would Japan have to increase her military expenditures to maintain such a possession, but she might also incur the potential danger of China and Russia embarking upon a war of revenge. In these circumstances, it might be more judicious for Japan to adopt a conciliatory attitude.' The United States took a similar view. Only Italy declared a willingness to support Japan.

With the Russian fleet now standing at Vladivostok, the Japanese Government yielded up southern Manchuria and with it Port Arthur. The Japanese public was outraged. In an Imperial Rescript issued to his people, the Emperor Meiji counselled his subjects to 'endure the unendurable', a phrase to which his descendant Hirohito would return in August 1945. A sense of bitter humiliation and a thirst for satisfaction penetrated deeply into the nation's consciousness, recalled thereafter whenever foreign Powers sought to deprive Japan of the fruits of military accomplishment.

The hypocrisy of the Western Powers was all too evident. Within three years, German troops had landed at Kiaochow Bay, occupied Tsingtao and extorted a ninety-nine-year lease on both. Then Germany obtained rights to construct two railways across Shantung Province and won important mining concessions. The Russians, meanwhile, concluded a secret

* Quoted by G. M. Berger (ed. and trans.) in Mutsu Munemitsu, *Kenkenroku: A Diplomatic Record of the Sino-Japanese War, 1894–1895*, Tokyo University Press, Tokyo, 1982, p. 282. Prince Lobanov had become Foreign Minister of Imperial Russia in March 1895.

alliance with China in 1896, aimed against Japan, in consideration for which China gave Russia rights to construct the so-called Chinese Eastern Railway 925 miles across North Manchuria, cutting 600 miles off the Trans-Siberian line to Vladivostok and making possible Russian economic domination of northern Manchuria. Then the Russians demanded and obtained mining rights and the huge Yalu timber concession in Korea, installed Russian military and financial 'advisers' and sought a naval base at Masanpo, directly opposite the Japanese island of Tsushima. The Russian battlefleet was sent to occupy Port Arthur and Dairen (Talien-wan/ Dalny) in December 1897 and extorted twenty-five-year leaseholds which provided the Tsar with his first ice-free ports in East Asia. In March 1898 the Russians obtained the right to build a branch railway from Harbin to Port Arthur and a leasehold on the entire Liaotung Peninsula so recently retroceded by Japan to China. The whole of these railway zones were aggressively patrolled by Russian gendarmerie. It was plain beyond contradiction that the Tsar contemplated nothing less than the virtual annexation of Korea and Manchuria, which were to be secured by the iron rails to Vladivostok and European Russia. Far to the south, the French, too, were carving out their pound of flesh, winning a ninety-nine-year leasehold on Kwang-chow Bay together with railway rights for a line to run between French Indo-China and Yunnan-fu. Britain obtained a ninety-nine-year lease on the New Territories at Hong Kong. A host of other projects and proposals appeared: the 'Celestial Kingdom' was disintegrating, unequal to the western onslaught, and on the horizon, half-way across the Pacific, the United States annexed Hawaii and took possession of the Philippines, raising the prospect of American imperial designs in East Asia.

While Japan redoubled its efforts to build up its military and naval resources and its domestic economy, the Japanese Government also strove to reach some kind of accommodation with the Western Powers. Seeking first to protect its interests in Korea, an agreement was concluded with Russia which on the face of it recognized Korean independence and safeguarded the Japanese commercial and industrial foothold in Korea. Both signatories promised to refrain from interference in the domestic affairs of Korea. Neither side was to send military or economic missions to Korea, and the two sides were to abandon any plans to construct defence facilities on Korean soil. Nevertheless, given the fact that China was now in no position to contest the issue, the Russo-Japanese agreement had the effect of establishing Korea as a condominium of the two contracting parties, neither of whom expected to abide by its provisions for long.

U S S R

MONGOLIA

Kuril Is
(Chishima)
1875

KARAFUTO
1905

Harbin

MANCHURIA
(MANCHUKUO) 1932

HOKKAIDO

Mukden

Pailingmiao

Peking

KOREA
(CHŌSEN)
1910

HONSHŪ

Tsinan

Tsingtao

Hwang-ho

Tōkyō

Nanking

Hankow   Shanghai

SHIKOKU

KYŪSHŪ

Yangtze-kiang

Bonin Is   1876

C H I N A

Ryūkyū Is
1874-9   1891

Amoy

Swatow   TAIWAN
(FORMOSA)
1895

Canton   Hong Kong

Haiphong

HAINAN
1939

Mandates 1919
Marianas Is
Caroline Is
Marshall Is

PHILIPPINE IS
(USA)

P A C I F I C

O C E A N

IMPERIAL EXPANSION OF JAPAN
1875-1939

■ *Japanese Empire 1870*   ▦ *Manchuria (1932)*
▨ *Japanese expansion to 1932*
▧ *Additional extent of occupation to 1939*

0   300 km
0   200 miles

Meanwhile, Chinese popular outrage over the nation's devastating defeat by Japan and over the ensuing western scramble for the spoils reached boiling-point. An uprising, known to history as the Boxer Rebellion, broke out in Shantung in 1898 and soon threatened to engulf the Manchu dynasty. However, the imperial régime skilfully deflected the public's anger away from itself and against the outside Powers. The unrest grew in seriousness and intensity under banners reading 'protect China, exterminate foreigners'. A number of missionaries and Chinese Christian converts were murdered, churches and warehouses were destroyed and European residences in Tientsin and elsewhere were attacked. Finally, the riots reached a climax in June 1900 after the German Minister to China was murdered. Chinese government troops joined the mobs and attacked the foreign legations in Peking with the apparent aim of annihilating the 'foreign devils'. A siege ensued in which a small force of only 458 legation guards and assorted foreign volunteers narrowly prevented the legation quarter from being overrun.

An international expedition, spearheaded by 12,000 Japanese troops, who made up more than half of the total force, was hurriedly assembled, captured Tientsin on 14 July and fought its way to relieve the foreign legations in Peking on 14 August 1900. The Chinese surrendered, agreed to punish those held to be responsible for the outbreak, permitted the foreign Powers to establish strong garrison forces along the railway to Shanhaikwan, and consented to pay the victors an indemnity twice the size of that imposed by the hated Shimonoseki Treaty. The conduct of the Japanese contingent was remarked upon by observers as being especially praiseworthy and well-disciplined, in sharp contrast to the deplorable inhumanity displayed by all of the other foreign forces, who engaged in widespread rape and looting. The German contingent, however, conducted itself with particular bestiality surpassed only by the Russians, who, while showing reluctance to participate in the relief of the legations, took independent action elsewhere, murdering thousands of civilians and, under the pretext of protecting the Chinese Eastern Railway, pouring an estimated 100,000 Russian troops into Manchuria, thereby occupying virtually the whole country. While the other international expeditionary contingents departed after the conclusion of a general settlement with the Dowager Empress, the Russians remained firmly in possession of Manchuria and demanded Chinese recognition of its status as a Russian protectorate. The other Powers prevailed upon China to reject these demands, but Russian forces continued to infiltrate into North China in large numbers. St Petersburg strongly resisted international appeals to follow the example of the other Powers by effecting a rapid withdrawal:

thus hatched the *casus belli* of the Russo-Japanese War which followed in 1904–5.

In these incidents nearly all the ingredients of international politics in East Asia up to 1945 (and even beyond) are already plain. Japan perceived that events were presenting it with an extraordinary opportunity: Japanese were to speak, until their final defeat in 1945, of 'Japan's hour of destiny', the fleeting opportunity of which they must take advantage. In East Asia, in the Japanese view, any further advance of the Western Powers into East Asia must be checked: in the long run, there must emerge a hegemony of either Japan or China, and the concept of co-existence seemed to have no place.

In general, in the comparison between the two, Japan was the weaker Power. The immense size of China, the antiquity and impressiveness of its civilization, its latent economic superiority, must in the end prove decisive – or be harnessed by the alien intelligence of the West. All the warlike qualities of the Japanese people and the advantages of geographical position could not prevail against such illimitable potential. But over the short period, in a time of instability and of unnatural weakness of China, Japan would have the advantage of stealing a march on China, of becoming, despite the historical disparity between the two, the stronger partner (if only some compromise could be reached with the Western Powers); and then, if Japan was willing to rely on its will and on the use of force, it could count on maintaining for an indefinite period the advantage which it had. Japan would stake all upon its ability to repress by force the natural event of a revival of Chinese power – or its obvious alternative, the military and economic consolidation and re-extension of western imperial interests throughout East Asia.

From that determination came the events which led Japan to its fateful participation in the Second World War. Japan's resolution to stake all its future upon the employment of force came to determine most things in the life and domestic achievements of its gifted people.

It was an audacious resolution, and a rather horrifying one. It meant choosing to act against what many abroad regarded as the progressive forces of the age, and allying with the darker tendencies, which were never far below the surface. It involved Japan in courses of action which gradually led to its having a reputation for cruelty and insensitivity, and it coarsened the emotional life. Inevitably Japan turned away from the more delicate things in its civilization. Japan had chosen to follow *Bushidō*, 'The Way of the Warrior' (of which more anon) and to concentrate its interests on making itself feared as the ogre of the Far East. Japan was dazzled by its feudal past, and did not sufficiently take note of the fact that military effort in the new conditions of industrialism was quite unlike that of Japanese tradition. Bushidō in the twentieth century was to be unlike that of the days of the Samurai and feudal lords (*Daimyō*). With fevered resolution Japan found itself impelled on the road of national brutality, and this was hard because in a part of their minds, the Japanese, like the Germans and Americans, desire to be loved, and find it difficult to understand when their actions make them monstrously unlovable.

The contrast between this alarming and determined imperialism, and the natural diffidence of a great many Japanese, perhaps the majority, has often been commented on. The Japanese have a tendency to be abnormally apologetic for themselves and unassertive. As a people, they reprobate individualism. It strikes the Japanese as selfish. This trait is one of the most pronounced in the Japanese character, and is at the root of much that is peculiar in politics, in ethics, in Japanese tradition. It explains why they have rarely produced great assertive figures to take charge of the affairs of the nation individually.

But the very modesty of individual Japanese explains much of what was horrible in recent Japanese history. When the fashion for national aggressiveness set in, few people had the decisiveness, the resolution and the courage to oppose it. What was the individual Japanese doing in taking it on himself to resist the rush of the whole people, even if their direction was to the Gadarene lake? This artistic people, when its emotions were touched, was capable of a national behaviour which was arrogant, demanding, fierce and sinister in the extreme. A naturally diffident people became ready to sweep aside all the restraints which stood in its way. But the fact that there was another side to Japan, another aspect to the machine of conquest, needs to be kept constantly in mind if Japanese action is not to be a continuous puzzle.

It was some time before this hardening of the Japanese attitude towards China became plain. This is often forgotten: it is wrongly assumed that the Japanese hostility became rigid much earlier than in fact it did. For a long while Chinese and Japanese had viewed each other with natural affection. Japan remained, in a peculiar way, tied to China by linguistic, cultural and religious connections. The two languages were distinct from one another, but the Japanese had borrowed thousands of Chinese characters, could write Japanese in these and incidentally found them exceptionally valuable in rapidly assimilating complex scientific and technical innovations imported from the West in recent times. This proved a powerful bond of attachment. In the modern period many of the leaders of Chinese nationalism had been inspired by modern ideas by residence as students in Japan. They looked back on that period with nostalgia. Japan, where the conditions of life were not so very different from China's, was for these young men the convenient forcing house and museum of western attitudes, the place where western institutions were on show but had not become too uncomfortable, and where life was not a leap in the dark. Moreover in Japan there still survived, by habit and as the result of conviction, the consoling sense that China was a land with a magnificent past.

A belief that Japan could be the natural protector of Chinese nationalism, and that together the Chinese and Japanese peoples might discomfort the western world; the fascination of the Chinese at discerning the Japanese methods of surviving in the dangerous world and getting level terms with its horrific visitors: these facts tended to postpone an inexorable break between China and Japan. The Chinese and Japanese still preserved a special feeling for each other, even when the Japanese were behaving most brutally and insensitively. For a long while the Chinese had the instinct that they should be patient, and that the day might come when the temporary clouds between the two countries would disappear and that Japan would become useful to them. They cherished Japan's successes, as, for example, its victory in 1905 in the Russo-Japanese War, as a matter for the common pride of Asians.

In the end, the relations between China and Japan took a turn for the worse, and became cooler. Events on both sides contributed to this. Chinese nationalism became more unrestrained and irresponsible: it revealed more clearly its ultimate goal. Japan set itself with more determination to thwart reviving Chinese ambition; and the internal events in Japan had rendered inactive the groups which fostered understanding and indulgence. Relations became colder; but only disastrously so during the 1930s. When this happened, much of the warm regard of each country for the other, especially among the more traditional classes, still continued in latent form. It was suppressed, but it was always there just below the surface, an imponderable factor in the situation of East Asia.

While this national resolution was slowly forming as the response to the circumstances of the time, it should be remembered that the circumstances were different from those of today. Japan made a disastrous choice, which was to lead to untold retribution and havoc, but at the time of its first moves toward empire building its decisions did not appear so eccentric. In the later part of the nineteenth century, force was still the final tool in the conduct of international relations; all countries accepted this, and Japan was not peculiar. Britain's conquest of India still stood out as the brazen example of what imperialism might succeed in doing. The only deterrent was in the calculation of consequences, and these were at that time clear of such devastating things as the atom bombs, or even, for the most part, of the horrors of wars of attrition.

For all its apparent modernization, many features of the Japanese state continued to be very different from those of the West. In contrast with the Western Powers, Japan, though it wore the trappings of a modern state, continued to be at least mentally attached to the Middle Ages. This accounted for its often bewildering reaction to the situation in which it found itself. It explains frequently surprising recourses to the methods of the past. They did not represent an abrupt move to reaction by the Japanese, as they were apt to be interpreted by the West. Rather they were the intrusion into modern ways of the instinct of an earlier day, which had never died completely in Japan. Japan, though suitably made up for the part of a contemporary Power, was never quite at home in the modern world; it was wearing a kind of fancy dress, and the West dimly recognized the fact. The West was never entirely at home with Japan, for it sensed a certain eerie mystery, as of a survivor from a past civilization.

The psychological drama behind Japan's attempt to prevail by force, and especially behind the attempt to prevail over China, is exceedingly interesting.

Throughout their history the Japanese have always exhibited symptoms of schizophrenia, exemplified in their attitude towards China. Japan admired China, and simultaneously it despised it; it was tied to China and yet yearned to be free. Its attitude combined the pious reverence of a child towards a grandparent with the disrespect which eventually led to war with its cultural ancestor. For the civilization of Japan, though ultimately it was due to the Japanese spirit playing upon the various influences which went into its making, was, in its remote origin, derived from China. From China came the initial impulse, and the Japanese could never put this out of their minds. On one hand they accepted, in an excess of self-abasement, the traditional Chinese view of the Japanese as being a race of 'deformed dwarfs'; on the other, they felt themselves superior, and proclaimed themselves with neurotic insistence to be the children of the Sun Goddess – 'the race of Yamato' – and destined to rule the entire world, even a world as powerful, rich and wide as their extended knowledge of the nineteenth and twentieth centuries proved it to be. This ambivalence and the unreality behind so much of Japanese action – together with the extremes of violence alternating with extremes of self-control – are the key to understanding a great deal of East Asian history.

The relations with China always preoccupied the Japanese. Even when Japan was led, via China, into war (which few people in Japan really desired) against the United States, Britain and finally Russia, it was essentially a by-product of this great absorbing interest. When Japan went to war against the US and Britain, it was because the West intervened between Japan and its victim China. In a sense, Japan was perfectly sincere in claiming that it wished to protect China: it was protecting it from the western aggressors so that it could be preserved intact for Japan's benefit.

However, it must not be supposed from this description that Japan acted monolithically. For a country as consensus-orientated as was Japan, there were always surprising divergencies from the norm. From time to time there rose movements which altered the policy of the Government, and even at times seemed to offer the prospect of a reversal of policy. But, seen in perspective, Japan's drive on China continued with little interruption throughout the period.

CHAPTER 2
Japan in International Affairs

JAPAN followed this resolute policy of establishing its ascendancy over China for half a century down to 1945. It was hampered in its execution by the jealousy of the Western Powers, which believed that they had a monopoly in exploiting China. In asserting itself in China and the Pacific Ocean, Japan ran the risk of increasing opposition from these Powers. It had discovered early that they would not willingly leave it in peace to bully China: not because they were sympathetic to China, but because they objected to Japan's rise.

In pursuit of its purpose, Japan had to resort to one of the oldest devices of diplomacy. Ringed by a group of unsympathetic powers, Japan set itself to split their united front, to woo one of them as its ally and advertise its useful role in return for patronage. If it could enlist the friendship of one of the larger Powers, for which it was prepared to pay a price, it reckoned on being able to hold in check the others, and to avoid being compelled by them to forgo advantages at China's expense (as had happened in 1895).

Where could it find the friendly patronage? Which Great Powers could it woo away from the conventional attitude of suspicion of Japan as an upstart? Above all, how could Japan supply a Great Power with an inducement to take certain risks to gain its friendship? These problems exercised Japanese statesmen at the turn of the century.

Opinion was divided. It was generally agreed that the extreme enemy of Japan, the frustrator of all its schemes of advance, was its immediate neighbour, Russia. Nevertheless one school favoured an apparently direct appeasement of Russia, and, when it had the upper hand, began negotiations which might have found a way for Japan and Russia to co-exist. Another school wanted an alliance with Germany. Already Japan felt the attraction of Germany; in its programme of modernization it had borrowed from Germany the outline of its Constitution, and also it had copied much in the organization of its Army. In the formative years of Japan's foreign policy Japan had soundings with Germany which looked towards a much closer link.

But eventually another school prevailed. It was the group which was inclined to rely on the Japanese Navy. Japan was a group of islands; it was a maritime Power; it felt that it was obeying its predestined fate in accepting a maritime solution of its problems. It did so by throwing in its lot with Britain. Japan, perched offshore of the land mass of Asia, was aware that its conditions of life were very much the same as those of Britain, which was similarly an island nation offshore of the land mass of Europe. The geopolitical attractions of an alliance with Britain were reinforced by a strong emotional reaction in Japan. The political attitudes of the Western Powers since the enforced opening up of Japan to foreign trade in the middle of the nineteenth century had been marked by galling restraints on its mainland explorations, for instance, in the restriction of its spoliation in China in the war of 1894–5, and in some quarters by a cultural insensitivity, of which the term 'yellow peril' was an example. The British readiness to come to an understanding not only promised a political alliance of real value but also wiped out a sense of previous humiliations and produced a response of warm friendship in Japan. Thus in 1902, there was concluded the Anglo-Japanese Alliance, which gave Japan the partner which it sought.

The Alliance was an event of fundamental importance in Japanese history. The complicated diplomacy which preceded and followed it are a clue to all that happened in East Asia. History had taken hold of Japan, and placed the Japanese eventually in a position from which their nation drove on, blindly, but with a certain exhilaration, to its fated part in the Second World War, and to doom. Too much attention cannot be given to these events by anybody wishing to find out what really happened. With one eye turned towards Pearl Harbor, and, what lay beyond, to Hiroshima, the complexities of these years must be unravelled.

From the Japanese point of view, the desire for an Anglo-Japanese Alliance sprang from the expectation that the final disintegration of China was imminent and that a major conflict between Japan and Russia must ensue from Russia's ever-increasing military and political power in the region. Still impressed by the vigour and resourcefulness of British imperialism, which the whole world regarded as the most highly evolved imperial system in history, a powerful faction within the ruling Japanese oligarchy came to believe that Japan's only means of protecting its own security and achieving relatively modest objectives on its own East Asian doorstep lay in reaching an effective military and political alignment with Britain. This view, in the end, prevailed against others who regarded such steps as premature, or who instead perceived that the British Empire was passing into a period of appeasement and decline rather than of driving ambition, and who therefore desired that Japan should avoid hazarding all on an alliance with an irresolute, diffident Power but rather seek a rapprochement with Russia aimed at establishing an East Asian condominium between just the two of them. The Russophils had been more influential than those who pressed for an alliance with Britain during the decade that followed the Triple Intervention, but the impetuosity and aggressiveness which characterized Russian penetration into Manchuria, Korea and North China gradually tipped the balance.

At the same time, the British, feeling the harsh condemnation of the world over the Boer War, and fearing any potentially hostile combination of the European states in a world of uncertainties, began to seek alliances: the time had come to choose sides. Approaches were made to Russia in hopes of detaching it from an alliance with France: the British proposed what would have amounted to an Anglo-Russian condominium that would take in most of China, the Balkans and the Middle East. These breathtaking overtures were misunderstood by the Russians, however, and so the moment was lost. Britain then turned to Japan, the sole remaining rising military Power in East Asia. At first it seemed that a Triple Alliance might be possible between Britain, Japan and Germany to further their individual interests in East Asia. This prospect faded as the Germans neglected to pursue the matter, and in January 1902 the first Anglo-Japanese Alliance was concluded.

That Alliance was in effect a neutralizing arrangement so far as Japan was concerned. The two Powers declared that their motives were to maintain the status quo and general peace of 'the Extreme East', particularly with reference to 'the Empire of China and the Empire of Korea', and in securing 'equal opportunities in those countries for the commerce and industry of all nations'. It went on to acknowledge Britain and Japan's special interests in China and, revealingly, recognized that Japan 'is interested in a peculiar degree politically as well as commercially and industrially in Korea'. They agreed that 'it will be admissible for either of them to take such measures as may be indispensable in order to safeguard those interests if threatened either by the aggressive action of any other Power, or by disturbances arising in China or Korea' – which in other words gave them a free hand to do what they liked within their respective spheres of influence. The Treaty next provided that if either of the two partners became involved in war with a Third Power, the other partner would remain strictly neutral and endeavour to dissuade other states from joining in the fray against its ally. However, if these efforts proved unavailing and 'any other Power or Powers should join in hostilities against that ally, the other High Contracting Party will come to its assistance, and will conduct the war in common, and make peace in mutual agreement with it'.* The Treaty had a nominal five-year term but with provision for its indefinite extension in the absence of any notification to the contrary.

The effect of this upon Japan was that probably it would be relieved of the prospect of war with more than one adversary. The Treaty virtually guaranteed that the neutrality of the other Powers was likely to be assured. For example, under the protection of the Treaty, Japan could safely make war on Russia, being reasonably assured that it would not be assailed by any Power which otherwise might be inclined to come to the aid of Russia. British power, promising war against any ally of Russia, or any combatant of Japan, was enough to secure the neutrality of all other Powers. So, by a minimum use of actual force, the danger of war against several countries simultaneously was very much reduced.

The Russians and French were outraged by the Anglo-Japanese Alliance and in March 1902 issued a joint declaration opposing it. But some vestiges of caution remained intact in St Petersburg, and in April 1902 the first positive result of the Alliance could be perceived when a Russo-Chinese Accord was announced which provided for a staged withdrawal of Russian troops from Manchuria. Its first phase was concluded without difficulty a month later. But the Russians soon appeared to have had second thoughts about continuing with the process. Fresh Russian units flooded into southern Manchuria to areas where no Russian forces had penetrated before, and the Russians began to establish themselves in strength near the mouth of the Yalu River, directly across the Korean frontier.

The British, United States and Japanese Governments protested. They were unavailing. A diplomatic resolution of the crisis was sought in vain. Finally, Japan gave Russia a deadline. It expired, unheeded.

Seen from the Russian perspective, there was a ghastly inevitability in the progression of events leading to the Russo-Japanese War. Once the Maritime Provinces had been acquired, it seemed a natural step to build a railway to bind the ends of the Empire together. That in turn produced demands for concessions in Manchuria and Korea and, then, led to attempts to seek ice-free naval and commercial ports in the East. All of this required huge investments of capital, and that in turn had to be protected. Japan stood in the way: her opposition could not be tolerated. The Anglo-Japanese Alliance brought matters to a head. Those who advocated conciliation were overborne by jingoistic voices on both sides War, finally, appeared to become inescapable.

* International Military Tribunal for the Far East (IMTFE), Defence Exhibit 2292, Text of Anglo-Japanese Alliance, 30 January 1902.

On 6 February 1904 Japan severed diplomatic relations with Russia and launched a surprise attack upon the Russian Far Eastern Fleet two days later. A number of Russian warships were sunk, scuttled or badly damaged at Chemulpo (the port of Seoul, capital of Korea) and at Port Arthur. The remainder fled back to harbour and were bottled up in Port Arthur.

This first of Japan's great wars also set what many have regarded as a precedent of undiplomatic conduct. Japan began it by a surprise attack on the Russian Navy: it dispensed with a declaration of war. This point has been exaggerated beyond all proportion by virtually all commentators, but it is not difficult to place within its proper context: when a British survey* conducted in 1883 reviewed 'all the circumstances under which hostilities have been commenced by different countries against others, prior to a declaration of war, from the year 1700 to 1871', it could enumerate fewer than ten conflicts where hostilities had been preceded by a declaration of war during that period compared with 107 cases where no such declaration had been pronounced. Every one of the European Great Powers – and the United States – had 'engaged in such transactions again and again'. Even where there had been declarations of war in the past, it had been exceptional for a state to declare war with the intention of preventing its enemy from being taken by surprise (a point to which we shall return later). Thus Japan's freedom to launch a surprise attack against the Tsar was not fettered by customary international law, and no international agreements to refrain from undeclared war existed until a convention was signed at The Hague in 1907 (where it would evolve as a direct result of the Russo-Japanese War). Moreover, even those who framed the 1907 Convention did not intend to prohibit surprise attacks but merely to clarify a sense of the seriousness, justification and responsibility for such a conflict.

In view of the appalling record of barbarism which the Japanese soldier so richly came to deserve in later years, it is also worth pausing to reflect that in this war, as in the Boxer Rebellion a decade earlier, Japan's treatment of prisoners and scrupulous regard for international conventions on clemency were exemplary. Foreign observers attached to the two opposing sides in considerable numbers likewise remarked upon the high standard of medical services and hygiene that they found on the Japanese side compared to the Russian side's deplorable neglect of such matters. Given the ferocity of the fighting, the inhospitable climate, and the ap-

---

* J. F. Maurice, *Hostilities without Declaration of War: An Historical Abstract of the Cases in Which Hostilities have Occurred between Civilized Powers Prior to Declaration or Warning from 1700 to 1870*, H.M. Stationery Office, London, 1883.

palling losses suffered by both sides, Japan went to extraordinary lengths in caring for the wounded and ill, and for captives for whom it was responsible. Japanese and western commentators alike comprehended that there was a considerable difference between the humane and civilized conduct of the Japanese and that of other peoples.

The watching world was surprised at Japan's temerity in challenging such a mighty antagonist, and was astonished at Japan's survival. The Russians, handicapped by the Trans-Siberian Railway's single track and scarcity of rolling stock, strove to bring up fresh troop reinforcements, munitions and supplies while trying desperately to complete the final hundred miles of track round the southern shores of Lake Baikal. The Russians began the conflict with 110,000 regular troops and 30,000 railway guards in the war zone. The Japanese began with 180,000 men in the field and dispatched another 30,000 to Korea with the outbreak of hostilities. As the war progressed, these large opposing forces were heavily reinforced. The Russians transported a further 210,000 troops out to the operational theatres of the war (which still left Russia with more than four million trained soldiers and militiamen in reserve or deployed elsewhere within the Russian Empire). The Japanese Army comprised fewer than 250,000 men under arms at the beginning of the conflict and had only 400,000 in reserves, but Japan threw its full weight into the war as it developed, managing to maintain a local superiority in forces throughout the conflict. The campaign was characterized by gross incompetence within the Russian command and by brilliant recklessness on the part of the Japanese (who showed a breathtaking disregard for the expenditure of human life, repeatedly launching massed assaults against heavily fortified and entrenched positions). The besieged Russian garrison at Port Arthur finally surrendered in January 1905. Elsewhere, a succession of mammoth battles, involving more than a quarter of a million men on each side, culminated in a final battle which took place in March for possession of Mukden. It ended with a shattering defeat for the Russian forces, which then withdrew northwards in disarray. The Japanese by now were too exhausted to pursue their enemy and so let them go.

Several weeks later, a classic victory by Admiral Tōgō over the Russian Baltic Fleet in the Straits of Tsushima annihilated what was left of the Russian Navy. Ten years before, Tōgō had captained the man-of-war which sank the British merchant ship *Kowshing* at the beginning of the Sino-Japanese War. Now he confirmed his position in the pantheon of Japanese naval heroes. In the greatest naval battle fought since Trafalgar, four Russian battleships were lost and four captured out of a total complement of eight; seven cruisers out of twelve were sunk; five destroyers out of nine were sent to the bottom; one cruiser and two destroyers reached the safety of Vladivostok, and several other vessels fled to the safety of foreign ports where they were promptly interned. The only losses sustained by the Japanese during the battle were three torpedo boats. It was a victory almost beyond comprehension, and it led the Russians to accept the good offices of the United States (extended by President 'Teddy' Roosevelt following a secret approach to him by the Japanese Government). An armistice was agreed and serious peace negotiations were opened. All of this was to be recollected by the Japanese as they calculated their chances of following up the projected attack on Pearl Harbor in 1941 – or the Battle of Midway in 1942 – with a negotiated peace settlement.

The world was astonished at Japan's survival. The Russians had lost every engagement of the war and yet Japan's victory was less complete than popular legend might suggest. Japan was exhausted and grasped at peace after eighteen months of war. The conflict cost Japan more than 86,000 dead and an additional 6,700 reported missing or taken prisoner by the Russians, who in turn suffered 43,300 dead and 39,500 missing or taken captive. Japan was in no position either to sustain such losses in future or to carry the financial burden of continuing such a war.

Although the Japanese military and naval victories were spectacular, the Russians had time on their side. In the peace negotiations conducted at Portsmouth, New Hampshire, the Russians proved effective negotiators and stoutly resisted a number of the Japanese demands. Russia finally agreed to acknowledge 'the paramount political, military and economic interests of Japan in Korea', and transferred to Japan Russia's Kwantung Leased Territory on the Liaotung Peninsula, including Port Arthur and Darien, together with a railway zone extending along part of the Russian-built Harbin to the Port Arthur branch of the Chinese Eastern Railway from Changchun ('Hsinking') to the sea. The Japanese failed in their efforts to acquire the whole of Sakhalin Island, which had served as a remote Russian penal colony, but secured possession of special fishing rights and its southern half (land which Japan had occupied following the battle of Tsushima). Title to all Russian property and interests within these territories passed to Japan, but the Japanese were unable to extract a separate indemnity to offset their war expenditure. Japan was in no position to demand to annex Manchuria, though it might seem to have gained the right to do so. The two sides agreed to restore Manchuria to Chinese sovereignty and administration. But Japan was given the right to safeguard the South Manchurian Railway zone with Japanese troops. This was fateful. From this military base, the power of Japan was to spread over to the mainland and came to menace all China. As a first step, taken in December 1905, Japan and China concluded a separate Treaty of Peking by which the Empire of China reluctantly consented to the terms of the Treaty of Portsmouth and at the same time agreed to permit Japan to extend the railway network eastwards to Korea.

The Japanese public, however, long remained unaware of how near Japan had come to exhaustion and ultimate collapse during the war against Russia: that is not the sort of information any nation reveals at such times. Accordingly, the terms of the Treaty of Portsmouth fell far short of what the nation had expected. The political parties in the Imperial Diet reacted with bitterness and consternation. Riots broke out on the streets of Tokyo, suppressed by armed troops at the cost of a thousand casualties. Martial law had to be declared, there was a general curtailment of such tender liberties as the Japanese public had come to enjoy, and the Government finally had to resign.

The second Anglo-Japanese Alliance, concluded secretly in London a month before the restoration of peace with Russia, was in some sense a compensation for the disappointments clearly pending for Japan at Portsmouth. The new Alliance was not announced until after the Treaty of Portsmouth was signed in September 1905. One obvious departure from the terms of the 1902 Treaty was the new Agreement's recognition of Japan's paramount position and right of control over Korea (with the rather cynical proviso 'always that such measures are not contrary to the principle of equal opportunities for the commerce and industry of all nations').* The new Alliance also differed from the old in placing the protection of India on an equal footing to the defence of the special interests of the respective powers in 'the Extreme East'. It was a potent warning against any Russian threat to the British Raj in India. The most critical difference of all was that the two parties now determined that an 'unprovoked attack or aggressive action, wherever arising' from even a single enemy state upon either of the two signatories would bring the other signatory into the conflict. Another indication of the trust which both sides reposed in their relationship was that they doubled its term to ten years (or longer, should neither side give notice of its abrogation).

The British public received word of the new Anglo-Japanese Alliance with delight. The Government and Opposition parties alike committed themselves to dependence upon three cardinal principles which would

---

* I M T F E, Defence Exhibit 2293, Text of Second Anglo-Japanese Alliance, 12 August 1905.

henceforth underpin the defence of the British Empire: establishment of a close harmony with the United States, improvement of relations with France, and a confident trust in the extended Alliance with Japan. These were popular policies.

Within Japan, however, the mood was different. The spectre of the Triple Alliance had risen from the past: news of the extended Alliance could not wash away a sense of grievance and shame. Once again the nation seemed to have been deprived of the fruits of Japan's military and naval exploits through a combination of the ineptitude of her civilian bureaucrats and a conspiracy of the foreign Powers. The truth, however, was that the execrated bureaucrats had done all that was humanly possible – and that the goodwill of the Americans and the British saved Japan from far greater humiliations and the spectre of a war of attrition that Japan could never win.

Meanwhile, at the outbreak of the Russo-Japanese War, Japanese troops had moved rapidly to occupy Seoul and spread across Korea. Afterwards, Korean independence was all but erased, and the concessions which the Tsar's agents so audaciously had secured were cancelled at a stroke by the Korean Government to appease the Japanese. Over the next three years, the Japanese occupation authorities tightened their stranglehold upon the country as the Japanese made effective use of that freedom of action which they had secured in their treaties with Great Britain, Russia and China. Finally, during July 1907, Japan decreed the disbandment of the Korean Army. In violent revolt, the Koreans rose up in the name of their lost autonomy, if not for their independence. The Korean régime had been arbitrary, tyrannical and corrupt, but this was a rising against a totally alien foe, a national rather than a factional cause. Yet it was a hopeless struggle. Well-seasoned Japanese troops fought back with ferocity and after a vicious struggle emerged victorious. A purposeful, forcible attempt to assimilate the country began, lasting until 1945. In August 1910 Korea was annexed to the Japanese Empire, which suffered only occasional pangs of indigestion afterwards.

The arrogance and roughness of the Japanese occupying authorities multiplied the pre-existing fear and hatred which the Chinese, Taiwanese, Manchurian, Korean and Sakhalinese indigenous populations already felt towards their new masters. As Japanese immigrants arrived to assume the functions of bureaucrats, managers, entrepreneurs and colonists, Japanese control, relentless and thorough, was exerted throughout their new domains. There was little if any hope that the Japanese would be content with a temporary occupation of alien soil: they dreamt of eternity and called it 'cooperation'. It left a legacy still palpable today.

The demands of life within the modern world were vastly greater than this formerly self-sufficient island race appeared able to sustain without exploiting the resources of its newly acquired imperial outposts on the Asiatic mainland and on islands beyond the horizon. Security and hubris required vastly increased military expenditure. Foreign markets were beginning to close to Japanese manufactured goods, but the Japanese people were developing an appetite for overseas trade and western consumer products.

The extent of this economic, colonial and military transformation was beyond the expectation of the British statesmen and officials who had negotiated the terms of the first or even second Anglo-Japanese Alliance. By 1911 Russia had restored good relations with both Japan and the British Empire. In a sense, the Anglo-Japanese Alliance coupled with the outcome of the Russo-Japanese War had forced the Tsar to abandon any dreams of establishing his hegemony over East Asia. At the same time, trouble was brewing just beyond his European borders. There were war scares and unrest in the Balkans and in North Africa. Anglo-German naval rivalry had reached such a pitch that it seemed most unlikely that either of those two Powers could afford the expense of a protracted stalemate. The temper of public opinion, the inability of nations to increase their expenditure on armaments indefinitely, and the rigidity imposed upon mobilization plans circumscribed by the manpower, munitions, provisions and railways that now were regarded as essential in modern warfare all contributed to a chilling certainty that a second European War of some dimension was bound to occur sooner rather than later. Meanwhile, considered from the point of view of naval relations between the Great Powers, it had become a basic principle of naval strategy that a 'fleet in being' seeking command of the sea should be concentrated against its principal enemy rather than allow itself to be divided (a lesson taught by the popular American naval theorist Alfred T. Mahan and reinforced by the recent Russo-Japanese War). Conditions in Europe required the British fleet to concentrate in Home Waters during peace as well as in war. Protection of British imperial interests in East Asia now appeared to depend upon support from Japan.

At the same time, American concern was hardening into opposition as Japan endeavoured to squeeze the Western Powers out of all of Japan's recent territorial acquisitions in the process of assimilating colonial domains encompassing some ·3 million square kilometres (an area more than three quarters the size of Japan Proper). Under the terms of the second Anglo-Japanese Treaty, Japan was entitled to expect backing from the British Empire if any serious conflict with the United States should develop (as might happen, for instance, if the United States Fleet ever backed up American diplomatic protests by staging a naval demonstration in the Western Pacific). Moreover, at this moment British and American negotiators were seeking to formulate an Anglo-United States Treaty of General Arbitration. There seemed very real justification for hope that far from aggravating relations between Japan and the United States, a new Anglo-Japanese Alliance would help to prevent serious trouble from arising between them.

Thus the Anglo-Japanese Alliance was revised in 1911 * and effectively became redirected to meet the threat of war against Germany and its allies while underscoring the happier relations which both signatories now enjoyed with Russia and their desire for harmony with the United States. It was not a charter for aggression.

Despite the unpleasant side of Japan's increasing strength, the Alliance served Britain in the same way that it served Japan. In effect, it provided that the British interest in East Asia would be protected in case Britain became involved in war in Europe. If that happened, Britain would rely on Japan to keep the British Empire and its interests intact in the Pacific. And so it happened when Britain had to fight the first European War. The Treaty was not quite perfectly observed, at least in spirit. Some Japanese, influential ones, could not help speculating on what Japan might do if Britain should lose the war, a possibility which they did not seem to see with regret; and the positive aid Japan gave was less than might have been expected of an honourable ally had Britain, in fact, not asked her to do less still. But concerning the effect of the Treaty as a whole, Britain was content: in the years ahead, British admirals, treasury officers and cabinet ministers often lamented its demise.

When the European Powers initiated the Great War, Japan declared war on Germany. Its action in doing so was prompted by loyalty to its ally but also by an expectation that the War would offer opportunities to strengthen Japan's position in East Asia and to avenge losses imposed upon Japan at the time of the Triple Intervention. Although the Chinese had declared their neutrality at the outbreak of the War, the Japanese launched a land offensive across Shantung Province and, with British naval support, laid siege to the German port of Tsingtao, which finally capitulated in early November. The Japanese forces then established control over the remainder of Germany's Shantung Leased Territory. In doing so, they seized the railway zones that traversed the Province from

* IMTFE, Defence Exhibit 2294, Text of Third Anglo-Japanese Alliance, 13 July 1911.

Tsingtao to Tsinan, the Chinese provincial capital, and gained Japan the distinction of employing military aircraft for the first time in the history of warfare. After the campaign ended, Japanese security forces were left to police the railway zones. Peking sought the return of these railways to Chinese administration and, when its efforts failed, unilaterally announced the abolition of the Shantung war zone and requested the withdrawal of all foreign troops from China.

The balance of forces in the East was disturbed by the Western Powers being engaged in war in Europe – which for the western countries was a kind of civil war. The eastern countries made their calculations accordingly. China's audacity would have seemed unthinkable in previous years, and in the short term it misfired badly. Japan, in turn, seized its opportunity and secretly presented China with virtually an ultimatum, the notorious Twenty-One Demands, a document prepared in advance by the Japanese Foreign Minister in consultation with junior officials and sanctioned by other Cabinet Ministers for use on the first such occasion that might present itself.

Acceptance of the Twenty-One Demands would have ended even the circumscribed independence of North China: it would have transformed it into a Japanese protectorate. The pattern of probable events had been made clear in Korea. China was saved when both the scheme and the methods adopted by the Japanese Government came under sustained attack from all sides but especially from three distinct directions: a diplomatic intervention by the United States; apprehension expressed in Japanese military circles (particularly when it was proposed to dispatch further military forces to China in order to secure Peking's compliance), and condemnation by three of the *Genrō*, the last surviving oligarchs of the Meiji Era, who emerged from the shadows to curb what they regarded as a gross abuse of power and trust by the Foreign Minister and the Prime Minister. It is not likely that any one of these sources of pressure was strong enough on its own to force the Japanese Government to water down the Twenty-One Demands. As matters stood, however, the Japanese Government was compelled to drop its most objectionable terms, which would have granted Tokyo an exclusive right to select military, economic and political advisers to 'assist' the fledgling Chinese Republic; obliged China to purchase more than half of her munitions from Japan; established Japanese control over Chinese arsenals; authorized Japan to build more railways on Chinese soil, and even provided for the creation of a joint police command within areas designated by Japan. There were other demands which the Japanese Government was unwilling to abandon.

Helpless still, China was forced to acquiesce in four other sets of

'Demands', which conferred upon Japan control of the extra-territorial rights in Shantung formerly extorted by Germany; extended Japan's leaseholds in Manchuria from twenty-five years to a period of ninety-nine years and guaranteed Japanese subjects the right to own land; gave Japan a foothold in Inner Mongolia; forced China to concede Japan control over the exploitation of iron and coal resources in Central China, and barred China from ever again ceding any island, harbour or bay along her coast to any Third Power.

At a stroke, these concessions endowed Japan with rights and interests in China which were in no way inferior to those acquired piecemeal by all of the other foreign Powers who had enforced their claims there during the past three quarters of a century. The Japanese Government felt, indeed, that the Twenty-One Demands would open a new era of 'cooperation' with China that ultimately would free both of them from interference by the Western Powers: Japan was giving China the 'freedom to say yes' in what promised to be a unique scheme for the future interdependence and mutual advancement of the two countries. Seen from the Chinese side, of course, the Twenty-One Demands excited the just wrath of every Chinese, who already regarded Japan as their most loathsome foreign enemy. Efforts were made by later Japanese Governments to appease China by extending huge loans and bribes to the Chinese authorities, and these had some effect. But Japan's inept mishandling of the Twenty-One Demands thoroughly discredited her in the eyes of the world. Above all, it strengthened American opposition to Japan, attracted great sympathy for China (which had been noticeably rare in previous decades), and was one instrumental factor in Britain's subsequent decision to abandon the Anglo-Japanese Alliance.

Meanwhile, Japanese naval forces had moved swiftly at the outbreak of the First World War and established their control over the German island territories in the Pacific Ocean, including the Marshalls, the Marianas, Palau and the Carolines. Japanese naval escorts protected ships carrying troops and supplies bound for the European War and the Japanese main fleet acted as a deterrent that shielded Australia and New Zealand from enemy attack. As the War developed, Japanese cruisers and destroyers were sent into the Mediterranean and were assigned to the exceptionally arduous and dangerous escort and patrol duties necessary to combat the menace of German submarines there.

Japan more than met its obligations to its ally during the First World War. Strictly speaking, Japan had no duty to take part in the War. The Anglo-Japanese Alliance of 1911 specifically applied only to 'the consolidation and maintenance of the general peace in the regions of Eastern

Asia and of India', not to what might have been limited to a European War. No precise military obligations had been spelt out in the Anglo-Japanese Alliance anyway, but it had never been anticipated that Japanese forces would serve in any European theatre of operations.

The Japanese felt, indeed, that they did everything which could be asked of the Anglo-Japanese Alliance, given the constraints placed upon them. Throughout the two decades which it lasted, that Alliance stood as the cornerstone of Japanese policy. Upon that rock, Japan safely took the first steps to the establishment of its Empire. The irony was that the extension of this Empire was to lead Japan into the most disastrous war of the 1940s, and war with its former ally. It pressed ahead with imperial enterprises when jangled events had deprived Japan of the British alliance and had transformed Britain into an enemy, or a wished-for victim. It is no wonder that the Anglo-Japanese Alliance was, by old-fashioned and conservative Japanese, looked back upon with melancholy regret. It represented the time of safety. It was an instrument which had brought Japan respect, growing power and few doubts or perplexities. It was a tower of strength to Japan psychologically. It had been the dependable way, felt the solider elements in Japanese society, amid other kalaeidoscopic attractions, and Japan had been wise not to forsake it.

The issues in East Asia grew more complex and divided. One of the most serious problems to arise was the Siberian Intervention, which grew out of the chaos of the Russian Revolution of 1917. For a time it appeared that the Revolution might spill over into Manchuria and Korea. At an Allied conference meeting in December 1917, General Foch pressed for an invasion of Siberia. The idea met with a cool response from Britain and the United States. The Japanese, however, began to study the respective advantages and disadvantages of intervening on their own. In the following month, the British came round to the French idea and suggested the possibility of seizing Vladivostok in order to safeguard the huge Allied war supplies – some 600,000 tons – that lay stockpiled there. Within a fortnight, two Japanese cruisers and a British cruiser reached Vladivostok harbour and dropped anchor to await developments.

The British asked the United States to reconsider the French proposal and suggested Japanese occupation of the Trans-Siberian Railway. President Wilson flatly rejected the idea. Even ruling circles in Japan, however, were divided on how far they should venture in attempting to halt the advance of bolshevism: it was arguable that direct intervention might prolong the war or lead to an Anglo-Russian reconciliation and possibly provoke further trouble after the eventual restoration of peace. On the other hand, Japanese occupation of Eastern Siberia and the Maritime Provinces was an attractive notion in its own right.

Eventually the arguments in favour of military intervention became irresistible after the Czech Legion, striving to escape from Russia in a mass exodus via the Trans-Siberian Railway, was caught up in a hopeless tangle of international (dis)agreements, orders and counter-orders. The trains were stopped: time passed, and the 70,000 Czechs gradually lost patience, strung out in troop trains over a distance of 6,000 miles of track from beyond the Volga to Vladivostok. Trotsky ordered his Red Army to disarm the Czechs and utilize them as conscript labour battalions. The Czechs intercepted his messages and fought their way out, capturing the great port of Vladivostok and holding the eastern sections of the Trans-Siberian Railway. As fighting continued, the Czechs moved back into the interior and allied themselves with the White Russian and Cossack armies operating right across Siberia to the Urals. It was their military effectiveness more than their predicament which persuaded the Western Powers and Japan to act in 'support' of the Czechs.

In July 1918 British, Chinese, Czech, French, Japanese and United States representatives at Vladivostok declared that the Allied Powers would henceforth assume responsibility for the safety of the area. British troops began coming ashore on 3 August, followed a week later by the Japanese. An American division arrived and so did smaller French and Canadian contingents. Although the British troops soon made their way as far westwards as Irkutsk, the other Western forces scarcely made their presence felt. The Japanese, however, dispatched some 70,000 troops, a force vastly greater in number than the other Powers had sent: it was more than a little reminiscent of the Boxer Rebellion except that on this occasion the barbaric behaviour of the Japanese troops is said to have been indistinguishable at times from that of their adversary. After extraordinary adventures, the Czechs finally extricated themselves from Russia in good order and in April 1920 embarked on their evacuation ships at Vladivostok. All of the national contingents of the Allied Expeditionary Force then withdrew except for the Japanese, who stayed.

The Japanese Government endeavoured to recall its troops from Russia but the Japanese Army refused to concede. The Japanese Cabinet found itself unable to prevent the Army from extending its military operations into northern Sakhalin. Eventually, however, the Japanese contingent bowed to the inevitable and returned home in October 1922. Nothing could turn the episode into a triumph. On the contrary, the disobedience of the Army set an evil precedent. The Japanese public, far from rejoicing in the achievements of its forces, distanced itself from the Siberian campaign. Militarism, until the outbreak of the Manchurian Incident a decade later, had become thoroughly unpopular in Japan for the first time in the nation's modern history.

Meanwhile, at the Paris Peace Conference which had opened in January 1919, Japan's standing as a Great Power was confirmed when it took part as one of the 'Big Five' nations who arrogated to themselves the overall design of the post-war settlement. In the main, the Japanese delegation emerged from the Peace Conference having achieved most of its demands, including succession to the rights formerly held by Germany in Shantung and a South Seas Mandate to administer the islands north of the Equator which Japan had seized from Germany during the war. All of these gains were achieved in the teeth of efforts to prevent them. Japan also won one of the coveted permanent seats on the Council of the League of Nations. However, Japan signally failed in its attempt to persuade the Powers to add a clause to the League of Nations Charter establishing the principle of racial equality in the affairs of member states. The proposal attracted the support of China, Czechoslovakia, France, Greece, Italy and Poland but was defeated after it was strongly attacked by Australia and the United States (in the end, Britain, too, sided with the antipodean representatives notwithstanding its affectionate regard for the Anglo-Japanese Alliance). Voices in Japan had prophesied that rivalry between the 'white' and 'coloured' races of the world would escalate into a struggle for world domination following the Great War. The portentousness of Japan's failure to gain acceptance of the racial equality clause was not lost upon the Japanese. Nevertheless, it has to be said that the matter was considered a relatively minor and mischievous distraction by the four other Great Powers, who no doubt were prompted by domestic racial prejudice but also had regard for the discrimination and prejudice to which the Koreans, Taiwanese and Manchurians were subjected under Japanese rule.

The Treaty of Versailles did not silence those who opposed Japan's continental ambitions. Japan had taken the precaution of securing an agreement with Russia in July 1916 sanctioning Russian domination of Outer Mongolia in exchange for formal Russian recognition of Japanese influence in China, but that achievement was nullified by the Russian Revolution. Similarly, Japan had signed the Ishii-Lansing Agreement of November 1917 which seemed to give recognition to Japan's claims on mainland China, though in vague form. However, the Chinese kept the Shantung issue alive, steadfastly refusing to sign the Treaty of Versailles on the grounds that China had conceded to Japan's wartime demands only under duress. This line of reasoning had little to commend itself to foreign governments. It is difficult to think of more than half a dozen territorial disputes or border adjustments resolved by any means other than 'unequal' treaty or conquest to the disadvantage of one side or another: these are practices in which all states have engaged, and, as the reader will agree, there were abundant local precedents for Japan's extra-territorial demands upon China. Yet in this instance the Chinese complaint enjoyed a sympathetic reception in countries such as the United States, where popular sentiment was already aroused against Japan's aggressive behaviour.

The mood of the American public was growing increasingly hostile towards Japan and antagonistic towards the European Powers, too. The first phase of American antagonism towards Japan had coincided with the racial tensions which erupted in California at the turn of the century and from thence spread to every state westwards of the Rocky Mountains by the time of the First World War: it is impossible to exaggerate the outrageousness and popularity of the xenophobia and race hatred so manifest on the Pacific slopes during that period. The second phase took account of Japanese subjugation of Korea, Taiwan and 'Karafuto' (Southern Sakhalin) but mainly developed out of the earlier phase and in response to the Twenty-One Demands. When the Koreans rose again in revolt during 1919 and the Japanese acted promptly in restoring order, the violent measures adopted by the Japanese Army to suppress the rebellion further weakened Japan's position abroad.

However, an entirely new phase of bitterness and rivalry had already become apparent during the first European War. The United States Navy had felt its own strength, and with this development America became less inclined than formerly to share the seas with other Powers. The United States Government declared its policy to build the most powerful fleet afloat, and the United States Navy Department unveiled a programme capable of achieving that objective by construction of a navy both numerically and qualitatively superior to any of its rivals. The British Admiralty showed its determination to keep ahead of the Americans (or at least its resolve not to be left behind). This state of affairs posed a more pressing threat to Japanese independence and development than anything which had occurred since the Meiji Restoration. Japan turned its hand to the construction of warships which arguably were the most sophisticated designs in the world. Complex naval arms rivalries between many of the Powers were threatening to run out of control, but nowhere was this more likely to give rise to another world war than in the Pacific. The costs of naval rearmament on this scale were astronomical: each of the Powers began to reflect that it might be cheaper to reach a naval accord with its chief rivals than to risk financial ruin.

Great changes were coming over the whole world. The instincts of imperialism had begun to subside in all the countries involved, Japan excepted; the climate of opinion was changing, and there was a reconsideration in many countries of their long-term objectives. In all lands, the doubts of the liberal intelligentsia were undermining the former certainties. It was even asked whether it was certain that imperialism in certain countries really paid; whether the profit from the economic rampage over China was equal to the costs and dangers of keeping China down. There was an unfamiliar readiness to receive politely the advances of Chinese nationalism. Above all, the instinctive resort to force showed signs of waning; there was more readiness to treat China as other countries were treated.

In these new circumstances the British decided to terminate their Japanese Alliance; and thereby struck a heavy blow at Japan's sentiment and security. On balance Britain considered that the Treaty had come to have disadvantages which outweighed its attractions. The immediate motive for not renewing it was pressure from the Canadian Government, which in turn reflected opinion in the United States. The chief reason for Britain's acquiescence to American pressure to break the Anglo-Japanese Alliance was the belief that, if Britain was faced with a choice between American goodwill and that of Japan, the decision must go in favour of Anglo-Saxon solidarity. Every aspect of the issue was meticulously analysed in Whitehall and in consultation between the Prime Ministers of the British Dominions. Far more careful consideration of what was involved took place behind closed doors in London than anywhere else in the world: that was an inevitable result of the unequalled governmental efficiency of Great Britain. Yet perhaps few such fateful decisions have been made with so little national debate, and with such small public realization of what had been done, and what it meant for the future.

The ending of the Treaty confirmed that the world was to divide upon racial lines. By rebuffing Japan, this event compelled Japan to recognize itself as being on the Asian side. It confirmed the tendency of Japanese and westerners to see the tensions of this part of the world as consisting in the polar opposition of the white and the yellow races. Japan, cast out again from the inner ring of Powers which had the last word in world affairs, would in the end seek to overthrow this same inner ring. It would do so in the name of the equality of races. In its manoeuvres it could no longer be assured of the neutralization of most of the Western Powers; and undoubtedly it would make a commotion in seeking to forward its interest in a world grown more hostile to it.

As a compensation for the old Anglo-Japanese Alliance, Japan had to content itself with an agreement for limitation of naval power, in which Japan's status as one of the greatest naval powers in the world was recognized. The Japanese Government, weakest of the three, appreciated that Japan had little option but to do everything possible to restore a semblance of international goodwill. Thus Japan suffered the mortifying experience of coming to the Washington Conference, convened by President Harding a few months after his inauguration, and of being obliged to sign a series of interlocking agreements that gave away a good deal of what the Japanese people believed they had earned during the recent Great War.

In a Four Power Treaty with Britain and the United States (joined by France at the last minute after pressure by the American Secretary of State), Japan was compelled to give up the protection of the Anglo-Japanese Alliance in favour of what amounted to a quadruple non-aggression pact respecting one another's 'rights in relation to their insular possessions and insular dominions in the region of the Pacific Ocean'. This Treaty also vaguely provided for mutual consultation – but not arbitration – in the event of any of the signatories finding themselves in a dispute that seemed insoluble by normal bilateral diplomacy.

In a separate Washington Five Power Treaty with Great Britain, the United States, France and Italy, Japan undertook to abandon its own naval expansion programme and to accept an inferiority of six tenths of the tonnage permitted to the British or Americans in capital ship and aircraft-carrier displacement. At the same time delegates also established limitations on the size and armament of capital ships and aircraft-carriers and agreed to observe a ten-year 'building holiday' during which no new capital ships would be laid down. In naval arithmetic, that left the Japanese Navy no margin of superiority against either of its two foremost potential enemies in its own home waters.

The one major concession which the Japanese delegation wrung from the other representatives was a promise to maintain the present balance of power by refraining from the construction of new naval bases and fortifications in the Western Pacific and by renouncing the right to increase their existing naval repair and maintenance facilities in the region. The United States only accepted this proposal on the understanding that it did not extend to Hawaii and islands contiguous to the Western Hemisphere, but Guam, Midway, Western Samoa, the Philippines and the Aleutians were effectively condemned to helplessness and lost much of their potential value as staging areas or main fleet bases. Britain excluded the Canadian offshore islands, Australia and its dependencies, New Zealand, and above all Singapore. Hong Kong, however, was left unprotected. The British also agreed to surrender their leasehold on the Shantung port of Wei-hai-wei to China as an inducement to the Japanese to do likewise with Japan's special interests elsewhere in that Province. Japan promised to demilitarize the Kurile Islands, 'Karafuto', Formosa, the Pescadores and the Japanese Mandated Islands. The whole of French Indo-China was excluded from the Treaty (not that France ever seriously contemplated its defence). These voluntary undertakings were intended to reduce the risk of conflict in the Pacific. If it ever became necessary for Japan to defend herself against an attack by either one of the Anglo-Saxon naval powers, any fleet hostile to Japan would have to leave secure fleet repair and revictualling facilities thousands of miles behind. This arrangement compensated the Japanese to a considerable degree for the inferiority which she had to accept in relation to the size of her fleet compared to that of the United States or Great Britain.

The Japanese Navy had hoped to establish its right to indisputable mastery of the Western Pacific and so free Japan to reconstruct East Asia with little regard for either British or American sensitivities. The Japanese delegation at Washington had the wisdom to leave such schoolboy dreams behind, but the Naval Treaty did force the Japanese Navy to revise its strategic thinking and fatally compromised the design of its heavy war-ships: emphasis was placed upon their speed and armament with little attention to cruising range and crew accommodation. The same defects also became evident in some other classes of ships as well. This in time – as we shall see – was to lead to their comparatively early exhaustion and inefficiency when deployed in the punishingly long and far-flung naval campaigns of the Pacific War.

The Washington Conference contemplated a period in which Treaty Ports and extra-territoriality in China would be no more. The Powers professed to be willing that China should eventually be admitted to the comity of states as an equal, and welcomed the signs of modernization. The instrument embodying these agreements, called the Nine Power Treaty, was for twenty years a memorial of the limitations put upon Japan from having a free hand to decide the shape of the Far East. Japan joined with all of the remaining Powers interested in the Pacific (apart from Russia who bitterly objected to being excluded) in pledging itself to respect China's integrity and independence. The principle of the Open Door, which the Americans regarded as holy writ and others privately regarded as sanctimonious nonsense, was endorsed by China for the first time and publicly reaffirmed by all of the other Powers, who also denied that any of them would henceforth seek special rights, privileges, monopolies or preferences in China 'which would abridge the rights of subjects or citizens of friendly states' there. Although there were provisions for mutual consultation in the event of breaches of these undertakings, the Nine Power Treaty had no specific provision for 'collective security' or for mutual guarantees. In Japan the change of mood in the Powers who were party to the Treaty was received with consternation, which would have been greater if most Japanese had not regarded it as hypocrisy. Nevertheless, Japan did agree to withdraw its garrison from Hankow and, in a separate Sino-Japanese Treaty, restored Shantung to China (while retaining a short-term interest in the Shantung railway zone which would ensure that Japan did not suffer any financial losses from the reversion). Sino-American efforts to restore China's position in Manchuria were blocked by Britain and Japan, but the Powers agreed to terminate the Allied Intervention in the Russian Civil War. There were many other achievements during the Washington Conference: we need not consider them in detail.

All in all, there was a remarkable blend of *realpolitik*, self-sacrifice and compromise at the Washington Conference. It produced nine treaties and twelve international resolutions. The nations represented there seemed determined to avoid a repetition of the events which had culminated in the calamity of the Great War: they gave expression to a common desire to mark the end of an epoch and the beginning of a better, more peaceful world. For a time it appeared that the 'Washington Treaty System' would operate in the way its authors had hoped. The Washington Conference itself had a profound moral influence everywhere, established a precedent in successful arms control negotiations, curbed Great Power rivalries in East Asia and resolved a number of troublesome issues. Nevertheless, it dissatisfied the naval advisers of each of the Governments concerned and effectively concentrated those Governments' attentions upon their unremitting conflicts over other matters affecting peace and stability in East Asia.

Within the admiralties, treasuries, foreign ministries and cabinets of nations, the processes of administration continued much as before. The Washington System fell far short of satisfying those unreconstructed ultra-nationalists of every hue and country whose exaggerated visions of manifest destiny always seem to be intertwined with paranoiac apprehension. It is this which finally led to the downfall of the Washington System.

Scarcely before delegates returning from the Washington Conference had unpacked their bags and souvenirs, the United States Supreme Court pandered to public prejudice and shamelessly ruled in November 1922 that Japanese were ineligible for United States citizenship through naturalization. One year later, the Court also ruled that the States of California and Washington were entitled under the Federal Constitution to deny Japanese the rights to own or lease land. A further step embittering relations took place in 1924 when the United States Congress smashed the 'Gentleman's Agreement' that had underpinned Japanese-American relations since 1907, and passed an Exclusion Act which barred Asiatics, including Japanese, from any hope of being accepted as immigrants. About the same time Australia became notorious for a White Australia Policy. Canadian hostility against Japanese immigration was no less vocal. These developments, more than any others, convinced the Japanese that, whether they wished it or not, the great world of contemporary history insisted that they were to be Asian; Japan would take them at their word and would seize the Asian leadership.

Japan, having been disowned by its partner among the Great Powers, was thereafter condemned to a restless search for an ally which would offer her the same security as Britain had done. Although Japan persisted in efforts to revive Anglo-Saxon goodwill towards Japan, it was an exercise in futility. Many Japanese continued to believe that cooperation with China was not only possible but offered East Asia's ancient civilizations their only hope for survival against the onslaught of western wealth and technology. Japanese efforts to supervise the recovery of China had been thwarted by China's unwillingness to cooperate and by the intervention of other Powers. Japan was induced to retreat. It was still lacking in self-confidence. It had not yet developed the willingness to outrage the rest of the world. But the stage was being set for the more determined confrontation from which Japan would not back down so easily. The Chinese would be goaded into stubborn effort to defend their revolution and the recovery of their vital power. Japan would be lured by the attractions of a dangerous new ally in the West which some factions would calculate would give Japan the security which its Government and people had sought. Others imagined that an alliance with Russia offered Japan better protection than no alliance at all. Japanese decision-makers indeed responded to this impulse, overcame their animosity towards the Soviet Union sufficiently to recognize the régime in 1925, and sought to explore opportunities for closer economic relations. But communist agitation within Japan, Korea, Manchuria and China made the Japanese shy away from more intimate political connections with Russia. As Japan cast around during the first decade after the Great War, its neuroses of alarm and resentment deepened and became always more dangerous. Far more was at stake than a struggle for the mastery of China, but nevertheless in a sense it was true that all the Powers concerned would drift in the end into a war that came from the complications arising out of this fatal competition.

CHAPTER 3
The Japan Which Struck

AT the start of hostilities between two countries it is customary to take stock of their rival strength. Japan, both in its own eyes and in the eyes of the rest of the world, began the conflict, of which the first phase opened in 1931, with overwhelming advantages. Most eye-witnesses to the initial clash would have been astonished if they had had a glimpse of what it would eventually grow into. It was expected that Japan would settle the quarrel in a small-scale colonial war, such as the world had been accustomed to in the recent past.

Japan had reason for its confidence. It was a modern state, recognizably like the states of the western world. It had a formal constitution like a western country. It was indeed a copy of these, and it included such institutions as a constitutional monarchy, a cabinet, a civil service, and two houses of parliament with rather more than consultative powers. It had, moreover, a modern industrial structure. Its achievements in making a success of a western-style economic system is one of the wonders of East Asian history, the more remarkable because the traditions of Japan had appeared to tell against commercial success. The ethos of Japan remained unbusinesslike. There was, fairly widespread, a deep contempt for money. But this had not prevented the Japanese from setting money to do its work.

The state machinery was strong. Its administration, even if there was much corruption, was reasonably well organized. Though Japanese institutions were apt to strike the westerner as being odd and haphazard in the way they were run, they produced the result intended: they had the secret of effectiveness.

The national unity, which had been so conspicuous in the war with Russia nearly three decades earlier, had not been undermined as Japan entered on a more sophisticated life in the 1930s. Its people, in spite of an increase in wealth, continued to be easily regimented. The success of the Government in doing this was due to the extraordinary competence and ubiquitousness of the police, which was one of the traditional features of administration in Japan. For centuries the police had been harrying the Japanese people. One of the victims of modern extremism was the curious, nonconformist cults of Japanese Buddhism. The police seemed to be infuriated by their existence, and persecuted them severely.

Though there were the beginnings of social unrest and of a Communist Party, this was as yet scarcely reflected in Japan's political life. Dangerous ways of thought were appearing among students – in themselves a surprisingly large class – and there was a dedicated, but very small and ineffective left-wing movement: but though this was enough to give nightmares to the police, and to the Army which played a special part in keeping the morale of the nation untainted, they could console themselves that they were dealing with an eccentricity rather than a serious threat.

Though Japanese is an exceptionally difficult language to learn, the population was almost entirely literate. Knowledge, especially technical knowledge, was advanced. The newly literate populace, which was so different from other populaces in Asia, did not band against the Government. Indeed, the Japanese people, though hardy and enterprising, remained extraordinarily docile to govern. They had an ancient tradition of turbulence, upheaval, and a readiness to make civil war: but these had become only a distant memory. Their martial quality had been mobilized, exclusively and entirely, in the national interest, and was embodied in the Japanese Army.

For the result of the war, much would naturally depend on the capability of the Army. The Japanese Army had had a various history, and had passed through changes since the days of the Meiji Restoration, during which it had been organized. In the 1930s it was a National Army, the product of universal military service. But though this was its origin, it stood apart from the nation in a rather sinister way.

The young men of the Army, when called to the colours, were trained in a manner which was calculated to ensure their obedience, to brutalize them, to make them unlikely to act like the rest of the Japanese people. They became docile instruments of the officer corps. Extraordinary stories leaked out of the barbarity of the system of military training. The Japanese Army was not the nation in arms – since it rejected much in Japanese life which might have made it more capable of self-control in the aftermath of battle – but it was the Japanese peasantry in arms. Such a force was dangerous because it was liable to be swayed by terrible spasms of inane and savage barbarism. The rigid discipline under which it was kept in Japan was suddenly set aside when it found itself under foreign skies and in different surroundings. The woes of the Asian continent wherever the Japanese soldier was to tread were to be proof of this.

The corps of professional officers, the centre of this military system, was drawn from the entire nation and, at least in theory, was not limited to certain parts of the country or certain social classes. In practice, the vast majority of soldiers sprang from rural peasant stock. In a sense most never left behind the poverty and deprivation of their backgrounds, living a Spartan existence throughout their years of service. Yet it did offer a unique escape from the rigid stratification of Japanese society outside. Boys who chose the Army as their career joined at the age of fourteen or upon completion of their compulsory primary education. Few would have been able to afford further schooling but for the Army. There they were trained in the numerous military schools. The most capable of them were selected through competitive examinations as officer candidates at the Japanese Military Academy. After some experience as junior officers, the brightest attended the Army War College and then graduated into the true élite of the Army as staff officers. With factionalism playing its peculiar part in Japanese affairs, their subsequent careers depended on the clique in the Army to which they attached themselves (a matter often predetermined by the geographical regions from which they originated).

Soldiers followed a certain conventional pattern in their lives, with somewhat different aims, interests and ethics from those of the majority of the Japanese people. They were less liable to be swayed by ordinarily changing ideas because their education had been distorted. The common soldier had no human rights and was subject to incessant oppression, brutality and cruelty from his superiors. Nevertheless, his was a better lot and an incalculably more interesting life than that of his family back home, where the struggle for daily existence made military life far more of an attraction or matter of the family's economic survival than it was for urban youth. The better sort of officers, having come mainly from much the same background or from military families, had a deep-felt sympathy for the plight of their men and an intimate knowledge of the conditions of privation which they had left behind. Likewise, conservative country folk who deplored the percolation of western influences into the lives of the young and into the policies of their Government, looked to the Army for reinstatement of the values of old Japan. At any rate, it was widely appreciated that the strength of the Army lay in the strength of the peasantry, in the strength of equal opportunity for advancement through ability, and in the strength (and weaknesses) of an army educational system that had to carry an enormous burden further and wider than in other advanced countries. From thence there was a natural tendency for the War Ministry and for the Army's powerful Inspectorate-General of Military Education to interest themselves in the indoctrination of youth throughout the nation – and in what Allied post-war prosecutors later termed 'the preparation of public opinion for war'.

The Japanese educational system, founded on liberal principles, became a tool for ultra-nationalist and militaristic indoctrination at about the time of the First World War. This was possible only because more than 90 per cent of the population had achieved literacy by the turn of the century, a lasting tribute to the Meiji educational system. Military training was made compulsory in schools, and by 1925 military officers were assigned to all middle and upper schools and to universities. Arrangements were made for local military education centres to cater for the majority of the populace who could not afford to continue their education past the minimum of primary school. Thus by the end of the so-called liberal decade of the twenties, an effective system for national indoctrination had been implanted and was in use.

This was particularly obnoxious because of the peculiar quality of Japanese militarism. This derived from the fact that, in traditional Japan, the use of arms had been a monopoly of a military caste called the *Samurai*. Officially the Samurai had been brought to an end soon after the Meiji Restoration. Nevertheless, the tradition which animated these professional soldiers continued to prevail in the modern Army, and became dominant in the period of national assertiveness which prevailed in the thirties. By and large, the Japanese Army officers of the professional, thorough-going kind guided themselves by a code of ethics called Bushidō, the Way of the Warrior. Bushidō prescribed the life of the soldier at all points. It proclaimed that his ultimate fate was to serve his master, and as the Imperial Institution had divine status, the valiant death of a soldier in the service of his Emperor was a kind of sublime super-nova of his bodily existence in which the fulfilment of perfect service was consubstantial with eternal righteousness and truth.

Bushidō laid down everything that was possible in the relation of one Samurai with another, the mutual obligations of paternalistic absolute lords and the total obedience of loyal knights. That same mantle of benevolence was to protect the weak and vanquished, and there was great concern that unfortunates and the wayward should be restored to paths of righteousness appropriate to their proper status. This should not be confused with tolerance, forbearance or respect for human rights. These liberal values were poles apart. Harshness, endurance, the carrying out ruthlessly of impossible orders, vengeance and the duty in circumstances of disgrace to commit *seppaku* – more vulgarly known as *hara-kiri* (self-slaughter by a peculiarly courageous and painful method of dis-embowelment) – were its subjects: it is helpful to appreciate that the Japanese regarded neither the heart nor the intellect but the bowel as the seat of the soul. The Way of the Warrior demanded intense self-control and preparation, a process which alone permitted the fusion of a spiritual ideal with human flesh and will-power to produce a mystical energy offered in the service of one's lord. It did not glorify unnecessary violence or mayhem but comprehended that the victims of either could find transcendence in death. Leadership, on the other hand, was both an instrument and function of the force of the code, produced out of an iron discipline and the effusion of a kind of tyrannical, overbearing love that did not admit of the vulnerability of the warrior. Not surprisingly, such esoteric teachings were corrupted and completely failed to meet the challenges of universal conscription and Total War against alien foes in the modern world.

Bushidō was a deeply fatalistic cult. Its parallels are perhaps to be found in old German sagas with their compounds of horror and doom, honour and absolutism. It is significant that the revival of the typical Bushidō outlook was associated with a type of politics such as that which prevailed amid the Nazis. The gloom and grimness of this tradition of Japanese militarism were symbolized in the deliberate drabness of the Japanese uniform. The Army was taut but without glitter. Alone among military Powers, Japan exhibited no military panache. Bushidō painted the heroic life as one which excluded frailty and which was directed to perfect service and success. This produced an 'attack spirit' which led to recklessness in rushing into conflict and to savagery in battle and afterwards. Surrender was punishable by death, and it was a disgrace to be taken prisoner alive. Nevertheless, most internecine Japanese civil wars – and they had been interminable until the twentieth century – had ended in a negotiated capitulation by the vanquished to the victor. It was the demonstration of superior force which imposed its own logic; it was not mass slaughter. Honour, then, was preserved on both sides. The reader may wish to recall these facts when contemplating the justifications commonly put forward for the use of atomic bombs at Hiroshima and Nagasaki in 1945.

Bushidō was a remarkably compelling code, abhorrent although aspects of it are when judged in terms of western values. It differed but was not incompatible with the fabric of mainstream Japanese culture. Honour, self-respect, the marriage of beauty and utility, and the avoidance of shame were of vital importance to Japanese in every walk of life, not merely ideals to which they paid little more than lip-service. Japanese traditionally loathe ostentation and regard egotistical self-advertisement as both despicable and unworthy: those who yield to such impulses incur scorn and ostracism. Simplicity and economy, on the other hand, are admired. Combining these factors, we begin to appreciate why Japanese militarism seems so curiously anonymous at a distance. It did not carry any 'cult of personality', as did most European and American brands of militarism. A consequence was that Japanese generals, interesting personalities though many of them were upon closer acquaintance, seldom attracted public adulation or popular glorification. The national heart neither venerated nor reviled them for their deeds. The public might feel pride, respect or satisfaction but rarely affection for them. Only within individual military units did loyalty, devotion and charisma find full expression – with the result that they often became the fiefdoms of gifted commanders.

The tragedy of Japan happened in dangerous ideas becoming so influential when, in the twentieth century, Japan possessed the power to make itself so formidable internationally. Japan's modern military machine was administered by men who took as serious guides to conduct a rigid social and ethical tradition quite out of date and barbaric. Of course, not all the officer corps lived by this code. Some were as civilized as the most progressive civilians – or as susceptible to blandishment and self-gratification. Many Japanese regarded the ideas of the Samurai as absurd, medieval, deeply irrational, frightening and frightful. It was not uncommon to regard the cult of Bushidō (if not the Samurai caste) as a plague in Japanese civilization which must be eradicated. But the fact that it was really an eccentricity made Japanese militarism the more difficult to keep under control, and it attached itself easily to wild and irresponsible aims.

Japan was strengthened for war by a peculiar psychology of its people: so strange and well-marked that the study of its evolution has become one of the standard exercises of East Asian history. This psychology proceeded from certain moral conflicts which the Japanese, almost to a man, accepted as axiomatic. A Japanese longs, before all other things, for a world organized on the principles of harmony. Harmony is only to be achieved when everyone fills his predestined place, and asks for himself neither too much honour, dignities and awards, nor too little. It is an outlook curiously like that of the European Middle Ages, at least in its theory. It is worship of 'degree, priority and place'. Above all, it is an outlook which detests anarchy. The simple fact which the Anglo-American democracies found hard to understand was the horror which the Japanese felt at an individual or group which had a clear conception of its own interests, as distinct and separate from those of the community, and which set out to realize them. In fact, that very idea was all but incomprehensible.

The state, to a Japanese, was itself a moral entity. The notion of *Kokutai*, the national essence or polity, is complicated but embraces absolute righteousness, truth and beauty – in short, all national virtue. It was inseparable from the Emperor-system. Private interests had no legitimacy except in the context of Kokutai. On the other hand, this also ensured that private interests, where they did exist, intruded into national concerns. Japanese ultra-nationalism, although it did not admit of private interests, derived its authority from an appeal to the internal moral fortitude of each individual and his inseparable identification with the national virtue. Resting upon a consensus of devotion to the Emperor and to the Kokutai, therefore, ultra-nationalism escaped the censorship of common sense in society as a whole. Little by little, this insane part of Japan succeeded in becoming dominant.

There was no sudden or diabolical transition from enlightenment to despotism. It is tempting to suggest that military, archaic Japan took captive twentieth-century, ingenious, civilian Japan, and swept it along towards the challenge to other civilizations of the world, which was the principal history of Japan in this time. Many historians have characterized the 1920s as liberal and democratic, and have condemned the thirties as a period of unmitigated terror and depravity. But the elements of modernity and reaction continued to exist side by side as they always had done; first one, then the other, moving back and forth into prominence. The images conjured up by Hugh Byas in a brilliant wartime book, *Government by Assassination*, are graphic, helpful and have proved durable, but recent investigators have struck a better balance between those who felt that only the *Sturm und Drang* of dark terror and brutality held centre-stage in Japan during the thirties and those, principally in Japan, who have been swayed by the romantic apologists of the period.

It is true that the period did produce violent domestic outbursts which appeared to threaten the social order of Japan. Assassination attempts cut down no fewer than three Prime Ministers and a host of other prominent officials and public figures. A number of revolutionary plots were exposed or briefly erupted into murder, melodrama and farce, but the scope of violence was strictly confined both by those who perpetrated such deeds and by those who apprehended them. Every one of the attempted *coups d'état* failed to achieve its ends. The plans of the conspirators, indeed, are remarkable not only for their boldness but for their deficiency in anticipating the consequences which would follow either from success or failure. They had not worked out detailed political programmes for change. They simply seem to have felt that the violence of their insurgency would itself provide an all-compelling logic for change to which the nation would respond satisfactorily.

The culprits, when caught, were regarded as misguided patriots, not traitors. It was recognized that they generally sought no personal gain, and indeed their heroic idealism and self-sacrifice attracted genuine public sympathy if not support. They were handled gingerly by the authorities. Some escaped punishment altogether, a few subsequently rose to higher command within the armed services, and others received light penal sentences. Yet all of the assassins and most of the other principals appear to have been dealt with severely by the courts, and some were executed. It is, perhaps, revealing that the greatest censure was reserved for those who had harmed the innocent, failed to act in a respectful manner towards victims and bystanders alike, or refused to do the decent thing by committing suicide afterwards. In these matters such terrorists had transgressed the code of Bushidō.

The Japanese nation was shaken by the terrorist crimes, some of which were appallingly bloody, but there was neither mass intimidation nor any sign of panic by people in authority. Paranoia did not affect the workings of the state, and attempts were made to accommodate or re-absorb rebels who atoned – although not necessarily the causes they espoused – within the political system. The broad political objectives of the terrorists were recognized as fundamentally revolutionary, not reformist. Yet there was no mass murder, no official or secret campaign of counter-terror mounted by the organs of the state, no private civil war between rival factions, no 'outlaw' category of 'non-persons', no exile system. The effect of the disorders was less than is commonly supposed.

A democratic state has the right to defend itself: whether it has the right to commit suicide is a question which arises from the history of Japan as well as that of Germany in the twentieth century. The Japanese Diet passed a peace preservation law in 1925. This was designed to combat the spread of communism, anarchism and other subversive doctrines after the First World War. The law attracted strong political support from the major parties and evidently met with a good deal of public satisfaction. A repressive 'Thought Police', the *Tokubetsu Kōtō Keisatsu*, or Special Higher Police, was created to enforce the law. It is tempting to regard such Orwellian developments as proof of tyranny. Yet these measures were the creation of a widely admired and democratic system, not the trappings of a police state. Later, it is true, the military gendarmerie (*Kenpeitai*) played an increasingly important role towards the same end. Both of these police forces struck terror into the hearts of their enemies and were not averse to employing beatings and other forms of torture. Yet the remarkable fact is that the Japanese always preferred to rely upon conversion (*tenkō*) rather than penal sanctions. They had inquisitors but no fiery *auto-da-fé*. Although tens of thousands of people were arrested on suspicion of harbouring or promoting 'improper thoughts' between 1925 and 1945, only one Japanese was executed for such crimes (late in the Pacific War). Westerners in Japan were terrified by ugly street demonstrations against them, which often were known to have been deliberately incited by the police, yet not one foreigner was killed during these incidents. Japanese communists were jailed, but, even during the most militaristic period, liberals and western-style internationalists suffered no more than denunciation and censorship. The mainstream political parties themselves went into eclipse from the middle of the 1930s, but the civil and court bureaucracies and their institutions remained in place and were not simply replaced by military absolutism or fascism.

The Japanese also had a sense of being under an immense obligation, which any amount of altruistic behaviour could never requite, to their family predecessors, to the Japanese Emperor as embodying the Japanese state, and to the Government of the day for making life tolerable. It was possible for a Japanese Government to make extreme drafts upon this sense of obligation, and a diffused sense of responsibility in general among its people, and to do so almost without limit.

In organization for war, the Japanese system was the stronger because of the Emperor-system with which the whole was covered. Though in actual fact the Emperor had, or at least exercised, little political power, as a figure-head he was of the utmost possible importance. The Emperor, as an institution, has now undergone change, probably permanent. It is true that the Emperor survived the war; but he was to lose, by contact with the realities of the modern world, so much of the mystique which at this period continued to surround the office that today some careful inquiry is necessary to recapture it. The Japanese Emperor is no longer regarded as a divine person. But in the 1930s it was widely accepted as axiomatic that he was of different stuff from ordinary humanity.

Immensely awe-inspiring, extremely sacred, the incarnation of all that was meant by the Japanese national spirit, remote, mysterious, never criticized in press or parliament – the Emperor Hirohito obviously possessed qualities which made him the ideal mascot for war. In fact the role of the Japanese Emperor, at least in its remoter origin, was as much sacerdotal and magical as it was governmental. It is significant that the Japanese word meaning to observe a religious rite is radically connected with the word meaning government. Simply to dwell in the same country as the Emperor conferred felicity, and laid on his subjects a readiness to endure sacrifice which recognized no limit.

The court of the Japanese Emperor was not notably military in its atmosphere. He existed as a man, as well as an idea, and it was hard for

him to live up to the position required of him by the theorists of the
Japanese state. It was strange to find that the Emperor Hirohito was a
mild-mannered, courteous prince, and that he lived in a court which was a
museum of venerated or picturesque objects. It was rather like the
entourage of a British monarch. It was decorous and somewhat dull: but
it was colourful – and was much more strongly marked by fragile aestheticism than is ordinary life in Japan. This was not really surprising,
because, in the long history of the Japanese monarchy, it had seldom been
associated with military leadership. Though in theory the Japanese
monarch was the supreme commander, in military matters as in civilian,
only the Emperor Meiji had taken this at all seriously. His successors,
including Hirohito, reverted easily to the more ancient attitude. Emperor
Hirohito was head of the state, he received reports from ministers, and
advised but played a strictly constitutional part. He did not sully the
office with politics. The court class clearly did not want war.

A basic cause of all the misfortunes in East Asian politics was the
fundamentally precarious state of the Japanese economy. Japan had
built up, especially during this century, an impressive industry, but was
at bottom a poor country. It lacked raw materials. Its chief asset was
its manpower, and it owed its economic advance to the organization of
this. Its people were strenuous, punctual, persevering, disciplined, adapt-
able: out of these talents, combined with a leadership capable of
putting these to use, there was constructed one of the most thriving
economies of the world. Japan threw itself with zest into imitating the
western countries.

Starting in the early days of the Meiji Restoration, Japan built up its
industry, and the rest of its economy, systematically. Its constant impediment was that it had to build bricks without straw. But it succeeded.
The result was that the Japanese economy followed a particular pattern.
It imported almost all the raw materials for industrial use: iron, the rare
metals, coal, oil and, in the early days, machinery; it exported many of
the products of industry. The raw materials were sent to Japan, and the
Japanese people, organized in a great productive machine, processed these
and marketed the product. It lived thus upon the proceeds of being the
workshop of the East, but one to which the raw materials were delivered
from abroad, and one which was kept going by orders from abroad. This
was the basic pattern which shone through, although of course much in
the economy was exceptional to the system.

The broad lines of the Japanese economy were thus very similar to
those of the British economy in Europe. There were differences: Japan

never allowed its agriculture to become so small a part of the economy as did Britain when Britain concentrated on being the workshop of the world. Japan, unlike Britain, never took the decisive step towards *laissez-faire*, and never abandoned the direction of its economic destinies to blind economic laws. It never, to the same extent, was confident, as Britain was at the time, that the economic machine, if left to itself, would automatically right itself, whatever the predicaments to which it was exposed by adverse political circumstance. The Japanese Government had constantly in mind that Japan's prosperity was at the mercy of other countries allowing it unimpeded access to raw materials, and unimpeded access to markets for the sale of its products; and it sought, by countless means, to remedy this. Japan, like Britain and most other countries at the present time, had a continual anxiety from its balance of payments. It lived dangerously. It knew that it must export or die.

Its great industrial machine, and along with this, the remarkable nexus of mercantile institutions which it built up, all depended on the inward flow of raw materials, and on being able to find a foreign market for the finished products. If ever this process was interrupted, or seriously dislocated, Japan would be halted, its national talents would be wasted, its prosperity disappear, its nakedness be exposed.

Such a restless, dynamic society, explosive and always ready to seek new opportunities, uneasily aware of the narrow conditions for its survival, was not easy to fit into the world around it. It was constantly producing new situations: its nature, and its indispensable quality, was to be at home in constant vicissitudes. Though, as a military empire, Japan stood for a certain stability, it was really, though it would have denied this, the force making for constant instability in East Asia.

Arrogant although Japanese seemed to foreigners, there was nothing acutely xenophobic about either Bushidō or the civil structures of Japan. Quite the contrary. Nevertheless, these institutions could not fail to be affected by the intense international pressures upon Japan. Even the anti-foreignism of the Tokugawa period was no less adopted as an expedient than the borrowing of western technology, education and institutions which prevailed in Japan after the Meiji Restoration. In each case, these were responses to what were perceived as threats from outside (and who is to say that they were disproportionate to the degree of danger). In reacting against these alien threats, the Samurai tradition became subverted into a pessimistic militarism that was an amalgam of reactionary national politics and an inherent belief in the spiritual dignity of the Japanese race and cultural traditions. It found itself a rival to the civil apparatus of a modern state in seeking to protect and act on behalf of the Imperial System.

The civilian bureaucracy and the economic infrastructure of Japan were not consumed by the coercive forces and atavistic spiritualism of militarism. They continued to operate side by side, each harnessed and constrained by one another. Policy did not evolve from tyranny. It evolved from a consensus of opinion, part of Japan's historical sense of community, which took into account pressures for radical action, the perils of insubordination and *faits accomplis*. The need and desire to achieve an orderly consensus were profoundly felt by the public at large and by all decision-makers in particular. Their problem was that efforts to compromise with extremists could not produce policies which any external observer would regard as 'moderate'. Astonishing although it may seem, Japan did remain a land of law and order throughout the years leading up to the Pacific War. Nevertheless, the processes of cause and effect in international relations guaranteed that Japanese policies tended progressively to become more and more outrageous. When the democratic institutions of Japan finally failed, it came about neither as a concession to indigenous terrorism nor even to institutionalized military indoctrination and subversion: it came about as a direct response to the emergency of war.

As the twentieth century proceeded, it became a fixed idea in Japan that the country was in great peril, and the Japanese felt their economy to be ever more insecure. They had had the experience of entrusting themselves to be carried forward by the great expansion of world trade, and had been taught by successive trade cycles to fear disaster. The grave effect of the world depression on Japan after 1929 strengthened the case of the Army for finding a military solution to economic dangers. Japanese exports were halved within the space of two years. While industrial wages declined by nearly a third, rural incomes dropped by two thirds. The price of raw silk fell by 65 per cent within a year of the Wall Street crash. This deprived the agricultural class of its second main source of income and caused widespread distress in the countryside. As banks foreclosed on the small farms and businesses in rural areas, the Army, with its intimate connection with the Japanese peasantry, was greatly concerned. The younger Army officers were frequently drawn from the class of small landowners and viewed affairs accordingly. Big business, banking interests and the new political order of post-war Japan were blamed for their avarice, for their over-dependence upon foreign nations, and for the calamitous effects of this reversal in the country's fortunes. Steps were taken by the nation's civilian leadership which headed Japan back towards economic recovery more rapidly than any of her trading partners: given the nation's paucity of national resources, this was a considerable achievement.

Nevertheless, ideas of expansion through foreign conquest were gaining in popularity. Right-wing propagandists found a sympathetic response in meetings of patriotic groups, veterans' associations, chambers of commerce, farmers and even in the judiciary. In an early sign indicative of this change of mood, a former Chief Justice of the Supreme Court, Baron Hiranuma Kiichirō, who had served as a Minister of Justice shortly after the Washington Conference, founded one of the most powerful of all the extreme right-wing pressure groups, the *Kokuhonsha*, or National Foundation Society, as early as 1924, serving as its President between 1926 and 1936 (during the whole of which time he held office as Vice-President of the Privy Council): this particular society was dissolved when he became President of the Privy Council in 1936. Eventually he went on to become Prime Minister of Japan in 1939. Another example was Ōkawa Shūmei, one of the most notorious of all the ultra-nationalist propagandists, an intellectual who had specialized in Marxism and Indian philosophy after graduating from Tokyo Imperial University. Later, he headed the South Manchurian Railway Company's influential East Asia Economic Research Bureau, then became a professor with particular expertise in colonial economic enterprises. He was a money-spinning rabble-rouser. Many of his political books and pamphlets today might appear to be the ravings of a lunatic, but they were taken seriously enough by many of his countrymen at the time. He became one of the arch-terrorists of the thirties, and his association with other conspiratorial figures of the day runs like a thread through the decades. One cannot escape the fact that there was a great deal of continuity in these affairs. It was not simply a question of an old guard giving way to brash new men who were more inclined than their elders to seek violent solutions. Not surprisingly, however, there was an answering response from the Army, where ideas of expansion through foreign conquest began to be heard once again, not now primarily from the generals but from the young officers. The militaristic dragons within Japan had awakened from their slumbers.

If Japan were able to conquer the adjacent territory from which raw materials could be produced – such as Manchuria – and if it should obtain military control of some of the markets for buying Japanese exports, it could breathe at peace. It could have the assurance of maintaining its industrial greatness, of safeguarding the livelihood of the countryside and of solving problems of over-population. The peace, prosperity and progress of all Asia, as well as Japan itself, depended on this consummation. The Japanese military were able to argue that they supported not only a narrow national cause, but that they were crusaders for the whole of Asia. The well-being of the entire continent depended on the safeguarding of the Japanese economy. Only the western countries could think it an advantage that the Japanese talent should be thwarted.

This was the frame of mind behind the Japanese attempt to gain absolute control of China, and later, of South-East Asia. The Japanese believed themselves to be economically propelled. This does not mean that the war was an economic necessity, or that the Japanese soldiers who made it were economic puppets. But they made Japan's economic problems the justification of their military action, and, not insincerely, supposed themselves driven on by economic forces which compelled them to act as they did.

The Army's emergent views on economics became a matter of concern to the large mercantile institutions which dominated the economy of the country. These institutions, with plenty of money to spare, found that, in the condition of Japanese politics of the day, it was prudent to buy support wherever possible – not only from politicians in the Diet, but from soldiers and from the cliques involved in canvassing the plans of the Army. Whether this was *real* corruption or should be seen as merely betokening the close harmony desired by commerce, the fighting services and government in Japan is a point where many Japanese observers feel westerners misinterpret Japan. It was certainly less crude than the relationship between, say, American big business and government has tended to be. Undoubtedly the degree of corruption can easily be exaggerated: there were many honest senior Army officers, just as there were many incorruptible Cabinet Ministers, bureaucrats and Diet members. But the links between the Army, with its economic fixation, and the opportunist commercial interests, were well-established, widely ramified, and liable to influence Japan's politics in an irregular manner.

The gathering public discontent, which is inevitable in a difficult economic situation, expressed itself in growing criticism of the established organs of government, and of the regular methods of doing public business. The forces of radicalism became more insistent, and membership of extremist societies began to expand alarmingly. The famous 'Shidehara Diplomacy' of the later half of the 1920s had been little more than a re-articulation of the principles set forth in the Nine Power Treaty of Washington. But the post-war attitude of appeasement adopted by the Western Powers – of spinning out for as long as possible their period of privilege while eventually coming to terms with the changed world –

seemed hardly comprehensible in Japan. The harsh facts of the economic depression supplied the country with arguments for a 'forward policy' of expansionism.

In the late twenties a document called the Tanaka Memorial was in fairly wide circulation in Tokyo. It was a forgery, published by the Chinese in 1927, but like any successful forgery it had credibility. Baron Tanaka Giichi had served as War Minister at the time of the Washington Conference and more recently at the end of 1923. He became leader of one of the two main political parties of Japan in 1925 and, after a banking crisis and financial scandal in 1927 lost a rival three-party coalition a general election, he took office both as Prime Minister and Foreign Minister of Japan until July 1929. The document with which his name will always be associated purported to be a memorandum to the Throne presented by General Tanaka shortly after he became Prime Minister, and it outlined a plan to take military possession of all North China. It also proclaimed that 'In the future if we want to control China, our primary aim must be to crush the United States, just as in the past we had to fight in the Russo-Japanese War. But in order to conquer China, we must first conquer Manchuria and Mongolia. In order to conquer Europe and Asia, Japan must conquer China, and in order to conquer the world, we must first conquer Europe and Asia.' The document went on to declare that Japan must throw off the shackles of the Nine Power Treaty. Under the pretext of trade and commerce, the Japanese would spread their influence from Manchuria and Mongolia into the remainder of China. 'Armed by the rights already secured, we shall seize the resources all over the country. Having China's entire resources at our disposal, we shall proceed to conquer India, the Archipelago, Asia Minor, Central Asia and even Europe. But to get control of Manchuria and Mongolia is the first step if the Yamato race wishes to distinguish itself in Continental Asia.' What a mad adventure!

In truth, however, the 'Positive Policy' adopted by Baron Tanaka's Government bore very little relation to the so-called 'Memorial'. It was characterized by a somewhat bellicose style of 'military diplomacy', but it differed little in practice from the objectives pursued by Baron Shidehara and other 'moderates'. It did not include any blueprint for aggression. In fact, Tanaka did no more than deflect a military advance northwards by Kuomintang troops, who, preceded by a vanguard of propaganda agents, were seeking to crush the war-lords of North China and so round off China's political and administrative reunification. The result was an experience which boded ill for the future.

Within a year of coming to office, Prime Minister Tanaka had reached an informal understanding with Chiang Kai-shek which appeared to guarantee an acceptable standard of protection for Japanese residents in North China and scrupulous respect for Japanese rights in Manchuria. Although the Chinese were in a belligerent and confident mood, making no secret of their intention to re-establish a tight control over North China, they had their hands full in conducting their own private war: the Japanese position in Manchuria did not seem imperilled. Tanaka, who relied heavily upon Japanese financiers and industrialists to preserve himself and his party in power, was keenly aware that they strongly opposed any measures that would harm Japanese trade with China. The Army General Staff, for reasons of caution, also opposed any intervention in China. Thus Tanaka and the Army were inclined to feel that Chiang Kai-shek and his moderates ought to be given the opportunity to demonstrate that they could indeed be relied upon to protect Japanese residents and their interests in North China. This, it was hoped, would create stronger bonds of mutual trust and goodwill. Although there were dissenting voices on the sidelines, the Governments of both nations, in short, wished to avoid any conflict.

The War Ministry, unwisely, favoured intervention, and there was foolhardy political pressure upon the Cabinet from its party supporters in the Diet, who reminded the Government of its election promises to extend any protection necessary to ensure the safety of Japanese residents in China during time of trouble. Finally, reluctantly, the Japanese Government sent out an expeditionary force to Shantung and appear to have intended to withdraw it as soon as it had served its purpose by demonstrating that the Japanese were sincere in their determination to protect Japanese citizens in China. There was no intention of using this force in large-scale combat operations. It was simply a token force, and in fact its size made it something of a hostage to the well-disciplined armies which China then had so close at hand. It was a mistake. As that ancient seer Sun Tzu had warned, 'If not in the interests of the state, do not act. If you cannot succeed, do not use troops. If you are not in danger, do not fight.'

Unfortunately, the Commander of the Japanese division which landed in Shantung failed to resist the temptation to exceed his instructions. Seeking glory for himself – or more charitably for his Army – he proceeded to enter Tsinan, the provincial capital of Shantung, where there were more than two thousand Japanese residents. At the same time, a Kuomintang force also entered the city, possibly in ignorance or defiance of Chiang Kai-shek's orders. Both sides maintained strict military discipline and, their honour having been upheld, the Japanese decided to trust to the promises of the Chinese forces and began to withdraw. However, a purely accidental clash then occurred, frantic efforts by both sides to disengage proved unavailing, and fighting gradually spread across the city. A temporary ceasefire finally took hold, and the bulk of the Chinese forces departed, leaving only a comparatively small holding-force behind to maintain order. But the Japanese Commander and his staff felt that the inconclusive result of the fighting had undermined Japanese military prestige. The Army General Staff in Tokyo, abandoning their earlier caution, took the same view. Both were determined to resume fighting. The Japanese Cabinet caved in under the pressure, and reinforcements were ordered to the area. The result was that the Japanese gained the military victory they craved and won control of the city and surrounding countryside, subjecting the unfortunate Chinese inhabitants to a terrible occupation which lasted into the following year.

Japan's actions, of course, won for Chiang Kai-shek's forces a propaganda victory of incalculable value which far outweighed his temporary loss of territory. The whole episode, however, was designed as a limited operation and, though bungled from start to finish, it was defensive, not aggressive, in intent. It was certainly true that a rough and ready faction within the Japanese Kwantung Army, guardians of the South Manchurian Railway zone, wanted to seize North China once and for all. At that time, however, neither the Army General Staff in Tokyo nor the Japanese War Ministry supported such a scheme.

The events at Tsinan are especially significant for three reasons. It serves to remind us that the Japanese soldier yielded to no one in foolishness and was second to none in vanity. Although acting in defiance of superior orders has always been a characteristic of the Chinese way of warfare, this was the first occasion on which insubordination by Japanese troops deliberately invited war with a foreign Power. It was the first example of any Japanese Cabinet's acquiescence in pursuing a military adventure which it knew to be foolhardy. Although the Japanese commander at Tsinan was prematurely retired shortly after the Japanese forces were withdrawn, nothing constructive was done to prevent such a deplorable incident from happening again.

Always it was the northern part of the country which interested Japan. Though the nationalist ferment was happening in the south, and from South China came the impulses which were making China a revived power in world politics and a danger to countries such as Japan, even the forward bloc of Japanese imperialists was at first content that this should be left alone if Japan could cooperate with China in controlling the vast resources of manpower and potential economic wealth in the north. All the while, Japanese diplomacy and semi-secret organizations were busy spreading Japanese influence in China, softening up the Governors of the Chinese provinces where the Japanese sought to protect their own interests, and making propaganda to counter the effects of the nationalist ideas spreading from South China.

Many political groups in Japan, even those which declared themselves activated by generally liberal principles, found themselves in sympathy with the policy of containing Chinese nationalism. At least, few strongly resisted it; many, however, were inclined to regard a decisive countermove by Japan as being more of a dream than practical politics. But, as the country moved towards what was to be its great expansionist adventure in Asia, there began to appear sharp differences between the different sections of opinion. These were over the extent to which Japan should press China; over tactics, methods and timetables; over whether Japan should aim at direct conquest of Chinese territory, or some form of indirect control. As the critical period came nearer, the danger of collision with other Powers grew increasingly plain, and there was disagreement about how they should be confronted. In particular the Army and the Navy came into conflict. The Navy had favoured the old plan of advance behind the umbrella of good relations with the Anglo-Saxon naval Powers, and for long was cool or hostile towards Asiatic adventures. But the Navy fiercely resented what seemed to be the pusillanimity of the civilian Cabinets in tamely agreeing with the United States and Britain to Japanese naval limitation. It supported conspiratorial sorties which resorted to assassinations as a protest; and in this set the Army a fatal example to follow. The right wing in politics was also divided. There were differences between cautious conservatives and wild visionaries: between those who were carried away by a mythical view of Japanese history and those who interpreted the realities of the day with cool realism.

These differences became increasingly expressed in struggles between organized factions. In these, there took place the real conflict over the path which Japanese affairs were to take. In Japanese politics during these years the great decisions were not fought out in the formal seat of national debate, in the Japanese Parliament, but were made as the result of fierce factional dispute. There were factions within the Army, factions within the different sections of business, factions of the Navy.

Political life of this kind – a tussle between factions fought in a jungle fashion – proved very congenial to Japan. It was more comfortably Japanese than was the contest between political parties carried on according to rules in the Japanese Diet. It was natural for a Japanese to look to a faction and its fortunes for forwarding his interests. The faction was organized in such a way as to give free play to Japanese paternalism. In Japan there is a disposition to see all problems in terms of personal relationships rather than great political principles. This was more compatible with the breakdown of society into competing factions than it was with the struggle of political parties.

After the Russo-Japanese War, the Army had estimated that twenty-five divisions would be required to guarantee the Empire's safety. Subsequent events placed a severe strain upon the Army's strength, and during the First World War it had lagged well behind the military efficiency of other major Powers. After the Siberian Intervention, the critical number was reduced to twenty-one divisions. The comparative liberalism of the twenties led to a growing assertion of civilian dominance over military affairs. Financial considerations led the Government to cut back military spending from 49 per cent of its budget in 1921 to 28 per cent in 1927, a drastic reduction by any standards. Such a dramatic decline graphically mirrored the declining influence of the fighting services during the period. The Navy, of course, bore the brunt of much of the cut-back and accordingly the Washington Naval Treaty spared a large part of Japan's financial assets. At the same time, the Army perceived its need to effect a modernization programme to improve its efficiency in modern warfare. Four Army divisions were axed, and some of the money saved by demobilizing no fewer than 38,000 troops was spent on mechanization, Army aviation, an anti-aircraft regiment and specialist communications training establishments.

These developments, however, were accompanied by a shift in underlying assumptions, within the Army in particular, which ultimately played a crucial role in reversing the trend of civilian dominance. The War Ministry appreciated that the recent European War had shown that in any future hostilities, Japan would have to depend upon the 'total mobilization' of the nation's economic, political and military resources. In a sense there was a convergence in doctrine between the European and Japanese defence staffs. By 1929 the Japanese Army had worked out the apparatus and at least an outline of contingency plans required for coordination of all the civil, military and economic strength of the nation in an emergency. Although resisted by some Army and reservist die-hards, these arrangements and doctrines received widespread support within the Army, and in time they became an administrative basis for authoritarian control over the civil power during the period which lay to the future. Whether this should be regarded as a process achieved by usurpation rather than by mutual consent is a moot question to which we can supply no definitive answer. Nevertheless, it is clear that the civil power felt itself under compulsion to comply with what the Army demanded and that the Army seized almost every opportunity open to it to extend its grasp over the machinery of politics.

In 1931 Japan's conviction of its manifest destiny, its need for economic recovery, the restlessness and ambition of its political leaders, especially of the Army, converged. The year seemed to be the predestined time for action. The place for action was Manchuria.

Manchuria consisted of three provinces which were an integral part of China, but were not part of old China. It lay to the north of the Great Wall which had been built to shelter China from barbarian raids. It was the home of the Manchus, which had been the barbarian tribe which in 1664 had penetrated the defences, overthrown the Ming dynasty, and substituted for it the Manchu dynasty which had continued until 1911. Towards the end of its life, this dynasty nearly lost its original homeland to tzarist Russia. It had the mortification of proving powerless to protect it, and of seeing Japan wage the Russo-Japanese War to put an end to Russia's penetration of Manchuria instead of protecting it itself. As the result of that war, Japan did not annex Manchuria, but China did not recover its full and unconditional control of it, and Japan enjoyed special privileges.

The South Manchurian Railway Company, a corporation owned by the Japanese, had much authority and excessive control in the region. The railway company was operated by the Japanese in an expansive mood, and was used by them to build Japanese political power. It grew from being simply a railroad undertaking, operating the line which ran from north to south as the spine which held Manchuria together, into a general trading organization with vast interests in the development of the country: and it took on political functions which in turn led to Japan having to maintain a force for the defence of its employees.

In the civil war in China which followed the fall of the Manchu Empire in 1911, Manchuria suffered rather less than the rest of the country. A gifted common labourer turned bandit, named Chang Tso-lin, was able to build up power with which he took over the territories. He recognized that in these provinces he could survive only if he had the protection of the Japanese, or, at least, that he could not flourish against Japanese wishes. He chafed at Japanese interference, but he submitted, and governed Manchuria, in all that was essential, as a Japanese puppet. In his maturity, and perhaps in response to stirrings in China, he became restive.

He also had held a part of China south of the Great Wall. From there, in 1927, he was driven out by the expansion of the Kuomintang. The Chinese Nationalist challenge had come in that part of China where Japan had become dominant. In Manchuria, Japanese capital was making very substantial profits, and it had become the lodestar for Japanese economic expansion. Manchuria itself scarcely resembled the primitive and neglected hinterland which the Japanese and Russians had coveted since the beginning of the century. Japan was faced with the decision whether to acquiesce in China's re-establishment of its control – in which case the Chinese pronouncements and record left no reasonable doubt that they would terminate Japan's privileged position, at once or after a few years – or would stand and fight.

Chang Tso-lin himself was at first determined to resist. He tried to rally the people to join him in his struggle to exterminate the communist-tainted Nationalists. The Japanese Foreign Ministry wanted to warn both sides that Japan wished to remain neutral but must insist that no armed soldiers would be permitted to cross the Manchurian frontier. The 'Old Marshal' should be advised privately that it was time for him to retire (he was, in fact, only fifty-five years old). Prime Minister Tanaka, however, took the view that both peace and Japanese interests in Manchuria would be best protected by a continuation of Chang's rule north of the Great Wall.

In a crucial Japanese Cabinet debate, the Prime Minister's arguments prevailed. The Government decided to advise Chang to withdraw into Manchuria and issued instructions for the Kuomintang to be assured that Japan would forestall any attempt by Chang to interfere in China's affairs again. At the same time, Japanese military authorities were given to understand that they should turn something of a blind eye towards attempts by Chang's forces to smuggle their weapons back into Manchuria: they might well be necessary to contain any disruption by anti-Chang forces in Manchuria. This was to prove a fateful decision.

The Chinese Nationalists accepted the solution offered by the Japanese, but Chang, foolishly, for some months clung to a vain hope that he might be able to work out something better. In the end, perceiving the morale of his forces fast crumbling and that he could not block the Nationalist Armies from seizing control of North China, Chang agreed to the Japanese Government's plan and ordered his troops to retreat into Manchuria. The Japanese Government's plan appeared to be working.

In the course of his evacuation of his southern territory in 1928, the train in which Chang was travelling was blown up, and Chang Tso-lin perished. It was widely supposed at the time that the Japanese had found him unsatisfactory as the Japanese agent for resisting the Kuomintang and had murdered him. This does the Japanese Government less than justice. The truth was, if anything, more disturbing to the few who knew it. A small cabal of Kwantung Army officers, none above the rank of colonel, took strong exception to Prime Minister Tanaka's instructions that Chang's forces need not be disarmed at the frontier. They had plotted the assassination in hopes that it would provide an excuse to impose Japan's direct rule over the whole of Manchuria by force. Neither the Army General Staff nor the Kwantung Army's top brass knew anything about the plot in advance. Rather more surprisingly, even the hawk-eyed Kenpeitai surveillance officers appear to have been ignorant of it beforehand.

The murder of Chang Tso-lin failed to bring about the immediate military and political transformation which its authors desired, nor were they more successful in other bombings which they perpetrated afterwards in hopes of achieving the same ends: neither the Chinese nor the Japanese were prepared to embroil themselves in a wider conflict. The Japanese Government made an endeavour to discover who had been responsible for these outrages. A secret report was prepared by the Kenpeitai, named the guilty men and demanded their punishment. The Emperor wanted them severely punished, too, and went to unusual lengths to make his wishes known. The Government, embarrassed by the affair, also wanted to put the culprits on trial. The Army General Staff, however, took the view that full disclosure of the facts would tarnish the prestige of the Army to an unacceptable degree. Moreover, no one could doubt that the villains of the piece had been motivated by a sincere sense of patriotism. The Army connived with right-wing elements of Tanaka's own political party in the Imperial Diet while at the same time the Government came under fire from the Opposition benches. Powerless to take any constructive action, Tanaka and his Government were forced to resign. Accordingly, the Kenpeitai Report was suppressed, the insubordination went unpunished, and, officially at least, the facts surrounding Chang Tso-lin's death remained mysterious. Thus, although Tanaka showed considerable moral courage in striving to effect a genuine reconciliation with China during the last remaining months of his premiership, the Chang Tso-lin Incident became another of the stepping stones leading the Japanese Army into chronic instability and disorder: one conspiracy was following another, each designed to force the hand of successive governments and to present them with *faits accomplis*.

Chang Tso-lin was succeeded by his thirty-year-old son, Chang Hsueh-liang, a golf-playing, self-cured opium addict whose engaging personality disguised his huge will-power and immense intellect. He was much closer in touch with the mood of China south of the Wall than his father had been. To what extent was not realized by outside observers (although the Japanese Government was well aware of it): most people were astonished when he formally accepted the sovereignty of the Kuomintang over Manchuria. It was a recognition of the power of the national idea. Chang Hsueh-liang appeared to have admitted that the day of the war-lord was passing. Chinese nationalism had coerced him into accepting its claims to dispose of Manchuria as Chinese soil, and of himself as a Chinese subject. But the 'Young Marshal' also had to contend with attempts by the Japanese Government to dissuade him from siding with the Nationalists. Using their threats and fair words (knowing also that Japanese troops had murdered his father), he appeared to be tempted by the promises of Japanese emissaries, buying time to secure the best possible terms from the Kuomintang. He described his aims as 'autonomy and compromise'. He achieved both. But though Chang himself submitted to the pretensions of the Kuomintang when he had wrung as many concessions from them as his position allowed, the Japanese did not fail to notice that Chang's apparent acquiescence to his enemies firmly buttressed his personal authority in Manchuria (in much the same way as King John's feudal submission of England to the Pope was a supremely astute move calculated to confound enemies moving in for the kill).

It was a challenge to Japan, which successive Japanese Governments were obliged to resist but could not be seen to do so directly. Accordingly, the Tanaka Government, while still clinging to power but irreparably damaged by the shockwaves from Chang Tso-lin's murder, made no protest when the Kuomintang flag was unfurled in Manchuria. Yet the Japanese made it perfectly clear that they would brook neither interference nor disregard for their treaty rights in Manchuria, and in this determination the Japanese civil and military authorities were united but only in this.

The incoming Japanese Government, under the direction of Prime Minister Baron Hamaguchi Osachi and Foreign Minister Shidehara Kijūrō, altered the emphasis of Japan's foreign policy from one of bilateral Sino-Japanese rapprochement to a wider design of multi-lateral cooperation in which not only Japan and China but the Western Powers would work together to create new conditions for peace, development and prosperity in East Asia. This strategy, known to history as the 'Shidehara Policy', was given a boost by renewed civil strife in China during 1930, which led to a number of atrocities against foreign residents. For a short time the Western Powers turned away from their individual efforts to seek better relations with China and decided that to dispel the chronic disorder in their relations with China, the foreigners must sink their differences and endeavour to achieve solutions based upon their common interests.

The Army in its entirety mistrusted the Shidehara diplomacy in relation to China. As we shall see in the next chapter, such policies opened deep ideological chasms within the Japanese naval establishment when the Government accepted appalling risks to her security for the sake of an international accord on naval arms limitations. That kind of split and the grave constitutional crisis which it provoked did not occur in the Army. The Shidehara Policy was regarded as particularly woolly-minded and abhorrent by the men who fancied themselves as the well-honed cutting-edge of the Japanese Army, the Kwantung Army Headquarters staff, who evolved a final blueprint for the military conquest of the whole of Manchuria.

The Japanese War Ministry, too, made contingency plans to ensure that Manchuria did not slip from Japan's control. As the Tanaka Memorial had anticipated, the War Ministry's prime consideration was the importance of Manchuria in the event of any future war against the Soviet Union or, come to that, against the United States. There was nothing especially sinister in this: such ideas were no more than the common currency of Japanese ultra-nationalists in those days. The War Ministry conceived a three-step plan to deal with the Manchurian situation. In the first instance, it was not proposed to go beyond the Japanese Government's existing policy of insisting that the Manchurian authorities must have scrupulous regard for the holy writ of Japan's treaty rights and interests. If this policy failed, however, the next step would be to install a régime favourable to Japan. If this did not produce the desired result, then the ultimate solution would be the military conquest of Manchuria (and possibly its incorporation into the Japanese Empire). While this may seem to differ little from run-of-the-mill contingency plans routinely produced by the military planning staffs of other nations, even without benefit of hindsight this particular draft plan could be regarded as a fairly bald scheme for aggressive imperial expansion, for in every important aspect the War Ministry's plan conformed to the pattern of Japan's handling of the Korean problem years before. That is scarcely surprising. Japan had few other precedents to draw upon from her own direct experience, and many senior officials within the War Ministry and Army General Staff had been involved personally in the subjugation of Korea during their careers. Indeed, the two successive Chiefs of the Army General Staff during this period each came directly from previous postings as Commanders-in-Chief of the Korean Army. The likelihood of the military taking independent action unauthorized by the Cabinet developed almost into a certainty when the Army General Staff, having already established a broad measure of agreement with the War Ministry, sent a senior emissary to Manchuria in November 1930 for a meeting of minds with key staff officers of the Kwantung Army Headquarters.

By August 1931 the Army General Staff, the War Ministry and the Kwantung Army's strategists all knew more or less what they were prepared to do, but they spent the whole of that month seeking to agree on the details and timing of their plans for solving the Manchurian problem by direct military action. The War Ministry and Army General Staff in Tokyo wanted to delay matters until the spring or summer of 1932, not only to ensure that they would have time to complete all necessary preparations but also because it seemed prudent to await the inevitable downfall of the Wakatsuki Cabinet before embarking upon such an ambitious campaign, especially since the Opposition Party and the press were becoming increasingly demonstrative against the Shidehara Policy in relation to China and Manchuria. The Kwantung Army, however, or rather the small clique within it who were privy to the plot, were determined to take action in September 1931.

The general political blood pressure was rising fast. The Japanese were particularly bellicose following an outbreak of trouble at Wanpaoshan, west of Changchun (Hsinking), where antagonism between about 400 Korean immigrant farmers and local Chinese peasants bred violence for which the Chinese authorities refused to accept responsibility. This incident in turn produced a chain reaction of anti-Chinese riots within Korea itself, resulting in death and injury to several hundred Chinese. In a further incident that also took place during June 1931, a Japanese Army Intelligence officer, Captain Nakamura Shintarō, was murdered together with his three aides while on a secret foray into northern Manchuria: while the circumstances remained mysterious, it was widely conjectured during the summer that Chang Hsueh-liang's men were responsible (indeed, a regimental commander of Chang's Reclamation Army was arrested and charged with the offence a few days before the Mukden Incident which began the Manchurian Affair). The Wanpaoshan and Nakamura Incidents stiffened the resolve of those who were predisposed to seek a military solution of the Manchurian problem. Yet by September 1931 it was plain that a diplomatic resolution for each of these problems was in prospect. That scandalized those who aspired to a forceful, 'forward' policy, men who saw no other remedy to the underlying malady of Sino-Japanese rivalry in Manchuria.

The precise timing of the Mukden Incident, however, was decided by a handful of perhaps half a dozen Kwantung Army hot-heads who were fearful that their own immediate superiors as well as the desk-bound Army bureaucrats of the Army General Staff and War Ministry were now at best half-hearted and at worst positively hostile towards the plot. These fears were amply justified. What they did not know was that War Minister Minami Jirō had been called to the Imperial Palace for an audience with Emperor Hirohito on 11 September and was told by Hirohito in no uncertain terms that Army discipline – particularly in the Kwantung Army – *must* be restored. The newly appointed Commander-in-Chief of the Kwantung Army, Lieutenant-General Honjō Shigeru, was a solid, highly respected soldier who previously had kept his political opinions to himself. But during the informal inspection tours which he undertook immediately after his arrival in August, he had lost no opportunity to lecture his officers and men against rash actions. His chief of staff, Major-General Miyake Mitsuharu, who had been impressed for some months by the Army General Staff's determination to avoid trouble in Manchuria for the time being at least, learned that the conspirators wanted to act in late September and tried to nip the matter in the bud: Miyake forthrightly refused to authorize any provocative actions and secretly cabled Army authorities in Tokyo that 'the present situation was becoming very delicate' and required 'extensive personal talks'.

Tokyo caught Miyake's meaning and an emergency conference was convened, attended by the top generals of the War Ministry and Army General Staff. Bearing in mind the Emperor's attitude, and strong warnings given to Minami even more recently by Foreign Minister Shidehara, the generals decided that the Chief of the Army General Staff's Operations Division, Major-General Tatekawa Yoshitsugu (who had attended the meeting), should proceed at once to Manchuria bearing personal letters to Honjō from Minami and the Chief of the Army General Staff, informing Honjō of the Emperor's wishes and instructing Honjō to prevent any unauthorized incident. Tatekawa, however, secretly let it be known to the conspirators what his mission was designed to achieve – and that he intended to take a roundabout route which would give the conspirators a few days' grace before he would see Honjō and Miyake. Upon receiving this news, the conspirators promptly moved the date of their plans forward by ten days.

A Kwantung Army officer of the Special Services ordered a Japanese railway maintenance worker at swordpoint to set and explode small explosive charges which blew up 31 inches of the South Manchurian Railway downline just north of Mukden at about ten o'clock on the night of 18 September 1931. So little damage was caused that the speeding southbound express from Changchun, approaching the site a few minutes later, was seen to sway and lurch sideways over the gap but carried on without halting and reached Mukden Station punctually at 10.30 p.m. Nevertheless, this small blast, which the instigators of the plot and the Japanese Government afterwards blamed upon Chinese saboteurs, led within hours to the Japanese military occupation of Mukden and to the outbreak of full-scale military operations elsewhere.

Major-General Tatekawa, having arrived in Mukden dressed in civilian attire in the late afternoon before the Incident began, claimed to be 'worn out' from his journey, and dined with several of the leaders of the plot. Their ringleader, Colonel Itagaki Seishirō, the Senior Staff Officer of the Kwantung Army, takes up the story:

He did not incline to mention his business immediately, except a few words to the effect that the superiors were worrying about the careless and unscrupulous conduct of the young officers. I answered that there was no need of worrying if that was the business, and remarked that I would hear him at leisure the next day, because he seemed tired out.*

Tatekawa took his ease that night at a geisha house, passing out from rather too much sake. He awakened to the sounds of gunfire as Japanese soldiers swarmed across Mukden. He staggered to the door and into the waiting arms of military guards, who took him back inside, admonishing him that it was dangerous outside and they were there to see that he came to no harm.

Meanwhile, Major-General Miyake, hearing news of the Mukden Incident shortly before midnight, called together his staff and rang Honjō, who had retired for the evening (he was then in his bath). Among those who hurriedly gathered at the Kwantung Army's Headquarters that night was another one of the principal architects of the plot, Lieutenant-Colonel Ishiwara Kanji, the Kwantung Army's brilliant and sardonic Operations Chief, who tells us:

Then appeared the Commander of the Army, after a careful study the whole staff arrived at the following conclusion: 'The expected worst has unfortunately come owing to outrageous acts on the part of China; the limit of patience is reached. There is no knowing how the situation may aggravate even during this night unless we take a resolute measure to chastise the enemy. There is no time to lose. We must resolutely mobilize the whole strength of our military might to seal the fate of the enemy within the shortest possible time.'

* R. J. Pritchard and S. M. Zaide (eds.), *The Tokyo War Crimes Trial*, 12: *Transcript of the Proceedings in Open Session*, Garland Publishing, New York, 1981, p. 30261.

When I expressed my opinion as the operational officer to General Honjō to that effect, he meditated a few minutes with his eyes closed, and then, judging from the general situation, he made a final decision, saying resolutely, 'Yes, let it be done on my own responsibility.' We were all silent with deep emotion . . .*

Honjō and his staff then briefed themselves as well as possible. Honjō issued fresh orders and counter-orders, deploying his forces throughout Manchuria: Ishiwara had his hands full trying to keep the old general in line without disclosing the true nature of the plot (which aimed at nothing less than committing Japanese forces to such an extent that there could be no turning back). Finally, Honjō left Port Arthur with most of his staff shortly after 3 a.m., reaching Mukden in time for lunch. It was all a bit late by the time Major-General Tatekawa finally handed over his messages to Honjō on the night of 19 September.

Long before that, Consul-General Morishima Morito was summoned to the headquarters of the Japanese Military Special Services Mission in Mukden barely forty-five minutes after the outbreak of the Incident. When he began to remonstrate with Colonel Itagaki and his officers, it was soon clear what the Japanese Government was up against, as Morishima told the International Military Tribunal for the Far East fifteen years later:

I insisted that there was no question involved of interference with the right of military command but rather that I was certain the matter could be adjusted amicably through normal negotiations and that the latter course would be advisable from the viewpoint of the interests of the Japanese Government. At this point in the conversation, Major Hanaya† unsheathed his sword in an angry gesture and stated that if I insisted upon interference with the right of military command, I should be prepared to suffer the consequences. He stated further that he would kill anyone who endeavoured to so interfere. This outburst on the part of Major Hanaya broke up the conversation, and I returned to my headquarters to make a full report, which I did.‡

As it happened, the West was dealing with a British financial crisis, which led among other things to the British naval mutiny at Invergordon. That in turn drove Britain from gold and prompted the devaluation of the pound. But that did not influence the Japanese: it would have run against

* ibid., 9, p. 22119.
† Major Hanaya Tadashi was Acting Head of the Japanese Army's Special Services Organization in Mukden during the absence of his chief, the 'Lawrence of Manchuria', Colonel Doihara Kenji (who was then in Tokyo receiving fresh orders to reach a settlement of the Nakamura Case on terms which had dismayed the Kwantung Army's young dissidents). Hanaya was another one of the key figures behind the Mukden Incident.
‡ ibid., 2, pp. 3020–22.

the entire history of Manchuria for Britain or any of the other Western Powers to mobilize naval forces against Japan in opposition to actions ostensibly taken in defence of treaty rights and interests. The Japanese Army stood forward as the undisguised makers of its policy towards China and sent units throughout southern and central Manchuria. The Japanese Government, with obvious misgivings by some of its members, was dragged along in its wake.

While Japanese diplomats assured foreign statesmen that the military operations were only a temporary expedient to restore peace and order and that Japanese troops would be withdrawn at the earliest possible moment, the advance of Japanese military forces in Manchuria continued scarcely without pause. Most international observers simply concluded that the Japanese Government was cloaking its naked aggression with sweet words that only compounded the sense of treachery and deceit, but in fact the Japanese civil authorities were striving desperately to restrain the Army. The War Ministry and Army General Staff were divided among themselves and unable to regain control of the Kwantung Army machine. Many senior officers were unwilling or unable to intervene. Some, like Major-General Tatekawa, had always been sympathetic to the conspirators. Others, including War Minister Minami, regarded this unauthorized military adventure with grave misgivings and alarm but felt obliged to support their men while military operations continued in the field. It seemed scarcely possible for them to do otherwise since the Kwantung Army, joined by forces of the Korean Army, defied orders from Tokyo and advanced inexorably from victory to victory.

The Japanese public, conscious of the strength of modern armaments, and for a long time inclined by the experience of their early victories to underrate China's power of resistance, put their complete confidence in the use of force: they regarded the war light-heartedly and with rejoicing. Their levity recalls the comment in *Coriolanus* of the Volsces greeting war:

> Let me have war, say I. It exceeds peace as far as day does night:
> it is sprightly, waiting, audible, and full of event: peace is a very
> apoplexy, a lethargy, deaf, mulled, sleepy, insensible.

They would have been wiser to reflect on the comments of Thucydides at the beginning of the Peloponnesian War in ancient Greece. He makes a wise envoy argue that war is so full of accident and so difficult to control that one should always embark on it with deep anxiety, even if the results seem assured. Thucydides writes: 'Consider the vast influence of accident in war before you are engaged in it. As it continues it generally becomes an affair of chances, chances from which neither of us is exempt, and whose event we must risk in the dark.' But Thucydides was a Greek, no Tatekawa, and not much read in Tokyo.

CHAPTER 4
The China Which Was Struck At

THE notable advantage of Japan in the 1930s was that it was a relatively well-organized and modern state attacking, in China, a society which was still in the early stages of adopting modern institutions. At the time, Japan's resolve to subdue China did not seem absurd or incredible. It faced, it is true, a huge adversary. That China was immense, and had unlimited manpower, might well have daunted it. Japan had only one fifth of China's population. But there were many factors which told against China's deployment of its potential strength, and which made Japan's ambition seem less absurd.

There was the economic position. China had a totally inadequate industry for making war. Except for coal, with which China was bursting, it was generally short of accessible raw materials. Initially it had a pitifully small steel industry. Its equipment for generating power was completely insufficient. Its railway system had great gaps. Its roads, for modern needs, were, for the most part, terrible. It had no system for enlisting its scientists, who were produced in some quantity in the gifted Chinese race, in its war effort. Its population contained far too many illiterate peasants, far too small a middle class, for its economy to be properly organized. Such was the technical side of China's capacity for war-making. The facts encouraged aggressors against it.

In China the state did not have the same reality as it had come to have in Japan. China, in spite of chaos, held together as a society, but this was because of the natural cohesiveness of families and clans. The principles of its unity were of very ancient origin. The family, and not the state, was the centre of loyalty. In a day when the Japanese were becoming, in form at least, more and more like the typical nation-states of the West, the Chinese continued to be rather archaic, to breathe the air of the ancient world, to be sceptical of the overriding claims of the state upon the individual. It is true that, from these very qualities, China drew on a massive strength – something primeval – with which it could confront Japan. But, equally, it was at a deep disadvantage.

In an effort to redress this weakness China put its faith in nationalism. In doing this, it followed the pattern of all the peoples of Asia. Nationalism was their support. Peoples responded to it, and it gave them an impetus which propelled them past crises which would otherwise have overthrown them.

Nationalism was an astonishingly simple force. For all its surprising lack of intellectual content, it produced in country after country the same result. Nationalism brought in new considerations, and a man was given by it new motives by which to govern his conduct. It burst the narrow confines in which men had been content to see the affairs of the world. It made a man feel that he belonged to and had objectives in common with the whole community, and not simply his own family. The majority of the Chinese people espoused nationalism with passion. Few were untouched by it. Its wings beat strongly in all recent history. It was the central, compelling force of the times. It was the root of the war, just as religion was the base of events in the Thirty Years War in Europe.

Of course it happened that nationalism, great as was the stir which it made, loudly as it raised its voice, often had to compromise. Too often it came off second best in China at this time in a struggle with the quiet voice of family obligation. It was seldom that the claims of the nation would totally prevail over the more ancient social ties. Throughout the period, this was true of China, as it was also of most other agrarian societies. All men, or nearly all men, acted in ways which proved that the family was still the centre of their interest. Society was simply a federation of families. To keep this in mind is to understand many things about the modern history of Asia. Yet, by and large, nationalism prevailed in China in the 1930s. It was the force which animated politicians, and gave them the power to make China perform tasks which would otherwise have seemed impossible.

At the start of the war with Japan, China was governed by the quintessential national party, the Kuomintang. The Kuomintang had its origin in a number of societies, more or less secret, which had worked to overthrow the Manchus. As a single party it dates from 1912. When the old régime fell, the Kuomintang was not yet strong enough to claim the succession. It came, however, to power in Canton, and raised an army. With this, and with the support of the relics of the old system of government, it had made good its authority, subduing the warlords who had divided up the inheritance from the Manchus. It gradually became the dominant power throughout the country. But in doing so, it compromised, abandoned large parts of its revolutionary programme, and took care to make itself acceptable to the social classes which had great traditional authority in Chinese society. It took in tens of thousands of

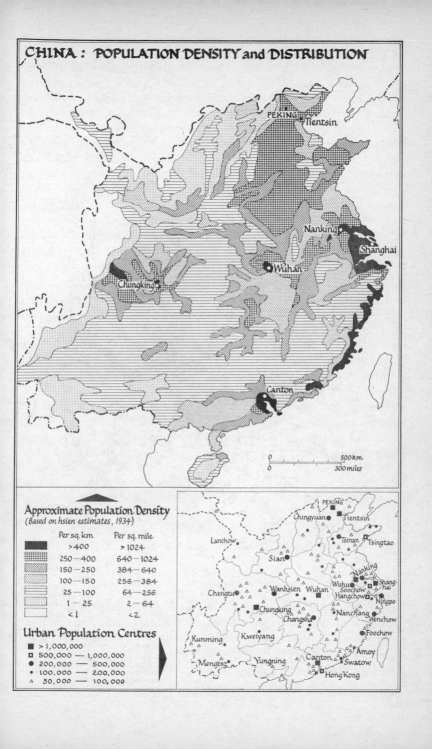

CHINA : POPULATION DENSITY and DISTRIBUTION

PEKING
Tientsin

Nanking
Shanghai

Wuhan

Chungking

Canton

0   500 km
0   300 miles

Approximate Population Density
(Based on hsien estimates, 1934)

	Per sq. km	Per sq. mile
	>400	>1024
	250—400	640—1024
	150—250	384—640
	100—150	256—384
	25—100	64—256
	1—25	2—64
	<1	<2

Urban Population Centres

■	> 1,000,000
▫	500,000 — 1,000,000
●	200,000 — 500,000
•	100,000 — 200,000
△	50,000 — 100,000

PEKING
Chingyuan   Tientsin
Lanchow   Tsinan   Tsingtao
Sian   Nanking   Shang-hai
Chengtu   Wanhsien   Wuhan   Wuhu   Soochow   Ningpo
Chungking   Hangchow
Changsha   Nanchang   Wenchow
Kunming   Kweiyang   Foochow
Mengtsz   Amoy
Yungning   Canton   Swatow
Hong Kong

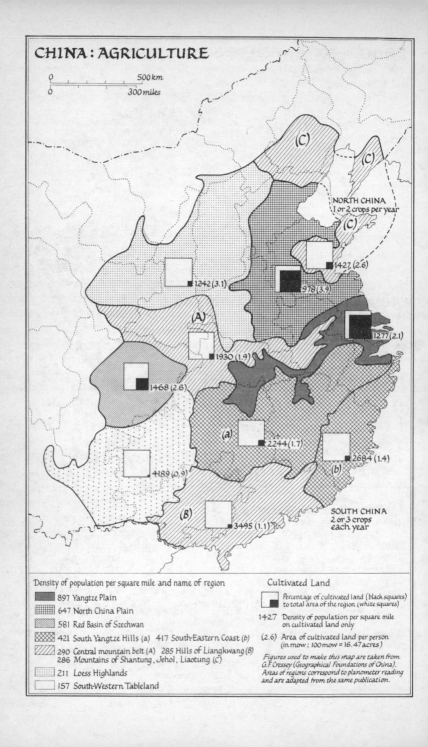

CHINA: AGRICULTURE

0 — 500 km
0 — 300 miles

(C)

(C)

NORTH CHINA
1 or 2 crops per year

(C)

1242 (3.1)

1427 (2.6)

978 (3.9)

(A)

1277 (2.1)

1930 (1.9)

1468 (2.6)

(a)

2244 (1.7)

2684 (1.4)

4189 (0.9)

(b)

(B)

3495 (1.1)

SOUTH CHINA
2 or 3 crops
each year

Density of population per square mile and name of region

▓ 897 Yangtze Plain

▦ 647 North China Plain

▨ 581 Red Basin of Szechwan

▧ 421 South Yangtze Hills (a) 417 South-Eastern Coast (b)

▨ 290 Central mountain belt (A) 285 Hills of Liangkwang (B)
286 Mountains of Shantung, Jehol, Liaotung (C)

░ 211 Loess Highlands

□ 157 South-Western Tableland

Cultivated Land

■□ Percentage of cultivated land (black squares)
to total area of the region (white squares)

1427 Density of population per square mile
on cultivated land only

(2.6) Area of cultivated land per person
(in mow; 100 mow = 16.47 acres)

Figures used to make this map are taken from
G.F. Cressey (Geographical Foundations of China).
Areas of regions correspond to planometer reading
and are adapted from the same publication.

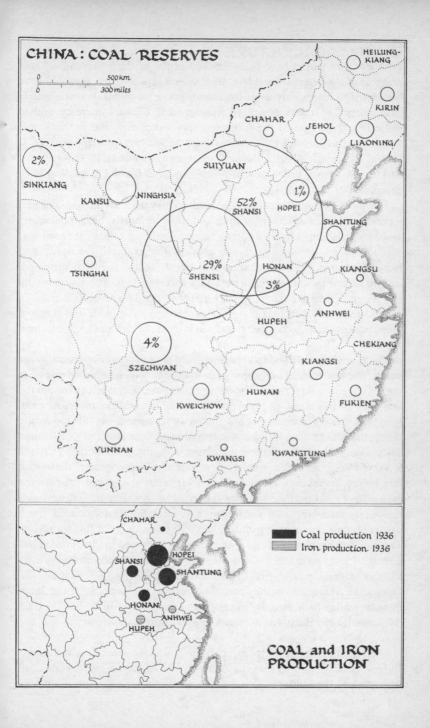

CHINA: COAL RESERVES

0 ———————— 500 km
0 ———————— 300 miles

HEILUNG-
KIANG

KIRIN

CHAHAR   JEHOL   LIAONING

2%
SINKIANG

SUIYUAN

KANSU   NINGHSIA

52%
SHANSI

1%
HOPEI

SHANTUNG

TSINGHAI

29%
SHENSI

HONAN
3%

KIANGSU

HUPEH

ANHWEI

4%
SZECHWAN

CHEKIANG

KIANGSI

KWEICHOW   HUNAN

FUKIEN

YUNNAN   KWANGSI   KWANGTUNG

CHAHAR

SHANSI   HOPEI
SHANTUNG

HONAN   ANHWEI
HUPEH

■ Coal production 1936
≡ Iron production 1936

COAL and IRON
PRODUCTION

members who would have been shocked at the modernizing radical programme of the original founders. By the time Japan struck, it would have
been hard to say exactly what the Kuomintang stood for. It was a purely
national party. It was dedicated to advancing China's interests, and to
protecting these against the foreigner, Japan included, and in this it was
ferocious. But beyond that, it was hard to see any principles which it
followed, except feathering the nests of its many members. Its Government
had to rule over a hotch-potch of interests, and for this a succession of
compromises was necessary.

The party brought together the rural gentry and urban bankers and
merchants, bosses of secret societies and trade unionists, brokers, soldiers
and bandit leaders. Its attitude to the particular questions it faced was
determined by expediency. Some classes, for example landlords and
bankers, were more powerful socially than others, and the party mirrored,
instead of trying to modify, the existing social system. The Kuomintang
was a comprehensive party, never a party of genuine revolutionaries. In
general the party had become more conservative the older and larger it
grew, because each group that it included strove, before all else, for its own
survival.

The Kuomintang liked to represent itself as a progressive, avant-garde
party. The westernized and sophisticated classes, which made up one of its
influential parts, advertised it as being democratic. Certainly it was, in the
intention of this wing, to be aligned with the progressive forces of mankind. But the enlightened part of the party leadership was all too aware
that it sat with colleagues who were anything but liberal and democratic.
They also had to reconcile their claim with the blatant fact that the
Kuomintang operated a single-party system of government, that (with
one temporary exception to be described later) it did not tolerate the
existence of rival parties, and that it carried on government – if only as a
temporary measure – as a Kuomintang dictatorship. It announced that it
would become democratic in future but it fixed no date for this transition.
The dictatorship aspect of the Kuomintang was to give many of its leaders
a sense of unity with the Axis countries of Europe. It embarrassed greatly
the pro-American and pro-British circles, which were very powerful
among the Shanghai businessmen who formed the support of the Kuomintang with which westerners came most readily in touch. But they did
not count in the party for as much as was supposed.

The Kuomintang, from its earliest days, owed its strength to the Army.
In fact the Kuomintang was the Army. Its being, ethos, performance, all
depended on the military. This was the outstanding fact about it, and the

paradox is that this fact was never grasped by western observers. The westerners in China, in dealing with the rise of nationalism, commonly met and negotiated with the middle-class and civilian members of the party. Chinese militarism had a bad name, and the middle class, who struggled against it, were ready to assure the foreigner that their party – the Kuomintang – stood for the complete supremacy of the civilian element, which was what the West desired to hear. The westerner, in this and other matters in which the Kuomintang was interested in misleading him, too easily accepted the expurgated version of Chinese reality. After all, the civilians were often highly articulate and convincing. By contrast, the generals were for the most part ill-educated, and even the best of them trained in very poor military academies. The westerner seldom understood how the decisions as to power were taken in the Kuomintang; he did not understand how the mind of the generals moved. And yet for a true appreciation of Chinese history at the time, the politics of the generals were the essential study.

The Chinese war-lords never stopped being war-lords. Republicanism was to that extent a veneer, democracy a debased and irrelevant concept in the day-to-day existence of peasant, landlord and soldier. National identity, however, was a mystical concept – xenophobic, utopian, mercenary and feudal all alike.

How, then, was the Kuomintang 'Army' made up?

The Kuomintang Army was a painful thing to contemplate, especially in the early days of the Chinese revolution. The southern forces had a far better reputation than those of the north. From the late 1920s, the Kuomintang hired several bands of gifted German military advisers, led first by the redoubtable Max Bauer, Ludendorf's right-hand man during the First World War; then successively by Hans von Seeckt, architect of Germany's post-war *Wehrmacht*, and by Alexander von Falkenhausen, perhaps the most courageous of them all. They sought to improve the equipment and organization of the Chinese Nationalist Army and, above all, to create cadres of the type that made both the *Wehrmacht* and the professional British Indian Army so effective when it became necessary first to train and afterwards to lead vast conscript armies into battle. But the situation in China was not exactly comparable. The few smart, well-drilled regiments which the Germans brought into being scarcely concealed that the dedication of the German instructors and their herculean labours were not equal to the politics, corruption and social upheaval of China. Organization of the whole Army continued to be dreadfully poor. The Kuomintang Army generally appeared as much a rabble as did the army of the Revolution in France in the years which followed 1793. But for a time that had incarnated the spirit of the Revolution. In the same way, in an oriental and haphazard fashion, these soldiers were the true spirit of the Chinese revolution.

The Chinese Army was an army of mercenaries. The leaders of the Kuomintang were content, unlike the Japanese, with raising an army by payment, as China had always done. This was peculiar for an army which was the instrument of revolution: a political force is more usually raised by making service compulsory. But China could raise a force of millions, at incredibly little expense, so overcrowded was the land. There were far more men than there was equipment. There was a rudimentary general staff. The financial administration of the Army opened the door to corruption: the pay for whole regiments was made to colonels, who were left to fix the pay scales and conditions of service with their men. They were divided in their allegiance between the central and the provincial authorities, and between the centre and local generals, who were little more than respectable bandits. A Japanese, taking note of their indiscipline, had little cause to be anxious about them.

The weakness of the Chinese Army reflected the essential backwardness of the social system. It was an army which was raised from the peasantry. This peasantry had so many just causes of grievance against the holders of power in China that it could not be relied upon to fight with any tenacity. Here is the key to the life of the country, here the explanation of all the events which have since followed.

The Kuomintang could not trust the rank and file of the Army, and this lay at the core of the frustration of Chinese nationalism. The party, which claimed essentially to be the party of the nation, evolved a policy for which it could not expect the support of a sufficient part of the Chinese nation.

This was the most important fact about China in 1931. It leads to an examination of the realities of Chinese society.

The trouble of China at this period was that it was virtually without an effective administration. From this proceeded many of the peculiarities of Chinese society.

The Government issued enlightened decrees – hence the good reputation internationally of the Kuomintang. But there was no civil service to give effect to them; no government with an effective will; almost anarchy. The apparatus of the Chinese administration was adequate when it was worked by educated and dedicated men; but the spirit of the times had forced these into retreat. A rapid and appalling worsening took place. The machinery of government fell into decay. There was an abundance of officials, but these were not bound together in any articulated system. They stood out, but each acted on his own, without giving the impression of orderly administration. Most offices became objects for purchase. The magistrates and assistant magistrates, having bought their posts, set themselves to exploit their office to recoup themselves. They taxed remorselessly, and they sold justice. They were venal and incompetent in the performance of their principal functions which should have been to protect the people against those who always appeared to prey on them in the times of decay of government. In the atmosphere of general decline, the elements of society which felt themselves naturally strong organized themselves and usurped the functions of government. Usually this meant groups of landlords: in many areas they raised an unofficial militia, which terrorized the countryside and ran the locality: it seized grain from the peasants at low prices, intervened to back up the money-lender in exploiting the farmer, carried out a forced loan on the people to meet the Government's demand for troops, put down forcibly the resistance of the bolder spirits, supported all kinds of obnoxious practices, such as protecting the opium trade, and gave more or less open protection to bandits. Sometimes the local bosses found themselves on different sides in support of different claimants on governmental power; and the pressures on the rank and file of society were thus doubled.

In spite of all this, it is important to remember that the Chinese peasant, if the whole circumstances of his life are considered, still probably enjoyed, at least at the start of this period, the best life of any peasant in any country in the world. China was in decay politically; it was in mortal danger from the Powers around it; but for a long while the degree to which this affected the peasant, and the number of peasants whose lives felt the consequences, can be exaggerated. China had begun to fall to pieces, but this process had not yet reached a stage where, for the mass of the people, it discounted the other advantages of Chinese civilization. If the miseries over so large a part of the rest of the world are borne in mind, if the misfortunes and the quality of life caused by creeping industrialization are weighed up by the observer, the balance is tilted and the virtues of Chinese life appear very shining. The worst man-made calamities which the Chinese had to fear were famine and the insecurity of life due to there being no adequate rule of law. On the other side, he enjoyed the protection of the family, of public opinion, and the many things which are summed up in the term 'Chinese civilization'. At any rate, the peasant was not dissatisfied with his lot.

He would have been surprised to learn that he was pitied. The decay of

China he regarded as a passing phenomenon: he must wait, be patient, and all would come well again. Misery was to break over him, but civil war, its root cause, did not become endemic until the middle of the second decade of this century. The checks and balances which limited arbitrary powers, the pressure of public opinion, still operated, and did not cease to do so until the break-up of society had proceeded a long way.

At the centre of life in China, there was, like a canker, the question of the ownership of the land. China had always been rent by a great schism. It was divided between the peasants who owned some land and the peasants who were landless. The schism was the fundamental one in Chinese life: from this division of the population, and all the facts incidental to it, there have followed, almost from the beginnings of Chinese history, many of the characteristic trends of its society and politics.

In 1931 five out of every six Chinese lived by agriculture: and the proportion had remained more or less constant throughout history. From his relation to the land depended most of what was significant to the status, to the life itself, of the typical inhabitant of the country. Land ownership gave a man the entitlement to a share in the good things of civilization. Without land he was virtually an outlaw. Education, which was the key to social advance and to status, was firmly in the hands of the landed. They controlled the village school. Without going to the school, there was no way of progressing upward on the educational ladder, and of taking advantage of the opening of careers to talent, which should otherwise have been a unique benefit of the Chinese social order.

A peculiarity of the Chinese agrarian system was that in spite of the social importance of land ownership, there was no rich landed class. There was nothing comparable to the Junkers, or to the landlords of eighteenth-century England or Ireland. There were a few excessively rich landlords, usually the product of families which had recently done extremely well in state service: but these were the exception, and were like fish out of water in the rural society. The landowners in China were very numerous, but each possessed land on a scale grotesquely small, and did nothing to make these privileges less painful to the landless labourers, and to the masses in the country districts who were totally unprivileged.

The division between the rural gentry and rural proletariat was exceedingly sharp and brutal. The landless were powerless: they were at the mercy of the landowners, who were also local officials, money-lenders, or merchants. (The only alleviation of their position was that if, by a miracle, they chanced to prosper economically, society put no obstacles in the way, legal or otherwise, of their acceptance.) The situation is now the constant theme of Chinese communist propaganda. Its contention is that in Chinese society one part has lived off and mercilessly exploited the other part. The classic film *The White-headed Girl* represents very well the plight of the exploited class. Possibly their state of wretchedness is exaggerated, but not very much. In all China's long dynastic history, behind all the civilization and elegance of life, the reality was that it was the arena of a permanent class war. China has been permanently divided between two classes, one of whom has had nothing to lose but its chains, and has, through the centuries, sat down constantly with appalling in-security. The Chinese landowners bled white the masses of the people. As it had been since the beginnings of time, so it was still in 1931.

This tension was reflected in the politics of the period. The Kuomintang, as it developed, came to be completely monopolized by the landowning class. Though it had originally had place for eccentrics, for deracinated Chinese, for émigrés who were the product of a different social system, it underwent a change as it spread widely throughout China, and was adapted for purposes of the class struggle. The landless were denied membership, or at least denied any office of power. The Kuomintang régime was essentially a landlord régime. The Kuomintang official or politician was bound together in a kind of freemasonry with most of the Army officers. They all belonged to the exploiting class; they banded together against the landless. Any threat to the landed interest and the landlords closed their ranks, however much they might struggle and be divided over other matters; and as a result the landless mass had no escape, except to contract out of society, and take to a bandit life. Brig-andage was thus endemic over every province of China; in China, alone among civilized countries, banditry was talked of as an everyday condition of life, to which the poor might resort from time to time as a matter of course. The provinces never had a police force which could cope with this stream of malcontents.

The nature of the Kuomintang had grave consequences in the organ-ization of the Army. Most of its rank and file were drawn from the landless class: on the other hand, all of the officers were from the landed. The officers were well enough contented with the policy of the party. The rank and file could not be. Thus there was always a sense of grievance in the Army, and a sense of incipient revolt. The Army might for a time be made loyal – by occasional bounties, by the popularity of some local commander. But over the long run the Army remained sullen and of uncertain temper. It saw no reason to fight wars, or to incur danger, and found the lure of military life to lie in the plunder which was traditionally the reward of its exertions.

Here the contradiction at the centre of the Kuomintang – to use a Marxist phrase – became obvious. It was a party which, born out of revolutionary civil war, should have been carried forward by the Army. But its leadership, after the early years, took fright, and did not countenance the Army playing with revolutionary ideas such as the expropriation of the landlords. The Army ceased to be revolutionary. Discipline was called in against radical sentiment. By this action, the Kuomintang ceased to be a genuine revolutionary force in Asia.

The social disruptiveness, which was the inevitable result of such a social system, was increased by a tendency which has always existed in Chinese society and which from time to time in Chinese history bursts out and determines the affairs of the country. This is a very deep sentiment among the Chinese people towards anarchy. This is found among all classes, landed and landless, and goes with Taoism and Buddhism, two religions which have always been popular in China. There is a deep distrust of government as such: the typical Chinese has an insuperable scepticism about its benefits, and a temperamental optimism about the chances of regulating life without the recourse to official paraphernalia. For the three decades after the fall of the Manchus, this instinctive trend in the country was powerful, especially among the landless. The rise of the Kuomintang happened essentially as a reaction to this, and was marked by a revival of Confucian ideas and the notions of the more realist figures of Chinese civilization. But at this time, the natural and amiable inclination of the Chinese towards anarchy was not yet passed. It weakened considerably the reformist aims of the Kuomintang.

The inclination of the Kuomintang rank and file to mutiny, and the dissent of much of the country from a social order dominated by the rural gentry, were expressed in the rise of a rival nationalist party and government, that of the Chinese communists. From the early 1920s, China had seen both the nationalist Kuomintang, and, though it was at first very weak, a Communist Party which also appealed to nationalism, though it claimed to be internationalist. The Chinese Communist Party was founded in 1922 by members of the intelligentsia. In its first months it had been a study centre for fostering the readings of Marxist writings. These had had a great boom in interest due to the revolution in Russia; before that, Marxism had been practically unknown. The achievements of communist government in Russia gave Communism a great prestige in China: and Communism in China also began to receive direct aid from Russia: Moscow began to direct its disciples. The doctrine spread widely, and the Communist Party began to be of some consequence. At this time the Kuomintang still retained some of the radicalism of its early days, and a section of the party was not averse to some of the communist ideas. It looked with envy upon the support which Communism was gaining, and was prepared to collaborate with the communists in return for the accession of strength which this might bring to a coalition. In the mid-twenties, the two parties collaborated in advancing their common cause against the war-lords. Together they established the Kuomintang power, sketchily it is true, throughout China.

But the communists, with their Marxist beliefs, were not a safe ally for such a party as the Kuomintang. The communists were real revolutionaries, determined that one branch of political thought alone should prevail. The Kuomintang was a comprehensive party. Though it was itself a dictatorship, it was in reality much more a federation of parties, and it attempted nothing like the rigid thought control of Communism. Gradually it became clear to the Kuomintang that, by the understanding with the communists, it was nursing a viper in its bosom. It drove them out of the alliance.

The breach occurred in 1927, at the moment when the great port of Shanghai fell to the Kuomintang. This brought the vast accession of the economic backing of bankers and great commercial interests. The Kuomintang judged that its strength from this was worth much more than the strength which an alliance with Communism could bring it. It was willing to sacrifice the former association, which brought it a certain mass backing, to the new partnership, which brought it the immediate, tangible economic strength. It seized, shot and arrested as many of the communist leaders as it could lay hands upon. In Shanghai it used the secret societies, which were its habitual allies, for rounding up the known organizers of the Communist Party. It included in this purge a number of radical Kuomintang members of whose sympathies it felt unsure. Radicalism withdrew from the Kuomintang. From the time of the coup in Shanghai, the Kuomintang was definitely a conservative and right-wing party.

In retrospect it is obvious that these events in Shanghai were of great importance for Chinese history. But at the time they were not appreciated fully. The western observers, in particular, saw them as a blood-letting which strengthened the Kuomintang. The Kuomintang was, at this period, in the ascendant, and there was no comparison between it, and its sudden great prestige – its recognition as the legitimate government of China, and the millions of dollars with which it was watered by Shanghai business – and the communists, who led a hunted life, and who only appeared in the news as the comrades of China's notorious bandits.

The Communist Party took years to recover from this blow. In the interval the Kuomintang appeared supreme. But the communists survived, and reorganized. Their earliest actions, on recovering the zest for a campaign, had been frittered away in trying to organize secret anti-Kuomintang centres in the towns. They were under the influence of the Russians, and the Russians, from the experience of the October Revolution, considered that the only way of making revolution was by inducing the industrial proletariat to take action. But such a tactic was entirely impossible in China: the towns did not dominate political life, industry was too small, the powerful armies could move in to suppress them. From the futility of these tactics, they were saved by the genius of several rising young figures, one of whom was Mao Tse-tung. He was the discoverer of the way to make Communism an effective power in China. From 1928 he had shifted the effort to the rural areas. He laid claim to have discovered the power of the peasantry. He used the slogans of land reform to raise revolutionary armies. Through Mao Tse-tung the communists became again a power in China, however modest was their strength at first in comparison with that of the Kuomintang.

The communists, by making alliance with local bandit chiefs, managed to organize a small opposition government in the heart of the Chinese countryside. This was the famous Kiangsi Soviet, the first communist government in China. It owed its being and its survival to the general disorder sweeping China. But their ability to create a government was to have vast consequences in the direction of Chinese affairs. It meant that the radicalism which was endemic in China was being provided with a practical programme. It is true that in the past there had often been a ferment of desperation in the country, but it had remained always without an effective organization and effective ideas to attach itself to. The masses were ripe for revolution, but their emotions were never attached to some cause worthy of them. For example, the Taiping Rebellion, in the middle of the last century, was a far more significant revolt than is today in general understood, and came near to overthrowing the Manchu Government: but the Taiping acted under an ideology which was unworthy of their rebellion. It was a half-crazy messianic movement, which borrowed most of its ideas from the corrupted teaching of Christian missions. The movement failed because the Taiping did not offer a régime which, in the country's judgement, was comparable to that of the imperial régime.

It was now different. In Kiangsi, the communists had set up an actual government. It had teachings, organization, slogans, all of which attracted classes which were deeply hostile to the Kuomintang. It provided the standard round which they could rally. They had been able to set up on Chinese soil a soviet government which had become the centre of revolutionary action.

At first the Kiangsi Soviet had simply the sympathy of the dispossessed and alienated masses elsewhere in rural China. It was conscious of waves of sympathy which washed round it, but it was unable to bear any effective support to its well-wishers. Other soviets were established, too, but they had a more ephemeral existence. Over vast areas of the country, the Kuomintang was still unchallenged. Nevertheless, by founding the Kiangsi Soviet, and keeping it alive, the communists had kept open the possibility that one day they would eclipse the Kuomintang, and that, one day, the support of the country, still given to the Kuomintang, would be transferred in bulk to them.

At first, the significance of these events was overlooked by the outside world. Very little was known about them; the communists were underrated as a danger to the Kuomintang. The Japanese had a livelier appreciation than the westerners, but it was supposed that they were so much interested in blackening the face of the Kuomintang, as a disorderly, untrustworthy government, that their concern could be regarded as routine propaganda. Chiang Kai-shek, the military leader of the Kuomintang, judged however – rightly as events were to make clear – that the danger was acute and deadly. He threw a cordon round the communist district, and kept up a constant pressure upon it. He proclaimed that, if the communists were not extirpated, they might grow into a force which would eventually overwhelm the Kuomintang. They might transform all the existing politics in the Far East.

All this was eventually to prove a correct forecast. Chiang Kai-shek, who had received a very limited education, who was the product of rural China and who was obviously outshone in intellect by the *haute bourgeoisie* of the Kuomintang to which he had been linked, was found to have perceived the realities of China more correctly than did his more sophisticated colleagues, trained in the universities and banking houses.

Chiang not only judged events. He set himself to try to influence how these would move. It was his will which determined that at first the threat from Japan should be given less weight than the threat from the Chinese communists. As a result, the head-on clash between Japan and China was delayed for some years. He had a civil war on his hands, whose issue would be of greater consequence than that of any war between China and Japan. Therefore the civil war loomed far larger in his mind than a national war. The civil war came first.

Chiang Kai-shek was therefore in the unpopular position of demanding that Chinese should concentrate on fighting Chinese. He neglected to take account of the fact that Chinese national feeling demanded that Chinese should fight Japanese. Even though there were plenty of wealthy and propertied Chinese, who saw that Communism was a real threat to their interests, they were held back and checked by nationalism from whole-heartedly acting upon calculation. The majority were ashamed to do what calculation directed.

CHAPTER 5

Naval Conflict by Methods Short of War

AT the Washington Conference, Japan had refused to entertain the idea of accepting a 10:10:6 ratio on any categories of naval vessels apart from capital ships and aircraft-carriers. Japan took the position that any agreement as to other classes would have to concede to Japan at least 70 per cent of whatever number the British and United States insisted upon maintaining, especially in heavy armoured cruisers (regarded as the most powerful of the unregulated classes of warships). This determination, together with a protracted dispute between Britain and America over the tonnage and calibre of cruisers which they wanted, unfortunately scuppered any chance of reaching a comprehensive régime of naval arms limitations or reductions – extending to all classes of ships – as part of the Washington Naval Treaty.

In fact, Britain continued to boast the most powerful fleet afloat. The United States Navy failed to achieve its dream of a 'navy second to none' because the American taxpayer and United States Congress refused to pay for it. The elected representatives of the American people found better things to do with money than build warships. They nevertheless saw nothing wrong with striving for naval dominance in international relations. American statesmen scarcely would admit it, but the two reasons underlying their demands were first of all an overweening national vanity and, secondly, a strong expectation that there was more likelihood of war against Japan than against any other Power. Thus the United States wanted to reconstruct its Navy with that specific contingency in mind. Having enshrined the Washington standard of naval strength in capital ships and aircraft-carriers, the United States was determined to compel Britain and Japan to accept the same 10:10:6 ratio as a general rule and particularly intended to concentrate upon the construction of a cost-effective number of heavy cruisers designed for fleet work (it had very little interest in routine trade protection duties).

Britain's Royal Navy, too, regarded the contingency of war against Japan as 'the general basis on which preparations are made'. War against the United States was ruled out by successive governments as a matter of national policy simply because there was no longer even the remotest chance of British victory in such a war. A war against Japan, however, could be waged and won. No other potential antagonist posed any serious threat to Britain's mastery of the seas. Thus it was that even before the more turbulent era of the 1930s, the United States and Britain had each examined every aspect of the eventuality of war against Japan in studies which were protracted in length and, one should say, refined to the point of exhaustion, in fleet exercises and war plans.

The British saw the primacy of Japan's threat to their Imperial security in the context of Britain's unique dependence upon the preservation of safe sea communications between those constituent parts of the Empire which were its vitals. For this purpose, light cruisers were perfectly adequate to form the connective tissues for imperial defence – and were also the only affordable means for achieving that end, given the large number of vessels (seventy) which the Royal Navy claimed to be necessary. Even that figure of seventy light cruisers related solely to the hypothesis of a single-handed war against Japan, one in which neither side had the benefit of allied naval support. Unfortunately, since light cruisers were no match for heavy cruisers in offensive armament and armour protection, it was plain that the Japanese would require vessels to meet the threat of any new heavy cruisers built by the United States, thereby outclassing the vessels which the Royal Navy wanted to build instead. The only one of the three Powers in a position to give way without compromising genuine national security was therefore the United States.

The Japanese had not neglected their naval reconstruction in the aftermath of the Washington Naval Treaty. Japanese naval construction in the aftermath of the Washington Conference had but one prime objective: Japan's total ascendency over the United States Fleet in any future contest that might be fought in the waters of the Western Pacific. This was purely a regional, not a trans-oceanic, policy. And so successful were the Japanese naval construction programmes that by the late 1920s, Japanese naval experts recognized that they could afford even to reduce their naval strength for the sake of an agreement with the United States and still retain a modest margin of safety, provided that Britain and the United States did not ask for too much.

At the Geneva Naval Conference of 1927 the United States took the view that 'Equality with Britain is the sole basis on which a just treaty limitation can be imposed.' Having said that, they reiterated their demand for the construction of a new generation of heavy cruisers rather than light ones, a position which the Royal Navy was bound to regard as unfriendly if not antagonistic. The Americans' apparent hostility to Britain was to some extent in surrogation for the thinly disguised paranoia which the United States harboured against Japan. Japan, genuinely desiring international arms reduction, strove mightily to prevent a breakdown between Britain and the United States and did her best to seek a compromise which would benefit all. Unfortunately, the United States remained obdurate and American press reports of private Anglo-Japanese conversations revived all the old paranoia which the United States had exhibited in the run-up to the Washington Naval Conference seven years before. The British and Japanese did succeed in reaching accord, but their efforts to bring the United States into a rational frame of mind proved totally unavailing. It was an experience which embittered naval relations between the British and United States navies for years afterwards.

These things develop a momentum of their own. The apparently irreconcilable objectives of the United States and British delegations contributed to what the chief British delegate deplored as 'mischief, friction and ill-will'. The 1927 Geneva Conference – which like all such so-called 'disarmament' or 'international arms limitations' negotiations belong to a special category of 'war by other means' – produced fresh anxieties and engendered animosity through the very processes of addressing hopes and needs. In this case emotions became so over-wrought in the conflict between naval delegations that certain key officials, admirals and government ministers on both sides began to regard the development of actual hostilities between Britain and the United States as a serious possibility. The Japanese public were pleasantly surprised by reports of this Anglo-United States rivalry at Geneva, for it seemed to lift the threat of Anglo-American collusion against Japan. Their rejoicing turned to dismay a few months later, when the United States announced plans for a huge naval expansion programme.

This came about partly due to the fact that Anglo-American rivalry and antagonism actually worsened still further during the year following the collapse of the Geneva Naval Conference. The immediate occasion was a clash between the two nations during deliberations of the League of Nations Preparatory Commission for the forthcoming General Disarmament Conference scheduled to take place at Geneva. The Americans believed – quite wrongly – that 'perfidious Albion' was seeking arrangements with the French against the United States. The Americans, not for the first time, were exceptionally ill-informed and misled by half-baked and malicious press reports, and by efforts of the United States naval establishment to manipulate the zephyrs as well as the prevailing winds of American public opinion. No democratic government finds it easy to separate 'arms control' from 'military appropriations' and 'economic priorities'. In naval arms negotiations foreign offices tend to aim at an agreement, any agreement. Admiralties want a limitation but insist upon maximizing their special requirements. Treasuries are invariably interested in economies in naval strength. Nevertheless, the American budget process and military procurement interests are singularly complicated if not ungovernable, and that, perhaps, was the root of the problem.

In fact, there had been nothing underhand in Britain's negotiations with the French, nor in the earlier discussions with the Japanese. Yet as a result of these affairs, the American and European Governments were driven further apart. Such was the seriousness of the rift and exchange of recriminations that only the exercise of considerable efforts by President Coolidge and Prime Minister Baldwin halted the downhill slide of Anglo-American relations by snatching the issues from the hands of the feuding naval experts and rebuilding political common sense.

By 1930 the Japanese Naval General Staff had good reason to be content with the Washington Treaty system, which had enabled them to concentrate their relatively slender resources on heavy cruiser and submarine development. Thus, unknown to the United States Navy, Japan achieved a qualitative superiority over the United States in these classes of ships and a *de facto* numerical ratio considerably in excess of that for which they asked at the bargaining table.

Matsudaira Tsuneo, the Japanese Ambassador in London, welcomed Prime Minister Ramsay MacDonald's suggestion of a new naval arms limitation conference and, as a contribution towards ensuring its ultimate success, proposed that it be preceded by a settlement of the parity dispute between Britain and the United States and by agreement between Britain and Japan concerning Japan's strategic requirements. The need for greater moderation in the American demands was acutely felt, both by Britain and Japan. The United States had eighteen heavy cruisers, and Japan had twelve. Britain had fifteen and wanted no more. But if the United States insisted on increasing her heavy cruiser strength to twenty-one or even twenty-three (as she showed every sign of doing), then Japan would certainly insist on a 70 per cent ratio, thus increasing her number to fourteen. That would leave the Royal Navy dangerously insecure in Far Eastern waters. Accordingly, it was all too clear that unless the Japanese could reach some understanding with Britain beforehand, the British were likely to have no option but to side with the Americans in denying the Japanese the 70 per cent figure which they were so convinced was essential to Japan's security.

Seeking to strengthen his hand, Prime Minister Hamaguchi arranged for a review of Japanese defence policy at the official residence of the Navy Minister, attended not only by his entire Cabinet but also by leaders of the less liberal opposition *Seiyū-kai* (literally, the 'Party of Political Friends') and members of the Privy Council. Even some of his friends, however, had serious misgivings about the extent to which the 70 per cent ratio had become non-negotiable. When Navy Minister Takarabe suggested that an Imperial Conference be called to decide upon Japan's aims and then unite public opinion, Court circles initially favoured the idea. But the last of the *Genrō*, wise old Prince Saionji Kinmochi, succeeded in quashing it: 'Do nothing of the kind,' he told Takarabe. 'In diplomacy, one does not burn his bridges or show his hand.' Nevertheless, Hamaguchi won a great deal of credit at the time when he held a press conference and revealed his Government's determination to adhere to the 70 per cent ratio in heavy cruisers at the very least. Addressing the Diet, he declared:

Our claim . . . is based upon the practical necessity to make our defence secure against foreign invasion. We offer no menace to any nation, we submit to menace from none. On that fundamental principle, it is our desire to seek a naval agreement satisfactory to all the parties concerned.*

This was not hyperbole. It was pre-eminently sane, the minimum to which any nation aspires if it possesses the wit and means to survive as an independent state. It did not go down well in Washington, DC, however, where the United States Government was equally determined that the Japanese must submit to an extension of the Washington Conference's 60 per cent ratio in all classes of warship. What the United States feared was that it might someday find itself unable to enforce its will upon Japan if the Japanese were to run amok in China (or even the Philippines). The American position, as Gregory Bienstock pointed out in the mid-thirties, was that 'unless America is able to carry the war into Japanese waters, she will lose it'.† But to put it another way, unless America could carry the war into Japanese waters, there was most unlikely to be any resort to war in the first place.

At the London Naval Conference of 1930, Britain and the United States finally found ways to overcome their most serious difficulties. They then joined in common cause against Japan. Although Britain did induce the United States to moderate the xenophobic and unreasonable attitude of the United States to a slight degree, the Japanese were the only participants who, for a second time, sought a reduction rather than merely a limitation in naval armaments. Moreover, as Captain C. Varyl Robinson,

* Speech before the Imperial Diet, 21 January 1930, as quoted in Takeuchi, *War and Diplomacy in the Japanese Empire*, Chicago, 1935, pp. 289–90, and cited in J. B. Crowley, *Japan's Quest for Autonomy*, Princeton University Press, Princeton, 1966, p. 44.
† G. Bienstock, *The Struggle for the Pacific*, Kennikat Press, Port Washington, New York (reprint of 1937 edition), 1970, p. 242.

the British Naval Attaché assigned both to Tokyo and to Peking, privately observed shortly before his return to England, Japan alone among the naval powers had based her policy solely on her minimum defensive requirements rather than leaving a margin sufficient to pursue a successful naval offensive. Baron Shidehara, confirmed internationalist though he was, reportedly likened America's behaviour to that of a rich 'spoilt child', who could afford to squander unlimited resources on armaments if it should please it to do so. Nevertheless, once the British and American delegations had reached agreement, the Japanese could make little headway in protecting their own interests. Prime Minister Ramsay MacDonald afterwards reported to King George V that 'From beginning to end, the two delegations [Britain and the United States] worked in complete harmony. To all intents and purposes they were one team.'* Even allowing for exaggeration, this nevertheless shows the very real dangers to which the Conference exposed the Japanese. When a compromise was reached in the end, it therefore came as a relief to the Japanese as well as to the British and American delegations – and privately most circles within the Japanese Government admitted that they had achieved more than for a time had seemed possible.

In some respects it can be argued that the 1930 London Naval Conference actually reduced the real security of each of the major naval Powers. France, who attended the Conference but tried to wreck it, and Italy, who also found herself in an untenable position, both refused to sign the Treaty. So far as Britain was concerned, the effect of the Treaty was that she was able to adhere to her present strength of fifteen eight-inch calibre cruisers while building an additional 90,000 tons (fourteen ships) of light cruisers and at the same time increasing her strength in auxiliaries and conducting an extensive modernization programme for her existing fleet. The United States increased its strength by three eight-inch gun cruisers and five light cruisers, although it was agreed that construction of these vessels would be deferred until the mid-thirties. More importantly, the Americans became entitled to construct 346,811 tons of new vessels, including seventeen heavy cruisers, to replace older ships. Japan, by contrast, was not permitted to construct a single new heavy cruiser and was permitted only 50,769 tons of new construction in all other categories of warship put together. Thus although Japan gained a 70 per cent ratio in six-inch calibre (light) cruisers and in destroyers together with parity in submarines, she was restricted to 60.02 per cent of the American heavy

* S. Roskill, *Naval Policy between the Wars: II, The Period of Reluctant Rearmament, 1930–1939*, Cassell, London, 1976, pp. 65–6.

ruiser strength. These figures gave Japan an overall entitlement to 69.75 per cent of the American gross tonnage figure but the appearance of an improvement in ratios over Washington Conference levels was illusory. The real effect of the London Naval Treaty was that Japan had to concede in principle her right to a hegemony in the Western Pacific which she had enjoyed in practice since 1905. After agreement was reached, the Head of the Japanese Delegation, Wakatsuki Reijirō, sadly but soberly remarked, 'Suspicions and misunderstandings will only be deepened. This is what the Japanese Government views with the most serious concern.'* Indeed, the bullying tactics of the American Secretary of State, Henry L. Stimson, towards the Japanese during the Conference begs comparison to that of Adolf Hitler towards the Austrian Chancellor, Dr Kurt Schuschnigg, on the eve of the Austro-German *Anschluss*.

All of this contributed to the gradual determination of Japanese ruling circles to turn away from such negotiations in future, or at least not to subject themselves to the likelihood of such humiliating consequences. At the same time, the London Naval Treaty had left the British and United States navies inadequately prepared to meet their very real national defence requirements in the decade ahead. In the short term, however, the worst effects of the Treaty were visited upon Japan. In particular it brought about the resignation of the Chief and Vice-Chief of the Naval General Staff, the retirement of the Navy Minister and Vice-Minister, an assassination attempt upon the life of Prime Minister Hamaguchi (who suffered a lingering death as a result of wounds inflicted by a right-wing fanatic) and the political ruination of his *Minseitō* (Democratic Party). These events all cast a shadow over the ensuing years. As the gifted Admiral Katō Kanji told Prince Saionji's ubiquitous secretary, Baron Harada Kumao:

It's as if we had been roped up and cast into prison by Britain and America. When I and my kind have gone, it will be you [Harada] and your kind who must bear the brunt of it. Since there's no fixed national policy, it follows that the programme for national defence will also vacillate. This is indeed disturbing . . . What has caused me the gravest concern recently has been the activity of those about the Throne.†

At this point we must digress momentarily to explain that the Japanese Navy had become a house divided against itself. In Japan, the Emperor exercised 'Supreme Command' (*Tōsui*) through the Army and Naval General Staffs together with the Supreme War Council (a kind of panel of

---

* Crowley, op. cit., p. 65.
† Harada Diary entry for 28 April 1930, as translated in T. F. Mayer-Oakes, *Fragile Victory*, Wayne State University Press, Detroit, 1968, p. 111.

elderly umpires who, when requested to do so by the Army or Nava
General Staffs, advised the Emperor on important military and nava
policy issues). On the other hand, the Emperor exercised his organizatio
and administration (*Hensei*) of national defence through the War an
Navy Ministries. The Army and Naval General Staffs, according to D
Minobe, the distinguished Japanese constitutional scholar to whom th
ruling élite now turned for guidance, were entitled to *participate* in defenc
planning and rightly 'should be given every serious consideration by th
Government'.* Nevertheless, Dr Minobe continued, the General Staffs 'd
not at all have the right of decision'. Traditionally, the Naval General Sta
had far less power than the Army General Staff. Executive power in th
Navy rested almost exclusively with the Navy Minister in time of peace
Senior members of the Naval General Staff chafed at being condemned to
position of perpetual inferiority to the 'prima donnas' of the Navy Ministry
They envied the far greater power of their Army counterparts. Thus whil
the Navy Ministry had broad powers as the 'administrative' side of th
Navy, the Naval General Staff was confined to 'operational' or 'staff
duties defined in the narrowest possible sense. The Naval General Sta
tended to be less moderate than the Navy Ministry, just as the Arm
General Staff was more imbued with an offensive spirit than the Wa
Ministry. All of these organs experienced difficulty in resisting the influenc
of more radical elements within the officer corps, but clearly the Nav
Ministry was far more fortunate in this respect than the others.

The Navy as a whole was a much more moderate service than th
Army. On most issues even the Navy General Staff felt some temptatio
to seek a form of compromise. It did not really identify itself with th
arcane feudalistic ethic which had proved so attractive to the Army. A
one time the Navy had been administratively subordinate to the Army. I
ancient times its prime functions were to transport the Army, to maintai
the Army's lines of communication, and to preserve the Army's freedom
of manoeuvre. But the modern Japanese Navy cherished its independenc
from the Army. It had adopted western values as well as Europea
practices with far less modification than its elder brother service. It wa
also much more élitist. It drew its officer corps not from poorly educate
peasant youth but from upper- and middle-class young men straight from
the universities, and it was susceptible to the same kind of class conscious
ness as that which afflicted the officer corps of the United States Navy
and Royal Navy. The naval officer was typically far more familiar with
international affairs, more technologically sophisticated and, generally

* Mayer-Oakes, op. cit., pp. 112–15.

speaking, more cosmopolitan than his Army compatriots. At the same time, the Navy was much smaller. Its officer corps was only a fifth the size of the Army's, and its political influence, rarely more than, say, a third of the Army's, shrank further still during the London Naval Treaty controversy. In the past, the Navy had prided itself on its internal cohesion. The disciplines of life at sea helped to preserve the Navy from the ravages of political storms and social upheaval ashore. In any case the Navy lacked traditional ties with the agrarian-cum-revolutionary radicalism so deeply implanted within the Army. And looking across the horizon and in foreign ports of call, the Navy had reason to know and greatly respect the strength of the Royal Navy and United States Navy, understood the economic capacity of their respective countries and saw little advantage in entangling Japan in China at the expense of good relations with the western democracies. Perhaps equally significant, there were as yet no foreign naval Powers towards whom any Japanese naval officer could look for assistance if unbridled national passions should erupt into war.

These considerations particularly affected the older generation of naval officers: Admiral Ōkada Keisuke, Navy Minister in the preceding Cabinet and a future Prime Minister; Admiral Count Yamamoto Gonbei, also a former Navy Minister, who had twice been Prime Minister; Admiral Saitō Makoto, three times Navy Minister, now Governor-General of Korea for the second time, subsequently another Prime Minister: all of these and others were strong supporters of the Treaty faction. The talents of men like these were considerable, and so was the esteem in which they were held by the Genrō and palace officials. Yet the fact remains that the most able men of the Naval General Staff were bitterly resentful of their continuing subordination to the Navy Ministry, and in that sense the London Naval Treaty came as merely the last straw. As Katō Kanji complained:

Before the Government dispatched the instructions to the delegation in London, they ought to have listened to our views on this matter; and yet when I wanted to present explanations at meetings of the Cabinet, I was prevented from attending . . . They are altogether defiant of the General Staff. It would have been acceptable if they had allowed me to have my say and then had given me to understand before the instructions were sent that there was no alternative after considering the matter from various angles. But they didn't even do that. The very issuance of the instructions shows a disregard for the Navy General Staff and is equivalent to ignoring the prerogative of Supreme Command. Can I stand by and allow decisions on the national defence to be made in this way?*

It is scarcely surprising that this sense of genuine grievance struck a

* Harada Diary entry for 5 May 1930, as translated in Mayer-Oakes, op. cit., p. 121.

responsive chord outside the confines of the Navy. The main parliamentary opposition party (*Seiyū-kai*), Hiranuma's *Kokuhonsha*, the Naval Reservist Organization and the combined services' Military Club, all joined the band-wagon. This mésalliance could not stop the Treaty but it forced the 'moderates' into adopting means which only reinforced the determination of the dissidents to redress the balance.

It is within this context, then, that we may note the sentiments expressed by one of 'those about the Throne' in reply to the efforts by the Navy's diehards, Admiral Katō Kanji in particular, to throttle the London Naval Treaty before it could be ratified: the venerable Grand Chamberlain, Admiral Suzuki Kantarō, drily commented,

It behoves the Chief of the Naval General Staff as the Emperor's chief staff officer to be more discreet and circumspect. It is highly reprehensible to drum up popular support for his own notions and then to try to push them through because of the public opinion thus aroused. Only the mediocre could clamour for 70 per cent or nothing. He who is Chief of the Naval General Staff must be able to utilize whatever strength is allotted to him; whether it be 60 or even 50 per cent that may be decided upon. It may be that Katō is too obstinate and emotional. So it seems to me.*

Prime Minister Hamaguchi's successors, alas, were not nearly so prepared to brave the demands of Japan's fighting services. Baron Wakatsuki, who took charge after a short caretaker period during which Baron Shidehara was Prime Minister *pro tempore*, had to yield to the expedient of promising to consult more closely with the Army and Navy General Staffs in any future matters affecting national security. After the London Treaty crisis, the right of 'supreme command' was much more jealously guarded than before – and was upheld by the preponderance of Japanese public opinion. Moreover, the Naval General Staff had learned the lesson that it would need to maintain the support of public opinion against the bureaucrats and officials who, having outmanoeuvred them in securing ratification of the Treaty, could no longer be trusted. Meanwhile the Japanese, like other top-class naval Powers, secretly bent their backs to the task of planning ways of circumventing the régime of naval limitation treaties to prepare for the likelihood that no satisfactory arrangements would be achieved by the time that all the existing agreements were due to expire at the end of December 1936.

There were many within the Army as well as the Naval General Staffs who were alarmed by the success of the bureaucrats and party politicians in railroading the London Naval Treaty through the Supreme War

* Harada Diary entry for 28 March 1930, as translated in Mayer-Oakes, op. cit., p. 103.

Council, the Cabinet, the Privy Council and the Imperial Diet. The whole affair had raised constitutional issues of the gravest importance, unresolved issues which struck at the heart of the military's independence and direct responsibility to the Throne on matters relating to Army as well as Navy control over the means available to them in the execution of national defence policies in the widest sense. When Prime Minister Hamaguchi had advised the Emperor to sign the Treaty against the wishes of his Naval General Staff, he tugged at the lynchpin which enabled the military and civil arms of government to work together, and his actions were thus contributory to a natural reaction, the sabre politics of the 1930s. Nor can one overlook the significance of the fact that the political ferment surrounding the London Naval Conference had coincided with the world depression. This increased pressure on governments to find solutions but it also added to the xenophobic sense of grievance which the ignorant, foolish and mad felt against foreign Powers.

Finally, it is worth stealing a last look at the Army's key role during these 'disarmament' controversies, for it not only helps to illuminate the constitutional relationship between the defence services but also may help to dispel the common misapprehension that the Japanese Army was invariably hamfisted in relation to the affairs of other government departments which affected the 'national polity'. Had the Army taken strong exception to the London Naval Treaty, it lay within the power of both War Minister Ugaki Kazushige and the Army General Staff to force the issue by his resignation, at one stroke bringing down the Cabinet and the Treaty. At the time, Ugaki was seriously ill in hospital. The pressures exerted upon him to resign were great. For a very long time, he stoutly resisted these pressures, confiding to Navy Minister Takarabe (another courageous man), 'This disarmament is a Navy matter and the Army has no share in or knowledge of it. A joint Army-Navy meeting would be quite superfluous. The Navy alone must handle it.' * As the matter dragged on for months, it began to appear that Ugaki would have to yield to the mental and physical strains. His Cabinet colleagues and Prince Saionji then prevailed upon him to appoint his Vice-Minister to deputize for him as War Minister *ad interim*. Constitutionally, this was another unprecedented step, but another hurdle had been surmounted. Whatever may have been Ugaki's motives (and there were many who felt that he would one day make a first-class premier), the Japanese Army General Staff as well as Ugaki had resisted a marvellous opportunity to join forces with the rank and file of the Naval General Staff in seeking to bring about

---

* Harada Diary entry for 9 June 1930, as translated in Mayer-Oakes, op. cit., p. 147.

the collapse of the Government and possibly to establish in its stead a new political order based upon the apocalyptic and hyper-nationalistic authoritarian principles which Katō Kanji and many of his adherents held dear. Whatever the dangers on the horizon (and they were manifold) Prince Saionji's voice tells us how determined were those who struggled against the rising tide of pessimism: while ratification of the London Naval Treaty was still far from assured, he declared:

Today, when new impetus has been given to peace through the new agencies devised after the Paris Peace Conference, agencies based on a spirit of peace for the promotion of human welfare, no nation should have offensive armaments. In a word, then, may we talk of weapons for defence, but nowhere can anyone today talk of weapons for aggression. These may seem to be wholly new schemes and principles, but if we go back a little further, we find they have a long and splendid history. This is what Jean Jacques Rousseau advocated so long ago. Men are not beasts; hence they should cease chewing each other up. For the welfare of mankind, let us preserve peace: this is the spirit that has come forth as the new principle today since the Peace Conference. Both the disarmament treaties and the Anti-War [Kellogg-Briand] Pact stem from a fine long-developing tradition. There's no intention of using treaties to threaten or reduce a particular nation's armaments. On the contrary, these treaties should be considered as undertaken for the sake of human happiness which can come from a spirit of the love for peace.*

His words express the well-nigh universal aspirations of the human race, but the tensions and accidents of history are no illusion, and the breadth of his vision is mocked by the horror and torment of the years that were still to come.

* Harada Diary entry for 13 June 1930, as translated in Mayer-Oakes, op. cit., pp. 158–9.

CHAPTER 6

The Great Manchurian Adventure

IN September 1931 the Japanese Army operations in Manchuria rapidly developed beyond the South Manchurian Railway zone. The movements of the Kwantung Army after the bomb incident (which the Chinese were not slow to accuse them of contriving) were so systematic, orderly and comprehensive that they obviously had been considered long in advance. Army field commanders were openly flouting normal civilian controls, and the Japanese Government floundered in the wake of events, responding sluggishly to news from the front.

The Japanese quickly overran Manchuria. Efforts both by the Japanese Government and Lieutenant-General Honjō, Commander-in-Chief of the Kwantung Army, to contain the affair and to restrain the advocates of a 'forward policy' were unavailing, and as Honjō's own orders were disregarded and his officers led their forces across Manchuria, the private doubts in Japanese official circles were laid aside amid scenes of public jubilation. Although vastly outnumbered 20:1 by Chang Hsueh-liang, the Manchurian armies were routed by the Japanese. In the fighting, only one of Chang's generals, Ma Chan-shan, resisted skilfully. Originally he seems to have been relatively well-disposed towards the Japanese until it became obvious that the Japanese wanted him to step down for another Manchurian war-lord, Chang Hai-peng, to become the provincial governor of Heilungkiang. Ma showed, by his field tactics, that he had studied the teaching of the old Chinese military texts on how to feign and double-cross. He won momentarily a great deal of popularity in the national press of China by the 'successful' action which he fought on the Nonni River. The importance of his actions was exaggerated. It was a campaign of delay. There was precious little fighting. He received no support, either from other Manchurian generals or from the Chinese central Government, which did not use its forces to support him. This is far from difficult to understand. Ma had regular forces twice as numerous as the total numerical strength of the Japanese troops then in the whole of Manchuria, his tactical position was more secure than his ability to seize the offensive, and the main struggle at the Nonni River bridges was anyway not a direct contest between 'the Chinese' and 'the Japanese' but between the assembled forces of two rival Manchurian generals, one of whom was favoured

by the Japanese. As the subsequent report of the League of Nations
Commission of Enquiry pointed out, the feuds between rival generals and
their gangs were a critical factor in the unfolding of these and other
events.

The complete evacuation of Manchuria by the troops of Marshal Chang Hsueh-
liang, practically without striking a blow, was not unconnected with the internal
conditions of China south of the Wall.*

A full appreciation of the Japanese achievement in Manchuria can be
approached only through an understanding of the immense geographical
obstacles which had to be overcome by the Japanese forces. Chang Hsueh-
liang not only had governed the whole of Manchuria, a country extending
900 miles in length and the same in breadth (encompassing some 380,000
square miles of territory, much of it mountainous, equivalent in size to
the combined area of Germany and France). His rule also extended to
control of the province of Jehol, an adjacent fiefdom which added a
further 60,000 square miles to his domains and which left him in military
command of the northern approaches to Peking beyond the Great Wall.
While it is true that railway construction in Manchuria was far more
developed than that of China Proper in 1931, communications were difficult and depended chiefly upon river and road traffic. Many of the rivers
in Manchuria were navigable only by small craft at the best of times and
all were generally frozen between October and March each year. With
winter temperatures well below freezing throughout the land for six to
eight months of the year, followed by summer temperatures rising to 38°
C (100° F) in conjunction with widespread monsoon floods over many
parts of the country, the climatic environment of Manchuria varied from
bad to intolerable, certainly utterly inhospitable to the alien Japanese
invaders.

By January 1932, however, the Kwantung Army, exploiting the divisions between Chang Hsueh-liang's lieutenants and supported by units of
the Korean Army, had established a complete mastery over the whole of
South Manchuria and had made serious inroads into Russian-dominated
North Manchuria, too. Most of the time the Kwantung Army struck first
and informed Tokyo afterwards. As Prime Minister Wakatsuki recalled
afterwards:

It was the unanimous sense of the Cabinet that these operations in Manchuria
must cease immediately and War Minister Minami agreed to put this Cabinet
policy into effect with the Army at once. However day after day expansion con-

* *The Report of the Commission of Enquiry into the Sino-Japanese Dispute*, Chūō Korou,
  Tokyo, n.d. [October 1932], p. 100.

MANCHURIA
Economic and Strategic Significance

+++ Railways built 1932   + + 1932–45
— Roads in use / under construction

0 _____ 300 km
0 _____ 200 miles

U S S R

Trans-Siberian Rly.

Amur
International boundary
Provincial boundary

Argun

Manchouli

Dailai Nor (L. Hulun)

Buir Nor (L. Peir)

NGOLIA

HAHAR

K H I N G A N

Hailar

Nunchiang

Heiho   Blagoveshchensk

Khabarovsk

Birobidzhan

Pei-An

H E I L U N G K I A N G

Tsitsihar
Angangki

Hailun

Chiamussu

Great Khingan Mts

Lesser Khingan Mts

Tailai

Nonni

CHINESE

Sungari

Harbin

Ussuri

L. Hanka

EASTERN RLY.

Hsinking
(Changchun)

Kirin

K I R I N

Suifenho

Voroshilov
(Ussuriysk)

Tungliao

Laoha

Liaoyuan

Tunhua

Hunchun

Vladivostok

J E H O L

Sungari Res.

Tumen

Liao

Chihfeng

Mukden
(Fengtien)

Yalu

Jehol
(Chengteh)

Liaoyang

F E N G T I E N

KOREA
(CHŌSEN)

Antung

Sea of
Japan

entsin

SOUTH MANCHURIAN

Port Arthur
(Ryojun)   Dairen

---

ustrial
ources
Centres

alfields
on Ore
uminium shale
agnesite
olybdenum
dro-electricity

Tsitsihar

Hokang   Fuchin

Chiamussu

Sungari

Paichengtzu   Harbin

Mishan

Hsinking

Kirin

Ssupingkai

Tunhua

Vladivostok

Tumen

Sungari Res.

uhsin

Fushun

Erhtaochiang

o

chou   Anshan   Niusintai   Yalu
Penhsihu   Chitaokou

Hulutao

eiling

Antung

Yellow
Sea

300 km
0 _____ 200 miles

Dairen

Human
Resources

Main areas of
Japanese
Agrarian
Colonies

Population density per square mile
▨ 280   ▨ 75–150   ▥ 12–25
▨ 225   ▦ 50–75   ░ <12
▢ Areas of Korean Agricultural Settlement

tinued and I, the Prime Minister, had various conferences with General Minami. I was shown maps daily on which Minami would show by a line a boundary which the Army in Manchuria would not go beyond, and almost daily this boundary was ignored and further expansion reported, but always with assurances that this was the final move.*

War Minister Minami strove to make excuses for the continuing disobedience of the Kwantung Army. He also strove, in vain, to reason with that Army's headquarters. The Army General Staff, meanwhile, may have had an underlying sympathy for the objectives of the Kwantung Army, but it issued a stream of orders intended to bring operations to a halt. There was some discussion as to the feasibility of cutting off military expenditure on the Kwantung Army, but this came to nothing when it was pointed out that such a course would produce an extremely dangerous situation for all concerned. The efforts of the authorities in Tokyo to stem the tide of the Japanese advance continued up to the end of 1931. The Kwantung Army was outraged, for instance, when the Army General Staff took exceptional steps to order the immediate evacuation of Tsitsihar, lynchpin for the control of the whole of North Manchuria, in mid-November 1931. Later still in November, after riots broke out in the northern Chinese city of Tientsin in the wake of political activities fomented by the Kwantung Army's ubiquitous secret service agents, the Army General Staff in Tokyo not only refused a request by the North China Garrison Army for reinforcements but also demanded that the Kwantung Army withdraw 150 miles back from the Chinchow area on the alluvial plains of south-eastern Jehol (where it had planned to advance on the pretext of seeking to relieve the garrison forces at Tientsin). That was about as much as any Japanese central authorities could have done towards reimposing control upon the troops in the field, for it was appreciated that all moves of this kind not only undermined military discipline in Manchuria but provoked extreme political unrest at home.

Caught in this cleft stick, the Wakatsuki Cabinet finally collapsed in mid-December 1931, at which time the moderate General Minami was put out to pasture and replaced as War Minister by the much more charismatic figure of Lieutenant-General Araki Sadao, who recognized together with Prime Minister Inukai Tsuyoshi and the Ministers of Finance and Foreign Affairs that in the absence of a 'fixed policy' by the new Government it would be powerless to prevent the further spread of hostilities in Manchuria. Araki convinced first his senior

* Pritchard and Zaide, op. cit., 1, pp. 1556–72, *passim*, and 1592.

ministerial colleagues and then the rest of the Cabinet that the only practical alternative to a drift into chaos was for the Government itself to resolve to occupy the whole of Manchuria together with Jehol, Chang Hsueh-liang's last foothold north of the Great Wall. As the Imperial Diet was not in session, the matter was submitted directly to the Privy Council which reluctantly consented to the plan and approved the necessary expenditure.

The first experience of Japan's adventure in the conquest of mainland China did not impress much of the outside world. What the Japanese would do in Manchuria had been awaited with some curiosity. Some countries had been ready to be tolerant. The development of Manchuria under Chang Hsueh-liang and his father before him had been arbitrary and exploitative. The Changs were reported to have kept a standing army of 300,000 men, greater than the regular forces of the Japanese Empire. They had created a huge munitions factory $1\frac{1}{2}$ miles long by half a mile wide, said to be the largest arsenal in the world after the old Krupp complex in Germany. Some foreign experts estimated that more than 85 per cent of Manchuria's state revenue of 133 million Chinese dollars for the fiscal year 1930 was spent on Chang Hsueh-liang's brand of militarism. The exploitation of Manchuria's rich natural resources had been devoid of imagination or enterprise. It would not have needed any exceptional skill in administration for the Japanese to do better. What they achieved, however, was little short of miraculous.

Japan decided to govern indirectly through friendly Manchurians rather than to establish direct administration. Thus far the choice was wise. We must not underestimate the change of attitudes which the Japanese had to undergo as they moved from being a mainly introspective, homogeneous race and culture to become the guiding spirit of a polyglot empire, from thence establishing a wholly new regional system. There were several mechanisms which effected these changes. We have seen how Japan after the Meiji Revolution had adopted and adapted western ideas and technology with quite extraordinary vigour and discernment. This was but one mechanism. Another mechanism by which the transformation was accomplished has been seen by some oriental observers to be little more than an exaggeration and adaptation of traditional Buddhist religious precepts that were held in common in nearly every territory that came under Japanese sway until 1945.

The concept of 'racial harmony' (*minzoku kyōwa*) between the Japanese and other Asiatic peoples first attracted attention in the late 1920s, when it was nurtured in Japanese intellectual circles in Manchuria and Mongolia. It was soon a topic for animated discussion everywhere among the Japanese settlers, and it became especially fashionable among second-generation Japanese residents in Manchuria who had known no life outside that of their adopted country. It was rather a natural expression of the attempts of these Japanese pioneers to achieve some enduring balance and stability in their relationship with the Mongolian, Manchurian, Chinese, Korean and White Russian populations that were more firmly ensconced in the area. At the root of the doctrine was a notion that bears a passing resemblance to that of the brotherhood of man in that it was certainly predicated upon a thirst for peaceful co-existence and co-prosperity. It was not, however, a doctrine indistinguishable from that preached by the Author of the Sermon on the Mount. It was no programme for racial equality nor for racial integration. On the contrary, it soon developed into a self-conscious programme for a social and economic re-stratification of Asian society by race. From the beginning, the Japanese in Manchuria perceived that their own special rights and privileges could not be preserved, much less extended, if Manchuria and Mongolia were subducted into the turmoil of Chinese politics. Yet there was ample scope for enlarging upon Japan's share in the development and exploitation of Manchuria and Mongolia if the region could be made a 'floating world', regulated by its own autonomous government yet responsive to pressure waves generated by Tokyo and by local Japanese special interests as well as by legitimate Chinese interests. This was not only a political and cultural imperative for the many Japanese who embraced such ideas. It was above all a question of their economic survival.*

Even at the earliest stage in the evolution of the idea of *minzoku kyōwa*, Japanese residents in Manchuria and Mongolia were thinking in terms of severing the ties that bound *Manmō* (Manchuria and Mongolia) to China Proper. But at that stage a purely Sino-Japanese 'racial harmony', nothing that need embrace other races, too, was favoured as the proper means to attain that end without recourse to military force. That soon changed. By 1930, as the effects of the world depression were felt in the region, a new sense of urgency was imparted as acutely vulnerable Japanese enterprises found themselves subjected to especially severe attacks. The anti-Japanese movement as a whole (to which nearly all the indigenous peoples of China, Manchuria and Mongolia responded wholeheartedly) and the discriminatory economic policies of Chang Hsueh-liang's régime in particular, gravely prejudiced the Japanese communities notwithstanding

---

* Hirano Ken'ichirō, 'Racial Harmony: A "Cover-Up" Ideology for a Puppet State', in *Proceedings of the British Association for Japanese Studies*, VI:1, *History & International Relations*, Sheffield University Press, Sheffield, 1981, pp. 92–7.

1 *Top left*: The Shōwa
Emperor of Japan, Hirohito,
riding his favourite white
horse

2 *Top right*: The railway
carriage in which the 'Old
Marshal' of Manchuria,
Chang Tso-lin, was killed by a
bomb in 1928

3 *Bottom*: The assassination
of Prime Minister Hamaguchi
Osachi at Tokyo Central
Railway Station in 1930

4   Japanese terrorists in court
Top: Members of the
'Ketsumeidan' (Blood
Brotherhood)

5   *Bottom*: Army cadets
involved in the 15 May
Incident

6 The Manchurian Incident (1931–4) *Top left*: Site of the explosion outside Mukden that signalled the start of the Manchurian Incident in September 1931

7 *Top right*: Warlord Chang Hsueh-liang, the 'Young Marshal' of Manchuria

8 *Bottom*: A star witness for the prosecution: 'Mr Henry Pu-Yi', last Emperor of China and ex-'Emperor of Manchukuo', stands with the Chief Prosecutor of the IMTFE, Joseph Keenan

9 The 26 February Incident,
1936 *Top*: Japanese Army
rebel troops occupy the
grounds of Tokyo's
Metropolitan Police
Headquarters

10 *Bottom*: Rebel troops
cover the approach to the
Hibiya Crossing, near the
Imperial Palace, Tokyo

11 *Top*: Japanese marines,
landed from the fleet to quell
the Army rebels, advance
through a waterside district of
Tokyo, 27 February 1936

12 *Bottom*: Lukouchiao, the
'Marco Polo Bridge'

13 The China Incident,
1937–45 *Top*: Horse-drawn
artillery

14 *Bottom*: Japanese artillery
in the battle for possession of
the Chinese quarter of Tientsin
in August 1937

15 *Top*: The great North
Gate of Taiyuan, capital of
Shansi Province in North
China

16 *Bottom*: Japanese forces
enter Nanking, led by their
triumphant Commander-in-
Chief, General Matsui Iwane

17 *Top left*: A not
uncommon scene from China's
'Middle Kingdom' in those
days

18 *Top right*: Japanese
soldiers are photographed
using bound Chinese prisoners
of war for bayonet practice

19 *Bottom*: A column of
Japanese troops belonging to
the Kwantung Army

the latent strength of the South Manchurian Railway and of the Japanese military forces garrisoned in the vicinity.

Many of those who could afford to do so left the Asiatic mainland and returned home to Japan. Others less fortunate found the attitude of the Japanese Government singularly unhelpful. As one spokesman for the Manchurian Youth League poignantly observed, 'With the basis of our life destroyed by lawless Chinese officials and with no place to return to, we are treated like enemies by the so-called sovereign of Manchuria and like stepchildren by Japanese statesmen.'* Some form of self-reliance and unity obviously was required, and Japanese residents in Manchuria and Mongolia began to contemplate the creation of a Manchurian state genuinely independent of Japan, if that should be the only way to protect their persons and livelihoods. 'In this way,' as Hirano Ken'ichirō has pointed out, 'the Japanese residents in Manchuria separated themselves from Japanese imperialism, the main target of Chinese nationalism, and at the same time identified themselves with the other racial groups living in Manchuria.'†

By the following year, 1931, the sense of abandonment which Japanese residents in Manchuria felt towards their motherland had become more acute. When the South Manchurian Railway announced plans to close its central teachers' training college, the plight of the Japanese expatriate community became desperate. In short, the idea of racial harmony had gained a widespread popularity among Japanese residents in Manchuria over the course of several years before the outbreak of the Manchurian Incident. Thus came to hand, ready-made, a fit instrument for the purposes of the Kwantung Army. It gave the militarists within that Army a blueprint for the political mastery of an entire country. It was a concept within the capabilities of the comparatively small military force under their command. And it was familiar to the tens of thousands of Japanese civilians who regarded that country as their own. Manchurian politicians and generals could be bought and sold by the sackful. By accumulating such sackfuls, Manchurian political institutions, internal allegiances and external relations could be transformed, and when they were transformed, the Japanese would emerge as a race of managers.

The structural side of the concept of 'racial harmony', indeed, was no less important. From the early years of the century, successive Japanese governments and private venture capitalists had promoted the commercial and industrial development of Manchuria and had used the influence

* ibid., p. 93.
† ibid., p. 95.

which their economic success brought them in seeking a special, and rather corrupt, relationship with the Manchurian civil bureaucracy. It was a relationship neither so very different from that which had existed in Korea prior to its incorporation into the Japanese Empire, nor in any way superior to the practices of the European merchant adventurers who had sapped the native energies of half a dozen continents during the previous half-millennium. Now the Japanese came to believe that it was imperative that the lingering apathy of the rural masses in Manchuria should be preserved. It was noted that the Manchurian peasantry traditionally were unmoved by affairs of state and by international relations. What mattered to them more were family, clan and local interests, which in turn were bound up in autonomous feudal relationships between landlords and tenants which had survived for centuries. So long as these traditional cultural values and constraints could be preserved intact, the indigenous population would pose no threat to Japanese economic or political enterprise.

Accordingly, it seemed to be in Japan's interests to cultivate relations with the Manchurian landlord class and for this purpose to stress their common interest in Manchurian autonomy. It must be remarked upon that though thinly populated overall, the country did include nearly $34\frac{1}{2}$ million inhabitants. Fewer than 3 per cent of the population consisted of Manchus by race. Fully 90 per cent were Chinese. That formed a not inconsiderable number of potential antagonists to pacify and police. Fortunately for the Japanese, the bulk of the Chinese were recent immigrants from North China with little love for the southern-dominated Kuomintang, so the Japanese cultivated local and particularist sentiment on fallow ground. Since direct imperialism had acquired a bad name even in these remote regions by 1931, even the most ardently imperialistic Japanese could not hope to overcome this unless they succeeded in wrapping up reality in some more acceptable political form. Aside from the influential Japanese circles in Manchuria to whom the authorities looked for guidance, there were many in Japan who strongly believed in Pan-Asian ideals. For these and other reasons which we shall probe shortly, the thrust of Japanese policies towards Manchuria in the period following the military conquest of the country made a direct appeal to the sentiment of 'Manchurians' in general and especially of those conservative or reactionary elements within the country who inevitably possessed great power and influence in such a society.

Thus, in 1932, the Kwantung Army unwrapped its own plan for the creation of a radical state which was designed to secure the political autonomy of the Kwantung Army within all of the domains it now controlled and also to give comfort to the Chinese of the old days of the Empire. It was called 'Manchukuo', the state of the Manchus. To administer it, there were invited a number of families of the old régime, especially those who had been identified by the Kwantung Army's secret service as friendly to Japan. The Kwantung Army's 'Lawrence of Manchuria', Colonel Doihara Kenji, went south to discuss the situation with Aisin-Gioro Pu-Yi, known universally by his nickname of 'Henry', conferred upon him by his English tutor. Pu-Yi, who in infancy had been deposed by the Chinese Revolution of 1911 as the last Manchu Emperor of China, was persuaded to become the titular head of this new state as a willing tool of the Japanese. No doubt the two sides had differing expectations regarding the true meaning of 'cooperation'.

'Henry' Pu-Yi was an extraordinary creature, undeflected by thought but not by ambition, whose admirable personal traits are difficult to discover. When he was brought before the International Military Tribunal for the Far East by hulking Soviet guards to stand as a star witness for the Prosecution in the early weeks of the Tokyo Trial, Pu-Yi wildly accused the Japanese of attempting 'to enslave the people of the whole world, and they started it with their experience in Manchuria'.[*] He seemed notably short of gratitude for the favours that the Japanese had bestowed upon him. From the witness-box he recalled his visit to meet Emperor Hirohito in Tokyo during 1940, long after Japanese military, political and economic authority had been established in Manchuria, and however much the seriously discombobulated Pu-Yi sought afterwards to distort the facts, what he conveyed to listeners spoke volumes about the harmony which the Japanese had hoped to establish with Manchukuo. Accompanied by his Japanese military aide-de-camp, the Manchu Emperor had been received by Emperor Hirohito with every sign of goodwill. As a token of his esteem, Hirohito gave him two of the three treasures vouchsafed as sacred to the Japanese throne (a sword, a piece of jade and a mirror). Young Pu-Yi received the sword and the mirror. According to ancient Japanese legends, the magical sword had been discovered by the brother of the Sun Goddess, Amaterasu Omikami, who had descended to earth to hack to death an eight-tailed serpent. The sword, found inside the monster's eighth tail, was thereafter renowned as the Excalibur of Japan. According to Pu-Yi, Hirohito also related how Amaterasu Omikami had given the sacred mirror to her grandson, the first Emperor of Japan, and his heirs, 'and told them that when you see this mirror, it is the same as when you see me'.[†] Pu-Yi took the two symbolic treasures back to

---

[*] Pritchard and Zaide, op. cit., 2, pp. 4005–7, 4011.
[†] ibid., p. 4010.

Manchuria. He told the post-war Allied court, 'That was the worst humiliation that I have ever faced.'* The Prosecution, although it never disputed the authenticity of the divine talismans, chose to regard this episode as evidence of a plot by Japanese war leaders to impose Japanese state shintoism upon Manchuria, and from thence throughout China and beyond, 'to control the minds, the souls, the wishes, the movements of the people'.† In fact there was no such grand design, no such uniformity of ambition, and years after the trial Pu-Yi confessed that he had lied during his testimony to save his own skin. Nevertheless, the anecdotal story just described does betoken the Japanese Empire's conception of the seriousness of its commitment to the struggle in which it was engaged on the continent. The sacred insignia offered to him by Hirohito effectively elevated Pu-Yi to a transcendental brotherhood between the two rulers and their realms, and it is therefore quite wrong to suppose that the Japanese conceived that Pu-Yi regarded the episode as symbolic of Japan's subjugation of Manchukuo into slavery.

Meanwhile the Chinese Government, from its capital in distant Nanking, had reacted to the Mukden Incident and its aftermath by playing the card which it hoped would relieve it of danger without its being driven to resolute action. It appealed to the League of Nations. The League's prestige as a peacekeeping machine had been growing in Europe. During minor European disputes in the previous dozen years, the Council of the League had at times intervened when peace was threatened. China was led to think that it might do so over Manchuria, too. The League had never yet been engaged in restraining a Great Power, and this was the task it was now set. Undoubtedly the Kuomintang leaders, though realist enough in home affairs, showed themselves surprisingly ingenuous in supposing that textbook methods of collective security could be followed, with effective results, in checking Japan.

Possibly the Kuomintang politicians were misled by a number of western enthusiasts who abounded in Nanking and Shanghai, and who were later to be joined by refugees from the rising storm in Europe. It had become a matter of prestige among the Chinese to become the patrons of expatriate dilettantes. A great (and venal) banker like T. V. Soong derived face from their permanent employment on his staff. This was reminiscent of a classical period in Chinese history; in the days before the establishment of the stable military empire, when China consisted of a group of

* ibid., pp. 4010, 4174.
† ibid., pp. 4006–7. The words are those of the Chief Prosecutor, Joseph Keenan.

warring feudal kingdoms, roving scholars offered themselves to the Chinese kings, who gladly employed them. Now, as then, the scholars, though cosmopolitan, had more influence on policy-making than most of the regular politicians. They were often dangerous or erratic advisers. Disillusioned by the western record, many of them made a cult of the Kuomintang because it was an apparently revolutionary power which was willing to experiment with new methods. They urged China to attach its fortunes to League procedures.

The League was embarrassed by the confidence shown in it. The skies were darkening over the world: the economic crisis had set in, and the Great Powers looked with alarm at being called to do anything which could further unsettle the world's economy and might even lead to military conflict between themselves and the Japanese. Faced with awkward problems from the rise of Germany, and yielding to the advice tendered by their general staffs, Intelligence experts and economists, the Governments of the leading Powers were more concerned with what they could do to take the danger out of these problems by diplomatic fiddles than they were ready to risk ships, troops and treasure on some quixotic and hazardous experiment in a course so doubtful (and possibly misbegotten) as that of protecting China. The Foreign Ministers who composed the League Council therefore agreed that the situation was far too dangerous for them to gamble by a concerted resort to armed intervention against one of the Great Powers. They used the customary expedient. They appointed that international Commission of Enquiry to which reference has already been made. It was presided over by an Englishman, Lord Lytton, who had been Governor of Bengal and was the grandson of the Victorian historical novelist, Bulwer Lytton.

The Japanese military and the Japanese civil service, although often at cross-purposes and mutually antagonistic, worked uneasily with the tentacles of the South Manchurian Railway which were everywhere. Together they were supreme in Manchukuo. The Japanese, though they had little racial feeling compared to Europeans, were very arrogant: peoples who were subject to them saw their follies, feared their excesses, but secretly tended to despise them. Many Japanese showed their worst qualities in the lands they ruled. In Japan itself there were people of intellectual and moral distinction: but the Empire had proved a catalyst, sifting out men of coarser fibre from the finer sorts.

There was so much to be done. Since its inception the South Manchurian Railway had constructed no fewer than twenty-five company towns, complete with district steam-heating schemes, together with scores of schools, colleges, technical institutes, a university, hospitals and a public health system second to none. By 1931, largely due to the enterprise of the SMR, there were 240,000 Japanese residents in Manchuria. Now ambitious efforts were rekindled in Japan to attract Japanese settlers from farming districts on the Japanese mainland. The cost of this programme was shared between the SMR and the Japanese and Manchukuoan Governments. The scheme was administered initially by the East Asian Industrial Development Company and then successively by the Manchurian Colonization Company and the Manchurian Colonial Development Company established specially for this grand purpose. The Kwantung Army drew up plans for settling five million colonists within twenty years, but between 1932, when the programme began, and 1937 fewer than 5,000 braved the hardships in the five isolated settlements chosen for the first experiment: fewer than 70 per cent of them overcame homesickness, endured the harsh climate and survived the fearful toll taken by infectious diseases and Manchurian bandits. It was a complicated scheme, however, and much progress was made. The infrastructure of training centres, land development, road construction, sanitation and hydro-electric power was ambitious in the extreme. By the outbreak of the Pacific War in December 1941, more than 100,000 new Japanese settlers, including women and children, lived in some 200 agricultural communities scattered over the Manchurian hinterland. One unforeseen consequence of this rapid development was that a marked labour shortage resulted in the rural communities of Japan Proper. Had the twenty-year programme developed as originally planned, it has been estimated that it would have cost Japan and Manchukuo ¥ 10 billion in treasure to complete. Small wonder that the Japanese Ministry of Finance and the Manchurian authorities were reluctant to proceed.

Meanwhile, other Japanese came out to Manchukuo as managers or trained technologists. Many of them were prepared to spend the balance of their careers in the service of the new state. Less admirable were many of the floating population of leech-like personalities who came to get rich quick. These camp-followers were the worst exploiters. One way or another, by 1939, the total Japanese population of Manchukuo had climbed to 837,000.

The dross found its way into many of the agencies of Japan's foreign ventures. Soon they began to make a reputation which was to be a lasting impediment to the further spread of their rule. There were complaints of arbitrary actions, arrests, executions. Notwithstanding pledges in 1932 by the Manchurian puppet régime and by the Japanese authorities in Tokyo promising to respect the Open Door principle, occidental investors and trading concerns found themselves tied down under masses of Japanese red tape and pettifoggery or were squeezed out altogether.

One Japanese publicist for the new régime wrote with greater candour than one might suppose he intended: 'The Open Door, as a practical matter, can be enforced only where law and order are maintained by stable and honest government.'* Western diplomatic protests met with indifference and inactivity. Manchukuo became a closed market for Japanese manufactures. And so whereas at one time all of the SMR's rolling stock had been American made, now the SMR relied upon its own workshops at Dairen, Mukden, Hsinking, Harbin and Tsitsihar to manufacture and repair the equipment it required. Meanwhile other branches of the SMR concentrated upon the creation of integrated traffic systems involving port development, inland waterways, road networks, even shipbuilding. The machinery of government was used to promote the interests of the SMR and fostered a multitude of subordinate economic enterprises. Working together, the Japanese and Manchurian authorities built up an impressive road system in a country that in 1932 was conspicuously lacking in motor transport. In the nine years between 1932 and the Pacific War, Manchukuo doubled its road mileage to 70,000 km. At the same time military and civil airfields were constructed throughout the country and regular airline services developed between all of its principal cities. Telecommunications developed with similar speed: the size of the telegraph network trebled in the six years between 1933 and 1939. All of this was achieved while other experts unified the currency, reorganized customs collection, reformed and centralized the internal revenue services, and modernized the banking system. Conservative monetary policies were instituted by the Government of Manchukuo acting in concert with gifted Japanese economists. It was an intrinsically competent and efficient system which they devised, far more equitable than that which it replaced, but it fell hard upon the entire population.

Above all, it depended upon continuing Japanese capital investment and purchasing power. Japan became increasingly dependent upon Manchuria for basic raw materials. Gold mines opened up. Forests covered 36 per cent of the country and the timber industry thrived as never before. New coal and iron ore finds all helped to buoy up Japan during a period of increasing adversity. Japanese investment mounted. It came to more than ¥4 billion between 1931 and 1940. After a time, surplus Japanese capital began to dry up as Japan became enmeshed in the China Incident and slowly drifted towards the Pacific War from which there

* Kawakami Kiyoshi, quoted in James A. B. Scherer, *Manchukuo: A Bird's-Eye View*, Hokuseidō Press, Tokyo, 1933, p. 117.

would be no turning back. Inflation began to bite as the Government of Manchukuo became obliged to borrow in order to meet current expenditure. Nevertheless, inflation never approached the levels that it did in unoccupied China. Japanese investment in Manchukuo during the whole period between 1931 and 1945 has been estimated at no less than ￥9 billion – an astonishing figure. That quite transformed a country of which it truthfully had been said for centuries: 'Manchuria produces two crops, soybeans and bandits.'*

Japan created in Manchukuo a state welfare system of a type never before seen in East Asia. Nevertheless, there were huge social costs in producing the economic miracle of Manchukuo, costs which beggar any attempt to describe the depravity underlying official policy.

Throughout Manchuria, Inner Mongolia and North China, Japan used its political influence and financial muscle to further all kinds of economic activity, some very detrimental to the indigenous populations. In particular it fostered the opium trade.

Opium had first become an issue in East Asia at the beginning of the previous century. The British, in forcing the trade upon China, had sought to counter the fact that China bought too little from the West, and thereby caused an adverse balance of trade, by creating a new Chinese want, opium. It was grown in great quantities in India, and could easily be shipped to Canton. The Chinese Government protested, and pointed to its duty to protect the Chinese people from the effects of the drug. Two wars had to be fought to overcome its moral objections.

The subsequent history of opium contains a number of unexplained matters. Why did the country as a whole take to opium smoking? What were the effects of the drug upon people's efficiency? Why was the habit, which had been so widespread a few years earlier, checked so completely and with such ease when China eventually had its communist revolution? In the 1930s this ultimate solution of the problem was still far off. Opium had long ceased to be an article of western import: it had become instead a major Chinese product, and though it was not legalized, it was consumed everywhere throughout East Asia. The Kuomintang régime in China and the Manchurian warlords in their domains to the north drew from its trade a revenue which was outside the ordinary state budget, which was unpublished, but which was the most important item in the financing of their respective armies. The Japanese systematically set about cornering this market.

The evidence must speak for itself. According to reports by United

* ibid., p. 93. Manchukuo produced 60 per cent of the world's soybean supplies.

States customs officers, amply confirmed by Japanese and Chinese witnesses at the Tokyo Trial, narcotics abuse in Manchukuo was used to stabilize the national budget, support the Kwantung Army's swollen establishment and maintain 'law and order'. It was an extraordinarily cynical process. The practice of opium smoking, previously encountered mainly among the business and professional classes, saw a meteoric rise. Whereas less than twenty opium dens operated in the Chinese quarter of Antung, for example, prior to the Mukden Incident no less than five hundred were in business within the Japanese Concession there. By July 1932 the number of these establishments in the Chinese city had increased to more than eighty while 684 were licensed in the Japanese Concession. Out of a population of 130,000, over 20,000 had become addicts, and with profits at more than 600 per cent, it was estimated that the revenue derived from this traffic was worth $6.48 million* that year for this one city alone. Even in the surrounding rural areas, the number of addicts rose to approximately 15 per cent of the population. Networks of Japanese and Korean houses of prostitution and bars of every description were augmented by retail opium shops, smoking dens, heroin dens, even pawn shops which exchanged opium for clothing and other personal property.

Opium, as it was usually taken in China and Manchuria, is a comparatively mild drug, and the Chinese addiction to it probably did them no great harm. A quite different effect, however, is produced by the derivatives of opium: heroin and morphine.

The Japanese set themselves to flood the provinces of North China and the lands beyond the Great Wall with heroin and morphine. Partly they did so because of the very high profits obtainable, partly they had in mind the destructive effects of these two drugs. Their use would corrupt the population, cause them to become apathetic, and weaken their will to resist.

One Japanese agency alone was discovered to be dealing with 200 lb of morphine a day in the early part of 1932. This explosive growth continued. The number of opium addicts in Antung and its environs doubled to 40,000, 25 per cent of the population, in the single year of 1933. Unofficial estimates suggested that $19 million was wasted on drugs in that one small locality in that year. Much of that was 'illegal' rather than licensed, yet the total sold by the state Opium Monopoly Bureau in its first year of operation amounted to $33 million, a mighty surplus over the $5 million in receipts estimated in the Manchukuo national budget for the fiscal year

* For all practical purposes, the Manchukuoan yuan or dollar was at parity with the Japanese yen, worth more or less 28.6 US cents apiece.

1932–3. The scourge continued to grow. So did the population of Antung and similar areas. The number of addicts there increased to 340,000, a third of the total population, by December 1934.

Farmers were encouraged to grow opium as part of the Kwantung Army's pacification programme in the countryside. While farmers who grew food crops were eligible for state loans of 5 cents an acre at 7 per cent interest per annum, those who grew poppies could borrow up to 33 cents an acre at 2.3 per cent interest. The poppy tax set at $1.66 to $2.32 in Chang Tso-lin's day was reduced to 83 cents an acre in 1934. But even as the farmers stampeded to produce poppies, the state monopoly purchasing officials cut the producers' profits so savagely each year that many of the farmers found themselves unable to repay their loans and so had their lands confiscated by the Japanese. Still, legal and illegal cultivation of poppies continued to spread as the years passed. Legal cultivation increased by 17 per cent from 133,333 acres in 1936 to 156,061 acres in the following year as demand continued to outstrip supply despite an officially admitted importation of a further 41,335 lb of opium into Manchukuo from the Korean Monopoly Bureau in 1936. Annual opium production in Korea was stepped up to meet that demand: in February 1937, the Director of the Korean Monopoly Bureau declared that it would increase from 57,870 lb to 82,670 lb per annum: 70 per cent of that would go to Manchukuo. Other imports came in from Turkey, Persia and elsewhere.

In mid-1937 the League of Nations Advisory Committee on Traffic in Opium and Other Dangerous Drugs focused the world's attention upon what was happening. As one speaker declared:

We should not be far short of the mark if we said that 90 per cent of all the illicit white drugs of the world are of Japanese origin, manufactured in the Japanese Concession of Tientsin, around Tientsin, in or around Dairen or in other cities of Manchuria, Jehol and China, and this always by Japanese or under Japanese supervision.*

For a time the press was full of stories of the trade, of the protection illegally given the traders by the Japanese Army and Navy, and of the unfortunate inhabitants reduced to fawning submission to morphine and its paraphernalia. The world, startled by Japanese cynicism, reacted more deeply against it than Japan perhaps foresaw. The West, which had the opium wars on its conscience, was more scandalized by the Japanese re-enacting the events of the buried past than prepared to hail them as brothers in crime.

By the end of the 1937 season the Japanese were driven to promise

* Pritchard and Zaide, op. cit., 3, pp. 4697–8.

reforms. They were heartless, empty promises. The harvest in Manchukuo alone that year amounted to a staggering 2,800,000 lb of raw opium. In 1937 the state monopoly budgeted $29,025,000 for the purchase of raw opium and recorded sales of $47,850,000. In 1938 it authorized an expenditure of $32,653,000 on raw opium and received $71,045,200 in revenue. By 1939 the cost rose to $43,470,000 and sales reached $90,908,400. The scope for racketeering in such a climate was virtually unlimited. This was an entirely new instrument of Total War, and it set the pattern for Japanese occupation forces elsewhere. Most disturbing of all, however, is the well-documented fact that this policy was approved and promoted not only by the Kwantung Army, by the Japanese Army General Staff and by the Japanese War Ministry but by the Japanese Cabinet as well.

Meanwhile, a handful of rogue Japanese industrialists began to pour capital into the exploitation of huge, newly discovered coal and iron ore reserves and then into prodigiously profitable investment in virtually monopolistic enterprises, keenly monitored and sheltered by the Kwantung Army, such as Ayukawa Gisuke's *Nihon Sangyō* Company (better known as Nissan) and the great Manchurian Heavy Industries Company which he founded in 1937. The latter became all-powerful within its sphere of activities, hiving off interests which had formerly been the exclusive preserve of the far more paternalistic S M R. All of this greatly worried many of the giant financial and industrial combines on the Japanese mainland, such as the colossal family firms of Mitsui, Mitsubishi and Sumitomo, who not only showed a marked reluctance to invest in Manchuria but feared the emergence of potential competitors and tried in vain to persuade successive Japanese Governments to seek the orderly development of a purely complementary Manchurian economy under totally civilian direction.

The close collaboration between Japan and Manchuria, without doubt oppressive to its opponents, was welcomed in many quarters as an alternative to political disorder and economic instability. There had been an amazing drive towards modernization affecting one of the most backward frontiers on earth. The huge importation of Japanese capital and entrepreneurs had made it possible. The thousands of Japanese 'advisers' who forced themselves into every nook and cranny of the land guaranteed that there could be no resistance. These developments and the cost of the expanded military appropriations necessary to underwrite the whole endeavour increased the burden of defence expenditure to which the Japanese nation was already committed in the naval rearmament programme which successive Japanese Governments all regarded as an essential defence requirement in an uncertain world. The inevitable result of all of these commitments was to force the Japanese Government and taxpayer into an economy geared for war production. This in turn led Japan to reconsider its trading relationship with the rest of the world. Non-essential trade was sharply curtailed and strong preference for home-produced goods instead of the allure of foreign manufactures took root in the hearts of Japanese consumers and traders: it has remained a marked characteristic of Japanese society to the present day.

These new economic practices rapidly improved Japan's balance of payments notwithstanding the depths of the great depression in the world at large. By as early as 1933 Japanese expenditure on armaments produced a boom economy in which most Japanese rejoiced. Japanese exports cut through the international economic doldrums and by 1936 had surpassed the record levels of 1929 by 60 per cent. Japan soon dominated the world market in cheap textiles of good quality, undercutting not only the recovery and historical ascendency of Britain's Lancashire cotton mills but also the emergent textile industrial exports of India which on the eve of the depression had risen to prominence in the market stalls of Africa, Asia and South America.

The true cost of Japan's military adventures on the Asiatic mainland, however, worried Japanese economists from the beginning. As a number of them foresaw, Japan found itself unable to escape a progressive dependence not merely upon the territories which it had conquered but also upon war materials imported from the United States. As imports of non-essential goods declined, strategically important commodities became an increasingly high percentage of Japanese imports. They were also politically sensitive. For the time being, this proved to be little problem. Isolationist sentiment in the United States counteracted the influence of those Americans who sought to intervene in the relations between Japan and her continental neighbours. The United States Secretary of State's proclamation of the 'Stimson Doctrine' of 'non-recognition' of territorial changes achieved by the use of force failed to move that pragmatic economist President Herbert Hoover during the nightmare of the great depression, and after 1932, when Franklin D. Roosevelt occupied the White House, the attention of the United States administration was at the very least distracted by events in Europe, by his grand strategy aimed at improving relations with Latin America, and by efforts to effect an economic and political transformation within the United States itself. The United States had its finger on the jugular vein of Japanese military expansion so long as Japan had no other source for vital strategical commodities. Given the disparity in economic and material resources of the Japanese

Empire compared with those of the United States, the Japanese Army appreciated that means should be sought to neutralize or to woo the United States away from its moral support for the Kuomintang. Since it appeared highly improbable that Japanese reassurances or efforts to appease the Americans would suffice so long as Japanese ambitions on the continent were unfulfilled, diplomatic and even military links with Nazi Germany and fascist Italy became increasingly attractive means of holding off the threat of intervention by the Anglo-Saxon Powers.

A particularly nauseating sanctimoniousness did arise in certain American and European political circles. Stripped to essentials, the cry was in support of 'Collective Security and the League'. It depended upon a willingness by powerful states to hazard their own forces in support of economic and diplomatic pressure upon aggressor states. However, the human, material and financial costs of any such actions inherently bite back hardest at those Powers whose unswerving devotion to the cause is essential if success is to be achieved. Selflessness of that kind, always a rare commodity, generally disappears from the scene when the aggressor is a first-class Power and the issues are 'exceedingly complicated' – as they plainly were in this case.

A policy of forceful intervention commanded too little support to become a realizable possibility. The United Kingdom alone among members of the League of Nations possessed in the Royal Navy the means to enforce whatever sanctions might have been instituted, and there were good reasons to doubt suggestions by the American Secretary of State, Henry L. Stimson, that the United States stood ready to share the burden of any concerted sanctions to force Japan out of Manchuria. How would such sanctions be enforced? In this instance they could be made effective only by interposing naval forces between Japan and the Asian mainland or between Japan and her outside sources of supplies. What would any self-respecting nation do to defend itself against the first (or only) ships that might be mustered against it? The choice for such a nation was stark. It could lie low and wait for the tempest to subside, leaving the supporters of 'Collective Security' with egg on their faces and with no stomach for another such venture if further steps should be taken by the aggressor following the inevitable disbanding of such an expensive naval operation. Alternatively, it could sink or damage the interfering vessels, at the besieged nation's selected moment, close to that nation's own repair and supply depots, and far – very far – from the white knights' bases.

Thus it was that British public and official opinion about the Manchurian Incident mattered more than the views of any other Third Power including the United States. The *Manchester Guardian* alone among prominent British newspapers argued that Japanese complaints in Manchuria were entirely unjustified. Most of the press held the contrary view, believing that the Japanese had a strong case against the Chinese. Wags among old China hands declared that the only thing worse than a Japanese victory would be a Chinese victory. Such attitudes remained prevalent throughout the crisis and were not confined to conservative press and political circles. The former Liberal Foreign Secretary Lord Grey, for instance, told an audience at the Central Hall, Westminster, on 11 December 1931, 'Japan had a strong case in Manchuria, where her interests were being threatened by lawlessness, and if Japan had submitted her case to the signatories of the Covenant and the Pact [of Paris], it would have been the business of those signatories to see how the remedy could be applied.'* Even Lord Lytton long shared the same view, at least until February 1933. He then told an audience in Manchester, 'Let me say to the partisans of China that the case of Japan *vis-à-vis* the League may be a weak one, but the case of Japan *vis-à-vis* China is a strong one.' He developed this theme in an interview with the *Daily Herald* a few days later: 'Japan has a case. She has a very strong case on merits. But she has no case at all for the action she has taken.' While the Pact of Paris may have been violated, as all conceded, that was not yet regarded as tantamount to law-breaking. More importantly, it was far from clear that Japanese actions were in breach of the Covenant of the League of Nations. The Japanese Government had been trying for months to gain redress for its grievances from the Chinese central Government at Nanking and had shown great patience in the face of long-continued provocation. The *Daily Telegraph* in London, for one, suggested in October 1931 that 'The right of a government to protect its interests against barbarism and anarchy is a well-recognized one, and if Japan is studious to keep within it, her position is a strong one.'

Thus when the League of Nations Council demanded the total withdrawal of all Japanese troops as a precondition to negotiations for the settlement of the dispute, many people in Britain – and virtually everyone in Japan – felt that this was to ignore reality and to prejudge the Japanese case. Moreover, when the League Council decided to affix a deadline for that withdrawal, that was seen – quite rightly – as a new obstacle to the resolution of the dispute, and as an insufferable slap in the face for the Japanese, who were already exceedingly resentful and irritated by the

* R. Bassett, *Democracy and Foreign Policy: A Case History, The Sino-Japanese Dispute, 1931–33*, Frank Cass & Co., London, 1968, p. 32.

double standards of certain Western Powers. Mindful of the history of the area, this reaction by the Japanese was entirely appropriate. In a sense, therefore, League interference actually helped deliver the Japanese nation into the hands of hotheads who had no time or thoughts save for action.

The Army's Manchurian adventure proved far from disappointing. The Japanese, despite their excesses, were slow to abandon the hope of sincere or large-scale cooperation with the Chinese. The Japanese embraced the idea of Sino-Japanese cooperation with such fervour that it seemed only logical to crush the influence of those that opposed it. The driving spirits of the Kwantung Army and kindred forces within the Army General Staff and War Ministry, far from meditating upon means of ending Japanese control over Manchuria, became increasingly interested in the provinces of China itself south of the Wall, at least in the provinces of the northern half of the country. The grass may not have seemed greener in that valley than it had turned out to be north of the Wall, but it was nevertheless green. It became fashionable in Japan for ambitious young officers to seek service in the Kwantung Army. Others of the same stamp chose to seek their future in the much smaller China Garrison Army and to build up their military experience while acquiring detailed local knowledge from the vantage points of places such as Peking, Tientsin and Shanghai, which were certain to acquire a critical importance if relations between the Japanese Empire and China were to degenerate into Total War. The hopes of these military adventurers grew, and it was in the nature of things that they were not deterred by the unfortunate end to which some of their colleagues came simply because the Chinese had grown anxious about the Japanese Army's secret service.

While the Lytton Commission was preparing its report, the crisis took a new turn. The shock to China had been deeper, spread quicker and produced more results than many in Japan had expected. Events passed out of control. A commotion among the Chinese people, not any specific action by the Chinese Government, was the unexpected factor. A boycott of Japanese goods took place, which was partly spontaneous, partly organized by Chinese secret societies, and fully exploited by the competing political activists of rival Kuomintang and communist factions. Violence broke out in Shanghai as a result of the boycott and in consequence of street demonstrations that grew out of a curious mésalliance between religious extremists belonging to the Japanese *Nichi-ren* Buddhist sect and a few Kwantung Army *agents provocateurs* sent there to distract attention from events in Manchuria. Large-scale riots soon developed. Terror was met by counter-terror.

All of this provoked Japan to land a token force of about 700 marines on 28 January 1932 with the task of doing no more than protect the city's 30,000 Japanese residents and the large commercial stake which they had built there over the decades. They met with something like the resistance of a Popular Front. Panic spread through the Japanese community. The Japanese Minister in China was Shigemitsu Mamoru. In all but name he was Ambassador: as befitted China's third-rate status in the international world, few countries dignified their chief representatives in China with the rank of Ambassador, and Japan was no exception to this practice. Shigemitsu came to the conclusion that the only way to save Japanese residents and the beleaguered marines from annihilation from the now frenzied mobs was to request his Government to call up large-scale re-inforcements. Even the post-war Tokyo War Crimes Tribunal absolved him of any guilt for his part in the affair. The Japanese Cabinet agreed with Shigemitsu's assessment, and a marine brigade of 10,000 men hur-riedly embarked the next day on a squadron of fast destroyers which set sail from Japan under the command of Vice-Admiral Nomura Kichisa-burō, a man later fated to serve briefly as Foreign Minister of Japan in the critical months following the outbreak of the European War in 1939, later still as Japan's forlorn Ambassador to the United States between November 1940 and the Japanese attack on Pearl Harbor. The marine reinforcements rapidly found themselves unable to cope with the situation despite gunnery support at point-blank range from Japanese warships which had steamed up the Wangpoo from the Yangtze fifteen miles downstream. Lieutenant-General Ueda Kenkichi, until recently Com-mander of the China Garrison Army maintained by Japan in North China in conformity with the old 'Unequal Treaties', was ordered by the Army to proceed from Japan with the Ninth Infantry Division to rescue the marines. Unexpectedly, even Ueda's division proved unable to tip the balance. Two more divisions had to be sent from Japan, this time under the overall military command of ex-War Minister General Shirakawa Yoshinori.

The Chinese 'defence' of Shanghai, improvised on the spur of the moment, was impressive. This was one of the first demonstrations in modern times of which the world took effective notice, that the Chinese, or some of them, were a martial people. Hitherto the Chinese had fought their wars by often incompetent professional armies or under bandit chieftains, operating from books of rules which, though they might give occasional apt counsel as they had done on the Nonni River, were hope-lessly out-of-date. The people, who were sceptics by tradition, expressed their contempt for all things military. But in this, as in so much else,

China was changing, and the Powers in contact with it grudgingly took notice of the fact.

The resistance was at first hampered by the ambivalent, cautious, luke-warm attitude of the Chinese Government. Perhaps by accident, there happened to be garrisoned, on the outskirts of Shanghai, a rather wayward left-wing unit of the Chinese Army known as the Nineteenth Route Army. This force was commanded by Tsai Ting-kan, an ingenuous, simple-minded man who had breathed in the simple slogans of the nationalists (and also, it appeared, of the communists). This officer, whose military training had been elementary, and who had received no indoctrination politically, and his troops, simple peasants with the most ordinary equipment, stiffened the resistance of the rest of the Chinese. As two more Chinese divisions, the 'China Bodyguard Army', joined the struggle for control of Shanghai, the significance of the fighting increased. Large parts of the International Settlement were destroyed and the Chinese suburbs beyond were ravaged.

It must be stressed that the initial Japanese military aims were modest, and operations in Shanghai were conducted in the early stages with relative self-restraint. Japan was doing no more than acting fully in conformity with the old extra-territorial rights which Japan as well as the British Empire, France, Italy and the United States possessed in the International Settlement. In the beginning, Admiral Nomura even anticipated that a restoration of orderly conditions in Shanghai by his marines would be welcomed by the other international contingents in the city: the British had sent in their own troops to quell similar disturbances as recently as 1926. Whatever the moral issues underlying the whole affair, and not-withstanding the activities of provocateurs on both sides, there was cer-tainly no intention on the part either of the Japanese Government or of the Army General Staff to 'punish China'. Except within the headquarters of the Kwantung Army, the issue was seen in Japanese high circles as entirely one of 'self-defence'. As the struggle continued, however, each side inflicted hideous atrocities upon their enemies. Japanese conduct especially became remarkable for its extreme cruelty. The dispassionate historian must reject the judgement of the Tokyo Tribunal 'that the real purpose of the Japanese attack was to alarm the Chinese by indication of what would follow if their attitude toward Japan continued, and thus break down resistance to future operations. The Incident was part of the general plan.'* It is nevertheless indisputably correct that:

The needless bombing of Chapei [a squalid Chinese suburb tucked in a corner between the western edge of the International Settlement and the northern bounds

* Pritchard and Zaide, op. cit., 20: *Judgment and Annexes*, p. 49106.

of the separate French Concession], the ruthless bombardment by naval vessels, and the massacre of the helpless Chinese farmers whose bodies were later found with their hands tied behind their backs, are examples of the method of warfare waged at Shanghai.*

The fighting lasted until 3 March when the Japanese at last broke through to the open country beyond the city. The confidence of the Japanese military received a setback from the unexpected resistance, and from the international stir which the crisis had provoked. The good offices of the United States, Britain, France, Italy and officials of the League of Nations helped to effect an armistice. Chief credit for the settlement, however, properly belongs to the British Minister, Sir Miles Lampson, and to Minister Shigemitsu, the very man who had called for the marines at the end of January. It was he who persuaded the Japanese Commander-in-Chief at Shanghai, General Shirakawa, to order a ceasefire on 3 March, on the very eve of a meeting by the General Assembly of the League of Nations which was due to consider the crisis. Negotiations to achieve a lasting peace were fraught with difficulties, but the final breakthrough sprang from the personal courage of Shigemitsu. As he and other Japanese dignitaries stood on a reviewing stand at a parade to mark the Emperor's birthday on 29 April, a Korean nationalist threw a bomb which killed General Shirakawa, tore off part of General Ueda's foot, blinded Admiral Nomura in one eye, and killed the chairman of the local Japanese residents' association. Shigemitsu, too, was caught in the blast but refused to undergo life-saving surgery until a peace agreement was reached on 5 May. His own account of what happened was confirmed after the war by western diplomats and foreign correspondents who rallied to Shigemitsu's defence during the Tokyo Trial proceedings:

The text of the agreement having been drawn up at the British Consulate-General, the scene of the negotiations, the document was brought round to my bed in the hospital, where, racked with pain and in danger of my life, I managed to complete the numerous signatures required. I said then to Chang the Chinese Secretary: 'Relations between Japan and China must now enter a state of amity. I pray that this document may be the starting-point of future good relations between our two countries.' At that moment it was a question whether my life could be saved. The Chinese Secretary returned to the council chamber and in impressive tones disclosed my message. When all the signatures were completed, the operating table was wheeled in and one leg was amputated.

Peace having been restored, the Japanese forces were withdrawn from the Shanghai area and conditions returned to normal.†

* ibid., p. 49105.
† M. Shigemitsu, *Japan and her Destiny*, Hutchinson, London, 1958, pp. 78–9.

In fact, of course, conditions did not quite return to normal. Chinese morale everywhere was recharged by the stout resistance which their compatriots at Shanghai had maintained against crack Japanese troops for more than six weeks. It did not affect the outcome there or anywhere, but it gave the Chinese hope and gladdened the hearts of their friends.

Finally, the League of Nations Commission of Enquiry made known its findings, and as the British historian of Japan, Richard Storry, later remarked, these 'included a sympathetic explanation of Japanese grievances that was more compelling than anything put out by Tokyo'.* The Report by Lord Lytton's Commission was a thoughtful document. It cautioned that '[the] issues involved in this conflict are not as simple as they are often represented to be. They are, on the contrary, exceedingly complicated, and only an intimate knowledge of all the facts, as well as of their historical background, should entitle anyone to express a definite opinion upon them.'† After such a shot across the bows of public opinion, it is tempting to alter course, or heave to, for a discourse on the minutiae of the Japanese, Manchurian and Chinese claims and counter-claims. Happily, however, we need not dwell on the rights and wrongs that bemused contemporary observers were obliged to consider. It is sufficient to note that as a case study in international politics and in the misconduct of civil/military affairs, the period encompassing the Manchurian Incident and the foundation of Manchukuo is so rich, fascinating and, indeed, thought-provoking that we must regret the usual knee-jerk conclusion that Japan and its leadership were intent from the beginning upon nothing less than the complete subjugation of Manchuria and its incorporation into the Japanese Empire with as little fuss as possible. This is belied by the cracks that the crisis produced within the Japanese Government and its armed forces. It was understood, as articulated in the words of the Report of the League of Nations Assembly, adopted on 24 February 1933 (a month after Hitler's rise to power), that 'Past experience shows that those who control Manchuria exercise a considerable influence on the affairs of the rest of China – at least of North China – and possess unquestionable strategic and political advantages. To cut off these provinces from the rest of China cannot but create a serious irredentist problem likely to endanger peace.'‡ Nevertheless, the habit of disparaging the

* 'The English-language Presentation of Japan's Case during the China Emergency of the Late Nineteen-thirties', in *European Studies on Japan*, Paul Norbury Publications, Tenterden, Kent, 1979, p. 146.

† *The Report of the Commission of Enquiry into the Sino-Japanese Dispute*, op. cit., p. 166.

‡ *Sino-Japanese Dispute: Report adopted on February 24, 1933, by the Assembly of the League of Nations*, United States Government Printing Office, Washington, DC, 1933, p. 16.

military prowess of all oriental races died hard. From a sociological as well as from a military point of view, the most curious fact remains that western observers generally failed to appreciate the magnitude of Japan's feats of arms. There was still an inclination in many quarters to regard the Japanese as only marginally more civilized than the Chinese.

The Lytton Commission did not scruple to say that Japan had been an aggressor, though in polite and reasoned language, and though it held that China had itself been provocative, and was therefore in part guilty. The Report was accepted by the League Council by a vote of forty-two to one, unanimously but for the dissenting voice of Japan. It was too much for Japan to swallow. It may be uncharitable if not inaccurate to say that Japan objected to China, the parvenu, being treated as equal with Japan, which thought of itself as one of the established imperialist Powers of the world. Nevertheless, its reply was to resign from the League of Nations in March 1933.

The final scene was enacted at Geneva by the Japanese Ambassador, Matsuoka Yōsuke, a graduate of the University of Oregon, who was later to serve as President of the South Manchurian Railway between 1935 and 1939 and would thereafter reappear on the international stage as Foreign Minister of Japan. The drama was described as follows in *The Times*:

> Mr Matsuoka announced immediately after the vote that his Government found themselves compelled to conclude that Japan and the other members of the League entertained different views of the manner to achieve peace in the Far East, and were obliged to feel that they had now reached the limit of their endeavours to cooperate with the League with regard to Sino-Japanese differences. The Japanese then walked out in a body. They maintained the self-possession of their race to the last, but many of them are known to have been cleft in their emotions.

Their departure was seen with ruffled feelings by some of the officials of the League of Nations, who, while they recognized that Japan was aggressive, felt themselves obliged to state that, on the various international committees and agencies which the League promoted, Japan had been a most valuable member. The hearts of some of them were heavy at what they felt had been the driving out of Japan from associating with enlightened governments, and at the increased opportunity which this gave to all the darker forces at work in Japan.

The Manchurian Incident, or rather the failure of the League of Nations to find an effective means of enforcing the moral precepts professed by the majority of states, seriously handicapped the League's efforts to resolve subsequent international disputes elsewhere. No attempt was made by the League Council to organize sanctions against Japan, although

Japan's actions did not technically relieve it of the threat: but it is obvious that the Powers snatched at excuses eagerly. Also, by withdrawing from the comity of nations, Japan relieved the League of the effort to regulate internationally the privileged position of Japan in Manchuria, which the Lytton Commission had agreed that it should have. In fact, there was precious little that the League or any of its member states could have done to wrest the initiative from the hands of the Kwantung Army. Any economic, military or naval demonstration in support of China would only have undermined still further the efforts of moderate Japanese statesmen to bring the Japanese militarist factions under control. Moreover, China's domestic upheavals and disregard for the 'extra-territorial' rights of Western Powers had aroused considerable apprehensions among many foreign governments in the years preceding the Manchurian Incident. Small wonder, then, that a fatal inertia overcame international outrage particularly in those countries where the initial response of public opinion had been favourable to Japan, especially since Japan at first did not seem intent upon displacing western investment and commercial interests whether in North China or Manchuria. The protection of that investment and those interests had always been a matter of great concern to western governments and was one of the principal objects of their policies towards China and Japan. Now those governments perceived that a major change was taking place in the relations between Japan and the outer world. It was not so much a change in Japanese aims as in the preparedness of the Japanese to defy western opinion in seeking the furtherance of those aims. And so while the personal integrity of Japanese diplomats abroad remained in high esteem, the opinion spread throughout the democratic nations of the world that the Japanese Government was itself out of control or that it was content to carry out its true predatory plans behind honourable professions which it intended to breach. European dictatorships, by and large little involved in the East Asian crisis, nevertheless drew the lesson that the use of force could pay considerable dividends for 'have not' nations who possessed the will to grasp the meat they craved.

Robert Osgood, in a book entitled *Problems of Modern Strategy*, defined Limited War as a conflict 'fought for ends far short of the complete subordination of one state's will to another's and by means involving far less than the total military resources of the belligerents, leaving the civilian life and the armed forces of the belligerents largely intact and leading to a bargained determination'.* Berenice Carroll, another student of the

---

* 'The Reappraisal of Limited War', in *Problems of Modern Strategy*, ed. A. Buchan, Praeger Press, London, 1970, p. 92.

subject, observed that a war regarded by the aggressor as a limited campaign may seem to be a Total War to the power upon whose soil it is waged, especially if the defending power succumbs to the invading forces.* Still another expert, Arthur Marwick, suggests four tests by which Total War may be identified: it must involve whole populations; the organization of the home front is as critical an influence as that of the military front; it shall mobilize all of the resources of science, technology and propaganda available to each side, and it shall be an 'all out' and 'all-embracing' struggle.† Looking back over the development of the Manchurian Incident and its aftermath, it becomes evident that these events involved the whole populations of Manchuria and Japan. Japan as well as Manchuria was thrown into immense upheaval. This has been under-appreciated in most western historical accounts of the Greater East Asia or Pacific War, yet it is essential to grasp the fact that the Manchurian Incident marked not simply a military signpost pointing to a providential turn of fortune in a backwater territory encountered along Japan's road to Hiroshima. It was that but more. It changed the political and social geography of both countries, creating a political and economic breakwater in the historical evolution of East Asia which only the unprecedented tide of changes endured in 1945 would sweep away. Japanese historians have long recognized this. So should we. As Kipling reminds us:

> The toad beneath the harrow knows
>   Exactly where each tooth-point goes;
> The butterfly upon the road
>   Preaches contentment to that toad.‡

The Manchurian Incident and the transformation of Manchukuo into an industrial and colonial powerhouse had no real precedent in contemporary history. This experiment in colonial government by proxy deeply affected the Japanese, and it is instructive to link events there first with the China Incident and afterwards with the conduct and expectations of Japanese forces during the Pacific War. The Japanese were conscious of the fact that the Second World War, if it came, would be a Total War. They were keenly aware of their industrial and material shortcomings in comparison to the Western Powers. The Japanese counterpart of the 'Yellow Peril' was a nightmare in which the barbarian western hordes,

---

* *Design for Total War: Arms and Economics in the Third Reich*, Mouton, The Hague, 1968, pp. 9–36.
† *Britain in the Century of Total War*, Bodley Head, London, 1968, *passim*.
‡ R. Kipling, *Rudyard Kipling's Verse: Definitive Edition*, Doubleday, Garden City, New York, 1942, p. 26.

possessed of unlimited money and manpower, would inexorably sweep across Asia and the Pacific. The Japanese knew that they must rely upon their own mental fortitude, physical self-sacrifice and traditional values embodied in their 'national polity' to escape defeat (indeed, this helps us to explain the tenacity of Japanese resistance – and suicides – during the war). For many decades there had been a wide measure of agreement, one certainly not confined to political extremists, that in the event of hostilities with any Third Power, it would be vital to harness all of the energies of Manchuria as well as of the Japanese Empire.

In Manchukuo the Japanese developed the first economy anywhere since the end of the First World War to be mobilized and dedicated to Total War. By the same token, the scale of Japan's achievements in Manchuria went largely unnoticed abroad. The partnership, whatever its strains (and they were considerable), between the Kwantung Army and the South Manchurian Railway and its Research Department, technical institutes and training establishments, was hugely important in setting a pattern for the future both in Japan Proper and throughout Greater East Asia. Like some latter-day East India Company, the S M R possessed incalculable prestige and not inconsiderable influence. Yet there were other forces at work as well. It was a time of five-year plans and huge monopolistic enterprises, state-controlled in theory but run by highly entrepreneurial venture capitalists. One can find similar partnerships and attendant strains manifest in the South Seas Mandated Islands, in Japanese-occupied territories everywhere, in the Asian Development Board's activities in China and beyond, in the evolving relationship between the *zaibatsu* and the Japanese political parties, and in the emergence of what is often regarded as a kind of totalitarian, non-party police state (in imitation, so it is said, of European fascist systems). It is true that many Japanese felt attracted by foreign political systems – although whether by democratic or totalitarian solutions depended upon the taste of the individual. Yet to dismiss the Japanese as imitators is to underrate the far greater importance of Japan's own creativity and dynamism. Overriding all calculation, however, was a sense that the modern history of Japan inspired faith that somehow the Japanese would muddle through, and that their cause was just.

CHAPTER 7
China: Internal Revolutions and Foreign Policy

CHINA made a great impression upon the foreigners who came to assist in its modernization. Following his return from a period of service with the Chinese Government, one young Englishman wrote a long private report on the relations between China's internal affairs and foreign policy. The Head of the Far Eastern Department of the British Foreign Office read it and minuted, 'It tells one more about the subject than anything I have seen.'* In his opening remarks the reporter had observed:

In the nation as a whole, the proportion of persons with high natural gifts is at least as large as, perhaps larger than, that of other eastern or western peoples. It is true that, owing to poverty and to the social structure, the greater part of this talent is never brought to fruition: nevertheless changes in social institutions may well put China once again in the forefront of civilized nations. The developments in the Far East ought therefore to be of first-class interest to the rest of the world.†

The prime characteristic of modern China was the importance of the farmer and the rural situation. This did not mean that farmers governed the country or that the Government was in their interest. On the contrary, as we shall see later, there were few countries in the world where the farmer had less to say in the conduct of affairs: and this was one of the causes of China's troubles during this time. Nevertheless, it was, broadly speaking, true that though China was governed almost exclusively by townsmen, it was not events in the cities – for example, the sentiments of the town proletariat – which made China strong or weak: it was the events in the countryside. An overwhelming proportion, perhaps 85 per cent, of the Chinese population lived upon farms. If this peasantry were reasonably satisfied, the Government would be powerful: when the peasantry was against the Government, the Government, *vis-à-vis* its neighbours, was half-paralysed.

The second most noticeable feature was the high density of population in certain areas. To a perceptive observer at the time, Chinese history –

---

* F 7911/166/10, minute by C. W. Orde, 4 January 1937, FO 371/20252, preserved at the British Public Record Office, Kew.
† ibid., memorandum by Guy Wint, 15 December 1936.

though this is subject to controversy – could perhaps be given a cyclical interpretation in terms of cyclical changes in the size of population, bearing in mind that every such simplified interpretation can be only partially true, and that a full analysis would require many factors besides population to be taken into account. With increasing population there was increased pressure on the land; as a result farms would become smaller, rents, and the number of tenant farmers, would increase. Finally, the standard of living would sink so low that banditry would break out on a nationwide scale. In the confusion which resulted, a dynasty would fall, either from pressure outside or from internal weakness; there would follow prolonged civil war; eventually, as a result of violence, pestilence and starvation, the population would reduce to limits which would permit the majority of farmers to win such a living from the land as to place the attractions of peace and order above the more adventurous and uncertain life of banditry. This would enable the political power which happened at that time to be in the ascendant, to consolidate itself and to found a new dynasty; and with peace re-established, China would enter upon one of its periods of great literary, artistic and cultural productivity. Later on the population once more would increase, pressure upon the land grow, and revolt break out afresh. That was how things appeared to stand in the years which preceded the outbreak of Total War between Republican China and Imperial Japan.*

In spite of its apparently easy defeats, and in spite of its disappointments at Geneva, China did not lose face. In this Japan was disappointed. It had counted on its action being regarded in the public opinion of the world as an old-fashioned colonial operation, which, in the atmosphere of 1931, was still condonable. China, a manifestly unequal Power, was to be put in its place. But the world, to Japan's surprise, was not inclined to revise its previous impression that China was genuinely in revival, and to write it off as now discredited.

As soon as the fighting in China was checked by a truce, China resumed its continuous, painful steps towards recovery as a Power in world affairs. The Japanese became conscious, though at first they could scarcely credit it, that this Chinese ambition was now fostered by the former imperialists who had once treated it with so much contempt. In fact, Japan's determination to rise had now become so evident, and was seen with so much misgiving by other Powers, that it was natural for its rivals to

---

* Adapted from the private memorandum submitted by Guy Wint to the British Foreign Office, 15 December 1936: see above.

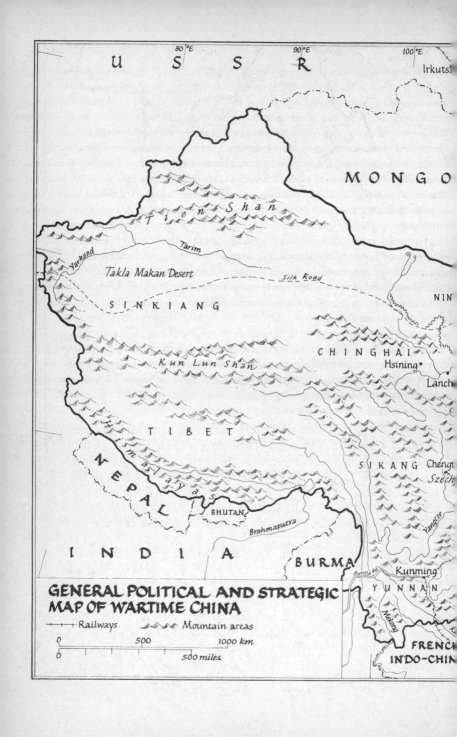

GENERAL POLITICAL AND STRATEGIC
MAP OF WARTIME CHINA

Railways Mountain areas

0   500   1000 km
0   500 miles

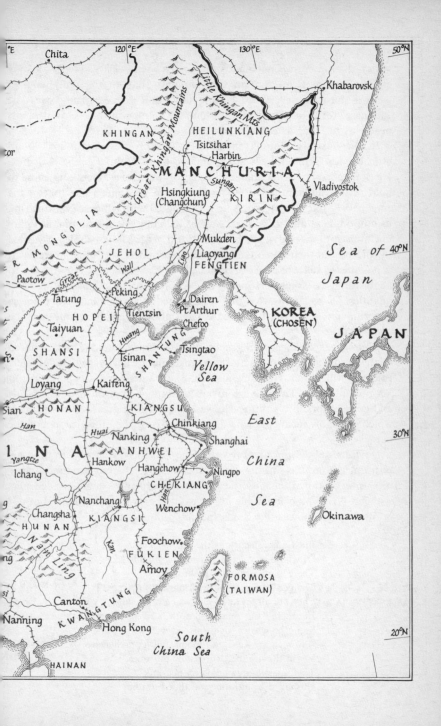

switch their interest benevolently to Japan's enemy. This slow, but lasting change was more evident in Governments than in the sentiments of western businessmen, who, by the old habit of consorting with the Japanese, for a long while had found the change in their Governments nearly as puzzling as did the Japanese.

In the next six years, from 1931–7, this progress continued. Domestically, for China, they were dominated by one man, Chiang Kai-shek. He drew ahead of his civilian colleagues in the Government and came to hold in the public mind of China a position very much like that of the emperors of old. By foreigners he was equated with Chinese Nationalism, its embodiment and its principal agent. Chiang was the dominant figure in China until the end of the Second World War. Many people forwarded the drama but their personalities remain shrouded. In China, however, it is possible to tell what sort of man Chiang Kai-shek was. An attempt to analyse and assess his personality is necessary, for, in understanding what qualities he had and why they established his supremacy in Chinese government, many of the obscure facts about China's régime may be made plain.

Chiang was the successful general of the Kuomintang. He had mounted on the shoulders of the party and come to dominate it. His special characteristic was will-power. He knew just what he wanted, and was never idle in his pursuit of it. This gave him an advantage over most of his rivals and competitors in Nanking. He was gifted with a great self-confidence, which probably meant that he despised most of the other leaders of the party.

Devious, subtle, resourceful – these he had to be if he was to hold his position among the shifting sands of Nanking. His outstanding quality was an exceptional tenacity: he got his way through single-minded persistence. His mind being made up, he would never change. In this, but not in other ways, he was like Shakespeare's Julius Caesar:

> But I am constant as the northern star
> Of whose true-fixed and resting quality
> There is no fellow in the firmament.
> The skies are painted with unnumbered sparks,
> They are all fire, and every one doth shine,
> But there's but one in all doth hold his place.
> So in the world: 'tis furnished well with men
> And men are flesh and blood, and apprehensive,
> Yet in the number I do know but one,
> That unassailable holds on his rank
> Unshaked of motion: and that I am he.

He had a chilling attitude to the issues of life and death. If an object could be obtained with comparatively little sacrifice, so much the better. But if its purchase should cost 100,000 lives, he was willing, with scarcely any hesitation, to pay the price. He would have regarded this attitude as realistic.

He was not especially clever, inspiring, good, proficient at public speaking or public appearance. He was the product of a provincial military college in China, and of a rather inferior Japanese education. With this background he was neither so well educated as to have eccentric views, nor so badly as to appear scandalously ignorant. Accordingly the middle ranks, the mediocre, served him well as the medium out of which he rose to fame. He had a poor imagination, but, as against this, an exceptionally good memory. He dissimulated, and always held back his real thoughts. His suspiciousness was boundless. But if he did not check this, he could point to it having served him well. He was habitually surrounded by so much deceit that only a carefully nurtured suspicion kept him aware of the plots of remarkable complexity which were the stuff of Chinese politics.

He had a flair for political manoeuvre, and was excellent at manipulating his colleagues. He knew, and was at home in, the labyrinth of Chinese affairs – in the secret societies, in knowing how to use money to build a personal empire, in knowing how to operate a front in politics, and what to say in public through that front. He had the political talent, which comes near political mysticism, for nearly always foreseeing how things would fall out, and for knowing what needed to be done in particular circumstances. This flair, which included judging a situation correctly – and not with the distraction of moral considerations – was perhaps the key to his success in politics.

He preferred to rule through the ubiquitous secret societies which were always one of the chief characteristics of China. Some of these societies were of ancient origin, had existed originally for respectable purposes, but had degenerated. Chiang took steps to bind the societies to himself. They secured discipline among their members by strong-arm methods, always secret. Chiang, being fundamentally uninterested in ideas, jumped at the opportunity of gaining China by means of authority in this twilight world, twitching a string here, a string there. The extent to which China, before the Communist Revolution, was a rabbit warren of secret societies, ramified with weird ceremonies and tied up at distant removes to Confucianism, cannot be exaggerated. They caught in their net all who mattered in the Government – bureaucrats, soldiers, businessmen. Because of these societies, Chinese public life was always shrouded in a certain mystery. Nothing happened in a quite straightforward way. In any transaction the trail at some stage went underground. Things could not be done without recourse to the secret society. And, more probably than not, Chiang would be involved.

If he never pursued lofty or exceptional aims, that meant he would be set on nothing he could not achieve. He kept his nose to the ground, and pursued ends which were strictly practical. He was cautious and did not expose himself recklessly to danger: but when danger found him, he could call forth the stoic courage of the better type of army officer to sustain him in it. Science and all the arts did not interest him. He became a Christian, and he used to read, and read again, familiar books: but he had no taste for new books. He was not speculative. He had no particular ideas about the way the world was changing, and probably was never in a position to understand this. When he did not understand a point, he was unwilling to speak, and became inscrutable.

He had the natural xenophobia of the uneducated man; but he had the wit to conceal this in his necessary dealings with foreigners. These found him puzzling, and they never established complete rapport with him. But some of them were very much impressed by the man, and agreed that he was dignified, not garrulous, and reserved. He had a cynical view of human nature. But by natural instinct he tended to consort with the type of man who was foreign to exceptional virtue. His cynical views thus proved correct, as far as those with whom he came into contact were concerned. His rancour and vindictiveness against his enemies were constantly spoken of. But probably this rancour proceeded from considerations of prudence, which taught him that a man who was once his enemy was likely to remain so, and that generosity had few conquests, rather than from bitterness of mind.

In private life he was rather dull, faithful by routine to his intimates, determinedly egotistical. In the wider circles of life, he had no friends. Those who knew him well agreed that he was neither particularly wicked nor noticeably squeamish. A study of the countless crises he survived, and his way of dealing with them, might be added as an appendix to Machiavelli's book.

He was not magnetic and not lovable, though he was sometimes loyal to his colleagues and was admired for this. To outer show, he appeared ascetic, and if, as his enemies alleged, this was a pose, it did not appear so to the mass of the people. His family were venal, but he himself was probably not open to accepting bribes: he more than tolerated such practices in others, especially as a means of exerting political control. He felt the pull of the past and he played round with Confucian ideas, and the somewhat austere and chilly teaching of Chinese conservatives, which ceased to be revolutionary and swung to the Right, was his guiding thought.

Yet that Chiang was in many respects a remarkable man cannot be denied; otherwise he could not have battled on, receiving countless checks, seldom achieving total success. Only his will and obstinacy were indomitable.

The interest of the nation was in reconstruction. The prime concern of Chiang Kai-shek was in fighting the communists.

Chiang was obsessed with the civil war. So were his principal bankers and backers within the Chinese oligarchy, right down to village level. The first shots of the communist wars were fired in Nanchang, the capital of Kiangsi. In August 1927 the garrison commander, Chu Teh, had revolted and declared for the communists. How many soldiers were involved in that rebellion is doubtful, but the number was probably not more than 5,000. Defeated, they retired to the south, met a powerful Government force, and, reduced to a tenth of their former strength, scattered.

Thus, almost unnoticed, began a war which, by the eve of China's life and death struggles with Japan, devastated great areas in one third of the provinces of China and cost the Central Government over a billion dollars. Hundreds of thousands of lives were lost, and the issue remained in doubt.

As we have seen, the communists occupied, and maintained, a soviet Government in part of the Kiangsi province and neighbouring territory. Between 1930 and 1934 they resisted five successive so-called bandit-suppression expeditions, each of them more elaborate than the last. For a time, the heavy losses sustained by the Red Army were offset by new recruits inducted into their ranks in large numbers. Some came from the local farming communities, some from deserters from the Kuomintang forces. In 1930, when the communists made their first big gains, their armed forces do not seem to have numbered more than 20–30,000 men. Between 1931 and 1934, their number increased to 120,000 regular troops. In addition to their regular army, the communists also disposed of large numbers of militia men, not so well trained or equipped but playing an important part in guerrilla warfare.

The communists promised the expropriation of the gentry and the redistribution of land. The only experiment with communal ownership of land was made upon a small scale, persisted in for one year, and officially declared a failure. On the whole, there can be no doubt that, as a device for enlisting the support of the masses, the policy pursued was shrewd and

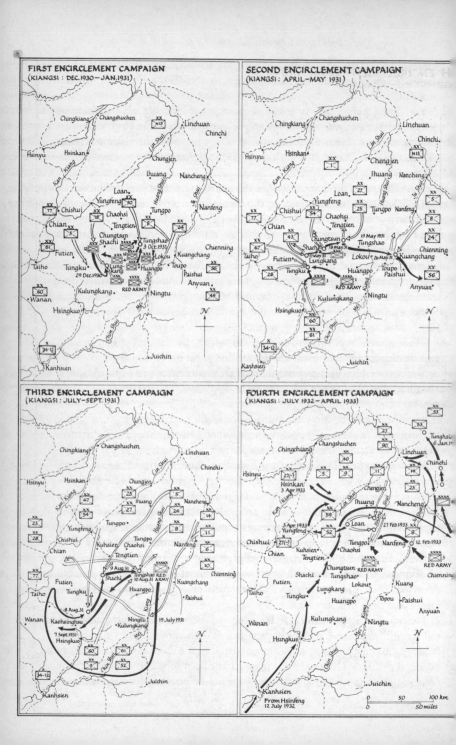

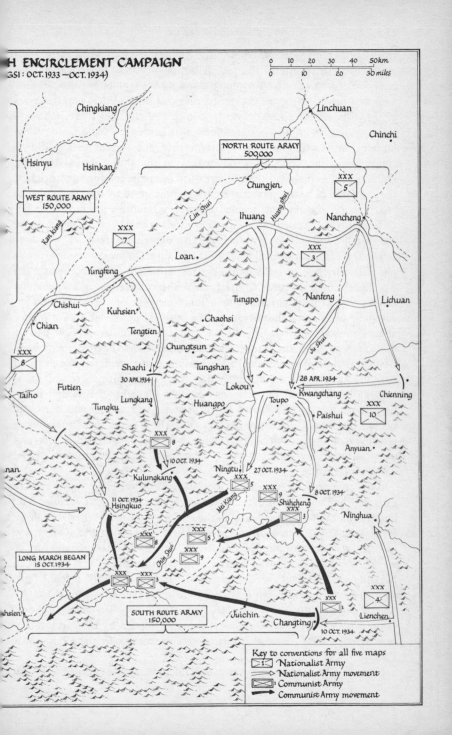

H ENCIRCLEMENT CAMPAIGN

GSI: OCT. 1933 – OCT. 1934)

0   10   20   30   40   50 km
0   10   20   30 miles

Chingkiang

Linchuan

Chinchi

Hsinyu

Hsinkan

NORTH ROUTE ARMY
500,000

Chungjen

XXX
5

WEST ROUTE ARMY
150,000

Ihuang

Huang Shui

Nancheng

Kan kiang

Lin Shui

XXX
7

Loan

XXX
3

Yungfeng

Chishui

Tungpo

Nanfeng

Lichuan

Kuhsien

Chaohsi

Chian

Tengtien

Chungtsun

Ju Shui

XXX
8

Shachi

Tungshan

30 APR. 1934

28 APR. 1934

Chienning

Taiho

Futien

Lungkang

Lokou

Kwangchang

Huangpo

Toupo

XXX
10

Paishui

Tungku

Anyuan

XXX
8

10 OCT. 1934

Ningtu

27 OCT. 1934

XXX
5

Ninghua

nan

Kulungkang

Mei Kiang

XXX
9

8 OCT. 1934

Shihcheng

11 OCT. 1934
Hsingkuo

XXX
3

XXX
8

Chin Shui

XXX
5

LONG MARCH BEGAN
15 OCT. 1934

XXX
9

XXX
1

XXX
5

XXX
4

SOUTH ROUTE ARMY
150,000

Juichin

Changting

Lienchen

hsien

10 OCT. 1934

Key to conventions for all five maps

▷1   Nationalist Army
▷   Nationalist Army movement
⊠1   Communist Army
➤   Communist Army movement

successful. Families whose sons had enlisted in the Red Army were given preferential treatment in the redistribution of land. Moreover, it was linked with a tax reform effort that did not merely replace one tax collector with another and produce greater income but rather led to real increases in the disposable income of most people. The effect of these policies – strange for a communist programme – was to create a society of yeomen farmers, small capitalists. At the same time, the communists instituted compulsory education for the indoctrination of children and adults alike. Other activities included the organization of credit cooperative societies, the provision of health services (greatly handicapped by the lack of drugs, instruments and modern, trained physicians) and an attempted social-ization of trade. Added to this was a cry for the expulsion of the Japanese – a sure-fire formula for winning massive popular support.

The foregoing is the bright side of the picture. On the debit side must be put the restriction of individual liberties – though it may be questioned whether the poorer classes enjoyed much liberty under the old régime; the arbitrary system of government; a large element of confusion and in-competence in the administration; the ruthless destruction of property and of monuments of ancient China; and – the most discreditable part of the soviet record – the massacres and persecutions. These atrocities are well attested. In many villages of Kiangsi there was a field left uncultivated and shunned by the inhabitants: this was the execution ground. It is, however, fair to add that the war against the gentry, although in no way restrained by the soviet Governments, was rather willed by the people than dictated by communist officials. Behind the slaughter lay centuries of oppression and pent-up bitterness. Significantly, recruits were attracted by the Red Army rather than by the politics of the Communist Party.

As is common in revolutions, the terror was directed as much against those within the ranks of the revolutionaries as against their enemies. The death penalty was imposed, and in the majority of cases carried out, upon officials detected in corruption; disobedient soldiers of the Red Army, soldiers who looted, minor intrigants. Death was even the penalty for lax work. For example, during a time of flood, labourers engaged in dyke building were warned twice for idleness, and on the third offence were shot. The ruthless proscription of supporters diverging from the party line recalls, and during those years surpassed, the achievement of Adolf Hitler. In 1934 an internal political crisis was ended by the execution in one week of 4,300 persons, most of them members of the Communist Party.

Some of the leaders enjoyed a special pre-eminence, especially Chu

Teh, the Commander-in-Chief, and a political organizer named Mao Tse-tung. Chu Teh appeared to be of a type not unfamiliar in Chinese history: born into a wealthy landlord family, by the time he had reached middle age he had shown an aptitude for life as a successful war-lord, enjoying the pleasures of corruption, the dissipations of opium-smoking and responsibilities which are said to have included nine wives and concubines. An admirer wrote:

> One might have thought he had everything he desired: wealth, power, love, descendants, poppy dreams, eminent respectability, and a comfortable future in which to preach the proprieties of Confucianism. He had, in fact, only one really bad habit, but it was to prove his downfall. He liked to read books.*

Chu underwent the first of several conversion experiences: 'Disembarrassing himself of his previous encumbrances, he went to Shanghai and joined the extremist wing of the Kuomintang.'† He then left the country to take up political studies among Chinese students in Hanover, Paris and Moscow. While in Germany he became a member of the Communist Party. He returned home late in 1925 and was appointed Chief of the Bureau of Public Safety in the provincial capital of Kiangsi. After raising the communist rebellion against the Kuomintang in Kiangsi, he became a man of a somewhat Rabelaisian turn, living in a very democratic way, and receiving from his followers unbounded devotion, both because his picturesque character appealed to their imagination and because of his genuine care for their well-being. So much legend grew up round him that it is hard to sort out true from false. He was said to be a man of quickly changing moods. Like King Saul, he was given to fits of extreme depression; at other times, like Cromwell, he was inclined to play the buffoon. He was known to order massacres on the grand scale. He was said to live in one room, eat the same food as the common soldier, and drew the regulation wage of a private – $3 a month. Alone among the important figures in China, he is said to have refused the protection of a bodyguard. Chu Teh, though sympathetic to the farmer and the grievances of the poor, did not belong to the doctrinaire wing of the party. Leadership there fell to Mao Tse-tung, an ex-schoolmaster, around whom as much legend grew as round Chu Teh.

Mao came from Hunan, a province noted for the energy and fiery temper of its inhabitants. Son of a poor peasant family, his early career need not detain us. In many characteristics – in his secrecy, and in a

---

* Edgar Snow, *Red Star over China*, Gollancz, London, 1937, p. 355.
† F 1113/1113/10, China Personalities Report by Sir A. Clark Kerr, 19 December 1940, FO 371/24699, British Public Record Office, Kew.

certain indirectness – he was typically Chinese; it was said that he took none of his collaborators into full confidence, and was unwilling that they should be in too close touch with one another. When confronted with opposition, he rarely compromised, but veiled his opinion and, in the end, by subtle manipulation, usually carried his point. He was an orator. His characteristics, which were of significance for the fortunes of the Kiangsi Soviet and the travails of his movement thereafter, were an inflexible attachment to principle and a talent for organization. The first of these qualities kept the agrarian rebellion upon communist lines and caused its leaders to pursue something like a consistent policy; the second ensured that an administration, a more or less ordered community, emerged from the storm of revolution, and that the Red Army was fed and supported from the civilian side in such a way as to make it the formidable power which it became.

These and one or two others were the great names among the communists, but in Kiangsi Chu and Mao were certainly not dictators. Not only did they have to give way to each other, but frequently also to other members of the Central Committee of the Chinese Communist Party. It was the Committee which governed; Chu and Mao were the most prominent of its members, but they were not all-powerful.

During most of the time they were in Kiangsi, the communists were able to import supplies from the outside world. The territory between Kiangsi and the sea was held for some time by the Nineteenth Route Army, the force which distinguished itself in the defence of Shanghai against the Japanese. Somewhat radical in its leanings, the Nineteenth Route Army adopted towards the communists a neutrality which was distinctly benevolent, and made no difficulty about the passage of arms and ammunition from the ports of Swatow and Amoy. But the principal source of ammunition was the Government forces. Until the traffic was detected, large quantities could be purchased from corrupt junior officers in the Government Army; moreover, deserters from the Government side usually brought their equipment with them; and the Red troops referred to Government soldiers as 'our ammunition carriers'.

Nevertheless, the communists never obtained heavy armaments such as big guns or tanks; for a time they possessed two aircraft, but they were not extensively used. The weapon on which they most relied was the machine-gun. Operating on interior lines in the early years, their tactics then were those of guerrilla war. Its elements were ambushes, sniping, surprise attacks at the hour when the morale of their opponents was lowest, and propaganda among the enemy forces (perhaps the most formidable of all their weapons). One of their chief assets was the support received from the population; in many recaptured districts the Government troops were received with a hostility suitable only to a foreign invader, spied on, harried and delayed in every possible way. Another was the speed of movement of the communist forces. Marching as a rule by night, and maintaining contact by means of radio, they would arrive in overwhelming force against an objective, before the Government, infinitely better supplied and much superior in numbers, knew that it was even threatened. As time passed, the communist forces became increasingly professional in their training, and guerrilla warfare gave way to the tactical deployment of the Red forces in large conventional formations.

In fact the communists proved to be far more successful than the Kuomintang in the mobile warfare which characterized the earlier expeditions, but inexorably the tactical skill of the Red forces was overcome by the immense firepower and numerical strength of Chiang's armies.

As is the way in warfare, the communist tactics eventually called forth new tactics on the other side which checked them. It was not, as might have been expected, the employment of aircraft which defeated them. Aircraft, though they played some part in the Government campaigns, never proved a decisive weapon. Since the Red troops moved by night, it was difficult to detect and bomb their columns, and the Government was unwilling to drop bombs upon civilian villages. The weapon which the Government and its German advisers discovered to be a deadly one was the blockhouse. Fortified by machine-guns, these were able to command the surrounding countryside and were practically invulnerable to any force which, like the communists, lacked artillery and suitable aircraft. The communists, in their turn, attempted to erect their own blockhouses to stem the Government advance, but their constructions were easily destroyed by gunfire. Guided by his German military advisers, and backed up by artillery and air support, Chiang's armies systematically advanced, carving up the countryside with a new road network, protected by chains of thousands of blockhouses in ever-decreasing circles, depriving the communist leadership of any hope of maintaining its grip on its soviet base. From that time on, communist raids into Government territory became almost impossible: the ground which the Government recovered was held effectively, and little by little the national troops pressed forward until finally the communists gave up the fight.

In the Fourth Encirclement Campaign during 1932, the Hupeh-Honan-Anhwei Soviet was forced to evacuate through the mountains, fleeing westward in disorder to the comparative safety of Szechwan, where they made the best of a temporary respite. Finally, in October 1934, the Central (Kiangsi) Soviet was squeezed out by the Kuomintang. Exhausted, squabbling among themselves, the communists had no option but to take flight or face annihilation. In more attractive terms, the time had come for a move in a way which has become classic in Chinese communist strategy: one step back in order to prepare for two steps forward. It was regarded at the time, however, not as a moment of impending victory or grand strategic opportunity but rather as a desperate struggle for day-to-day survival:

The Central Committee of the CCP, the Government, the Red Army, their personnel and dependants fled, with the Kuomintang forces on their heels. This was only the beginning of the worst disaster in the history of the Chinese communist movement. The Red political power which controlled some 300 *hsien* (counties) at one time in Kiangsi, Hupeh, Honan, Hunan, Anhwei, and Fukien, was almost totally wiped out. The revolutionary movement appeared to be on the verge of extinction. The defeat split the Chinese communist leadership both in China and Moscow and gave rise to serious internal disputes.*

Ninety thousand survivors broke through Chiang's lines and made an astonishing march, in which their columns again and again repelled or evaded the troops sent to block their way, from Fukien and Kiangsi to the Tibetan borderlands in the far west of China. Chased by Chiang's forces, the communists then made their way northward and up to the remote and mountainous province of Shensi at the north-west frontier between China Proper and Inner Mongolia, on the northernmost approaches of China to the Soviet Union. The Long March covered a distance of 6,000 miles and virtually wiped out the Red Army. The number which reached the relative safety of the north-west a year later was 20,000.

By this fantastic march the communists associated themselves with all that was remarkable in Chinese military history. Out of their struggles emerged a cohesive party leadership and an exceptional sense of political and social unity. They captured the imagination of the country in a way that was quite disproportionate to their size and their real importance. Arrived in Shensi, they set themselves to build a new soviet Government, as they had had before in Kiangsi, one which was milder than the Kiangsi model and which did not automatically frighten off all the propertied class of peasants. It made more appeal than had the Kiangsi model to rational feeling, less to class warfare. Moreover, it was hallowed by the record of legendary deeds of the communists in the transit force which had crossed eighteen mountain ranges and forded twenty-four rivers from Fukien and

* Kataoka Tetsuya, *Resistance and Revolution in China: The Communists and the Second United Front*, University of California Press, Berkeley, 1974, p. 12.

Kiangsi to their new home. When they took up the cry for war against Japan, they were heard with increased respect throughout China.

It must not be supposed that the communists had a monopoly of reform activities. The National Government, in fact, embarked upon a plan of economic development which, though on a small scale compared with the effort in such countries as Soviet Russia, nevertheless, both by its scope and success in execution, surprised many experienced observers. The programme covered the whole country, and it was therefore much more difficult to carry out than that of the communists, which was confined to a relatively small area. Moreover, in judging the results, it must be remembered that the greater part of the resources intended for reconstruction were swallowed up in the civil war.

The National Government postulated that, without law and order, economic development was impossible and that the first use of its resources must be the creation of an efficient police system. This involved many difficulties, one of the chief of which was the problem of identifying persons in country districts. To all inquiries from outside, villagers presented an unhelpful and united front. To remedy this state of affairs, the Government revived a part of the ancient administrative machinery of China, first invented eight centuries before but allowed to fall into disuse during the past hundred years. This was called the *pao chia*. Every ten families were grouped into a unit called the *pao*; every ten paos formed a *chia*. All members of the pao must be registered, and every person in the province must wear on his clothes a label showing to which pao he belonged. Each pao and each chia had a headman, appointed by the Government. When any person was wanted by the police, the pao to which he belonged had to produce him, otherwise the members were held, in theory, collectively responsible for his misdeeds. It was a far from perfect system of control but it was on the whole very serviceable as a police measure. It also made the creation of an efficient militia possible and that, in turn, was frequently employed in public works construction such as the creation of motor roads, dyke building and irrigation projects. At the same time, improvements in medical services, agricultural methods, free education, the revival of the silk, cotton and tea industries, the creation of a cooperative movement, and a genuine opium-suppression campaign were all given enormous attention by both the military and civil authorities. Western observers noted that the principal defect in this reconstruction effort was that it did not include a drastic reform of land ownership and tenure. The second defect in the programme was its rigidly authoritarian structure. The third defect was the inability of the National

Government to override the reluctance of the gentry to carry out the redistribution of power and influence rapidly and efficiently. These defects, of course, were intertwined with each other.

Meanwhile, Chiang Kai-shek himself had grown in strength, consolidating his executive control over the political forces of the Kuomintang. Of the four groups which combined to make the Kuomintang revolution, the communists and farmers had been eliminated from a share in the Government; the educated, bourgeois group was relegated to a very inferior position: left to administer national finance in the interest of the Army but otherwise disposed to ignore constitutional principles, checks and balances, and confined to commerce, industry and learning, and the Army, under General Chiang, was really supreme. His Army was master of nearly all China.

Chiang Kai-shek, indeed, did not consider that he had suffered a setback. Militarily, he had won. His reconquest of the Kiangsi soviets had taken four years. It is, however, necessary to be very cautious in interpreting this as a reflection upon the national armies. It is not only that, in guerrilla warfare, the regular forces tend to be at a disadvantage, nor that the Government was distracted by the Japanese question. There were also matters of policy involved. For it is easy to understand that the communist war gave to the military authorities the opportunity to build up, test and experiment with, a national well-equipped Army upon a modern basis. The years 1932 and 1933 were spent in this undertaking, and operations were carried out with only a fraction of the national forces. When the whole might of Chiang's Army was turned against the communists in 1934, the result was a foregone conclusion.

The military cohesiveness of Chiang's nationalist forces depended upon his ability to command and enforce the personal allegiance of the warlords who fought under the nationalist banner. It was on this that his political and military authority ultimately rested, but he also attended to building up an élite section of the national army to set an example under his direct control. This was the section which had been trained by German military advisers since the expulsion of a Russian advisory team in 1927. These advisers, with establishment levels of around forty to seventy men, were led by men such as Colonel Max Bauer (1927-9), Colonel Hermann Kriebel (1929-30), Lieutenant-General Georg Wetzell (1930-34), General Hans von Seeckt (1934-5) and General Alexander von Falkenhausen – some of the most illustrious and experienced military officers of the time. They succeeded in adapting themselves to the manners of the more military Chinese, and spoke significantly about the warlike qualities of the Chinese under proper leadership. In startling contrast with the hordes of ragged Chinese troops in their tattered uniforms which were all too familiar in China, occasional khaki-clad regiments were now to be seen, very smart, alert, marching with precision: the élite of the Kuomintang. Its numbers were to rise to 300,000 men. Eventually the German military advisory group, acting with remarkable independence from Berlin but strengthened by a treaty which Chiang had negotiated with the German Government, began pressing Chiang to break off his campaigns against the Chinese communists and to march against the Japanese instead.

Throughout this period, German armaments manufacturers eagerly shipped up-to-date weaponry to Chiang Kai-shek's forces. As time wore on, this was subject to countervailing political pressures within the Third Reich and compromised German-Japanese relations, but the fact remains that in the year preceding the Anti-Comintern Pact, for instance, almost 60 per cent of German arms exports went to China (20 million Reichsmarks, 113 times the value of German exports to Japan). The Chinese contracts therefore became important in building up the military production of Nazi Germany.

The British and Americans had no doubts that they were being made scapegoats by the Japanese, whom they found entirely unreceptive to suggestions that the Japanese should address their complaints to their German allies. The discomforture of the Japanese was acute, but they were unable to accept the loss of face that would have resulted from any loud objections to Berlin. They did make their displeasure known, but for a prolonged period little notice was taken by the German arms exporters and their governmental patrons. As the disparity between German military exports to China and Japan became increasingly embarrassing, efforts were made by the Germans to adopt a 'policy of balance' between the two sides. This compromise solution proved to be unstable. Eventually Joachim von Ribbentrop and his cronies, who opposed the Chinese connection, overcame those who wished its continuance, ordered the German military mission to return home and forced German arms suppliers to tear up their Chinese orderbooks. Nevertheless, according to British and American Intelligence estimates, German and German-occupied Austrian and Czech arms factories continued to supply up to 75 per cent, and even more, of all foreign military equipment and ammunition sent to China from abroad throughout the first two years of the China Incident. When the decision to stop this traffic was taken in April 1938, the Reich Ministry of Economics calculated that the loss sustained by the German armaments industry from cancellation of contracts already signed amounted to 282 million Reichsmarks. Nevertheless, reliable reports indicated that a significant quantity of military supplies continued to flow from Germany and its satellites to China. It is indicative of the importance of this connection that in the first shipment of war materials to pass all the way up the fabled Burma Road into Free China in December 1938, there was German and Czechoslovak machine-gun ammunition valued at $112,000. At the same time a Norwegian steamer unloaded 1,300 tons of Italian arms and ammunition at Rangoon. These were by no means isolated instances. So much for the solidarity of Axis collaboration with Japan. The British Cabinet even took the extraordinary step of instructing British naval and customs authorities to turn a blind eye towards a German freighter due to unload a contraband shipment of arms at Hong Kong in the week following the outbreak of the European War.*

In everything, things began to go well for China. Its great weakness had been disunity, and the lack of a modern political structure. Now, very slowly, and largely by means of the tortuous, devious policies of Chiang Kai-shek, which he pursued with resolution, China's political unification made progress. The Kuomintang prevailed in new provinces: the war-lords who survived had their powers reduced: the central Government of Nanking found new ways of undermining them, and of making new contact with the people by new institutions. Chiang Kai-shek, alert, like the Japanese of the earlier generation, to take advantage of borrowing what seemed to him relevant from abroad, took over various devices from the contemporary example of Hitler for reinforcing his personal ascendancy. The country began to be studded by a secret organization called the Blue Shirts, whose members were pledged to advance his interest: this included thugs, but also highly respected professors from Peking University, who felt that the desperate needs of the country required that Chiang should be supreme. During this period there was only one retrograde moment when a nationwide unrest among Chiang's opponents led to an outbreak of civil war on the old pattern: but this was soon stopped by diplomacy.

In 1935 the Kuomintang, advised and assisted by experts lent to it by the League of Nations, France, the United States and the Bank of England, greatly enhanced its prestige when it introduced a new currency throughout the whole country: and held it more or less stable for the first time in the history of China. The new system replaced the silver standard which had been made unworkable by the financial policy of the United States. Franklin D. Roosevelt's Government, under pressure from senators advancing the interests of silver producers, had raised the price of silver,

* R. J. Pritchard, *Far Eastern Influences upon British Strategy towards the Great Powers, 1937–1939*, Garland Publishing, New York, 1987, pp. 96–8; J. P. Fox, *Germany and the Far Eastern Crisis, 1931–1938*, Clarendon/LSE, Oxford, 1982, *passim*.

and, ignoring Chinese protests, created a deflationary spiral of about 30 per cent between 1931 and 1935 which drove China to seek another basis for its currency. The success of the Kuomintang in bringing a fiat currency into areas which it had previously occupied by military means alone was the best sign of the consolidation of its authority. It gave both the Kuomintang and China a fillip: and braced it to face the approaching war. Britain, by giving aid in this reform, had shown that it considered the new China worth taking risks for, and that it was willing to develop its East Asian policy on the hypothesis that China was becoming stable.

In these years an additional person of the drama was beginning to play an interesting and much publicized part. This was Madame Chiang, whom Chiang had married, as his second wife, in 1927. She was one of three ambitious and remarkable sisters, one of whom was the widow of Sun Yat-sen, the leading spirit among the founders of the Kuomintang, who had died in 1924 and was revered as a national hero. One of her brothers was T. V. Soong, the banker, Kuomintang politician and Minister of Finance between 1928 and 1933. Her other sister married the fabulously wealthy H. H. Kung, seventy-fifth lineal descendant of Confucius and Minister of Finance from 1933 to 1938. Madame Chiang supplied the female influence, which recalled to Chinese, who are extremely historically minded, many parallels in the dynastic histories of the past. In a way this increased their tendency to see Chiang as being like one of the founders of past dynasties. But, though her influence on Chiang was considerable, it must be seen for what it was, and not misinterpreted. She was not responsible for developing any new qualities in him: the stubborn will, which had made his place initially in the Kuomintang, was all his own. Madame Chiang, who was American-educated (as were all five of her brothers and sisters) and in temperament had become more American than Chinese, was his window on the United States. Through her, the relations of China and the United States became closer than they would have been without her. Madame Chiang gave her husband a glamour, an interest, which he could not have hoped for himself in American eyes. She was a forceful personality, wilful and dogmatic, and, though she lacked great political wisdom, she had an intelligence which made her a useful intermediary with foreigners. Some observers regarded her as a very wicked lady, misguided, corrupt and selfish in the extreme. Others, such as Sir Stafford Cripps, saw more wholesome qualities. Chiang's use of his wife was skilful, and she, in turn, probably possessed more power and influence than anyone else of her sex in the world at that time, apart, perhaps, from Eleanor Roosevelt.

In 1934 Chiang Kai-shek, assisted by his wife, launched what was called a 'new life movement'. This was not very popular: it was the subject of mirth among foreigners and the sophisticated classes of urban China. It was an attempt to revive the ancient Confucian virtues as the spiritual basis of the new state. Confucianism had been repudiated soon after the revolution which overthrew the Manchus; but a void had been left, and the Kuomintang lacked a spiritual basis on which to build the new order. Confucianism was not really a religion; it was a code of ethics which from earliest times had been accepted as the ideal of the Chinese people: it served throughout history as the powerful pillar of the state, and the fact that in China this role was performed by ethics, which in other states was performed by the great organized religions, has been one of the characteristics and fateful elements of Chinese civilization. Confucianism performed the unlikely part of presenting in a fossilized form the ethical outlook and views of the feudal society which was the state of China two thousand years ago. Attitudes which would have been appropriate in a good Chinese feudatory continued to be advocated, though the society which gave rise to them had long since changed. Confucianism urges submissiveness, demands reverence to the old, deplores a headstrong attitude in individuals, prizes the rites of courtesy, assumes that the business of women is to obey in all things. The task which the Chinese set themselves was to reinstate Confucianism, without allowing a too evident Confucian control of all the institutions of public life.

The new life was to be puritanical. A gloom settled over Chinese society. Nevertheless, by dint of propaganda, by the use of all the Government machinery for indoctrination, by the use of various Army bureaux for its propagation, and by manipulation of all the Government powers of patronage, a not unimpressive Confucian revival began to make headway in China. The change in the intellectual climate of China, with the substitution of a rather narrow Confucian dogma for bland scepticism, was one of the notable features of the time.

In the middle thirties the sense that China was recovering, which increased Chinese self-confidence at home as well as affecting the policies of all the powers concerned in the region, caused the Chinese to feel an increasing resentment at Japan's constant pressure upon them. In 1934 Japan, its ambitions enlarging after the conquest of Manchuria, was demanding that an area, carved out of China's northern provinces, should be declared autonomous, and that the writ of the Government of Nanking should cease to run there. Obviously the calculation was that in a short time it would pass under the control of Japan. The activities of Japanese agents caused a wave of indignation, and this was particularly strong among the students of Peking. Peking was always the seat of three or four universities, and their pupils, partly because of the regard which China traditionally paid to scholarship and to the learned life, enjoyed peculiar prestige. They were buoyed up by memory of the great demonstration which they had made fifteen years earlier against a particularly corrupt Government because of its craven acceptance of foreign demands; this had never been forgotten by the Government or by the students themselves; they had come to think of themselves as the custodian of the nation's conscience; they felt themselves morally obliged to be the nation's barometer. The Japanese overstepped the limit. Pressed too hard, the students erupted, in December 1935, in a great demonstration against the Chinese officials who were subservient towards the Japanese.

Those who had the good fortune to be present on this occasion felt, even if obscurely, that they were taking part in a historic action. The beauty of Peking in the freezing mid-winter, the sense of great issues happening which could only be dimly seen, the foreboding and the excitement, the sense of returning power and rising might in the Chinese people – of a people long oppressed feeling strength to quell the brute and boisterous force of the oppressor – all this made a memorable event in the history of China's ancient imperial city. Even though Peking at this time was demoted, and had temporarily ceased to be the capital city, the students must have sensed the drama of its being the setting for this great demonstration that marked China's national resurgence.

The growing nationalist temper was directed in part against Japan: in part against Chiang Kai-shek, because, though he was the military leader of China, he declined to act as its champion. Instead of calling China to arms he continued to sit in Central China, and called for the national attention to be riveted there, to wars for the eradication of communism. In doing this, Chiang began to be regarded as almost a traitor to the Chinese nation. China, or at least its intelligentsia, was ready to go to war, but it felt that one hand was tied behind its back by the Generalissimo of its own armies, or at least was engaged in keeping down the peasantry – an action which the younger, generous section of the nation did not desire at all, and was only necessitated because the landed interests of the Kuomintang required it. How long would these interests continue to control Chiang? When would he become responsive to the will of the younger and more virile section of the nation?

One point stands out sharply. That is, that China, being preoccupied with so many domestic problems, was very ill-placed to deal with foreign aggression. The conflict in the countryside between the gentry and the peasants, which is a normal occurrence in Chinese history at periods of two or three centuries, was then in an acute phase. It was made more bitter because of the distress of the farmers due to the dislocation of the rural economy which resulted from the increased trade with western nations. The contact with the West had led also to the emergence of new classes, the commercial plutocracy and the urban proletariat. The conflict between them increased the social tension; and it introduced to China a medley of new ideas and new conceptions, which profoundly influenced the behaviour of the intelligentsia and began also to influence the behaviour of the masses which, since they were in many cases conflicting, added to the confusion of affairs, caused divided aims and rendered quite uncertain the course which China was ultimately destined to take. As we have seen, a Government, composed of a bloc of the military, the plutocracy and the rural gentry, held with some security the cities and commercial centres. But in many parts of the countryside it confronted either open or potential revolt. Moreover, there was division within the Government itself on personal grounds but also between the faction standing for military and semi-fascist government and the faction standing for a more liberal development.

The policy of General Chiang Kai-shek, of basing the unity of China on his personal authority, was, successful though it had been to date, a source of weakness; for though China in the brief span of ten years had made great progress in modernizing its government, and though public opinion stood for the unity of the country, that unity was a tender plant. For unity to be consolidated other than in the figure of Chiang himself, it seemed to China-watchers that the country needed twenty years of peace during which the new institutions could take root and a system might be perfected by which political power could be shared or transferred without domestic combat or violence. The position thus appeared far too delicate for the Government to enter a foreign war except as a last resort. The patience of Nanking; its willingness to make concessions; its anxiety – in spite of a very real patriotism and a determination to recover lost territory in the future – to find some *modus vivendi* with Japan; its politic readiness – in spite of its own sincere anti-Japanese sentiment – to suppress the manifestation of it by its citizens; all of these impulses for some years seemed to westerners not only comprehensible but wise and prudent. Eventually, however, pressure for change became irresistible.

While Chiang Kai-shek's best forces were employed in the war against the communists, a very brief and humiliating campaign took place in which Japan conquered the province of Jehol, which was part of Inner Mongolia, and incorporated it into Manchukuo. This mopping-up operation was conducted by the Kwantung Army. The Japanese Cabinet in Tokyo, the Army General Staff and even the Emperor attempted to frustrate it but to little avail. Jehol was historically of interest as it had been a vast hunting preserve of the Manchu princes when these ruled in Mukden. After the Japanese invasion had breached the Great Wall itself, an armistice known as the Tangku Truce was concluded between China itself and Japan on 31 May 1933. Among its provisions was an agreement to establish a 5,000-square-mile demilitarized zone within the adjacent province of Hopei, ending at the Great Wall. Chinese forces eventually withdrew even from the vicinity of Tientsin, the Shanghai of the north and gateway to Peking. The principal benefit of the Tangku Truce for China was that it enabled the Kuomintang to strengthen its hold upon the nation as a whole. The Truce itself did not address the question of the status of Manchukuo nor its relations with the northern lands which still maintained an allegiance to China.

Nevertheless, the Tangku Truce laid the groundwork for Japanese agents to foster autonomy movements throughout the whole of North China, not merely among the Mongols of Chahar, Suiyuan and Ningsia along the borderlands north of the Wall but in the northern provinces of China Proper, including Hopei, Shansi and even Shantung. One reason for these preparations was to secure the Japanese rear in Manchuria against a Chinese surprise attack in the event of serious trouble with the Soviet Union. Another reason was that the Kwantung Army was eager to exploit the 'inexhaustible' iron and coal reserves of Shansi.

If we dilly-dally, these resources will end up in British or American hands. If we keep saying this and that about so-called international ethics, and if we yield the road to others by saying 'after you, after you', the one who will be left holding the bag is Japan. Therefore, while Europe and America are preoccupied with situations in their own countries, and while their circumstances are such that they cannot interfere with the Orient, it is of vast importance and a very good opportunity to get North China into the hands of Japan.*

Exhilarated by their unbroken string of successes, the Kwantung Army was not immune from the temptation to extend their imperium as far as lay within their power. Peking itself, the historic capital of the Middle Kingdom, was now within their sights. The dangers were obvious.

*

* *Harada-Saionji Memoirs*, 23 June 1935, recording report from Sakatani Kiichi about the views of Itagaki Seishirō and other leading figures in the Kwantung Army.

During the two years that followed the Tangku Truce, the Chinese gave way to further demands imposed by the Kwantung Army while Tokyo ran hot and cold. In an address to the Imperial Diet on 22 January 1934, Foreign Minister Hirota Kōki proclaimed a Japanese Monroe Doctrine in East Asia: 'Japan, serving as the only cornerstone for the edifice of peace in East Asia, bears the entire responsibility. It is in this important position and vast responsibility that our foreign diplomacy and national defence are rooted.' In remarks to the foreign press on 17 April 1934, the Head of the Foreign Ministry Information Bureau, Amō Eiji, repeated the substance of Hirota's words and indicated that Japan had no intention of tolerating foreign interference in the bilateral relations between China and Japan. While Hirota's statement had passed off without much comment, western governments, driven by public outrage, responded to the Amō Declaration with howls of protest. Hirota's attempt to pour oil over these troubled waters proved unconvincing.

In July 1934 a 72-year-old admiral, Okada Keisuke, replaced the even more venerable Viscount Admiral Saitō Makoto as Prime Minister of Japan. Saitō himself arranged the succession to signify his Cabinet's united distaste and alarm over the Japanese Army's unchecked activities on the continent. There was an obvious continuity between the two Cabinets: the War, Navy and Foreign Ministers were all retained and Saitō's Minister of Agriculture and Forestry was elevated to the portfolio of Home Affairs with all of its police and public order functions. Nevertheless, the new Cabinet, like its predecessor, felt obliged to support the *faits accomplis* of the Japanese Army in China as well as in Manchuria. Foreign Minister Hirota, indeed, pursued diplomatic initiatives which closely dovetailed into the efforts of the Army to consolidate its gains in the region. In March 1935 the Soviet Union finally sold its Chinese Eastern (Trans-Manchurian) Railway to 'Manchukuo' after two years of haggling with Hirota over the price. *Pace* Clausewitz, this was (aggressive) war by other means. It also struck a responsive chord in the Manchurian popular memory, for as recently as 1929 Marshal Chang Hsueh-liang had tried to wrest the CER from its Russian railway guards, lost an ensuing campaign when the Soviet Union dispatched an expeditionary force into northern Manchuria, and been forced to abandon his pretensions in exchange for the withdrawal of the Soviet troops. Ever since the Japanese military conquest of the whole of Manchuria, however, Russian control over the CER had become untenable. The sale of the CER marked the end of an era.

Then in June 1935, following the murder of two pro-Japanese Chinese journalists, General Ho Ying-ch'in, Head of the Peking Military Command, yielded to grotesquely disproportionate demands pressed upon him by the Commander of the Japanese North China Garrison in Tientsin, Lieutenant-General Umezu Yoshijirō, and endorsed the secret Ho–Umezu Agreement promising to evacuate Kuomintang troops and abandon all political activity in the province of Hopei. The Japanese Government in Tokyo was unaware until late in the day how far Umezu had exceeded his authority, but there was considerable satisfaction at the outcome once the crisis had passed. By degrees, the Chinese were learning the Japanese definition of 'cooperation'.

At almost the same time, another trifling incident took place in Chahar during which four Japanese soldiers were held at gunpoint for four or five hours by Chinese troops. Former War Minister General Minami Jirō, now Commander of the Kwantung Army, ordered the head of his Special Services Agency, Colonel Doihara Kenji, to negotiate a settlement of the incident that would satisfy the honour of Japan. Late in June 1935 the outcome, known as the Ching–Doihara Agreement, spoke volumes concerning the nature of the pressures which the Japanese were ready to impose. Unable to appease the Japanese by a token punishment of the Chinese officers responsible, General Ching Teh-ch'un, the Chinese Army commander in Chahar, unwillingly evacuated his military forces from the province, agreed that all political activity by the Kuomintang within the province should cease forthwith, prohibited further Chinese immigration into northern Chahar, and banned all anti-Japanese activities within the province.

Within two months of the Ho–Umezu and Ching–Doihara Agreements, Prince Teh, a Mongolian chieftain who had striven for some time to carve out an autonomous government north of the Great Wall, overcame his apparent reluctance to accept Japanese assistance. General Minami promised him money and lent him two battalions of cavalry to help the Prince extend his control from Suiyuan province into northern Chahar.

On 5 August 1935 Foreign Minister Hirota advanced several general guidelines which he believed should govern Japan's relations with her continental neighbours. He lost no opportunity to repeat these 'Three Principles' in the months that followed: first, the Kuomintang must suppress all anti-Japanese pronouncements and activities, end China's subservience to European and American interests, and take positive steps towards friendship and cooperation with Japan; second, China must accept Japan's special relationship with Manchukuo, cooperate with Manchukuo in economic and cultural relations, and, ultimately, grant formal diplomatic recognition to the independence of Manchukuo; third, China must collaborate with Japan in Chahar and adjacent territories to obliterate communist influence in areas bordering Outer Mongolia. At the time, Japanese military factions and business circles were obsessed by the fear that Communism might spread from Russia to China. There was some foundation for these fears, given the close connection between the Chinese communist movement and the spread of 'anti-Japanism' across the length and breadth of China.

A Five Ministers' Conference of the Japanese inner Cabinet (chaired by Prime Minister Okada and attended by his War, Navy, Finance, Foreign and Home Affairs Ministers) reviewed the situation and reached the conclusion that Japan should give strong support to other autonomy movements in North China, thus progressively undermining the Kuomintang's efforts to unify the whole country. Three days later the midwives of the Kwantung Army attended to the birth of the East Hopei Anti-Communist Autonomy Council within the demilitarized districts defined by the Tangku Truce of 1933. In early December the Kuomintang responded by establishing the Hopei–Chahar Political Council, headed by General Sung Che-yuan, who undertook the thankless task of attempting to effect a reconciliation. Contrary to the expectations of the Kwantung Army, Sung successfully steered a middle course between this Scylla and Charybdis.

In January 1936 the Commander of Japan's North China Garrison Army was instructed by his military superiors in Tokyo on how to deal with the situation in his area. A summary of those instructions, cabled by Foreign Minister Hirota to Ariyoshi Akira, Japan's first fully-fledged Ambassador to China in the modern era, accurately shows how naked self-interest tends to masquerade in altruistic clothes in such circumstances:

The principal objects to be borne in mind in dealing with the North China area are to assist the Chinese people in realizing a self-government in North China by themselves, and thus to let the people enjoy their lives and jobs peacefully; also to let them adjust their relations with Japan and Manchukuo, and thus promote the mutual welfare of these three nations . . .

Territorially speaking, the five provinces of North China will be made the object of that self-government, but we must be careful not to be too eager to embrace the entire area all at once. On the contrary, we should first aim at a gradual realization of self-government in Hopei and Chahar as well as in the Peking and Tientsin conurbations and we should aim at inducing the remaining three provinces to join with the other two voluntarily. Our advice and guidance to the Hopei–Chahar Political Council should be given through Sung Che-yuan for the time being, and self-government movements by the people should be encouraged in so far as they remain fair and just, and should make use of them in gradually realizing an actual self-government among the people of those two provinces, thus laying firmly the foundation of eventual self-government for all five provinces in North China . . .

With regard to the extent of that self-government, it would, of course, be better to let the people have as much liberty as possible, but for the present, we should aim at and endeavour for the realization of such a state as will leave no room for the Nanking Government [of Chiang Kai-shek] to carry out anti-Japanese and anti-Manchukuo policies, and by leaving the rest for gradual achievement in future, we should avoid too hasty a desire for an acquisition of independent powers.

With regard to the guidance to be given by us, we should endeavour principally to guide in the economic field, especially in finance, and also in military affairs, along with the education and guidance of the general populace; and in doing so, we should confine our guidance to the general line, leaving, as much as possible, the details to the task and responsibility of the Chinese people.*

The document goes on to explain these policies at greater length and to establish the importance of seeking cooperation from the Kwantung Army and close contact with Japanese military attachés, diplomats and naval officials stationed in China. Other messages, much more aggressive in expression, were to follow in the months ahead. More importantly, internecine political struggles and civil/military conflict once again rocked Japan. In North China, however, peace of a kind was maintained, uneasily, until July 1937.

Although it was not immediately apparent, a turning-point had been reached several months earlier in December 1936. The Young Marshal Chang Hsueh-liang, driven into a bitter exile from Manchuria, had found Chiang Kai-shek utterly unwilling to embark upon major operations designed to expel the Japanese from Manchuria and North China. On the contrary, Chiang attempted to pit the Young Marshal against the communist forces that had regrouped in Shensi. It was widely believed that Chiang confidently expected both sides to be badly mauled. In any event, the Young Marshal was appointed commander of the 'North-western Bandit-Suppression Forces'. His Manchurians, numbering 130,000 troops assisted by 40,000 local militia, were deployed across the central and southern areas of Shensi and Kansu provinces, showed themselves half-hearted against the communists, who operated from the more northerly districts. The campaign began well enough but soon began to run out of steam. The morale of Chang Hsueh-liang's forces drained away: two of his best divisions defected to the communists, weary of the

* Pritchard and Zaide, op. cit., 2, pp. 2721–6 [PX 215]. The text given here slightly rephrases the English translation admitted at the Tokyo Trial.

Chinese civil war, desiring only to push the Japanese out of Manchuria. The campaign ground slowly to a halt. By degrees, in the summer and autumn of 1936, the two sides found they had reached a common understanding and mutual respect. In June 1936 Chang met with an exceptionally astute young communist leader named Chou En-lai, one of Mao Tse-tung's most trusted lieutenants. It seemed pointless to fight one another: the time had come for all Chinese guns to turn against their common enemy. Chang did everything within his power to persuade Chiang Kai-shek to move in the same direction.

Chang Hsueh-liang made two fruitless journeys to Nanking simply to press his case. At the end of November, he wrote eloquently to Chairman Chiang:

For the period of nearly half a year, I have continuously laid before Your Excellency my principle and program of struggle against Japanese imperialism for national salvation . . . Now the war against Japanese imperialism is beginning . . . I have therefore waited patiently for Your Excellency's order of mobilization. To my greatest disappointment, I have so far received no such order at all . . . Pressed by the zealous sentiments of my troops and urged on by my personal convictions, I ventured to present my recent appeals, but Your Excellency instructed me to wait for an opportunity . . . In order to control our troops, we should keep our promise to them that whenever the chance comes they should be allowed to carry out their desire of fighting against the enemy. Otherwise, they will regard not only myself but also Your Excellency as impostors, and will no longer obey us. Now is exactly the right time. Please give us the order to mobilize . . .*

It was all in vain. Chiang was unmoved by the Young Marshal's pleas and warnings.

The tension came to a head in December 1936. Chiang flew to inspect the Manchurian troops at the Young Marshal's headquarters in Sian, the provincial capital of Shensi, accompanied by a large entourage and eighty bomber aircraft to see why no progress was being made in the 'bandit-suppression' campaign and to read the riot act.

From Chairman Chiang's point of view, the quality of the troops and their record as fighting men were both rather poor, and their employment had been a problem. Blockading is a tedious duty: the soldiers and officers felt themselves in a strange land; they desired only to be led back to their homes. So disgruntled were they that they fell easy victims to propaganda by the communists, whom they were supposed to be cutting off from all communications with the outside world. Rumour of this had reached

---

* Text released at Sian on 2 January 1937 following collapse of the mutiny: cited in T. A. Bisson, *Japan in China*, Macmillan, London, 1938, p. 162.

Chiang, but he did not realize how deeply the rot went. It is very strange that he should have ventured among such disaffected troops with no proper bodyguard. Not for the first or last time in his career, the secret police and Intelligence services, who were a major factor in his Government, failed him. He visited Chang Hsueh-liang twice at his headquarters in Sian, and on his second visit, on the first night, he was surprised while in a bungalow by a rising of the Manchurian officers. He managed to escape in the darkness and crawl up the garden, but he had hurt his back in getting away, and after a few hours he was discovered.

The Young Marshal had learned of the appointment of another general to take direct charge of the operations, and it was this which finally led him to break with Chiang, side with the communists and unexpectedly place Chairman Chiang and his entire entourage under arrest. Chang Hsueh-liang sent telegrams to Nanking. A period of suspense followed news of the kidnapping. The mutineers tried to negotiate Chiang's release in return for an undertaking that he would declare war on Japan. Chiang refused absolutely to enter into negotiations with them, and tried, though power was all on their side and he was isolated and defenceless, to over-awe them and compel them by superior strength of will to set him free. Chang Hsueh-liang appeared quite prepared to kill Chiang in the event of any attempt by the Kuomintang to mount an expedition to rescue their national leader. Afterwards it emerged that Chiang's life was spared mainly through the intercession of Chou En-lai, a man of great patience, tact and persuasion. Chiang, too, impressed his captor, who eventually wilted under Chiang's rebukes, and who, in consequence, became his protector against some of the more extreme officers, who would have shot him on the spot. Whatever may have been felt later about Chiang, his bearing among his captors compels admiration.

In the outer world, the Government in Nanking was extremely be-wildered. There were signs of a break-up, and some of the key personalities began to prepare for a struggle for the post which Chiang seemed to be about to vacate. In Tokyo, too, the Government had no plans for such an unexpected contingency. Britain and America likewise waited, consulting their runes.

The people with resolution were on the one side Chiang's dynamic and opinionated wife and his brother-in-law, T. V. Soong: and on the other side the leaders of the communists, who were only a few miles away. After Chiang's captors had drawn a blank in their efforts at compelling him to negotiate, they sent for Chou En-lai and the political officers of the communists. It has never been cleared up whether the communists had known beforehand of the plot. One view is that, immediately after the kidnapping, Moscow had taken a hand in the direction of events. There was radio communication between them and Yenan, the capital of the communists in Shensi province; and the policy of Moscow, which was itself under menace from Japan, had been to preserve, at whatever sacrifice this might be to ideological sense, Chiang Kai-shek alive as the most useful and strongest ally against Japan. The kidnapping threatened this policy, and the interests of the USSR. Simultaneously, Madame Chiang and her brother flew to Sian. By acting whilst others talked, they had intervened to prevent the Nanking Government from using its planes to bomb the mutineers. Such an action might have seemed justified, but it would probably have resulted in Chiang's immediate execution. His death might have suited the ambitions of some of the higher officers of the Nanking régime.

There were confused and secret deliberations at Sian. In the end the communists returned home, apparently convinced that Chiang would call off another large-scale offensive against their position in Shensi, which had been planned for the immediate future: and they seem to have been given some assurance that he would in future carry on a more lively defence against the Japanese. The communists were to be autonomous in the areas, not very extensive, which they actively held, and an attempt was to be made at associating a few communist dignitaries in the central Government of the Kuomintang. Chiang flew back to Nanking on Christmas Day, a free man, and accompanying him was Chang Hsueh-liang, who said that he repented of his mutiny and desired to make restitution. Certainly Chang seemed to have neglected to obtain reliable guarantees of his treatment, for on arrival at Nanking he was promptly tried and imprisoned for a ten-year term. But this was nothing more than a gesture to demonstrate the authority of the National Government, and the Young Marshal was granted a free pardon almost immediately afterwards.

It took several months before the significance of these confusing events could be understood, months during which the central political authorities met to consider the situation. The Chinese communists put forward a programme calling for an end to the civil war; the introduction of freedom of speech, assembly, organization, etc., and the release of all political prisoners; the convening of a national congress representing all parties, factions, military groups and organizations, to serve as a focal point for national talents in the interests of national salvation; the initiation of preparations for a war of national resistance against Japan, and amelioration of the living conditions of the Chinese people as a whole. In exchange for these the communists declared that they would abandon their attempts to overthrow the Kuomintang by force of arms; transform their so-called 'Soviet Government of China' and 'Red Army' into a loyal 'Government of the Special Region of the Republic of China' and a 'National Revolutionary Army' subject to direct control by the Chinese central authorities; accept a democratic system of universal suffrage within the 'Special Region'; end the expropriation of landlords, and commit the communist movement to the service of the anti-Japanese united front.

The Government and the Kuomintang's political leadership, however, threw out the proposals put to them by Chang Hsueh-liang and the communists. Communists and their collaborators were declared to be anathema to the state. There could be no compromise with those who spread communist subversion, nor with any group whose activities undermined national unity. The Sian rebels had engaged in treasonable sedition; their resort to force nullified the terms which Chiang Kai-shek had been obliged to accept during his captivity. The Young Marshal, indeed, seemed to have struck the death knell of the 'common front' strategy. One foreign observer, listening perhaps too much to the opinions of well-connected Chinese politicians and bureaucrats, wrote at the time that the Young Marshal's 'foolhardy action . . . called down upon him the wrath of the vast majority of the Chinese people and robbed him of what little prestige he still possessed'.* Following his pardon, Chang retired to Fenghua in Chekiang province south-east of Nanking: far from Chang's Manchurian homeland but near to where Chiang Kai-shek was recovering from his injuries at his home outside Ningpo. The Young Marshal's disaffected troops were transferred to the provinces of Honan, Anhwei and Kiangsu, where they were integrated into the forces of the Central Government but retained their own officers. There they were kept out of trouble, and were well positioned to move forward against any attempt by the hated Japanese to seize control of Shantung or Shanghai.

The Sian Incident had been dramatic: and was also fateful. It might as easily have ended in an opposite way. Chiang Kai-shek might have been executed by the communists or his captors: the history of Sino-Japanese relations would in that case certainly have developed in a different way. It throws light on the intelligent and subtle mind of the communists, whose roughness of manner had hidden their talent for diplomacy. They must have calculated that Chiang alone could lead China into war: and they were content to use him, and the huge and growing armies of the Kuomintang, for this purpose. Ostensibly Chiang agreed to this; he accepted

* F 2835/829/10, Record of Leading Personalities in China, by B. E. F. Gage on behalf of Sir Hughe Knatchbull-Hugessen, 7 April 1937, F O 371/20999, British Public Record Office, Kew.

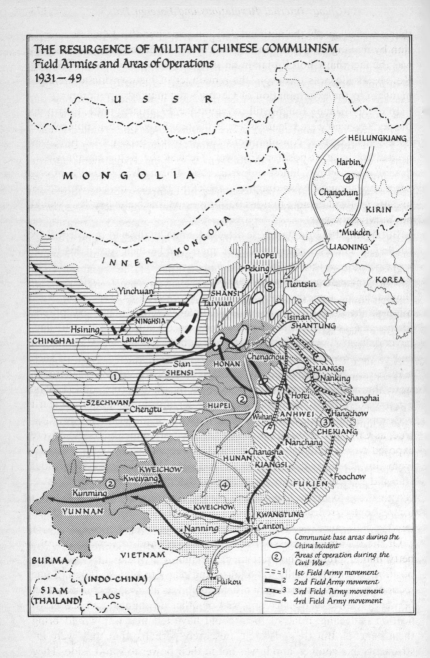

THE RESURGENCE OF MILITANT CHINESE COMMUNISM
Field Armies and Areas of Operations
1931—49

U S S R

MONGOLIA

HEILUNGKIANG

Harbin

④

Changchun

KIRIN

Mukden

LIAONING

KOREA

INNER MONGOLIA

HOPEI

Peking

⑤

Tientsin

Yinchuan

SHANSI

Taiyuan

Tsinan

SHANTUNG

Hsining

NINGHSIA

Lanchow

CHINGHAI

Sian

SHENSI

HONAN

Chengchou

KIANGSI

Nanking

②

Shanghai

①

Hofei

SZECHWAN

Chengtu

HUPEI

②

ANHWEI

Hangchow

③

CHEKIANG

Wuhan

Nanchang

Changsha

HUNAN

KIANGSI

KWEICHOW

Kweiyang

②

④

Foochow

FUKIEN

Kunming

KWEICHOW

YUNNAN

Nanning

KWANGTUNG

Canton

BURMA

VIETNAM

(INDO-CHINA)

SIAM
(THAILAND)

LAOS

Haikou

Communist base areas during the
China Incident

② Areas of operation during the
Civil War

===1 1st Field Army movement

▬▬2 2nd Field Army movement

▦▦3 3rd Field Army movement

▭4 4th Field Army movement

that it was allegedly the national decision to respond to Japanese aggression by making war. One of the great curiosities of the next four decades was the fact that Chou En-lai, in no small measure the saviour of Chiang Kai-shek's life, was to devote the remainder of his own life and statesmanship to the extermination of Chiang's régime and reputation.

In reality Chiang fought still to temporize, to procrastinate, to trip up the persons who were relentlessly pressing him forward, to complicate the issues, to drag new considerations to the front. In any case time was needed to make dispositions for war. He was the Reluctant Dragon – dragon because all Chinese emperors (and Chiang was virtually an emperor) are thought of as dragons – reluctant because he was warned by his sure political instinct that his position – and much else besides – would not survive the war.

But in July 1937 the Japanese attacked, and Chiang had to accept their challenge. The assessment which he made, and which forced his hand, was probably as follows.

The students, and the university professors, so vastly influential in the China of that day, so exaggeratedly more important than their numbers or physical power made credible, were, with few exceptions, for resisting. They compelled the country as a whole to take a stiff line, beyond what it would otherwise have thought possible. Also, for an end to patience – though it was hard to speak of a solid voice of such a disparate class, and one not used to having its views considered – were the army officers as a whole, underneath the top commanders. They were variously derived: many were corrupt; but the national spirit was apparent, in varying degrees, in most of them. The same was less true, as Chiang knew well, of some of the senior commanders, who were exposed to the blandishments of the Japanese, whose attitude changed from time to time according to the inducements offered to them, and who did not constitute an inspiring leadership. However, in 1937, most were willing to fight. The landed gentry, while not exactly enthusiasts for resistance, reflected the mood of China: their patience was strained beyond endurance.

Of the true middle class – the native bankers and money-lenders, the petty manufacturers, the craftsmen, the minor civil servants – the disposition was fairly solidly nationalist, and ready to oppose Japan. Some sections were less forward than others; there was always the contradiction between defence of their commercial or other advantage, and the gratification of feeling: none of them could have felt that war would bring them benefits. But they also felt, obscurely perhaps, that they were instruments in a conflict, and it was not in their power to stand aside. They may have deplored their fate, but most of them, while privately desiring to be left in peace, were ready to follow the national path. The merchant guilds, which played a considerable part in the organization of economic life, had been very prominent in the organization of the resistance in Shanghai in 1931. It was indicative of the part which national sentiment was to play in the organization of the people in the Chinese war effort.

More individualist and more cynical was the attitude of the great bankers and financial magnates of the Treaty Ports. Some of them, indeed, were with the war party: many had greater political regard for the security of their possessions.

The masses of people – the poor peasantry, the unskilled workers of the towns – the people who were to bear the main burden of the war in hardship and toll of life – were not consulted, and their opinions would have been taken as being of little weight. But among these, so far as they were informed, the temper was apt to be nationalist, and strongly nationalist. In the Asia of the past generation, it was always remarkable how news circulated, and how accurate the reports tended to be which circulated in the back streets and urban slums. The temper of the vast anonymous mass could not be overlooked.

CHAPTER 8

Japan: Internal Revolutions and Foreign Policy

THESE years, 1931–6, had been, for Japan also, a period of relentless pressure towards a formal war with China, which had come to be regarded as inevitable. Japan's descent into Avernus, during the six brief years since the Manchurian Incident, and the corruption of its political system were rapid. Most of what happened prepared Japan for the part it was later to play. In this time Japan took, with great speed, a series of plunges which ensured that, when the Pacific War came, it was fought in a spirit that surprised the world by its barbarity.

Historians often despair at the fact that close examination of the web of historical events reveals it to be both intricate and seamless. Convention and the need for coherence force us to impose conceptual frameworks which assist us, imperfectly, in our efforts to describe the processes and events that form part of the history we seek to define. It is as well to recognize, however, that some of our conventional ideas concerning the Manchurian Incident, the China Incident and the Pacific War are hopelessly inadequate. As Ienaga Saburō, a distinguished and controversial Japanese who has had a profound effect upon Japanese historiography concerning 'Japan's Last War', writes:

The six years of intermittent military action and political intrigue after the Manchurian Incident suggest that 1937 marked a new phase of a war already well underway. It is impossible to delineate the major 'incidents' as separate crises; in fact, it is probably more accurate to treat events from 1931 on as a single conflict.*

A rapid deterioration set in among most of the national institutions. It had the obvious effect of easing the path to war, and it harmed the spirit of the country profoundly. When there was a lull in the development of external events, the crisis deepened internally. The process can be traced from point to point. In Manchuria, in 1931, the decision to act had been made by the Japanese Army. It dragged the civilian Government in the wake of its *fait accompli*. The precedent was alarming, and was regularly

* Ienaga Saburō, *Japan's Last War: World War II and the Japanese, 1931–1945*, Blackwell, Oxford, 1979, p. 70.

acted upon by the Army in the years which followed, and accepted by the nation. No successful revolution took place, and no change of institutions was necessary: the civil service continued to operate, and remained comparatively unpurged. But in the Government of the day, with a constitution all too precise, it was enough that one of the controlling forces should shift the balance of power in the administration for the whole nature of government to change. The civil authority from time to time ceased to intervene in matters which were properly its concern, and left these to the Army. It was a species of anarchy.

This uneasiness, vague but pervasive, increased the danger of war. Many Japanese, fearful that the military, which they felt was already beyond control, might now move towards the acceptance of all kinds of radicalism in Japanese internal affairs, thought that its giddy mind would best be occupied by foreign quarrels. Many voices were raised in open opposition to this trend, but gradually, by the Kwantung Army's successive *faits accomplis*, the critics were overborne.

Following hard on the success of the Kwantung Army in establishing its ascendancy throughout Manchuria in the years 1931–4, as we have seen, there was but a short step to its covert involvement in the political affairs of the buffer zone comprising Hopei, Chahar and even North China itself. In the end, this involvement became increasingly open, and Japan found itself with no option but to continue with its expansion in China, by peaceful or other means, despite the obvious inconsistencies in pursuing an aggressive foreign policy while complaining of Japan's isolation in foreign affairs. At the same time, having announced its withdrawal from the League of Nations, Japan now felt itself even more vulnerable than before to the constant and predictable winds of international disapproval for her actions and policies.

In these years there also took place a distinct shift in the religious life of the country. Attention was less on the compassionate, often intellectually subtle, religion of Buddhism; more emphasis was given to the religion which had co-existed with Buddhism for many centuries – Shintō, superficially a rather simple form of animism and worship of the symbols of state. Some of its adherents were inclined to take its cosmogony literally. Others found it more satisfactory as an extended metaphor. A Japanese scholar has noted that 'The myth is essentially beyond science.'* Many western observers, who knew next to nothing about Shintōism, believed that it had no intellectual corpus to it. It certainly is true that it was

---

* Anzu Motohiko, quoted in Jean Herbert, *Shintō: At the Fountain-Head of Japan*, Allen & Unwin, London, 1967, p. 230.

neither readily perceptible nor translatable into Aristotelian terms. Like the Japanese language itself, it was highly symbolic and ambiguous, even vague. It must not be thought of as having no substance, however, for its efficacy can be seen from its social impact, from its political achievements. That these were purposeful, however, is doubtful, nor was it by accident that the circumspect authors of the Meiji Constitution had regarded Shintōism as an unsatisfactory organizing principle for modern Japan but borrowed some of its underlying assumptions.

In some ways it became ill-advised for a Japanese to diverge by however little from the norm in behaviour, sentiment or thought. Japan had never been kind to the pronounced individual and Japanese society had eyed any departure from conformity with uneasiness. (Only those cases where experimentalism had been backed up by a reputation of extreme religiosity were exempted.) The increasing tension in political life made the Japanese dislike eccentricity even more severely. In the years preceding the end of the Japanese military venture, there was an increasing anarchy in Japanese literature and in all departments of creative life. Older generations of Japanese deplored the enthusiasm with which the youth of the country embraced alien imports such as baseball, football, golf, the cinema, jazz and ballroom dancing, all of which seemed to break down traditional Japanese cultural values. These, however, were fads, group obsessions, and they reflected a widespread sense of material well-being. Of true individualism, of the man with the social courage to stand up and denounce what society was doing, or the innovator who worked under the pressure of his *daimon* and ignored the praise or censure of the world, there was strikingly too much evidence.

All of this reinforced the desire of the Japanese to promote the cherished plurality of Japanese society, *Musubi* – a dynamic, vitalizing process in which all things bind themselves together. Strangeness and conflict were no enemies here: they could be utilized, not merely tolerated, by finding every manifestation a proper place and limited function, harmoniously helping to create and define the larger purposes of the whole community and nation. All of this is, of course, an extended image, a descriptive representation of birth and growth itself. Above all it depends upon constructs of compartmentalization, boundaries, and life-giving power. This concept, one of the basic concepts of Shintōism, had a strong grip on the people of Japan.

It is scarcely surprising, therefore, that people from all walks of life wanted the sublime reassurance that came from submitting themselves to what they perceived was a universal community of place and purpose under a truly all-encompassing organizing principle, the sacred Imperial

Will, made manifest in the *Kokutai* to which we have already alluded
This process, although it had formed the basis of the consolidation o
political authority following the Meiji Restoration, itself involved ₐ
suspension of critical faculties, a febrile casuistry which, during periods o
internal crisis, interfered with political judgement and made any exercise
of political leadership objectively irrational. Japan had been saved from
the dictation of a ruthless and flamboyant figure only because no such
figure had the ability to seize the Government. The tradition of Japan was
against individual leadership. Even in times of great crisis it required that
revolutionaries should act in committees. But the spectacle of the administration of a great empire ceasing altogether for a few days, and great
offices of state being hawked round by captains and majors, caused all
lookers-on to marvel and to shudder.

The national temper began to be touched, but only touched, by hysteria
Thought control, imposed by the Government, meant the virtual interruption of all forms of rational thinking. An official version of Japanese
history, drawing on fairy stories and full of absurdity, was made to prevail
it became dangerous to publish more serious matter. Dr Minobe Tat-
sukichi, the much respected Japanese professor, had been hounded from
his job in 1935 because radical circles found it unforgivable that he had
stated in a book on political science that the Japanese Emperor was an
organ of the constitution. The Emperor was too sacred to be defined. The
deification of the Emperor, which had been resurrected from the Japanese
past, grew now to absurd proportions, and was especially ironical because
it was known to be distasteful to the Emperor himself.

Nevertheless, consider these manifestations of the country's malaise
within some sense of proportion. Whatever the tendency of certain factions and special interest groups to pursue courses of action which were
fundamentally irrational, and whatever the temptations of hindsight to
perceive the national life itself as ineluctably hysterical in the years which
we know ended in the catastrophic disintegration of the Japanese Empire,
the Land of the Rising Sun was not without subjectively reassuring
features that eased the political and moral transitions through which the
country passed. As the distinguished Israeli historian Ben Ami Shillony,
an acknowledged authority on the development of Japanese extremism
and political terrorism, has observed:

Throughout the decade Japan remained a land of law and order, despite the
eruption of occasional 'incidents'. It was governed by its constitutional institutions: the Emperor, the Cabinet, the civilian bureaucracy and the military high
command. There were constant frictions among them and periodic outbursts
from below, but the system did not break. *Gekokujō*, or the rule of the higher by

the lower, was a popular phrase with writers, but it very rarely materialised in reality. The special blend of pragmatism and fanaticism, which had characterised Japan in former times, continued to characterise her in the 1930s.*

Indeed, one may go even further: the same qualities that led Japan into the Greater East Asia and Pacific Conflict were to sustain it through the years of travail that followed, and were to prove receptive to the adaptations imposed upon Japan during the Allied Occupation in the post-war period.

The number of terrorist incidents multiplied. Some were simply lunatic in conception and execution, such as the assassination of Prime Minister Hamaguchi Osachi by Sagoya Tomeo at Tokyo Central Railway Station in 1930. Sagoya was a member of the 'Blood Brotherhood', one of many right-wing jingoistic associations, clubs and societies that proliferated in Japan. It is ironic that these organizations were bitterly divided, for one idea shared by most of them was the notion that the entire Japanese people were an extended family. Elaborate schemes were concocted in attempts to establish common ground between them. These efforts generally collapsed, abandoned because of the paranoia and testiness of their respective leaders. This in turn left a legacy of failure, disappointment, recrimination and even fratricide.

A growing number of prominent political and military figures became involved. The so-called March Incident of 1931 was, in Professor Maruyama's pregnant phrase, 'born in the dark and buried in the dark'. It was the product of a conspiracy in which prominent members of the *Tōseiha* (of which more anon), notably Lieutenant-General Ninomiya Harushige, Vice-Chief of the Army General Staff, Major-General Koiso Kuniaki, the powerful Chief of the Military Affairs Bureau at the War Ministry, possibly Colonel Nagata Tetsuzan, Chief of the Army Affairs Section under Koiso, and certainly Major-General Tatekawa Yoshitsugu, Chief of the Intelligence Division, were all deeply involved. Tatekawa was the general whom we find stumbling drunkenly outside on the night of the Mukden Incident six months later. Individuals such as these – and many of the junior officers who called upon them to rise up in the name of national integrity – were genuinely talented and privileged. They were motivated not so much by further personal ambition as by alarm at the drift of national policy and discontent over the quality of Japan's civil administration.

They fell under the influence of disaffected officers who belonged to the *Sakura-kai*, the radical 'Cherry Blossom Society', a secret fraternity of

---

* Ben Ami Shillony, 'Myth and Reality in Japan of the 1930s', in *Modern Japan: Aspects of History, Literature and Society*, ed. W. G. Beasley, Allen & Unwin, London, 1975, p. 88.

fewer than one hundred junior officers, none over the rank of Lieutenant-Colonel, formed in September 1930 by the notorious Lieutenant-Colonel Hashimoto Kingorō, a gunnery officer, then serving as Head of the Russian Desk at the Army General Staff after his return from an overseas posting as Military Attaché in Turkey, determined to model his activities upon those of Kemal Atatürk. The *Sakura-kai* was created as a 'discussion group' for the furtherance of his brand of crypto-fascist radicalism, identified more broadly as the *Seigunha* or Army Purification Faction. The *Sakura-kai* was his own personal instrument: it had no rulebook or membership fees. His recruits were drawn from the War Ministry, the Army General Staff and from military training establishments and forces garrisoned within the vicinity of metropolitan Tokyo. Hashimoto's plan called for close collaboration with a similar secret society of Navy officers, the *Seiyō-kai* (Stars and Ocean Society). He also sought and won the support of that indefatigable propagandist, Professor Ōkawa Shūmei, whose acquaintance we have already made.* War Minister Ugaki Kazushige, too, was tainted by the affair, although his real attitude towards it, like that of Nagata, remains obscure.

At a restaurant in Tokyo, Dr Ōkawa concocted a plan for a mass public rally to be held outside the Imperial Diet building in protest against anti-labour legislation. Amid ugly scenes, the Diet would come under a mock attack. Troops would rush to the scene, seal off the building and restore 'order'. The Cabinet would be compelled to resign. War Minister Ugaki would be called upon to form a reform Cabinet, sweeping away the corrupt party political machines. Hashimoto expressed enthusiasm for this plan, provided Ōkawa obtained Ugaki's personal blessing. Later that night, Ōkawa reported that Ugaki was willing to take part. He asked Hashimoto to obtain a supply of practice grenades to add convincing sound-effects during the disturbances which were to lead to the military coup. Hashimoto encountered difficulty in obtaining these and approached Major-General Tatekawa, until recently his immediate superior, who gave Hashimoto a letter of introduction to the Commandant of the Army Infantry School which overcame all obstacles. He in turn handed the grenades over to Major-General Koiso, who took them away for safekeeping. When Dr Ōkawa was put on trial in 1934 on charges of sedition, he testified that 'Koiso, taking charge of everything, told me that since there would be the danger of being discovered if too many fussed about it, we should pretend to have suspended it on the surface, and that I should represent the civilians and that he would represent the Army.'

* See p. 65.

Ugaki, however, evidently had second thoughts, the ever-vigilant *Kenpeitai* stood by, and the March Incident was nipped in the bud.

Seven months later, just a few weeks after the Manchurian Incident began, Lieutenant-Colonel Hashimoto went a step further. He had begun to feel that if civilians were involved, leaks would inevitably occur that would frustrate any attempt to overthrow the existing order. Together with one of his friends, Captain Chō Isamu, and Major Nemoto Hiroshi, Head of the China Desk at the Army General Staff, Hashimoto plotted a *coup d'état* known to history as the October Incident. Ostensibly they acted to prevent the Government from restraining the Kwantung Army's rampage through Manchuria. Nevertheless, there is evidence that at the time Hashimoto had neither met nor established any liaison with Itagaki, Doihara, Ishiwara or the other Kwantung Army officers principally involved in the outbreak of the Manchurian Incident. In any event Hashimoto was conscious that there were good grounds for supposing that a harmony of views existed between them. Hashimoto's plans began to assume fantastically grandiose proportions. The number of individuals involved rapidly increased. The plotters made preparations for mobilization of the First and Third Infantry Regiments of the Imperial Guards Division. The headquarters of the Army General Staff and the War Ministry were to be surrounded. Senior officers were to be coerced into declaring martial law. Naval aircraft from Kasumigaura Naval Air Training Centre would launch bombing attacks against key targets. A coordinated assault would be mounted against the Prime Minister's official residence during a meeting of his Cabinet with the intention of murdering all those in attendance.

Although there are conflicting accounts about what happened next, it appears that War Minister Minami and Vice-Minister of War Sugiyama learned of the plot about a week before it was due to take place. They were unable to bring the insurgents to their senses. The two then turned to Lieutenant-General Araki Sadao, a former President of the Army Staff College whom the rebels admired as 'a man of unimpeachable character'. Hashimoto and his conspirators regarded Araki as a model soldier and wanted to install him as Prime Minister. Minami and Sugiyama now asked him to sort out the mess. Araki's response was somewhat ambiguous: he, too, was deeply enmeshed in factional politics within the Army (as we shall see), and Hashimoto's plans caused him no little embarrassment. Minami asked the *Kenpeitai* to step in before the incident could take place. This time, however, the potato was too hot to handle. The forces of law and order achieved what must have seemed to be the best outcome to which they could aspire under the prevailing circumstances.

Those at the heart of the dispute were placed in protective custody for a short time. They were not charged with the commission of any offence, nor were the careers of most of them blighted (although Hashimoto himself, promoted to full colonel in 1934, was relegated to the reserves and never rose higher in the next eleven years of peace and Total War). Inconceivable as it may seem, there was scarcely any serious criticism of the idealistic patriotic fervour which had impelled the rebels to resort to force. Fainthearts and realists alike were fatally compromised. In a footnote to this incident, Hashimoto, Chō and their *Seigunha*, having been inspired by General Araki's eloquence in the past, now began slowly to turn against him, regarding him as a charlatan. Over the course of the next two years, there would gradually emerge a new, loose coalition of interests, bound together only in its opposition to Araki's *Kōdōha* group. It would absorb the *Seigunha* and become known to its enemies as the *Tōseiha*, or Control Faction.

Meanwhile the politics of terror, born out of despair but nurtured by success, continued to enjoy a vogue among radical groups. In December 1931 the charismatic General Araki was promoted to War Minister in a shrewd manoeuvre to bring order to the Army. Araki succeeded in this and then went on to dominate the Cabinet.

Araki's popularity among many junior Army officers remained high, and they were anxious to do nothing that might spoil his hopes of bringing about the political reforms they wanted by peaceful means. Their counterparts in the Navy, however, had never felt inclined to regard Araki as a national saviour. Despite opposition from the young Army officers, the Navy group decided to go ahead with a plan to kill a considerable number of leading statesmen and business magnates.

Inoue Nisshō, a half-crazed Nichiren monk, who prior to taking up holy orders had spent years in Manchuria as a secret agent of the Japanese Army, led a clandestine civilian gang that called itself the *Ketsumeidan* (the 'Blood Brotherhood', or 'Dare-Devil Bunch') and provided its members with what passed as spiritual guidance. He allied his movement with that of the young naval officers and even lent the conspirators his temple for an arsenal. In February 1932, Araki, who had been kept informed of developments, prevailed upon the young Army officers to have nothing to do with the plan. He did nothing to denounce the plot but the Naval General Staff caught wind of it and appeared to have averted it by a timely transfer of certain naval officers to sea duty. Unfortunately, this failed to prevent others from attempting to carry out the plan. Nineteen thirty-two became known as 'The Year of Assassinations'.

The 'Blood Brotherhood' Incident of early February 1932 was a lineal descendant of Sagoya's actions two years before. Inoue decided to act independently of both services. He selected a hit-list of twenty victims. His followers simply drew lots, a different assassin for each target. The first to be slain was Inoue Junnosuke (no relation to the turbulent priest), a former Finance Minister known to be strongly opposed to the Manchurian Incident. His death was followed by the murder of Baron Dan Takuma, Managing Director of the Mitsui business empire. Following police investigations, Inoue Nisshō and the other main culprits in the 'Blood Brotherhood' gang were soon arrested. After a trial they were convicted and Inoue himself was sentenced to life imprisonment; he was subsequently freed in 1940 as part of a general amnesty and later resumed an active political life with the help of his old disciples after the withdrawal of the Allied Occupation in 1952.

By tradition, Japanese Cabinets governed as long as they retained the confidence of their two armed services Ministers. The resignation of an unhappy War Minister or his Navy counterpart could force the downfall of a Cabinet. Civilian Ministers, however, could do the same. The most telling case was that of an ambitious Minister for Home Affairs, Adachi Kenzō, who in December 1931 compelled the Wakatsuki Cabinet to resign by refusing either to attend the Cabinet or to resign his office. Adachi had wanted to promote a Government of all the talents, modelled perhaps on Ramsay MacDonald's National Government in Britain and led, he evidently hoped, by himself. His own ambitions foundered, but his actions led directly to the first minority Government ever to be formed in Japan since Prince Saionji's introduction of party politics into National Government shortly after the turn of the century.

The new Prime Minister was Inukai Tsuyoshi, 75-year-old leader of the opposition *Seiyūkai*, who rejected calls for the formation of a Cabinet of National Unity in which both parties might participate. Inukai did not lack courage, and he took to heart the Emperor's injunction to resist the military's interference in Japan's domestic and international affairs. Five months later, he was dead, assassinated by another cabal of radical officers who carried out the 15 May Incident.

The terrorists had struck again, after a brief pause, mounting their unsuccessful *coup d'état* on 15 May 1932. This time it was the turn of the junior naval officers, who joined forces with an even more feckless band of radical Army cadets that had fallen under the influence of civilian ultranationalists including Dr Ōkawa and Tachibana Kosaburō. The naval officers and the Army cadets kept a Sunday rendezvous at the Yasukuni shrine, embarked in a pair of taxis to the official residence of Prime

Minister Inukai Tsuyoshi, and simply walked in unchallenged. The operation was bungled, the intruders lost their way, but they finally found and murdered the 77-year-old Premier. Leaving the building, the terrorists killed two guards. They made their way to the *Kenpeitai* Headquarters and gave themselves up. In the confusion, the remainder of the Cabinet had escaped harm. Meanwhile, a second squad of naval officers threw grenades at the house of Count Makino, the Lord Keeper of the Privy Seal. Makino himself may have been warned of the attack by Ōkawa, who regarded the old man with affection and even had hopes that Makino could be prevailed upon to be Prime Minister after the revolution. In any event, this attack caused no fatalities. A third group lobbed bombs at the Metropolitan Police Headquarters, again to little effect. Tachibana and his agrarian reformists carried out an elaborate attempt to black out Tokyo's electric power supply system but their bombs failed to wreck their targets. Finally, one of the Army's leading young radicals was shot and wounded by one of Tachibana's supporters for having been instrumental in withdrawing support for the plot six months before: it was a breathtakingly ill-conceived revenge attack which further cemented relations between the Army Young Officer movement and the Army top brass at the expense of future collaboration between the extremist factions of the two armed services. Once again, the leaders identified by the authorities were handled with kid gloves and respect for their lofty motives. The murderers of Premier Inukai declared at their trial that their motive had been to protest against the Japanese ratification of the London naval agreement which the Japanese Government had incurred much displeasure by accepting. It was to be the last constructive agreement for peace that a Japanese Government was to be allowed by public opinion to make. War Minister Araki issued a public statement proclaiming:

We cannot restrain our tears when we consider the mentality expressed in the actions of these pure and naïve young men. They are not actions for fame, or personal gain, nor are they traitorous. They were performed in the sincere belief that they were for the benefit of Imperial Japan. Therefore, in dealing with this Incident, it will not do to dispose of it in a routine manner according to short-sighted conceptions.*

Well may we marvel at his words. With the passing of time, however, opinion within the Young Officer movement was gradually hardening in its appreciation that Araki was too moderate for their taste, and began to think in terms of even more independent action.

* Maruyama Masao, *Thought and Behaviour in Modern Japanese Politics*, Oxford University Press, London, 1963, p. 67.

The culprits showed no remorse for their actions. They had every reason to believe that the reactions of their superiors to the March and October Incidents of 1931 had indicated that direct action was a not unwelcome response to civil corruption and indolence. The cynical opportunism of senior officers was an important element in creating a climate in which mass terrorism by young officers could flourish. The mechanism was a well-established Japanese tradition, one to which we have already referred in passing, known as *Gekokujō*, that phenomenon involving the subordination of senior officers by junior officers – the tail wagging the dog. It is not, perhaps, the frequency of its occurrence which is important. What is more significant is the fact that it led to very widespread displacements of authority and political judgement when it did occur. The same process had manifested itself in the development of the Manchurian Incident.

Following the 15 May Incident, those apprehended by the authorities were arraigned on a variety of charges including murder and sedition. The proceedings were held in public and received unprecedented publicity. Although Japan was by no means given to civil liberty and to the unfettered freedom of the press, on this occasion no attempt was made to impose either effective state censorship or any discernible self-restraint by the news media.

The rebels took full advantage of the occasion to proclaim the righteousness of their cause. Their patriotic motives elicited popular sympathy. The country was in a political ferment. None of those found guilty were executed. The penal sentences imposed by the courts were, under the circumstances, exceptionally mild. The leader of the Army Cadet group, Gotō Terunori, together with his ten military co-defendants, was court-martialled. They each received four-year prison terms. They were freed on parole within the year and were pardoned soon afterwards. Koga Kiyoshi and Mikami Taku, the two principal ringleaders of the naval faction, were sentenced by a naval court martial to fifteen years' imprisonment. Their followers received sentences of thirteen, ten, two and one year's imprisonment respectively. Pardons were granted to all of them by 1940. The civilians involved in the Incident were treated more severely by the civil courts. Tachibana Kōsaburō was singled out and sentenced to a term of life imprisonment. In Hugh Byas's evocative phrase, the 15 May Incident had been carried out by 'adolescents straying in a pink mist'. That mist was no more remarkable than the corrosive fog which enveloped the due processes of law and order.

In the following year, there was another hare-brained plot, known as the *Shinpei-tai Jiken*, or 'Heaven-Sent Troops' Incident. It was concocted by the Patriotic Labour Party and the Great Japan Production Party, both right-wing labour organizations which had links with the russophobic Amur River Society. This plot had no direct links with the Young Officer movement, but among the ringleaders were an Army Lieutenant-Colonel and a Navy Commander by the name of Yamaguchi Saburō. The idea was that on the morning of 7 July 1933, Yamaguchi, a naval pilot, would take off in his aircraft, bomb the Cabinet at the official residence of the Prime Minister, blow up the residence of the Lord Privy Seal, Count Makino, and then attack the Headquarters of the Metropolitan Police. He would then land in front of the Imperial Palace. At that point a mob of 3,600 men, having converged seemingly out of nowhere, would assault the Metropolitan Police Headquarters. A handpicked group of men would then rush away to attack the Prime Minister's residence and assassinate any Cabinet Minister who might have survived the initial air attack. Other units would attack the homes of the presidents of the two main parliamentary parties, the residence of the Lord Privy Seal, the Japan Industrial Club (where it was hoped to kill a few *zaibatsu*), the headquarters of the left-wing Social Masses Party and a list of other hated targets. Still more units would smash their way into certain armouries to seize weapons and ammunition. The focus of the rebels would then shift to the Headquarters of the Industrial Bank of Japan where they planned to barricade themselves for a bloody last-ditch stand against the entire might of the Metropolitan Police. Evidently there was some thought that they might spark off a wider insurrection leading to Emperor Hirohito's replacement by his brother Prince Chichibu and the establishment of a new Government under Prince Higashikuni. There is not a lot that one can say about this plan except that the police arrested a number of the conspirators in time to prevent the Incident from occurring. Nevertheless, there is some significance in the fact that the plot would have involved the assassination of War Minister Araki as well as his other Cabinet colleagues, and this lends some credence to suggestions that his opponents were also aware of the plan, hoped to use it as a pretext to seize power, and may even have intended to provide the conspirators with arms.

After the murder of Inukai in 1932, no other political party leader was to become Prime Minister until the defeat of Japan. It was not immediately apparent, but the mould of Japanese party government had been shattered – and the fault lay not so much with the terrorists (although they were a proximate cause) but mainly with the parties themselves, together with the local regional political machines upon whom they relied for support.

It is notable that neither of the two mainstream political parties sought mass political support from the general public as a means of bolstering its claim to authority over its opponents. The system was corrupt, and looked it. Indeed, the political parties never truly reflected the aspirations and concerns of the Japanese public at large. The parties served to legitimize the views of élites more interested in power and patronage than in democratic values.

Paradoxically, the political parties were intended to provide a vehicle for national opinion. Constitutionally, the elected House of Representatives in the Imperial Diet was not designed to be a powerful branch of government. The Meiji oligarchs had confined its purpose to the expression of popular sentiment. It was not an instrument for actively governing the country. It could obstruct the imposition of unpopular laws, and it could initiate legislation of its own devising, but its will could be thwarted by the inactivity of the House of Peers or by a vote of the Privy Council. It lacked any real power to control the budget.

Moreover, the political parties were perceived by many circles in Japan as divisive, alien structures, incompatible with traditional Japanese values and above all inimical to the neo-Confucian harmony and benevolence that ought to extend from the Emperor to all of his subjects. As long as Japanese security was seen to depend upon a more or less cooperative relationship with the Western Powers, as had seemed to exist throughout most of the years between the Anglo-Japanese Alliance and the late 1920s, more reactionary forces were held at bay notwithstanding the enmity that existed between the political parties. During this period, indeed, the political parties between them not only gained real control in the House of Representatives but selected successive Prime Ministers, determined the composition of their Cabinets and exercised a commanding influence over government policies on most issues. From thence the power of the political parties was extended into the House of Peers, determined the composition and attitudes of the Privy Council, intimidated the civil service, and established uneasy partnerships with factions in big business, in the armed forces and even in the Imperial Court itself. All of this seemed to represent a new kind of stability quite different from the clan-based oligarchic factions of previous decades. None of this had any natural place in the Meiji Constitution.

In the end, the party politicians lost whatever credibility they pretended to have. They seemed to be yesterday's men. Few could command general respect. None appeared to have the vitality, imagination and flair that people trusted in old war horses like Admiral Saitō Makoto, Admiral Okada Keisuke and General Hayashi Senjurō, or figures such as the veteran Ambassador Hirota Kōki (a commoner) and the sophisticated Prince Konoye Fuminaro, last of the noble Fujiwara line: each of these men became Prime Minister, handpicked by the wily old democratic Genrō, Prince Saionji Kinmochi, who himself bitterly regretted the eclipse of the party system which he personally had introduced into Japanese society in the early years of the century. Now even Saionji appreciated that the leadership of the two great political parties of the mid-thirties was bereft of talent, criss-crossed with factionalism, utterly unfit for the daunting task of restoring a national consensus. The fact that after 1932 *both* main political parties – the *Minseitō* and the *Seiyūkai* – were committed to Japanese recognition of the puppet state of Manchukuo did nothing to relieve the anxieties of Saionji, who fervently hoped that the men he selected as Prime Ministers over the next few years had the strength of character and moral toughness necessary either to withstand the temptations of overseas expansion or, when that failed, to bring the political ambitions of the Army under control. If that strategy should fail, Saionji appreciated, then Japan was set on a course leading directly to its own ruination through economic collapse or through a collision with the Western Powers. Unhappily, the instruments through which Saionji attempted to manipulate the policies of the nation were unequal to his purposes.

Following the murder of Prime Minister Inukai in May 1932, Saitō Makoto was selected by Prince Saionji to take the dead man's place. He had been a full admiral since 1916, had served as former naval attaché to the United States before the turn of the century and then, as Vice-Minister of the Navy for seven years between 1898 and 1906, had been largely responsible for building the Navy which was to defeat the Russians in the Russo-Japanese War. He then had served as Navy Minister for a period of eight years until the beginning of the First World War. After the war he emerged from a period of retirement to serve as Governor-General of Japan between August 1919 and December 1927. He was very nearly the victim of a terrorist bomb thrown at his carriage, shortly after taking up that appointment but, undeterred, dedicated himself to the transformation of the Japanese colonial government from a military occupation to a civil administration. After attending the Geneva Disarmament Conference as a plenipotentiary in 1927, he took a well-earned rest. He was clearly a man of personal courage, and he later returned to Korea for a second stint as Governor-General between 1929 and June 1931 (a period when radical elements in the Korean Army were kept well under control). As one of Japan's most distinguished elder soldier-statesmen, he was a man of proven ability and experience; he had a reputation for being relatively liberal by Japanese standards; and he had shown phenomenal staying-power in the face of adversity. As Prime Minister, he also briefly reserved for himself the portfolios of Foreign Affairs (until July 1932) and Education (after March 1934). Nevertheless, the old man was tired. Two other figures, War Minister Araki Sadao and his Inspector-General of Military Education (Mazaki Jinzaburō), both leading figures in the Imperial Way Faction of the Army, dominated the policies of the Saitō Cabinet and were greatly esteemed by the same radical groups of Young Officers from whom the most recent crop of assassins had emerged. After presiding over Japan's recognition of Manchukuo, rejection of the Lytton Report, withdrawal from the League of Nations, and the approval of a huge arms procurement programme for the Navy as well as the Army, Saitō had proved a great disappointment to Saionji and the moderate elements in the country. In the end, however, Saitō only felt obliged to resign from office in July 1934 after his Finance Minister (former Prime Minister Takahashi Korekiyo), other members of his Cabinet and senior officials in the Finance Ministry were implicated in a sleazy bribes scandal involving the sale of stocks in a rayon company. His successor was another admiral, Okada Keisuke, who more or less unwillingly followed down the same path of compromise that Saitō had been forced to tread. A year later, Saitō himself was appointed Lord Keeper of the Privy Seal as a mark of the Emperor's affection, but the fire had gone out of his soul.

It should be said that corruption for some time had become much more blatant than before. Election fraud in particular had become a regular feature of Japanese political life, as had 'pork barrel' largesse and the sale of political offices to the highest bidder at local, regional and even national levels. The political parties did not exercise power autocratically, nor by means of any direct appeal for public support. Their authority survived only as long as they retained the allegiance of local political bosses at subordinate levels. This in turn meant that the political parties blocked efforts by the central bureaucracy to extend their power into local affairs.

Indeed, many bureaucrats found themselves unable to function at local or regional levels without surrendering their political initiative to the whims and personal interests of the local party bosses. As a result, discontent with the political parties spread laterally throughout the professional civil service apparatus as well as in the élite circles of the House of Peers (where political cant had begun to disrupt the clubby atmosphere of former times).

The whole system came crashing down under the weight of the Manchurian Incident and the international condemnation and isolation of

Japan which became a permanent feature of the nation's political life from 1932 until the end of the Pacific War. During this period, Japan turned gradually towards the military and civil bureaucracies to survive what was regarded universally as a period of national emergency surpassing anything in the country's previous history. The fact that both of these groups could claim legitimacy under the Constitution as mere servants of the Imperial Will also gave them authority as the constitutional embodiment and voice of that national essence, *Kokutai*, to which reference has already been made in Chapter 3. Added to that was the evidence, borne out in the years of maladministration, corruption and the demonstrable incompetence of many members of the Imperial Diet, that modern government was no place for bumbling amateurs: the reins of power should be in the hands of those best equipped by intelligence, training and experience to perform the functions of their offices. As the reputations of the political parties diminished, so did the ability of those parties to attract into their ranks men of experience and probity who might have led them through successive crises.

Parallel with the eclipse of the political parties and the rising importance of the military and civilian bureaucracies in the domestic as well as in the overseas affairs of Japan during the thirties, there took place in Japan an ideological splintering of the Army and the Navy but more especially of the Army. Although the situation was often more complicated, as we have already intimated, the factionalization of the Japanese Army officer corps is generally perceived as a struggle between two major ideological groups, each of which dispensed patronage and found outside supporters. The efforts of these groups to achieve supremacy in Japan shook the nation to its core.

The *Kōdō* group stressed obedience to the divine Imperial Will and sought to emancipate Emperor Hirohito from the baleful influence of effete, liberal-minded palace officials, the corrupt, materialistic accretions of twentieth-century parliamentarianism, and the bureaucratic and capitalistic opportunists who used the state to further their selfish interests. They yearned for a 'Shōwa Restoration' to usher in a new age of Imperial splendour. They saw themselves as the natural successors to the Samurai clansmen who had carried out the 'Meiji Restoration' in the previous century. Their vision of life in that future age was obscured by the misfortunes, maladministration and structures of the modern era. Only when all that was swept away would the one true path forward stand revealed in crystal clarity. Thus, so said one adherent of the Imperial Way: 'The punishment of evil men and the Restoration are the same thing.'* In terms of foreign affairs and military policy, however, the *Kōdōha* regarded war against the Soviet Union as inevitable and imminent. At all events it became a fixed star towards which all *Kōdōha* sought to steer Japan. From this phobic obsession with the Soviet Union (and the Comintern) sprang the demand of the Young Officer movement, with which the *Kōdōha* were allied, for the immediate spiritual reformation of Japan. At the moment, by contrast, it seemed prudent to avoid any military adventure against China. This consideration proceeded partly from the fact that the difficulties of overcoming Chinese resistance were regarded as considerable, and partly from a sense of kinship with the Chinese which members of the *Kōdōha* imagined the Chinese might be taught to reciprocate. By one means or other, however, the Imperial Way planned to embrace the Middle Kingdom: contrary to what is often supposed, the policy of restraint towards China was by no means unconditional. And when Kita Ikki, the most important ideologist associated with the movement, looked further into his crystal ball, he foresaw Japanese expansion beyond, as far as eastern Siberia and even, in due time, *Australia*.

Against the *Kōdōha* were ranged a number of groups which the *Kōdōha* tended to lump together under a pejorative label, the *Tōseiha* (Control Faction), in which a number of the elder generation of senior officers were allied to some of the young technocrats and brighter staff officers. Many of them rejected the spiritual mumbo-jumbo and traditional values promoted by General Araki and his cronies. Others felt that it compromised efforts to mechanize and introduce other technical innovations into the Army. The fixation of the *Kōdōha* about the Soviet Union worried those who wanted time to develop the economic infrastructure of Manchukuo rather than waste resources in a war for which they believed the nation would remain ill-prepared for a considerable period. Thus the *Kōdōha* harkened back to a mythical past but wanted radical changes overnight. The *Tōseiha*, arguably the more dangerous of the two groups in the long run, looked forward to a different kind of war, where all the resources of the modern state would be harnessed under unified direction: in two words, Total War.

The rapid eclipse of the *Kōdōha* began in 1934, when Araki resigned as War Minister, ostensibly due to ill-health but mindful of the animosity that he had generated within the senior ranks of the Army. As a naval Intelligence report on the Army, prepared within the Naval General Staff, observed rather drily:

* Muranaka Kōji, cited in Maruyama Masao, op. cit., p. 55.

While chanting effortlessly that he must promptly invest the Emperor's Army with integrity and abolish all cliques from the Army, War Minister Araki, in fact, built up his own large faction. The Imperial Army is not so generous as to permit this deed.*

In the aftermath of Araki's departure, the Vice-Chief of the Army General Staff, Lieutenant-General Ueda Kenkichi, had links with the Control Faction. Prince Kan'in Kotohito, the Chief of the Army General Staff, was personally rather favourable to it, too, while Major-General Nagata Tetsuzan, regarded as the 'brains' of the *Tōseiha*, now returned to the centre of power as Chief of the Military Affairs Bureau at the War Ministry after having being pushed out for a period by one of Araki's favourites to serve as a brigade commander. Nagata had first risen to prominence as the protégé of War Minister Ugaki in the ill-starred Cabinet of Hamaguchi during the great London Naval Conference controversy. He was an early advocate of Army modernization, the development of mechanized forces and research into biological and chemical weapons systems. He was dynamic, brilliant and thoroughly efficient. Araki's successor as War Minister, General Hayashi Senjurō, was greatly influenced by Nagata, who had set himself the task of rooting out adherents of the *Kōdōha* from all positions of influence in the Japanese Army. However, since Nagata himself had been implicated in the October Incident of 1931, it was a case of poacher-turned-gamekeeper. The main obstacle in Nagata's path was Mazaki, Ueda's predecessor as Vice-Chief of the Army General Staff and presently Inspector-General of Military Education. Mazaki was regarded as a lion by the Young Officer movement and the Imperial Way Faction. Nagata's schemes reached fruition, however, and Mazaki was forced to resign much against his will.

This signed Nagata's own death warrant. A lieutenant-colonel by the name of Aizawa Saburō decided that Nagata's actions in this and other matters had put him beyond the pale. He came up to Tokyo, made his way into Nagata's office, and murdered him with his sabre. The ensuing trial of the malefactor put Tokyo on tenterhooks. The defence used the occasion to ventilate the frustrations of the *Kōdōha* and to malign the reputation, and personal reputations of leading members, of the *Tōseiha*. Aizawa himself said that his sole regret was that he had failed to slay Nagata with a single blow of his sabre. For its part, the Control Faction, turning on those in the Imperial Way Faction whom they had recently

* Naval General Staff, Intelligence Report on the Military, 8 February 1934, cited in J. B. Crowley, *Japan's Quest for Autonomy: National Security and Foreign Policy, 1930–1938*, op. cit., p. 206.

been squeezing but had previously tolerated, determined to thwart further outrages by dispatching known *Kōdōha* troublemakers to the outer reaches of the Empire and beyond. Amid a general expectation of further outbreaks of violence, it had gradually become clear that the forces of discontent centred upon the First Division, which had been stationed in Tokyo for longer than scarcely anyone could remember. To defuse the situation, the First Division was ordered to proceed to Manchukuo. These steps, however, convinced leading elements within the *Kōdōha* that they must act in haste before the *Tōseiha* plans could be implemented and while the daily reports surrounding the public court martial of Aizawa still excited widespread national sympathy for the defendant.

In February 1936 the turbulence of the new Army reached its peak. There took place then an incident which embodied all the trends to violence of the time, and all the flouting of established political conduct. A plot was made by the younger officers in some of the most respected regiments. Plots, it will be gathered, were nothing new: it was the scope and audacity of this particular one which were original. The conspiracy was to murder the leaders of the Cabinet and the most respected elder statesmen who advised the throne. They intended to slaughter seven prominent individuals whom they regarded as representative of the reactionary elements of the country. These included the old Genrō, Prince Saionji (subsequently removed from the slate of intended victims); Prime Minister Okada; Finance Minister Takahashi; the Lord Keeper of the Privy Seal, Viscount Saitō; his predecessor, Count Makino; the Grand Chamberlain, Admiral Suzuki, and Mazaki's replacement as Inspector-General of Military Education, General Watanabe Jōtarō. A second deathlist was prepared in case any opportunities presented themselves during subsequent phases of the uprising. This list included the names of five individuals who were implicated in the terrorist plots of 1931 and the outbreak of the Manchurian Incident: War Minister Hayashi, Lieutenant-Colonel Mutō Akira, Lieutenant-Colonel Nemoto Hiroshi, Major Katakura Tadashi and Colonel Ishiwara Kanji. Then, as an act of unheard-of impiety, the conspirators planned to give an ultimatum to the Emperor for the appointment of a particular kind of Cabinet.

The disaffected troops finally mutinied on 26 February 1936, when they carried elements of the Imperial Guards Division with them. The usual mishaps and bloodthirsty scenes occurred, and it was notable that both the Metropolitan Police and the *Kenpeitai* were conspicuous by their absence in the opening hours of the Incident. The rebels occupied key positions in the city, including the Metropolitan Police Headquarters, the Ministry for Home Affairs and the War Ministry, holding them for several days. The death toll was far less than might have been expected. The number of troops deployed by the rebels was far greater than had taken part in any previous rebellion on Japanese soil since the Great Saigō had been put down by the forces of the Emperor Meiji. The terrorists who conceived the incident failed because their plot was prepared inadequately, and because some of the leading figures escaped their would-be assassins. But for some days the politics of Tokyo, which at the time was snow-covered, was divided between a barracks, which housed the rebellious officers who were waiting for high personages such as their erstwhile spiritual mentor Araki Sadao to throw in their lot with them, and the rest of the metropolis, variously (and nonetheless entirely accurately) described as strangely apathetic, quiet or stunned by the enormity of what had been done.

No attempt was made to inform, much less to appeal, to public opinion about what was happening in the early stages of the uprising. The rebel troops even failed to take the elementary precaution of seizing control of the national broadcasting system or mounting any other kind of propaganda. Their civilian supporters printed a couple of hundred copies of two or three bulletins which they composed during the first two days of the uprising, then, with breathtaking fecklessness, contented themselves with posting these to their supporters. Accordingly, the disturbances did not spread beyond Tokyo. Apart from what little the people of Tokyo garnered from rumours about the horrific series of murders at the beginning of the Incident, all that was visible was an unnatural calm and the sight of troops occupying key positions near the Imperial Palace, Government buildings and the like in the centre of Tokyo. While the rebels and the rest of the Army sought to find some peaceful solution to the crisis, the rebels felt that it would be only a question of time before their coup would receive the Emperor's own blessing. For some time Japanese troops outside Tokyo remained calm and obedient to military discipline.

Gradually, the assembled forces of the Government took stock of their position. Although the attitude of the bulk of the First Division remained unclear, the other division stationed in Tokyo, the Imperial Guards Division, largely remained in safe hands. Outside the metropolis, other commanders were very much opposed to the uprising. The factionalism with which the Japanese Army was riven made that certain. The struggle was not between military moderates and radicals. Many of those most keen to crush the rebellion had defied the central authorities when it had suited them: they included General Tatekawa Yoshitsugu, who now commanded the Fourth Division in Osaka, General Minami Jirō, now Commander-in-Chief of the Kwantung Army, and Colonel Ishiwara

Kanji, who was appointed to head the Operations and Communications Sections of the Martial Law Headquarters in Tokyo.

The Emperor himself was powerless during the crisis. His initial reaction was one of undisguised outrage at the actions taken by the rebels. He subsequently told his chief aide-de-camp, General Honjō Shigeru: 'They have killed my advisers and are now trying to pull a silk rope over my neck . . . I shall never forgive them, no matter what their motives are.'*

Having commanded his War Minister to smash the revolt without delay, the Emperor was at a loss to understand why his instructions were not carried out without further parleying. On the second day of the rebellion, the Emperor went further and told Honjō that unless the Army proceeded at once to end the mutiny, he himself would take personal command of the Imperial Guards and crush it. There seems little reason to doubt his resolve to carry out that threat if necessary. He and his palace advisers were also determined to oppose mounting pressures for the installation of a new Cabinet that might open the way for the rebels to achieve their aims. When the surviving members of Admiral Okada's Cabinet sent Home Affairs Minister Gotō Fumio to the Palace to suggest an interim Prime Minister, the Emperor appointed Gotō as Acting Prime Minister instead. Later, when Gotō returned to submit the collective resignations of himself and his colleagues, Emperor Hirohito informed Gotō that he would decline to permit any change in Government until his orders to end the uprising were carried out. News of this development finally reached the rebels on the night of 27 February, where it came as a shock. They had believed that they had hit upon a winning formula to achieve their demands by agreeing to return to their barracks if General Mazaki were to be appointed Prime Minister. The Emperor's opposition, in the end, sealed the fate of their fanciful Shōwa Restoration.

The decisive step, however, may have been the landing of strong contingents of marines backed up by the guns of some forty ships, which sailed into Tokyo Bay on 27 February, obedient to orders issued by moderate leaders of the Navy who were appalled at the gravity of the rebellion, concerned for the safety of the Imperial Court and incensed at the reported murder of two admirals (the Prime Minister, Okada Keisuke, and the Lord Keeper of the Privy Seal, Saitō Makoto) and the severe injuries sustained by a third (Suzuki Kantarō). Both the Army and the Navy shied away from an open confrontation, but the Navy was instrumental in forcing the military authorities to take positive action.

Finally the rebels recognized that their tide had run out. Their officers

* Shillony, op. cit., p. 173.

sent word that they would surrender their commands and commit suicide if ordered to do so by an Imperial Messenger. Hirohito, not wishing to dignify their actions, merely responded that if the rebels wanted to commit suicide then that was for them to decide. Stung by this rebuke, the mutineers decided to go down fighting. At the same time, the Cabinet, the General Staff and the Emperor were all determined that the rebel positions must be taken by storm. Throughout 28 and 29 February, military reinforcements poured into Tokyo from further afield. The city was cut off from the rest of the country. Civilians were evacuated from forward areas. Bombarded by Government leaflets, radio broadcasts and even an advertisement suspended from a tethered balloon, the rebels offered no resistance as the Army's tanks moved forward. Their morale utterly broken, the mutiny simply collapsed as the rebels came out, surrendered and returned to their barracks.

After all 1,483 surviving participants in the rebellion were interrogated, civilian as well as military, 124 were prosecuted. These included all nineteen of the surviving officers (two others had committed suicide), seventy-three of the ninety-one non-commissioned officers, nineteen of the 1,358 common soldiers, and a sorry lot of ten civilians. The remainder were set free on the grounds that they had done no more than to obey the orders of their superiors. The majority were returned to active service with the First Division and transported in disgrace to the outer reaches of Manchuria. The trials, held in camera, were conducted in an atmosphere of severity in great contrast to the trials of previous terrorists. There was no popular support for the accused, and senior officers who had felt some sympathy for their aims now kept their own heads down. The rumours that surrounded them added to public confusion and a pervasive sense of interlocking and countervailing conspiracies. After a considerable delay, there were some exemplary executions. Thirteen rebel officers and four of the civilians accused of major responsibility for the 26 February Incident were stood before firing squads. Five officers were sentenced to life imprisonment, another received four years, while forty-four NCOs, four common soldiers and one other civilian found guilty were sent to prison for varying terms. In subsequent proceedings against persons accused of collaboration with the active conspirators, the authorities managed to protect a number of influential individuals who had been favourable to the rebel cause. The natural tendencies of mainstream politicians to seek the support of influential cliques now led to the serious embarrassment of the *Seiyūkai*. The same tendencies had tempted large and vulnerable financial conglomerates to curry the favour of military or political circles, and many well-connected *zaibatsu* were implicated, notably Ikeda Seihin (the *de facto* head in the vast Mitsui empire, who was tipped off in time to escape the assassins on 26 February), Kuhara Fusanosuke (founder of the Kuhara Mining Company, partner and brother-in-law to Ayukawa Gisuke of Nissan and a man whose reputation abroad was thoroughly unsavoury)* and Ishihara Kōichirō (the President of the Ishihara Industries and Marine Transportation Company, who made his personal fortune as an importer of Malayan rubber and iron ore). Each of them attracted the unwelcome attentions of the police: Kuhara and Ishihara spent a period in protective custody. Ishihara was charged with conspiracy but was acquitted by the courts.

In the Army there were many leading figures, including some who harboured an honourable detestation of the wheeling and dealing that characterized the political and social life of Japan, who suddenly found themselves out of favour. Some of them retained sufficient influence to escape prosecution. General Mazaki Jinzaburō, who as Inspector-General of Military Education had been instrumental in exposing the leading rebels to the ideas for which they risked everything, was involved in the conspiracy up to his neck. He was indicted but won an acquittal. Retired General Saitō Ryū, who served as a middle-man between the *zaibatsu* and the plotters, was sentenced to five years' imprisonment. Other active sympathizers who were treated lightly included former War Minister Araki Sadao; General Kashii Kōhei, who commanded the Tokyo Garrison and was put in charge of the Martial Law Headquarters established to deal with the crisis; General Yanagawa Heisuke, Commander of the First Division until the eve of the Incident; General Hori Takeo, his successor; Major-General Yamashita Tomoyuki, Chief of the Research Bureau at the War Ministry, and General Murakami Keisaku, Chief of the Military Affairs Section of the Military Affairs Bureau, all of whom wriggled free. So, too, did War Minister Kawashima Yoshiyuki, who dithered throughout the crisis but at one point took the suggestion of Araki and other proactive generals and agreed to issue an official declaration supporting the aims of the rebels. Prince Chichibu, the Emperor's brother, had close ties with several of the leading Young Officers in the conspiracy, but by common consent the authorities turned a blind eye to his true role in the crisis. One disgusted onlooker, General Ugaki Kazushige, then Governor-General of Korea and one of the intended victims of the most recent crop of conspirators, remarked in his diary: 'How

* Kuhara's entry in the annual 'Report on Leading Personalities in Japan', compiled by the British Embassy in Tokyo, ends with the words 'He is an ambitious and unscrupulous person . . . a pure gangster and personally responsible for more than one murder.' F 4913/ 4913/23, Report by Sir R. L. Craigie, 2 April 1938, F O 371/22192.

disgusting it is to watch these rascals, holding in one hand the matches and in the other one the water hose, setting fire and putting it out at the same time, inciting the Young Officers, pleading their cause and then claiming credit for having put them down.'*

By contrast the authorities did not spare two of Japan's most notorious radical right-wing renovationists. The first was Kita Ikki, a one-eyed ascetic, fire-eating socialist turned Nichiren monk, whose most famous work, *An Outline Plan for the Reorganization of Japan*, banned in its unexpurgated form by the censor, called for the foundation of a revolutionary empire and was found among the personal effects of the rebels. The second was his disciple, Nishida Zei, once a promising young officer who had abandoned his career to pursue Kita's mystical vision of national and East Asian upheaval and reform. The evidence against them was weak and entirely circumstantial. It was afterwards revealed that their judges, however, decided to condemn them to death by firing squad in spite of the fact that the guilt of these two accused was not proven. Both men had been closely associated with Ōkawa Shūmei for many years.

This abortive revolution, by its radicalism, led to a realization that the Japanese Army, or part of it, was ceasing to be a conservator of the state. One of its causes was said to be the unfamiliar outbreak of political discussion among junior officers. This was partly the result of their becoming affected by Japan's economic problems. They were seeking solutions; they did not mind if these were radical. Hitherto the Army, to the comfort of the better-off classes of the Japanese, had seemed to connote safety, conservatism, stability. But they had to recast their thoughts towards what in Japan had been regarded as dangerous ideas. Some reflective onlookers noticed that, if the Army should turn towards Communism in its new adventurousness, it would have a good chance of putting the whole country on a communist footing. Japan, with its heavy industry, with its huge industrial population which was accustomed to strict discipline, and its underlying taste for violence, would be admirable material for a communist dictatorship to work on. The same was observed in the attractions which European fascism held for many Army officers.

The forces in opposition to the *Kōdōha* showed more diversity than might be supposed, especially in the period which followed the 26 February Incident of 1936. After the failure of that uprising, the influence of the *Kōdōha* simply collapsed. The surviving leaders of the faction

---

* Ugaki Kazushige, *Ugaki Nikki*, Asahi Shinbunsha, Tokyo, 1954, pp. 217–18, cited in Shillony, p. 203.

were isolated, consigned to the Reserves or sent off to remote corners of the Empire and Manchukuo. Generals Araki, Mazaki, Yanagawa, Obata and the rest simply ceased to exercise a dominant role. In their place Generals Umezu, Tōjō, Sugiyama and Koiso took control, and under the guise of protecting the nation from right-wing populist radicalism, they insisted upon taking steps which ensured that liberalism, too, would gain no headway.

The resurgence of the Control Faction after the 26 February Incident was coupled with a drawing together of the military, court administrators, civil bureaucrats and *zaibatsu*. The agrarian and social reformist impulses of the *Tōseiha* yielded to what was regarded by the established forces as a perfectly prudent concentration of the nation's resources on satisfying the requirements of the military. The Army leadership played upon the fears of the establishment, dwelling on their own alleged inability to restrain the *Kōdō* faction if progressively more militaristic policies were not adapted. In this way the *Tōseiha* did indeed become a controlling faction in the political affairs of the state, far beyond their ostensible constitutional responsibilities, especially in the realms of industrial development, fuel policy, labour, wage and price controls, financial policy, and the formulation of foreign policy. Heavy-handed legislation was passed concerning thought control, and jingoistic measures were introduced to ensure that militaristic values were inculcated in all sectors of education. The military utilized their power to select and replace Ministers at will, regulated only by their own sense of national priorities, collectivism, bureaucratic conceits and the inter-service rivalry between the Army and the Navy.

The outcome of the uprising therefore did nothing to restore a sense of balance to Japan. It frankly did not matter that only six days before the Incident, a national election had been held which had returned a liberal *Minseitō* majority to the Imperial Diet. It is a measure of the rebels' disinterest in any popular mandate that they acted before the outcome was even known. It is a measure of the *Tōseiha*'s victory that the outcome was irrelevant. After the incident, Hirota Kōki was selected as Prime Minister and General Terauchi Hisashi was chosen to be his War Minister. The new Finance Minister, Baba Eiichi, submitted a greatly inflationary budget and the Government set its sights on the national mobilization of heavy industry. Ten months later the uneasy working relationships in the Government came unstuck. War Minister Terauchi took offence when a member of the Imperial Diet, Hamada Kunimatsu, accused the Army of seeking to establish a dictatorship in Japan. Terauchi, enraged by this slur, required Prime Minister Hirota to prorogue the

Diet. Hirota refused on the grounds that the outcome of another election was uncertain. Terauchi promptly resigned, and the Army ensured
that no other suitable candidate could be appointed. The Government thereupon fell from power, more or less bearing out Hamada's
prophecy.

A further period of instability followed. The Emperor invited General
Ugaki Kazushige to form a new Government only to find that Ugaki was
blocked by the 'Three Chiefs Council' of the Army (the War Minister, the
Chief of the Army General Staff and the Inspector-General of Military
Education), who felt quite rightly that he was determined to put a brake
upon the rapid expansion to which they were becoming accustomed.
Since the Hirota Cabinet had bowed to Terauchi's demand for the
reinstatement of a once-discarded provision of the Meiji Constitution
that War Ministers must be selected from general officers on the active
service list, the Prime Minister-designate effectively depended upon the
grace and favour of the Army (and indeed the Navy) to fill his Cabinet.
Ugaki had no choice but to return his mandate to the Emperor.

Instead, former War Minister Hayashi Senjurō formed a new
Government in early February 1937. Two months later, seeking a popular
mandate for a pattern of non-party government which he sought to
legitimize, Hayashi called a snap election, the fourth since 1930. He
abandoned any attempt to woo the political bosses and their party
machines. Instead he offered the electorate a new party, the *Shōwa-kai*.
His bombastic, barrack-square behaviour did not go down well, however,
and the election gave the two main political parties a massive vote of
confidence against the militaristic Hayashi. The two regular parties won
359 seats in the Diet with a tally of more than 7 million votes. The *Shōwa-
kai*, by contrast, won nineteen seats with just over 400,000 votes, and
another splinter party also backed by the Army, the *Kokumin Dōmei*,
fared even more poorly. Thus the democratic instincts of the people (or
the effectiveness of the party machines) remained surprisingly undimmed
throughout the turbulent years that were to culminate in the outbreak of
the China Incident in July 1937. Nevertheless, despite very outspoken
criticism by members of the Imperial Diet concerning the drift of the
nation towards militarism, the increasingly jingoistic and reactionary
tenor of Japanese Governments was echoed in the mass media and, inevitably, was soon reflected by the general population.

On the whole, the Japanese showed little aptitude in their propaganda,
particularly where it was intended for foreign parts. In great contrast to
the Chinese, they not infrequently created greater misunderstanding and
hostility towards themselves than had they left well alone. It was not a

new problem: the Japanese had lost even the propaganda war with Tsarist Russia during the appeal to foreign opinion in the run-up to the Treaty of Portsmouth. In October 1934 the Japanese War Minister produced a famous pamphlet urging the creation of a centralized organ responsible for the dissemination of information and propaganda. One result of such pressure was the creation of the *Dōmei Tsūshinsha* (the United Press Agency) in June 1936 followed a month later by the establishment of a Cabinet Information Board, which was succeeded in turn by a Cabinet Information Division in September 1937 and upgraded to a Cabinet Information Bureau one year before Pearl Harbor. Whatever its name, these Cabinet organs were intended to manipulate the news and gradually fell under the control of military censors. At the same time the news apparatus became increasingly cumbersome, unreliable and an exasperation to foreign correspondents, who learned to place no reliance upon the factual accuracy of Japanese official statements as the years passed. Japanese goodwill missions likewise failed to achieve the positive impact upon foreign countries which exponents of these missions desired. Cultural exchanges often proved only slightly less counter-productive in the short term, and by the late 1930s only the short term mattered.

Public awareness of the irresponsibility of Japan's continental adventure was less pronounced in Japan than it was abroad. In part this was due to the imposition of censorship involving all forms of press and broadcasting media. Even Japanese street theatre, notably *Kamishibai*, or picture-postcard theatre productions akin to Punch and Judy shows, were subject to close examination by thought control police and so, like the cinema, played safe. There were other factors, too, such as the Army's step-by-step extension of the military training and indoctrination into Japanese schools, universities and factories. Then there was the matter of the economy.

Elated by the successes of the Japanese Armies, first in Manchuria and afterwards in Inner Mongolia and North China, initial worries in Japan about foreign reactions gradually subsided into mixed resentment and indifference when the West failed to take effective action. Industrial production in Japan by 1932 had returned to 98 per cent of its 1929 record, compared with corresponding figures of 84 per cent for the United Kingdom, 72 per cent for France, 67 per cent for Mussolini's Italy, 53 per cent for Germany on the eve of Hitler's accession to power, and 53 per cent for the United States at the commencement of the Roosevelt years. By 1933, therefore, the Japanese, buoyed up by defence expenditure, could regard the depression as a thing of the past. The illusion persisted for a surprisingly long period of time. Eventually the Ministry of Finance, excusing its own failure to operate within prudent monetary practices, as time wore on adopted the phrase 'quasi-war economy' to express the higher priority given to the development of Japanese military preparations for war rather than the demands of the civilian economy. In essence, the Japanese gradually were forced to recognize that what their British counterparts characterized as 'the Fourth Arm of Defence', financial stability, was something that Japan could not afford, and this added point to the importance of seeking concrete economic benefits from Japan's dependencies on the Asian mainland. As the country ground through its gears towards Total War, the mobilization of the Japanese economy was plain to see, together with the cracks caused by its disfunctioning. The mortal danger to which this exposed Japan was well understood. Japan's reliance upon the West for more than 90 per cent of its petroleum supplies meant that the liberty of Japan to wage war on the continent or anywhere else was subject to the goodwill of the United States and its friends, as the following table of Japanese petroleum imports in 1936 demonstrates:

Source	1,000 tons	%
United States	3,043	65.79
Netherlands East Indies	991	21.43
British North Borneo	301	6.51
Manchukuo	73	1.58
North Sakhalin	26	0.56
Others	191	4.13
Total	4,625	100*

Nevertheless, Japanese public opinion gradually appreciated that Japan was caught in an international crisis from which there could be no escape, and even began to develop a fatalistic sense, shared with many abroad, that war with the West as well as China might be unavoidable.

It was a world in which rearmament was becoming the order of the day. Recognizing the danger of a naval arms race against the combined strength of Britain and the United States, Japan demanded parity with each of them, with the object of making it impossible for the Anglo-Saxon countries to blackmail Japan. Thus the hard evidence of Japan's irremediable dependence upon foreign imports of strategical raw materials was ignored by the Japanese during what were to become their last naval

* Adapted from Hosoya Chihiro, 'Miscalculations in Deterrent Policy: Japanese–U.S. Relations, 1938–1941', *Journal of Peace Research*, V:2, 1968, p. 114.

arms limitation discussions prior to the Pacific War. Their demands were thwarted, however, and in a major miscalculation by its Navy, Tokyo thereupon closed its eyes to the factors which had impelled Japan to accept previous humiliations, and withdrew from the 1935–6 London Naval Conference. The Army and the Navy, with a carelessness born of distraction, drove along through the night, mechanized now, on the road to Total War.

CHAPTER 9

The War Resumed: The Outbreak
of the China Incident

THE second phase of the war began in an obscure skirmish between Japanese and Chinese troops at Lukouchiao, 'Black Moat Bridge', a site not far from Peking, better known in the West as the Marco Polo Bridge, after the Venetian explorer who had regarded it as one of the most beautiful in the world. During the night of 7 July 1937 some of the 15,000 Chinese troops in the region of Peking exchanged rifle-fire with a portion of the 550-strong Japanese garrison at Fengtai, which was carrying out night manoeuvres in open territory north of the bridge, an area long favoured for such purposes by the foreign garrisons guarding their respective legations in Peking under the terms of the Boxer Protocols. The Japanese reported the incident to the mayor of Peking, General Ching Teh-chun, at around midnight and expressed particular concern about the fate of one Japanese soldier who appeared to be missing and was presumed to have been taken captive.

Formal permission was requested for a company of Japanese troops to conduct a search for the missing man in the little fortified town of Wanping, which was also an important railway junction on the main line to Paoting and Hankow (and thus to Central China). Ching, however, denied this request and offered instead to send a joint investigating commission into Wanping to make any necessary inquiries. This was agreeable to the Japanese and suitable arrangements were made. In the meanwhile, Ching took the precaution of ordering the Chinese Army town commander at Wanping to repel any Japanese troops who might attempt to take matters into their own hands. These precautions were well-taken, for eight truckloads of Japanese troops turned up outside Wanping at 3.30 a.m. in an effort to enter the town and were forcibly repelled by the Chinese. While these events were in progress, it is said that the missing man, whose fate was ostensibly the main source of concern, added to the embarrassment of the Japanese by turning up at his unit two hours after his absence was first discovered, apparently having been led astray that night by nothing more than his sexual desire.

In response to the fighting at Wanping, however, each side rushed a battalion of reinforcements to the scene. The Japanese reinforcements, only a few hundred men strong, came not from Tientsin, fifty miles away, where the main elements of the Japanese North China Garrison Army were based, but like the Japanese troops already on the scene, were drawn instead from the 450-man Japanese Legation Guard, which was the only other Japanese force in the Peking area apart from the battalion based at Fengtai. All parties concerned recognized the gravity of the situation, which threatened to erupt into another Manchurian Incident.

The Japanese were in a particularly vulnerable position: virtually the whole of the North China Garrison Army, which altogether comprised little more than a single infantry brigade, had been deployed away from their various depots in field exercises ever since 6 June and was therefore in no immediate position to render practical assistance to the detachment at Wanping. Moreover, the asthmatic Commander-in-Chief of the North China Garrison, General Tashiro Kan'ichirō, had fallen victim to a serious heart-attack a fortnight before (from which he died on 16 July). In Tashiro's absence, his Chief of Staff, General Hashimoto Gun, exercised effective control of the North China Garrison and gave clear instructions to Major Ichiki, the battalion commander sent to Wanping, that no action must be taken pending a thorough review of the situation. Hashimoto also made it known that he intended to seek a peaceful resolution of the matter without delay.

And as hindsight soon overlaid the confusing reports issued at the time, the myth grew that the China Incident, as it came to be called, was the product of the same kind of conspiracy as had provoked the Manchurian Incident six years before. On the contrary, Japanese policy on the eve of the China Incident had been in a state of flux. Even the Kwantung Army was hesitant at taking action in China Proper, for as the Chief of Staff of that Army, one Tōjō Hideki, advised Vice-Minister of War Umezu Yoshijirō and Vice-Chief of the Army General Staff Imai Kiyoshi in June 1937, the Japanese Army's greatest concern remained Russia, not China:

Judging the present situation in China from the point of view of military preparations against the Soviet Union, I am convinced that if our military power permits it, we should deliver a blow first of all upon the Nanking régime to get rid of the menace at our back.

If our military power will not permit us to take such a step, I think it proper that we keep a strict watch on the Chinese Government that they do not lay a single hand on our present undertakings in China until our national defence system is completed. We will thus wait for the Chinese Government to reconsider.

We should not take the initiative to become friendly with the Nanking Government, which has no intention whatsoever of adjusting diplomatic relations with Japan, for, judging from their national characteristics, such a step will only aggravate their disdainful attitude towards Japan.*

The Chinese, in fact, desired peace no less than did the Japanese but were determined to resist any further Japanese aggression on a major scale, and on 8 July Chiang Kai-shek ordered four Nationalist divisions into the area. Although the evidence suggests that this move was probably designed as a precautionary step, it was regarded by the local Japanese commander at Wanping as highly provocative. Unfortunately, despite efforts by the Japanese representative on the *ad hoc* Sino-Japanese joint commission to restrain him, Ichiki threw caution to the winds and committed his battalion to a charge against the Chinese positions on 9 July. The attack failed. Three days later, six Kuomintang divisions were moving northwards. The situation was complicated by the fact that under the Ching–Doihara Agreement reached with Japan in June 1935, no troops under Kuomintang command were supposed to be in the North China provinces of Hopei and Chahar, which formed an autonomous buffer between Manchuria and the Nationalist Chinese further south.

Although Japan had intended for some years to establish political control or at least economic hegemony in North China, neither the Japanese military command in China nor the authorities in Tokyo were intent on seeking any trouble at that moment. The Japanese Government in Tokyo and Japanese military commanders in China made herculean efforts to isolate the conflict and avoid further provocations. Meanwhile, cool heads prevailed elsewhere. Hashimoto himself ordered his top aides to open negotiations with senior Chinese officials in Peking and flew there himself the next day, determined to put an end to the trouble. The Army General Staff in Tokyo backed up Hashimoto with orders to settle the matter; agreement was reached by bureau chiefs from the Navy, War and Foreign Ministries on the policy to be adopted in handling the dispute; and the recommendations made by these bureau chiefs were approved by the Japanese Cabinet as early as 8 July. On that basis the Chinese and Japanese negotiators soon achieved an interim local truce agreement.

Troops from other Japanese garrisons in North China, including every available man at Tientsin, were brought into the area, but rumours of major reinforcements from Japan's Kwantung and Korean Armies were

---

* IMTFE, PX 672, Telegram 670, marked Ultra Secret, Urgent, from Tōjō to Umezu and Imai, 9 June 1937. Taking the document out of its full context, the Prosecution at the Tokyo War Trial read only the first paragraph into the *Record of the Proceedings*: see Pritchard and Zaide, op. cit., 4, pp. 7336–7.

without foundation. On 11 July the Japanese Cabinet announced the mobilization of three divisions in response to Chinese troop movements, but late that evening the plan was cancelled when news came of Hashimoto's satisfactory agreement with Ching. For the next month the Japanese sent no fresh troops into the area from outside China. But a stalemate developed in negotiations for a withdrawal, and matters were not helped by Chiang Kai-shek's 'Kuling Declaration' on 16 July, in which he effectively tore up the Ching–Doihara Agreement and proclaimed his determination to re-establish China's historic territorial unity and sovereign rights. The thousands of Japanese troops and civilians legally present in China under existing treaties were at risk of being massacred by the many times more numerous Chinese regular and militia forces moving forward.

In 'efforts to save the situation', another far-reaching agreement was hammered out between the Head of the Japanese Foreign Ministry's East Asiatic Affairs Bureau, the Chief of the War Ministry's Military Affairs Bureau and the Navy Ministry's Chief of the Naval Affairs Bureau on 23 July. Like other documentary evidence from the period, it puts paid to the suspicion of onlookers that Japan's string of military victories in the early stages of the China Incident stemmed from a well-laid plot to take over the whole of China in one fell swoop:

1. As long as there is no big change in the situation, we stick to our policy of settling the incident on the spot and of non-expanding the incident, and stop further sending of troops.
2. To voluntarily and speedily evacuate our reinforced troops out of the Great Wall when we see for sure the possible conclusion of a local agreement and feel safe.
   Remark: We consider we can be sure of the possible carrying out of the local agreement when the forces of Feng Chi-an [a local Chinese commander] have completely been moved to Paoting.
3. To declare the purport of No. 1 and No. 2 at a good opportunity.
4. To begin negotiations with the Nanking Government for adjusting our relations with China immediately after the time for evacuating our troops is fixed.
5. In the negotiation for adjusting the relations of both countries, matters will not be biased by past circumstances, and these matters should be rapidly considered by the three ministers [Foreign, War and Navy Ministries] to work out a good plan.*

---

* IMTFE, PD 1634–L, *Aide-mémoire*, 23 July 1937. This Prosecution document was not tendered in evidence at the Tokyo War Trial.

Unfortunately, even these extraordinary efforts were unavailing. By late July further incidents were occurring with increasing frequency and seriousness. In many of these exchanges, the Japanese came out much the worse for wear. Within the space of a few weeks, at first sporadic, later general, fighting spread through all North China, and reached Shanghai. As far as can be discovered, none of the main Japanese generals, and certainly not Chiang Kai-shek, wanted war at this particular moment: and peace efforts were made constantly. But the situation was out of hand. The Chinese communists, who were now formally reconciled with the Kuomintang, used every opportunity to drive their allies on to war. The decision was forced by relatively junior officers in command in the field. The situation became virtually irretrievable after 25 July, when the Chinese, manning the ancient defences of Peking, trapped three hundred Japanese troops as they passed between the inner and outer gates of the city while returning from Fengtai to the Japanese Legation in the city: some of the Chinese guarding the gates found the temptation irresistible, swung the gates shut behind the Japanese, and raked their victims with withering grenade and mortar fire. Order was soon restored and the surviving Japanese were permitted to continue on their way, but this incident naturally provoked further outrages on both sides. Three days later, the Japanese Forces at Fengtai exacted their revenge, marched into Peking and made short work of Chinese resistance. Compulsively the fighting spread. The top commanders on both sides saw this and made futile efforts to check it, and excused themselves from all responsibility.

The situation became so tense by early August that the Japanese Cabinet agreed to take the precaution of sending an expeditionary force into China with the intention of protecting Japanese property and covering the withdrawal of Japanese civilians. It must be stressed that Japan did not intend to open a larger campaign at this stage, although obviously these reinforcements would be essential if Japan should find itself at war with the much larger forces that China was now bringing forward. Nevertheless, Japan's reinforcements had an electrifying effect on the Chinese, who were enraged at what they understandably interpreted as a Japanese design to extend the conflict. Too many Chinese and Japanese preferred to go to war rather than endure insults to their respective national honour.

The two years which followed were the chief phase of slaughter in the war between China and Japan: then came a renewed period of lull. The conflict was still separate from the Armageddon which was being prepared in the West, and at first remained a separate war when the explosion

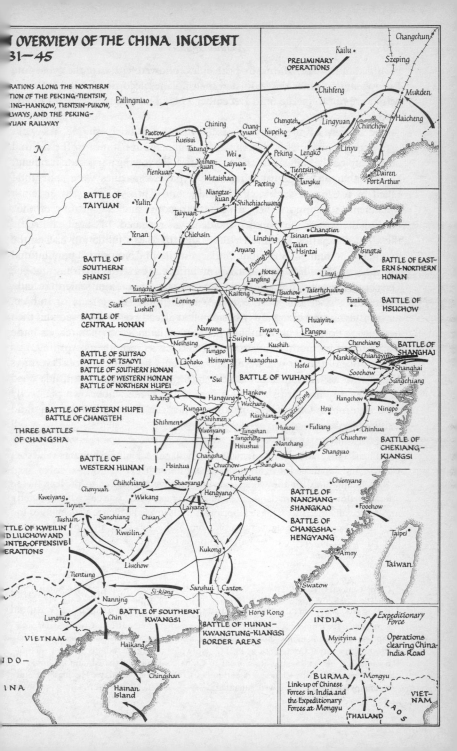

OVERVIEW OF THE CHINA INCIDENT
31—45

RATIONS ALONG THE NORTHERN
TION OF THE PEKING-TIENTSIN,
ING-HANKOW, TIENTSIN-PUKOW,
LWAYS, AND THE PEKING-
YUAN RAILWAY

N

PRELIMINARY
OPERATIONS

Changchun
Kailu
Szeping
Chihfeng
Mukden
Chengteh   Lingyuan
Haicheng
Kupeiko   Chinchow
Linyu
Pailingmiao
Paotow
Kueisui   Chining   Chang-   Peking   Lengk'o
yuan
Tatung   Wei   Tientsin
Yenmen-   Laiyuan   Tangku
Pienkuan   Su·   kuan
Wutaishan   Paoting   Dairen
Port Arthur
BATTLE OF
TAIYUAN   Yulin   Niangtze-
kuan
Shihchiachuang
Taiyuan
Yenan   Chiehsin   Linching   Tsinan   Changtien
Anyang   Taian   Hsintai   Tsingtai
Hwang-ho   BATTLE OF EAST-
BATTLE OF   Hotse   Linyi   ERN & NORTHERN
SOUTHERN   Langfeng   HONAN
SHANSI   Yungchiu   Kaifeng   Tsuchow   Taierhchuang   BATTLE OF
Sian   Tungkuan   Loning   Shangchiu   Funing   HSUCHOW
Lushih
BATTLE OF   Nanyang   Suiping   Huaiyin
CENTRAL HONAN   Neihsing   Fuyang   Pangpu
BATTLE OF SUITSAO   Tungpo   Kushih   Chenchiang   BATTLE OF
BATTLE OF TSAOYI   Laohoko   Hsinyang   Huangchua   Nanking   Chiangyin   SHANGHAI
BATTLE OF SOUTHERN HONAN   Sui·   Hofei   Soochow   Shanghai
BATTLE OF WESTERN HONAN   BATTLE OF WUHAN   Sungchiang
BATTLE OF NORTHERN HUPEI   Hankow   Hsu
Ichang   Wuchang   Hangchow   Ningpo
BATTLE OF WESTERN HUPEI   Kungan   Kiuchiang   Chinhua
BATTLE OF CHANGTEH   Shihmen·   Shihmen   Hukou   Fuliang   BATTLE OF
Yuenyang   Tungshan   Nanchang   CHEKIANG-
THREE BATTLES   Tungcheng   Chuchow   KIANGSI
OF CHANGSHA   Hsiushui   Shangyao
BATTLE OF   Changsha   Shangkao
WESTERN HUNAN   Hsinhua   Chuchow   Chienyang
Chenyuan   Chihchiang   Shaoyang   Pinghsiang   BATTLE OF   Foochow
Kweiyang·   Tuyun·   Wukang   Hengyang   NANCHANG-
Tushun   Sanchiang   SHANGKAO
TTLE OF KWEILIN   Chuan   Laiyang   BATTLE OF   Taipei
D LIUCHOW AND   Kweilin   CHANGSHA-
UNTER-OFFENSIVE   HENGYANG
ERATIONS   Kukong
Liuchow   Amoy   Taiwan
Tientung
Si-kiang   Swatow
Nanning   Sanshui   Canton
Lungmi·   Chin   BATTLE OF SOUTHERN
VIETNAM   KWANGSI   Hong Kong
Haikang   BATTLE OF HUNAN-
KWANGTUNG-KIANGSI
JDO-   BORDER AREAS
Chingshan
INA   Hainan
Island

INDIA   Expeditionary
Force
Myitkyina   Operations
clearing China-
India Road
BURMA   Mongyu
Link-up of Chinese   VIET-
Forces in India and   NAM
the Expeditionary   LAOS
Forces at Mongyu   THAILAND

occurred in Europe. Naturally both sides followed with care the events in Europe, and at times they adjusted their policies accordingly. But the two wars were not to merge until December 1941. There were four years to go before that.

The history of these first years of fighting is fairly simple. As was expected, Japan quickly overcame the organized resistance in the north, and occupied the railway lines and the cities. Following a separate incident at Shanghai on 9 August, when two Japanese marines were shot and killed by a Chinese sentry, the Japanese and Chinese both sent in reinforcements to support their existing garrisons, and the history of the landing there after the Mukden Incident was repeated. In Shanghai itself, the Chinese resisted for seven weeks, and there was jubilation in China. The stakes were high: Shanghai, the largest city in China with a population in excess of $3\frac{1}{2}$ million people in normal times, was swollen with refugees. Overhead the two sides waged the first air war on a major scale that had taken place since the First World War (although the effects of Italian aerial attacks on Abyssinian tribesmen had already been observed and the destructive power of air bombardment on undefended civilian targets had been proved by German aviators at Guernica as recently as April 1937). The lessons of this air war were watched keenly by occidental observers in China with less than dispassionate detachment: their general attitude was voiced by a senior British naval officer at the scene whose own personal association with China went back to his birth in Shanghai as the son of a British physician:

We on the spot share the disgust with which all the foreign inhabitants view the Chinese and Japanese for fighting their main battle here.

It is humiliating for the white man not to have the power to prevent these inferior yellow races from damaging and making use of the fine city which he, and most especially the British, have laboriously built up and which is such an asset to the Far East. There are signs, however, that both sides have attempted to spare foreign property. On the other hand, both use the [International] Settlement as a 'base of operations'.*

* China General Letter 16, Observations on the Sino-Japanese Conflict by Vice-Admiral Sir Charles Little, Commander-in-Chief, China Station, 14 September 1937, Adm. 116/3682, British Public Record Office, Kew. As a young midshipman, Little was present in Hong Kong when the Chinese leased the New Territories there to the British Crown. Later, as a captain, while still in his thirties, he was a member of the British delegation at the Washington Naval Conference in 1921–2. Notwithstanding the bluntly racialist tone of his remarks, his sentimental attachment to China continued unabated, and his home in Sussex was filled with Chinese art antiquities to the end of his days. His loathing and contempt for the Japanese were boundless.

At this point the undeclared hostilities suddenly exploded into a Total War of appalling ferocity. By the end of the month, Japanese armies began pouring into China, smashing the inefficient and often corrupt Chinese forces. Gradually the truth about the Chinese Armies became known in the outer world, which had at first been inclined to credit that China had become better organized than it was in fact. The Chinese command organization went to pieces. Soldiers went into battle as part of a modern military formation, but this usually broke under strain, and they became pockets of fighting men. Hence came much of the nightmare quality which made this one of the most awful periods of China's recent black record. Administration was primitive, corruption was extreme and pervasive. Army medical services and hospitals scarcely existed, and soldiers who were only slightly wounded usually perished. Volunteer medical aid began to appear from the sympathetic countries of the West, but all that its doctors could do was to add to the swelling chorus of lamentation.

Improvising a guerrilla warfare, the Chinese discovered in one or two isolated battles a military prowess which China's friends afterwards took too much for granted. But at Shanghai, on breaking through in the end to open country in early November, the Japanese advanced rapidly up the Yangtze River Valley and converged upon Nanking, 200 miles to the west. Swinging southward, they captured the important river port of Wuhu, fifty miles upstream. On 13 December they occupied the Chinese capital without difficulty.

Chiang Kai-shek and his Government had withdrawn to Hankow. In the last fortnight of December 1937, after they had lost Nanking, the slaughter and atrocities were far worse than in 1931. It was the history of an earlier time, of the Mongol ravages of Asia, of Timur and the cold terror he spread – a horror which his name can even now evoke in Central Asia. There are lurid tales of Timur sacking a city. If an army dared to oppose him, Timur built up a pyramid of skulls of those he slaughtered. He camped in a tent of scarlet canvas outside the towns he besieged, thus symbolizing the massacres he intended to carry out. The ferocity of the Japanese likewise amazed the world. The massacre was done for the most part by Japanese conscripts, unfamiliar with war, perhaps neurotically working out of their system the extreme repressions in which they had passed so much of their lives. Some Japanese officers in other centres wept with shame and indignation when they heard details of the carnage.

Chinese burial parties afterwards counted upwards of a quarter of a million dead: some of the dead may have been tallied more than once, and more accurate estimates, if indeed they do exist, are no less subject to controversy. In any case, the burial rolls that were compiled are a sufficient measure of the extent of the catastrophe. There were many eye-witnesses who survived: against all odds, there generally are survivors of such events. They told of scenes of systematic arson, of looting on an unbelievable scale, of mass rapes in hospitals, in exclusive Chinese women's colleges, in many of the twenty-five refugee camps dotted round the city, in residential districts. And there was worse, as Captain Liang Ling-fang of the Chinese Army Medical Corps, for instance, was to testify at the Tokyo War Crimes Tribunal after the surrender of Japan:

We were given orders to stay in Nanking and take care of the Chinese wounded, and stay there after the Japanese took the city. We found that the Red Cross was no protection, and therefore dressed in civilian clothes, and we were in a refugee camp when the Japanese took the city. On the sixteenth, we were ordered by the Japanese to proceed to Shsia Kwan, on the bank of the River Yangtze, in Nanking. I estimate there were above 5,000 who were marched four abreast, and the line was a $\frac{3}{4}$ of a mile long. When we arrived there we were placed in a line near the River, and on either side of the line there formed and in front of [the] line were machineguns and Japanese soldiers, with the machineguns pointing at the line. There were two trucks carrying rope, and men were tied five in a group with their wrists tied below their backs, and I saw the first men who were shot by rifles in such groups and who were then thrown in the river by the Japanese. There were about 800 Japanese present, including officers, some of whom were in sedan automobiles . . . We [had] started from the refugee camp about five o'clock in the evening, arrived at the bank of the River about seven o'clock, and the binding of the prisoners and shooting kept up until two o'clock [in the morning].*

Liang's body still bore the marks of his ordeal; his testimony was corroborated by other witnesses. The episode that he described was by no means an isolated occurrence. In post-war Japan, there has been an observable tendency to regard tales such as Captain Liang's as exceptional or exaggerated. At the time, Japanese who were there had no such illusions.

The effect was profound in other countries of the world. At first the news of the outrage was censored, but ultimately it got into the world's press. Anxious though they were to avert their gaze from Asia, because of their preoccupations in Europe, the countries of the West found themselves distracted first by Shanghai, then by the events at Nanking, and were appalled by seeing a foretaste of what might soon be everywhere. From then on, the Japanese Army was held to be uncivilized, savage and terrible. The incident became known as the Rape of Nanking, and frenzied

---

* Pritchard and Zaide, op. cit., 2, pp. 3369–75 [PX 250, Sworn Statement by Captain Liang, dated 7 April 1946].

atrocities which the Japanese Army committed there, although no different in kind from what was to happen elsewhere, were on a scale quite unmatched anywhere else during the Greater East Asia and Pacific Conflict.

World opinion had favoured the Chinese side from the beginning of the war, but even those who most admired China or most despised Japan came to wonder how long China could endure the Japanese onslaught. Foreign condemnation was ineffectual in these early years, however. Without the benefits of Germany's substantial military mission and supply programme to China, and without Britain's amorphous but indispensable economic empire within China, which provided, respectively, the basis of Chinese defence and financial stability in the early years of the war, there seems little doubt that Japan would have won the China Incident absolutely.

The Japanese Cabinet itself was bitterly divided over future policy almost from the very beginning: there were suddenly vast new territories to administer, a frightening financial outlook, and a war which patently neither the War Ministry nor the Army General Staff could control. In a sense Japan's policy-making machinery went to war with itself. The Army repeatedly promised the Cabinet and the Emperor that the military advance would halt at one specified objective after another. Each time it was found that additional territory was desired to protect previous gains, and each time it was clear that immoderate elements within the Army were set to act as they themselves determined.

The Japanese certainly believed that they gave China generous opportunities to negotiate a peace settlement. The war was nearly six months old before the Government in Tokyo abandoned the limited aims which they had held when the fighting had started. A considerable number of peace feelers were extended either directly to China or indirectly through serious approaches to Germany, Britain and America. The Americans showed a marked reluctance to become involved, but the British, and more especially the Germans, took their opportunities far more seriously. Even Italy and France occasionally served as intermediaries in the furtherance of peace negotiations. But if Japan was eager to conclude a peace settlement, its leaders were rarely prepared to offer genuinely conciliatory terms to the Chinese once Japan's ascendency in the war became clear. The often hamfisted quality of the Japanese proposals was itself a product of the political turmoil that existed within the upper reaches of the Japanese military and political leadership: those who offered such proposals not only had a natural tendency to adopt positions which would be acceptable to most of the Japanese policy-making élites but also had to take account of the damage which any offer of over-generous concessions would do to their continuing political influence at home.

While the frustrations experienced by the Japanese began to manifest themselves in an increasing unwillingness to treat with the Nanking Government at all, the Japanese began to explore the possibility of linking the Japanese and Korean domestic economies with those of Occupied China and Manchukuo. On 22 December 1938 Prime Minister Konoye Fumimaro made a major radio broadcast to the world in which he proclaimed Japan's determination to create a 'New Order in East Asia': 'The spirit of renaissance is now sweeping over all parts of China and enthusiasm for reconstruction is mounting ever higher,' he declared, and he went on to urge the people of China to embrace a three-fold programme based upon 'neighbourly amity, common defence against communism, and economic co-operation'. He utterly failed to anticipate that in demanding the right to station Japanese troops at predetermined places throughout China and in the designation of Inner Mongolia as 'a special anti-communist area', the Chinese understood that he intended nothing less than the complete domination of China. One must appreciate the elements of continuity that existed between this manifesto and the historical trends of Japanese military campaigns and political schemes north of the Great Wall prior to the outbreak of the China Incident. Not for the first time was the Japanese definition of 'cooperation' profoundly different from the meaning which other countries ascribed to the word. Most foreigners – including the Chinese – were utterly amazed that the Japanese Prime Minister could close such a speech with what appeared to be sentiments of either unsurpassed self-delusion or unmitigated hypocrisy:

If the object of Japan in conducting the present vast military campaign be fully understood, it will be plain that what she seeks is neither territory nor indemnity for the costs of military operations. Japan demands only the minimum guarantee needed for the execution by China of her function as a participant in the establishment of the new order.

Japan not only respects the sovereignty of China, but she is prepared to give positive consideration to the questions of the abolition of extraterritoriality and of the rendition of the concessions and settlements matters which are necessary for the full independence of China.*

Yet in efforts to explain his motives to American interrogators after the Pacific War, Prince Konoye insisted that he had intended his speech as a genuine contribution to mutual understanding and goodwill: it was *not* Japan's purpose to annex China. Japan, as the stronger economic, military and even political power, naturally expected 'to take leadership

---

* Joyce C. Lebra, *Japan's Greater East Asia Co-Prosperity Sphere in World War II*, Oxford University Press, Kuala Lumpur, 1975, pp. 68–70.

in the development of a unified Far East'. But that was not regarded by the Japanese as tantamount to the destruction of Chinese sovereignty. His broadcast had been intended as no more than an enunciation of moral or political principles. The objectives set out in his speech could have been achieved with goodwill and good faith on both sides through cultural and economic ties rather than by armed conquest. In the end, he declared, the high principles underlying his speech were betrayed firstly by his own military, which corrupted his benevolent political aims by means of military force, and secondly by the Government of Chiang Kai-shek, which proved equally unresponsive to his overtures. Whether this rather confused but popular Prime Minister ever truly expected anything less, however, must remain something of an enigma. What is clear is that Konoye's 'New Order in East Asia' projected nothing less than the alignment of the entire political and economic resources of China in support of the domestic and international aspirations of Japan. Expressed in terms of Total War, that could have provided Japan with an incalculable increase in strength against any of her potential adversaries.

China managed, just barely, to withstand wave after wave of Japanese attacks during the first two years of the China Incident. Despite losing her principal cities, rivers and thousands of miles of territory, China survived. As each successive catastrophe was endured, China's self-confidence in itself emerged to strengthen China's historic contempt for its barbarian invaders. The few Chinese voices raised in support of a negotiated settlement with Japan found precious little favour. They were either eased out of positions of authority or isolated by Chiang Kai-shek. By the end of 1937 there was no possibility of a return to the *status quo ante bellum*: the human cost of the fighting had become too terrible for that. It became evident that the very success of the Japanese armed forces was acting as an impediment to peace. When Prince Konoye, the unhappy Japanese Prime Minister, decided in January 1938 to offer no more peace compromises after the collapse of a particularly important German mediation attempt, he laid particular stress on the bitterness which the Chinese must feel after having lost 700–800,000 soldiers in barely six months of war. Japan's own war dead were thought to number only 50,000. This may have been an over-estimate of the losses of the one, and an under-estimate of the other. Yet there was a great gap between the losses on both sides. Later Prince Konoye, one of the most remarkable ditherers ever to hold the premiership of Japan in the twentieth century, changed his mind several times and made further peace efforts, but he and other Japanese leaders remained anxious about the effects which possible peace negotiations would have on Japanese Army and civilian morale: with an Army

CHINA FIGHTS ALONE 1937—41

of 1,600,000 men fighting on behalf of the Emperor, it was argued that the nation had an obligation to the tens of thousands of Japanese war dead, who would never rest until Japan gained victory. Moreover, so far as Prince Konoye and his intimates were concerned, offering to come to terms would only be interpreted as an admission of Japan's underlying weakness which would create financial panic in the Japanese money markets and would inflict a major blow to Japanese morale. To this argument Prince Chichibu, the Emperor's younger brother, retorted, 'How much longer do they think that Japan's financial strength will last anyway?'*

The death toll grew, and the Chinese continued to lose many times the number of casualties that the Japanese suffered. Looking back, the British Embassy in China observed in an annual report: 'Measured in terms of human anguish, there has probably never been, even in the long history of Chinese suffering, such a year as 1938.'† The spirit of China was transformed in the process; an angry and increasingly resolute China faced Japan with implacable hatred.

Worries about the threat of Soviet mischief-making on the northern frontier, concern about Japan's relations with the Western Powers (and particularly Britain), and mounting evidence that the military and economic strength of Japan was unequal to the conquest of Chinese resistance all brought home to most members of the Government, to virtually the whole of the General Staff and to the War Minister, as it did to other influential circles such as the *zaibatsu*, that some kind of rapid settlement of the China Incident was imperative for Japan's well-being. But it did not happen. Chiang had set his face against peace; he was prepared to endure a long war because he and his supporters could have survived nothing shorter, and so the war dragged on. The American Ambassador in Tokyo, Joseph Grew, likened Japan's war with China to the fable of Brer Rabbit's struggle with the Tar Baby: the more fiercely the Japanese forces thrashed the Chinese, the more firmly the Japanese attached themselves to their victim, and when the Japanese did try to disengage themselves, they found themselves ensnared, stuck firmly to the Chinese.

In 1938 there was much fighting in North and Central China. The fighting tended to concentrate along the main arteries of the country, which were its railways, rivers and canals. China possessed 225,000 miles of canals, and as one well-qualified western scholar observed in the

* *Harada-Saionji Memoirs*, Part XIV, Chapter 260.
† F3662/53/10, Annual Report on China for 1938 by Archibald Clark Kerr, 28 February 1939, FO 371/23443.

mid-thirties: 'If forty canals were dug across the United States from east to west, and sixty from north to south, their total mileage would be less than that of the canals in China.'* In the spring, in an effort to halt the Japanese advance, Chiang ordered the breaching of the Yellow River dykes. This slowed but failed to halt them, but it was estimated that a million peasants drowned in the flood which resulted. It began to be clear what torment had been let loose on the world. There was heavy fighting: the Chinese engaged in positional warfare, and did not use guerrilla tactics.

Some divisions showed the result of their having received German training from Chiang Kai-shek's German advisers. In the Battle of Taierchwang, near the border between Kiangsu and Shantung Provinces, the Chinese won a temporary triumph in April which purchased a six-week delay in the advance of the Japanese upon Hsuchow, the junction of the important two Tientsin–Pukow and Lunghai railways, but the moral and strategic effect of this solitary victory were minor in comparison with the fighting that began to distract the world in the next few months at Changkufeng against the Russians. While fighting raged at Changkufeng, the Japanese advance through Wuhan Province in Central China slowed down but did not falter. After the Changkufeng Incident came to an end, Japanese reinforcements hastened to the Central China front, and the Japanese juggernaut, to no one's surprise, once more picked up speed.

In October, the Japanese, in the south, took Canton and its hinterland. Canton was the original base of the Kuomintang; its capture was significant, as it seemed to symbolize striking at the root of the Kuomintang. It also left the Japanese in possession of the hinterland surrounding Hong Kong, hitherto the principal avenue for German and other western arms imports intended for the Chinese Republic.

In the same month the Japanese, advancing up the Yangtze, had taken Hankow, last of the fabled Three Cities of Wu. This was not an easy victory, as many successes had been. Chiang Kai-shek's administration, with all the impedimenta of government, was forced to withdraw once more. This time, having learned something at least, the Kuomintang moved a thousand miles up the Yangtze to Chungking, the principal town (though not the capital) of the remote province of Szechwan, which bordered on Tibet, and which since 1935 had been prepared by Chiang as the national capital in an emergency. Chiang was now following what proved to be his masterplan for the war: to trade space for time; to care little for losses of territory (or manpower) provided the centre of resistance remained intact; to put faith in the huge distances and population of

---

* Scherer, op. cit., p. 14.

China, and to hang on in spite of defeats (and administrative incompetence or malfeasance).

Chungking was well beyond the gorges in the Yangtze, which are one of the beauty spots of China. To attack Chungking was to involve the Japanese in such problems of logistics that Chiang was safe there. The Japanese did not follow him further.

A very long pause set in. Japanese communications and supply lines grew lengthy and cumbersome. The prospect of a stalemate once again brought fear to the Japanese. There were few signs of public discontent, and official misgivings were muted. Despite deep gloom in Japan's Imperial Household and the Ministries of Finance and Foreign Affairs, ways seemed to be found to avoid the great threats of bankruptcy and international economic or armed intervention in the war by outside Powers. Senior naval officers, especially Navy Minister Yonai Mitsumasa and Navy Vice-Minister Yamamoto Isoroku, had opposed the war from the beginning and were unflagging in their efforts to moderate excessive Army demands for the commitment of more and more of the nation's resources to the military conquest of Chinese resistance. But beneath this thin crust of sensibility lay a core of middle-ranking naval officers who had control of the Naval General Staff and who were altogether too eager to exploit the war in China through a desire to support their common cause with their counterparts in the Army and through a wild ambition to 'facilitate future air-raids' against Hong Kong and other bastions of western power in East Asia. Even the Japanese Army found these Navy hotheads somewhat frightening and recognized that such men might bring the Army into conflict with Britain and America as well as the Army's traditional foes, China and Russia. A compromise was reached. Thus far the Army had been successful on the battlefield even if victory proved ever elusive. So long as naval appropriations suffered no harm, the senior naval leadership of Japan tolerated the maintenance of the Japanese Army's war in China until such a time as a truly favourable opportunity to end it might appear.

Japan took stock of what it had gained. After only a few months of war, the Japanese had captured most of the important river systems which formed China's economic arteries. By the end of 1938 they also possessed nine-tenths of the Chinese railway system and controlled the entire coastline of China under a tight blockade. In a technical sense little remained of China worth conquering by Japan at the end of 1938. Such heavy fighting was not to happen again, even when this war was eventually swallowed up in the Second World War, and when China's weapons were much strengthened by aid from its allies, mostly flown over 'the hump' of northern Burma. All the important battles appeared to have been fought and won. Japan could be content with consolidating her position and mopping up isolated pockets of resistance. Japanese morale predictably reached dizzying heights, and so did Japanese political ambition.

Superficially Japan had conquered territory which contained 170 million people. China had lost its principal seaports, the Chinese Navy had ceased to exist, and the Japanese mounted very effective naval patrols round the entire seaboard of the country from Manchukuo to French Indo-China. China depended henceforward for foreign supplies on two routes. The first was an earth road from Russia through the huge province of Sinkiang (Chinese Turkestan), which had been used for centuries as part of the ancient Silk Route linking China with Central Asia; in more recent times it had been used by the bandits of Sinkiang, a no man's land, and by Chinese communists as their back alley to the Soviet Union. The other was a new road, 350 miles long and completed only in 1938 by 200,000 coolies, from the city of Kunming (formerly Yunnanfu), provincial capital of Yunnan and the communications hub of south-west China, to the south, where it ended at Lashio in northern Burma, providing access to roads leading south to the Bay of Bengal at Rangoon. Both roads were very long, poorly constructed, virtually impassable by motor vehicles during the rainy season between June and November, and liable to traffic blocks at the best of times. The difficulties of the logistics and terrain were formidable. When pack animals instead of motor vehicles were used, it took about sixty days to transport military supplies from Rangoon to Kunming via the Burma Road. For a time China had been able to use the port of Haiphong, in Indo-China, but the French authorities ran hot and cold depending upon the attentions of the Japanese, and the bridges were destroyed which carried the French-owned railway line linking this port with its terminus 550 miles away at Kunming, where it connected with roads and canals to Chungking and the whole of South and Central China.

Unfortunately for the Japanese, the stalemate in China which had emerged in late 1938 grew more serious during the next year as the Nationalist régime continued to survive. By 1939 Japanese military forces seemed to have reached the limits of their power in China. No appreciable advances were made in the central regions of China, and events on the periphery had a significance far larger than the war against the Nationalists. Hainan Island was taken after an unopposed invasion on 10 February, which frightened the French into reducing the trickle of war supplies which flowed north from Haiphong in Indo-China to Kwangsi

Province in Free China. A larger expedition all but completed this object in November after landing north-west of Hainan on the Chinese mainland at Pakhoi and easily advancing north to Nanning. Neither of these campaigns materially advanced Japanese efforts to end the war in China, but the seizure of Hainan marked an important step towards the Pacific War. It was occupied in the vain hope of satisfying the ambitions of activists in the Japanese Naval General Staff who wanted to wrest control of the South China Seas from the British and so pluck from European hands the fabulous riches of Malaya, the Netherlands East Indies and French Indo-China. Thus the move into Hainan revealed how far the authority of moderate, pro-western senior leaders of the Japanese Navy had slipped. The advocates of Japan's 'Southern Advance' wanted to secure Asia's back door against the West, but in pursuing that strategy the Japanese invited more trouble than they could handle.

The notorious arrogance of Japanese soldiers, while often not much greater towards foreigners in China than towards Japanese civilians at home, inevitably led to international incidents. As Japanese casualties in China reached approximately half a million men during 1939, scapegoats were sought. Although Japanese officials never ceased to bicker among themselves, they found common cause in blaming Britain, France and the United States for Japan's failure to achieve victory in China. The expeditions to Hainan and Pakhoi reflected this general tendency, and so did crude reprisals against western property and commercial interests in Occupied China. These measures were effective locally but encouraged Britain and the United States at least to resist further encroachments on their treaty rights in China. There were frequent incidents on the Yangtze River involving confrontations between Japanese and western gunboats, and a particularly alarming confrontation occurred at the International Settlement on Kulangsu, an island lying off Amoy in the vicinity of Formosa. Japanese troops landed there on 23 May 1939 in search of Chinese terrorists. This resulted in a rapid concentration of British, American and French warships at Amoy, and all three countries promptly landed separate shore parties each equal in size to the Japanese contingent. Tension lessened only when the British and French forces withdrew at the outbreak of the European War. The Japanese and Americans then negotiated a mutual withdrawal of their marines in mid-October.

Notwithstanding the Kulangsu Incident and provocations on the Yangtze, Japan discounted the danger of armed intervention by the West. Indeed, the Japanese Army had developed no contingency plans for war against either Britain or the United States at this time, and the Japanese Navy had no detailed plan, yet, for war against an Anglo-American coalition. The Japanese had the satisfaction of believing they knew how Britain and America would react in the event of a war. The Japanese Embassy in Washington, DC, had secured a copy of War Plan Orange, the United States contingency plan for a war against Japan, and the Japanese Government knew the substance of British naval war plans, which had been obvious in general outline ever since construction of the Singapore Naval Base had begun in the aftermath of the First World War. Japanese cryptographers had cracked the British diplomatic codes and had the benefit of monitoring, among other things, how far apart the British and Americans were.

So long as Japan left Hong Kong to the British and avoided all but the occasional outrage against British or American nationals in China, the Anglo-Saxon Powers seemed unlikely and indeed unprepared to mount the kind of combined effort necessary to impose their will by naval means against Japan. Short of a world war, the Japanese Navy was capable of defending Japanese interests and even extending Japanese influence in the waters of the Western Pacific Ocean and South Seas. The China Incident did not adversely affect Japan's naval strength in the Western Pacific. On the contrary the training received by Japanese naval airmen under combat conditions in China was invaluable and allowed the Japanese to improve their aircraft far more rapidly than would have been possible in peacetime. Likewise, the war in China gave Japan the opportunity to develop amphibious operations into a new art several years ahead of any other nation. In traditional areas of naval construction, Japanese naval architects had managed to evade the restrictions of the Washington and London naval limitations treaties, which expired in 1936, and by means of four naval replenishment plans kept pace qualitatively, as well as quantitatively, with rapid British and American naval expansion programmes. The result was that by 1939 Japan was impervious to either (but not both) of the British or the United States navies in the Western Pacific and most of the China Seas.

Nevertheless, Japan had a well-justified fear of Anglo-American economic encirclement. There was disturbing evidence very early during the China Incident that Britain wanted American support for a programme to impose an early end to the war at Japanese expense through joint economic countermeasures against Japan. Later, strong pressure groups in the United States lobbied for similar ideas. Tokyo could not hope to resist such a programme for long.

Over 40 per cent of Japanese exports and more than half her imports were with the United States. Japan's balance of payments' situation was precarious, and her financial future was a hostage to the vagaries of

American public policy. Although Government controls in Japan succeeded in limiting Japanese imports to essential materials, the trend over the first two and a half years of the China Incident was for Japanese exports to fall sharply while imports from the United States continued to rise. Traditionally, Japan had been dependent upon the British Empire and the United States for vital strategical raw materials ranging from tin, nickel and zinc to oil, iron and steel. The British calculated that a bilateral embargo on Anglo-Japanese trade would hurt the British Empire more than Japan, but it was evident to all that confiscation of Britain's considerable assets in Japan would not begin to compensate Japan for the losses that Japan would suffer if Britain and America both imposed sanctions against the Japanese economy. This difficulty for Japan increased substantially when the European War began in September 1939: alternative sources of supply for some strategical goods vanished along with an important segment of the Japanese export market. Meanwhile, Yen-bloc countries such as Formosa, Korea and Manchuria absorbed an increasingly high proportion of Japanese industrial output while contributing a disappointingly low proportion of Japanese war production requirements. Self-sacrifice by Japanese consumers permitted the war to continue indefinitely, but it was universally accepted that Japan had no margin of safety against the firm application of Anglo-American economic sanctions.

Within China Proper, however, there was no more large-scale fighting of transcontinental dimensions for five years. For much of that time it might have been supposed that the war had petered out. Yet a staggering 40 to 50 per cent of Japan's entire national budget was appropriated for defence purposes, and the nation was resolved to fight for victory.

Japan suffered its first reverses in the occupied districts in the north. Its control of the railways and towns did not give it control of the rural areas. It began to feel severely the effects of communist guerrilla warfare. At first the Japanese generals had supposed that they had the measures for repressing the communists, and, for a time, little was heard about the communist armies. This was to the dismay of the friends of China who had built up extravagant hopes on the reconciliation between Chiang and the communists. Eventually, though, the stubborn resistance of the communists began to take a toll. To have overcome it, to have attempted a stricter control which would have eliminated this, would have cost many millions of troops, which the Japanese could not afford. China had begun to draw the advantages from one of its assets, size. Because the Japanese could not pacify the vast area of Hopei, Shantung and Shensi provinces, which they had overrun, they constituted themselves as a target for guerrilla action.

Chiang Kai-shek sat in his fortress at Chungking and waited. The city, though not beautiful like Chengtu, the capital of Szechuan, was fitted for its purpose. Rainfall was heavy, and the clouds which overhung it for weeks on end, together with surrounding mountains which made it difficult to approach, prevented it from being an easy target of attacks from the air. It was bombed heavily for a time, but later was left in peace. The city was large, and had once been affluent. Chiang's task was to keep his Government in existence, to survive the plots against him, to plot against others – to continue to be regarded as the symbol of nationalism. Alas, though wartime propaganda made the reputation of Chungking as a heroic centre of resistance, a long, slow demoralization set in among the Kuomintang establishment, the inevitable result among an army and bureaucracy condemned to too much idleness, and this proved in the long run too much for Chiang Kai-shek to combat. The Chinese of the Kuomintang and the Army staff were a different people from the particularist Szechuanese, who resented their impact on their ancient provincial culture. Relations between them and the local people deteriorated steadily. 'Down-river gangsters' was the term used for Kuomintang officials by the Szechuanese people. Internal rot was the price the Kuomintang paid for the tactics of masterly inactivity.

Chiang Kai-shek was resting his hopes, not on the Kuomintang Army, but chiefly on foreign aid, principally American aid, which his diplomats in the United States tirelessly sought. Certainly there was abundant American goodwill to China, based chiefly on the vast American missionary enterprise there. It seemed that China, before the war, had been willing to reconstruct its society according to American ideas, and this seemed to impose on the United States the obligation of protecting it internationally.

As far as China was concerned, Japan for a time now turned its back on battles and daring campaigns, and engaged in political warfare and in political intrigue. The only military action was a single attempt in June 1940 to force the Yangtse gorges, which ended at Ichang. Japan decided that to carry on the war was to bring complication after complication, and, from now on, explored ways to end it. From this time, 1939–40, the Japanese Army sought peace in China as constantly and assiduously (though maladroitly) as it had once welcomed war. It was out of the question to arrange to annex the vast territory it had overrun, and to rule it directly as the British used to rule India. The need for civil servants would be immense, beyond anything which Japan could supply. It turned in consequence to indirect rule, to organizing North China as a puppet state (similar in general shape to Manchukuo), which would be under the rule of a single man or body of men upon whose loyalty they could rely, because it would be clear that, with Japanese aid removed, they would collapse.

Their first thought was to use Chiang Kai-shek himself. If they could have detached him from his nationalism, and made it worth his while, Chiang would have proved an excellent puppet. He would have had a full and apparently contented life hunting down communists. Realizing how greatly an alliance with Chiang would serve them, understanding that this was indeed the crisis of the war, the Japanese used the utmost finesse to bring it about. But neither the secret emissaries whom they sent tirelessly to visit him, nor the German and British Ambassadors who proposed mediation, brought the Japanese any hopeful news. Chiang had little room to manoeuvre in. He had made his way to the top of the Kuomintang, but he had become a prisoner of the national movement, which would have broken him if he had sought to betray it. Chiang, who knew the dark corners of China's political life, and availed himself of the services of its inhabitants, knew well what agents it would employ.

Furthermore Generalissimo Chiang Kai-shek, who was the heart and soul of Chinese unity against Japan, probably never expected any peace to emerge from these discussions. Chiang demanded nothing less than Japan's unconditional withdrawal from China: he only departed from this basic position when he evidently hoped to throw Tokyo off course while Japanese armies were sweeping towards one particularly important objective or another. For the most part, Chiang disdainfully rejected Japan's efforts to seek a compromise based on present realities, and he made use of western good offices to further China's international propaganda campaign rather than to achieve a negotiated end to the war. Not only did the Chinese mistrust the Japanese peace offers but they had also come to regard resistance to Japan as a necessary precondition for the survival of Chinese nationalism. In addition, the Japanese terms were often poorly expressed due partly to the vagaries of the Japanese language and partly to fears that enemy morale might recover if it became known beforehand how small were Japan's fundamental desiderata.

Reluctantly the Japanese decided on alternative plans. After several experiments with Chinese puppet régimes of little significance, they set themselves to persuade certain respected nationalists, who were opposed to Chiang Kai-shek, to form a Government which had all the outward shape of the Kuomintang, and which the Japanese could substitute for the official Kuomintang. They had resort to one of the most distinguished members of the Kuomintang, who had been almost a founding father of the party.

This man, Wang Ching-wei, one time Vice-President of the Kuomintang republic, had previously built a career on the leadership of the left wing. He had never exhausted the fame which he had gained by being involved in a plot in the days of the Empire to murder a Manchu grandee. In private, his views were anything but radical and he had married a very wealthy wife, who came from a family of Singapore millionaires. But his political talents had been acceptable to the revolutionary branch of the Kuomintang. After the fall of Canton and Hankow he seems to have accepted the Japanese argument that further resistance was useless, and to have argued that China, by recasting its foreign policy, could still come to terms with Japan which would be mutually advantageous. At Chungking, he conferred at length with Chiang Kai-shek. Though no record exists of their conversation, it is known that the two men debated in full the Japanese peace offer.

In December 1939 he recognized his failure, and left the capital. The Japanese were willing to see in him the best substitute head of a cooperative Chinese Government. He had the aura of a major politician. He had the record of being a persistent rival of Chiang Kai-shek. Mostly Chiang had succeeded in keeping him out of office, and, when Wang Ching-wei had manoeuvred so that he compelled Chiang to share power with him, Chiang was suspected of a hand in the mysterious shooting which had removed him from office. The Japanese acted with resolution. Wang's name, the prestige of Nanking city, the attraction of the Kuomintang – renamed by Wang the Reformed Kuomintang – all these were used to give the new Government such prestige as it could have in a Nanking which remembered vividly what it had been made to suffer.

The Government came into being in 1940. A fairly long list of landholders, industrialists, former officials, diplomats out of employment, politicians who had ruined their prospects with the official Kuomintang, came to see if the vistas opened up under the new administration appeared brighter for them. Many were recruited for the régime. Many of the more or less respectable Chinese nationalists had begun to find the régime of the Reformed Kuomintang very beguiling, especially since it reconciled nationalism with the prospect of opting out of the war. Wang Ching-wei's Government was a copy of the genuine Kuomintang. Its constitution was much the same; it contained the complications and intricacies which had puzzled all those who tried to follow Chinese politics. Its methods of administration were much the same.

In administration the régime was slightly less corrupt than had been expected. It did little that was outwardly disgraceful. As the head of a puppet Government, camouflaged for the general public in the colours of nationalism, Wang Ching-wei did neither more nor less than was expected of him: he fought for China's interests while being ready in the last resort to yield to Japan's superior strength. In China he played the same part as Marshal Pétain in France. But Wang's Government never succeeded in living down the sense of national shame in which it was born; never managed to take independent life; it remained a creature of the Japanese; it never became a serious body internationally. From the point of view of a historian detached from these events, the chief points worth under-scoring are that the Japanese did put a great deal of energy into cultivating local régimes as part of their search for a peaceful solution to the China Incident; that Free China's sole unifying force in local as in national government was Chiang Kai-shek's personality cult, and yet that there were many Chinese who took immense risks to seek some kind of com-promise based upon a mixture of *realpolitik*, personal ambition and their sense of Pan-Asian brotherhood.

Meanwhile the pretence that the war was a joint one, of the Kuo-mintang and the communists against Japan, was wearing thin. The Chinese communists, in the regions which they had overrun in the north, maintained a lively propaganda against the Japanese. Guerrilla warfare was their special art. There was also activity by guerrilla bands who fought in the name of the Kuomintang. But the pretence, which had been built up immediately after the Sian Incident, that the armies of the communists were to be fused with the armies of the Kuomintang under some kind of common command, never became a reality. The communists had no intention of surrendering the sole command of their Army. That was their most effective instrument in Chinese politics, and they would hold on to it. The communists relied on their Army to win them new territory, and to retain what they had; and they could scarcely trust their old enemy, the Kuomintang, with any recognized power to dispose of this force.

A subtle, concealed, very bitter struggle was resumed between the Kuomintang and the communists. Everybody who was interested in Chinese politics saw the danger of revived civil war taking shape. The Kuomintang, without entirely dropping the mask of the common front, was alert to the spread of communist power, and tried to guard against it by maintaining, as far as it could, an inner blockade of the regions which the communists ruled, including an embargo on all medical supplies. The most competent and orderly section of the Kuomintang Army was in fact left permanently at Sian, where its sole duty was to watch and over-awe the communists. The communists directed their fire equally against the Kuomintang and the Japanese.

Sometimes the struggle became too obvious for decency between apparent allies. Each side had its own territory. Sometimes the communists would move into a Kuomintang region: the Kuomintang would drive them out by force. At such times the hollowness of the partnership became plain. There was a particularly flagrant example of this in 1941 when the communist Fourth Route Army was ambushed by patent treachery, and fighting flared up on a large scale. The communists lost several generals in the course of this affair. But even at such times both the communists and the Kuomintang tried to put limits to hostilities. An important part in keeping peace at least formally was played by the communist representative at Chungking, who was Chou En-lai, saviour of Chiang, destined in the next decade to become Prime Minister of China. A competition was being fought out between the two Governments, to determine which of them, in the harsh conditions of war, had the better spirit to endure. The war was proving a hothouse, and had brought on the decision which otherwise might have taken half a century to deliver. All the data were to the discomfiture of the Kuomintang. The communists, who began as very much the weaker, became a steadily greater force.

Meanwhile a part of the horrors which had overtaken the Chinese people became known to the West – to a West which was bracing itself to face its own agony. The full terrors of war broke over the Chinese towns and countryside. They had gradually become accustomed to civil war during the thirty years of breakdown of ordered government. In much of the country, the old magistrates had left. The armies of the war-lords had harried the villages, seized their grain, and sometimes carried off the young men and women. But all this was as nothing compared with what befell in the years after 1936. One estimate puts the number uprooted from their homes by the war as 50 million. The Chinese are as a rule greatly attached to their villages, and will not forsake a home which contains the graves of their ancestors. Many of the cherished customs of the village – the sweeping of the family graves, ceremonial meals eaten over the tombs – are connected with tomb-rites. Now a great wrench had loosened the population from its hold. China dissolved from people living in orderly, extremely conservative patterns of life, into a maze of people wandering aimlessly from village to village. They sought food, protection, shelter. All China seemed to be restlessly on the move. Any representation of its people at this time shows them trudging from place to place, carrying their belongings with them. (A similar nightmare befell persons who were compelled to see the sights in post-war Germany.) How many perished in this time will never be known. Their plight made them powerless to escape the scourge of famine and the scourge of the other terror of the

Chinese countryside, flood. One by one, the very ancient annual ceremonies in the villages, which gave Chinese life its admirable quality and
its deep sense of continuity, were given up. Life became especially hard
for the old, the class which Chinese civilization was notorious for
revering.

Colour, richness and elegance disappeared from China. Everywhere
people went dressed in simple cotton clothes, either because they had been
impoverished, or because the slightest display of luxury was an invitation
to plunder. The pleasantness and decorum of the life of the Chinese upper
classes, which had already been much shaken for a hundred years by the
impact of the West, descended to a new calamitous level, as society gradually disintegrated. Only in such protected centres as Chungking was the
attempt made to live in accustomed Chinese style.

A similar break-up of society had taken place in France at the end of
the Hundred Years War, and in Germany during the Thirty Years War.

Early on in this period there had taken place one of the most unlooked-
for emigrations in history. As we have seen, the universities of China had
a precocious development. In wealth, in their standing in society, by the
personal eminence of their staff, both Chinese and also the core of expatriate foreigners, they were ahead of the standards which universities
might have been expected to reach in the country, and were suited for a
society such as China might have evolved two or three generations later.
In consequence of this, much of the most advanced, the purest, and
certainly the most disinterested nationalism of the day was nursed to life
within their walls.

Most of the universities were on the seaboard in the path of the Japanese
invasion. They were one of its special targets, because the Japanese, being
themselves an East Asian people, understood (though Japan did not share
this characteristic) the extraordinary influence which the Chinese intelligentsia had over the rulers of the nation. The Chinese student was alone
among the student class of the world in not feeling, or feeling much less,
an acute sense of frustration. Why should he? The nation hung on his
moods, was willing to follow him in his attitudes to Ministers and public
affairs. Since he was so influential, the student buoyed himself up: and
the conditions he put up with in student life, the squalid poverty, were
felt to be the necessary price of privilege. Besides it was spread equally
over the whole student body. Let them reduce the pride and aspiration of
the intelligentsia, the Japanese told themselves, and they would have gone
a long way in subduing Chinese nationalism. Under Japanese domination,
the universities knew that they would face a purge, and the conditions of

the new life would be quite intolerable to them. Rather than suffer it, many of the university communities moved off by spontaneous resolution, and trekked from the coasts to new sites far in the interior.

Chinese learning was pulling up its stakes and seeking out a territory where it might exist in freedom; and, as the price to be paid for this, live a life less gilded than before. The professors and their assistants, the student body, and university servants, all sought a home where they could continue their life with less harassment. Previously, Chinese scholars had not taken kindly to manual work; now they voluntarily undertook the hardship of the journey, the uncertainties of what awaited them, and a life of toil. It was the more surprising because these learned societies had to leave palatial premises, which had been given them by millionaires and foreign philanthropists, and had to fit their academic life into camps which had been made available to them as exiles. Throughout their vicissitudes they had safeguarded their libraries and the equipment of their scientific laboratories. Many of them transported these across the rivers and mountains of inland China.

During the war years the Chinese intelligentsia continued their studies diligently. In view of the way in which learning was regarded this turned out to be the most useful thing which they could contribute to China's war effort. They had firmly aligned themselves with the decision to resist Japan, and by their action in seeking voluntary exile they increased their prestige in the eyes of the people. The scholars and the mass of common people came closer together.

The universities, in deciding on their odysseys, were influenced by the example of the Chinese communists on the Long March. From this time there began to grow up the great sympathy of the Chinese scholar class for the communists. The scholars felt themselves being blown along by the same hurricane which had swept together the communist insurgents throughout China: and as the leadership of the Kuomintang began to falter, they began to look to the communists for an alternative. They did so with more eagerness because when they had migrated in the cause of freedom, they found that, when they eventually reached the security of the interior, they were regarded with suspicion by the Kuomintang, and that their freedom was interfered with by an irksome secret police. The campus was invaded by an army of spies.

The reliance on the secret police by Chiang Kai-shek to maintain his exaggerated political role was a departure from Chinese tradition. Before Chiang, China had known periods of despotism; but the despot had, to a remarkable degree, avoided the organization of a secret police as the instrument of tyranny. Even in the last years of the Manchus the

Government, though repressive, had avoided the creation of an organ specially for Intelligence and coercion. Therefore the collisions which now became frequent between the literati and the secret police offered the more provocation because the Chinese had not been accustomed in the past to think of the police as a necessary evil.

The writings of Chinese academics became full of woe; they had exchanged the persecution of the Japanese for the supervision of the police. It was less efficient, less rigorous, but it was deeply offensive. The grievances thus sown were to bear fruit at the end of the war. Without the moral approval of the scholar class, the Chinese communists would never have been able to impose themselves so successfully on the Chinese nation.

CHAPTER 10

International Alarums: Japan and Appeasement

'A war postponed may be a war averted!'* – Anthony Eden

BETWEEN 1931 and 1939, while facing military aggression committed or threatened by Germany, Italy and Japan, the foreign policy options of the western democracies were reduced to a choice between three dangerous strategies – or traditions – each with historical roots: 'Appeasement', 'Resistance' and 'Isolation'. The British tended to favour the well-trodden pathway of Appeasement, a policy based upon 'moderation' and conciliation which had served Britain's perfectly respectable selfish aims throughout most of the preceding century or more. By concessions to the territorial, economic or even ideological ambitions and conceits of powerful potential enemies, Britain hoped to lead their governments away from 'gangsterism' (to borrow Anthony Eden's word for it) and back into the modalities of peaceful international relations which so favoured British ascendency in the world.

'Resistance', a policy superficially opposite to 'Appeasement', involving steadfast confrontation against aggression, was favoured by France and some elements in the United States throughout most of the inter-war years (although practised more in the breach than in the observance). While Resistance may take 'peaceful' forms (for example, economic sanctions or non-recognition of territorial or political change), it carries with it an implication that war (for which France and the United States, as well as Britain, were generally unprepared) is preferable to surrender in matters of immutable principle. Lacking sufficient strength to defeat the forces ranged against them, any policy of British, French and even American resistance to German, Italian or Japanese aggression had to be predicated upon effective rearmament or, at the very least, upon the acquisition of powerful, dependable allies. Failing that, as Prime Minister Neville Chamberlain

---

* Quoted in K. Feiling, *The Life of Neville Chamberlain*, Macmillan, London, 1947, p. 320, or, as Winston Churchill wrote in his final volume of *The World Crisis* in 1931, 'A war postponed is a war prevented', cited in M. Gilbert, *The Roots of Appeasement*, Weidenfeld & Nicolson, London, 1966, p. 155.

avowed as late as January 1939, 'In the absence of any powerful ally, and until our armaments are completed, we must adjust our foreign policy to our circumstances.'* Unfortunately, there were practical difficulties which undermined British and French attempts to rearm or to attract the kind of allies they required: as the British Chiefs of Staff warned their political superiors in December 1937, more than three years after the rearmament programme began and while the greatest crises were yet to befall, it was the risk of a two- or three-enemy war which was of prime concern:

The outstanding feature of the present situation is the increasing probability that a war started in any one of these three areas may extend to one or both of the other two. Without overlooking the assistance which we would hope to obtain from France and possibly other allies, we cannot foresee the time when our defence forces will be strong enough to safeguard our trade, territory and vital interests against Germany, Italy and Japan at the same time . . . they could not exaggerate the importance from the point of view of Imperial Defence of any political or international action which could be taken to reduce the number of our potential enemies and to gain the support of powerful allies.†

The underlying difficulty was that by the time the western democracies awoke to the challenge of Japanese aggression in Manchuria during 1931, neither Britain nor France had sufficient means to defend their respective vital interests and the United States plainly lacked the political will to do so. The effects of the economic depression placed severe limitations on the ability of any of the three to make good their military deficiencies. Too little rearmament would be ineffective; too much (or even enough) would bankrupt the soundest European economy. Prominent among the circumstances of the western democracies which differed from those of Germany, Italy and Japan was that the latter were intent upon drawing upon the resources of neighbouring economies through aggression (as in fact occurred in Manchuria, China, Austria, Czechoslovakia, Poland, France, the Netherlands and so forth). If they could be prevented from achieving their objectives, however, the economies of Germany, Italy and Japan were more vulnerable than the better balanced economies of the western democracies. The problem was that an *unanswerable* rearmament programme (that is, any programme which potential enemies could not match, step by step) would require *time* – purchased at great expense by international concessions or ignored only at great economic, political or military peril.

* Letter to Mrs Morton Prince, 16 January 1939, cited by Feiling, p. 324.
† CID 1366-B, Report by the Chiefs of Staff entitled 'The Strength of Great Britain Compared with Certain Other Nations as at 1 January 1938', 12 November 1937, CAB 4/26, British Public Record Office, Kew.

Even if governments did their sums correctly, an adequate scale of rearmament, if produced too soon, would doom a nation's armed forces to obsolescence in time of war. If, contrariwise, rearmament proceeded at an inadequate level or set out to achieve its designed results over too long a period, a crisis might occur or a war indeed might be lost before deficiencies could be overcome. As General Maxime Weygand, Inspector General of the French Army, declared in a review of French defence policy in mid-January 1933, less than a fortnight before Hitler swept to power in the German polls:

If we leave questions of this magnitude without examining or solving them, we shall be led inexorably day by day, under the pressure of budgetary necessities, political influences or international blackmail, to take measures which will gradually drain our national forces of their substance. They will become merely a façade and will not be in a condition to fulfil their mission at the hour of danger.*

In Britain, rearmament received its initial impetus first from the Manchurian Incident. Only later, after Hitler's rise to power, did attention begin to shift towards regarding Germany as the greater peril. In the process, time was lost. Yet the arguments in favour of limiting defence expenditure in the midst of a worldwide economic depression were plain enough, and so it took both the unbridled exercise of Japanese military might in Manchuria and the political changes in Germany to force the British Government to abandon the principle of Winston Churchill's 'Ten-Year Rule', imposed by him as Chancellor of the Exchequer in 1928, 'That it would be assumed for the purpose of framing the Estimates of the Fighting Services, that at any given date there will be no major war for ten years.'† Thus while French politicians, who were deaf to the sound of battle on the Asiatic mainland and responded to the economic crisis by actually *cutting* French expenditure on rearmament, the British authorities took the first steps in the opposite direction, although the faith of the British Treasury in orthodox economic doctrine severely limited the scale of what London attempted. In both countries, resources of skilled manpower, productive capacity and their ability to maintain financial credit abroad were crucial. Throughout the 1930s the French economy teetered on the brink of insolvency while at the same time the intense pacifism of the French public and the volatility of French domestic politics made a nonsense of long-range economic planning and rearmament policy.

* A. Adamthwaite, *The Making of the Second World War*, Allen & Unwin, London, 1974, doc. 2.
† N. H. Gibbs, *Grand Strategy* vol. I: *Rearmament Policy*, HMSO, London, 1976, pp. 55–64.

The importance of preserving Britain's purchasing power played a vital role in a country completely dependent upon overseas supplies for its survival: as Sir Warren Fisher, the immensely powerful Permanent Under-Secretary of the Treasury (and Head of the Civil Service), pointed out in a paper circulated to the Cabinet with the first Report of the Defence Requirements Committee in April 1934, raw materials and food 'are only produced within this country in negligible quantities and therefore have to be secured from other countries who will not, of course, give us them, and, when our international purchasing power is exhausted, will not continue indefinite credits to us'.*

Judged by orthodox economic standards, not only were financial strength and economic stability seen to be essential in peacetime economic recovery from the great depression but in time of war they would assume even greater significance – as what the British Treasury and strategical authorities termed 'the fourth arm in defence', no less important than the three fighting services and 'without which purely military effort would be of no avail'.† Although Britain and France felt they had little chance of coming out victorious in a short, sharp war, they believed they stood an excellent chance of eventual success against the military strength (and economic vulnerability) of their potential enemies in a long war. The point was put well by Sir Thomas Inskip, Minister for the Co-ordination of Defence, in December 1937:

The maintenance of credit facilities and our general balance of trade are of vital importance, not merely from the view of our strength in peacetime, but equally for purposes of war. This country cannot hope to win a war against a major power by a sudden knock-out blow; on the contrary, for success we must contemplate a long war, in the course of which we should have to mobilize all our resources and those of the Dominions and other countries overseas . . . We must therefore confront our potential enemies with the risks of a long war, which they cannot face.‡

Against Japan, particularly, Britain's economic advantages were believed for many years to be decisive. With time, however, these 'advantages' seemed less obvious and Britain became more and more stretched by the effort to establish the means to defend the Empire against the

---

* M. Howard, *The Continental Commitment*, Temple Smith, London, 1972, p. 135. See also G. C. Peden, *British Rearmament and the Treasury, 1932–1939*, Scottish Academic Press, Edinburgh, 1977, p. 91; D. C. Watt, *Too Serious a Business*, Temple Smith, London, 1975.

† C P 316(37), 'Defence Expenditure in Future Years: Interim Report by the Minister for Co-ordination of Defence', 15 December 1937.

‡ ibid.

combination of enemies confronting it. In practice, the arguments in favour of seeking coercion by the application of economic measures short of war were never as attractive as some of its advocates supposed. There were times when the British Foreign Office was inclined towards sanctions, but in general most professional observers shared the view expressed by one in relation to Japanese aggression at the outbreak of the China Incident in 1937, that 'the principle to be applied to the whole problem is essentially simple: half-measures are far worse than useless and full measures mean war'.* Equally, a strategy based upon deterrence – involving the threat rather than the use of force – had little to recommend itself to the British or the French if their adversaries were demonstrably better disposed to deter them from using it.

Both the British and French Governments during the 1930s aimed in very different ways to establish adequate defences at what they regarded as the highest level which could be maintained indefinitely. Added to the costs of constructing modern armaments were enormous costs of maintenance, training and manning them. To turn resources of manpower and production towards military ends too soon would adversely affect the reconstruction of national prosperity, social welfare, and all manner of foreign confidence and domestic support. All across the British political spectrum, responsible leaders shared these sources of concern, differing only by degree.

It bears emphasis that in so far as the international alarms of the day were concerned, and Britain's capacity to respond, the whole machinery of government was held together by finely interlocking networks of committees through which a mere handful of brilliant civil servants and their military counterparts worked hard to educate Ministers and formulate national policy. The British Civil Service and especially its most senior officials, was much better informed than Government Ministers, backbench Members of Parliament, the public and even the press. For the most part, Ministers soon fell in step with their professional advisers in their individual respective Government departments. Above all, however, British military and foreign policy-making initiatives generated within separate departments were filtered and refined by their passage through a structure known as the Committee of Imperial Defence. Underneath the Committee itself were more than a hundred inter-departmental sub-committees of greater or lesser importance or duration, and the membership of most of these sub-committees was composed of officials who genuinely shared a desire to work harmoniously with their opposite

* F 8142/6799/10, Minute by Gladwyn Jebb, 8 October 1937, FO 371/21015.

numbers in their sister departments or services. Thus debate, obstructiveness and paper-pushing made it almost impossible for solitary Ministers to carry out measures that lacked the collective support of the system. On the other hand, when there was a common purpose (and reaching that often involved a great deal of personal energy from its contributors as well as a readiness to compromise) the collective efforts that could be harnessed by this system made it the most efficient, although not necessarily the swiftest, governmental powerplant in the world. The significance of this cannot be overstated, for it gave to British policy-making a semblance of rational coherence and intelligence that was missing in other countries. In particular it provided a great contrast with the anarchy that prevailed in dictatorships like Germany or Italy where competing chiefs scrambled to catch their leader's eye and favours, and it also was the envy of popular democracies like that of the United States where institutionalized 'checks and balances' between the executive branch and Congress were an encouragement to continuous guerrilla warfare between independent-minded government departments who were only too eager to 'leak' sensitive information that would embarrass one another.

In any event, the personalities who dominated the British political scene during the years leading up to the Second World War did agree, in the words of a warning given the British Cabinet and Committee of Imperial Defence by the Chiefs of Staff, uttered in their 1933 Annual Review of Imperial Defence and repeated at regular intervals thereafter, 'The accumulation of deficiencies ... is very heavy, and if we are to be ready for grave emergencies, a steady increase in certain of our estimates over a number of years is essential.'* The will was there. The two questions of unlimited complexity were What could be done? and Would it be effective?

Not until the late 1930s, with the shock of successive international crises and a growing appreciation of Keynesian theory, did the idea of public borrowing for rearmament gradually become respectable in the absence of viable alternatives: when as British Chancellor of the Exchequer Neville Chamberlain first suggested the idea of a 'National Defence Contribution' scheme in his budget speech of April 1937, there was enormous public outcry against this 'tax on recovery', and as the value of the French franc and of sterling plummeted, Parliament forced him to abandon the idea on 1 June, only five days after he had become Prime

* CTD 113–B, Chiefs of Staff Review of Imperial Defence, 12 October 1933, CAB 4/22.

Minister. While subsequent efforts to employ deficit financing proved more successful, the vulnerability of the British and French economies to financial panic fully vindicated their Governments' concern about financial stability: during the fifteen months between the Austrian Anschluss and the Tientsin crisis in June 1939, more than £300 million worth of gold – 40 per cent of Britain's total reserves – was lost, and Britain's balance of trade went into a steep decline as 25–30 per cent of the raw materials imported by the country were diverted to arms production rather than for exports.

By this time the point had been reached where Britain genuinely could do no more: as the First Lord of the Admiralty, Sir Roger Backhouse, wrote in November 1938, 'The trouble is . . . that we are now trying to take on more than we are really able to . . . and we simply cannot produce more than we are doing.'* Britain's arms factories were working to full capacity, but Treasury comparisons with the national debts per head of population in various countries at July 1939 gave equal cause for concern:†

	£s
United Kingdom	172
United States	64
France	57
Italy	52
Germany	33
Japan	11

As the Treasury informed the Cabinet, 'unless, when the time comes, the United States are prepared either to lend or to give us money as required, the prospects of a long war are becoming exceedingly grim'.‡ When the growing weakness of the nation's financial position was explained to the Cabinet, Oliver Stanley, the President of the Board of Trade, remarked to his colleagues that 'There would, therefore, come a moment which, on a balance of our financial strength and our strength in armaments, was the best time for war to break out.'§

From that point of view it was fortunate that war broke out in August 1939. A few months later, at about the turn of the year, the precarious balance between the nation's impending insolvency and the demands of

---

* Backhouse to Sir Percy Noble, 14 November 1938, Adm. 205/3, cited in Peden, op cit., p. 152.
† T 175/115, Internal Treasury Memorandum, cited in Peden, p. 192.
‡ CP 149(39), Cabinet Memorandum by the Treasury, CAB 24/287, cited in R. P. Shay, *British Rearmament in the Thirties: Politics and Profits*, Princeton University Press, Princeton 1977, pp. 279–80.
§ CC 36(39)2, Cabinet Minutes, 7 May 1939, CAB 23/100, cited in Shay, op. cit., p. 280.

rearmament was acknowledged by no less an authority than Keynes himself, the very apostle of 'deficit financing'. Writing from his chambers in Cambridge University at the invitation of the British Government in December 1939, he warned that unless the United States could be persuaded to back the British war effort not with loans but with outright grants, the United Kingdom would be bankrupt within six months. His letter was intended to galvanize the Americans into taking action to rescue Britain, but it provides stark and unequivocal evidence that the financial control and rearmament programmes of Britain in the pre-war period were by no means so mismanaged, inadequate, ill-conceived or unsophisticated as the majority of the critics of 'Appeasement' generally suppose. In time the United States came to underwrite the expenses of British rearmament (although this was accompanied by a liquidation of British investments in the United States). Yet the pre-war administrations of Baldwin and Chamberlain had never been in a position to request, much less to expect, such help from their most powerful potential ally. It was, indeed, by no means facile of the Committee of Imperial Defence to expect that Britain would have to pay its way, and that the maintenance of the financial strength of the Empire was an essential defence requirement.

Constraints upon British and French budgets and rearmament were thus governing factors in their foreign and defence policies which, even divorced (as they could not be) from isolationist sentiment and widespread resolve 'never to go to war again', would have made military intervention abroad a lunacy for France after 1936 and a reckless course for Britain before the end of 1939. As Chamberlain's successor at the Exchequer, Sir John Simon (who had been Foreign Secretary during the Manchurian Incident) summed up Britain's dilemma a few days after the Anschluss in March 1938:

At the present moment we are in the position of a runner in a race who wants to reserve his sprint for the right time, but does not know where the finishing tape is. The danger is that we might knock our finance to pieces prematurely.*

This brings us to the question of France's conception of her potential enemies, for we must remind ourselves that France considered herself as a European rather than as an essentially inter-continental imperial power. Home defence against Germany was her paramount concern in the face of which other considerations such as the defence of her overseas territories paled into insignificance. France's interest was to maintain the somewhat artificially contrived position of French dominance in Europe

---

* CC 13(38)3, Cabinet Minutes, 14 March 1938, CAB 23/92, cited in Peden, op. cit., p. 66.

with which she had been left at the end of the First World War. French
hatred and suspicion of Germany, compounded by the failure of the
Treaty of Versailles to quell her fears of German resurgence once the
United States had withdrawn from active participation in continenta
European affairs, led France to strive to throttle German aspirations
towards the revision or revocation of the most draconian measures
embodied in the Versailles *Dictat*. France therefore adopted every
measure it could in resistance to German economic, military and political
recovery, and in doing so frantically negotiated mutual reinsurance
treaties with most of Germany's continental neighbours. Ultimately this
policy fell in a shambles as the French Foreign Minister was forced to
appreciate that

such a policy is not practicable, for it assumes first of all that the participants are
in fact, all allied among themselves. The result of the present situation is not only
weakness. It also results in the concentration on France of any attempt made
against peace [*sic*, by Germany only!], France being – and how inadequately – the
only link between countries which would be inclined to oppose such an attempt.*

A permanent alliance with Britain – or one with the United States –
would have provided the basis for a different policy where trust and
mutual respect could have been allowed to develop, but neither of these
potential allies was prepared to underwrite French paranoia against
Germany no matter how well-grounded it might have been in past experience. Locarno was briefly regarded as a satisfactory first step, but
when Britain's reluctance to commit herself further became clearer, France
considered her next best course to be a negotiated marriage of convenience
with Mussolini since, without Britain, the French Government believed
that the only way to cope with Germany was to gain Italian backing, or at
any rate a sufficient improvement in Franco-Italian affairs to permit
French military might to focus its undivided attention upon the frontier
of Germany. In pursuing this relatively short-lived courtship of Italy,
French diplomats found themselves at odds with the British over
Abyssinia *and* unable to prevent Il Duce from listening to Hitler's sweet
nothings. Italy scooped up Abyssinia, and Hitler in turn seized his moment
– and the Rhineland – while France remained unprepared, irresolute and
isolated. In the same way, France tried to avoid involvement in the
Manchurian Incident (leaving Britain to shoulder the burden of any action
taken by the League of Nations), the Spanish Civil War (where even Leon

---

* *Documents diplomatiques français, 1932–1939*, 2nd series, *1936–1939*, vol. II, Paris, 1964,
doc. 372, transl. in Anthony P. Adamthwaite, op. cit., doc. 34.

Blum's Popular Front Government refused to be drawn into open conflict with Franco), the China Incident (during which the French often echoed the protests of Britain and the United States in Tokyo against Japanese actions but nevertheless successfully dissociated themselves from the two Anglo-Saxon Powers), and the Italian conquest of Albania (which occurred in the immediate aftermath of the German occupation of Prague in the spring of 1939). All these were for France merely distractions from the central issue which was her powerlessness to resist German aggression but her humiliating inability to tolerate it.

In contrast with France, Britain saw herself as the island anchor of a global empire, perhaps the only truly 'world power' and certainly unique in placing her 'imperial interests' above all others. When the Manchurian Incident broke, the British Chiefs of Staff were joined by the Treasury and senior diplomats in warning Ministers against becoming involved. The British Ambassador in Tokyo cabled that 'Tension here is so great that a false step might cause the Japanese to take some action which would render war with the Powers almost inevitable.'* The Chiefs of Staff painted a grim picture of the Empire's vulnerability to Japanese attack, suggesting that 'the political reaction in India and the various colonies' should give pause for thought, and quoting with approval the Ambassador's view that reaching an accommodation with Japan 'may well entail ... fewer military commitments than thwarting her'.† The Treasury declared 'that in present circumstances we are no more in a position financially and economically to engage in a major war in the Far East than we are militarily'.‡ Under these pressures, it is not surprising that the British Government did no more than lend its moral support to the Lytton Report.

When the shock of these events pushed Britain into rearmament, the nation's strategical authorities naturally concentrated upon the danger of war with Japan, the only first-class military power then threatening Britain's imperial survival. As technical experts pondered how to deal with Japan, they gradually found themselves forced to consider the question of Germany. By 1934, although still working from the premise of the Chiefs of Staff (as expressed in their annual Reviews of Imperial Defence) that 'the defence of possessions and interests in the Far East' continued to come before 'European commitments' and 'the defence of India' in terms of the balance of strategical risks, the British defence establishment as a whole (in which Treasury and Foreign Office interests

* Cited in Howard, op. cit., p. 97.
† ibid.
‡ ibid.

were strongly represented alongside their Army, Navy and Air Force counterparts) formally recognized that the danger posed by German rearmament would eventually surpass that of Japan.

The combination of these two potential enemies was so grave that the British Government's professional defence advisers vehemently opposed making any defence preparations whatever against Italy: there was no way in which Britain and her likely allies were in a position to cope with three enemies at once. Yet no sooner had this doctrine been accepted by the Cabinet than the Abyssinian crisis caught Britain by surprise and brought Italy and the United Kingdom to the brink of war. This, then, formed the background to the Hoare–Laval Pact aimed at nipping the crisis in the bud, and it greatly limited the ability of the British Government to give full vent to the nation's growing sense of outrage by formulating a programme of economic sanctions or military reprisals against Mussolini's antics whether in response to the Abyssinian campaign, the operation of Italian 'pirate' submarines during the Spanish Civil War in 1937, or the Italian conquest of Albania.

As the Chiefs of Staff warned in 1937 and constantly reminded Ministers thereafter:

The chief danger which imperial defence has to face at the moment is that we are in the position of having threats at both ends of the Empire from strong military powers, i.e., Germany and Japan, while in the centre we have lost our traditional security in the Mediterranean owing to the rise of an aggressive spirit in Italy accompanied by an increase in her military strength. So long as that position remains unresolved diplomatically, only very great military and financial strength can give the Empire security.*

The situation worsened rather than improved. Naturally, the three fighting services vied with one another for the resources which the country could spare on rearmament, and attempts were made to cut through the nation's tangled defence requirements by applying Occam's razor: 'Are we to put Germany or the Far East first?' wrote the British Air Minister privately to the Minister for Co-ordination of Defence as late as October 1937:

I assume finance precludes our taking both in our stride. No doubt production does, too. It is for the Cabinet to lay down where the great danger lies and where we should concentrate. This of course directly affects both the Admiralty and the Air Ministry. If we have to make provision for the Far East that means

---

* COS 560, Chiefs of Staff Review of Imperial Defence, 22 February 1937, CAB 53/30, cited in Pritchard, *Far Eastern Influences*, op. cit., p. 8.

a great increase in the fleet. It also means aircraft, which can only be provided in the fairly near future to the detriment of the home position.*

Yet the principal difficulty facing British Ministers and their professional defence advisers was that they simply could not ignore the threat to their imperial security from Japan while dealing with events nearer to the United Kingdom. Much was done to rearm, but the military strength of the British Empire was dissipated by the nation's inability to focus upon a single potential adversary. Viewed from London, the rearmament efforts of those enemies seemed to outpace those of the British Empire. The leadership of Britain's potential enemies faced similar difficulties but not over such extended lines of communication.

Underpinning and foreshadowing the foreign policies pursued by the Chamberlain Government during the closing years of the decade lay a revised list of strategical priorities prepared by the Chiefs of Staff in February 1937, and these were scarcely modified before the outbreak of the Second World War: in place of the three-fold liabilities outlined previously, five critical objectives were itemized and ranked in their importance: (i) the maintenance of imperial communications (and that implied good relations with the Dominions as well as a high regard for the welfare of the Colonial Empire); (ii) security of the United Kingdom against German aggression (a modification of Britain's traditional opposition to the hegemony of any one power in Western Europe); (iii) the protection of imperial interests in East Asia (where concern about Japan's encroachments had now completely supplanted the worries about Chinese jingoism which had been expressed by British officials in earlier decades); (iv) the stability of the Mediterranean and Middle East (made more difficult first by the expansion of Italian power and more recently by the outbreak of the Spanish Civil War), and (v) the Russian threat to India. In hindsight some of these contingencies appear far-fetched or fantastic. At the time, however, they crippled Britain's sense of initiative and self-possession.

In the view of His Majesty's Government, involvement in any other issues could only be risked in the knowledge that it would diminish the nation's ability to respond or to survive threats to Britain's vital imperial interests. 'The broad principles on which our Empire strategy has always been based should not be forgotten,' warned the Chiefs of Staff (whose expertise no Government could ignore without running appalling risks), 'nor should the lessons of history be overlooked. The greater

---

* Uncirculated Note concerning DP(P)12, October 1937, RAF Expansion Scheme file, Wier 19/18, Wier Papers, Churchill College, Cambridge, cited in Pritchard, *Far Eastern Influences*, op. cit., p. 48.

our commitments to Europe, the less will be our ability to secure our Empire and its communications.'*

It is scarcely surprising, therefore, that formal military pacts and other alliances were often considered but generally ruled out by Britain's policy-makers, who regarded most such treaties as inflammatory or self-deluding. In the British view, states should be expected to act in their own self-interest. The need was to find the common denominator of self-interest with potential allies that would make formal pacts unnecessary. In the absence of a common basis for such understandings, the prospect of concluding empty alliances with weak and unavailing allies held no charm for the United Kingdom, for while some outsiders saw only the benefits of 'collective security', the British Government appreciated only too well that there was rarely security in the collective. Meanwhile the self-governing British Dominions, whose role and influence tends to be underrated, expressed strong and vocal opposition in public as well as in private against any moves which might involve them in another European holocaust. The security of the greater part of the Empire as well as of the majority of the Dominions was threatened more directly by Japanese expansionism than by German or Italian adventurism.

The only potential ally strong enough to warrant Britain adopting a policy of 'Resistance' against Japanese aggression, the United States, ex-hibited a marked unwillingness to take a full share of the risks. Although sympathetic to Britain's plight, the United States had no wish to become involved in war unnecessarily. Notwithstanding public statements to the contrary, dating from posturing by the American Secretary of State at the time of the Manchurian Incident, Henry L. Stimson, right up to the period of the Munich Agreement and on to the outbreak of the European War in September 1939, the United States privately rebuffed repeated British overtures for consultation and collaboration against all three of the main potential enemies facing the British Empire. While Roosevelt used various incidents as a means of 'educating public opinion' to their common danger, Chamberlain's gradual appreciation that 'it is best to count upon nothing from the Americans but words' expressed only the simple truth.† On the other hand, as the Chiefs of Staff forecast in February 1939, in the kind of three-enemy war which by then looked the most likely prospect,

The British Empire would be threatened simultaneously in Europe, the Medi-terranean and the Far East by an immense aggregate of armed force, which neither our present nor our projected strength is designed to meet, with France as

---

* C P 218(36), Cabinet Memorandum by the Chiefs of Staff, cited in Howard, op. cit., p. 102.
† Feiling, op. cit., p. 324.

20 The *Panay* Incident, 12
December 1937 *Top*: The 450-
ton, 191-foot gunboat USS
Panay settles into the waters
of the Yangtze after being
bombed and strafed by four
Japanese naval aircraft

21 *Centre*: The passengers
and crew of the USS *Panay*
abandon ship and take to the
gunboat's motor launch

22 *Bottom*: HMS *Ladybird*
and the USS *Oahu* arrive at
Shanghai with the USS *Panay*
survivors and the bodies of
those who had been killed in
the attack

23 'Britain possesses what Japan wants and what no other country has – a dominating position in China' *Top*: With government encouragement wall posters appeared during the Tientsin Incident in the summer of 1939

24 *Centre*: HMS *Ladybird* lies in dry dock at Shanghai after bombardment by Colonel Hashimoto Kingoro's artillery in December 1937

25 *Bottom*: The Tientsin Incident, June–August 1939

26 *Top*: A band of Chinese
communist partisans, fleeing
from Kuomintang 'Bandit
Suppression' campaigns, trek
over a pass on the Long
March in search of refuge

27 *Bottom*: Four major
leaders of the Chinese
Communist Party:
Mao Tse-tung, Chou En-lai,
Po Ku and Chu Teh

28 *Top left*: A Japanese
political cartoon

29 *Top right*: Chinese troops
display German light machine-
guns against the backdrop of a
Chinese communist flag

30 *Bottom*: Marshal Chu
Teh, greatest military genius
of the Chinese Communist
Party, poses at the door of an
ambulance donated by the
Chinese Laundry Workers of
New York

31 *Top*: A camel train, following the ancient Silk Road to China, carries across Sinkiang supplies sent through Soviet Central Asia

32 *Bottom*: Russian tank troops rest during a lull in the fight against the Japanese at Nomonhan, May–September 1939

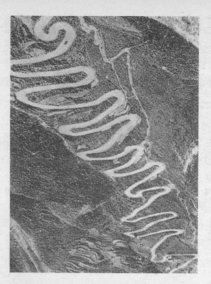

33 *Top left*: The Sino-
American-built Ledo Road
links India, across the
southern slopes of the
Himalayan mountains and
dense jungles, with the Sino-
British-built Burma Road to
China

34 *Top right*: The U S Army
and Chinese coolies, often
working in difficult terrain
without mechanized vehicles,
construct the Ledo Road

35 *Bottom*: A convoy of
Chevrolet trucks, carrying
British markings, stands
against the backdrop of a
Hindu temple in Rangoon

36 A caterpillar tractor of
the US Army Engineering
Corps clears the way for a
convoy of supply trucks
travelling on the Ledo Road

37 *Top*: Chinese troops
disembark from an American
transport aircraft at Myitkyina
Airfield in northern Burma

38 *Bottom*: War-torn
Chungking, capital of Chiang
Kai-shek's régime

our only major ally. *The outcome of the war would be likely to depend on our ability to hold on to our key positions and upon other powers, particularly the United States, coming to our aid.**

Under the circumstances, the thought was harrowing.

If Japan was isolated economically, diplomatically and militarily during the first two and a half years of the Sino-Japanese War, the position of the British Empire was scarcely more enviable. Unlike the United States, the British had vital interests in the Far East. Those interests stood directly in the path of Japanese expansion. Japan could not hope to operate in China without appropriating the use of British-owned railway stock, interfering with British control over Chinese maritime customs and the salt gabelle, upsetting British merchant trading monopolies, and in many other ways disturbing Britain's nearly 50 per cent share in Chinese commercial affairs, a level of investment worth perhaps £500 million at 1937 prices.

Meanwhile Japan had been making itself conspicuously disliked by the classes which had no interest at all in residing in East Asia, but made their living at home in trade. For them, Japan mattered simply because of its commercial policy. In the thirties, this became increasingly competitive. To avoid its national destitution and starvation, Japan balked at nothing in efforts to increase its exports. Under this compulsion, it became notorious as the country hunting for markets, successfully snapping up the old markets of older countries, ruthlessly underbidding, successfully dumping.

Japan, in short, was feared and disliked by everybody in an established position in world trade, who saw its activities with dread. This dislike of Japan for commercial reasons was carried over into an irrational anti-Japanese prejudice. Feeling tilted over and became pro-China and anti-Japan; it was reinforced by a modish fashion among the intelligentsia for all things Chinese. Nevertheless, commercial competition was at the root of the sentiment.

Though feeling was shifting among even local businessmen from being pro-Japanese to being pro-Chinese, the British were resolved to go to great lengths to preserve their formal neutrality. All eyes in Britain were on the European continent. Through it all, however, as we have seen, there remained a constant and interdependent preoccupation in the cloisters of Whitehall with the strategical threat posed by all three of Britain's potential enemies: Germany, Italy and Japan. Their hesitations

---

* DP(P)44, Defence Plans (Policy) Committee Memorandum by the Chiefs of Staff: European Appreciation, 1939–40, 20 February 1939, CAB 16/183A, cited in Pritchard, *Far Eastern Influences*, op. cit., p. 138.

and preoccupations were rooted in an understanding of the world as it was, which was not the world that impatient amateur strategists and wishful thinkers thought it ought to have been.

The day was long past when Britain could afford to defend all her territorial and commercial outposts, and now for the first time in their history the British were confronted by a first-class threat to the eastern half of their Empire, while facing a similar threat in Europe. British defence experts had long anticipated that, in the absence of a two-hemisphere fleet, the next world war could bring about the downfall of the British Commonwealth of Nations at the hands of Japan and Germany: 'Australia, New Zealand, India, Burma, the rich colonies east of Suez and a vast trade would be at their mercy, and the eastern half of the British Empire might well be doomed,' predicted the Defence Requirements Committee.* Since Britain could not afford to build the forces required to give her real protection, it followed that unless sufficient allied support could be found, Britain would have to reach some kind of settlement with Germany or Japan. It was argued at the time that more economies in defence expenditure could be made by adjustments with Germany than with Japan; successful appeasement of Germany would do much to solve Britain's Far Eastern crisis.

Britain's peril in the Far East was one of diplomatic as well as strategical isolation. During July and August 1937 the State Department excused itself from participating in British initiatives to mediate the Sino-Japanese conflict and offered the lame excuse that it did not want the Japanese to feel 'that there is any form of collusion' between the British and Americans. The British wanted something far more definite: a commitment on the part of the United States to share all the risks of a firm policy in the Far East.† At first the British toyed with the idea of imposing sanctions against Japan in the early days of the war, but Chamberlain came to regard sanctions with deep loathing: in view of Japan's unbroken string of victories, 'economic sanctions are not likely to be effective in time to stop the war, and the experience of the Abyssinian affair shows that if unsuccessful they would leave behind them an evil legacy of ill-will and suspicion', he wrote in October. Suppose that Britain, America and the Netherlands East Indies imposed sanctions: 'If the sanctions seemed likely to become really effective Japan

* DRC 37, Third Report of the Defence Requirements Committee, 21 November 1935, CAB 16/112, British Public Record Office, Kew.
† The discussion which follows is based largely upon Pritchard, *Far Eastern Influences*, op. cit., pp. 69–91.

would be rendered desperate. Suppose she then made a sudden or unexpected attack on the possessions of one of the three sanctionist countries?' Were the other two Powers likely to defend the nation which was attacked? Chamberlain had his doubts, since on 5 October 1937, the very day of Roosevelt's famous Quarantine Speech calling for the isolation of aggressors, Under-Secretary of State Sumner Welles had informed the British that 'this country intends not to be drawn into any armed conflict'.

Chamberlain was convinced that 'the only way in which the war could certainly be brought to a close at once would be by the expressed determination on the part of . . . the U.S.A. and H.M.G. to use an over-whelming force to bring compulsion on Japan'. Since the United States specifically rejected all offers to bring Japan to her senses by 'superior sea force', Chamberlain reluctantly concluded that Britain could take no risks on the strength of Roosevelt's rhetoric alone: 'In the present state of European affairs with two dictators in a thoroughly nasty temper, we simply cannot afford to quarrel with Japan, and I very much fear, there-fore, that after a lot of ballyhoo the Americans will somehow fade out and leave us to carry all the blame and the odium.' The Government's chief advisers in the departments concerned were agreed on this point. The Foreign Office, for instance, described British efforts to build an Anglo-American front as a 'sorry failure'; the defence departments had no confidence in Britain's ability to impose sanctions against Japan at a time of great European uncertainty and no assurances of American support; the Treasury view was summed up tersely by its permanent head, Sir Warren Fisher, who remarked: 'However much we denuded European waters our fleet could not hope to defeat Japan in her waters. And we should be at mercy in Europe. The U.S.A. would fail us at the critical moment even in the Far East. Still more would she fail us in our conse-quential danger in Europe.'

Although tempted time and again to dispatch the British battlefleet to Singapore, on each occasion Britain backed down because American support could not be secured and Britain could not afford to present Japan with any economic or naval challenge that might involve Britain in a single-handed naval war. The strafing of the British Ambassador in China, Sir Hughe Knatchbull-Hugessen, in August 1937; the repeated aerial and artillery bombardment suffered by British enclaves in China; Japanese abuse of British property and interference with trade: all of these created a succession of nasty but minor incidents. Similarly, there were incidents between the Americans and the Japanese, which stirred up the blood of the Americans and the hopes of the Chinese. The war was fought at Shanghai in a vastly overcrowded place, and inevitably the bystanders were hit. But the Americans, the British and the French in the area were divided about their policy, and nothing much was done.

Then in mid-December 1937, Japanese Army and naval forces attacked five western warships on the Yangtze: the HMS *Ladybird* and HMS *Bee* were damaged and the USS *Panay* was sunk. That rogue Japanese Army artillery officer, Colonel Hashimotō Kingorō, whom we have already encountered and who was now in charge of the invasion forces at Wuhu, had ordered his guns to open fire on the two British gunboats passing upstream: long afterwards it was confirmed at the Tokyo War Crimes Trial that his intention was to provoke a war with Britain that would lead to the eradication of British influence from China. On the very afternoon of Hashimoto's initiative, the USS *Panay*, an American gunboat, was bombed and sunk after successive attacks carried out by nine Japanese naval fighter aircraft, twelve dive bombers and three high-level bombers. Whether some of the Japanese commanders desired to frighten the United States away, or whether the bombing was a mistake, remains a matter of historical controversy. Those aboard the *Panay* were convinced that the identity of their vessel was clear to the attacking aircraft; however, the attack was carried out by three inexperienced group commanders who had arrived from Japan only eight days before. According to a post-war account by one of the attack leaders, the *Panay* Incident was simply a blunder from start to finish, one which horrified all the Japanese concerned when the facts became known. Reports from the survivors suggested that far from trying to render assistance, the Japanese made every attempt to hunt down and destroy those who had escaped from the vessel, who underwent a harrowing ordeal before they finally reached safety. In the same incident, moreover, two other British gunboats had also been attacked from the air but fortunately had escaped injury. The Japanese forces involved had exhibited great persistence in following up all of these attacks, and the *Ladybird*, the *Bee* and the other two British gunboats were fortunate to escape the fate of the *Panay*.

The British Government, like the American, was infuriated by the affair. At first, Prime Minister Neville Chamberlain was prepared to take any action – including a resort to force if necessary – to halt further Japanese erosion of western interests in China. Despite the risk that such an act might precipitate a pre-emptive strike by Japan, the British battlefleet was prepared to depart for Singapore. The United States Navy was in a war fever after the *Panay* affair, but American policy was in disarray. Roosevelt refused to take any parallel or identical action with Britain which would involve the threat or use of naval power, and he unilaterally accepted Japan's formal apologies and a $2 million indemnity without prior consultation with Britain. Taken by surprise, there was hardly anything that the British could do in the circumstances.

The Americans, however, were not insensible to the need for some sort of collaboration if events like these were to continue. The Incident gave ammunition to those in the United States Navy who wanted to develop Anglo-American naval collaboration against the Japanese, and so Roosevelt, who fondly recollected his own part in such contacts during the First World War, had a few private words with the British Ambassador at the White House, accepted a long-standing offer by the British, and sent Captain Royal Ingersoll of the United States Navy War Plans Division to London for clandestine naval staff talks at the beginning of the new year. These discussions provided an opportunity for the two navies to do little more than exchange opinions rather than to coordinate policies because the Americans divulged little information and refused to make any strategical commitments of any kind. The tone of the conversations was tentative and speculative; as the British had expected, the Americans were friendly but finally had to admit that the United States Navy was not nearly so ready for war as the Royal Navy: the most that the Americans could offer at this stage was to consider the possibility of cooperating in a long-distance naval blockade of Japan to take place after the next incident. Early action, in short, was ruled out, although these conversations were to become only the first of many.

Meanwhile, the American public watched newsreel footage of the attack on the *Panay*, taken by a camera team aboard the gunboat while the Japanese aircraft had pressed home their attack, and as details of the Incident emerged and the findings of the US Naval Court of Enquiry were reported in the press, these powerful graphic images became firmly linked in the public mind with the outrages against the Chinese civil population at Nanking. The Americans were confirmed in their anti-Japanese frame of mind. The tide was running in support of the China lobby which was made up of businessmen, scholars, philanthropists, former missionaries, and other specialists on Asia. Eventually the China lobby was to become one of the powers in the land, but that time had not yet arrived.

The next incident happened sooner than anyone expected. Before Ingersoll could return to Washington, DC, two British policemen were murdered by Japanese soldiers at Shanghai in early January 1938. Once again, Britain, with an irate Neville Chamberlain at the helm, went to the brink of war: the fleet might have been dispatched to the Far East within days, and for a brief moment the will to take such drastic action was manifest. Washington was contacted again. But the Americans, as before, declined to advance one step or give any assurances: indeed, they suggested rather archly that Britain would do well to concentrate on dangers nearer to English shores. Pricked, nay, deflated, by this rebuff and afterwards distracted by the steady increase in European tension in the nine months preceding the Munich Conference at the end of September 1938, the British lost heart. Apart from an ill-judged intervention by Foreign Secretary Anthony Eden (the balance of whose mind was deeply disturbed for some weeks prior to his resignation on doctor's orders in February 1938), the British made no more serious efforts to attract American support against Japan prior to the outbreak of the European War. Confrontations between Japan and the Occidental Powers emerged during 1938 at Shanghai, Tientsin and along the Yangtze, not to mention the Changkufeng Incident on the Korean border with the Soviet Union, but it was evident that the Konoye Cabinet in Tokyo, then preoccupied with the prosecution of its war in China, was doing its best not to antagonize any of the third Powers unnecessarily. The only development that was particularly dangerous occurred when Japanese troops seized Canton in October 1938, following a timetable which the British had known about several weeks before Munich. At this point there was a grave risk that a war might have started through the injudiciousness of local Japanese commanders on the doorstep of Hong Kong. But the Japanese were careful, and the British, who recognized that they stood no chance whatever of rescuing the fabulously wealthy Crown Colony by any defence measures they might take in the event of hostilities, were no longer prepared to respond to anything less than extreme provocation. Without American cooperation, Britain felt powerless against the two most aggressive nations of the world.

The United Kingdom Government also explored the possibility of gaining assistance from the only other make-weight power who might have supplemented rather than dissipated Britain's ability to resist aggression in Europe and East Asia: the Soviet Union. When the Manchurian Incident took place, Soviet land and air forces were the most powerful in the world and were generally regarded as unified and well-commanded. At that time, however, it was unimaginable that the United Kingdom would ever welcome Soviet assistance in establishing a common defence against Germany. The prospect of Soviet naval assistance in enforcing sanctions against Japan was equally uninviting. Politically unreliable and even hostile, the Soviet Union made no secret of its ambition to export the Bolshevik Revolution abroad, and that was reason enough to avoid taking Moscow into British confidence on military as well as on political matters, particularly when the consequences of any collaboration between the two powers would be bound to heighten international tension and war fever. Britain's potential enemies were already aware, after all, that they were liable to a Soviet attack if their backs were turned; clear evidence of British complicity in a policy of 'encirclement' would have forced Britain's enemies to attack or face destruction. By the time Britain was morally certain that she was unlikely to be able to avoid war within the more or less immediate future, Stalin's great military purges were believed – almost certainly rightly – to have disembowelled the Soviet armed forces. From the end of 1936, therefore, Britain could not anticipate any help from the Soviet Union in the struggles ahead, although London was quite prepared to welcome whatever help Moscow might provide of Russia's own accord after the outbreak of hostilities.

As for an alliance with France, during most of the 1930s the general opinion in Whitehall regarded that prospect as having little to recommend it. A few francophiles, notably within the Foreign Office and War Office, took exception to this view, but on the whole the cost of a 'Continental Commitment', which would have been the inevitable consequence of any meaningful alliance with France, was not regarded as commensurate with imperial self-preservation at a time when the globe was dominated by a loose alignment of great potential enemies. Even before the advent of Hitler to power, that commitment would have required of Britain the creation of an army incomparably larger than what those responsible for Britain's defence believed the nation could afford at a time when Britain already was fully stretched to meet what experts in Whitehall regarded as the Empire's minimum requirements in naval and air forces. London's objective in Europe as in East Asia was rather to foster international economic development and peaceful political evolution. Should Britain find itself at war with Germany, no one believed that France would stand aside. Just as Britain did not expect to dictate to the French how to deploy their huge land forces and whatever small British contingent might join them, so the British did not accept that the French would have any choice but to accept British direction when it came to war at sea. Premature disclosure to Paris about British naval war plans would only shock the French (and possibly lead to leaks of information) after the French appreciated Britain's resolve to abandon the naval defence of the Mediterranean to the French in order to dispatch the British fleet to the Pacific if Japan joined in the fighting as Britain expected. In maintaining her freedom of action for as long as possible, Britain gained rather more than she lost by delaying prior consultation with France about the forging of some kind of common strategy. Imperial defence had to come first. In fact, what the newly appointed Deputy-Chief of the Naval Staff, Admiral Cunningham, found to his amazement just after Munich was that apart from war plans against Japan, 'there were no naval plans at all'!*

The French, however keen to make an alliance with Britain, saw British imperialism as an obstruction to the development of a postive programme of opposition to German aggressive designs. At best the French regarded Britain's imperial defence priorities as a flimsy excuse for inactivity which had the effect of feeding Germany's boundless appetite and development while abandoning the possibility of playing any constructive role in policing the peace of Europe (although not the world) in support of France: as Edouard Daladier, the French Prime Minister at the time of Munich, confided several months afterwards to the American Ambassador in Paris, 'England had become so feeble and senile that the British would give away every possession of their friends rather than stand up to Germany and Italy.'† By contrast France, as the sympathetic contemporary historian Arnold Wolfers wrote in 1940,

may initially have acted only from fear of another German invasion, [but] her policy of security had led her to become the champion of the *status quo* and of the entire order of Central as well as of Western Europe. Her anxiety was, therefore, that of a nation with responsibilities truly continental in character and extent.‡

When in December 1938 the French looked round and counted the divisions which Appeasement had 'lost' to them (or so they felt) in Central Europe, they derided Britain's precious forces and demanded of her '*un effort du sang*'.§ Shamed and made desperate by events, Britain soon obliged. France did not.

The setting in of the war in earnest brought a decisive change in the attitude of the westerners. Sentiment, which among some classes in Britain, for example, had for some time been anti-Japanese, hardened; and it spread throughout most sections of the people, at least of those, admittedly a minority, who thought it necessary to take a view about such a distant part of the world.

The change was marked in the early period of the China Incident.

* Cunningham of Hyndhope, *A Sailor's Odyssey*, Hutchinson, London, 1951, p. 195.
† Adamthwaite, op. cit., doc. 67.
‡ A. Wolfers, *Britain and France between Two Wars*, Norton, New York, 1966 (reprint), p. 20.
§ Howard, op. cit., p. 126; Peden, op. cit., p. 182.

Westerners with foreign contacts, especially the businessmen resident in the Far East, had on the whole been well disposed to Japan. Japan professed to be the champion of foreign business interests. It claimed to be taking steps – in putting down bandits, in removing the Chinese officials who were the bane of traders – which the other countries had taken it upon themselves to do from time to time in the past and which they would have continued to do had they the resolution to stand up for their interests without regard for distractions elsewhere. Chinese xenophobia was the enemy of all who had to do with China. And, for a long while, Japanese action received a great deal of sympathy from certain sections of westerners.

This view continued to be held, at least until the China Incident merged with the Second World War. Not only a section of the business world but many of their diplomatic and military counterparts maintained their regard for Japan. They became progressively smaller in number as the years passed, but they still remained powerful in influence. They thought that no comparison was possible between the Japanese – clever, energetic, industrious, above all disciplined and punctual – and the Chinese, who, if they were clever, had all the faults which went with political impotence; who were corruptible, were voluble in justifying the inexcusable, were argumentative without being convincing to many of the western representatives whose opinions mattered in the propounding of their respective national responses to the developing East Asian Conflict. These westerners, from the less admirable specimens to some very astute observers indeed, liked the Japanese way of life, Japanese discipline and Japanese customs: though it should be noted that most of the things they admired were regarded by educated Japanese, who had continued to revere many standards from their past, as vulgar. They liked the solidity of the buildings in western style which the Japanese had put up. Some of the westerners even felt that the Japanese had very sensible ideas about the status of women. A few of its would-be admirers understood the genius of Japan to be aesthetic, non-intellectual, and non-acquisitive, were inclined to excuse the dramatic passions within Japanese society as but redeemable manifestations of temporary enthusiasms, and, taking the culture as a whole, saw that while it cultivated the art-forms of force it strove to avoid the necessity of any resort to arms. These considerations, however, were merely the contentious reflections of the few, and were of no concern to pragmatists.

Of great significance was the fact that the admirers of Japan were not unchallenged among the guardians of western interests in the East. A rival section of western residents in Treaty Ports had backed the rise of the new China. From among these there was, it is true, not at first a strong condemnation of Japan. Most of these people felt, secretly if not openly, that China had been moving too fast and too far, and that chastisement by Japan would bring it to reason. A series of murders and outrages had occurred in previous years: and Nanking did its cause no good by obvious deception and the pretence that it could not unravel the circumstances.

Western businessmen were less far-sighted, less impersonal than their Governments. They had also a sense of racial superiority, although some had abandoned it in the case of Japan, since the Japanese had demonstrated that they could not be pushed around. Business was conscious of the great advantage of living in concessions under an extra-territorial régime. It lamented the fact that negotiation had begun for their abolition, and that many concessions had already been surrendered: it saw itself vitally threatened. There were some men of vision among them, who looked ahead and saw the future; but these men were rare. American businessmen in spite of their general liberalism and of the pro-Chinese sentiment of many of their countrymen, were endowed with more than their share of the same temper as their European counterparts.

However, as the great offensive of the Japanese began to take shape and its direction passed from the Japanese civilian, whom the western businessmen used to know, into the hands of arrogant generals, with whom they did not feel at home, they began more and more to change their minds. The fear grew that it was the Japanese, not the Chinese, who would chase them out of the concessions. Japan was spending its blood and treasure to make China into a place fit for a person to live in; but the Japanese intended that it was to be a Japanese businessman, an agent of the Mitsui and the Mitsubishi, not the foreigner – whom the Japanese regarded as more undesirable than the Chinese. The western traders or industrialists saw that if they lost the protection under which they were living, they would not have a very long tenure of life. By controls, by subsidies, by taxation, by withholding permits to move their capital and profits out of the country, Japan would be able to drive them away in a brief time, and in less than ten years, perhaps, the concessions would be no more.

Thus the change of attitude had become almost universal, and the businessmen of the West who regarded the East were as anxious as the Chinese when in July 1937 the fighting began in earnest. At least they could console themselves that there was an end for the time being to the negotiations for the return of the concessions. The Chinese defence of Shanghai happened before their eyes, and the destruction which the Sino-Japanese conflict threatened to bring upon that city outraged more than it terrified westerners who witnessed it. An epitome of western reactions to this earliest phase of the war can be found in a succession of reports sent to London by the Commander-in-Chief of the China Station, Vice-Admiral Sir Charles Little, who watched the battle from his flagship. Reviewing the harrowing events of October 1937, he wrote of 'inexcusable carelessness and lack of control of subordinates, the use of modern weapons which have outstripped in their rapid evolution the until recently medieval brains that try to control them'.* A month later, as the Japanese moved forward to lay siege to Nanking, Sir Charles remained preoccupied by the lessons of the battle at Shanghai:

Depressing and nerve-wracking as the active military operations carried on round the defence perimeter . . . have been for the British community at Shanghai, they have always clung to the idea, fostered by the events of 1927 and 1932, that as soon as the 'cease fire' was sounded, somehow or other 'business as usual' would be the order of the day.

Of course there are exceptions and far-seeing people realise, as I am afraid it is the regrettable truth, that with Japanese domination, added to the blocking of the Yangtse and the reduction of trade at all the 'Treaty' ports, the troubles of Shanghai are only really commencing. It is already evident that with their narrow-minded, petty-fogging ideas, the Japanese mean to assert their rights, qua rights, in the Settlement, to possess themselves of everything they possibly can Chinese or destroy it and to squeeze and hinder the Foreigner.

With a broader outlook on the future and a magnanimous policy towards Foreign interests the Japanese are in a position to gain for themselves the respect and almost the gratitude of Foreigners, to their ultimate great advantage. For the Japanese though, such a far-sighted course is impossible! †

The Chinese did not lose hope of entangling foreign powers, including Britain, in the war as it moved through its successive stages. In August 1937, as the events took place that Sir Charles Little witnessed, two Japanese aircraft, perhaps unaware of who was their prey, machine-gunned from the air a motor car on the way from Shanghai to Nanking. In it was Sir Hughe Knatchbull-Hugessen, known as 'Snatch', the then British Ambassador in China. He was seriously wounded, and for a few days this nearly fatal accident, to which we have already alluded, caused an electric tension. But the British could do little more than protest, given that the Japanese military and civil authorities were plainly horror-struck by the event (and that none concerned was as keen to report the

* China General Letter 18, Report of Proceedings of the Commander-in-Chief, China, for the period 4–31 October 1937, 15 November 1937, Adm. 116/3683.

† China General Letter 19, Report of Proceedings of the Commander-in-Chief, China, for the period 1–30 November 1937, 14 December 1937, Adm. 116/3683.

circumstances of the 'accident' as eagerly as they were prepared to offer the British financial compensation for it). The incident was closed by an exchange of notes that were meant to save everybody's face. (Sir Hughe thus goes down in history as a diplomat who was nearly murdered and started a war. 'Snatch' is remembered also as the Ambassador in Turkey who had the plans of the Second Front filched by his valet who gave them to the Germans: Fortunately, the Germans could not credit their good fortune and assumed that false information was being planted on them.)

Moreover, that succession of incidents to which we have already referred involving Japanese attacks pressed home against western gunboats on the Yangtze, followed by the Rape of Nanking after barely six months of warfare, raised western discomfort to an acute level, purging for a time whatever cynicism the western businessman and his guardians might have striven to cultivate.

Western military and diplomatic observers nonetheless never lacked confidence in their ability to act far more objectively than their business compatriots in dealing with the Chinese and Japanese. The great western financial and commercial houses of the East, together with their trading associations and other pressure groups, ceaselessly plied their Government contacts with local tittle-tattle, opinions and representations. This certainly helped to condition the attitudes of western consular staff towards individual Chinese and Japanese personalities with whom they came into contact. The indomitable moral and physical courage of these merchant princes in the face of Japanese discrimination, persecution and threats cannot but excite one's admiration, and their correspondence, preserved in the records of the China Association, the Swire Archives and elsewhere, like the Fugger newsletters of the sixteenth century, offer historians useful insights into the local conditions experienced by agents of the various companies. Broadly speaking, the foreign tycoons in China showed far more fortitude than, say, the British community in Malaya or Burma. But western businessmen, like their missionary counterparts, had a negligible influence upon the course of the evolving western strategical relationship with Japan and China during these years.

The British Ambassador in Tokyo, Sir Robert Craigie, fought out a battle on what should be British policy towards the war with Sir Archibald John Kerr Clark Kerr, the successor to Knatchbull-Hugessen in China. Clark Kerr had spent most of his career in the Middle East, North Africa and in a cluster of South American banana republics. He was what can be delicately described as an acquired taste. He also had pronounced left-wing views, which were in favour of Britain supporting China on grounds of plain international morality. China was weak, was being bullied, and, he thought, should be protected. On this, at least, he had the advantage of reflecting the sentimentality of most of the western democratic nations of the day.

Craigie, in Tokyo, possessed one of the keenest intellects in the British diplomatic service of his day. He was fully convinced of the benefits which Britain had derived from the Anglo-Japanese Alliance, as long as this had existed. He saw the best hope in working for a revival of the spirit of Anglo-Japanese friendship which had marked the period of that Alliance. He was to a great extent conditioned by his lifelong knowledge of naval affairs (his father and both grandfathers had been admirals in the Royal Navy). His expertise in British naval arms control policy formulation was unsurpassed: he had been involved with the subject ever since attending the Washington Naval Conference, and he knew that throughout the years since the First World War its ultimate success or failure had always turned upon the (in)security of the various powers in the Pacific region. Moreover, he came to his duties in Tokyo after having served with distinction as Head of the American Bureau of the Foreign Office: he knew the political temperature of Washington, better than almost anyone in Whitehall, and his career was strongly influenced by his marriage to a Southern belle. He had also spent a sufficient period of service in the British Department of Overseas Trade to have reinforced his better than average sensitivity to Britain's commercial interests abroad. Although a man of his calibre would have made quite an impact upon the relation of the British Empire to the China Incident in any event, he was able to give effective voice to the pro-Japanese views of the British Embassy.

Unfortunately for Craigie, his critics made capital of the extent to which he made use of contacts served up to him by his military attaché, Major-General F. S. G. Piggott: Whitehall wits coined the word 'Piggottry' to describe those who shared the general's peculiarly romantic view of Japanese history. There is no doubt that Piggott's uncritical adulation of Japanese militarism did much to undermine his Ambassador's effectiveness at home.

The divergent views of the two British representatives, at Chungking and at Tokyo, inevitably clashed with vigour in the telegrams and reports. Those who took part in this conflict were convinced that the issue was of first importance. They did not fail to recognize that the attention of London was often otherwise engaged, and that their respective views were not treated very seriously within the Foreign Office. Yet in higher circles still, within the apparatus of the Committee of Imperial Defence and the Cabinet itself, the views of both men, but especially of Craigie, commanded attention. Time after time, however, they mainly contributed to a palpable sense of unease, malaise and vacillation: and so for the most part the voice of one or the other was used to nullify that of his opposite number.

Although Britain continued to adopt a policy considerably stiffer in the Far East than in Europe, there were major attempts to reach a limited understanding between Britain and Japan in the summer of 1938. In part these discussions, which were held in Tokyo between Ambassador Sir Robert Craigie and Foreign Minister Ugaki Kazushige, dealt with a formidable list of outstanding claims and complaints against Japanese behaviour detrimental to British interests in China. The Japanese countered this list with a demand that Britain should cease to support Chiang Kai-shek and should 'cooperate' with Japan in developing China. The British flatly refused to accept these suggestions, and the talks led to no significant improvements in the situation. Failure to reach an agreement led to an undermining of moderate elements in the Japanese Cabinet and the fall of Foreign Minister Ugaki, a man genuinely well disposed towards the Western Powers.

By 1939, as the clouds of war darkened steadily over Europe, many businessmen in East Asia recognized that their bright day was over: and that, once the Treaty Port system was disbanded, it would not be set up again. In this year there was a humiliation of occidental businessmen and other residents in Tientsin which profoundly affected the climate of official opinion in western capital cities. The European War was about to begin, although there were hopes in many quarters that Hitler as well as Mussolini could be deterred from further aggression. The British Government seemed preoccupied with that, and so far as the ever-speculative press reports of the day could discern, there was little faith or hope that the British authorities were prepared to do much for their countrymen in Shanghai or Tientsin.

In fact, however, the long-standing friction between the Japanese and the British at Tientsin escalated into a major international incident. To some extent the French Concession in the city was also drawn into the affair. Over the past few years, the diplomatic storm created during the Tientsin Crisis has become recognized as an important development in the breakdown of order that accompanied the China Incident and preceded the European War. Between June and August 1939 it even threatened to become the proximate cause of the next world war. From the perspective of Anglo-Japanese relations, the Tientsin affair was regarded – by all of the countries concerned – as far more serious than the machine-gunning of the hapless British Ambassador to China at the outbreak of the China Incident, or even the Japanese air attacks and artillery bombardments directed against British gunboats on the Yangtze in December 1937. Indeed, the only Anglo-Japanese confrontation during the China Incident which really compares with that at Tientsin was the Burma Road dispute in the darkest days of 1940 (to which we shall return in due course). Nevertheless, its peaceful outcome, coupled with the outbreak of the European War only a week and a half after pressure upon the British and French Concessions at Tientsin was relaxed by the Japanese, has led many historians to overlook or to doubt that both Britain and Japan had been determined to stand fast if the diplomatic negotiations failed or in case a direct military clash had ensued. In particular, Japanese commanders at Tientsin, as well as military and civilian leaders in Tokyo, assumed that London was bluffing in issuing warnings that the British fleet – or at any rate a major part of it – might depart for the Pacific if the situation deteriorated. A closer examination of the evidence, however, leads to completely different conclusions. So important are the wider implications of this struggle that it is worth examining in some detail.

First, the reader must appreciate that the whole issue pivots around what Britain planned to do in case of war. As is now widely known, Britain's contingency plans long envisaged the immediate dispatch of the main fleet to Singapore in the event of hostilities against Japan. The risks attendant in actually taking such a step were self-evident, and it is a common error to conclude that there was never much danger that the British Government would ever have been willing to take such a course, unilaterally, whatever the provocation. In the end, private reservations within the minds of military planners may exert a powerful and perhaps decisive influence in the formulation and execution of national defence and foreign policy. There is some truth, after all, in the cynical view that the art of contingency planning – in which the defence services contrive to establish plausible justifications for the construction of the most formidable forces which they feel their political masters can be persuaded to underwrite – is altogether a different matter from putting into execution operations which planners privately regard as wholly unrealistic. Not surprisingly, there were acrimonious differences of opinion within the British Foreign Office, the War Office, and – most importantly of all – the Admiralty during the period that culminated in the Tientsin Crisis. During the eight months between Munich and the unexpected eruption of the Tientsin dispute in June 1939, there occurred two 'palace revolutions' within the Admiralty. The importance and depth of these 'revolutions' and their effect upon British strategical policy towards Japan during the

Tientsin affair are comparable in significance to the eclipse of the *Kōdō* Group in Japan on the eve of the China Incident.

The two bodies that actually made Britain's war plans, the Chiefs of Staff and their Joint Planning Sub-Committee, began a sweeping re-evaluation of their strategical assumptions shortly after Munich. The basic assumption underlying their traditional 'Appreciation' of what to expect in case Britain became involved in hostilities in East Asia was no longer remotely tenable – that is, the idea that 'The European situation makes us entirely confident that European Powers will remain strictly neutral, and will not take advantage of our commitments in the Far East to prejudice our interests in other parts of the world.'*

Certainly the Admiralty needed no prompting by anyone before re-considering Britain's basic naval strategy. Admiral Chatfield, Britain's Chief of Naval Staff from the beginning of the decade, had never wavered in his determination to protect the East Asian half of the Empire with the main fleet in any war against Japan. However, he lost most of his influence over the Admiralty when he replaced the unfortunate Sir Thomas Inskip as Minister for the Co-ordination of Defence after Munich. The new Chief of Naval Staff, Sir Roger Backhouse, wasted no time in clearing the Admiralty of his predecessor's predilections by reorganizing key Admiralty departments. The Plans Department he left intact, but he invited Admiral Drax, the brilliant and acerbic former Commander-in-Chief, Plymouth, to advise the Admiralty on war plans as an independent voice before moving on to be principal A D C to the King (Backhouse's own previous posting). Drax shared the rising discontent of many senior line officers and relished his new appointment. Within a short period, he effectively smashed axioms which had governed naval policy for many years. Writing in mid-January 1939, Drax observed:

In our war plans, so far as I can ascertain, no details have been worked out for any offensive operations of major importance either by the Home or Mediterranean fleets . . . I venture the opinion that, if Japan joins our enemies, we should incur very great risks to the heart of our Empire if we dispatch our fleet too early to the Far East. The only hope for the Far East is, not to get active help from America (that, alas, is asking too much) but at least to persuade the USA to move their whole fleet to the Pacific in order to 'keep the Japs guessing' and delay their entry into the war.†

* DP(P)S, 14 June 1937, CAB 16/182, British Public Record Office, Kew. The importance and context of the Tientsin dispute are discussed at greater length in Pritchard, *Far Eastern Influences*, op. cit., pp. 127–68, from which the following discussion borrows freely.

† Memorandum by Admiral Sir Reginald A. R. Plunkett-Ernle-Erle Drax, 20 January 1939, Drax 2/19, Drax Papers, Churchill College Archives, Cambridge.

These views coincided with Backhouse's own. The new Chief of Naval Staff thought the Japanese fleet was too powerful to oppose while Britain was refitting her older vessels and behind schedule in building new ones, particularly if Britain should have to fight Italy as well as Germany in the West. That seems plain enough to us, but it was a radical notion at a time when Britain's Navy was the strongest afloat. With the significant exception of the Director of Plans, Captain Danckwerts, who clung to Britain's traditional policies and was roundly rebuked by his superiors, sentiment within the Admiralty shifted behind the First Sea Lord in opposing the dispatch of the fleet to the Far East.

Meanwhile, higher authorities dealt with the implications of Far Eastern naval strategy. They met to consider a new appraisal prepared by the Joint Planning Committee (including the errant Captain Danckwerts) on behalf of the Chiefs of Staff Committee (including Admiral Backhouse). The document was called the 1939/40 European Appreciation.

In late February 1939 the Chiefs of Staff endorsed the Joint Planning Sub-Committee's draft. When it reached the Committee of Imperial Defence (on which Ministers sat with the most senior officials responsible for the Empire's security), the Ministers were stunned. For the first time, the strategical authorities had provided the Government with a grand review of a war against Japan, Germany and Italy in combination, no holds barred. The distinction which hitherto had existed between a European War and a Far Eastern War was blurred to an extent which was quite novel. Even were peace between Britain and Japan maintained, British interests in East Asia would soon wither away during a general European War. If Japan stayed out, the force of Anglo-French naval and economic power would be superior to that of Germany and Italy, but enemy army and air forces would surpass those of the Allies. Even so, once any European War began, a significant proportion of Britain's military and air strength would have to be diverted immediately to the Pacific and to staging points along the route there as a precaution against Japanese attack. Moreover, as the Chiefs of Staff already were aware, air squadrons in the East must have the latest types of aircraft: notwithstanding critical shortages of modern aircraft in Britain's metropolitan forces, nothing less would suffice against Japan.

If Japan formally entered the war alongside Italy or Germany, a British fleet strong enough to hold Japan must proceed to East Asian waters at once: again, no half-measures would contain the Japanese. This finding, too, coincided with what the Chiefs of Staff themselves had declared in recent advice to an Expert Committee on the Defence of India (which

Chatfield had chaired): 'We feel it right to point out that, while by force of circumstances we are bound to take risks in assessing the minimum defence requirements in certain parts of the Empire, we should not be justified in doing so at Singapore.'* It followed that in the light of more recent developments, including the Japanese occupation of Hainan and the Canton area of South-East China (surrounding Hong Kong), 'any alteration to our general naval plan of operations is unlikely. Far from any probability that naval dispositions can enable us to dispense with the military and air force requirements [in Malaya], their presence becomes all the more essential.'† Nevertheless, once the fleet departed for the Pacific, Anglo-French control in the Mediterranean could be expected to vanish after a short struggle. German and Italian influence over South-East Europe would mushroom. Enemy access to oil and other essential supplies in the western theatre would be greatly facilitated. The Middle East would tumble into the Axis camp. Thus the attitude of Japan would determine the degree of British ascendency or retreat throughout the Mediterranean and Middle East. If the war escalated into a three-enemy rather than a two-enemy conflict, then Anglo-French forces, alone, stood no reasonable hope of victory without the intervention of other Powers, particularly the United States.

When the Committee of Imperial Defence considered the European Appreciation in late February 1939, the First Lord of the Admiralty, Lord Stanhope, revealed the first signs of the change of heart in naval circles by suggesting that perhaps one or two capital ships would be enough to deter Japan from any adventure against British territory, considering Japan's own fear of attack by Russia or the United States. Prime Minister Chamberlain hesitated. Chatfield managed to stave off changes in policy for the moment. A select Strategical Appreciation Committee (SAC) was established to examine the Appreciation further.

From the first meeting of the SAC, an open feud existed between Backhouse and Chatfield. Chatfield argued that Britain's position had not deteriorated so much that it was impossible to protect the East Asian interests of the Empire. True, Italy was now regarded as a probable enemy in addition to Japan and Germany, but that was less important. Admiral Backhouse, however, thought that this made a tremendous difference. Britain's modernization was lagging. The Japanese fleet was fully modernized. Would any squadron that Britain might send be 'capable of acting as a deterrent'? Backhouse now called into ques-

---

* COS 805, 14 December 1938, CAB 53/42, British Public Record Office, Kew.
† ibid.

tion the very idea of a Far Eastern squadron, but Chatfield remained adamant: even if Britain found herself at war against all three potential enemies, 'We should have to send a fleet to the Far East ... If we sent seven [capital] ships, that would still leave us with six at home, which, with the seven French capital ships, would be a reasonable force. We must do this, or risk the Empire.' *

At this point, William Strang, representing the Foreign Office at the SAC, interjected that France had not yet heard officially of Britain's intention to send any fleet to the Pacific in certain eventualities. On the contrary, France had been told that Britain's contribution to the common cause would be mostly by air and sea. In French eyes the decisive theatre was Europe. Backhouse seized upon this as an additional reason for trying to knock Italy out of the war at the start, a complete reversal of previous strategy. This tipped the balance. The War Office and Air Ministry were enchanted by the prospect of an easy victory over Italy, and the SAC agreed that the French should be told that in the event of war an early offensive was envisaged by Britain against Italy with French cooperation. The SAC also decided 'that it is undesirable, if it can be avoided, to make any further communications to the Dominions as to the limitation in the size of the fleet' that might be sent to the East in case of trouble with Japan. These recommendations were condemned by Chatfield, who continued to demand political solutions that would avoid war against all three enemies at once. But if world war was inevitable, then he would prefer to abandon the Mediterranean rather than Britain's imperial obligations in East Asia: 'It would be better to lose the Empire by fighting than by default,' he said grimly. 'In the first case it would be an honourable defeat; in the second case it would be a disgrace.' †

As Minister for the Co-ordination of Defence, Chatfield ordered the Admiralty to present their views in writing to the SAC. This formal demand caused uneasiness in the Admiralty: they were uncertain what the SAC – and particularly Chatfield with his formidable mastery of naval affairs and political infighting – would do with the Admiralty's reply. Backhouse's new Deputy Chief of Naval Staff, Sir Andrew Cunningham, therefore emphasized that strategical circumstances could change rapidly: it might not be wise to commit the Admiralty to any specific policy 'until we are able to judge how the war is going'.‡

---

* SAC 4, 28 February 1939; SAC 1(39)1, 1 March 1939; SAC 2(39)2, 13 March 1939, all in CAB 16/209, British Public Record Office, Kew.

† ibid., SAC 2(39)2.

‡ Backhouse to Stanhope, 30 March 1939, Adm. 1/9897, British Public Record Office, Kew.

Taking a less cautious view, one in keeping with his maverick position, Admiral Drax wrote a detailed account of measures which he believed met the twin threats of war in Europe and in East Asia. Although he expressed a willingness to send a small detachment of ships to the Pacific at the outbreak of hostilities against Japan, he set two tests to establish whether any major transfer of forces should take place:

(a) that our main fleet in the Far East can do more towards rapidly winning the war than if it is kept in Europe;

(b) that the 'holding force' we have sent East is failing to maintain its object, and therefore there is real danger that the Japanese may shortly do us some vital damage.*

In Admiral Drax's estimation, neither precondition was liable to occur within the first six months of war. He closed with an emphatic warning: Britain's unconditional policy to send the main fleet to the Pacific in the event of a conflict with Japan 'constitutes a grave danger to the Empire and might easily lead to its complete ruin'.†

Drax's memorandum did impress the Admiralty: that much is clear. His detailed but bold proposals encouraged the First Lord to complain that the nominal Director of Plans, Captain Danckwerts, 'seems to afford the Navy no opportunity of helping to win the war and to be purely defensive'.‡ Backhouse himself went so far as to write in an internal Admiralty minute that 'It would certainly be very serious if Singapore fell to the Japanese but it would not necessarily mean, in my opinion, the loss of our Eastern Empire for all time.'§ He preferred to stress the shattering effect which the loss of Egypt and Suez would have upon British prestige round the world. Backhouse's thoughts and those of the new men he had brought into power with him departed so radically from Britain's traditional naval strategy that the Admiralty decided to return the vaguest possible written answers to Chatfield and the SAC. It was an old and favourite tactic of the Admiralty when faced with outside threats to its authority. Even Lord Chatfield found himself unable to grapple with a policy which was so non-committal. In oral explanations, the Admiralty convinced the SAC – and more importantly convinced Neville Chamberlain – that it was time to abandon in all but name Britain's long-standing guarantees of naval protection to the Pacific Dominions against Japan.

---

* Memorandum by Drax, 16 March 1939, Adm. 1/9897.

† ibid.

‡ Minute by Stanhope, 2 April 1939, Adm. 1/9897.

§ M.01188/39, Minute by Backhouse, 24 March 1939/Adm. 1/9909.

It should not be supposed, however, that the victory of Backhouse's men in this, the first of our two 'palace revolutions', was totally convincing. A gulf continued to exist between the Admiralty and the Far Eastern experts at the Foreign Office, where G. G. Fitzmaurice (an admiral's son) complained that the Admiralty displayed 'such a fatuous degree of complacency and ignorance of Far Eastern realities that sometimes I think we ought to let them know'.* The Permanent Under-Secretary at the Foreign Office, Sir Alexander Cadogan, privately called Admiral Cunningham 'King Half-wit' and Stanhope an 'exhibit'.†

The War Office, too, raised doubts about the new course set by the Admiralty, criticizing a recent paper from the Admiralty which suggested that Japan would rather bide her time and digest China than launch an unprovoked war against Britain. The War Office disagreed: 'Japan has been led on politically by her expanding military objectives until she is uncertain where to stop both politically and militarily. It is not certain what the extent of her present object is, as the Japanese are themselves uncertain how far to go.' ‡ Notwithstanding the recent recommendations by the SAC, the War Office insisted that 'Our general policy is already fixed – to retain our hold on Singapore at all costs and to do what is possible to protect our interests in China. This should be a sufficient guide to our actions whatever course Japan may adopt.'§ Clearly, remarks such as these demonstrate something of the extent of the residual influence of the Chatfield or Far Eastern school. The revival of that faction a month later, therefore, may seem less surprising in view of the fact that in the Foreign Office, in the War Office, and even in planning circles at the Admiralty itself, there remained a well of sentiment throughout this period which tapped a sense that Britain had to defend imperial interests in East Asia more or less irrespective of dangers elsewhere.

Meanwhile, the extra naval power which it was now policy to use in Europe, once the Committee of Imperial Defence and the SAC had agreed to ignore the risks of war against Japan, momentarily appeared to offer a chance for changing the European strategical balance. Against Italy, in particular, the fleet might enable Britain to deal Mussolini such devastating blows that he could not survive. Before this prospect was recognized as an illusion, British defence planning grew increasingly muddled during the spring and summer of 1939, and Ministers took

---

* F 2798/471/61, Minute by G. G. Fitzmaurice, 28 March 1939, FO 371/23544.
† D. Dilks (ed.), *The Diaries of Sir Alexander Cadogan*, Cassell, London, 1971, pp. 169, 176.
‡ War Office Memorandum regarding JP 415, unsigned, 22 May 1939, WO 106/131.
§ ibid.

political decisions, such as Britain's new commitments to states already on the brink of collapse in Central Europe and the Balkans, without the benefit of sound strategical advice.

These new undertakings seriously compromised Britain's already weak position in East Asia. While attention remained focused upon Europe, Britain's newly revised global strategy – which depended upon an ability to maintain a naval offensive in the Mediterranean from the outbreak of war – began to fail its first major trial at Tientsin.

Although Britain and France had squabbled with Japan over complex local difficulties at Tientsin almost since the start of the China Incident in July 1937, the situation had remained deadlocked due to gross mishandling by both sides. To bring further pressure upon Britain (and, indirectly, France), the Japanese had imposed a makeshift blockade in mid-December 1938, curtailing entry and exit and restricting commercial traffic between the British Concession and the outside. These measures continued until General Kuwaki, the Japanese Army commander at Tientsin, was replaced by the relatively pro-British Lieutenant-General Honma Masaharu, who had been the Japanese military attaché in London at the height of the Manchurian Incident. In early February 1939 Honma temporarily relaxed the controls, much to the relief of the British.

Then, in the first week of March, Honma's soldiers began erecting barricades and live-wire entanglements, completely surrounding the British and French Concessions. Ostensibly this was in self-defence, counteracting the activities of 'anti-Japanese' elements operating from the relative safety of the Concessions. The British and French troops were brought to combat readiness.

Although weak in military terms, morale remained high in the British Concession. Evidently the French garrison was equally resolute. Brigadier A. H. Hopwood, Officer Commanding the British Forces in Tientsin, tried to improve the static defences of the British Concession and was determined to stand fast over British rights no matter what consequences might ensue. The War Office was sympathetic to Hopwood's stance and – astonishingly – derived some comfort from the view that 'What will weigh with the Japanese . . . is not the degree of strength of the local garrison but the fact that if they start a fight it means war.'

If Honma was proving an unpredictable quantity in his new role as commander of the Japanese Garrison at Tientsin, so were his two immediate superiors. It was more than coincidental that the original blockade in December 1938 had occurred as General Sugiyama Hajime became Commander-in-Chief of the North China Area Army in place of General

Terauchi (who went back to Tokyo to rusticate as a 'Supreme War Councillor'). Sugiyama's second-in-command, Major-General Yamashita Tomoyuki, likewise, had been appointed Chief of Staff of the North China Area Army only recently, and in high Japanese circles it was known that he had little care whether war with Britain resulted or not. This uncompromising attitude, in fact, was welcomed by the War Ministry and by the Army General Staff in Tokyo, who reasoned that Britain would try to avoid war but in any event posed no serious obstacle to Japan. At worst, war with Britain would align Japan with Germany at a moment when a European War already seemed imminent.

The next stage occurred when the manager of the Japanese-sponsored Federal Reserve Bank at Tientsin, who had just been appointed Superintendent of Customs, was assassinated by a Chinese terrorist. After being invited by the municipal authorities to assist, the Japanese helped to conduct a series of searches throughout the Concession. A number of arrests were made, and it was in the course of these that four Chinese detained by the British were accused by the Japanese of complicity in the deaths of three Japanese soldiers. Without conclusive proof to substantiate these charges, the matter languished until June, by which time Honma had grown weary of Britain's failure to comply with Japanese demands. The Japanese insisted that all four of the suspected terrorists should be surrendered to them. The Japanese also required that the British should hand over the precious silver reserves which the canny Kuomintang Government had deposited in British banks within the Concession: acceding to this Japanese demand not only could be expected to demoralize the morale of Chiang Kai-shek's supporters but might also have precipitated a catastrophic collapse in the value of his régime's currency and a strengthening of the Japanese puppet régime headed by Wang Ching-wei. Pressed to accept these and other radical demands, the British, perhaps predictably, refused: and in consequence the Japanese imposed a close blockade of the British Concession on 14 June 1939. People still went in and out but at the cost of an exhausting wait and a humiliating body search of men – and women – by the Japanese Army. A smile of appreciation went through Asia, even in countries which approved of China and were against Japanese militarism. The Japanese, it seemed, were effectively putting down the mighty from their seats, and scattering the proud. The Taipans, as the heads of firms were called, could not see their way ahead through the gloom. Perishable food stocks fell to 10 per cent of normal supplies, and rice disappeared altogether. At the same time, the Japanese Foreign Ministry demanded a reversal of key British policies concerning the China Incident as Japan's price for lifting the blockade. Ugly anti-British demonstrations were staged in Tokyo with official approval and with the active connivance of the Metropolitan Police (acting on instructions from the powerful Japanese Ministry for Home Affairs). Reports reaching London suggested that the police might allow the British Embassy to be stormed by mobs. Even moderate organs such as the *Oriental Economist* abruptly reflected this darkening mood. London was unclear whether those orchestrating these events wished to force Britain into war or merely into a humiliating loss of prestige (on the evidence of Baron Harada Kumao and Marquis Kido Koichi, it appears that Japanese honour would have been satisfied by minor British compromises in June but that a month later the situation was too exacerbated to allow for any simple resolution of the crisis).

Britain responded to the Tientsin Crisis in three ways. First, diplomatic exchanges were begun at Tientsin, later extended to formal exchanges between Ambassador Sir Robert Craigie and Foreign Minister Arita Hachirō. Eventually these conversations covered all major points of friction between the two countries. Second, to the despair of Britain's strategical advisers, the issue of commercial and financial reprisals against Japan was reopened in Whitehall. Third, the Tientsin Crisis made a nonsense of Britain's recent changes in defence strategy, which, as has been seen, were predicated upon the assumption, now, that war would begin in Europe and then spread to East Asia rather than the other way round.

Although Japanese policy was not as monolithic and unambiguous as London supposed, Britain's first reactions to Honma's blockade verged upon panic. 'Pug' Ismay, Secretary to the Committee of Imperial Defence, privately informed Lord Hankey's son, Robin, at the overwrought British Embassy in Warsaw, that 'For the moment all our eyes are on Tientsin instead of Danzig.'* The Foreign Secretary, Lord Halifax, closeted himself with his advisers: 'Had to spend half the day holding H[alifax]'s hand,' wrote Cadogan in his diary on 15 June.† When Halifax emerged, he met with Prime Minister Chamberlain and Lord Chatfield to discuss the question of retaliation and dispatching a battle squadron to the Pacific. The Commander-in-Chief, China Fleet, had cabled that 'Tientsin may develop into a case of giving in to such an extent that we virtually lose the Concession or of making a *casus belli*. I have never before suggested I required reinforcements but am reluctantly forced to the conclusion.' He asked for 'a squadron of two or three capital ships accompanied by

---

* Private Letter, Ismay to Robin Hankey, 16 June 1939, Ismay IV/Han/20, Ismay Papers, King's College [London] Centre for Military Archives.

† Dilks, op. cit., pp.186–8.

a cruiser squadron and a destroyer flotilla' to augment his slender forces.*

The Cabinet Committee on Foreign Policy was advised by the Foreign Secretary that

the present situation at Tientsin has revealed the policy of the Japanese to eliminate or vastly diminish British interests and prestige in China as a means to the attainment of her long-term objective of establishing her control over the whole of East Asia and the formation of a closed economic bloc between Japan, China and Manchuria, which would in turn place her in a position at some later stage to pursue ambitions to southward at the expense of the British Empire.†

Lord Halifax went on to inform his ministerial colleagues that 'the situation with which we are faced has reached an acute stage, and whereas up to date we have been able to allow our future course of action to wait upon events, the necessity to do something to counter the Japanese plan has now become imperative'.‡ Oddly enough, the Foreign Office rejected a policy of inaction on the grounds that it would weaken Britain's political position relative to Germany and Italy as well as against Japan.

At the behest of the Prime Minister, Chatfield asked the Chiefs of Staff for advice, admitting that 'we can only strengthen our position in the Far East by weakening our position in Europe and therefore the main decision is a political one'.§

At first sight, it might appear that the answers to Chatfield's questions were plain enough after the Government's recent acceptance of the naval strategy promoted by Backhouse and Cunningham. However, at the beginning of June, before the arrival of the warnings from the Commander-in-Chief, China Fleet, there began another major shift of power in the Admiralty which had the effect of enhancing the influence of the Admiralty's Plans Division. Now gravely ill, Backhouse retired in June as First Sea Lord and was replaced by the more traditionalist Sir Dudley Pound, while Admiral Tom Phillips, a former Director of Plans and an adherent of the Far Eastern School, became Deputy Chief of Naval Staff, relieving Admiral Cunningham, who went out to take Pound's place as Commander-in-Chief of the Mediterranean Fleet. Significantly, Danckwerts remained Director of Plans, and Drax, who had left the

---

* F 5800/176/23, C-in-C, China Fleet, to Admiralty, 13 June 1939, FO 371/23556, British Public Record Office, Kew.
† FP (36)95, 16 June 1939, CAB 27/627, British Public Record Office, Kew.
‡ ibid.
§ COS 300(39)1, 16 June 1939, CAB 53/11, British Public Record Office, Kew.

Admiralty to become ADC to the King at the beginning of April, no longer counter-balanced the orthodoxy of the Plans Division. All of this meant that difficulties which Chatfield had encountered with his immediate successors at the Admiralty might now be overborne. Certainly Chamberlain himself did not now regard the case against dispatching the fleet as unanswerable. The lesson to be derived from this is that policies cannot be divorced from personalities.

Haltingly, over the next few weeks, the issues became clear: the Tientsin Crisis threatened the very survival of British influence in East Asia; the Empire could not abandon its position there; only the dispatch of naval reinforcements to the Pacific would deter the Japanese; any fleet sent to the Pacific must be able to accept a main fleet action against the whole Japanese fleet if pressed; the dispatch of such a battlefleet to the East would involve the abandonment of Britain's naval control in the Mediterranean. No efforts must be spared to reach a compromise with the Japanese in the Craigie–Arita talks, but orders were issued that the fleet must be ready for immediate service in August in case events turned for the worse.

There were soon indications that Hitler might be taking advantage of the Tientsin Crisis. Henry Pownall, the War Office's chief planning officer, recorded in his diary, 'Things are beginning to thicken at Danzig. Rather earlier than we thought, but it may be that the Tientsin affair has caused Hitler to accelerate his tempo.'* It was also clear that the Germans were seizing upon the propaganda value of the Tientsin dispute in efforts to persuade the Japanese Government to conclude a military alliance with Germany, and there were reports from Egypt that the Germans were interpreting the incident 'to show that Orientals can insult Englishmen with impunity and that the British Empire is too enfeebled to react. Effect on Oriental mind is most damaging.' †

In the weeks after suggestions voiced by Admiral Pound opened the way to a reconsideration of a large fleet movement to the Pacific in the event that the negotiations with Japan failed to produce a satisfactory result, the second tide of changes continued to roll through the Admiralty in the wake of Admiral Backhouse's departure. The new Deputy Chief of the Naval Staff, Tom Phillips, used his influence in efforts to sweep away Admiral Drax's formulations. Drax's genius and daring earns our respect, and he had a natural flair for battle action. Tom Phillips, although perhaps equally gifted, was a complete contrast: a thorough master of detailed

* H. Pownall, *Chief of Staff*, vol. I: *1933–1940*, Leo Cooper, London, 1972, p. 209.
† Alexandria Telegram 397, 26 June 1939, copied to the War Office in WO 106/126, British Public Record Office, Kew.

staff-work, who, in between appointments in the Admiralty's Plans Division during 1930–32 and 1935–8, had served as Chief of Staff and Flag Captain to the Commander-in-Chief, East Indies, during 1932–5, where the prime mission had always been to move out to Singapore in case of trouble with Japan. It is hardly surprising, therefore, that Phillips now maintained that the Tientsin emergency proved the importance of re-articulating key elements in Britain's traditional naval strategy:

1. Make it clear that we cannot have three fleets.
2. Point out that Home Waters are vital and a sufficient force must always remain there.
3. If a fleet is sent to the East, it must be of sufficient strength.
4. As a corollary to the above, if the situation arises, H M G will have to choose between the Far East and the Eastern Mediterranean – this choice must depend upon circumstances and the progress of the war and must be made at the time, e.g., is Singapore invested, etc.
5. All references to a 'flying squadron' in the East to be omitted.*

One might recall these words when the time comes to consider the fate of the singularly unfortunate detachment of two battleships that Phillips was destined to command in December 1941, sunk by the Japanese off the coast of Malaya only two days after the outbreak of the War in the Pacific.

Throughout July came conflicting reports on the advantages or not of taking retaliatory steps against Japan. The British Senior Naval Officer at Tientsin told London that he wished to mount armed guards with Lewis guns aboard all British vessels in his area, with authority for 'forcibly preventing stopping and boarding'. He remarked, 'Armed conflict might result from [the] above, but it is considered that opposition would not be serious and that incidents would remain local.'† The British military, naval and air attachés in Tokyo, however, were far better informed. They strongly opposed provoking even slight clashes during this sensitive period, and in a joint message to London they agreed

In the event of our inability to meet Japanese desires at forthcoming conference resulting in increased Japanese pressure and further inimical action against our interests in the Far East, we are convinced that Japanese military and naval confidence, reinforced by present exacerbated state of public opinion, is such that retaliatory action on our part is more likely to act as an incentive to open hostilities on their part, than as a deterrent.‡

* M.06226/39, Minute by Phillips, 5 July 1939, Adm. 1/9767, British Public Record Office, Kew.
† Senior Naval Officer, Tientsin, to Commander-in-Chief, China Station, 20 July 1939, W O 106/128, British Public Record Office, Kew.
‡ ibid., Military Attaché, Tokyo, to War Office, 15 July 1939.

With such reports in mind, London came under great pressure to increase British land and air forces in the Far East. The Chairman of the Chiefs of Staff, Sir Cyril Newall, indicated that his Committee now 'were mainly exercised about the situation in the Far East. The prospect of a successful outcome to the [Craigie–Arita] negotiations did not appear very hopeful.' * In the end, combined pressure by the Chiefs of Staff, Admiral Chatfield in his capacity as Minister for the Co-ordination of Defence, and Sir Robert Vansittart as a spokesman for the Foreign Office, proved irresistible: the Committee of Imperial Defence voted to give Malaya two squadrons from Metropolitan Bomber Command, two further RAF squadrons from India, together with an Indian Army infantry brigade and support units.

On 24 July Neville Chamberlain announced in the House of Commons that Craigie and Arita had reached a formula which might lead to improved understanding with Japan and thus permit the two countries to negotiate a settlement of the Tientsin dispute. At once, it is true, these negotiations eased what the Prime Minister called 'the stripping, searching and slapping' of British residents in Tientsin, but even he recognized that 'The attitude of the military in China itself, especially at Tientsin, Peking and Shanghai, remains intolerable, provocative and offensive.' † The anti-British demonstrations in Tokyo showed signs of abating somewhat, but no one could predict what changes might lie in store should the pace of negotiations falter and so exasperate the Japanese even more.

The ensuing suspense grew so palpable that on 2 August 1939 the British Chiefs of Staff discussed whether full war precautionary measures should be taken. They finally decided that further reinforcements should be sent to East Asia without delay if conditions deteriorated – but not yet. Much would depend upon whether the reinforcements had to meet the demands of a Far Eastern emergency or to act as a barrier against the spread eastwards of tension now arising in Europe. Either way, the next few weeks might prove critical.

Across Whitehall on 2 August, Lord Halifax was informing the Cabinet that 'the situation in the Far East was now causing him more anxiety than the position in any other part of the world'.‡ When one considers that Britain was then only one month away from war against Germany, the Foreign Secretary's remarks gives one pause for thought. Halifax explained that Japan insisted that general policy matters concerning the

---

* CID 367(39)1 [DP(P)], 21 July 1939, CAB 2/9, British Public Record Office, Kew.

† NC 18/1110, Neville Chamberlain to Hilda Chamberlain, 30 July 1939, Chamberlain Papers, Birmingham University Library.

‡ CC 40(39)4, 2 August 1939, CAB 24/100, British Public Record Office, Kew.

whole gamut of Anglo-Japanese affairs should be reviewed during the Tokyo conversations about Tientsin. These wider issues, originally excluded at Britain's request, might lead to an open breach in relations between the two countries. Since Sir George Sansom, in whose wisdom Halifax placed complete confidence, counselled that Japan merely wished to extort the best possible terms from Britain at the Conference, the Foreign Secretary suggested that Britain could afford to harden her approach to the Japanese. If relations continued to worsen so that further action became necessary, then Britain should denounce her commercial treaty with Japan – as America had done when the Craigie–Arita formula was announced. This would allow Britain and Japan to conduct further negotiations over a twelve-month period of grace and, in the Foreign Secretary's estimation, would be less likely to provoke military reprisals than an embargo (which would probably evolve into a naval blockade). Two days later, speaking in the Commons, Neville Chamberlain warned the world not to assume that Britain was incapable of establishing decisive naval superiority over Japan in the Pacific: 'we have such a fleet here, and in certain circumstances we might feel it necessary to send the fleet out there. I hope no one will think that it is absolutely out of the question for such circumstances to arise.' One can make of these words what one will. Not surprisingly, the mood in the Foreign Office verged on black despair: a member of the over-worked Far Eastern Department recalled afterwards that several of his colleagues collapsed under the strain. As far as the British Government was concerned, the outcome of the Tientsin Crisis, whether compromise or Pacific War, was up to Tokyo: in the face of Japanese blustering, the British Government had decided to stand fast. Nevertheless, judged by their own usual assumptions, normally cautious figures in the British Government responded to the threat of war in 1939 with apparent irrationality, a predisposition to bring matters to a head regardless of consequences. Although the country was better armed now than at any time since the end of the First World War, the international situation was virtually beyond hope of repair, and the dread prospect of a three-enemy war loomed dead ahead. In contrast to the winter of 1938–9, the later summer of 1939 was remarkably devoid of useful speculation about the strategical consequences of Britain's perilous course. The defence authorities, particularly the Admiralty, nevertheless remained worried about what effect the Tientsin Crisis might have upon the European situation. New operations plans written following Britain's strategical shifts in the spring of 1939 had not been received by British commands overseas when the Tientsin Crisis first blossomed in June. Out of necessity, the Navy temporarily suspended their new operations plans and returned to their earlier war plans for the fleet (based largely upon the 1937 Far East Appreciation by the Chiefs of Staff, which had been discarded as obsolete by the country's strategical and political authorities in the spring of 1939). While high-level policy concerning the future dispositions of the fleet remained undecided, up-to-date amendments to the Naval War Memorandum (Eastern) were not even sent to the Commander-in-Chief, China Station, until 15 June (the day after the Tientsin blockade was imposed by the Japanese) – and even then these were suspended for a day on 20 June while the policy questions hung in the balance. Relevant modifications to the Naval War Memorandum (European) were sent to naval commanders abroad only on 4 August. Therefore the actual fleet instructions in the hands of Britain's naval commanders overseas during most of the summer of 1939 remained predicated upon a task which the Admiralty wanted to abandon as hopeless only a few months before – the dispatch of the fleet to Singapore in the event of a conflict with Japan.

Finally, on Friday, 4 August 1939, British naval commanders worldwide were told how the Admiralty planned to distribute British naval forces if Japan joined the Axis in a world war against Britain and France. In essential respects, Britain's new plan conformed to suggestions which Chatfield had made at the worst of the initial Tientsin war scare. Indeed, it departed little from Admiral Pound's reaction to Chatfield's criticisms of the position taken by the Chiefs of Staff at the beginning of the crisis. In short, it meant a return to Britain's traditional posture, since it envisaged that control of the Mediterranean by the Royal Navy might be sacrificed in order to send the main fleet to Singapore while retaining a smaller force of six capital ships in Home Waters to contain the Germans. The new plans stopped short, however, of reviving one vital doctrine which the Chiefs of Staff had led the Government to abandon in the spring, namely, that there must be no hesitation in reinforcing Britain's imperial position in East Asia at full strength to the detriment of Britain's position in the Mediterranean. The ultimate strength of Britain's Far East Fleet would depend upon political decisions that Ministers could take only after war was joined.

As it happened, these developments during the China Incident forced London to choose either to accept the risk of Japanese belligerency against the British Empire without making proper provision for it, so that Britain could wage an intensive war against Italy with no immediate regard for the consequences in East Asia and the Pacific, or, alternatively, to reserve the forces believed necessary to resist Japan, renewing efforts to ensure that Italy was kept out of the German camp permanently. Notwithstanding ominous news that German-Italian Naval Staff talks were taking place throughout the summer, the grave crisis at Tientsin forced the British to adopt the second course. After having dallied with the idea of pre-emptive action against Italy in the event of war against Germany, London now chose appeasement rather than confrontation with Italy. This attitude persisted beyond the Tientsin Crisis because the success of the policy could be seen. A result was that upon the outbreak of war against Germany, the British Government's latest thinking on the future distribution of British naval forces worldwide showed the degree to which strength in the Mediterranean had been reduced to skeletal proportions compared to the size of battlefleet once contemplated for a Mediterranean offensive.

The two power-shifts, or 'palace revolutions', in the British Admiralty during 1939 demonstrate beyond peradventure that, at least in relation to the threat of war against Japan, national policy evolved around the actual strength of Britain's defence system and the views of Britain's strategical authorities. These same two revolutions also show the limits of the influence of strictly military factors: outside developments in Europe, especially the Nazi-Soviet Pact and the crisis over Danzig, ultimately proved far more important and seem to have developed without too central a regard in London for Britain's imperial defence liabilities in East Asia and the Pacific.

By the end of August 1939, international conditions had undergone a complete transformation, and Tokyo was reeling in confusion. The Japanese Foreign Minister, Arita Hachirō, was ready to reach a limited agreement with Britain despite the power of the Army, but on 21 August the Craigie–Arita Conversations were suspended at Britain's request. Britain's resolute defiance of Japan might have uncovered the instability and weakness of Japan in any event, and it is worthwhile remembering that Japan had to consider the consequences of Roosevelt's decision to abrogate the Japan-US Treaty of Commerce and Navigation at the height of the Tientsin Crisis, a matter which was reason enough to make Japan pause. As it happened, both of these events occurred while Japan was suffering serious military reverses in its major border conflict with the Soviet Union at Nomonhan, and thus the startling announcement of the Nazi-Soviet Pact on 23 August, which completely undercut the foundations of the Anti-Comintern Pact, constituted a final blow which no government in Japan could have survived. Under this succession of shocks, the Hiranuma Cabinet fell in Japan, and both the immediate danger of an Anglo-Japanese War and the prospect of substantial gains for Japan from the European crisis abruptly receded.

Nevertheless, the Tientsin affair is immensely important in the story of the approach of the Pacific War, for it marked the end of two centuries of British dominance in East Asia. Above all, the Tientsin Crisis was the last time Britain independently defied Japan without the clear prospect of active American intervention. An Anglo-Japanese war was averted only narrowly in 1939 – and perhaps only by the coincidence of outside events. Never again did Britain maintain any illusions about exerting decisive influence in East Asia. With the outbreak of war in Europe, western authority passed irretrievably from Britain to the United States. In some ways Tientsin was an embarrassing hiccup in Britain's imperial responsibilities, which Britain did try to ignore after the spring of 1939. Ultimately, Britain did concentrate upon Europe rather than upon the Far East. Yet it is important to establish that Britain, however muddled, was neither bluffing nor blustering at Tientsin, and that the momentous collapse of British influence in East Asia which followed the outbreak of war in Europe was nothing short of cataclysmic, even if the effects of that cataclysm could not be assessed fully until the summer of 1940.

Before leaving the Tientsin Crisis behind, one should appreciate the restraint shown by the Japanese Garrison at Tientsin. In the last analysis, they could have seized the British and French Concessions at Tientsin at any time. It must have been tempting. The consequences of such a simple step hardly bear thinking about.

CHAPTER 11

India and the Conflict

AT the time of the clash between China and Japan, the surprising fact in the rest of Asia was that most of it was under western government. Much of India, for example, had been under British rule for 150 years. Nearly all the rest of the region had also passed into the empires, or spheres of interest, of one European Power or another. Two ancient, but comparatively small, countries, Persia and Thailand, were the only exceptions. They owed their preservation to uncommon adroitness, aided by the fact that in each case two foreign Powers were competing for dominance over their territories.

From the beginning of the 1920s India, the heart and core of this series of subject countries, had made a resolute and persevering effort to throw off western rule. It was a fair deduction that, if it succeeded, an end would be put to the lesser imperialisms of Europe in Asia. Their circumstances were in some respects dissimilar: their end would be the same. All Asia would be free. Moreover India had so central a position in Asia, was a country with such prestige and resources, that the way in which it reacted to the issues of the time would have the deepest consequences for its neighbours. An account of the war requires therefore that the affairs of India should be followed, that its quarrel with Britain should be recorded, that the degree at different times of its pro-Japanese sentiment should be remarked, and its role in Japanese strategy examined. It demands also an inquiry into the different quality of British imperialism from Japanese which made the British Empire, even in its decay, by contrast so durable.

The major part of India was conquered by Britain between 1757 and 1820. The form of conquest was straightforward military annexation, but of a somewhat unusual kind. The conquest was not premeditated by Britain. A British trading company, the Honourable East India Company, had begun to trade peaceably in India. It was sucked into intervening in the management of Indian affairs by the anarchy which followed the downfall in the eighteenth century of the Moghul Empire. Out of its activities, the British Government, which had gradually assumed control of the political responsibilities of the Company, eventually found itself the master of a great military empire.

The British Raj was unique in having been set up by a people which used no large standing army of its own countrymen for the purpose Alone among governments which pursued an active imperialist role Britain operated with such a small army of its own that its aims seemed derisory It was much too small for Britain to have played any notable part on the continent of Europe, and it might have seemed too small to undertake operations on other continents. The Empire was won, not by British forces in the main, but by dexterous political manoeuvre, and by the Indian forces who chose to fight on the British side in a situation where there were several claimants for their arms. The East India Company, which was in India for trade, became, to all intents and purposes, one of the native powers between which India was divided; and from being one of these native powers it became gradually the paramount native state. It raised and paid for native armies which won for it territories for which it had to provide an administration: and this, though informed by British concepts, continued in many respects the traditional administration. The predominance of the Company was due primarily to the coherent political organization which it imported into India. It was also due, initially, to superior military technique, but when other native powers through foreign advisers imported the technology, it was due to superior discipline and organization.

Those statesmen of the Company who had conceived the policy, and saw where it tended, had usually to draw along their reluctant colleagues, who were always saying that a trading company had no right to be considering policies which would thrust upon it unwelcome political responsibilities. Nevertheless the bolder spirits prevailed, and they succeeded in their manoeuvres with startling ease. Thus Britain, which was five thousand miles away, found itself with an Empire which it had never, in its deliberate moments, set itself to acquire. It had gained it with the minimum military force; and it held it by the stiffening effect of a garrison of British troops which, in normal circumstances, amounted to no more than 60,000 men. It would have been impossible with such a puny force to have held down a genuine national movement, and to have ruled India by the sword. British Government thus rested, in the deepest sense, upon the consent of the people to be governed. Its continuance depended on the tacit ballot that this government afforded benefits which the majority of the people accepted, either from apathy or from general appreciation of it.

The reason why the British had made such an easy conquest of the country was that for the most part a stubborn defence was never encountered. The country changed hands while the peasantry, from which a popular army would have had to be recruited, looked on. This followed an old tradition of India. Observers of the country from earliest historical times had often exclaimed with wonder at the detached attitude of the peasantry, who went on with agricultural tasks, ignoring a pitched battle of their betters which might be taking place a few hundred yards from them, and on which their destiny depended. Not all the conquests were as easy as this. The East India Company had to fight hard, for instance, against the Marathas and Sikhs, who both had organized military kingdoms of a formidable nature. But even with them, the kingdoms were the armies: once these were defeated the East India Company had no more to do: there was no great popular resistance to wear down. Popular feeling against the foreigner interfering in the political affairs of the country is mainly a product of the twentieth century.

In this take-over of India there was no intention on the part of the British to produce a social transformation. As regards forms of society, the British were willing to leave things put. This was in some part due to the fascination and esteem which Indian life, in all its astonishing variety, exercises over the spirits of those who encounter it. It was also due to the realization that any interference with existing customs was likely to cause trouble. For example, the British were at first reluctant to give any countenance to Christian missionaries. Later, with the growth of evangelism in the nineteenth century in England the resistance to missionaries was partly eroded; but the mutiny of 1857, which stemmed from the mistaken belief of Indian soldiers that the British intended to force Christianity upon them, demonstrated the wisdom of non-interference. Thereafter social change was on the whole carefully refrained from. Profound social changes did, in fact, take place, but these were the inevitable result of the impact of a modern, highly industrialized society, such as Britain became, on an archaic, predominantly agrarian one. They were part of a world-wide trend, and not peculiar to the relations of Britain and India.

It was in the sphere of politics and administration that the struggle for sovereignty developed in India, and it was here that interesting forms were evolved. Nearly all the strains of thought in political philosophy in Britain during a century and a half found at one time or another reflection in the institutions of India. At the end of the eighteenth century the main preoccupation was to protect the individual citizen against arbitrary power, and to put government in the shackles of regular procedure controlled by courts. Then for a while the dominant interest was the philosophy of utilitarianism. One Governor General, Lord William Bentinck, was a close disciple of Bentham, and for forty years James Mill, and his son

John Stuart Mill, held key positions in the office of the East India Com pany. Certain questions were endlessly discussed, for instance, the case for direct administration by the British and the case for indirect administration; the duty of the government to promote change, and its duty to shield people against too rapid change; the virtues of control from above and the virtues of self-government; and the discussion resulted in action, or in some cases inaction – for instance, after the mutiny of 1857 there was no extension of direct British rule. Some of the shrewdest minds in Britain, from Victorian times to the late 1930s, found the Indian Government more malleable to ideas than society in the West. A philosophically inclined visitor to India towards the end of the nineteenth century said that a trip there was like re-living his life as a student of politics at Oxford.

The civil service in British India became remarkable for its quality. In the kingdoms and empires of the sub-continent in the past, the central governments found it traditionally very hard to get anything done. Their acts might be sporadically vigorous and imaginative, but the sum total of their deeds was slight: it disappeared quickly in sand. The Indian Civil Service, first instituted by the British, and then increasingly operated by both British and Indians, gave India for the first time an instrument by whose means government could carry out reforms which were pushed through to the end. Such was the prestige, the intelligence, and the standard of service to the community of this body of men that, even when the freedom struggle was at its height, distinguished Indian families, including the Nehrus, sent some of their sons into government service while others were operating in the opposition movement. The ideal of the Indian Civil Service was to gain willing acceptance of the policies and actions of the Government. To be compelled to use force at all was, therefore, regarded as a mark of failure; and its excessive use was rarely forgiven. This was a reflection of the fact that from the beginning of the Raj the number of Englishmen in India was far too small for them to govern the country arbitrarily and with incessant use of force. In the last years of British rule the British members of the administrative class of the civil service numbered less than a thousand, and in the subordinate services they hardly existed, whereas the population of India by the beginning of the war had swollen to 350 million, or one sixth of the population of the world.

Although, through the British period, government was carried on chiefly by the civil service, India was also by stages equipped with free institutions. Because Britain, in the grip of nineteenth-century liberal ideas, knew only one way of being politically constructive, it instinctively introduced into India representative councils and assemblies and the whole apparatus of liberal democracy. At the beginning these councils were largely consultative, but they contained seeds which grew, and which decided that the struggle for freedom in India would take the form of a demand for parliamentary rule.

Constitutional reforms in India were partly a response to, and partly they stimulated, the Indian national movement. That the transition from subjection to independence in India came in the end with such remarkable ease and restraint on both sides was due chiefly to three things: the liberal institutions set up in India by the British; the genius of Mahatma Gandhi, for many years the leader of the national freedom movement; and the quickening of a new age in Asia, and new ideas and a new type of British personality in India, as a direct result of the Japanese War.

On the Indian side, a vital factor in the struggle for independence was the emergence of a new Indian middle class. This class adopted English as its language, and owed its existence to the mass of institutions which the Raj fostered. Some members of it adapted themselves so phenomenally well to English culture that they became, to all intents and purposes, Englishmen. They lived in English style. They spoke English in their homes. Perhaps there is no comparable case in modern history of a class taking over so completely and with such ease the culture and language of another people: the parallel in the past is the assimilation of Latin culture by the provincials of the Roman Empire. Not that these families lost all touch with India; the women especially carried on the old Indian tradition, and in the deeper layers of the mind, the Indian structure persisted. But in practical action most of the men thought, felt, acted like Englishmen, and made very much the same value judgements. This victory of an alien personality was seen at times as a doubtful advantage to India; its psychological effects were frequently lamented by the social group in which it took place; but in the long run such fusions of culture are prized by the countries in which they occur, provided the assimilation is complete. The most surprising instance of this deep westernization is usually masked. Gandhi, the man under whose leadership the independence of India was achieved, a man who always stressed that he was a Hindu, the heir of the Hindu tradition; who wore Indian clothes, or very few clothes at all in the manner of Indian holy men, was nevertheless profoundly influenced by ideas from Britain. Equality of citizens, non-doctrinaire socialism, his apotheosis of the individual conscience, his social experimentation, prohibition, feminism, nationalism itself – this was the British tradition, not perhaps of government, but of radical non-conformism. Here, it might be said, was an example rare in history, of Rome making Greece its captive, not vice versa.

This westernized Indian middle class, though numerically very small became immensely important, and in the eyes of the rest of the world, it *was* Indian, spoke for India, represented India. As it matured, it inevitably took to nationalism, and the Indian patriot became the most typical example of the nationalist in his time. He was the most eloquent in denouncing imperialism – often in admirable English prose. He demanded the most fiercely to be liberated. He was the most confident, and with reason, of being able to operate by himself the institutions amongst which he had passed his life. Some years before the First World War, Indian nationalism was already vigorous. At first the nationalists had been divided between revolutionaries and constitutionalists. The revolutionaries, who carried on old Indian traditions of romantic protest, wanted root and branch overthrow of British rule, and terrorism seemed to be their best instrument. By contrast, the constitutionalists did not expect to end British rule by a lightning stroke; but by forming political parties, by entering the representative assemblies, by propaganda, and by accepting and operating the political systems which Britain had set up, they expected to be able to bring enough pressure to bear on the Government to make their voice felt in its decisions. They were buoyed up and encouraged by the support which they received from radicals in Britain. This active lobby in Britain for Indian independence was an important factor convincing Indian nationalism that constitutionalism would give results. After a time, terrorism lost its glamour, and the majority of nationalists opted for constitutional action, or only mildly unconstitutional action; and, with aberrations at times when crises came to a head, they remained faithful to this course.

On the British side there were, at times, explosive strains. There were, occasionally, violent men in the civil service and in the Army, and until the end the danger existed below the surface that in an emergency they might react brutally. Once violence had started it would have grown by its own momentum and both sides might have drifted into open war. An outrage occurred shortly after the First World War in the massacre at Amritsar. This town in the Punjab was the scene of demonstrations in which mobs got control of the city and martial law was proclaimed in the area. An Indian assembly convened in defiance of an order, was caught in a walled space, with inadequate exits, and a British general, General Dyer, ordered troops to open fire. As a result, nearly four hundred unarmed people were killed. That this atrocity should have taken place, and even been approved by a section of British opinion, was a shock to Indian leaders. But there were denunciations in London; those in Parliament were led with much force by Winston Churchill. The repudiation by the British Government of General Dyer was one of the factors which strengthened Indian nationalism in its belief that it could win freedom by relatively restrained means.

The chief organ of the freedom movement, the Indian National Congress, was led during the crucial years by one of the most extraordinary figures of history, Mahatma Gandhi. Gandhi's outstanding qualities were a combination of a peculiar gentleness with inflexible determination; his religious temperament, natural in an Indian, was allied with a practical ability, unusual in seers, to shape events to some extent in the light of his understanding. Gandhi made Indian nationalism self-confident; he fed it with imaginative ideas and moral fire. Avoiding the dreary tactics of terrorism and guerrilla warfare, he perfected the weapons of civil disobedience and non-violent resistance. Some of his methods, at first, struck his lieutenants in Congress as too ingenuous; for instance, Gandhi proposed a famous march to the sea, to defy the law and make salt, on which there was a very light tax. Congress regarded it as a useless demonstration and agreed to it only in order to humour him. But it set India alight, and demonstrated a method of inducing popular uprisings which was to be of first importance to Congress in their later campaigns. He pursued his ends undeviatingly, but discriminated about means; thus, in the greatest of human traditions, he made politics a branch of ethics. The moral reason for all his major decisions was clearly laid in view, and even if a sophisticated onlooker might sometimes have thought that he deceived himself, and that the moral judgements on which he based his actions were sometimes the flexible handmaids of political experimentation, his concern with principle was authentic, never hypocritical, and it affected those who dealt with him. An English judge, sentencing him on one occasion to a prison term 'for sedition', addressed Gandhi, as he stood before him in the dock, in words which illustrate the effect he had on his political opponents:

It would be impossible to ignore the fact that in the eyes of millions of your countrymen you are a great patriot and a great leader. Even those who differ from you in politics look on you as a man of high ideals and of noble and even saintly life . . .*

The whole character of Indian history in this period is the collusion, unspoken and hardly admitted, between the British power and Gandhi. For thirty years they fought each other, but cooperated tacitly in preventing the fight from getting out of hand. Both acted as if guided by the maxim of Machiavelli that you should treat your enemy as if he may one day become your friend. Because of the phenomenon of Gandhi's

* B. R. Nanda, *Mahatma Gandhi*, Allen & Unwin, London, 1958.

personality, a momentous struggle for freedom was fought, resolutely on both sides, but with an almost cheerful cordiality on both sides, and in a way which enabled both sides to be reconciled and to cooperate when it was over.

The climax of the struggle before the war was the civil disobedience campaign of Congress in 1930. Civil disobedience covered a variety of activities aimed at bringing government to a standstill – strikes, boycotts of British goods and services, and especially of foreign cloth, non-payment of taxes, and massive demonstrations, which were remarkably non-violent in the main, but on a scale large enough to alarm the authorities. The police took prisoners on a large scale: the prisons were overflowing, and special camps had to be organized. By these means the British Government in India felt that it had been able to prevent revolution and to maintain its power. But the years 1931–2 marked a watershed. The Government realized that although a rebellion had been broken, it could not repeat the operation, and that, if it tried to do so, it would strain too far the allegiance of the Indians in the civil service and the police. The issue from this period became the timing of the programme for self-government. While some of the diehards among the British held back on grounds of prestige, in other quarters in England and in British India there was anxiety on the more reasonable grounds that India was full of centrifugal and communal strains, and too hasty a withdrawal might lead to breakdown of government.

Congress, on the other hand, regarded the Government of India Act of 1935 as insufficient, although they were about to give it a trial. This Act had been thrashed out in a series of monumental deliberations in London, in which Mahatma Gandhi had taken part as the representative of Congress. It provided for parliamentary government and democratically elected Indian Ministers both in the central government at Delhi, and in the provinces. It retained, however, a British authoritarian element in two vital subjects: foreign affairs and defence. The demand of Congress at this time was for full Dominion status.

On 3 September 1939 the war began between Britain and Germany, and India was declared by the British Government to be also at war. It had no adequate cause of dispute with Germany to justify this declaration, and the Indian leaders said so forcibly. Nehru, it was true, and the more liberal leaders of Congress, shared the sense of outrage at Nazi misdeeds which was experienced by similar leaders in Europe. Nehru, while visiting England in the previous year, had written in the *Manchester Guardian* criticizing the policy of appeasement towards Germany. Gandhi, writing in his own newspaper, *Harijan*, after war broke out, expressed condemnation of Hitler and moral support for Britain and France, although as a pacifist he also condemned the fighting. The more reactionary Indian leaders were indifferent: not that they would have condoned Germany's brutalities had they credited them, they wrote them off as inventions of British propaganda. But since no attempt had been made to consult Indian opinion through any representative institutions, how, asked the Indians, could there be any sincere talk of a war for democracy when the war was begun in such an undemocratic way? As a result, the Congress Party resigned from the Government, withdrew from the eight provincial Ministries which it held, and recorded its extreme disapproval of all the acts of British officialdom.

Yet India did not protest very effectively against the German War. Several divisions of its Army fought in the Middle East, gaining battle honours of which even Indian nationalists were, paradoxically, rather proud. In one province of India the war was genuinely popular. This was in the Punjab, which was traditionally the chief recruiting ground for soldiers, and where the provincial government had not considered resigning. The Punjab actively demonstrated in favour of the war, and regarded as enemies those who were lukewarm in its service. Surprisingly accurate knowledge of the ups and downs of war strategy began to circulate in Punjab villages. Elsewhere the war, simply as war, began to appeal to the so-called martial classes. Anything to do with it – news about it, the social and economic changes consequent on it – interested them as trenching on their monopoly in life.

But by the rest of India the war was treated with indifference: with neither the excitement caused by the sense of genuine change in the air, nor with the alarm caused by the knowledge that India was compassed about by real dangers, some of which might soon hit India very hard. The fact that the war was to be enlarged, that a new enemy was at hand by means of whom the war would be transformed, that through no initiative of its own India was to be placed in its vanguard, and that invasion was to be a very near possibility, would jerk it out of its previous apathy. It would go to bed at night and get up in the morning with war at its elbow, instead of viewing it academically at a safe remove. The extension of the war would be the signal for a new phase of the freedom struggle to begin.

CHAPTER 12

The Magnetic North

THUS far the war had chiefly concerned China and Japan. Japan was aggressive towards China; considerations of how far this affected Japan's relations with other countries were peripheral. But from this time onwards, Japan's relations with the Great Powers became the prime concern of its Government. The war between China and Japan became increasingly difficult to limit to a private war; Japan was faced with problems, rising out of this war, each one of which caused it to consider afresh its policy towards other Powers. Sometimes it experimentally remoulded its policies towards them, only to change them again, with all the repercussions which such instability led to. Japan's policies became very uncertain. No settled principles guided its action.

Actually, since the days of the Anglo-Japanese Alliance, Japan had pursued a wavering foreign policy, spreading everywhere a diffuse suspicion. It had no sure base in a firm agreement with a greater Power. But until a late period, it seemed that its special, inexorable opponent was Russia. Suspicion of and hostility towards Russia governed its designs. One product of this attitude of mind had been the signing by Japan of the Anti-Comintern Pact with Germany in 1936. This was an alliance which somewhat nebulously pledged the partners to resist the infiltrations of Communism, and, in a secret clause, bound them to withhold aid from Russia should either party be involved in hostilities with the USSR.

As we have seen, there was special meaning in Japan regarding Russia as its hereditary enemy. Russia, as the perpetual threat, had penetrated into the folklore of the people even before Commodore Perry's expedition in 1853 signalled the opening of Japan's modern period of history. Ever since the end of the nineteenth century, Japan had regarded Russia as the Great Power against which it was destined to fight for survival. In 1904–5 it had fought the first round; it was convinced that it would have to fight again. The Siberian Intervention not only reinforced that conviction but also demonstrated the rapidity with which Japan could and often did find itself isolated and abandoned by its erstwhile allies. The serious strains which developed between the Army and the civil Government as a result of that crisis were to recur in the future, but this time the civilian Government, using one of the anti-imperialist swings in public opinion which at the time alternated with moods of aggressive nationalism, had prevailed in restraining the military. The Army felt that it had been ordered to drop its legitimate prey when it had been certain of it, and the sense that the civilian Government could not be trusted continued to weigh with it.

After Manchukuo came into being in 1932, Japan stationed there a large part of the Japanese Army. This did not disguise the fact that the eyes of the Japanese Army were focused upon Russia. Much of its training and manoeuvres were made with Russia as the ultimate adversary. Preparations were made to meet the danger of a full-scale Russian invasion; even more elaborate contingency plans were devised for a repeat performance of the Siberian Intervention, this time to be a wholly Japanese offensive against the Soviet Union. Russian belligerency was no less marked, and the exchanges between the two countries became increasingly explosive.

By 1938 2,800 separate armed clashes between the Russians and Japanese had been recorded and their successive repercussions provided the General Staffs of both countries with a perennial headache from which they had no relief in the years leading up to the wider conflict which engulfed the whole of East Asia and the Pacific. Since the rivalry between Russia and Japan is in many ways as important as the struggle between China and Japan in the tragic sequence of events that ended with the defeat of Japan in 1945, we must not overlook the significance of this interminable tension and succession of military clashes. Each was a cautionary tale. If details of most of them are unmemorable, their continuity was not. Three of the incidents had particular significance: the Amur River Incident, the Changkufeng Incident and the Nomonhan Incident. They foreshadowed special features about Total War which affected the perceptions and expectations of all the Powers in the Second World War.

During late June to early July 1937, on the eve of the great Sino-Japanese war that we call the China Incident, Japan and Russia fought the 185th in their series of inconclusive Manchurian border clashes at a site seventy miles down the Amur River from Khabarovsk. This is roughly the same area over which the Russians and the People's Republic of China fought similar actions decades afterwards. The Amur River Incident with which we are concerned, however, exposed serious Russian weaknesses in the wake of the first Red Army purges to affect East Asia. The Incident began when Russian troops landed on several disputed islets lying in the middle of the Amur River and took off a few Manchurian gold miners whom they accused of trespassing. Soviet gunboats then exchanged fire with nearby

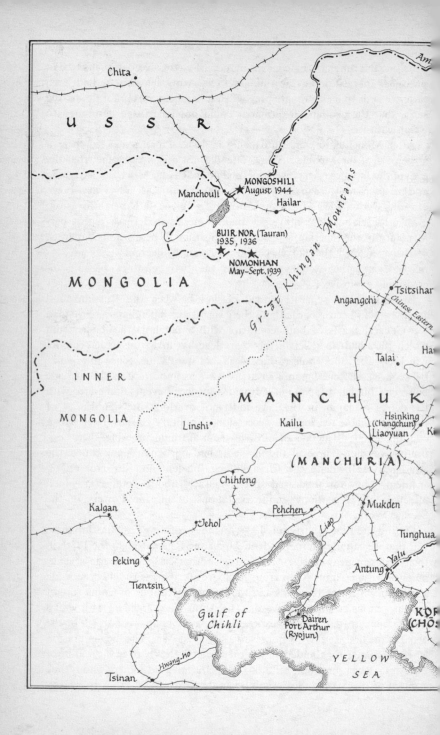

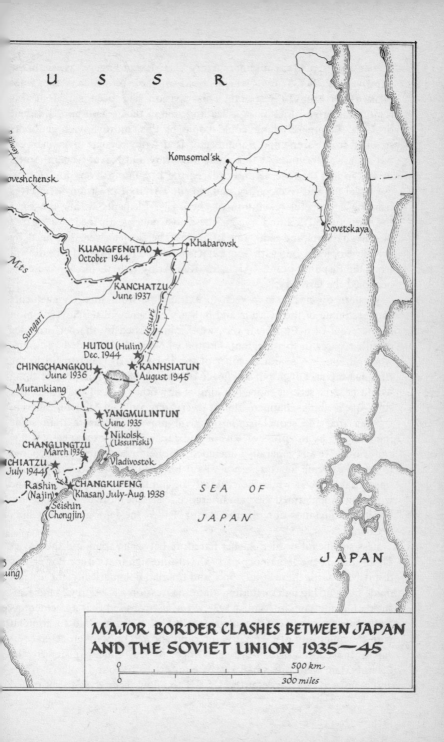

U S S R

oveshchensk

Komsomol'sk

Khabarovsk

Sovetskaya

Komile

Mts

Sungari

Ussuri

KUANGFENGTAO
October 1944

KANCHATZU
June 1937

HUTOU (Hulin)
Dec. 1944

CHINGCHANGKOU
June 1936

★**KANHSIATUN**
August 1945

Mutankiang

YANGMULINTUN
June 1935

Nikolsk
(Ussuriski)

CHANGLINGTZU
March 1936

Vladivostok

CHIATZU
July 1944

Rashin **CHANGKUFENG**
(Najin) (Khasan) July-Aug. 1938

Seishin
(Chongjin)

SEA   OF

JAPAN

JAPAN

ung)

MAJOR BORDER CLASHES BETWEEN JAPAN AND THE SOVIET UNION 1935—45

0   500 km
0   300 miles

elements of the Manchukuoan Army. The Kwantung Army, with the approval of the Army General Staff in Tokyo, ordered the First (Tokyo) Division to respond. This division had been exiled in this remote hinterland for taking a leading role in the 26 February Incident of 1936. Before anything could come of this, more Soviet gunboats steamed to the scene and a number of Red Army regular divisions were put on a war footing. At this point the Army and Naval General Staffs in Tokyo lost their nerve and ordered the Kwantung Army and Japanese naval air and river patrol units in the vicinity to restrain themselves pending a peaceful resolution of the crisis. Elements within the First Division turned a blind eye to these instructions, opened fire on the Soviet gunboats and sank one of them. The Soviets were outraged by this development but with some alacrity agreed to a mutual withdrawal from the disputed points. After the Red Army retired, the Japanese re-occupied the territory.

Western observers, ever keen to extrapolate from such engagements some estimate of the attitude and military efficiency of the Soviet Union in the event of a European war, were unimpressed by the performance of either party in this incident. On the whole it was regarded as 'somewhat puzzling'. A senior member of the Far Eastern Department in the British Foreign Office put his finger on the problem: 'This sort of thing would be very serious indeed in almost any other part of the world, but such queer things happen almost every day on the Manchu-Siberian frontier that the sequel to the incident may be no more than some mudslinging by the press of Russia and Japan and an exchange of a few rude notes.' It was generally concluded that neither country was prepared to adopt extreme measures, nor was it likely that either would gain the upper hand. Thus while the scale of the fighting was considerable, the world was not alarmed. Such indifference seems the more remarkable now given the juxtaposition of the Amur River Incident and the China Incident.

Less significant border clashes flared up between Japan and the Soviet Union during the remainder of 1937 with no sign that either Power was disposed to settle these affairs once and for all. Diplomatically, the Soviets made faces at Japan, concluding a non-aggression pact with Chiang Kai-shek's Kuomintang in August 1937. *Pravda* advertised that agreement as 'collective security', but the plain fact was that Russia had to contend with the animosity of Germany, too, and showed only token defiance of Japan. Indeed, the British Foreign Office advised Prime Minister Neville Chamberlain that 'one small ray of comfort to be found is the extreme and expressed reluctance of the USSR to allow themselves to get mixed up in the [Sino-Japanese] dispute. This allows us to hope that the dispute, if it develops, will be confined to China and Japan and that other Powers will not be dragged in.'*

As Japan sent more and more troops deep into China, the Soviet Union read the handwriting on the wall and began to reinforce its military forces in the East. The West privately counted this a blessing. It ought to make the Japanese more circumspect. There would be no need to encourage this development: Russia would strengthen her defence lines in her own interests, not because it might gain Moscow new friends. British air Intelligence experts – who in retrospect proved more perceptive (except in relation to Japan) than critics have credited – put Soviet front-line air strength at 4,000 aircraft, but 75 per cent of those aircraft reportedly were obsolescent. Soviet aircrews were regarded as badly trained, inefficient and very poorly led. No evidence could be found that Russia then believed that air bombardment of Japanese cities was practicable, although it was generally observed that 'the threat, slight as it is in reality, has altered the whole of Japan's strategical outlook and has created a most powerful deterrent to a Japanese attack on any part of Soviet Russia'.† On the eve of a European weekend crisis during mid-May 1938, French Intelligence suggested that Soviet pilots sent into action at Hankow and elsewhere in Central China were winning a string of victories against the Japanese. The British, however, discounted such reports. The difference in viewpoint between the two Powers in East Asia mirrored their respective (dis)inclination to welcome offers of Soviet air support for Czechoslovakia. In terms of what the Soviet Union could do to help preserve British, French and American interests in East Asia, London, at least, took the attitude that there were no significant developments up to the first anniversary of the birth of the China Incident. The French, who had less at stake anyway, remained slightly more hopeful if not optimistic. Both Powers, like the United States, recognized that for the time being the Japanese were in a position to do more or less as they liked in China although not, perhaps, further afield.

Then, late in July and throughout most of August 1938, a major battle erupted at Changkufeng, on the banks of the Tumen River west of Lake Khasan at a spot where the frontiers of Korea, the USSR and Manchuria meet some seventy miles south-west of Vladivostok. Changkufeng was

* Unnumbered FO note for Chamberlain, 10 August 1937, Premier 1/314, British Public Record Office, Kew, cited in Pritchard, *Far Eastern Influences*, op. cit. p. 93.
† File II A/1/37, item 37/12, Report by Squadron Leader Pelly (A.I.2.c), 4 November 1937, AIR 9/23, British Public Record Office, Kew.

one of the highest in a range of ancient volcanic peaks. It was possible to peer from its summit across intervening marshlands to Posyet Bay, fifteen miles distant, where the Soviet Union had begun constructing new submarine pens and air bases at the port of Novokievsk (Kraskino). Southwest of Changkufeng, about eleven miles away, lay the Japanese port of Rashin (Rajin), where transport vessels unloaded troops and supplies bound for the northern frontiers of the Japanese Empire. The railways, and the port of Rashin as well, were within sight of the ridge of the Changkufeng Hills. Observers there would encounter no difficulty in monitoring the bulk of Japanese railway traffic to the north. There were other vantage points from which the two sides could scrutinize each other. Changkufeng was not unique. However, possession of these crests affected the security of adjacent promontories which the two sides occupied along the same frontier.

Historians and political scientists have made much of this border incident. They have linked it to the great Soviet purges and the efficiency of the Red Banner Front armies. They have drawn conflicting conclusions about how it fits in with what are surmised to have been Soviet and Japanese intentions before, during and after it took place. They have argued over the manner in which the campaign was conducted and the scale of forces employed on both sides. They have inferred contradictory conclusions about the peace negotiations which followed in its wake. They have suggested that it demonstrated the ability or the inability of Japanese authorities in Tokyo and in the field to control the activities of their forces. They have even used it to advance various theories about wider conspiracies to wage aggressive war.

Almost everything about the Changkufeng Incident has been shrouded in mystery. The incident has long been appreciated as an event ranking in importance with, say, the far better known incidents of the German march into the Rhineland, the Italian conquest of Ethiopia, the American occupation of Iceland, or the Japanese advance into Indo-China with the acquiescence of the Vichy régime. Like each of those affairs, the Changkufeng Incident gave rise to accusations that one side or the other was guilty of systematic aggression.

The Soviet purges had decimated the Russian officer corps by the summer of 1938. Russian commanders everywhere were jittery. The initial Soviet occupation of the Changkufeng heights may have been prompted by the defection to Japan of General G. S. Lyushkov, the Commissar of the NKVD (Stalin's dread secret police) responsible for the whole of Soviet East Asia. In mid-June, Lyushkov's dramatic escape across the Manchurian frontier in full-dress military uniform, replete with medals,

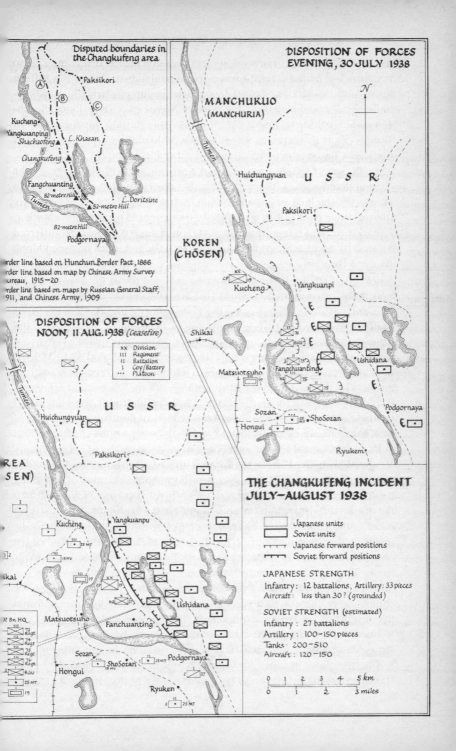

Disputed boundaries in the Changkufeng area

Paksikori

(A) (B) (C)

Kucheng
Yangkuanping
Shachaofeng ▲
L. Khasan

Changkufeng ▲

Fangchuanting ▲
82-metre Hill
Tumen
▲ 52-metre Hill
L. Doritsine

82-metre Hill
Podgornaya

─·─ order line based on Hunchun Border Pact, 1886
─··─ order line based on map by Chinese Army Survey
ureau, 1915–20
···· order line based on maps by Russian General Staff,
911, and Chinese Army, 1909

DISPOSITION OF FORCES
EVENING, 30 JULY 1938

N

MANCHUKUO
(MANCHURIA)

Tumen

Huichungyuan

U S S R

Paksikori

KOREN
(CHŌSEN)

CP
Kucheng

Yangkuanpi

Shikai

Matsuotsuho

Fangchuanting

Ushidana

Podgornaya

Sozan
ShoSozan
Hongui

Ryukem

DISPOSITION OF FORCES
NOON, 11 AUG. 1938 (Ceasefire)

xx	Division
III	Regiment
II	Battalion
I	Coy/Battery
···	Platoon

Tumen

U S S R

Huichungyuan

Paksikori

REA
SEN)

Kucheng

Yangkuanpu

Shikai

Matsuotsuho

Fanchuanting

Ushidana

Sozan
ShoSozan
Hongui

Podgornaya

Ryuken

32 Bn HQ
73 Regt.
74 Regt.
75 Regt.
76 Regt.
BGU
25 MT
19

THE CHANGKUFENG INCIDENT
JULY–AUGUST 1938

☐ Japanese units
▭ Soviet units
⊤⊤⊤ Japanese forward positions
⊤⊤⊤ Soviet forward positions

JAPANESE STRENGTH

Infantry: 12 battalions, Artillery: 33 pieces
Aircraft: less than 30? (grounded)

SOVIET STRENGTH (estimated)

Infantry: 27 battalions
Artillery: 100–150 pieces
Tanks: 200–510
Aircraft: 120–150

0 1 2 3 4 5 km
0 1 2 3 miles

forced the Soviets to effect a thorough reorganization of their forces and a tightening of their border security arrangements. Within weeks the Kwantung Army's ever-vigilant signals Intelligence monitors were to intercept and decode Russian military communications that provided the Japanese with an inkling of the trouble ahead. Shortly thereafter, the Soviets began to construct fixed defensive lines and reconnaissance positions on Changkufeng.

As the area formed a sector of the Manchukuoan frontier, it was only natural that the Kwantung Army should take a keen interest in its defence. However, local features of the terrain, better lines of communication and the fact that four out of every five inhabitants were Korean (and thus regarded as Japanese rather than Manchukuoan subjects) dictated that defence of the area should fall within the jurisdiction of Japan's Korean Army, whose major responsibility was the preservation of civil order in Korea. At first the Korean Army was inclined to adopt a watchful but undemonstrative attitude towards the Russian moves. Subjected to ridicule and accused of timidity by the Kwantung Army, the Korean Army Staff wired Tokyo that while the Russian action was clearly illegal, it had little immediate bearing upon offensive operations which Japan was preparing against Hankow and elsewhere. It would not be prudent to conduct a precipitate counter-attack while the China Incident was in full flood: 'This Army is thinking of reasoning with the Soviets and requesting it to pull back, directly on the spot . . . In case the Russians do not accede in the long run, we intend to drive the Soviet soldiers out of the area east of Khasan firmly by use of force.'

Imperial General Headquarters in Tokyo considered the matter calmly. It agreed with the Korean Army that the border should be kept under close surveillance and that no hasty action should be taken. If attacked, however, the Korean Army was to press forward at once, seize control of the disputed territory and on no account cross beyond what Japan recognized as the legal frontier. There was no policy of subterfuge or aggressive intent in this: the purposes of the Japanese high command were clearly unprovocative and as moderate as any self-respecting nation could permit itself. Through spontaneous impatience or unendurable provocation, however, Japanese officers at the scene sent out an unauthorized 'reconnaissance force' which resulted in a pitched battle for possession of the heights. The Japanese prevailed. In the weeks that followed, the Russians vainly attempted to re-establish themselves on the hills. The struggle intensified, but each successive Russian onslaught failed.

The emergency had arisen while the Korean Army was unusually weak. It normally comprised only two infantry divisions, but prior to the

Changkufeng Incident one of these, the Twentieth Division, had gone to take part in the China operation (leaving only a skeletal force at its depot in Korea). Fortunately, Lieutenant-General Suetaka Kamezō, commander of the remaining Nineteenth Division, giving vent to his mortification at long being held in reserve, had imposed an exceptionally arduous training regimen upon his troops that already had earned his division a reputation as one of the crack forces of the Japanese Empire. On the other hand, there was virtually no armour in Korea and only two air regiments (fewer than a hundred aircraft) in the entire country. Japan's experience in Manchuria and China had shown that any attempt to bring up reinforcements during a conflict was likely to lead to a mutual escalation of the fighting and to a vitiation of efforts to produce a negotiated settlement. The outlook was bad.

Once fighting developed, the world was confused by the evident scarcity of trustworthy reports from the battle zone. There was open disbelief about the veracity of information dispensed by Moscow and Tokyo. Western sentiments were summed up in a note which circulated in the British Foreign Office while the struggle was continuing: 'both Russians and Japanese are such accomplished liars and so addicted to all forms of bluff and bluster that one can be sure of nothing in this strange affair.' One curious difference was repeatedly remarked upon. The Soviet press was increasingly hysterical. The Japanese, in great contrast, took pains to underplay the strategical importance of the dispute. Each side, however, claimed to have suffered early setbacks followed by victory against almost overwhelming odds. British and American editors simply printed opposing accounts side by side under sensational headlines. The *New York Times* commented:

It isn't easy to guess what is going on. It is still more difficult to guess why it is going on ... In all the mystery and madness only one thing is clear from this distance. What takes place in the Manchurian frontier is not a mere border incident. It fits somehow into the great pattern of irrational forces moving behind events that involve Europe and Asia in an 'indivisible' struggle.

The little war of Changkufeng was no skirmish. Cramped within a radius of little more than one mile, an élite division of Japanese infantry, backed by a growing volume of artillery support but lacking any air or armour protection, was committed against a force three times as large and comprising no fewer than twenty-seven battalions of Soviet troops, 120–150 aircraft, 100–150 batteries of mostly heavy artillery, and massed tank assaults, often employing waves of 50–60 tanks, from Soviet armoured forces variously estimated at 200–500 tanks. Japanese military planners had long anticipated that in any war against the Soviet Union they would have to overcome odds of three to one. They expected to win. Here was a test case. Suetaka's under-strength division of barely 7,000 men faced the cream of the Soviet Far East Army, reputed to be a cut above the standard of the Red Army's European forces. By the time the guns were stilled, more than 40,000 men had been deployed by the two sides either directly in the fighting or acting in support. The intensity of the struggle can be gauged by measuring these numbers against the 70,000 troops which the Japanese would commit to the entire Malayan campaign and the roughly 43,000 utilized in the capture of the Philippines in 1941–2. Nevertheless, even experienced observers generally had no clear idea as to who started or even won the battle.

The truth was that both sides were badly mauled. The number of tanks, guns and aircraft which the Russians committed to the battle awed the Japanese but revealed a lack of imagination and common sense in terms of tactics and results. The performance of the Soviet infantry showed up badly against the initiative, efficiency and tenacity displayed by the Japanese. The effectiveness of the Red Army's artillery, although more impressive, by no means matched the standards set by the Japanese. Only 3 per cent of Japanese casualties were victims of aerial bombing compared to 37 per cent hit by shellfire. A neutral war correspondent at the scene who had fought on the Western Front in the First World War remarked that 'the Russian Army do not appear to have learnt anything of the art of war'.

The Japanese, who won the ground and held it, also had reason to be frightened. Although jubilant at their military victory, they knew how narrowly defeat had been averted. They were appalled not only by the rapidity with which the incident had developed but also by its sacrificial cost. The Japanese Army air force was not yet the superbly balanced instrument that it was to become in future. It was in no position to conduct air operations simultaneously in China and Manchuria. The Korean Army was desperately short of aircraft and first-class fliers, and Japan could not afford to be drawn into an air war that would prejudice the struggle underway in China. Military prudence as well as the political will to avoid any general escalation of the fighting compelled the Japanese to keep their own aircraft out of the skies and at airfields far from the scene. The Japanese gunners at Changkufeng, although able to engage the enemy at up to point-blank range, were seriously outnumbered and came perilously close to complete exhaustion of their ammunition. In these circumstances their technical superiority to the much-vaunted Russian artillery was scant comfort. The infantrymen fared little better:

their officers suffered exceptionally high losses and the exertions of the Nineteenth Division left it a spent force. The Japanese logistical system had repeatedly broken down, unequal to the demands placed upon it. This was serious. The main railway line between the port of Rashin and Hsinking (the imperial capital of Manchukuo and northern terminus of the South Manchurian Railway) ran within two or three miles of the battle line. In normal times troops embarked at Tsuruga on the west coast of Japan could cross the Sea of Japan and arrive at Hsinking via that railway within seventy-two hours. The Changkufeng Incident therefore exposed fundamental weaknesses in Japan's strategical position against the Soviet Union.

Fighting in such a confined space as Changkufeng and in such large numbers produced heavy casualties on both sides. The Japanese lost more than 500 dead and nearly 1,000 wounded. Although the Russians failed to overrun the Japanese positions on the eastern banks of the Tumen River and the absolute physical annihilation of the Nineteenth Division was narrowly averted, the human energies and material resources available to the Korean Army were all but consumed by the conflict. Estimates of Soviet casualties vary wildly, but the best guess is that the Russians suffered perhaps as many as 1,200 dead and more than 4,000 wounded. The Japanese set a pattern for the future by taking no prisoners. The casualties which each side suffered, while deeply disturbing to both, were minuscule compared to what Russia and Japan would lose when next they met on the battlefields of Asia.

The Changkufeng dispute was not settled by force of arms alone. Emperor Hirohito himself had already taken steps to express his unmistakable desire to see the Incident brought to a close and had insisted from the beginning that the forces committed to the battle must not advance into Russian territory. He had administered a strong rebuke to his War Minister, Lieutenant-General Itagaki Seishirō (the same man who had been one of the architects of the Manchurian Incident), and the Army Chief of Staff, the venerable old Prince Kan'in Kotohito, for seeking imperial authority to permit the Nineteenth Division and several divisions of the Kwantung Army to commence offensive operations against the Soviet Union if that perchance should seem appropriate to the Army General Staff. This was more than the Emperor was prepared to tolerate, and knowing that the Army's demands likewise were regarded as absurdly dangerous by Foreign Minister Ugaki Kazushige (himself a retired full general) and by the Navy Ministry and Naval General Staff, the Emperor forcefully expressed his abomination of the Army's propensity for embroiling itself in such incidents. From the

Army's point of view, the approach to the throne was therefore not only ill-conceived and ill-timed but heaped shame upon Japan's Imperial General Headquarters. Kan'in and Itagaki left the imperial presence completely shaken, convinced that their careers were in tatters and reflecting that they might have to atone for their misconduct by forfeiting their lives. In typically Japanese fashion, however, the Emperor sent word after them to say that he was content to retain them in the positions that they had so abused: divine benevolence could extend to those who saw the error of their ways.

Under the circumstances, the only way out was for the Japanese to abandon the field to the Russians or face the possibility of repeated counter-attacks by ever larger Russian forces. The Japanese Ambassador in Moscow, Shigemitsu Mamoru, was instructed to seek an immediate end to the conflict. The Russians seemed remarkably indifferent to his pleas, adding to the concern felt by the Japanese side. Any faint-heartedness felt by the Russians during the Amur River Incident was dispelled at Changkufeng by battlefield Intelligence coupled with high-level information acquired by Richard Sorge from a member of his spy ring who was a confidant of Prime Minister Konoye Fumimaro and in a position to observe the deliberations of the Cabinet close at hand. The certainty of the Russians that the Japanese authorities in the field and at Tokyo were determined to reach a rapid settlement of the incident at virtually any price laid the groundwork for the transformation of a military defeat into a Russian political triumph.

In the end, Ambassador Shigemitsu, with the full support of Foreign Minister Ugaki, agreed to surrender all of Japan's tactical gains. That, and the ability of the Japanese central authorities to control their troops on this occasion, impressed military planners, diplomats and their political masters abroad, who evaluated the slender information which had filtered through to them from the Changkufeng Incident. Many drew the ill-founded conclusion that Japan's wayward field commanders were only given their head when it suited the military authorities in Tokyo. In fact, the truth was almost precisely the opposite.

Odd though it may seem today, one theory which gained currency in Britain and elsewhere at the time was that the Japanese had bowed to German pressure in acquiescing to the only terms that Russia was prepared to accept: it was believed that the German Government had been so intent on resolving the Sudeten problem in Czechoslovakia that they had exerted all their influence upon Japan's military leaders to persuade them that it would be most unwise of Japan to start another major war prematurely. There was very little substance in this: Germany had no such influence over

Japan. Rather more accurately, Western doubts about the Soviet Union's military capabilities were abundantly confirmed by the events at Changkufeng. The tactical victory of the Korean Army showed that Japanese soldiers were just as able to stop a European Power (at least in a strictly limited war) as they had been in 1904-5. However the strategical lessons learnt from Russia's massive build-up during the fighting were that Japan could ill-afford to embark upon such adventures lightly and that Japan must liquidate the China Incident with all possible speed. Nearly everyone was convinced that Japan would scarcely be so foolhardy as to attempt any major offensive against the Soviet Union as matters stood. That being so, Russia might safely take a greater interest in European power politics for as long as Japan remained preoccupied in China. In each of these ways, then, the Changkufeng Incident provided a classic example of how events in East Asia were seen by the West to have a profound influence upon the stability of Europe.

Meanwhile, the Soviet Union gnawed its wounds. The celebrated and experienced Marshal Vasilii Konstantinovich Blyukher, who had risen from being a common soldier in the First World War to the command of the Red Army forces that had come to prominence during the Russian Civil War, and who afterwards had seen the Japanese out of Vladivostok in 1922, was obliged for the second time to bathe in the poisoned political waters of military defeat. In the mid-1920s he had been lent as a military adviser to Sun Yat-sen's young Chinese Republic. Under his tutelage, Chaing Kai-shek had embarked upon the northern campaign that had taken the Nationalist Armies to the gates of Manchuria. But when Chiang had turned against the communists, the man whom the Chinese had known by the name of 'General Galen' had been forced to flee. Afterwards, he had become virtually count palatine of Eastern Siberia. Now, having taken personal charge of the Red Army's operations at Changkufeng, Marshal Blyukher's second disaster proved fatal. Removed from command, he was executed by 9 November 1938. He had been living on borrowed time. General Lyushkov had given his Japanese and German interrogators information which linked Blyukher with anti-Stalinist circles within the Soviet Union. This Intelligence was fed back to Moscow by Richard Sorge in late October or early November 1938. Whether Blyukher would have survived the purges anyway is doubtful. More reliable and even more distinguished soldiers than he had perished in that lunatic bloodletting.

After the defeat of Japan in the Pacific War, fresh evidence concerning the operations at Changkufeng was put forward at the Tokyo War Trial by Soviet prosecutors. A parade of eye-witnesses, some lavishly decorated as 'Heroes of the Soviet Union' for their part in the action, tendered what purported to be incontrovertible proof that the Japanese first began the incident, were repulsed with heavy losses, thereafter continued to attack Soviet defensive positions along the disputed frontier, and treacherously took command of the heights only after a ceasefire had come into effect. The stories told by these Soviet affidavits and witnesses dovetailed together. They were packed with lies, but the Defence failed to rise to the challenge of producing evidence which would refute the Soviet claims. Due to lack of initiative and possibly lack of information such as a larger defence team might have amassed, the Tokyo Trial proceedings bogged down over the issue of conflicting Chinese and Imperial Russian versions of maps which neither side convincingly authenticated. In fact, the area had always been a no man's land, dotted with a few scattered Korean hamlets whose inhabitants cared nothing for frontiers and who had conducted seasonal religious sacrifices atop Changkufeng for centuries. The wooden stakes marking the original border had mostly rotted away long since, or been scavenged for firewood or been re-sited any number of times by over-zealous border guards. By 1938 there reportedly remained an average of one undisturbed marker for every twenty-five miles of frontier along a meandering line roughly 400 miles long. There were no markers at all within miles of Changkufeng. That was a suitably anonymous pretext for what is now seen as one of the classic limited wars of modern times. It was an archetypal antithesis, perhaps, to Total War, and yet nations stood eager to apply its lessons, imperfectly, on an unimaginably larger scale.

The following year, there was yet another of these incidents. The young turks of the Japanese Army believed that Japan was progressing. The Kwantung Army, recalling the imagined loss of face which it had endured when forced by Tokyo to restrain its subordinate units at the time of the Amur River Incident, distanced itself even further than before from the cautious policies promoted by the Japanese Government and the Imperial General Headquarters. Moreover, after analysing the Changkufeng Incident, Kwantung Army Headquarters was convinced that the Korean Army had bungled the affair and had been insufficiently aggressive from the start. So far as the bright sparks of the Kwantung Army were concerned, the only proper way to respond to Russian incursions was by the application of overwhelming force. Interrestingly enough, the Russians had come to much the same conclusions about the Japanese.

The Soviet Union laid a trap for the Japanese, a trap which seems to have been intended from the outset to teach the Japanese a punishing lesson. This incident occurred 700 miles away on the fringes of Outer Mongolia, where in the spring of 1939 a series of border incursions by cavalry units of the puppet Mongolian People's Republic culminated in an attack on 11 May 1939 by a force of seventy or eighty troops who crossed the Halha River and clashed with a Manchurian Army garrison a few miles to the north-east, at the Manchurian town of Nomonhan. The Kwantung Army, chafing at restraints imposed upon it by the General Staff in Tokyo ever since the Amur River Incident, was restless. In April 1939 the Commander-in-Chief of the Kwantung Army, General Ueda Kenkichi, had assembled his corps commanders to inform them that henceforward 'where the border lines are indistinct, the defence commander shall determine a boundary on his own'. As far as he was concerned, they could feel at liberty 'to invade Soviet territory temporarily, or to decoy Soviet soldiers and get them into Manchukuoan territory'.* It is unclear whether the trespass on 11 May 1939 stemmed from these instructions (which directly contradicted standing orders of Imperial General Headquarters). In the event, the local divisional commander ordered a Kwantung Army cavalry regiment to support the local Manchukuoan forces. When the Mongolian horsemen withdrew across the Halha, the Kwantung Army ordered its own cavalry to pursue and destroy them. A thousand infantrymen from the Kwantung Army's Sixty-fourth Infantry Regiment were dispatched to back up the cavalry. The trap claimed its first victims. The Japanese cavalry regiment was all but destroyed and the Japanese infantrymen narrowly avoided the same fate. Enveloped by Mongolian tanks and artillery before they had moved away from the river crossing, the Sixty-fourth Infantry Regiment were routed. This defeat was regarded by the Japanese as humiliating in the extreme, but no immediate steps were taken to avenge their defeat. For their part, the Russians issued an official warning that, by virtue of its defence treaty with Mongolia, Moscow would treat any further incidents on the Mongolian frontier as direct aggression against the Soviet Union.

By 18 June reports were received which indicated that Soviet forces had advanced once more across the frontier, driven back the Manchukuoan garrison forces (which may indeed have provoked them), and had bombed three major defensive positions to the rear. Within the Kwantung Army, a debate ensued during which it emerged that some staff officers were

* Cited by I. Hata in J. M. Morley (ed.), *Deterrent Diplomacy: Japan, Germany and the USSR, 1935–1940*, Columbia University Press, New York, 1976, p. 159.

inclined to take no action pending the outcome of Anglo-Japanese diplomatic conversations that were attempting to resolve the Tientsin Crisis and other outstanding sources of friction between Britain and Japan. Other voices, however, were raised in favour of inflicting an immediate blow against the Soviet Union sufficient to teach the Kremlin to avoid any further trouble with the Kwantung Army. The hotheads prevailed.

The Russians were far from blind to what the Japanese wanted to achieve at Nomonhan. Master spy Richard Sorge's top Japanese agent remained privy to the Japanese Cabinet's fervent desire to avoid war against the Soviet Union at virtually any price. The same agent also acquired detailed information from the South Manchurian Railway concerning the size and order of battle of the forces available to the Kwantung Army. Another Japanese in Sorge's employment toured the battlefront as a press correspondent, interviewed top-ranking Japanese military commanders at the scene, outlined the limited objectives of the Japanese forces and reported upon the numerical strength and types of Japanese aircraft and armoured fighting vehicles which had reached Nomonhan. Still other agents in Sorge's network passed on information about Japanese troop movements, the mobilization and state of readiness of Japanese air and armoured formations, and the strength of every unit which either had been committed to the battle or which might be in a position to take part in any full-scale offensive. Sorge himself learned from his contact with German military attachés and others that the Japanese had no intention of using the Incident as a pretext for a general invasion of the Soviet Union. The Kremlin may simply have chosen to disbelieve or to discount Sorge's Intelligence on this occasion. Moscow may have feared that the Nomonhan dispute was bound to escalate into a wider conflict unless drastic counter-measures were undertaken. On the other hand, the dispute provided a tempting opportunity to pay off a few old scores.

Kwantung Army Headquarters resolved to administer a crushing defeat upon the Russian and Mongolian forces by utilizing virtually all the rapid deployment forces of the Kwantung Army: the Twenty-third Infantry Division, nearly the whole of the Second Air Group, two regiments of light and medium tanks, a regiment of mechanized artillery, and an infantry regiment borrowed from the Seventh Division. This produced a force of some 15,000 men comprising three infantry battalions, 120 anti-tank guns, 70 tanks, 400 vehicles and 180 aircraft, leaving elsewhere only sufficient strength to safeguard the remainder of Manchuria. At this point the Soviet and Mongolian forces in the vicinity of Nomonhan were only less numerous than the Japanese, disposing of 12,500 men, 23 anti-tank weapons, 186 tanks and 266 armoured cars. Recalling recent experience and the Kwantung Army's formidable reputation as Japan's most battle-hungry military command, the odds appeared to be stacked heavily in favour of the Japanese. The War Ministry in Tokyo did hesitate to sanction an adventure which could contribute nothing to the China Incident (which was continuing to sap the nation's military and economic strength), but the Army General Staff felt justified in giving General Ueda its full support for the operation. War Minister Itagaki, who had retained a fondness for the 'forward policies' of the Kwantung Army ever since he had joined the conspiracy to assassinate Chang Tso-lin in 1928 and went on to engineer the Manchurian Incident in 1931, now decided to override the objections of his ministerial staff and gave his approval to the plans submitted by the Commander-in-Chief of the Kwantung Army. Significantly, however, General Ueda felt obliged to conceal his intention to open the campaign with an air offensive against the Russians: he was not the kind of man to shrink from the fact that a major air offensive, even if justified as a pre-emptive strike, was bound to provoke the Russians beyond measure. His worry was that revelation of his intentions would heighten the concern of those in Tokyo who wanted to avoid any serious escalation of the conflict: premature disclosure might prompt even the hawkish Army General Staff to abort the whole affair. When news of Ueda's secret intentions did come to the notice of Tokyo, his worst fears were abundantly fulfilled. A telegram was sent to Ueda ordering him to stay his hand pending the arrival of an emissary from the Army General Staff.

After considering the matter, the Kwantung Army staff responded by resorting to a trick which had served them well in early stages of the Manchurian and China Incidents: they advanced the date of their operations and pounded the Russian air base of Tamsagbulag before Tokyo could stop them. The returning pilots jubilantly claimed to have destroyed ninety-nine enemy aircraft in aerial combat and a further twenty-five on the ground. Tokyo was faced with yet another *fait accompli*.

Imperial General Headquarters in Tokyo was outraged by this latest example of the Kwantung Army's irresponsible and insubordinate attitude. The Emperor, too, was infuriated and demanded that General Ueda, if no one else, should be brought to book. Kwantung Army Headquarters, unrepentant, politely invited Tokyo to leave the fighting to the men at the scene. The Army General Staff and political authorities in Tokyo could do little else. They did force the Kwantung Army to suspend attacks against the Russian air bases, but air combat missions continued over the war zone. At the beginning of July, the Kwantung Army's Twenty-third Infantry Division crossed into Outer Mongolia. They were met by several hundred Russian tanks. At first the Japanese seemed destined to repeat their performance at Changkufeng. More than a hundred enemy tanks were set ablaze. But the Russians held, forcing the Japanese to withdraw across the river after less than two days of combat. Meanwhile, further south, a Japanese tank offensive was launched across the Halha River. After losing forty tanks, the momentum of the attack faltered and the Japanese again had no option but to withdraw. By this time more than half of the tanks deployed by each side had been put out of action after only a few days of combat. The Japanese were in a far worse position than the Russians to sustain such crippling losses. Moreover, the Japanese were alarmed to find that their own medium tanks were easily penetrated by Russian anti-tank guns and that Russian armour was proof against cannonfire from Japanese tanks. Most of the Russian tank losses to date had been due to grenade attacks pressed home by Japanese infantrymen who lacked effective artillery support. In an effort to remedy this imbalance, the Kwantung Army scoured its depots across the length and breadth of Manchuria and managed to gather together nearly a hundred heavy guns to bear upon the Russians. Their gunners laid down a barrage of some 15,000 shells a day and another Japanese offensive began.

The Russians replied with even heavier counter-fire. The Kwantung Army once again had to break off the engagement. The Army General Staff in Tokyo was ready to concede the victory to the Russians then and there, but the Kwantung Army was determined to continue. Then, unexpectedly, the Russians sent their bombers 200 miles deep into Manchuria. The Kwantung Army redoubled their efforts to raise the ban imposed by Tokyo on air strikes upon the Russian air bases. Imperial General Headquarters, however, flatly refused and intimated that the Kwantung Army was reaping a harvest which it richly deserved.

The Chief of Staff of the Kwantung Army, Lieutenant-General Isogai Rensuke, was summoned to Tokyo and on 20 July was told in no uncertain terms that the Kwantung Army must do everything within its power to bring the Incident to an end. If it should prove impossible to resolve the dispute by diplomatic means, then Tokyo would have to order the Kwantung Army to withdraw beyond the boundary now claimed by the Soviet Union. General Isogai was incensed by these instructions, flatly refusing to consent to them. In the end, however, he grimly agreed to convey the wishes of Imperial General Headquarters back to his Army Headquarters in Manchuria (where they were ignored).

By 21 July Japanese Intelligence reports were accurately predicting that the Russians would open their own offensive in a month's time. The Japanese anticipated, however, that the Kwantung Army could absorb whatever punishment that the Russian and Mongolian side might inflict. The military and political authorities in Tokyo remained as disturbed as formerly at the capricious behaviour of the Kwantung Army, and this certainly contributed towards their unwillingness to reinforce the units already engaged in the campaign. One trainload after another ferried fresh Soviet troops and up-to-date weaponry along the Trans-Siberian Railway. They disembarked and moved up to their assembly points beyond the Halha. In the early part of August, Tokyo reluctantly consented to a lifting of the ban upon air operations over Outer Mongolia: it was a purely precautionary measure, not an escalation of the conflict. News of this soon reached Marshal Zhukov. Then bad weather obscured Japanese aerial reconnaissance over the battlezone for a fortnight. The Russian commander seized his opportunity. The trap was sprung.

Rank upon rank of armoured vehicles backed by massed infantry and coupled with close air support (now far more effective than at Changkufeng) churned through the Japanese and Manchurian lines. Only when the weather began to clear did the Japanese discover to their horror that they were caught in a pincer movement by three infantry divisions and five tank brigades while Zhukov held two further divisions in reserve. This was four or five times the numerical strength of the faltering Japanese and Manchurian forces who were powerless to resist the Russian and Mongolian onslaught. The Japanese lines simply crumpled beneath the weight of the enemy attack. Within little more than the span of a week the remnants of the Japanese and Manchurian forces fled back across the Halha and beyond until they reached what was indisputably Manchurian soil. The Russo-Mongolian forces did not yield to any temptation to follow in hot pursuit. They settled down along the line of what they asserted to be the proper frontiers of the People's Republic of Mongolia and began to fortify it. This was Changkufeng turned upside down.

Deluded by the thought that Japanese divisional and company commanders at the scene had shown insufficient initiative, that courageous individual actions by common soldiers had somehow parried the Russo-Mongolian forces which (by this reckoning) must have lost any stomach for further fighting, Kwantung Army Headquarters decided to risk everything on an immediate, all-out riposte. Four more divisions as well as all the heavy artillery and quick-firing weaponry left in Manchuria were to be thrust into a counter-attack which was planned to open with a week of relentless night attacks from 10 September. The purpose of this whole operation was not merely to erase the Soviet gains by driving back the Russian and Mongolian armies. That was merely a preliminary objective. It was to be expected that military operations would have to break off for a season of suspended animation in the winter months, but Kwantung Army Headquarters planned its autumn offensive to herald nothing less than the opening of a general war against the Soviet Union in the following spring. Understandably enough, Imperial General Headquarters in Tokyo blenched. It was a perfectly ludicrous scheme. The Kwantung Army was told to abandon it at once.

Many considerations affected the outcome. Events were moving swiftly in international affairs and the chronic internal wrangling of Army politics grew if anything more important. War in Europe was imminent. Hitler's preparations for the attack on Poland, completed since June, had been suspended while the Russo-Japanese conflict at Nomonhan developed. Then, just as the Soviets launched their offensive against the Kwantung and Manchurian Armies, news came of the Nazi-Soviet Pact. The groundwork for that had been well prepared months before, but the Japanese had been duped by the Germans into discounting evidence of what was afoot. The threat of a Russo-German War now abruptly receded, leaving the Japanese completely isolated and exposed. No Japanese Cabinet could have survived such a shock. The Hiranuma Cabinet duly fell on 29 August 1939.

War Minister Itagaki was replaced by the less mercurial General Hata Shunroku, who had last fought the Russians during the Russo-Japanese War of 1904–5. Hata knew what kind of difficulties would confront Japan in its efforts to seek a negotiated settlement of the dispute: he had taken an active role in negotiating the Russo-Japanese Convention of 1925 by which Japan and the Soviet Union first established normal diplomatic relations in the aftermath of the Siberian Intervention. Furthermore Hata, who had been Commander-in-Chief of the Japanese Expeditionary Forces in Central China in the wake of General Matsui's disgrace after the Rape of Nanking, was acutely conscious of the quagmire into which the Japanese had slipped in China, and as if that were not enough to make him more cautious than Itagaki as War Minister, Hata had been engaged as Chief ADC to the Emperor in May 1939 on the eve of the Nomonhan Incident and thus knew the earnestness with which Hirohito yearned for peace.

However well suited Hata may have been for the onerous tasks which lay before him, neither his appointment as War Minister nor General Abe Nobuyuki's selection as Prime Minister could be made without the endorsement of the Army General Staff. That approval was willingly granted, thus setting the seal upon the realignment of national politics that now took shape. The Army General Staff appeared to have taken to heart the painful lessons administered by Zhukov's battalions, and Japan emerged from the Nomonhan Incident with a consensus between Imperial General Headquarters and the Government which had been conspicuously absent in the recent past. General Abe and his Cabinet were committed to ending the war as soon as possible, and on 2 September, as early news of the German invasion of Poland reached Japan, the Japanese Army General Staff decided to wait no longer but to break off the Nomonhan Incident by effecting a unilateral withdrawal.

The peace negotiations for which neither Japan nor the Soviet Union had shown enthusiasm between mid-July and late August, were rekindled by the Abe Government in early September. On 16 September an armistice was signed, sparing the Japanese Army General Staff the embarrassment of having to implement its decision of 2 September. All concerned recognized that the ceasefire confirmed the comprehensiveness of the Kwantung Army's military defeat. Detailed discussions held over the months which followed led step by step to further concessions by the Japanese, who finally yielded to the Russians virtually every bone of contention. The end result was marked by a formal accord signed on 18 July 1940: the Japanese diplomats, as usual, were obliged to accept the obloquy of a defeat which quite properly should have been reserved for the military alone.

The military, meanwhile, found other scapegoats, too. Matters were patched up so as to disturb the system as little as possible. Nothing like the great debate over the Washington Treaty System was to be allowed to fragment the Japanese military and political establishment. General Ueda Kenkichi, the ill-fated Commander of the Kwantung Army, and his Chief of Staff, General Isogai Rensuke, were simply replaced by less volatile men. Ueda was never again to be re-employed by the Army. He was so well buried that when he re-surfaced to give evidence at the Tokyo War Trial after the war, nobody even remembered to ask him about what he might recollect of the Nomonhan Incident. General Isogai, after years of disgrace, had the dubious honour to be resurrected as Governor-General of Hong Kong from January 1942 until the war was all but over. He, too, excited no curiosity from either side at the Tokyo Trial: the Nomonhan Incident was a chapter which both sides wanted to forget, except in abstract formulations, and yet it had been one of the most significant armed clashes in the modern history of East Asia.

In geographical terms, the Nomonhan Incident had covered a far wider front than the Amur River and Changkufeng Incidents: it had spread out over an area roughly forty miles wide and eighteen or twenty miles deep. That scarcely accounts for its true significance. It is conventional to judge the relative importance of armed conflicts in terms of their human and material costs. Altogether the Kwantung Army and its protégé, the Manchurian Army, sent 56,000 troops into battle at Nomonhan. It cost Japan and Manchuria 8,440 dead and 8,766 wounded, a devastating 32 per cent casualty rate. The veteran Twenty-third Infantry Division, which had borne the brunt of the fighting, suffered 11,000 casualties, three quarters of its original strength. One can only guess at the strength of the Soviet-Mongolian side but certainly after the opening rounds it was both qualitatively and numerically superior to the forces disposed by the Japanese. It is said that the Russians and Mongolians sustained about 9,000 casulaties. Moscow never disclosed the true figures. The real significance of the Nomonhan Incident, however, extends beyond its human and material balance-sheet. To a great extent it was to determine the shape of the Total War that was yet to come.

From this point onwards the Kwantung Army, although previously regarded as the toughest and most audacious military force in East Asia, simply ceased to exert any decisive influence upon history. To all intents and purposes, it suffered a paralysing stroke at Nomonhan. It withered away and, by 1945, survived only in a twilight of senility which left it incapable of resistance when the Russians came to bludgeon their way across Manchuria. In a larger sense, the Nomonhan Incident provides us with a salutary demonstration of how limited military operations can affect the overall strategical balance between rival nations. It forced the Imperial Japanese Army to abandon any further serious design to mount a northern offensive to secure control over Eastern Siberia. The more bold and radical elements within the Army began to consider the merits of a southern advance instead. That was a strategy dear to certain middle-ranking cliques in the Imperial Navy with whom they were in contact. It was regarded by the Navy's more level-headed upper echelons as pie-in-the-sky, a mere nostrum that admittedly had served to justify ever-greater naval expansion over the years and in the past had helped to curb the hotheads who up to now had wanted to swarm across the Russian frontier. However cynically the Navy's most senior commanders may have paid lip-service to the southern advance idea in the past, it had been merely as a theoretical framework rather than as a blueprint for aggression. Now they and their civilian counterparts found themselves unwillingly drawn along by impatient junior officers who demanded deeds and despised masterly inactivity.

The lull in the north lengthened. The Kwantung Army and the Russians continued to probe each other, but the frontier gradually fell quiet. The small-scale incidents, the constant shooting and skirmishes, the espionage and incitements, which had from the start seemed natural to the relationship between these two Powers, dwindled. That is not to say that either side knew peace. At the Tokyo War Trial, Soviet Prosecutors would accuse the Japanese of having violated the frontiers of the Soviet Union on 49 occasions in 1940, 136 in 1941, 229 in 1942 and 414 in 1943. The Soviets would also charge the Japanese with having flown over Soviet territory on 56 occasions in 1940, 61 in 1941, 82 in 1942 and 119 in 1943. In reply, the Japanese would claim that the Soviets had violated the frontiers of Manchuria on 151 occasions in 1940, 98 occasions in 1942 and so on. Whatever the accuracy of these figures (and they cannot be said to be reliable), we must not doubt that these borders remained exceedingly sensitive. There was plenty of rumour, and the outbreak of war on the frontier was still regarded as a very natural possibility by the Japanese. The psychology had not changed: Japan remained malevolent and insecure towards Russia. Russia was still regarded, with deadly cold hostility, as a national enemy, in a way in which China, even at the height of the war between the two Governments, was not. But it became clear that in one way Japan had changed its behaviour. Unless attacked in Manchuria, it was content to do no attacking. More importantly, a powerful current began to pull Japan towards some kind of détente with the Soviet Union. Some Army circles even spoke up in favour of an alliance between Germany, Japan and the Soviet Union. It was an absurdly unrealistic idea. A non-aggression pact between Japan and the Soviet Union, however, was a practical proposition. It came to pass in April 1941, by which time Japan was well on her way towards the Pacific War.

Although one cannot say that peace subsisted between Japan and the Soviet Union after Nomonhan, an unnatural silence descended upon their common frontiers while, in other parts of the world, fighting broke out with great savageness.

Part II

OCEAN CLASH

CHAPTER 13

The War Changes Its Character

THE key to Japan's policy was still the China Incident. With this up-permost in mind, Japan approached the matter of its relations with the western countries in the war which was beginning in Europe.

When the Japanese found that Chungking would not make peace with them, they became convinced that it was enabled to continue fighting, and was encouraged to keep up a hopeless resistance, because of the aid given to it by the Western Powers. In fact, China was complaining desperately at the shortage of war supplies. The aid that it received from the western democracies was a trickle, which the Japanese greatly exaggerated. They professed to be convinced, however, that only the severance of China's link with the democratic Powers would bring an end to the China adventure. The war was telling upon the Japanese, and most groups were anxious to be free of it. Some of them had begun to think that it had been too lightly embarked upon.

The outbreak of the war in Europe in 1939 seemed to give Japan its opportunity to bring pressure to bear upon the countries which persisted in maintaining relations with China. Japan, on the world stage, found itself in much the same position as it had been in the war of 1914–18. To the average citizen reading his daily newspaper in London, Berlin or New York, the direction which Japan might take had suddenly magnified its value greatly: to the guardians of his country's security and foreign policies, the onset of hostilities in the West by contrast actually diminished the regard which European nations were disposed to give to events in East Asia. The experts agreed that for Britain, especially, whether Japan remained strictly neutral or sided with the Axis Powers remained a life or death matter but there was precious little that the British Empire could do to affect Japan's determination of its course. Nevertheless, Japan saw that a new bargaining opportunity had opened up. There was an unfamiliar flexibility in its international relations. Out of the international situation, by blackmail or cajolery, Japan could expect to bend the attitude of other Powers in such a way as to place the whole of East Asia under firm Japanese hegemony.

Already from 1938 Japan, partly under the impetus of patriotic parties which increasingly dictated its policies, partly because of the weakening position of its rivals in East Asia, drifted into a steady widening of its powers in the region. The stage was being set for its collision with the United States. It became convinced that it was practicable to clear East Asia of American as well as of European influences. The United States, while avoiding territorial aggressiveness, had no intention of vacating its position and rights.

First, however, Japan sought to apply its growing power to complete the isolation of China, and thus to compel it to bring the China Incident to an end. Japan's force had, as its immediate objective, the task of cutting off the links which enabled China, though beaten in the field, to refuse peace.

Chiang Kai-shek, in his retreat to Chungking in far-off Szechuan Province, had two lifelines to the West. There was a road through north-west China, occupied by the Chinese communists, down which filtered a little oil from Russia, a quantity of obsolescent weaponry and some Soviet personnel. The Soviet Union's most important contribution to the defence of Free China was a programme intended to build up the Chinese air forces. The first Russian airmen and ground mechanics had begun to arrive at the end of October or the beginning of November 1937. The Soviets evidently had agreed to sell the Chinese about 300 aircraft immediately and to keep about 200 in flying condition thereafter. It is difficult to put this into proportion, but British air Intelligence experts reckoned that this was about the same order of magnitude as the entire strength of the Czech Air Force, which was then judged to be a fairly formidable force: despite the vast differences in the size of Czechoslovakia and China, air operations over China tended to be concentrated in relatively small zones so the comparison is not unreasonable. In any event, the Soviets continued to maintain a steady supply of about forty aircraft per month to China, and the total number of aircraft supplied had reached around 500 at the first anniversary of the China Incident. At that time, the Soviet air mission in China was estimated by foreign Intelligence experts to include about 150 airmen and 300 ground staff. In combat and in training they suffered heavy losses. Two flying schools were established at Hankow and Lanchow early on, with about 100 aircraft and fifty Soviet instructors. Due to the low efficiency reached by the Chinese trainees, however, the Soviets tended to pilot their own aircraft in special-purpose squadrons, except during the Battle for Hankow and over neighbouring frontline areas where Chinese pilots were preferred.

All in all, the effectiveness of the Soviet aid to China is easy to exaggerate although the size of the Soviet commitment was substantial. Looking on the positive side, French Intelligence reports early on suggested that the Soviet airmen were very accomplished fliers and had proved themselves blindly obedient to orders whatever the consequences. Other western Intelligence officers, however, suggested that the true picture was far from rosy: the officer corps of Soviet air forces as a whole showed a notorious lack of initiative, employed wasteful, inefficient tactics, and disgraced the high morale and fair skill displayed by individual Soviet pilots. The performance of the Soviet air forces at Nomonhan in 1939 had surprised the Japanese. Yet by 1940 reports reaching western air staffs spoke of the uneasy state of relations between Chinese air officers and their propagandizing Soviet 'friends'. Americans who had seen the Soviet pilots took note of their unclean, unkempt appearance, their now poor flying skills, their obsolete aircraft, their high rates of attrition and their reluctance to press home any attacks against the Japanese. The same American observers were highly impressed by the skill of the Japanese, their discipline and their fighting spirit.

But it was clear to anyone who was at Chungking at this time that, following the collapse of German military assistance to China, the channels of communication which were valued most highly were those of the Anglo-Saxon Powers. It was on these – first on a railway through French Indo-China which had its outlet at Hanoi, and later, after it was wrecked by bombing and by Japanese intimidation of the Vichy French régime, on an earth road through Burma, and still later on an air lift from Calcutta direct to Chungking – that Kuomintang eyes were riveted. The Japanese were right in supposing that as long as these remained open China would feel that it was not cut off from support from the West. However little was flowing at the moment, as long as the communication remained open, the hope endured in China that more might be made to flow. But always the hinge of China's fate depended upon these communications remaining open. (There were still one or two other avenues, too, such as minute quantities of weapons smuggled out of Hong Kong to guerrilla forces operating within Japanese-occupied territories, but these, although much appreciated, were far less important.)

Japan was well aware that the most immediate way to force an end to the war lay in interrupting these tenuous lines of communication. The Japanese put their trust in a turn in events making it appear more a matter of material interest to the West that the western goverments should extinguish their foreign aid to China. The disastrous defeats suffered by France and Great Britain in the spring campaigns of 1940 appeared to give Japan its opportunity.

In the middle of 1940, after the fall of France, when Britain was in its most desperate condition, Japan demanded that Britain should close the Burma Road. Given the European situation, Britain was in no condition to refuse. Churchill demurred but in the end gave way. At the time, expert opinion was divided as to whether Japan would seize upon the issue as a pretext to open hostilities against Britain's imperial outposts in East Asia. Through well-judged crisis management all that Britain lost and Japan gained was a modicum of prestige, and even that was soon reversed to the discomfiture of the Japanese: the British agreed to suspend traffic on the Burma Road for an indefinite time, then re-opened it after the elapse of only three months, a period which (as British diplomats then lost no opportunity of recounting to the amusement of others round the world) happened to coincide with the monsoon season during which the Road was impassable anyway. After that, the aid again flowed, though scarcely more than a trickle. It was enough to give China hope and helped to restore flagging American confidence in the determination of the British Empire to continue to do its utmost to resist Japanese aggression. As Lieutenant-Colonel Harry Creswell, the long-serving United States Military Attaché in Tokyo, reported in October 1940:

In a practical sense it is difficult to determine how important the Burma Road is to China and whether any large bulk of supplies is being moved over that route. This aside from the fact that it is the last Chinese outlet except through Soviet Russia.

From the Japanese standpoint, however, the road has become the symbol of foreign opposition to the success of Japanese operations in China, and as such has taken on an importance in their eyes at least as great as whatever real value it may have as a source of supply to China.

As in the case of many controversies which were formerly more or less limited to the Orient, since the start of the European War and the alignment of Japan with the totalitarian Axis, the Burma Road issue has become more directly linked with the larger issues involved in that struggle . . . From this standpoint, what may be the Japanese reaction to a re-opening of this road is difficult to foretell at this time. That it will only serve to worsen both Anglo-Japanese and American-Japanese relations, should both nations use the road for supplying the Chinese, is too trite to deserve mention.*

Emperor Hirohito, indeed, had been deeply pessimistic about the outcome of the Burma Road Incident even as the crisis was coming to a head. The British announcement of the suspension of traffic on the Road surprised him. On 11 July, a week before, he gloomily told Marquis Kido Kōichi, Lord Keeper of the Privy Seal, 'I am inclined to think that Britain will

* MID 2063–357/37, Comments on Current Events No. 36, by Military Attaché, Japan, Report No. 10216, 7 October 1940, by Lieutenant-Colonel Harry I. T. Creswell, MA, RG 165, Modern Military Archives, Modern Military Branch, US National Archives, Washington, DC.

reject our proposal for closing the "Aid-Chiang Route". In such case, will not the occupation of Hong Kong become necessary, and result in the declaration of war? If so, the USA would probably resort at least to embargo measures.' Both of them worried lest unrest within the Army should 'stir up unpleasant incidents'.* In the Emperor's eyes, at least, the British position in East Asia thus far continued to command respect.

This seems, in fact, an appropriate place to observe that Britain's paramount position in China until the Second World War has been forgotten by the British public – and never was properly appreciated by the American people at large. The Japanese, however, knew of its importance as well as did the Chinese. It is easy to be more impressed by memory of the decline of British influence than by an appreciation of its long persistence.

It is commonly believed that Britain was caught lamentably off-guard by the Japanese attack in Malaya and Hong Kong at the close of 1941. That, however, is simply untrue. The Japanese threat was taken extremely seriously by the British Empire throughout the inter-war years, and until 1939 the position of Singapore was regarded as one of the two keystones upon which the survival of the Empire depended (the other being neither Suez nor Gibraltar but nothing less than the security of the United Kingdom itself). Britain's system of imperial defence planning, preparations and precautions continued to be as exemplary during the European War as it had been beforehand. The Royal Navy, as it existed at the outbreak of the European War, however, had been designed to fight the Japanese while containing the German fleet. There were no margins for error: until war actually broke out, the best professional advice was that the country could afford nothing more. If the generals and airmen grumbled, it was in part because huge sums of money had been spent on the Navy rather than reserved for ground or air forces. If the Japanese threat could have been ignored, all three of Britain's fighting services would have been constructed along very different lines. As it was, the British fleet in September 1939 continued to be the largest in the world, as it had been for longer than anyone cared to remember. The war against Germany and Italy made offensive action against Japan impossible throughout most of the Second World War. The loss of Malaya and Singapore, the obliteration of Britain's naval forces on the China Station, and the sinking of the *Prince of Wales* and *Repulse* within a week of the outbreak of the Pacific War may have been events which were still to come but they were not unexpected by Britain's admirals. They had always warned that the survival of Britain's defensive position in the East depended upon the

* PD 1632 QQ, Entry from Kido Diary, 11 July 1940, IMTFE Prosecution Documents.

immediate dispatch of Britain's main fleet to Singapore at the outset
of hostilities – and that if the fleet that could be spared should prove
unequal to its task, the British Empire would wither away. That is not to
say that the United Kingdon always shrank away from war against the
Japanese. There had been times – notably in December 1937, January 1938
and during the development of the Tientsin Crisis in the summer of 1939 –
when Britain was exceedingly truculent and came within a hair's breadth of
responding to Japanese provocations by sending out the fleet, even though
knowing full well that such a step would commit Britain to war.

On the whole, however, the general tendencies of British policy in the
East throughout this period remained as they had been since the beginning
of the China Incident. In his epigrammatic way, Sir Robert Vansittart,
the former Permanent Under-Secretary for Foreign Affairs, had voiced
one strand of opinion quite succinctly in those days: 'Our policy', he said,
'is to let the Chinese win the war for us, but without our help.' To this the
Deputy Director of Military Intelligence at the War Office had retorted,
with some truth:

It would be more accurate probably to say, 'let the Chinese prevent Japan from
winning the war'. While this policy appears to have more chance of success than
one of making an arrangement with Japan, it will invariably result, I should say,
in our becoming heartily disliked by both parties.*

The Burma Road affair was an occasion during which, in contrast to its
handling of the Tientsin Dispute only a year before, Britain lacked any
military means to act unilaterally in opposing the will of Japan. Britain's
resort to nothing more than parlour tricks in order to regain the upper
hand on the Burma Road issue was admired, and it did gain Britain
sufficient time to adjust to the calamitous events which had just taken
place in Europe. But the Burma Road Crisis, and the stepped-up American
economic pressure upon Japan which counterpointed it, also served notice
upon the Government and people of the United States – and Japan – that
prime responsibility for the continued maintenance of western influence
in East Asia had now passed irretrievably to America.

Throughout these years, indeed, Japan had come increasingly to collide
with the other Anglo-Saxon Power, the United States. The clash with the
United States, which at first had seemed a passing incident of its China

---

* MI2/379, Jap IV, 3.B(a), Minute by Deputy Director of Military Intelligence, 25 June
  1938, to Director of Military Operations and Intelligence (through Deputy Director of
  Military Operations), covering copy of Foreign Office Despatch 305 [F4462/71/23] to
  Tokyo, 17 May 1938, WO 106/5469, British Public Record Office, Kew.

policy, swelled up until it came to dominate all Japan's foreign relations. The need to free itself from American pressure in its plans for the future of East Asia became an obsession with Japan.

Japanese relations with the United States had been worsening for years. They had taken a steady decline from the days of the Russo-Japanese War, at which time the United States had been very sympathetic towards Japan, and relations had been cordial. In those distant days the United States had the characteristic of not always appearing to base its sentiments in foreign relations so solidly on self-interest as did the other Great Powers. It gave more play to national feelings in favouring and disfavouring countries. America was temperamentally drawn to the underdog; Japan seemed to be a small Goliath.

Afterwards, as we have seen, the relations became less good as Japan became a great naval Power and a target as well as an apparent threat to the United States Navy and those sectors of the American public which sought to extend American domination across the whole of the Pacific. Simultaneously, the American enactment of the Japanese Exclusion Act of 1924, which forbade Japanese emigration to the United States, pursued with the maximum resolution and the minimum regard to sparing Japan's feelings, made Japan reconsider its sentiments towards the United States. To Japan, the United States had become the most insulting and insensitive of Great Powers, blocking Japan's path to progress and compelling the country to devote exceptional energies to its effort to escape the forces which seemed to be propelling her towards a collision against twin millstones of American naval and economic might.

When the Manchurian Incident had occurred, the United States had quickly disclosed a policy which it was to follow with remarkable consistency (although the executive branch of the United States Government was not entirely able to overcome temptations to do otherwise). It would have nothing to do with the League of Nations or – except at a uselessly superficial level – with collective attempts at restraining Japan as an aggressor. That was ruled out by the overwhelming strength of American isolation and by the notorious clumsiness of American policy-making machinery. American opinion was behind isolation as the only way of preserving the United States from involvement in war: and it was fondly believed by many that in isolating itself, the United States was cutting itself off from the possibility of influencing the course of world affairs. Many enlightened Americans chafed at this and, often at cross-purposes with one another, involved themselves in international conversations which hopelessly confused and exasperated foreign governments. But it was accepted by most realist Americans that the United States had no alternative in the state to which it had been brought by the many-sided propaganda to which it was subjected.

The United States was unwilling to draw the conclusion from its inactivity that it would acquiesce in the map of the world being redrawn by force. It declared that it would never recognize changes which were being brought about by aggression. There was, it must be admitted, something slightly ridiculous in the spectacle of the United States refusing to recognize the facts brought about by war, but declining to do anything to prevent these changes. It was living in a fool's paradise. But the policy was calculated to bear fruit in the future. By persistently refusing to recognize Japan's coups in defiance of international law, but obstinately declining to regard Japan as ever succeeding in closing a door, by leaving open every issue for regulation in the future, and by resisting all efforts made by Japan to equate its actions with those which had been taken by other Powers, including the United States only a few decades before, the United States managed to undermine, with surprising success, Japan's various steps at building its Empire and establishing its hegemony in adjacent territories.

The United States, however, was peculiarly self-distrustful. It had had, in the First World War, the experience of being drawn into the fighting partly, as it decided afterwards, against its better judgement. Probably, when the war was over, a majority of the people, if their opinion had been tested in a plebiscite, would have opined that the First World War was a mistake. If they had had a second chance, they would have kept out. They believed that America had been over-persuaded by subtle propaganda. And unmindful as they were of the difficult economic circumstances which afflicted their erstwhile allies, the Americans were deeply offended by the reluctance or refusal of those allies to repay wartime loans granted by American institutions and taxpayers. There was more than one way to become victimized by scheming foreigners. There were many in the United States who became intent on warning their fellow countrymen to beware of all plots to make America go further than the American people meant.

So, when the Second World War broke out, most Americans, though their sympathies were for the most part engaged against Hitler and his supporters, were firmly against American participation in the war. They were bent on saving the United States from itself. Just because they wished for Hitler's defeat, they were suspicious that the United States would come under pressure to depart from its neutrality: they therefore sought to provide against American force being employed in his overthrow, and urged that the United States should not be officially engaged in war. They went to extraordinary lengths in devising laws which would tie up the American executive, and prevent it from drifting into war. Of the fetters by which the United States bound itself, the most remarkable were the successive Neutrality Acts: laws which aimed at prohibiting the United States from engaging in commerce with either of the belligerents which might involve the country in warlike attitudes. The Neutrality Acts had been passed by successive sessions of the United States Congress in the teeth of opposition by the administration. It was made possible by the American Constitution, which sharply separates the powers and responsibilities of the legislative and executive branches of the United States Government.

Because of this resolution to maintain the peace, because of the peculiar institutions by which the American resolve was enforced, Japan was for some years protected to a large extent from the consequences of its actions. The Neutrality Act was a product of the fear of war with Germany, but Japan derived benefit from it. There had never before in world history been such a strange case of a Great Power deliberately tying itself up, and ensuring that in no circumstances should it act as it would have been natural for it to do. The consequences, the ways that the United States responded to pressure from Japan, were curious. True, it was possible for the American administration to thwart in various ways the intentions of the American Congress, but the laws were rigid, and there were limits to the degree to which they could be transgressed.

One must not forget, however, that few modern nations are as politically volatile as the United States. Its elected officials are quick to follow the whims and fashions of a free but often xenophobic press, which itself is conscious of its need to balance its duty to inform an unsophisticated electorate with its duty to satisfy its advertisers and investors. In this government of the people, by the people and for the people, charismatic national figures with little knowledge of foreign affairs and party hacks with an inadequate grasp of the history of events, wield an uncommon control over generals, admirals and career civil servants, a control which is often undeflected by the weight of professional advice or experience. Given the extraordinary responsiveness of the United States Government to the political will of its people, it may have been as well that by passing the Neutrality Acts the American people effectively curbed for some years their own susceptibility to wild changes of mood and unproductive swings of political direction.

Throughout that time, some powerful American personalities and groups were warning the country that Japan on the march was a threat to the security of the United States. Each Japanese thrust – the rape of Manchuria, the rupture with the League of Nations, the war with China which had spread far and wide since 1937, the blowing of the wind in Japan of a revolutionary assertiveness – caused the warning to be louder. American opinion became troubled. It had reacted with little force to the beginning of the crisis in 1931 when Japan had seized Manchuria; ten years later, Japan's moves were followed with tense interest by many people in the United States. At first the concern over Japan was largely regional, being found especially on the West Coast, which had trading connections with Asia. Eye-witness reports also began to filter back home from missionaries who told of their first-hand experience of the horrors of life in the Chinese war zones. Gradually concern became more wide-spread.

Fortifying this group of people who would have liked the United States to take an active role in Asia was the China lobby. This became for some years an influential pressure group in American politics. The active and practical minded found themselves in an open conspiracy to bring pressure to bear in Congress upon all matters in which Chinese interests were engaged. The curious thing was that in the United States this group was so intent and generated so much emotion. Other countries, Britain for example, had had sectional groups which, by the accident of their history, had been equally exposed to the lure of Chinese civilization, a force which habitually proved attractive to minds of a certain type. But a Chinese lobby, in the sense in which it was known in the United States, never operated in British politics.

Japan doubtless failed to give due weight to the importance of the China lobby in the United States. It always mistook American politics: that was one of its features. Japan had, it is true, some experts on the United States who were well-informed: but they were not attended to. Some Japanese, including men of considerable influence among those who made Japanese policies, believed, and acted on the principle, that the United States, whose soul was given up to commerce, could not prevail over a nation of Samurai warriors, whatever material advantages it seemed to possess. They misread American history. They took no account of the fact that, after the compromises and the prevarication of the democratic system, the United States had shown itself able to go to war, and to wage it with an obsessive stubbornness until its objectives were achieved.

As German soldiers posed for triumphant photographs in occupied Norway, Denmark, the Netherlands, Belgium and France (not to mention countries facing east), there seemed little chance that Hitler's invasion of Britain would be long delayed. Clear-sighted observers tended to regard his complete conquest of the United Kingdom as a foregone conclusion.

Matsuoka Yōsuke was then the Foreign Minister of Japan. It was a critical period in Japan's foreign relations; and he was a new and unusual man to handle them. He came from a different background from those who were normally appointed to that office. As an impressionable child of thirteen, he had emigrated to the United States with his family in 1893, when American prejudice against the yellow man was near its height. Seven years later, he graduated from the University of Oregon Law School as the twentieth century dawned. Within twenty years, he had returned to Japan and had risen to become secretary to the Prime Minister of his native land. Afterwards, he had made his reputation as a business executive, working for the South Manchurian Railway. He became a director of the Railway in 1920 and its Vice-President by 1927. In 1930 he had resigned from the Railway to enter a controversial period as the head of the Japanese delegation to the League of Nations. That culminated in the storm which erupted as he led his people out of the League during its condemnation of Japan over the Manchurian Incident. He returned to Japan where he basked in his national popularity and enjoyed a prosperous life as President of the South Manchurian Railway between 1935–9. Never one to shirk his duty as he saw it, however, he accepted Prince Konoye Fumimaro's offer of the portfolio of Foreign Affairs in September 1940. It was a fateful decision.

By temperament Matsuoka was rather like the type of man who, in an earlier generation, had made the Meiji Restoration. He was abrupt, conceited, gauche, and impatient of the respect for old men which Japanese civilization, being partly Confucian, has usually shown. He was exaggeratedly westernized, or at least he had adopted wholeheartedly the characteristics which he and other Japanese thought to be the essence of western culture. At the same time, in keeping with his life-long love-hate relationship with the English-speaking world of his youth, he was exaggeratedly xenophobic, and opposed to the limit what he saw as an increasingly dangerous Anglo-American conspiracy to encircle Japan as a step towards the consolidation of Anglo-American hegemony in East Asia.

He began his ministerial career by negotiating Japan's adherence to a Triple Alliance with Germany and Italy. The Treaty, signed in September 1940, was subtly conceived. It was primarily directed against the United States: it was intended chiefly to immobilize the United States and to deter it from too active intervention in East Asia and in Germany's wars in Europe. It stipulated that if any Power – and the United States was particularly intended – attacked one of the three signatories or, by giving economic aid, should threaten to affect adversely to them the conflict then taking place, the other two should come to its aid. The

United States rightly interpreted this as an attempt to put fetters upon its freedom of action, and a Japanese withdrawal from the Pact became one of its demands upon Japan. Superficially, to the western democracies, the pact was aggressive: but on the whole, it was intended by the Japanese Government and the European Axis as a means to prevent the spread of war. In that sense, the Japanese and their European Allies regarded the Tripartite Agreement as defensive: it was therefore consistent with that view that Matsuoka and his followers interpreted the vociferous American condemnation of the pact as a proof that the ultimate purpose of United States policy was nothing less than to overthrow the New Orders in East Asia and in Europe by force of arms at a favourable opportunity.

Matsuoka conducted his foreign policy on the principle of *sacro egoismo*. In the spring of 1941, filled with this spirit, he made a tour of Italy, Germany and the Soviet Union. Before he went he had been in favour of committing Japan up to the hilt for Germany, giving it his warm support and leading it to suppose that it would have Japan's military backing if it attacked Russia. He was convinced that Germany was the winning Power, and that only by being among Germany's associates would Japan gain in the eventual share-out of the world at a peace settlement. He was restlessly aware that Japan could pluck great profit from the disorders of the world, and he feared that if it sat still it might fail to gain them. The world would have shaken itself to pieces – to no avail, if Japan did not set itself to win advantage from the outcome.

In his travels, Matsuoka was reassured by the Germans that Hitler harboured no intentions of attacking the Soviet Union: Berlin was not in the habit of confiding its innermost thoughts to its friends. When Matsuoka afterwards arrived in Moscow, therefore, the natural cynicism of this archetypal capitalist found the cynicism of Stalin irresistibly congenial. Conversation with him left Matsuoka convinced that Stalin was the wily man who would sit by Hitler's grave, and was the statesman whose combinations of policy were the most impressive he had met. (Unfortunately, the extraordinary lengths to which Shigemitsu Mamoru, his sagacious Ambassador in London, went in efforts to persuade Matsuoka to visit Winston Churchill in war-torn Britain on the eve of the trip to Moscow were unavailing.) The meetings of Matsuoka and Stalin were especially fateful. They resulted in a genuine change of policy by Japan, one of the Great Powers of the world. Matsuoka, behind his front of self-assurance, proved more volatile than is usually the case with foreign ministers; and he was able to communicate his erratic intentions to the Japanese state. So impressed was Matsuoka with what he deemed to be Stalin's superior power that he proposed that Japan and Russia should sign a Non-Aggression Treaty. Stalin, who was already alarmed at German intentions towards himself, and would in the coming days find Japanese neutrality a pearl beyond price, was much gratified, and closed with the offer at once: through his highly placed agents in Japan, Stalin knew that he could count upon the Japanese to keep their promises to him (as indeed they did). Matsuoka, for his part, chose to ignore the fact that the record of the Russians in keeping to treaties was somewhat poor.

Stalin played on the rather crude imagination of this brash man. When Matsuoka left Moscow, Stalin the oriental potentate surprised everyone by coming to the railway station to take farewell of him. Stalin hugged him, and used a phrase about their both being Asian which was taken to mean that, as a result of the western countries' collective suicide in the war, the future hegemony, at least in Asia, belonged to Japan and Russia. Matsuoka was flattered.

The Non-Aggression Pact signed by Japan and Russia on 14 April 1941 caused surprise. It was one of the sensational events of the war. The Japanese Government, confronted with this astonishing decision by its Foreign Minister, had to take stock of the new position. Events – the dying down of tension on the Russo-Japanese border – had, it is true, been running in this direction; but it was a different matter for the Japanese Government to recognize that its antagonism to Russia, the most cherished and traditional part of its foreign policy, should be formally suspended. Previous diplomatic negotiations between Russia and Japan had been characterized by nit-picking over fine details, demands and counter-demands. There had been Russian claims concerning Sakhalin, disputes over offshore fishing rights, arguments over the boundaries of Mongolia. All of that was swept under the carpet: the Pact covered only the broadest of issues. In a joint declaration appended to the Treaty, the two countries even guaranteed to protect the status quo in Manchukuo and the People's Republic of Mongolia. And most curious of all, no reference was made to the continuance or otherwise of Soviet aid to China. None of the real differences between the two countries had been resolved. Under these circumstances, the durability of this Treaty was probably understood by both sides to be less important than its general tone and moral effect. The truth of the matter is that the Russo-Japanese Non-Aggression Pact had no real foundation except in mutual expedience.

There are in existence the minutes of the Liaison Conferences and the Imperial Conferences held during 1941, at which the new situation was exhaustively debated. These conferences were a unique feature of the Japanese Constitution. The Japanese Government had been so much split up, particularly the Service Ministries which had been freed from civilian control, that special conferences were needed to achieve the unanimity of conclusions which alone made the Japanese mode of government possible. The Liaison Conferences became the centre at which the vital decisions of policy were made: representing the Cabinet there were present the Prime Minister, the Foreign Minister, the Service Ministers and sometimes other key Ministers such as the Finance Minister and the Director of the Cabinet Planning Board; the fighting services were represented by the Chiefs and Vice-Chiefs of Staff of the Army and Navy. In support of them the Chief Secretary of the Cabinet, together with the Chiefs of the Military and Naval Affairs Bureaux of the respective defence ministries, acted as secretaries and 'explainers'. General Mutō Akira, an enlightened and rather virtuous Chief of the Military Affairs Bureau whose ultimate fate was to be hanged as a war criminal by the International Military Tribunal for the Far East, struggled to convey to that court some impression of what the Liaison Conferences were like: he spoke of the harmony that these comparatively informal meetings were expected to produce. After frank exchanges of views, compromises would be agreed so that both the rational development of government policy and the independent operational control of the services could be accommodated without any impairment caused by misunderstanding or crossed purposes. Mutō recalled that members sat in a circle around the Prime Minister:

There was no presiding officer, and every member spoke freely. And, therefore, at times there might be occasions when two men would start talking at the same time, for one member to be whispering to another while another one was speaking. Secretaries were constantly leaving and entering the room on such business as making telephone calls, to call in explainers, or to bring in documents.*

The Imperial Conferences, which were held more rarely, were much more formal meetings of the Liaison Conference in the presence of the Emperor and the President of the Privy Council (who acted as a moderator): these were held when especially momentous decisions were being placed on record. The Emperor sat enthroned upon a dais in front of a gold screen while below him, ranged round a rectangular brocade-covered table, the members sat facing one another: the Prime Minister, followed in turn by the Foreign Minister, the War and Navy Ministers, other Cabinet Ministers in attendance, and then the Chiefs of Staff, would each read prepared statements. The President of the Privy Council would then direct questions to individual members.

* Pritchard and Zaide, op. cit., vol. 13, pp. 30618–19; vol. 14, p. 33270.

[Each member] speaking at the Conference stood up in front of his chair and spoke, after bowing to His Majesty. During the Conference no one would enter or leave the conference room. Conferences were held in a very solemn manner.*

The Emperor normally remained silent throughout the proceedings and afterwards gave its conclusions his sanction, which were tantamount to inscribing the outcome on tablets of stone, once and for all.

The notes of these meetings during 1941 are fascinating to read. They show the bewilderment of high Japanese officials at Matsuoka's radical new policy – which was the virtual designation of Japan's hereditary enemy, Russia, as the successor of Britain as the traditional friend of Japan. They show their constant confusion in the kaleidoscope of the contemporary world, always casting round for a dependable ally, always disappointed in the search. They reveal their experimentalism, which is very Japanese. The discussions took place under the urgent sense that at the time the world map was being re-made, and that a golden opportunity had arisen for Japan to share in the general loot – an opportunity which Japan, by its ineptitude, might lose.

The sense is conveyed that the Japanese were out of their depth (in fairness one must add that so were all the other great nations of the world, truth to tell). Here are generals, admirals and high diplomats ruthlessly planning how to further Japan's interests at the expense of the rest of the world: and, though later it was found that this ruthlessness could bear heavy consequences, their deliberations occasionally seem oddly light-weight. The Governments of most other countries, however, fare no better when the records of their inner councils are examined under the historian's microscope.

For the immediate period, the main preoccupation of the Japanese Government was to get rid of Matsuoka. Clearly some Ministers and officials felt embarrassed by this colleague, who spoke with such un-accustomed and uncomfortable directness, not taking advantage of the ambiguities and vagueness of the Japanese language. The Japanese are accustomed to convey their meaning by indirect hints and innuendoes, and the whole of life is in consequence strangely inexact, not as if they did not dare to face the truth but rather that they appreciated that life itself, whether a bed of roses or weeds, is far from cut and dried. In the case of Matsuoka, the Japanese dignitaries, already thinking of an enterprise which was so audacious that they hardly dared acknowledge it, were constantly embarrassed by a Foreign Minister who called a spade a spade.

This is not to imply that Matsuoka's colleagues were reluctant to cut

* ibid., vol. 14, pp. 33269–70.

him to ribbons, even to the point of excoriating his recommendations in front of the Emperor: listen to what Hara Yoshimichi, President of the Privy Council, for instance, had to say on 19 September 1940, when Matsuoka sought approval from an Imperial Conference concerning the Tripartite Alliance which he had negotiated with Germany and Italy:

This Pact is a treaty of alliance with the United States as its target. Germany and Italy hope to prevent American entry into the European War by making this Pact public. Recently the United States had been acting as a watchdog in Eastern Asia in place of Great Britain. She had applied pressure to Japan, but she has probably been restraining herself in order to prevent Japan from joining Germany and Italy. But when Japan's position becomes clear with the announcement of this Pact, she will greatly increase her pressure on us, she will greatly step up her aid to Chiang, and she will obstruct Japan's war effort. I assume that the United States, which has not declared war on Germany and Italy, will put economic pressure on Japan without declaring war on us. She will probably ban the export of oil and iron, and will refuse to purchase goods from us. She will attempt to weaken us over the long term so that we will not be able to endure war. The Director of the [Cabinet] Planning Board has said that all available steps will be taken to obtain iron and oil, but the results are uncertain. Also, the Foreign Minister's statement shows that we cannot obtain iron and oil right away, and that in any case the amount will be restricted. You cannot carry on a war without oil. The capital in Netherlands East Indies oil is British and American, and the Dutch Government has fled to England, so I think it will be impossible to obtain oil from the Netherlands East Indies by peaceful means. I would like to hear the Government's views on this.*

In reply, of course, Matsuoka robustly defended his policy. But the criticism which he endured made no difference anyway, for at the close of the Conference Hara was obliged by custom to give Matsuoka the ceremonial approval which was required.

So we see that Japan's policy to ensure the neutrality of the United States and to end the China Incident on acceptable terms had two legs while Matsuoka directed the Japanese Foreign Ministry: the Tripartite Alliance and the Russo-Japanese Non-Aggression Pact which closed the back door to Japan. It was therefore inevitable that Matsuoka's days in office were numbered once the Germans attacked the Soviet Union in June 1941. In the end, to get rid of him, the Prime Minister Prince Konoye, and the whole Cabinet, had to resign; and it was thus reformed in July 1941 without him, but with a Foreign Minister who spoke the diplomatic language, and rescued his colleagues from contemplating

* I. Nobutaka, *Japan's Decision for War: Records of the 1941 Policy Conferences,* Stanford University Press, Stanford, 1967, pp. 9–10: Imperial Conference, 19 September 1940.

ing too directly the stark realities of the world as it was being made by their policy. More significantly, it was hoped that the new man would give Japan a better chance of success in negotiating a successful compromise in the diplomatic negotiations underway with the United States.

During Matsuoka's tenure as Foreign Minister, Japan had decisively altered course and set sail towards the Pacific War. Yet while the Tripartite Pact of September 1940 was his initiative and creation, the fundamental changes of direction sprang from circumstances that Japan either had nothing to do with or policies which it seemed only prudent to take in Japan's self-interest. Among the most influential of the external factors affecting Japan's perceptions of its opportunities was the success of the German spring offensive in 1940 leading to German mastery over the whole of Western Europe from Norway to the Pyrenees. And among the objectives which it seemed thoroughly rational for the Japanese Army to take at this juncture were the efforts which were made to establish Japanese military strength in French Indo-China so that Japan would be enabled to cut the Burma Road by force if necessary at the end of the Burma Road Agreement. Similar efforts were made by the Japanese Navy to ensure access to the natural resources of the South Seas. All of these objectives were supported by a wide cross-section of opinion in Japan.

By the summer of 1941, opinion in Japan had veered round to the view that Japan should strike south. No Japanese leader, military or civilian, truly believed that Japan could withstand a prolonged attack by the combined might of the British Empire and the United States, far less achieve total victory over the Allies in a struggle to the death. But the Japanese Government and people felt that they had little option but to take whatever steps were necessary to force the great Western democracies to accept the wisdom of leaving East Asia to attend to itself. Almost by definition that meant that sooner or later – and well-informed Japanese fervently hoped it would be sooner – Japan and the Western Powers would have to reach a negotiated settlement which would re-shape the political map of Greater East Asia and the Western Pacific. These ideas were by no means incompatible with Japan's progressive steps towards a Southern Advance.

To the south lay the vastly rich resources of oil, tin, rubber and other valuable commodities. This was the area of colonies: British, Dutch, French and American. If it seized them, Japan could hope for three results. First, it would free itself from the economic pressure of the western countries, which had shown themselves ready to threaten Japan with strangulation by economic sanctions intended to control Japanese expansion.

JAPANESE PLANS AND THE 'SOUTHERN ADVANCE', November 1941

| 0 | 1000 | 2000 km |
| 0 | 500 | 1000 miles |

100°E

130°E

160°E

60°

U S S R

Attu I.

MONGOLIA

Approximate limit
of Japanese
Objective Area

KWANGTUNG
ARMY

Kuril Is

40°

KOREAN
ARMY

J

CHINA
EXPEDITIONARY
ARMY

GENERAL
DEFENCE
COMMAND
(Homeland and
adjacent islands)

A

CHINA

P

A

N

Ryūkyū Is

20°N

Formosa

SOUTHERN ARMY
14th Army — to Philippines
15th Army — to Thailand
16th Army — to East Indies
25th Army — to Malay States

BURMA

Hong Kong

Luzon

Wake I.

FR. INDO-CHINA
THAILAND

PHILIPPINE
ISLANDS

Guam

MARSHALL IS

Truk Is

Palau Is

CAROLINE ISLANDS

MALAY STATES

0°

DUTCH EAST INDIES

Bismarck
Arch.

GILBERT IS

SOLOMON
IS

N

20°S

AUSTRALIA

Second, by making deadly war on these Powers, if that became necessary, it would crush the last hopes of Chungking and make it sue for peace. And finally, if Japan's western adversaries could be brought by successive shocks to acknowledge that the pursuit of victory over Japan made no sense in terms of western values, the Japanese would build up a new Greater Asia, a solid overseas buttress to the Japanese Empire which would guarantee future Japanese security and become the principal monument of the war. And there was the added advantage that Japan would no longer have to take account of the feeling of its Allies in Europe, whose influences had dangerously distorted the development of Japanese domestic politics over the years.

The birth of these new conceptions about Japan's Southern Advance was guided by the plan being presented, not as a military operation or crude imperialist activity, but as being a beneficent, world-regenerating liberating force in the East which was to be called 'The Greater East Asia Co-Prosperity Sphere'. It was to be a great enterprise, summoning under the protection of Japan the people of South-East Asia and of China, in which justice would reign and the needs of each would be promoted by what was done for the whole. The pride of Japan, the welfare of the world, would be satisfied in equal measure. The mixture of moral ideas, reinforced by a popular Confucianism, made a powerful appeal to the Japanese mood of the hour.

These ideas had been for some time in parturition. As early as 1938, as we have seen, Prince Konoye had proclaimed solemnly that the aim of the China Incident was not to conquer China but to win its cooperation. Looking at East Asia, seeing it threatened by Communism, he said that Japan hankered after a 'New Era' in the territory: a 'New Order' marked by harmony, universal cooperation, and, it was taken for granted, by the benevolent, organizing presence of Japan. Individualism, materialism, the power struggle, everything to do with Communism, were to be ruled out.

The ideas fructified in the next years: and as European imperial Powers all appeared to be toppling one by one, Japanese ideologues, economists and military strategists adapted, and came to apply, the ideas to a steadily widening territory. The 'New Order' was enlarged into the 'Greater East Asia Co-Prosperity Sphere'. In this the countries of Asia would re-orientate, even reconstruct, their economic relationships for their common good, escape from western domination, and be governed by what were thought of as essentially the ideas of eastern civilization. This meant an end to the long night in Asia during which western ideas had prevailed. It meant that an end would be put especially to everything which favoured

Anglo-American ideas and the British and American business presence. Reflecting as it did the aspirations of all the peoples of East Asia for independence from the West, it was to be an essentially cooperative movement. Naturally, given the circumstances of the day, East Asia would find itself for an indefinite period of time under strong Japanese leadership if not hegemony, perhaps in a closely linked federation of East Asian states; and everyone who accepted the 'New Order' more or less accepted this. It was marked by a recognition of the arrangements which Japan had organized, such as the quasi-state of Manchukuo, and the special zone of close Sino-Japanese collaboration.

One of the fascinating things learnt about the war by inquiries afterwards is the butterfly-mindedness of many of the imperialists in Tokyo. They were not dogged, implacable men, tied down to a single idea. They were resilient and receptive. Contrary to the general opinion, they did not make their plans far ahead, and in pursuit of short-term gains they were not unwilling to shift the immediate object of their enterprises and to change the details. So, in 1941, there took place the great movement which determined the course of the war: the shift of mental concentration from a land campaign against Russia, with armies locked together to see which would prevail, to a sea strategy, a joint operation of Army and Navy, which should have as its object the putting of western imperialism to its death, and which would be directed against the Anglo-Saxon Powers, not against the Soviet Union.

In 1941 the decision was not taken: what had happened was that the willingness had appeared to take a decision when a great crisis should happen. A great mental revolution was lived through. New possibilities were envisaged and welcomed by many but not by all. Emperor Hirohito summed up his understanding of the deep divisions of opinion that existed within the Government and Japanese High Command:

Premier Konoye seems to consider that the China Incident will not be settled easily, and favours advancing to the South at the cost of [a] reduction of the occupation area of China. In other words, he seems to be trying to divert the people's dissatisfaction, arising from the unsuccessful China Incident, to the South. The Army seems intending to advance to the South upon a good opportunity, leaving the China Incident as it is now. The Navy's opinion seems to be that unless the China Incident is settled first, we should not resort to force in the South.*

In the end the Government dithered but more or less came down on the side of the Army.

* PD 1632 RR, Entry from Kido Diary, 30 July 1940, IMTFE Prosecution Documents.

The Japanese people responded to this policy. Quite honestly and sincerely, many saw themselves, in opposing western activity in Asia, as emancipators fighting a battle against the dead hand of old-fashioned imperialism. They genuinely believed that the Japanese Government was altruistic, and that the Asian people, who objected to being saved by Japan, were simply misguided. There was little need for propaganda to prepare Japan for the war which it was risking with the United States. If ever a people has gone to war thinking it a just war, if ever a war has been thoroughly popular, so it was to be in 1941. There was little trace of an elaborate misleading of the people, save in estimations of Japan's slim chances of victory. In this, as in so much else, there were parallels between the thoughts of those who held power in London, in Paris and in Tokyo.

Having taken for granted the addition of Manchukuo and China Proper within its compass, which already stretched from Korea and Karafuto to Taiwan, the next territory which Japan was tempted to bring in to the Co-Prosperity Sphere was Indo-China. Its Government had been left helpless by the collapse of France. The only Power to which it could have looked for aid was Britain, but Britain, especially since Dakar, had become the enemy of France. Siam, now called Thailand by the Pan-Asian zealots who seized power there from elements who had been well disposed towards western countries, was incited to present ultimatums to France. Throughout 1940 and 1941, Japan was able to extract larger and larger concessions from French Indo-China for not swallowing it up entirely. By 1941 it had reduced the northern part of Indo-China to a protectorate; presently Japanese garrisons were admitted to the key areas further south; they came to occupy the centres from which they could strike at Malaya, Borneo and the Philippines.

Japan pressed on with this new policy regardless of the fact that on 22 June 1941 a separate war started between Russia and Germany. The German attack on Russia certainly did not take Japan completely by surprise; but Germany, in this as in several other matters of great consequence to Japan, acted without any consultation with the country which, since signing the German-Japanese Anti-Comintern Pact in 1936 and the Tripartite Pact of September 1940, was formally its ally. Seldom had an alliance been operated by a country with quite such painful, humiliating lack of confidential deliberation (although in fact Germany's disdainful treatment of Italy was just as bad). Apart from the psychological and political shock which news of Germany's invasion of the Soviet Union produced in Japan, the Japanese had not made sufficient military provision to enable them to enter such a war at that time. Proper mobilization against the Soviet Union would have taken time and, as Kido Kōichi pointedly told American interrogators after the war, 'if these preparations built up to a certain necessary point, it would [have] become a winter campaign for which Japan was not prepared'. Moreover, there was some doubt as to whether there was anything to be gained by redeploying Japanese forces for an offensive against the Soviet Union: 'The Germans were constantly informing the people here that the war against Russia could be completed within a very short time – a matter of three months or so.'*

Germany now began to press Japan to throw in its forces against the Soviet Union. It had previously indicated to Japanese diplomats, in boastful language, that should it at any time attack the Soviet Union, the campaign would be largely a police operation since Russian resistance would be swiftly overcome. The Japanese Government was inclined now to wait and see. The Kwantung Army, bogged down in China, was not in a mood to venture further afield without the prospect of specific advantage in the overriding aim of bringing China to its knees. Moreover, the pull of the Asian Co-Prosperity Sphere was now being strongly felt. In South Asia its opportunity and its natural sphere seemed to lie.

---

* USBSS No. 308, Interrogation of Marquis Kido Kōichi by the United States Strategic Bombing Survey, 10 November 1945, RG 343, Modern Military Archives, Modern Military Branch, United States National Archives, Washington, DC.

CHAPTER 14

The Negotiation Preceding War

IN December 1940, the United States Government, disturbed by the increasingly belligerent tone of the Japanese, had imposed an embargo on the sale of scrap iron and war materials to Japan. Hitherto it had put no hindrance in the way of trade with Japan, and China was able to argue, with reason, that Japan's operations, in the first three years of its warfare, had been made possible economically because of United States policy. The American Government took advantage of the rising temper of the US to act resolutely, but it still had to move cautiously. Its action was an attempt to halt Japan's military activity against China.

A new way of conducting diplomacy was being tried out: the method of using economic pressure to effect political ends. Ever since the covenant of the League of Nations was drafted, the efficiency of economic sanctions had been in dispute. They were tried out against Italy, unsuccessfully, and deliberately with so many imperfections that they were bound to fail (because that was the intention of some of the Great Powers which had been coerced by pressure of their electorates into taking part in the operation) at the Abyssinian Crisis. But, as enforced against Japan, in the peculiar conditions of the time, they had an indisputable effect. They suggested to President Roosevelt the line of government action which, because of the caution of public opinion, he would not have dared to propose that America should take by more political means.

Over 40 per cent of Japanese exports and more than half her imports were with the United States. Japan's balance of payments situation was precarious, and her financial future was in American hands. Although government controls in Japan succeeded in limiting Japanese imports to essential materials, the trend over the first two and a half years of the China Incident was for Japanese exports to fall sharply while imports from the United States continued to rise. Traditionally, Japan had been dependent upon the British Empire and the United States for vital strategical raw materials ranging from tin, nickel and zinc to oil, iron and steel. The British calculated that a mutual British-Japanese trade embargo would hurt the British Empire more than Japan, but it was evident to all that confiscation of Britain's considerable assets in Japan would not begin to compensate for the losses Japan must suffer in the event of joint

Anglo-American sanctions. This difficulty for Japan increased substantially when the European War began in September 1939: alternative sources of supply for some strategical materials vanished along with an important segment of the Japanese export market. Meanwhile, yen-bloc countries such as Formosa, Korea and Manchuria absorbed an increasing proportion of Japanese industrial production while contributing a disappointingly low proportion of Japanese war requirements. Self-sacrifice by Japanese consumers permitted the war to continue indefinitely, but it was universally accepted that Japan had no margin of safety against firm Anglo-American economic sanctions.

In July 1941 the Japanese extended their political control of Indo-China from the north to the south. Their motive was plain: the places Japan had demanded to occupy were those which the military experts regarded as essential for an operation to reduce South-East Asia. Japan had seized the opportunity of the desperate situation of the French in Indo-China, and of the inability of France, following its collapse, to give the local French Government any decisive aid. The American press digested the facts, debated them, and had seen that the damage, which might or must result to the security of the United States, was put before the American public. Even now the American will to peace, and the concern over its neutrality sentiment, remained strong. Its propagandists continued to warn that the United States was being led along the path to war by appeal to fear and sympathy. Many of them feared that the United States was being led by the back door of war with Japan into the war which they feared and opposed: war with Germany. In spite of the alarm which they expressed, President Roosevelt responded firmly in the crisis over Indo-China. He tightened very greatly the economic war which he had begun against Japan. He froze Japanese assets. He proclaimed what amounted to an embargo on Japanese trade in oil and steel, and in the next few months he issued executive orders which extended that embargo to cover scores of other commodities ranging from metals, chemicals and plastics to machinery, hides, skins, leather goods, vegetable fibres and manufactures, even wool.

This was a vital stage in the development of the crisis. The American Government had suddenly stiffened its policy. It did so to the surprise of many of the parties concerned, including the Japanese. It had moved somewhat in advance of the change in the mood of the country. It had taken steps which it knew to be desperately inimical to Japan.

The effects on Japan were immediate. It was especially susceptible to pressure from the oil sanctions. Japan had stored enough oil for two years of war. Denied the opportunity of replenishing these stores from the United

States, it had to recognize in the circumstances of the time that it could not gain oil from alternative sources of supply. The United States was immediately followed in its embargo by the British Empire and the Dutch in Indonesia: Japan discovered that there was no possibility of driving a wedge between them. Each month brought the prospect of the exhaustion of its supplies that much nearer. It knew that its aggressive policies, and Japan itself, must wither away when the time limit arrived – because the vital commodities which sustained them would no longer flow.

The United States during these months was in an extraordinary state. Roosevelt steered it resolutely on a course of economic strangulation so intense and so aggressive that it must result in war or the abject surrender of Japan to America's implacable demands. But Roosevelt did not make the decision publicly: and the majority of the American public, though more deeply stirred by Japan than in previous years, still wanted peace, not war. A certain amount of the exchange of views with Japan was behind the scenes: but much of it leaked to the public. In the last period before the final catastrophe American feeling had moved towards greater caution, so that an impartial observer, if he believed that the great decisions followed the popular will, would have said that the chances of the United States going to war were lessening, not increasing. But the country had the sense that it was in the grip of uncontrollable necessity. Like a sleepwalker, it moved towards war.

The President, though he believed that war was perhaps inevitable, was willing to test the possibility of curbing Japanese expansion without fighting: he would have abandoned larger projects if he could have gained acceptable guarantees of a reversal of Japan's policies in China and Asia generally. Such a degree of unreality has seldom been equalled by a Great Power. The outcome of American economic pressure was not certain. The United States might indeed have forced Japan into belligerent action, but against the British in Malaya and the Dutch in the Netherlands East Indies, not against the United States itself. The American Administration, handcuffed by the Neutrality Act, might have been helpless while its Allies in South-East Asia went down before Japanese attack.

By the later part of 1940 Prince Konoye's Government in Japan had already come to believe that a political settlement of the China Incident was possible only through American mediation, and it was for that reason as well as in response to the direct American economic pressure upon Japan that his Government began to send out signals indicating its desire to open the bilateral negotiations with the United States which finally began in the spring of 1941. After the war, American investigators asked Konoye to explain why Japan had not deployed against China the tremendous military power she was to display at the outbreak of the Pacific War. He replied that the Japanese had come to the conclusion that 'it was almost impossible to gain a decisive victory over China' and that Japan must commit itself to the real possibility of achieving a political settlement.

When Japan proposed a final effort to come to terms which would make the impending Pacific War unnecessary, Roosevelt, and his closest advisers, entered with some hopefulness on the negotiations. They did so with the more readiness because they knew (and nobody else then knew) that they had the great advantage of seeing into the mind of their adversary. The United States had got possession of Japanese ciphers (one of the most notable feats of code-breaking in history), and during these weeks no communications passed between the Japanese Embassy in Washington and its home base in Tokyo without the US Government being aware of it. The putting of the Japanese war machine into readiness, its dispatch into action, all took place under the eyes of the American Government, which knew that it was provoking Japan unendurably.

Unhappily, so highly did the Americans value this means of overhearing the conversation of its adversaries, so resolute was it to defend the secrecy of its knowledge, that the circulation of this Intelligence was rigidly circumscribed. Extremely few men were privy to it – President Roosevelt, Secretary of State Cordell Hull, Secretary of War Henry Stimson, Chief of Staff General George Marshall, and barely a handful of others – and all of them, to guard the secrecy, read the messages and destroyed them on the spot within sight of the bearer. They called it 'Magic'. Whether adequate advantage was taken of this unique knowledge at this stage of events is questionable. Undoubtedly intense precautions to guard security prevented it from being properly digested, and opportunities were missed. Later, after March 1942, summaries of 'Magic' intercepts were prepared and circulated together with background information to an ever-widening circle of Allied officers after the outbreak of the Pacific Conflict, and in terms of their sophistication, general strategical utility and extensive circulation, these summaries came to have immense practical usefulness in the overall conduct of war operations in terms of Total War. In this respect 'Magic' eventually had far more influence on Allied policy formulation than the famous 'Ultra' messages decoded by British cryptographers at Bletchley Park, which were made available in undigestible form as raw intercepts, never enjoyed a wide circulation and remained chiefly of tactical assistance.

In the conduct of the pre-war diplomatic negotiations with Japan, the United States rightly perceived that the interests of friendly Powers with East Asian and Western Pacific involvements were engaged. It informed

Britain, in particular, step by step of their progress. Churchill, for his part, offered no resistance, encouraged the United States to persevere, and blocked those within the British Government who wished to urge the United States into considering alternative policies towards Japan. Churchill, indeed, was less than clear-sighted about Japan. He tended to discount the conviction shared by many people in Washington – and London – that war was imminent. To the last, rather like Secretary of War Stimson, Churchill believed that Japan would probably back down: it must be said that the Greater East Asia and Pacific War surprised both men. Churchill, indeed, culpably neglected the defence of Britain's Eastern Empire prior to the outbreak of war in the East, even wilfully preferring to reinforce the air strength of the Soviet Union than to fulfil the sacred trust of self-defence. His crony, the newspaper magnate Lord Beaverbrook, persuaded Churchill that national prestige was better served by diverting Hurricane and Spitfire fighters to Russia than in shipping them to Malaya: the British Government then persuaded the United States that some of the obsolescent American Brewster Buffalo fighter aircraft which the United States had earmarked for the reinforcement of the Soviet Union ought to be sufficient to meet Britain's imperial air defence requirements in East Asia. It was important for the world to appreciate that Britain, too, was a first-class Power capable of making a significant contribution to the Great Patriotic War of the Soviet Union against their common foe in Europe. Not for the first time, nor for the last, Great Men, with their grand sense of occasion, refused to listen to the wise counsel of their aghast but too timorous professional advisers. Air Chief Marshall Sir Robert Brooke-Popham, then British Commander-in-Chief, Far East, whose Intelligence left much to be desired, said he was satisfied that the Buffaloes would prevail against the Japanese.

The vital negotiations were started through the initiative of some bumbling but well-intentioned amateurs of diplomacy, the clerics of the Catholic mission in East Asia known as the Maryknoll Fathers. Their intervention is an interesting story. On the one side they misunderstood and immensely over-simplified the complexity of the issues dividing Japan and the United States. They viewed the imminence of war with horror, and were convinced that, by taking diplomacy out of its accustomed rut, they could give men of goodwill on both sides the opportunity to turn their natural benevolence to useful account. In their opinion, in the new atmosphere which they tried to generate, matters which had appeared as great obstacles, matters which had in them the seed of war, would be found unexpectedly tractable and would shrivel away.

On the other side, their over-simplification of the issues, which they minimized for lack of adequate appreciation of them, led in the long run to increased confusion, and had the effect of making agreement harder to reach. They roused hopes on both sides by deliberately misrepresenting the exact nature of the demands being made. Thus they stirred up the expectations of a settlement which was found impossible when the exact terms of the other side were clarified. The possibility of an accord receded. It left disillusionment, and made the situation seem more hopeless than before.

The contribution which amateurs can make in complicated dealings between Great Powers is always apt to run into this difficulty. The work of experts is written off, and it is assumed that a fresh approach by fresh minds is likely to succeed: in the end it so often is found that the expert has the dreary and hard truth on his side. In the present case, the Maryknoll Fathers undoubtedly for a time raised hope in certain quarters in the United States and in Japan also, of being able to draft a kind of Monroe Doctrine for the Far East which would be acceptable to those circles in the United States which were anxious before all to secure peace. Determined men in Japan seized on this – in the Army and Navy as well as in court and diplomatic circles – and translated it into a draft agreement between the two Powers, which they sought constantly to put forward as the basis of negotiation. But their draft treaty revealed the insubstantial basis on which they proceeded. They would have been better advised to realize that in seeking an agreement of this kind they were bashing their heads against a stone wall.

The enterprise of the Maryknoll Fathers was a little like that of Swedish philanthropic interlopers who tried to come between Germany and the West in the years before the European War. They were prompted by goodwill: but their initiative did not achieve much.

The Maryknoll negotiations led on to official negotiations which began in July 1941. By November they had reached their climax.

Japan had begun them out of desperation, but it hoped little from them. The sanctions were pressing hard. It is true that there were powerful influences in Japanese Government circles which dreaded war, which were opposed to all the least fortunate tendencies which Japanese foreign policy had given rise to, and which snatched at Japan's peril to recommend that safety lay in retreat: these men, including high-ranking soldiers, sailors, diplomats, economists and courtiers, were quite sincere in wanting a rapprochement with the United States. But Japanese foreign policy was made now chiefly by generals and admirals who had come to the con-

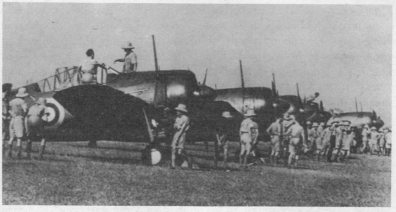

39 *Top*: 'Morning exercises on board troopship': green troops *en route* from Australia to Singapore in the mid-summer of 1941

40 *Bottom*: Sturdy but obsolete Brewster Buffalo aircraft, with R A F markings, were sent to defend Malaya during 1941 by the United States

While Aussies shed their precious blood, Ole man Roosevelt finds his selfish aims going according to schedule.

41 *Top*: A Japanese
propaganda cartoon

42 *Bottom*: Japanese troops,
supported by light tanks,
storm across the Johore
Causeway leading to
Singapore Island

43 *Top*: The battleship HMS *Prince of Wales*, the most modern capital ship in the Royal Navy, and the old battlecruiser HMS *Repulse* (obscured) reach Singapore on 2 December 1941

44 *Bottom*: The survivors of the sinking battleship *Prince of Wales* clamber over the side, rescued by the destroyer HMS *Express*

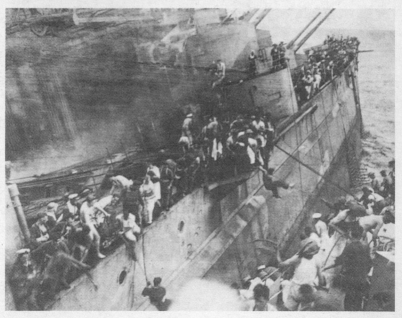

45 *Top*: Bicycle troops: the
Japanese intention was that all
Japanese troops without
mechanized transport would
travel by bicycle .

46 *Bottom*: The turret of one
of the 15-inch naval guns at
Singapore, photographed
during the war by an
Australian prisoner of war

47 *Top*: Under a flag of truce the GOC, Malaya, Lieutenant-General Arthur Percival (*right*), goes to surrender his remaining troops to General Yamashita Tomoyuki, the 'Tiger of Malaya', on 15 February 1942

48 *Centre*: The waterfront of Keppel Harbour, looking back at the General Post Office, the morning after Singapore surrendered and shortly before Japanese occupation forces arrived to take charge of the city

49 *Bottom*: The first Japanese occupation forces march into Singapore: in front of the General Post Office, 16 February 1942

50 *Top*: The heavy cruiser
HMS *Cornwall* sinks after an
attack by Japanese carrier-
borne aircraft off Ceylon,
April 1942

51 *Bottom*: Operation
'Ironclad', a British invasion
of Vichy-controlled
Madagascar in May 1942, was
intended to deny the island's
use to the Japanese Navy

52 *Top*: An American B17
bomber burns after a Japanese
air raid on Bandung Airfield
in Java

53 *Centre*: Australian troops
advance to recover Buna
during the two-year New
Guinea Campaign

54 *Bottom*: Strongly
influenced by contact with
Allied forces, bizarre 'cargo
cults' were to spread among
aboriginal tribesmen in many
parts of Papua, New Guinea
and nearby islands

55 *Top*: F-Force assembles at
Selarang Barracks, Changi,
before leaving for work on the
Burma–Siam railway

56 *Bottom*: Conditions in
Japanese prisoner-of-war
camps varied from bad to
atrocious during the Pacific
War. Here Dutch prisoners of
war 'take a day off work'
during the construction of an
Indonesian railway

clusion that war was the only policy which could effect sufficient change to offer hope of an acceptable negotiated settlement. They were being egged on by their exchanges of view with Germany, which in these months was urgent that they should embarrass Britain by attacking Singapore, and which supplied all kinds of information about how easy Japan might find this adventure to be. Contrary to the judgements of war crimes courts after the war, such men were not wicked or bloodthirsty. With troubled minds but the clearest of consciences they merely judged that sooner or later war would be inevitable, and that Japan stood a better chance by having the war then rather than later.

Many others in Japan took a contrary view, feeling that widening the East Asian War until it covered the whole of the Western Pacific and South-East Asia offered Japan no hope of victory, but that the United States might be brought to its senses, especially if Germany won the European War. Others were apprehensive that the Soviet Union posed a much clearer danger to Japanese security and believed that the survival of the Japanese Empire depended upon Japan's withdrawal from China as well as Indo-China. Scarcely anyone, however, believed that it would be realistic for Japan to abandon what were regarded as its responsibilities in Manchuria.

By November the United States was satisfied that general talks were fruitless. In this perception the United States Government was almost certainly wrong and, as British, Dutch and many individual American diplomats appreciated, the course which the American Administration pursued was singularly ill-conceived. However, the negotiations with Japan had been interrupted by a government crisis in Tokyo: the resignation of the sometimes moderate but hopelessly vacillating Prince Konoye, and his replacement in October 1941 by his own War Minister, General Tōjō Hideki.

No one believed that Japan was capable of winning a war outright against the United States: the purpose of any resort to arms would be to create the conditions which would permit Japan to extricate itself from the China Incident without submitting to American hegemony in East Asia. The Japanese Government had more or less lost its way. At an Imperial Conference held on 6 September, the Chief of the Army General Staff, General Sugiyama Hajime, recommended that Japan should go to war by mid-October if the outcome of the negotiations with the United States did not appear to be favourable. Tōjō took the same view. The Chief of the Navy General Staff, Admiral Nagano Osami, remarked that 'We can successfully oppose the United States in war for a period of two years. Any longer conflict would tend to be unprofitable for Japan.' The

Emperor himself emphasized his own hope that his Government would pursue peaceful negotiations energetically. His Government tried and failed. Now it was Tōjō's turn.

Tōjō was a military man, not in the highest position of control of the Japanese Army but a product of fashion, diligence and rather fine staff work. He had no special political ideas or standing, but represented in general certain unfortunate attitudes which were common among Army officers who had spent their careers engaged in Japan's military adventures on the Asiatic mainland: contempt for Britain and the United States, faith in what he regarded as the superior qualities of his native culture, willingness to take extreme risks against appalling odds, ignorance of the politics of the world. But Tōjō was also astute enough to recognize the underlying volatility of Japanese domestic politics and knew from personal experience the realities of Japan's predicament in China. He had been active in the Manchurian Incident but had done his level best to prevent the outbreak of the China Incident. His concern about the danger of war against the Soviet Union was acute. The Government which he led was serious in its aim to achieve a breakthrough in its negotiations with the United States, but Tōjō and his supporters were determined to end the policies of drift which had characterized the interplay between Japanese domestic political factions and had been manifest in the country's foreign relations with potential friends and foes for many years. Tōjō had acquired a well-deserved reputation for decisiveness. He also believed that only the manifestation of firmness on the part of Japan stood any chance of motivating the United States Government to seek a just resolution of the China Incident and any other disputes at issue with Japan.

Accordingly, Tōjō and his Cabinet more or less resolved in principle to go to war against the combined forces of the United States and its Allies; his Government nevertheless was ready to see whether anything would be offered by the United States which would make war unnecessary. Twice a deadline for a breakdown of the negotiations was fixed and later postponed. The absolute decision for war was not made until very late in the day. Even then, and until the end, the fleet, which was to deliver the first blow, was ordered to leave room for calling off its operations, so that it could return to Japan with peace preserved.

The Japanese did not seek to rely in their negotiations upon tactical threats or bluff: the negotiations begun by the second and third Konoye Governments and continued by Tōjō's Government were no idle game and the Japanese understood that oriental subtlety was wasted upon the kind of American gangbusters and coarse political hacks who did as much as America's career diplomats and xenophobic military advisers to influence the American President's conduct of American foreign policy. The negotiations were conducted in Washington, DC, because the Americans wanted it that way.

To lead the Japanese team, Admiral Nomura Kichisaburō, once a leading moderate in the inner counsels of the Navy, then called briefly from retirement to be Foreign Minister of Japan during the difficult months that followed the outbreak of the European War in September 1939, was chosen to be the Japanese Ambassador to the United States in January 1941. His appointment was meant to provide reassurance to the United States that the Japanese Navy itself fully supported the efforts of Japan's diplomatic corps to restore satisfactory relations between Japan and the United States. Recognizing his own limitations in the field of diplomacy, however, Nomura sought to obtain the assistance of a first-class professional Ambassador to provide him with help, someone who could guide him through the treacherous waters of diplomacy up the Potomac. The seriousness of the situation was so evident to the authorities in Tokyo that they sent him Ambassador Kurusu Saburō, formerly a Japanese consul in Chicago, later an Ambassador to Belgium (1937–9) and to Germany (1939–40). Kurusu seemed to be an ideal Special Envoy. He knew and liked America, he had an American wife, and, as the man who had signed the Tripartite Pact in Berlin on behalf of Japan, he could indicate to the Americans how truly insubstantial Japan's relations were with the European Axis Powers. A rather slick but well-intentioned banker named Ikawa Tadao, a crony of Prime Minister Konoye, who knew the United States well, was added to the team as an 'unofficial' participant. And backing up Nomura, Kurusu and Ikawa was a Japanese Army colonel, Iwakuro Hideo, who was sent in response to Nomura's request for a military aide who could advise him concerning the actual state of affairs in the China Incident. Iwakuro had been at the Army Affairs Section of the War Ministry's Military Affairs Bureau since 1938 and had headed it for the past couple of years. He had a reputation for excellent staff work, an even temperament and honesty. He had an intimate understanding about how the Army authorities viewed the history of the China Incident, but just as importantly he was chosen for secondment to the Japanese Embassy because he enjoyed the full confidence of Major General Mutō Akira, Chief of the Military Affairs Bureau, and Tōjō himself (who continued to hold the portfolio of War Minister after becoming Prime Minister).

Both Governments, however, handled the negotiations badly from start to finish. Neither Nomura nor Iwakuro recognized that their unofficial intermediaries had no standing with either the President or his Secretary of Staff. Nomura's command of English may not have been as poor as the Americans believed, but he certainly appeared to be exceptionally slow to grasp points of substance as well as of detail, and in any case he found particular difficulty in penetrating Secretary of State Hull's Tennessee accent and speech defects. Worse still, Nomura failed to keep his Foreign Ministry informed concerning precisely what Hull had to say regarding the manner in which the United States was prepared to receive the proposals being bandied about. Apparently he regarded Foreign Minister Matsuoka Yōsuke as so inimical to the peace negotiations that he deliberately sought to isolate the Foreign Ministry and win the general support of his Government by appealing to the Navy Minister and the Chief of the Naval General Staff. In this he did achieve considerable success, for Matsuoka was becoming such an embarrassment that he was ditched from power in July 1941. His replacement, Admiral Toyoda Teijirō, was another amateur in diplomatic affairs but was also one of Nomura's long-standing allies. Long before then, however, matters had become so confused by Nomura's unorthodox and selective reportage that the Japanese Government was heartened by the impression that a draft understanding largely composed by Iwakuro was in fact an American initiative and that the encouraging Japanese response which eventually emerged in reply to that supposed initiative was regarded in Washington as Japan's first official proposals. Cordell Hull took the view that

As the document stood, it offered little basis for an agreement, unless we were willing to sacrifice some of our most basic principles, which we were not. Nevertheless, it was a formal and detailed proposal from Japan. To have rejected it outright would have meant throwing away the only real chance we had had in many months to enter with Japan into a fundamental discussion of all the questions outstanding between us . . .

Consequently, we decided to go forward on the basis of the Japanese proposals and seek to argue Japan into modifying here, eliminating there, and inserting elsewhere, until we might reach an accord we could both sign with mutual good will.*

Everything now began to go utterly haywire as the Japanese gained the misimpression that the United States had been acting in bad faith all along. That misimpression was never corrected. Eventually a critical stage was reached during July 1941, after the Japanese had decided to occupy

* C. Hull, *The Memoirs of Cordell Hull*, vol. II, Hodder & Stoughton, London, 1948, p. 1001, cited by R. Butow, 'The Hull–Nomura Conversations: A Fundamental Misconception', *American Historical Review*, 65:4 (1960), p. 834.

the southern half of French Indo-China – but before the Americans imposed a freezing order on all Japanese assets within the United States – when for a period Hull refused to have anything to do with Nomura. All of this had serious consequences in terms of Japan's continuous monitoring of the prospect of a favourable outcome to the discussions. Equally unfortunately, Nomura himself seems to have believed that failure of the negotiations would produce nothing more catastrophic than a break in diplomatic relations between Japan and the United States. He apparently remained utterly unaware that his Government was finding itself driven to the point of having no alternative but to initiate an all-out attack upon the United States and its British and Dutch handmaidens.

Believing, rather like the Japanese, that their adversaries understood only the meaning of force, the Americans anyway were unusually inflexible in their approach to the negotiations and failed to appreciate the extent to which the Japanese yearned for a reasonable compromise. Though preparing for war, the Government of the United States had scant regard for the military resilience of the Japanese and accordingly did not expect to suffer any mortal injuries or even unduly serious consequences from any miscalculations which might lead to war. America went through the motions of manoeuvring for peace, knowing full well that Allied sanctions would become progressively more debilitating for the Japanese. At the end of the day, however, the United States decided to offer Japan a final 'bargain'. The embargoes on oil, steel and long lists of other commodities, which threatened to cut not only Japan's freedom of action on the Asiatic mainland but its very independence as a nation, were to be lifted: in return, Japan would need to give territorial guarantees. But what? Over this there was a great deal of debate: and the United States consulted its friends abroad.

The first attitude was to let Japan down lightly. Withdrawal from Indo-China would suffice. It was hoped that this would lead on to a general withdrawal from the Asiatic mainland: but this was not to be rushed, and was not to be included in the immediate terms.

But here came in the China lobby. Chiang Kai-shek had been informed of what was to be offered. He was indignant: he reported it as unlikely that China would be able to continue to fight Japan. He telegraphed London and, as an unlikely partner, he enlisted Churchill in representations. Churchill, ever conscious of the importance of the American deterrent to Japanese aggression against the territorial and commercial interests of the British Empire, mildly suggested to President Roosevelt that the proposed *modus vivendi* seemed to offer Chiang 'a rather thin diet'. Meanwhile, all the China lobby was turned on to the

President and Cordell Hull, a cantankerous and notably inflexible Secretary of State. In the result they stiffened the terms and called on the Japanese to evacuate not only Indo-China, but the whole of China as well, including Manchuria. In return for this, the United States would rescind its oil embargo.

In the negotiations, Hull took a stiffer line than Roosevelt. The President had been willing to accept an invitation from the Japanese Prime Minister, Prince Konoye, while he was still in power, to negotiate personally. In an unprecedented step for a Japanese Prime Minister, Konoye offered to meet the President in Hawaii, risking everything (including the probable loss of his own life at the hands of Japanese political extremists) on the outcome. Remembering the fate of those who had aroused the fury of Japanese radical elements during the Washington and London Treaty negotiations, Konoye's proposal, which was evidently entirely his own although warmly welcomed by his Cabinet and Emperor, was exceptionally courageous. One wishes that it could counteract the unfortunate impression made by Konoye's otherwise rather uneven contributions to his country's political welfare, but alas it seems only to confirm the rather manic-depressive tendencies that we can discern in Konoye's behaviour. This, after all, was a man who was subject to extremes: when the political parties of Japan were troublesome because of the China Incident, he had abolished them at a stroke and created a peculiar non-party apparatus headed by something which he called the Imperial Rule Assistance Association. He was always starting balls rolling and then backing away. This time, however, Konoye would have had no chance to back away. It was a marvellous opportunity. Cordell Hull intervened, however, and killed Konoye's initiative stone dead. Konoye had gone so far as to propose that the two leaders should make a preliminary temporary pact under which Japan would agree not to make war on the United States even if American activities led to war with Germany in the Atlantic Ocean. This meant that Japan was prepared to repudiate its Tripartite Alliance with Germany and Italy. The purpose of that Alliance had been to deter the United States from intervention in the German War by the threat of collision with Japan. Konoye's offer demonstrates the extent to which Japanese high officials recognized that their association with the European Axis Powers had been a grievous miscalculation. Apparently Secretary of State Hull, however, felt that Konoye was offering an engagement which he would not be permitted to fulfil. It would appear that Hull also feared that President Roosevelt would give away too much to the Japanese.

Once the United States Administration had responded to the China lobby and Churchill's remarks, the possibility of any real *modus vivendi* receded to vanishing point. The Japanese, their backs to the wall, recognized the utter futility of any further talk. President Roosevelt made what appeared to be a final attempt at peace by appealing over the heads of politicians to the Japanese Emperor. But this action, though it may have been meant as a serious contribution to world peace, probably sprang more from the President's self-interested desire to go down well in the history books. Whether or not his motives were misunderstood, the President's final message to the Emperor was scorned and resented by the Japanese.

On 7 December Japan sent a note which recognized that the negotiations had failed. By the time it was delivered, the consequences of the recognition were also clear: the Japanese were bombarding Pearl Harbor, which they had decided to do if the negotiations ended in deadlock. It is interesting to find that the US Army Chief of Staff General George C. Marshall, when news of the bombardment was first given to him, is reported to have said incredulously that it must be mistaken: Japan would have bombarded Singapore, not American territory. This is unlikely to be a measure of the failure of the Japanese to wring final advantage out of the preoccupation of the American public with remaining neutral. It is merely consistent with the certain knowledge shared by those privy to the most secret British and American Intelligence that a major Japanese task force had been shadowed on its way towards the Malayan coast for days. Above all, it must be stressed that the inevitable consequence of the economic pressures imposed by the United States upon Japan, and of America's failure to pursue its diplomatic negotiations with appropriate vigour, flexibility and imagination, was that Japan finally had no alternative to the Pacific War other than submission to abject surrender. The fact of the matter is that it lay within the power of the United States and the United Kingdom to adopt policies towards Japan which might have avoided that war.

CHAPTER 15
The Bombardment of Pearl Harbor

JAPAN, goaded into decisive action, was unleashing against the world its other major force, its Navy. Hitherto Japan's Army had been the agent of its dynamism: it was the Army which Japan's neighbours feared, and it was the influence of the Army upon the Japanese Government that kept the world in anxiety. The Navy, which by tradition was preponderantly officered by men whose Samurai origin lay in clans different from those which were powerful in the Army, was highly conspiratorial: it had tended to deplore the rashness of the Army, and to favour much more cautious policies. It was conservative: it did not feel the same desire to intervene over the whole range of government: it had less connection, though it had some, with patriotic societies. In the Navy, the old feeling in favour of the Anglo-Japanese Alliance lingered on, and there was a nostalgic sentiment in favour of the older basis of Japan's foreign policy.

But the Navy, like all other institutions in Japan, was divided by factions. One faction had been captivated by the vision of the economic adventure in the South Seas, and by the Empire which it felt lay open for Japan, open to the touch of the Japanese fleet. This section began to think of a war with the British Empire, which it would have to overthrow, as inevitable. It thought, too, that a collision with the United States was certain, for the United States also was likely to block Japanese expansion in this direction. The Navy, or this section of it, gradually came to regard the Anglo-Saxon Powers as the inevitable enemy, against whom war was to be prepared.

This faction identified itself in the vital years with the 'Go South' movement. It naturally saw in this an opportunity to reinstate itself with the Army in the public esteem, and to clip the Army's wings as the instrument of expansion *par excellence*. The prevailing war, an Army-led war, between Japan and China, would be transformed and eclipsed by being converted into a predominantly naval war, fought by the Navy chiefly instead of the land forces, and with the adversary changed. The war would be in a different terrain, would involve huge distances, vast oceans, distant islands – in all of which, the Navy, and not the Army, would shine.

In calling into action the second of the great weapons of Imperial Japan, the Japanese Government was employing an instrument which had been untested for thirty-five years. The Japanese Navy had won its greatest triumph as long ago as 1905, and had, since then, not fought a serious action. As long as the Washington Naval Limitation Treaty had been in force, the West had been able to inform itself of Japanese naval construction: and Britain, making use of old ties, had kept abreast of Japanese naval thinking. But the link had been severed in 1935: the American and British navies felt themselves incompetent at assembling information about interesting new developments in Japanese naval construction: in 1941, it was a matter of speculation how the Japanese Navy would fare if pitted against those of the other Great Powers. A great spurt in construction of big ships had taken place at the end of the 1930s.

In the twenties and early thirties, while contact lasted, the Japanese Navy had maintained a large battle fleet. It possessed ten large battleships: it was known to have built four more subsequently, though the West was without knowledge of their details. In addition the Navy, from the beginning of the 1920s, had been interested in the air, and had built aircraft-carriers. This was the speciality, not of the Navy as a whole, but of a clique in it, whose most forceful member was a Japanese naval officer, Yamamoto Isoroku, who early on had been attracted by theories of air power. He was openly sceptical about the usefulness of battleships: he thought their value was chiefly prestige, and he compared them to the ancestral scrolls which were hung upon the wall of Japanese houses, proving the piety of their upkeep but not able to guarantee much to the present prosperity of the family.

Yamamoto had, however, a very difficult time in propagating his views. Most Japanese admirals regarded his insistence on air power much as British military officers regarded the use of the machine-gun before the First World War. Some made it a point of honour never to fly in an aeroplane themselves, and to discourage flying by their officers. Yamamoto got his way, largely by becoming commandant of a naval school which trained a considerable number of naval pilots: they were to be the heroes of the coming war. By a characteristically Japanese compromise Yamamoto secured, not the replacement of the existing Japanese Navy by one which was governed by his ideas, but the organization of a separate fleet, which was geared to the air, in addition to the orthodox battle fleet. There was no stringent testing of naval construction in Japan by political commissions from the Imperial Diet, which might have subjected this settlement to criticism on grounds of economy, and the debate over the strategical and financial questions which were at issue took place within much the same channels as we have examined in connection with the related problems of international naval arms limitation.

The air development of the Japanese Navy was one of the things grossly underestimated by the Intelligence of the Anglo-Saxon countries. In 1938 aeroplanes which had bombed Shanghai had flown direct from Kyushu in southern Japan and had returned without refuelling. In spite of the stir which this made at the time, the official judgement in England and the United States continued to be that Japan had made little progress in turning out skilled naval pilots.

Admiral Yamamoto, it should be noted, was not a firebrand. He knew and respected the West, its navies and its statesmen. For many years he had been pivotal within the moderate group, a true disciple of Admiral Katō Tomosaburō, and he had risked assassination in consequence. Yamamoto had risen high in the Navy, by great industry fortified by originality of ideas. He became Vice-Minister of the Navy and exercised a powerful influence towards moderation in the mid-1930s. In the middle of 1939 he was made Commander-in-Chief of the Combined Fleet, which removed him from the political centre of civil-military controversies, reduced the likelihood of his assassination, but confirmed his position as one of the three or four men who were responsible for planning naval operations. As relations with the United States worsened, he became convinced that, in the event of Japan being forced into war by the United States – as the Japanese thought – Japan should begin operations with a surprise attack on the US Pacific Fleet, which was stationed at Pearl Harbor. By doing so, the Navy would be repeating its attack, before the outbreak of war, on the Russian fleet at Port Arthur in 1904. Yamamoto had himself been present at that famous action, and had lost two fingers. The American plans for war were known to be that, upon its declaration, the United States Fleet should advance westwards from Pearl Harbor, and that the war would take the form of great naval engagements with the Japanese fleet in the Western Pacific. Yamamoto's plan was to make this impossible by destroying the American fleet, by surprise, before it could sail. As a professional sailor charged with advising his Government on great matters, he recommended it to borrow from Japan's mode of action in the past, and to deal a lightning blow. His advocacy of his bold plan was conditional upon the Japanese Government concluding that no means other than war was open to it. It was to be the desperate means for a desperate situation.

For the attack on Pearl Harbor, Yamamoto proposed to use his aircraft-carriers, and to carry out the destruction from the air. No coup of such magnitude had as yet been carried out: it was its boldness which surprised the world. A relatively small operation of the kind had been executed by the British when they had bombed Taranto with twenty-three planes: their success undoubtedly encouraged Yamamoto to proceed. He had the operation studied minutely, and torpedoes were manufactured which were suitable for attacking in shallow waters: the depth of water at Pearl Harbor was little deeper than it had been at Taranto although the speed, height, bombs, torpedo weights and number of aircraft which he would employ made the puny Taranto raid look primitive by comparison. The Pearl Harbor attack plan was conceived in January 1941. Detailed planning of the action to be taken began in June 1941. Yamamoto had the greatest difficulty in getting the consent of the very few naval colleagues whom he had to consult, but whose number was rigidly limited by the need for entire secrecy. An appreciation by the Naval General Staff was that success would depend on surprise, and that the chances of sailing a task force within reach of Pearl Harbor undetected were negligible.

Yamamoto, however, was finally permitted to proceed. His skill in advocacy was great, and it was one of the qualities which made him so conspicuous in the war and in the years beforehand. He assembled a task force of twenty-three surface warships (which included six carriers, two battleships and nine cruisers), a considerable supply force and twenty-seven submarines. In the middle of November, one month before the actual bombardment, this force sailed from Japan to Tankan Bay in the Kurile Islands; from there they approached Hawaii from the north, arriving within 220 miles of it on the night of 6–7 December. Though Yamamoto had supervised in detail the planning and rehearsal of the expedition, he did not accompany it, but remained at his post of command near Tokyo.

It was understood that the issue of success and of disgraceful and humiliating failure turned upon secrecy. The United States had been warned many times that the Japanese did not exclude an attack on Pearl Harbor. It was not supposed that the Americans were likely to be as extraordinarily negligent as proved in fact to be the case. The idea that the Japanese attacks on 7–8 December 1941 were dastardly acts should be laid to rest: the notion of a Japanese 'Day of Infamy' has outlived its usefulness. Surprise attacks, as we have seen, has been the customary practice of states throughout modern times: they were not the exception, but the general rule.

Japan took a formidable risk in relying on the friendless and empty seas of the North Pacific to protect its fleet from discovery. In other ways it had taken security devices which had in some measure deceived the Americans, and were an essential part of the operation. When its fleet sailed from Japan, the fact had been camouflaged by setting up a system of fake radio messages which stilled any American suspicions that ships were on the move. After some time, however, some of the American monitors

realized that calls to and from the aircraft-carriers, specifically, had
unaccountably ceased. They accepted that the carriers had been moved,
but made the wrong deduction that they had been sent south.

The Americans were already aware, from their interception of the code
messages between Tokyo and the Japanese Embassy in Washington, that
the Japanese were preparing for war in case the vital negotiations with the
United States ended in deadlock; and they assumed that the operations
would, in the first case, be directed only against Malaya, the Netherlands
East Indies, or the Philippines. With this inference, the assumption that
the disappearance of the aircraft-carriers meant a concentration of force
in the South Seas fitted excellently. That the concentration was at that
moment directed against Pearl Harbor never seemed to have crossed the
mind of anyone in authority.

In the summer and autumn months of 1941, both the Army and Navy
refrained from informing their commanders in Hawaii of vital information
affecting the likelihood of a Japanese surprise attack. It has been suggested
that President Roosevelt and his most senior military and naval advisers
were so involved in a gigantic attempt to lure the Japanese into an attack
on the United States, using the US Pacific Fleet as an opening gambit,
that they were ready to risk the consequences of 'surprise' at Pearl Harbor
rather than lose this opportunity to bring America into the Second World
War on the side of the British Empire. These are serious charges and thus
far the evidence offered in support of this conspiracy theory is exceedingly flimsy. The simplest explanation for the lapses that occurred is that
many individuals in the American forces at the time were accustomed to
sloppy, unprofessional staff work because the approved administrative
procedures were cumbersome, irksome and often unworkable: supervision
was capricious and poor. Officials tended to try to avoid taking personal
responsibility whenever possible. Record-keeping was often haphazard.
The fighting services were expanding rapidly and evolving. When pressure
mounted so did inefficiency.

What is certain is that there was no shortage of Intelligence information
about Japan's intentions. Much of the documentary evidence concerning
that information has since disappeared. It is charitable but probably safe
to assume that misguided efforts by individuals or by their departments to
cover up embarrassing omissions or misperceptions have lent undue
credence to those who promote the idea that the Federal Administration
was involved in treacherous activities.

Shortly after the Pearl Harbor Strike Force sailed from Japan, two
experienced radio operators aboard the Matson liner SS *Lurline* intercepted and logged a stream of radio traffic which they convinced them-

selves must have been exchanges between a Japanese fleet and Tokyo between 1 and 3 December. War was in the air, and the operators were naturally jittery. Upon docking at Honolulu, however, they immediately took their suspicions and radio log-book information to US Navy Intelligence. No action appears to have been taken.

Far away on the coast of California, an Intelligence officer working on routine Intelligence activities at the 12th Naval District in San Francisco learned that unusual radio transmissions were emanating from west of Hawaii. He telephoned contacts at the wire services and major shipping companies and from these contacts he and a young seaman were able to establish the approximate location of the mysterious signals. They then continued to monitor the position of the transmissions as its source, which they assumed to be a Japanese fishing fleet, continued on its course. It was actually Nagumo's carrier fleet. By the evening of 6 December the Americans had tracked it to a position only 400 miles north-west by north of Oahu, the Hawaiian island which contains Pearl Harbor. They speculated that if the force was the Japanese fleet, it would attack Pearl Harbor early the following morning. They were content to pass along the information to their Chief of Intelligence, an officer who, according to office chit-chat, knew President Roosevelt well enough to alert him personally and save the country. It was a plan of breathtaking naïvety. In any case, it is difficult to know how to regard these two stories: according to Japanese sources, Admiral Nagumo's forces maintained radio silence while on their way to Pearl Harbor.

On 2 December 1941 a Dutch Assistant Naval Attaché in Washington, in the course of a routine visit to the Office of Naval Intelligence, was shown a map plotting a Japanese fleet sailing west of Manila on its way down the South China Sea to the Gulf of Siam. Noting that two Japanese carriers were shown at a position half-way to Hawaii, he expressed his surprise. Four days later, on returning to ONI, he asked where the carriers had gone and was shown a position some 300–400 miles north-west of Pearl Harbor. He recorded this in his diary, reported it to his Ambassador and sent word to the Netherlands Government-in-Exile in London.

Dutch cryptographers, meanwhile, working with primitive resources in Bandung, Java, had managed to crack one of the Japanese consular codes. On 2 December they intercepted a message advising the Japanese Ambassador in Bangkok that Japanese surprise attacks on Hawaii, the Philippines, Malaya and Thailand were imminent and informing him of the famous 'Winds' signals giving notification of the attack. Upon receiving this information, the Commander-in-Chief of the Royal Dutch Netherlands East Indian Army, General Hein Ter Poorten, delivered the message, personally, to the head of the American military mission in Java, Brigadier-General Elliott Thorpe, who managed to cable the news to Washington through the senior US Naval Attaché, Commander Paul Sidney Slawson, and the American Consul-General in the Dutch East Indies, Dr Walter Foote, so as to arouse no suspicion from Japanese monitoring the air waves:

When crisis leading to worst arises, following will be broadcast at end weather reports:
1. East wind, rain, war with United States.
2. North wind, cloudy, war with Russia.
3. West wind, clear, war with Britain, including attack on Thailand or Malaya and Dutch East Indies.

The messages were duly acknowledged by Washington, where no notice was taken. Meanwhile, General Ter Poorten had asked the Dutch Military Attaché in Washington to convey the message directly to General Marshall, the US Army Chief of Staff, who dismissed the report out of hand. When the 'East wind, rain' message was transmitted, it was remarked upon; but the machinery for bringing this information to the attention of American military and naval commanders round the globe was tied up with red tape.

The British authorities, too, had learned of the impending attack. They had been informed by the Dutch Government-in-Exile, who had passed it on to the British Embassy in Washington. Although other hard evidence is lacking, it seems inconceivable that the British would have failed to bring the news to the attention of United States authorities at the highest level. There is, however, no hint of this in the public records, despite the fact that there is an abundance of documentation showing the flow of information between the two Governments concerning the Japanese convoy steaming down the South China Seas on its way to Malaya. The British Cabinet records for the period show that Britain's uncertainty about whether the Americans would become involved continued to exist right up to the eve of Pearl Harbor. Despite months, indeed years, of effort by the British and Dutch to secure a definite commitment by the Americans to join forces in war against Japan in the event of an attack confined to European possessions in the East, Roosevelt continued to be evasive to the last. To some extent his reluctance was explained by his concern that any such commitment might be leaked prematurely in the American press with dire political consequences. However, at the root of his concern was his apparent and possibly genuine inability to forecast how American sentiment and Congressional opinion would respond to such a guarantee:

it is now generally accepted that for some considerable time Roosevelt had lagged behind American public opinion as his country drifted into war. Prime Minister Churchill together with President Roosevelt had become fixed in his belief that only a policy of Anglo-American firmness towards Tokyo could deter Japan from embarking on a Pacific War. Both men recognized, however, that it was one thing to utter warlike cries to undermine the confidence of a potential enemy, quite another thing to plunge blindly into war.

On Friday, 5 December, a United States naval patrol vessel on station north of Hawaii lay in the path of the Japanese fleet. According to evidence put before the subsequent US Congressional inquiry into the Pearl Harbor Attack, the patrol ship unaccountably disappeared from naval records of ship movements and locations the next day: no explanations were given.

On Saturday, 6 December, after having lost contact with the Japanese convoy north-west of Malaya in the fog where the waters of the South China Sea merge with the Gulf of Siam, British reconnaissance aircraft reported elements of the Japanese fleet off the coast of Thailand. The force reportedly included thirty-five transports accompanied by eight cruisers and twenty destroyers: it actually comprised two battleships, eight cruisers and fourteen destroyers backing up a flotilla of nineteen transports carrying troops who had embarked at Hainan only two days before. The Commander of the British Far East Fleet, Vice-Admiral Sir Tom Phillips, who had played such a prominent role in the pre-war naval planning and war preparations of the British Admiralty, was then in Manila for consultations with General MacArthur and the Commander of the American Asiatic Fleet, Admiral Thomas Hart. Upon hearing this latest news, Phillips immediately flew back to Singapore to rejoin his fleet.

Half-way across the globe, the senior United States Army observer in Cairo was informed by Air Marshal Sir Arthur Tedder, Air Officer Commander-in-Chief of the Royal Air Force Middle Eastern Command, that there were firm indications that the United States would be attacked within twenty-four hours. Meanwhile, out in the Aleutians and Hawaii, word came that the reconnaissance flights of the Catalina PBYs were to be relaxed, allowing their crews a much needed rest after an exhausting period of high alert. The dawn patrols in the morning were reduced. According to testimony before the Roberts Commission, at the time of the attack only three Oahu-based naval patrol aircraft were in the air out of a total available strength of around fifty long-range naval reconnaissance aircraft.

The American monitors intercepted wireless messages between some

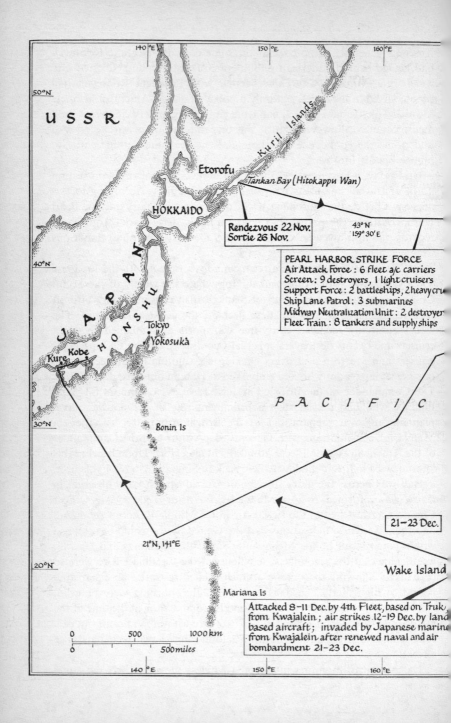

50°N

U S S R

140°E   150°E   160°E

Kuril Islands

Etorofu

Tankan Bay (Hitokappu Wan)

HOKKAIDO

Rendezvous 22 Nov.
Sortie 26 Nov.

43°N
159°30'E

J A P A N

40°N

PEARL HARBOR STRIKE FORCE
Air Attack Force : 6 fleet a/c carriers
Screen : 9 destroyers, 1 light cruisers
Support Force : 2 battleships, 2 heavy cru̶
Ship Lane Patrol : 3 submarines
Midway Neutralization Unit : 2 destroyer̶
Fleet Train : 8 tankers and supply ships

Tokyo
Yokosuka

HONSHU

Kure Kobe

P A C I F I C

30°N

Bonin Is

21–23 Dec.

21°N, 141°E

20°N

Mariana Is

Wake Island

Attacked 8–11 Dec. by 4th Fleet, based on Truk,
from Kwajalein ; air strikes 12–19 Dec. by land̶
based aircraft ; invaded by Japanese marine̶
from Kwajalein after renewed naval and air
bombardment 21–23 Dec.

0   500   1000 km
0   500 miles

140°E   150°E   160°E

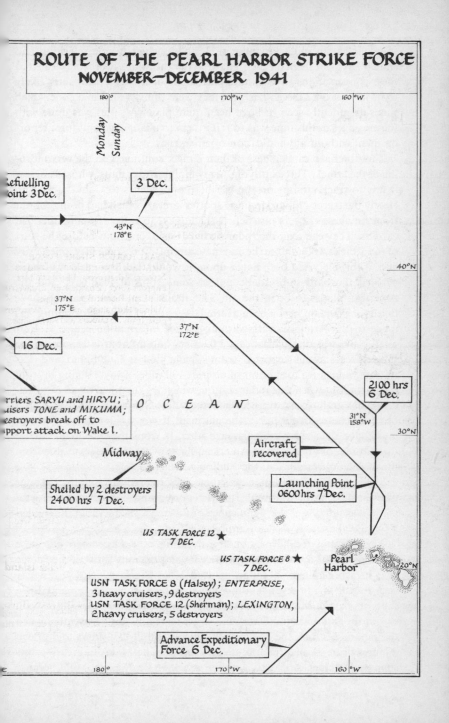

ROUTE OF THE PEARL HARBOR STRIKE FORCE
NOVEMBER–DECEMBER 1941

180° 170°W 160°W

Monday
Sunday

Refuelling
Point 3 Dec.

3 Dec.

43°N
178°E

40°N

37°N
175°E

37°N
172°E

16 Dec.

2100 hrs
6 Dec.

Carriers SARYU and HIRYU;
Cruisers TONE and MIKUMA;
Destroyers break off to
support attack on Wake I.

O C E A N

31°N
158°W

30°N

Midway

Aircraft
recovered

Shelled by 2 destroyers
2400 hrs 7 Dec.

Launching Point
0600 hrs 7 Dec.

US TASK FORCE 12 ★
7 DEC.

US TASK FORCE 8 ★
7 DEC.

Pearl
Harbor

20°N

USN TASK FORCE 8 (Halsey); ENTERPRISE,
3 heavy cruisers, 9 destroyers
USN TASK FORCE 12 (Sherman); LEXINGTON,
2 heavy cruisers, 5 destroyers

Advance Expeditionary
Force 6 Dec.

180° 170°W 160°W

source in Japan and a Japanese in Honolulu which were mysterious, and should have put them on their guard. After the attack it became clear that these conversations gave minute particulars of the American ships likely to be in port on 7 December. But they were thinly veiled in a code which was subsequently seen to have been quite plain. All that was done with the messages at this time was to refer them to a language unit for a report on them without any indication of emergency.

The American carelessness of their danger continued on the very morning of the attack. Three outlying Army mobile radar units, whose business it was to track aircraft on the northern approaches to Oahu, picked up clearly the traces of two Japanese spotter aircraft which had been sent out from Japanese cruisers just before the attack, to search for all American carriers. They came on the radar screen at 6.45, one hour before the start of the attack. At that time the Japanese aircraft were some fifty miles away and, if this alert had been acted upon, it would, late though it was, have enabled the battleships to be put in some state of readiness, and the American planes to be in the air. The attack would quite possibly have failed, or the main havoc been averted. A report of this radar sighting was made to the Army aircraft warning service information centre at Fort Shafter but was disregarded. At 7.02 a.m., half an hour later, one of the same three stations reported from Opana that it had found and was tracking a massive formation of aircraft 130 miles away, coming in from the north. But when this radar station, which was manned by an inexperienced but enthusiastic trainee, informed Fort Shafter of what had been observed, he was told not to be alarmed. It was assumed that the unit must have detected reconnaissance aircraft from the American carrier force at sea, or an incoming American flight of B17s which was due from the mainland in transit to the Philippines.

Similarly one of the Japanese submarines entered through the harbour gates at 4.50 in the morning. It was reported and hunted: but a general alarm was not given; the significance of the news, the fact that it heralded a full naval assault, was not appreciated.

At 1.15 a.m. local time, on the morning of 8 December, Japanese warships off the coast of Malaya fired Japan's opening shots of the Pacific War in a preliminary bombardment at Kota Bharu which left the way clear for the first of seven landings made by Japanese troops up and down the east coast of Malaya and Thailand over the next two days. In Hawaii, east of the International Date Line, it was 5.45 a.m. on 7 December when the Japanese struck the Malayan Peninsula, a full two hours and fifteen minutes prior to the attack on Pearl Harbor. The Malayan invasion was supposed to coincide exactly with the attack on Pearl Harbor, but because

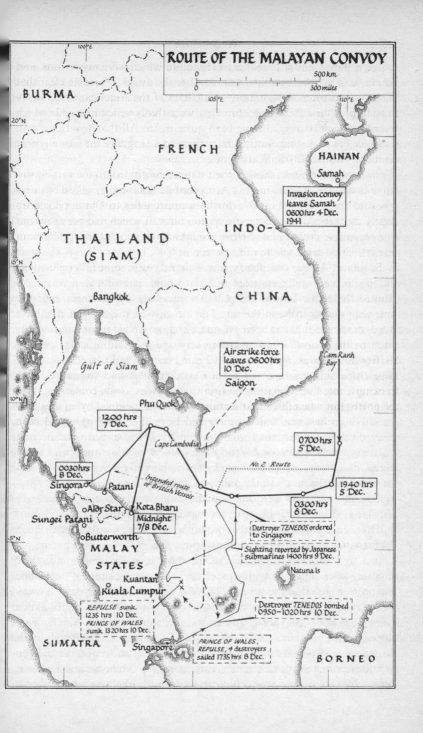

ROUTE OF THE MALAYAN CONVOY

0 ___ 500 km
0 ___ 300 miles

BURMA

FRENCH

HAINAN

Samah

THAILAND
(SIAM)

INDO-

Invasion convoy
leaves Samah
0600 hrs 4 Dec.
1941

Bangkok

CHINA

Gulf of Siam

Air strike force
leaves 0600 hrs
10 Dec.

Saigon

Cam Ranh
Bay

Phu Quok

1200 hrs
7 Dec.

0700 hrs
5 Dec.

Cape Cambodia

0030 hrs
8 Dec.

Singora

Intended route
of British Vessels

No. 2 Route

1940 hrs
5 Dec.

Patani

Alor Star

Kota Bharu
Midnight
7/8 Dec.

0300 hrs
6 Dec.

Sungei Patani

Destroyer TENEDOS ordered
to Singapore

Butterworth

MALAY

Sighting reported by Japanese
submarines 1400 hrs 9 Dec.

STATES

Natuna Is.

Kuantan

Kuala Lumpur

REPULSE sunk
1235 hrs 10 Dec.
PRINCE OF WALES
sunk 1320 hrs 10 Dec.

Destroyer TENEDOS bombed
0950-1020 hrs 10 Dec.

SUMATRA

Singapore

PRINCE OF WALES,
REPULSE, 4 destroyers
sailed 1735 hrs 8 Dec.

BORNEO

of an officer's error it took place ahead of schedule. There was no real harm done by this mistake: Britain and America were expecting the blow. The authorities in Hawaii, however, evidently remained unaware that the outbreak of hostilities in Malaya had occurred and took no special precautionary measures.

*Later that morning, a dispatch rider, carrying a detailed warning from General Marshall in Washington to General Short's Headquarters Command in Hawaii – a warning that had taken an unaccountable time to transmit on the telegraph – was forced to take shelter in a ditch while the raid on Pearl Harbor, which was accurately forecast in the document which he carried, was taking place round him. The warning never reached the authorities who, had it been brought to their attention a few hours earlier, could have taken effective action.

So the evidence, and plenty was at hand, of a coming coup at Pearl Harbor was allowed to pile up, and no counter-measures were taken. The United States was amply served by an acute Intelligence force and given warnings by its Allies. But what is the use of Intelligence if there is negligence and incompetence of mind-boggling proportions over its use and interpretation? What was necessary was that Admiral Husband E. Kimmel, who was in command at Pearl Harbor, and General Walter C. Short, who was responsible for the Hawaiian Defence Command, should have instituted air reconnaissance of all the seas around them: but this, after weighing the advice, and with the assent of their staff, they neglected to do. They believed that it was unnecessary. For nothing was done to alert them to the fact that conditions had reached a more critical stage than ever before. On the contrary, they knew nothing about the Purple codes and had been desensitized over a period of months by a long succession of warnings that Japan was seriously preparing for war. Afterwards, the two men were made scapegoats for the failure of others in Washington who were never court-martialled or punished.

Thus secrecy was maintained: the Japanese triumph was assured. To do Yamamoto justice, he had doubts about the propriety of what he was doing, and stipulated that the attack should not be made until thirty minutes after Japan had informed the United States that it considered the peace negotiations at an end. Thereby a punctilious correctness would be observed, even though by a hair's breadth. Actually the attack, when it came, preceded the notification, and to the outraged Americans it appeared as perfidious as Admiral Tōgō's assault had seemed to the Russians in 1904. But the Japanese had in fact tried to observe the conventions as well as the customary usages of war. The notification was in a bulky 5,000-word message which it took the Embassy much longer to decipher than had been foreseen in Tokyo. The U S Navy codebreakers on Constitution Avenue had cracked the message five hours ahead of the Japanese Embassy staff. It was in a way symbolical of how often the actions of the Japanese authorities were ruined by slovenly or incompetent work in their execution. It was Ambassador Kurusu, the professional diplomat, not Admiral Nomura, the amateur, who insisted on correcting the typing and wording of the Final Note, which in appreciation of its special secrecy was typed up by the Embassy's First Secretary, who was an inept typist, with the assistance at the eleventh hour of an equally inept translator. When the note was delivered, the blow had already been struck.

In the early hours of Sunday, 7 December, a last radio instruction came from Tokyo. By a quarter past six, the first wave of aircraft left the carriers. The flagship hoisted a flag reminiscent of the signal which Admiral Tōgō had carried thirty-six years before in his victory over the Tsar. The operation was the more hazardous because the Japanese possessed very sketchy information about the forces they were about to assail. It is a myth that they were well supplied by their Intelligence organizations about the American defences. They were uncertain to the end, for example, about whether the Americans had torpedo nets to protect their ships. They only had information, which they themselves mistrusted, about exactly what ships they were to encounter. One of their agents in Honolulu had warned them that the four aircraft-carriers which were normally with the Pacific Fleet were away from port that weekend. To catch the carriers was a vital objective. They had had in consequence serious thoughts of calling off the entire adventure at the last moment, or of postponing it indefinitely. Many of the decisions were made by guesswork.

The air attack force which the Japanese let loose was divided into groups of fighter planes, high-level bombers, torpedo-bombers and dive-bombers. Commander Fuchida Mitsuo, who led the first wave of the attack at the head of the torpedo-bombers, has put on record the sight which met him. It is quoted in John Deane Potter's book, *Admiral of the Pacific*:

Below me lay the whole U S Pacific Fleet in a formation I would not have dared to dream of in my most optimistic dreams. I have seen all the German ships assembled in Kiel Harbour. I have also seen the French battleships in Brest. And finally I have frequently seen our warships assembled for review before the Emperor, but I have never seen ships, even in the deepest deep, anchored at a distance of 500–1,000 yards from each other. A war fleet must always be on the alert, since surprise attacks can never be fully ruled out. But this picture down there was hard to comprehend. Had these Americans never heard of Port Arthur?*

* Quoted by J. D. Potter, *Admiral of the Pacific*, Heinemann, London, 1965, p. 98.

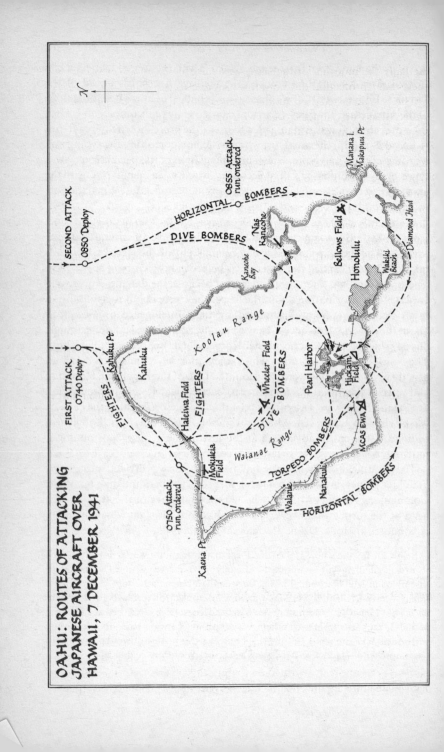

OAHU: ROUTES OF ATTACKING JAPANESE AIRCRAFT OVER HAWAII, 7 DECEMBER 1941

N

FIRST ATTACK
0740 Deploy

SECOND ATTACK
0850 Deploy

0855 Attack
run ordered

HORIZONTAL BOMBERS

DIVE BOMBERS

Kahuku Pt

Kahuku

Kaneohe Bay

NAS Kaneohe

Manana I.
Makapuu Pt

Bellows Field

Koolau Range

Honolulu

Waikiki Beach

Diamond Head

FIGHTERS

Haleiwa Field

Wheeler Field

Pearl Harbor

Hickam Field

DIVE BOMBERS

Waianae Range

0750 Attack
run ordered

Mokuleia Field

TORPEDO BOMBERS

MCAS EWA

Kaena Pt

Waianae

Nanakuli

HORIZONTAL BOMBERS

Actually the mooring of the ships was culpably unsafe. It was odd that their radar protection did not afford more effective safety.

The attack lasted two hours. In this short time the Americans had suffered loss or damage to eighteen battleships and auxiliaries, the destruction or damage of 349 aircraft, and had 2,345 sailors, soldiers and marines killed, 1,247 wounded and 103 civilians killed or wounded. By mid-morning the vast and impressive naval base, which had filled the United States with such confidence, was transformed into a huge ruin with flaming ships, a decimated garrison, and a monumental disorganization. The base from which the United States had counted on directing the war was a chaos enveloped in smoke. The Japanese were amazed at the extent of their success and at their enemy's unpreparedness. Nevertheless, they also noted with concern and respect the speed with which the Americans responded to the attack once it was underway. The second wave encountered very stiff and determined anti-aircraft fire.

To effect this slaughter, the Japanese had used 353 carrier-borne aircraft and the two cruiser-borne reconnaissance aircraft launched earlier. They lost fifteen dive-bombers and high-level bombers, nine fighter planes, and five torpedo-planes in combat, 8 per cent of their total strength, a figure which was surprisingly similar to average losses then being inflicted upon air raiding aircraft by alert defence forces in Europe. In addition a number of other aircraft were badly damaged or crashed on returning to their carriers, and more than twenty aircraft of these had to be written off. The total loss in Japanese naval personnel was fifty-five officers and men. The statistics, however, do not convey the full sense of shock which was felt throughout the world by news of the Pearl Harbor attack. It was the most spectacular triumph of the war. The Americans in Hawaii remained unaware throughout of the source of their attack, and the entire fleet sailed back in safety to Japan.

Impressive as were the results of the raid, humiliating as it proved to be for the American Navy, Japan fell just short of making it the crushing success it was meant to be. The Japanese, inexplicably, did not destroy the vast oil stocks and fleet repair facilities on Hawaii, or, at that stage, seriously consider whether it could seize them. America began the war with oil reserves at Hawaii which were almost equal to the entire supplies of Japan. Japan had them at its mercy: why they neglected to fire them remains inadequately explained. At one stage it had, it is true, been the Japanese intention to try to seize Oahu, and in that case the oil would have passed into Japan's hands. But this part of the plan had been quickly

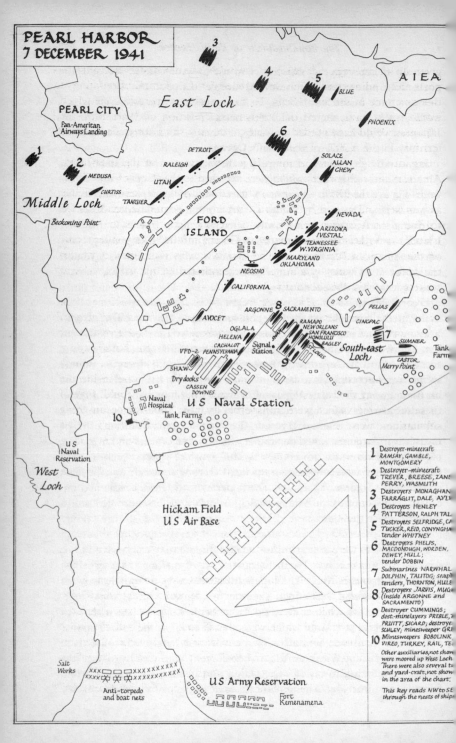

PEARL HARBOR
7 DECEMBER 1941

AIEA

East Loch

PEARL CITY

Pan-American
Airways Landing

BLUE

PHOENIX

DETROIT

SOLACE
ALLAN
CHEW

RALEIGH

UTAH

Middle Loch

Beckoning Point

MEDUSA

CURTISS

TANGIER

**FORD
ISLAND**

NEVADA

ARIZONA
IVESTAL
TENNESSEE
W. VIRGINIA
MARYLAND
OKLAHOMA

NEOSHO

CALIFORNIA

ARGONNE   SACRAMENTO

PELIAS

AVOCET

OGLALA
HELENA

RAMAPO
NEW ORLEANS
SAN FRANCISCO
HONOLULU
BAGLEY

CINCPAC

CACHALOT
VFD-2   PENNSYLVANIA

Signal
Station

ST LOUIS

**South-east
Loch**

SUMNER

7

SHAW
Dry docks

CASSEN
DOWNES

9

CASTOR
Merry Point

Tank
Far

Naval Hospital

U S Naval Station

Tank Farms

10

U S
Naval
Reservation

**West
Loch**

**Hickam Field
U S Air Base**

Salt
Works

XXXXX ☐☐☐ XXXXXXXXXXXX
XXXX ✕✕ ✿✿ XXXXXXXXXXX

Anti-torpedo
and boat nets

U S Army Reservation

☐☐☐☐☐
⌒⌒⌒⌒⌒   Fort
⊔⊔⊔⊔⊔⊔   Kemenamena

1 Destroyer-minecraft
  RAMSAY, GAMBLE,
  MONTGOMERY
2 Destroyer-minecraft
  TREVER, BREESE, ZANE
  PERRY, WASMUTH
3 Destroyers MONAGHAN
  FARRAGUT, DALE, AYL
4 Destroyers HENLEY
  PATTERSON, RALPH TAL
5 Destroyers SELFRIDGE, CA
  TUCKER, REID, CONYNGHA
  tender WHITNEY
6 Destroyers PHELPS,
  MACDONOUGH, WORDEN,
  DEWEY, HULL;
  tender DOBBIN
7 Submarines NARWHAL
  DOLPHIN, TALITOG; seap
  tenders, THORNTON, HULE
8 Destroyers JARVIS, MUG
  (inside ARGONNE and
  SACRAMENTO)
9 Destroyer CUMMINGS;
  dest-minelayers PREBLE, T
  PRUITT, SICARD; destroye
  SCHLEY; minesweeper GR
10 Minesweepers BOBOLINK
  VIREO, TURKEY, RAIL, TE

Other auxiliaries, not show
were moored up West Loch
There were also several tu
and yard-craft, not show
in the area of the chart.

This key reads NW to SE
through the nests of ships

given up as, among other reasons, it would have demanded troop transports and landing craft which were needed for the operation beginning at the same time in the South Seas. To have made the operation one which would really have altered the fundamental position of both sides, the Japanese would have needed not only to destroy ships but to have seized territory in the middle of the Pacific Ocean.

Japan did not include among its victims any one of the four major American aircraft carriers which were attached to the Pacific Fleet. These were to prove the decisive weapon in the subsequent struggle in the Pacific, as was well understood by Admiral Yamamoto. Fortunate accidents led to one aircraft carrier being away delivering some planes to Midway Island; to another delivering planes to Guam; another being under repair on the American Pacific coast. The fourth was, as was found out later, trailed for some hours by a large Japanese submarine, but, in the eventual contest with this, the submarine was sunk.

Pearl Harbor contained also one failure of the Japanese which was little noted at the time but which was to have a decisive effect. The plan of Yamamoto had included a submarine attack as well as one from the air: but this was as uniformly a failure as the attack from the air was a success. A special Japanese invention, the midget submarine, a minute submarine operated by a crew of two, was to be let loose inside the harbour among the battleships, and to work what havoc it could. Five of these submarines, which were transported by huge 2,000-ton ocean-going submarines, were inserted through the harbour gates: this was, to all intents and purposes, a suicide mission, for the chances of the crews being picked up again were, though it was just possible, exceedingly slight. In fact all the five midget submarines were destroyed and only one member of the crews survived, falling prisoner to the Americans. (Like most Japanese taken prisoner, he proved singularly talkative, and he disclosed useful information to the Americans.) In the subsequent share-out of the honours for the raid, the submarine commanders felt themselves neglected, and all the credit fell to the airmen. Subsequently, the submarine service was at a discount in Japanese eyes. No further plans were drawn up which devolved any great responsibility on it. Though attention had previously been given to the production of the midget, Japanese inventiveness swung away from the submarine and concentrated on other matters. Japan had begun the war with several very large and technically efficient submarines; they were subsequently engaged on colourful, hazardous action on the American coast and in the fighting at Guadalcanal; but they failed to keep their hold on the imagination of the public, which was fixed upon its navy pilots. So, in war, the issues can be decided by irrational judgement and politics. An unfair inference was that the Japanese Navy, though it possessed an incontestable genius in Yamamoto, did not have staff officers who were capable of recognizing that Japan possessed an asset which it was wasting; who were capable of evolving a strategy which would make use of this instrument; and who simultaneously had the ability to force their views on the attention of the faction-riddled Japanese High Command. What Yamamoto had done for naval aircraft, nobody seemed able to do for the submarine.

Was Pearl Harbor therefore really a success for the Japanese? Taking into account the whole course of the war, this has been doubted. The far from dispassionate or even-handed American naval historian, S. E. Morison, doubted this. He summed up the situation by saying that Pearl Harbor, for all the destruction which it achieved, was really an empty triumph. Looking at the careful Japanese plan which had been evolved for dealing with the expected offensive by the United States Pacific fleet advancing in the Pacific, he speculated that Japan would have done more wisely if it had waited for the attack, and contained it somewhere in the Marshall or Caroline Islands. By fleet action on these lines, Japan would have gained the best chance of surviving. Morison, in other words, believed that the war operations plan to which the Japanese Navy had adhered for twenty years until January 1941 was far more sound than Admiral Yamamoto's plans for the Pearl Harbor attack operation, which superseded it. Such a view may be hard to credit. Put at the most down-to-earth estimate, Yamamoto had gained eighteen months', or two years', respite for Japan, and, though the long-term prospects remained exceedingly black, he had insured that the typhoon should rage over Japan in two years' time, not rage at once. He gave the opportunity to his own war schemes, and to any others which Japan might produce, or, better still, to her diplomats and statesmen in their ability to work out a peaceable solution, to find a way of averting ultimate catastrophe. Here he felt there were genuine opportunities, making the mistake of assuming that his enemies still preferred peace to war. As for his own side, a close examination of the facts leaves one in no doubt that the Japanese recognized their mortal danger. One perceptive young Japanese historian has gone so far to argue that 'Not a single Japanese leader, either military man or civilian, believed that Japan could hold out against an Anglo-American combined attack for long, let alone achieve a sweeping victory over the Allies.'*

* Satō Ryozō, 'Japan's Entry into the Pacific War: A Reconsideration', *Senshū Jinmon Ronshū* (Collected Essays on Special Subjects in the Humanities), No. 30, Tokyo, March 1983, pp. 74–5.

One peculiar circumstance aided Japan at Pearl Harbor. It was to continue in some form throughout the war, and was to handicap American arrangements repeatedly. This was that the High Commands of the US Navy and Army at home were scarcely on speaking terms. The degree of discord varied from place to place, and depended in part on the accident of personalities engaged. But the tension was often an important fact of the situation: as it had been at Pearl Harbor, where there was the minimum cooperation between the Air Force, which in the United States was part of the Army, and the Navy. Much of the responsibility for friction lay with the Navy. The United States Navy existed in peculiar isolation from American society. It was self-sufficient and self-contained. It had its own politics, outlook, ethos. In war as in peace it was apt to think that its chief enemy was at home, in the rival services which entrenched upon its own liberty of action. The result was peculiarly catastrophic. Due to this self-imposed remoteness, the defence machinery creaked badly. Yet the United States Navy and its subordinate marine command was the country's only fully efficient fighting service at the outbreak of the war. Its training, weaponry and establishment were all capable of performing the tasks required of it. By comparison, the United States Army was clumsy, out-of-date, ill-equipped, under-strength and lack-lustre. It was scarcely surprising that the Navy regarded the Army with contempt – and preferred to rely upon its own people and their friends in Washington as well as overseas.

There were other defects in the American defence machine. All these stood out clearly at Pearl Harbor. The extension of peacetime bureaucratic controls went so far that the anti-aircraft batteries were obliged to indent for every shell which was fired. As the American wartime machine swung slowly into action, a great many blunders were discovered which had their source in this over-meticulousness of civilian control. It was the natural consequence of a long period of peace – and it was by no means peculiar to the United States.

If the sights are lifted beyond this war, it must be recorded that, by the shrewd blow delivered to the United States (which was so much larger than Japan) and by the superb secrecy which had been preserved in organizing such a complex operation, Yamamoto and Nagumo had given a boost to Japanese self-esteem, which would buoy the people up in future periods of national calamity. One day the Japanese triumph at Pearl Harbor will be regarded in a different light from that in which it was inevitably seen by the opposite side at the time; the memory of treachery will fade: it will stand out as a most memorable feat of arms.

CHAPTER 16

The War after Pearl Harbor

AN Imperial Rescript – the manifesto which is issued at great decisions of the Government – accompanied Japan's declaration of war, and read as follows:

We hereby declare war on the United States of America and the British Empire ... It has been truly unavoidable ... More than four years have passed since China, failing to understand the true intentions of our empire, disturbed the peace of Asia. Although there has been re-established the National Government of China with which Japan has effected neighbourly intercourse and cooperation, the régime which has survived at Chungking, relying upon American and British protection, still continues its fratricidal opposition. Eager for the realization of their inordinate ambition to dominate the Orient, both America and Britain, giving support to the Chungking régime, have aggravated the disturbances of East Asia. Moreover these two powers, inducing other countries to follow suit, have increased military preparations on all sides of our empire to challenge us. They have obstructed by every means our peaceful commerce and finally have resorted to a direct severance of economic relations thereby gravely menacing the existence of our empire ... This trend of affairs would, if left unchecked, endanger the very existence of our nation. The situation being such as it is, our empire, for its existence and self-defence, has no other recourse but to appeal to arms and to crush every obstacle on its path.*

Except for the blame it casts on China for the convulsion, this is an accurate statement of why Japan went to war. Japan states that it enlarged the war because it believed that only by doing so was it possible to wind up a smaller war with China. Its intervention in Indo-China, to which America had reacted so stiffly, had been undertaken for the same reasons.

War on such a scale as Japan now embarked on had come out of the inability of the Japanese Government to find any other means of dealing with a situation which had passed out of its control. It was due in the last resort to a failure of ingenuity. The war was not preceded by elaborate planning. There was no systematic scheme of operations against the United States and Britain, which laid down a timetable for successive undertakings. British and American war planners and Intelligence experts,

---

* This is the translation introduced into evidence by the Prosecution at the Tokyo War Trial: see Pritchard and Zaide, *Transcript of the Proceedings*, op. cit., 5 [PX 1240], pp. 10686–9.

considering their prospects in the eventuality of a war against Japan, had been virtually unanimous in affirming their belief that while the Japanese were meticulous in their staff work, their gifts of improvisation were of a low order. That was to prove another failure by the West to know their enemy. All the evidence which was to become available to the Western Allies at the end of the hostilities confirms that the war was a desperate venture, hastily decided upon: that it was conducted by a series of improvisations, however brilliant some of these were: that no elaborate plans were made of the assets, military and economic, of the Western Allies, and that no intelligent scheme existed for eroding them: that Japan was, quite literally, taking a great leap in the dark, and casting its faith into the keeping of a veiled Providence, which it had no reason to think would be kind.

Admiral Yamamoto, accomplished gambler and the architect of Pearl Harbor, summed up the attitude of those who took the decision to go to war:

What a strange position I find myself in now – having to make a decision diametrically opposed to my own personal opinion, with no choice but to push full-speed in pursuance of that decision. Is that, too, fate?*

To his sister, he wrote, 'Well, war has begun at last. But in spite of all the clamour that is going on, we could lose it. I can only do my best.' † And to a fellow admiral he wrote:

This war will give us much trouble in the future. The fact that we have had a small success at Pearl Harbor is nothing. The fact that we have succeeded so easily has pleased people. Personally I do not think it is a good thing to whip up propaganda to encourage the nation. People should think things over and realize how serious the situation is.‡

He had, at Pearl Harbor, fought a successful holding operation, which had bought time. But he knew, as well as anybody, that this time would pass, and that, if at the end of it Japan – and its ally Germany – had not found a way to peace, Japan would be ruined. He had said repeatedly that it was easier to start a war than finish one. However much territory the Japanese took, however many American battleships they sank, final victory almost certainly would elude them.

One way only seemed to offer hope. Japanese strategy should be to win, by the impetus of surprise, as much as it possibly could in the first six

* J. D. Potter, *Admiral of the Pacific*, op. cit.
† ibid.
‡ ibid.

months of the war. The only chance of a satisfactory peace would be to follow up Pearl Harbor by sinking the American aircraft-carriers: and then, from the triumphal height of that moment, to persuade the United States to negotiate peace. It might hope that Japan would seem to be in such a commanding position that its Anglo-Saxon enemies would be cast down by the difficulty of dislodging it. Though Japan's occidental enemies had potentially invincible power, they would be unwilling to make the exertion of mobilizing it, the more so since they would have been worn out by the war effort they were making against Germany and Italy. Japan, it should be remembered, occupied a naval position of great strength strategically. After the war of 1914–18, it had inherited from Germany the Caroline and Marshall Islands in the Pacific which, if thoroughly fortified (as they were to become), interposed a screen which would hamper the Americans in defending the Philippines or in advancing westwards towards the Japanese homeland. And in the South Pacific there were other considerations.

The Japanese, linked by blood to Polynesia as well as to Mongolia, Korea and China, have always exhibited a degree of interest in the South Seas and in that concept of manifest destiny which they called the 'Southern Advance'. The South Seas Mandated Islands, wrested by Japan from Germany during the First World War and conceded to Japanese control by the League of Nations, were a source of national pride as well as being a focus for economic exploitation. From a naval point of view, the strategical importance of the islands was immense. It was the view of the Naval Affairs Bureau that:

the South Sea Islands were so situated geographically as to constitute the bulwark of sea defence for Japan and hence we termed it the first line of defence for our country. We felt that if these islands fell into the hands of an enemy it would have meant certain defeat for Japan. Hence it was but natural that the Navy was desirous of installing on these islands or some of them such military defensive measures as would satisfy our need for security. Were it not for treaty restrictions we would have carried out defensive constructions on these islands with no hesitation.*

In the Covenant of the League of Nations there was a general prohibition against the establishment of permanent defences on mandated territories. The award to Japan of the islands formerly possessed by Germany in the South Pacific was contingent upon additional assurances that it would respect that prohibition. That the Japanese eventually broke these promises is not in dispute and, since the United States never joined the League of

* Pritchard and Zaide, op. cit., 11, pp. 26468–9: Affidavit [DX 2990] and Testimony by Captain Yoshida Hidemi, IJN.

Nations, has little significance in itself. A nation's self-defence was regarded as its paramount obligation and inalienable right. It was, however, important that in several treaties concluded during the Washington Conference in 1922, the Japanese repeated their categorical assurances that the Japanese Mandated Islands would not be fortified although, of course, it was plain that their freedom of action (like that of their rivals) would be restored whenever the agreements finally terminated.

Long before the expiration of the Washington Treaties, the British and Americans convinced themselves that the Japanese were in breach of their undertakings. Their evidence for this was merely that the Japanese declared the Mandated Islands off-limits to foreigners and strictly enforced the rule. The rest was rumour and speculation. Subsequently it emerged that the civil administration of the islands had been put into the hands of naval officers. They thoroughly surveyed the defence potential of each one, naval manoeuvres were periodically conducted there, and a number of facilities were erected which, strictly speaking, were not proscribed by the Treaties but might have raised a hair on an international lawyer's eyebrow: these included some rudimentary air strips, light harbour facilities and modest fuel storage tanks – all ostensibly for civil use in the economic exploitation of the islands though with their potential conversion to military use clearly in mind. None of these constructions nor a few temporary buildings built there constituted the kind of defended bases and fixed artillery emplacements proscribed by the Treaties. Even the limited development that did take place on the Mandated Islands prior to the outbreak of the Pacific War occurred only after the demise of the Washington Treaty System, and the contrast between what was built before the war and the defence installations installed there after Pearl Harbor provides some measure of the Japanese Navy's attempt to uphold its Treaty obligations.

The suspicions of the Western Powers were in fact groundless although understandable. The matter was explored by both sides at the time of the Japanese war crimes trials, and notwithstanding the International Tribunal's characteristically one-sided judgement to the contrary, the evidence produced by the Defence seems far more convincing than the case for the Prosecution. The myths and legends persist, but the formidable defence works constructed on these islands during the war itself should be regarded as a memorial to Japanese forward planning, engineering skill and efficiency, not to duplicity. Indeed it is clear that the policy of successive Japanese Governments and of the Japanese fighting services was to conform to Japan's undertaking not to fortify the islands, until a surprisingly late stage. It is a point worth setting straight, and the Summation by the Defence at the Tokyo Trial puts the issue squarely:

It was frankly admitted that after November 1941 the Navy decided for the first time to carry out the construction of defence works on the Mandated Islands. But it was not until after the middle of November that the construction corps left Japan for some of the islands. But this was only after conditions between the Western Powers and Japan had come to the danger point of explosion and it would have been militarily ridiculous for the Japanese Navy to have sat back quietly with folded hands.*

The Japanese defences in their Mandated Islands do merit comparison with the poor state of readiness that existed in British, American, Australian and Dutch island possessions in the Pacific in the years between the termination of the Treaties and the outbreak of war in the Pacific. The economic parsimony of the western democracies was responsible for the fact that they achieved less where development was permitted. The Defence, however, made another cogent point as well in summing up:

If Japan had entertained the thought of aggressive war against the United States, Great Britain or the other countries, surely [it] would not have waited until this desperately late day to begin such military construction on the life-line of Japan.†

The vast depths of the Pacific Ocean were in themselves a very strong defence. Japan could argue that the United States, confronted with the possibility of either a prolonged, arduous counter-assault, or with a generous peace offer by Japan – generous in the sense that it would not be against the United States' interest in any part of the world except East Asia – would choose the path of peace.

Of the chances of their ally Germany – who was little more, either then or later, than their nominal ally – they took a rather similar view: Gemany's long-term prospects were black, but it might find salvation in the war-weariness of the Western Allies. In this titanic world contest, one of the most curious things was the failure of Japan and Germany to cooperate. Their relations throughout were scarcely more than the conventional ones of peacetime association. Their relations were conducted by Ambassadors. The joint planning which essentially made up Anglo-American cooperation was almost totally absent in the wartime partnership of their rivals. There were joint commissions which Japan and Germany established to help coordinate their policies, but these were largely empty shells without much vital substance. When diligent spying

* ibid., 17, pp. 43209–10.
† ibid., p. 43210.

failed to discover any joint war plans by Germany and Japan, it was assumed at first that an unusually opaque veil had been woven to hide them. Not until much later did the real and simple truth become credible. No such plans had been brought into being.

Japan, unlike Germany, had no well-considered long-term war aims. In contrast to what Germany planned for Europe, Japan invested little effort in its projects for the Greater East Asia Co-Prosperity Sphere. The direction of the war on the Japanese side was too widely diffused among different hands for a clear national policy to become plain. Japan, even though it had hopes of limiting the war, was easily diverted away from the idea of a defensive war. By Pearl Harbor and Japan's initial victories, a situation had been created which made prudence difficult, and lured the Japanese on. It was as impossible to restrain its generals and admirals from further adventures as it is to prevent bulls from charging in a bull-ring.

In general, Japan followed a strategy remarkably close to that by which Mr Micawber governed his life. It was to take violent action, and then to hope that something or other would turn up, enabling it to escape disaster and to re-establish peace.

Japan had committed the error of all military Powers in dealing with the United States. It underrated grossly the willingness of the United States to bear the adversities of war. It despised it; and continued to do so throughout the war. Because in the course of every war the United States armies had begun badly, because its democratic institutions encouraged crude criticism and loose talk, because its people were not ashamed to harp upon considerations of material interest, the Japanese, like Hohenzollern Germany before them, too easily expected the United States to give up. They scoffed at the American commercial instinct, and they predicted that, in the grim struggle of war, this could never survive against the Samurai tradition.

But the nature of Anglo-Saxon democracy has often been its tenacity. This the Americans, and the British, have demonstrated clearly in chapters of their history. Confront them wth a desperate situation, give them disastrous leaders, let their economic policies be deplorable, saddle their public life with a rising rate of casualties; and they have generally become more stubborn. They can be implacable, and seemingly their pocket is limitless. They become pitiless and merciless, both to their enemies and to the civilian minorities among them who protest against a transfiguration of the values of life by the stubborn resolve to continue war. Passchendaele and the battlefields of the American Civil War are a terrible warning, which naturally militant people, but those untouched by the

traditions of Anglo-Saxon democracy, have never taken to heart. Once it
has taken up arms, and has suffered the blood-letting which warms its
temper, the democracy long ceases to understand the virtues of a peace
which is negotiated, and is satisfied only with the barren conclusion
spreading bitterness everywhere, of absolute victory. There have been
exceptions – the history of the Vietnam War was one, the adventures of
the United States in Mexico and elsewhere in Latin America have been
others – when public opinion has cast a decisive vote against foreign wars.
Britain, too, had her Boer War, and her scuttle from African and East
Asian conflicts after the Second World War may count as much the same.
Yet generally the Anglo-American democracies at war set aside all rules,
and, with a mood created by the tempest of the hour, work simply and
mechanically, grinding their way to victory. This was the tempest which
Japan was bringing down upon itself: more awful than any of its feared
typhoons.

It was to discover later that, terrible as a victorious democracy may be,
it has at least the virtue of quickly changing its temper when the goad of
war is removed. The resolution and implacability, which thrive during war,
are dissolved after a year or so of peace. Hence Japan, if it had dwelt on
past history, need not have been so miserably cast down by its total defeat.

If the Japanese despised the United States, Americans no less misunderstood the Japanese. Their mutual incomprehension is one of the
facts, tragic and at times comic, of the war. Throughout its course, anyone
visiting the United States was at once made conscious of the passionate
contempt, originally based on resentment, which was felt for the Japanese.
All the discreditable facts about them were remembered. All that made
Japanese civilization interesting was, as by system, forgotten. All Japanese
were lumped together as a misshapen, ugly, stupid, dwarf people. They
were like nothing so much as Mr Tolkien's orcs in *The Lord of the Rings*,
creations of a people of sheer malevolence and hideousness. One discreditable consequence of this racialist response was the public hysteria
which quickly developed on the West Coast of the United States for the
forcible internment of Americans of Japanese extraction.

Many Americans of a more reflective turn of mind were dismayed by
this outrage, but they were powerless in the face of the sensationalist press
and radio coverage which pandered to the prejudices of the majority.
With strong backing from local congressmen and other public figures,
notably from State Attorney General Earl Warren, who was then campaigning for the governorship of California which he won in 1943 (he
went on to earn a place in history as a Chief Justice of the United States
Supreme Court renowned for his then less than popular advancement of

the civil liberties of other minority groups), sufficient pressure was put upon officials in Washington, DC, to produce results. At first the Japanese-Americans were subjected to abuse, harassment and worse as individual American citizens 'took matters into their own hands'. Soon various curfews were imposed and Japanese-Americans were excluded from specified 'prohibited zones', which grew in number or extent over the first few months after Pearl Harbor until these unfortunates were barred altogether from the western third of Washington and Oregon, the western half of California and the southern quarter of Arizona. Then in June 1942, orders were given that led to further controls which effectively deprived all Americans of Japanese extraction of their liberty within any part of those four states.

Eventually, 119,000 were taken away to be concentrated at ten internment camps established for that purpose at remote, inhospitable sites (where they lived in terrible hardship and a significant number died from their privations). Forced to abandon their property and personal possessions or to dispose of their homes, businesses and smallholdings at give-away prices, there was to be no restitution of their property after the war. No real steps were taken by the United States Government to compensate Japanese-Americans for their losses until the early 1980s.

The supposed threat which was allegedly posed by these Americans to the national security of the United States was almost entirely imaginary – and was recognized as such by many of those who carried out the exercise: in that most sensitive of military districts, Hawaii, fewer than 500 persons of Japanese extraction were interned. Despite intensive surveillance by vigilant citizens, local police forces, the FBI and the Intelligence agencies of the defence services, not one Japanese-American was ever charged with the commission of an act of sabotage within the continental limits of the United States or Hawaii (although General John L. DeWitt, Commanding General of the Western Defense Command, who showed a keen interest in tightening his grip on the Japanese-Americans until their pips squeaked, remarked, 'The very fact that no sabotage has taken place to date is a disturbing and confirming indication that such action will be taken').* No similar measures were taken against the Italo-American or German-American ethnic communities in the United States or its overseas territories.

The British reacted in a no less extreme way. On going to war, Churchill wrote a quite sentimental letter to the Japanese Ambassador, but generally

---

* Cited by D. Swain Thomas and R. S. Nishimoto, *The Spoilage: Japanese-American Evacuation and Resettlement during World War II*, University of California Press, Berkeley, 1946, p. 5.

he shared the prejudices of his countrymen and of his American cousins. The stream of American feeling did not sweep the British along with it; the British had their emotions concentrated on the Nazis, and, except where they had powerful reasons for hatred from personal experience of Japanese camps or other atrocities, regarded the Japanese as a provoking irrelevance. These were differences of cultural styles, not of perception.

By its fateful decision Japan altogether changed the character of the war.

China, which until then had preserved the fiction that its war was no war but merely an incident, declared war on Japan on 9 December. It rejoiced in the United States being committed and saw the prospect of its operation being enlarged by American aid. All would have been denied to China by the isolationists of America had China declared war before America itself was committed to the struggle. So the declaration was a voluntary act by China. Events might have taken a different course if China had not thus regularized its American alliance. Similarly, on the same day that it declared war on Japan it declared war on Germany.

Why it did so is not clear. As Germany was under no obligation to declare war on the United States, and did so against its interests, so China was under no obligation to declare war on Germany. Apparently it did so out of a kind of contagion. It might be assumed that the countries were beset by madness.

From this time onwards, the direst and chiefly decisive part of the war was waged on sea and in the air. In fact the Japanese sea and air operations were probably the most spectacular in human history. It is true that the war with China continued desultorily, but the problems which compelled the attention of the wartime Japanese Governments had very little relation to those of the earlier period. Pearl Harbor meant a huge increase in Japan's enemies. It had against it the British Empire, in those days still a Super-power, as well as the United States. It had defied a great part of the world, and though it had at first won prodigious successes, the precariousness of its position was always plain, even to the Japanese man in the street.

In the whole of the latter part of the war, in the struggle of Japan with the Western Powers, Japan was by conviction as well as by circumstance compelled to appear as the liberator of the orient against occidental control. The role of the emancipator, which nationalists everywhere had first hopefully seen Japan as fulfilling in its victory against Russia in 1905, was now firmly wished upon it by the exigencies of the time. In India, in Indo-China, in Indonesia, in Burma, a tide was started which, if the Japanese had rightly worked with it, might have proved irresistible. In this new illumination the presence of the white man in Asia seemed a ghastly insult to the rights of Asian peoples. Even classes of people who had formerly been contented to work with the West hailed the new prospect of building the future of Asia upon Asian foundations.

The history of the war was to some extent a chronicle of Japan's lost opportunities: of a crusade which never got started; of a Japan which was so hampered by inner contradictions and by lack of a systematic blueprint that it was unsuccessful in rising to the occasion. As the war went on, many Japanese allowed it to become plain that they, at least, were bent on a simple predatory enterprise of the kind which had been supposed to have gone out of fashion with the passing of the nineteenth century. They failed to disguise in a plausible way that their interest was no higher than the transfer to Japan of the benefits enjoyed by western countries in the South Seas and in Asia. The ideology of the Greater East Asia Co-Prosperity Sphere, with its picture of an eastern world finding harmony under the protection of the Japanese armies, was far from being perfunctory for those who strove for it mightily. Yet for others it remained unconvincing amid the turmoil and the temptations of conquest which beggared the imagination of an island people. Opportunism, where it occurred, often overlay a deep-seated belief in *Hakkō Ichiu* (all-the-eight-corners-of-the-world-under-one-roof) rather than vice versa.

In three years, Japan, by a series of blunders, disappointed the hopes of Asia that it was the liberator. By extraordinarily insensitive action, hardline Japanese convinced Asian nationalists that so long as the war continued Japan could or would offer little or nothing to the peoples struggling to be free; and satisfied the national leaders that more was to be had from the European Imperial Powers – or from the United States – than from the victory of Japan. For this result, a part of the responsibility was due to the misconduct, repeated blunders, arrogance and stupidity, of the Japanese Army. Japan's imperial adventure was always associated with the Japanese Army: Japanese diplomats, civilians and captains of industry were of secondary importance. For reasons, one must look to the very sources of the Japanese Army's strength – to the social background, educational system, internal discipline and ascetic values of the Imperial Japanese Army, described earlier. The opportunities for a genuine new era in the region, which were made available by the daring and glittering achievements of Japanese arms, were flung away because the Japanese Army acted in the teeth of the inhabitants of the region, and came to be hated throughout Asia. It was defeated by Anglo-Saxon powers in military combat, but when this came about, few tears were shed by Asian nationalists at the result.

After Pearl Harbor, the war, or the China Incident and the European War, broadened out, and became a world war, in which nearly every country was engaged. It was more universal than the First World War had been. The greater part of the civilized world was drawn in.

There is a distinction, of kind as well as of degree, between a local war and a universal one. In a local war, there are boundaries to the general savagery. In general men can opt out of it: they, or at least some, can go to neutral territory. In a universal explosion, war is everywhere. The shortage of neutrals leaves man without refuge.

Ruskin, in a passage from *Praeterita*, describes the difference between a local war and a war which had got out of hand and swept the world: that of Napoleon. Of this war, Ruskin says that:

death was of another range and power; more terrible a thousand-fold in its merely physical grasp and grief; more terrible, incalculably, in its mystery and shame. What were the robber's casual pang, or the range of the flying skirmish, compared to the work of the axe, and the sword, and the famine, which was done at this time in all the hills and plains of the Christian earth, from Moscow to Gibraltar . . . Look on the map of Europe, and count the bloodstains on it, between Arcola and Waterloo.

So with this later convulsion; only the scientific progress with weapons of destruction made the havoc worse. What, in other ages, armies could bring about in a dozen years, they had now the capacity to do in a dozen days, or even hours.

The greater part of the civilized world was at war: little by little, in almost every country of the world, in great cities, and in most of the accessible villages, the sights and sounds of war were to become the commonplace of the age. In North America, in the Asian countries, in Australia, and in North Africa, the progress of the war became a grand preoccupation. In all too many centres of ordered life, centres which for more than a century had been famous for commerce or culture, the distant hum of conflict turned abruptly into the clash and commotion of sudden battle, to be followed often by the long tedium and horror of military occupation by an alien power. In all the world, only Central Africa and South America were relatively undisturbed.

The whole world moved senselessly in one direction or another, suffered and died in great swaths. Peasants and citizens of the huge Asian towns were caught alike. Many more perished from famine and disease than were killed by the armies.

This huge populace was informed about what was happening chiefly by local newspapers. Other media of communication scarcely touched it. Beyond Japan Proper and the Philippines, only the rare Asian village was, at the time, equipped with radio. For the townsmen, the radio set poured out propaganda, but in the towns the people largely discounted this, and put more faith in the printed word. From newspapers, and still more by word of mouth, word was spread, without which the Asian peoples would have supposed that there was no rhyme or reason in the convulsion of the world. It is hard enough to see how these instruments were sufficient for their purpose. Even though newspapers made their way into most of the villages, even remote ones in China and India, the number of people who could read them was very restricted. The war which had engulfed the governments had drawn in a mass of illiterate peasants. Those who could read found their talent even more highly regarded than in the past. They read in their newspaper and told the rest of the people what it contained. They and their village councils and headmen were the agents of the increasing self-awareness of the peoples of Asia during this time. But it is unlikely that many of them came to any conclusion about the events they contemplated more perceptive than that of little Peterkin on the battle of Blenheim two and a half centuries earlier:

> But what they fought each other for
> I could not well make out.

Part III

THE HIGH TIDE OF WAR

CHAPTER 17

Japan's Hundred Days

JAPAN, following its brilliant start in the new theatres of war, had the limelight in the times which succeeded. For the next three months it held the initiative in many different sectors. It concentrated on dealing with its new enemies, especially the United States and Britain, and it enjoyed a dashing period of cheaply won triumphs, rolling up the long established positions and colonial territories of the Western Powers in Asia. Its record was of almost unbroken success in the first hundred days of this war. This was to be a bitter recollection in Japan when its record ceased to be one of uninterrupted conquest, and the country faced the experience of endless decline.

Its first conquests were the remaining outposts of the western empires and of the United States in China. In some places, the defenders escaped into the interior or were evacuated by sea. Others were not so lucky. At news of the Japanese attack on Pearl Harbor, the Japanese demanded surrender of the British gunboat HMS *Peterel* at Shanghai. The British refused, and as the Japanese launch drew away Japanese troops along the Bund opened fire with small arms and artillery. The attack was soon over. The British ship caught fire and sank; its dead and dying crew were swept downstream in the retreating tide. A few survivors were rescued. The only remaining enemy warship, an American gunboat riding at anchor in the roadstead, lowered its colours and quietly surrendered without a fight. It was the end of an era.

Hong Kong fell almost immediately. A very small offshore island of China, useful for trade and for political action, Hong Kong had never been seriously prepared by the British for standing a prolonged siege, even in recent years when the situation looked threatening. It was ringed by Japan's armies and its fleet; it was without a hinterland of more than a few miles; its water supply was easily vulnerable; it was too far from a British base for there to be any possibility of reinforcing it. It never had a chance to survive, it was not expected to do so and it was surprising that it held out for as long as thirteen days.

The main feature of its siege was the confusion among the population, which was overwhelmingly Chinese. Many, though loyal inhabitants of

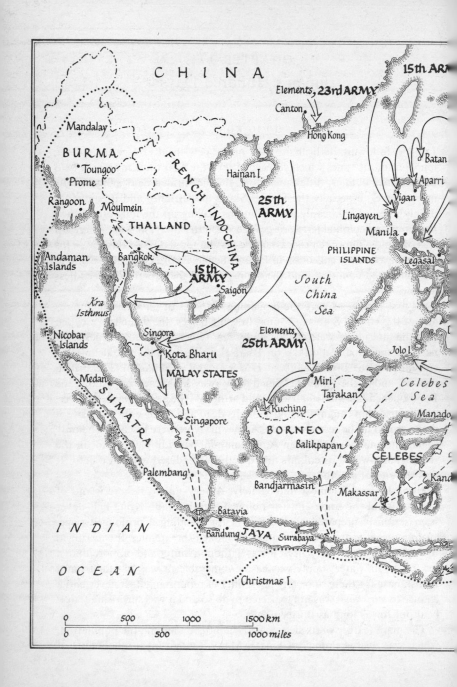

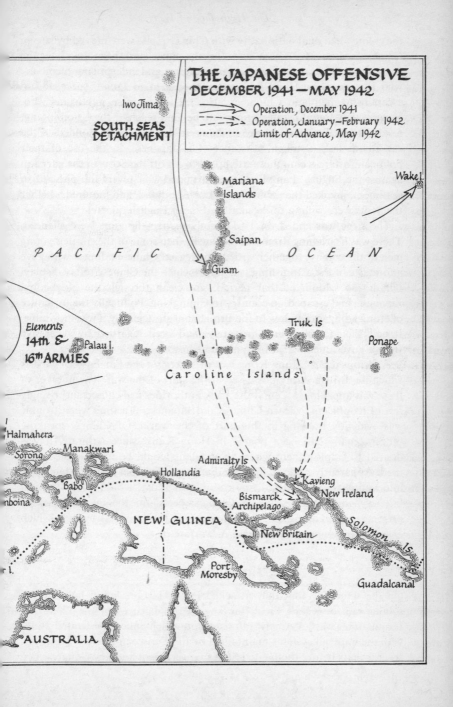

THE JAPANESE OFFENSIVE
DECEMBER 1941 – MAY 1942

→ Operation, December 1941
⇢ Operation, January–February 1942
⋯⋯ Limit of Advance, May 1942

Iwo Jima

SOUTH SEAS DETACHMENT

Wake I.

Mariana Islands

Saipan

P A C I F I C   *O C E A N*

Guam

Elements
**14th &
16th ARMIES**

Palau I.

Truk Is

Ponape

C a r o l i n e   I s l a n d s

Halmahera

Manakwari

Sorong

Admiralty Is

Hollandia

Babo

Kavieng

New Ireland

Bismarck
Archipelago

nboina

NEW GUINEA

New Britain

Solomon Is

I.

Port
Moresby

Guadalcanal

AUSTRALIA

the colony, had dual nationality with China, or else were moved by strong Chinese sentiments. These had for the most part been loyal to the Chungking Government, and its most active and enterprising members, who in consequence had become marked men to Japan, succeeded in escaping to mainland China; as also did the Chinese politicians who, because they found it safer to operate beyond reach of the Kuomintang, resided in Hong Kong. Many civilians in Hong Kong responded to the call for at least a token resistance. The Japanese, in the use of their political warfare techniques, attempted to set off the Scots in the garrison against the English. Pamphlets were dropped which were full of Scottish sentiment, invoked the memories of Loch Lomond, and inquired whether the Scots were willing to be sacrificed in an English quarrel.

The siege was ended on 19 December when the guns were silenced. There was heartening drama at the finish when some of the spirited young men of the colony, together with a one-legged Chinese admiral who gave a foretaste of the astonishing toughness which the Chinese today display, but did so seldom at that period, got clean through the blockading Japanese, and escaped up country to Chungking. Politically the forfeiture of Hong Kong was a blow to the British; but strategically it was inevitable. It had been foreseen and, privately, had been regarded by successive British governments as a foregone conclusion.

A serious loss at Hong Kong was of several of the Far Eastern experts which the British Army possessed at the start of the war. The number of these was appallingly scanty: the army authorities had caused surprisingly few of its officers to learn Chinese and Japanese at a time when trouble was evidently brewing in this part of the world. Of Chinese-speaking officers, many had been posted in Hong Kong, since naturally it was desired to employ them where their talents could be most immediately used. Apparently nobody foresaw that they would pass, after a few days, into captivity. The Army, for example in India, would be crying out bitterly against the famine of China experts, for the interrogation of prisoners, the reading of documents, or for the countless ways in which expertise in language is required in warfare.

THE PHILIPPINES

On the same day that they attacked Pearl Harbor, Japan had made a similar raid on Clark Field, the key to the defences of the Philippine Islands. This was an American possession which linked the United States with the imperial systems maintained by the European Powers. However, several years before the United States Government and key Congressmen had entertained serious doubts about whether or not the Islands were defensible or whether the Philippines should be granted 'Independence' merely in order to be 'neutralized'. Thus, effectively, the Philippines had been abandoned to their own devices rather than remaining a costly political and military encumbrance to the United States. As the risks from this process of estrangement mounted, leading Filipino politicians began to look elsewhere for defence guarantees, and the President of the Philippine Commonwealth, Manuel Quezon, sent feelers to the British Government in London offering to join the British Commonwealth and Empire in exchange for British protection. The British weighed up the risks involved and then secretly informed the Americans of what was afoot. By 1941, however, the American mood had changed and the United States was expected to defend it tenaciously. Although the real determination to hold fast in the Philippines came late in the day, the Philippine Commonwealth was not, like Hong Kong, regarded as expendable. With this attack, Japan launched upon the serious task of driving the white invader from the soil of Asia.

The Philippines are an island group off South-East Asia which for three hundred years had been the empire of Spain in this part of the world. They had passed into American possession – assisted in no small measure by a home-grown Filipino guerrilla rebellion against the Spanish crown – when the United States had defeated Spain in the Spanish-American War of 1898. It was a war which it was hard to justify: at first it seemed to show that the United States had given up its traditional stand against imperialism and was about to start on the acquisition of colonies. Its heart, however, was never in empire. No American literature had grown up around the Philippines; no class of Americans (except small groups of teachers, missionaries, West Point Army officers, businessmen, educators and planters) could claim to have the Philippines in their bones.

Thus it had been easy for Americans to compromise when they found that, among their new subject peoples, the Europeanized middle class of Manila was becoming inspired by the nationalism of the day. Americans had engendered no professional imperialists, in their adventure with ruling subject peoples. They could therefore readily conceive a constitution, which was a replica of the United States one, and could foresee that the Filipinos would make a success of this, and of governing their country without disaster.

By the time that Japan attacked, as a legacy of the period of doubts which Americans had held about the value of the Philippines in the past, the United States was already so well ahead with grooming the Philippines for liberation that all conceded that the Americans would not, after all,

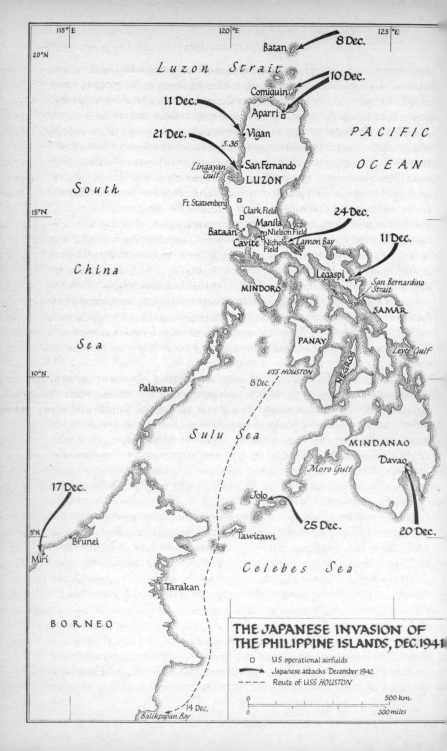

THE JAPANESE INVASION OF
THE PHILIPPINE ISLANDS, DEC. 1941

☐   US operational airfields
➤   Japanese attacks December 1942
---   Route of USS HOUSTON

0   500 km
0   300 miles

renege on their promises. Japan did not find in it a representative of imperialism at its most stubborn. More than six years before it struck, the United States had already passed a law which set a timetable for Filipino emancipation. This envisaged, however, that there would be a treaty between itself and the Philippines, regulating their defence.

By this treaty, the United States was to keep a moderately powerful Air Force, stationed at Clark Field. The rather sketchy chain of airfields throughout the islands was to be at its disposal. The United States also maintained a weak garrison of soldiers. When the war began, the defences were out of date; in part that was yet another legacy of the ill-fated Washington Treaty System which had expired in 1936. The communications between the islands were especially poor. The native Filipino Army, which was being trained by the United States, was only half ready.

The Japanese bombed Clark Field some hours after they attacked Pearl Harbor. Reports of what was happening there had reached the Philippines by radio. On receipt of the news, the Air Force – thirty-five bombers and seventy-two fighters – was alerted and had taken to the air. But the Japanese attack was delayed by dense morning fog. At lunch-time nearly all the American planes were grounded. While they were being serviced, lined up, while the pilots were being fed, the Japanese struck. Nearly a hundred American aircraft were destroyed in the air or on the ground.

Thus the war in the Philippines began with recrimination over an unnecessary loss. The American habit of concentrating its aeroplanes in formations which made the perfect targets had before this caused anxiety. Before the War against Japan, Duff Cooper, who had been appointed a few weeks before as Resident Minister in the British Administration of Singapore, was horrified at seeing them parked wing by wing at Clark Field and had pointed out to the Americans what a temptation they might be to the Japanese. Lest the apparent alarm of this former First Lord of the Admiralty and ex-Minister of War be mistaken for a general British reaction, it must be said that the reports of British air attachés exuded confidence in what they saw as General Douglas MacArthur's strategical understanding of East Asian defence problems and the American's willingness to learn from Britain's experience regarding the handling and deployment of aircraft. On the whole, British visitors to MacArthur's domain came away feeling that the defence of the Philippines was being far better attended to than they had previously supposed. The loss sustained in the Philippines, when it occurred, was anyway nowhere near as fatal as that at Pearl Harbor. Obviously the disaster had no deep influence on what followed. But the disgrace and the material damage had a very discouraging effect.

The raid was followed up by a landing of the Japanese Army. It came from Formosa, and the troops had been embarked some days previously. At first there was doubt as to whether the Filipinos, under American command, would resist the Japanese armies, which proclaimed they were bringing freedom. But this doubt was quickly dispelled.

The command in the Philippines was in the hands of General MacArthur. He was thenceforward to play the most conspicuous part of any commander in the Pacific War. A rather older man than most of his contemporaries, a general with an outstanding record in the First World War, a former Chief of Staff of the United States Army, he had been loaned by the United States Government to the Filipino Service to organize the future armies of the free Philippines. He entered with enthusiasm on this task. His father had been the first military governor in the American rule of the island. The relation of trust between him as generous patron of the Filipinos, and the Filipinos as loyal and grateful clients, caught his imagination. He believed that he had the knack and principle to do what other western soldiers and administrators had failed to do: to win the attachment of an oriental people. He was enabled to stand to his own Government in the position of a semi-independent power rather than a subordinate servant, a relation which suited him much better than a more regular one.

At the time when the Japanese struck, he had completed six years of a planned ten-year period on this task, and the Filipino Army had been brought to a stage of fair competency. Its worst impediment had been the multitude of languages and dialects which were spoken by the soldiers, which made it difficult for them to be organized under a single command. In the months preceding the war, it was, as part of the rather belated American preparation against the Japanese threat, reincorporated in the US Army. But when the invasion came, the plans, such as they were, for the defence of the Philippines were sketchy and completely shattered by the events of Pearl Harbor. The American intentions had proceeded from the axiom that the United States Pacific Fleet and Asiatic squadron would be intact, and would, at least within months, be able to come to the rescue.

MacArthur quickly appreciated that he could not check the Japanese landings. He met them with a scheme which had something of surprise. He gathered together his force, and withdrew into the historic fortress of Corregidor, on an island in Manila Bay, and into the peninsula of Bataan, on the northern side of the bay. Corregidor was one of the famous strong points in the East. It had first been built by Spaniards in the early years of their rule in the seventeenth century, and was heavy with history. But, though extremely picturesque – like Cyprus in the wars against the Turks or like a Crusader's castle – it had had nothing done to it in modern times to make it suitable for modern war. On the other hand Bataan was more serviceable. It was a strip of country covered by jungle and had been prepared by MacArthur for its role by the installation of concealed factories, supply depots and hospitals. In these two centres MacArthur had more than 50,000 troops (of whom only 6,000 men were of the regular American Army). He planned to withstand a siege by a Japanese Army numbered about 200,000.

MacArthur was at first optimistic that he would be relieved. Apparently, for a senior officer of the US Army, he was singularly out of touch with the ways in which the US General Staff thought in time of emergency. The explanation is simply that MacArthur had left Washington years before under something of a cloud. His prima donna behaviour, his fondness for the field marshal's baton that his appointment in the Philippines had brought him, did nothing to endear him to the American military and political authorities in the United States. He reckoned in terms of a six months' siege, for which he had stored ammunition, though his supplies of food were far less satisfactory. He refused to admit that the United States had been robbed by Pearl Harbor of all powers to relieve and reinforce its protégé. The United States might have lost its battleship fleet, but a great deal could be contrived with cruisers, destroyers and submarines. These ships remained in existence: they might have been used in relation to the Philippines. Actually the American Navy fought actively for the next few years in the Pacific without receiving any large new ships. But the will and dash had departed temporarily from the Navy. MacArthur, isolated in beleaguered Corregidor, did not grasp this fact. He adapted tactics of strategic defence when they were in fact pointless because the defence, however resolute, could look for no eventual reward in the early restoration of communications with the United States.

When MacArthur in the end faced the facts as they were, he seriously planned that the entire Bataan garrison should attempt a break-out, and should then filter away to southern Luzon, where they should wage guerrilla warfare. But the scheme, transmitted to Washington, was coolly regarded, and was never sanctioned.

The Japanese began their serious offensive against MacArthur on 29 December, when they let loose their aircraft against Corregidor. Surprisingly, both Corregidor and Bataan held out. The Japanese met their first check of the war. The resistance, unexpectedly prolonged, began to upset the larger Japanese plan. They had calculated that their forces would be quickly disengaged from the Philippines, and would be free to

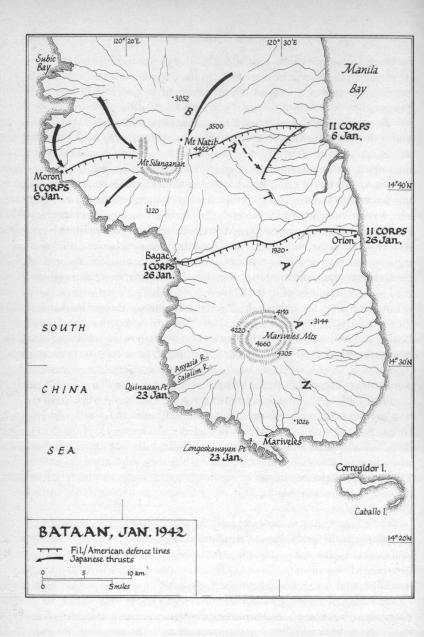

Subic
Bay

Manila
Bay

120° 20'E   120° 30'E

•3052

B

•3500

11 CORPS
6 Jan.

•Mt Natib
4422

Mt Silanganan

14°40'N

Moron
1 CORPS
6 Jan.

•1220

11 CORPS
26 Jan.

Orion

1920•

Bagac
1 CORPS
26 Jan.

SOUTH

•4193

•3144

4220   Mariveles Mts
        4660
        •4305

14°30'N

Anyasia R.
Salaiim R.

CHINA

Quinauan Pt.
23 Jan.

Z

•1026

SEA

•Mariveles

Longoskawayan Pt.
23 Jan.

Corregidor I.

Caballo I.

14°20'N

BATAAN, JAN. 1942

┬┬┬┬┬   Fil./American defence lines
➤   Japanese thrusts

0   5   10 km
0   5 miles

move on to the belt of coral islands which lay along the northern coast of Australia. From these they would be able to prepare for the invasion of Australia, and the cutting-off of its communications with the United States.

Their delay continued. At one time the Japanese were so badly placed – stricken with dysentery, beri-beri and other tropical diseases – that the Americans and the Filipinos, had they been able to launch an offensive, could have retaken Manila. But this did not put hope into the Philippine President, Mañuel Quezon. On 8 February he sent a telegram to Washington saying that the Filipinos were nearly exhausted, and proposing that, as the United States had been unable to fulfil its pledges of protection, it should immediately declare the Philippines independent, the islands neutralized, and the American and Filipino armies disbanded. Quezon, though mercurial and vain, probably regarded himself as personally loyal to the United States (for lack of any satisfactory alternative). Now, however, he judged it possible for the Philippines to take refuge in neutrality.

At the end of January the Japanese troops were heavily reinforced. Two extra divisions were moved in, together with heavy artillery groups. The Japanese offensive continued. It was marked by none of the brilliant improvisation which the Japanese were showing in Malaya, but the geographical circumstances and the calibre of their enemy commanders were vastly different.

On 22 February, the President of the United States sent a telegram to MacArthur, ordering him to leave the Philippines and to go to Australia to organize the war from there. He went unwillingly, half under the delusion, as is plain from the documents of the time, that he would be put in command of a mighty Army with which he would return to the Philippines. From this time onwards he developed a monomania about return. 'I will return' were his last words in transferring his Filipino command to General Wainwright.

The United States Navy had kept four speedboats intact. MacArthur had sent Quezon, the Filipino President, to Australia in a submarine, but preferred to travel in a motor torpedo boat. On the night of 11 March this little flotilla ran the Japanese blockade. The sea is vast; it is surprising how many times a blockade has been successfully broken. The speedboat in which MacArthur sat found itself at one stage in the shadow of a Japanese battleship, but in the darkness it failed to be aware of its prize. Certainly Japan would have done well to have intercepted this general, who, once away, responded, as if to a magnet, to the powerful drawing force of Japan. But when he returned it would be with an army.

With MacArthur gone, the Filipinos carried on their resistance for a month longer, but the spirit passed out of it. It was one thing to resist under MacArthur's command, and another under General Jonathan Wainwright. Although Wainwright was a valiant soldier, the American and Filipino defenders were conscious that they had been left in the lurch. On 9 April Bataan surrendered; on 6 May Corregidor. The defenders, the majority of them of the Filipino Army, were still a large force, and, as Japan was in future to show, a Japanese garrison would have been disinclined to surrender. But resistance seemed pointless when the Filipinos heard on the American radio that the United States was putting its energies first into the German War; and that, for the time being, it had written off the Philippines. The Filipino Army had fought with distinction when there was still reason for fighting and, with that reason gone, was entitled by all the conventions of war to surrender.

The garrison of Bataan and Corregidor met with a terrible fate for having been the first to throw the Japanese timetable out of date. They were shepherded into captivity in a march which earned the grim name of 'the Death March'. Most of the victims passed into the hands of the Japanese military police, the Kempeitai.

The other American island possessions in the Pacific had been able to offer very much less resistance. Guam was taken on 10 December after a spirited defence. Wake Island held out gallantly, but succumbed on 23 December.

MALAYA

Two and a half years before Japan attacked Pearl Harbor it began its assault on Malaya. This was to be one of the principal theatres of the war, the scene of what was probably its most brilliant campaign, and of disaster and disgrace for Britain which was to bring about the twilight of the British in Asia.

Malaya was a peninsula inhabited by Malay sultanates. Great Britain had extended its colonial rule over them in the nineteenth century while leaving formally intact the machinery of the sultanates; and the territory, with the great importance of its rubber, had become a major part of the British colonial empire. The rich and peaceful country had attracted the Chinese, who became a very large minority.

Malaya had a special significance for all the Western Powers with territorial possessions in the East. At the southernmost tip of the peninsula is the island of Singapore, the size of the Isle of Wight. In the early 1920s, with the ending of the Anglo-Japanese Alliance, Britain had determined to build up Singapore into a great naval fortress, and to make Malaya the vital centre of British power in the Far East. Singapore was to be a dockyard, a naval base, barracks and communications centre. It was to safeguard the communications with Australia and was the base from which the British Navy would operate to ensure that the Indian Ocean continued to be a British lake. The British, having decided to rely in the Far East on steel and reinforced concrete instead of on diplomacy, spent £60 million, which at that time was a very large sum, on the fortification of the base. When finished, it was regarded as one of the four greatest sea-fortresses in the world (the others being Pearl Harbor, Malta and Gibraltar). As we have seen, it was also regarded by British defence planners as one of the two keystones of British imperial defence (the other being metropolitan Britain) upon whose security the very existence of the British Empire depended. It would have such obvious military might that, while it stood, it would provide a guarantee of the continuity of British power and thus it would be looked to by all other British territories in Asia; nor was it without significance for France and Holland for the security of their empires in South-East Asia.

The plan was carried through. Singapore was completed. It seemed to double-lock the gateway of the Empire so that it was useless for an unfriendly rival Power, such as Japan, to dream of forcing an entrance. Japan might have been expected to be daunted by such prestige, and to avoid a direct attack on such an invincible place. It was to prove, however, that the complacency and false security which were generated about Singapore told against drawing up plans for a modernized, flexible defence of the system in case it should ever be challenged.

Almost unbelievably, a totally false estimate of its strength became general. It proceeded from an erroneous view of military reality, which was to prove so eminently disastrous that it is inconceivable how it could ever have been formed, or that, once it had come to determine the fixed lines of policy, it was allowed to continue for nearly twenty years un-challenged. There were two delusions. The first was that, as Singapore lay at the southern extension of 200 miles of jungle, it was militarily im-pregnable to land attack. Without any serious tests having been made in time, and as it turned out without any basis in reason, this fortress was given the certificate of virtual invulnerability. It was taken for granted that no enemy could carry on tank warfare in the hinterland of rubber plantations, and it was thought to be impassable, a region exempt from the manoeuvres of modern armies. The actual arrangements for the de-fence of Singapore were made from this misreading of fact. The rubber jungle was left undefended by human arts. Efforts made by the chief engineer of Malay Command, Brigadier Ivan Simson, to erect fixed defences, blow up bridges and lay down minefields were resisted by General Arthur Percival, his commander, who regarded such steps as these – and the civil defence efforts which were also Simson's responsibility – as counterproductive and bad for the morale of British troops, local politicians and the native races of Malaya. From over-confidence, the garrison of Singapore was lamentably inadequate; the roads were poor; no network of airfields was made which would have been adequate for a great Air Force; no great Air Force had ever operated from the Malayan Peninsula.

The second fatal miscalculation was that, as Singapore was to be a naval base, it would be threatened only in a great naval war. Singapore was envisaged as the centre of a titanic naval struggle, with a large fleet occupying her to capacity. The eyes of the world would always be on her, and those eyes would always look seawards. All the guns of Singapore would point seawards also. It was prepared with the most modern artillery which money could buy; but the guns were never in a position to fire effectively at an adversary who came by land.

Alas, it was never to play its part in a great war of the seas; its guns necessarily remained silent, for they were not the mobile things of a hundred years before. They were built in concrete and could not in a matter of days or weeks be re-adapted to a new kind of war. The traversing mechanisms of electrically fired long-range guns of the period were fitted with stops to prevent their crews fouling control cables or damaging adjacent batteries and other installations by the effects of the blast cones of these devastating weapons. Nevertheless, in the final days of the siege at Singapore, one or two of the guns were modified so as to fire above Singapore town at the Japanese on the Malayan mainland. In any case, the effect of fifteen-inch AP (armour-piercing) naval shells on moist jungle was less than edifying. Had these guns been equipped with HE (high explosive) shells or proximity fuses, they would have wrought terrible carnage upon the Japanese. Money spent on Singapore was largely useless, for the same reason as was the treasure of France which had been squandered on the Maginot Line; they succeeded in deterring one form of attack, and greatly reduced the danger of a surprise attack, but the generals whose duty it was to integrate these magnificent fixed defences into an overall flexible response to invading forces elsewhere proved unequal to the challenge of war.

In the opening years of the war – before Japan suddenly made its nature real and alarming to them – British people living in Singapore had had time to digest how deadly was their peril. Most of them did not do so. The old myths bore them up. They were cheered by the belief that the British Navy, though it was away in other waters, had power to neutralize the Japanese. They could still see the apparent strength of Singapore, which they thought would house its Navy, and did not grasp its essential weakness.

Only a few British soldiers during this time saw the ominous cracks appearing. One was Colonel Stewart, the commanding officer of a battalion of the Argyll and Sutherland Highlanders, who refused to accept the conventions which govern the training of garrison troops. Day after day the soldiers under his command spent their time in jungle training. The Argylls were considered eccentric; but in the end, Colonel Stewart formed the view that Singapore was not in fact surrounded on the north and east by a vast and easily defensible belt of jungle. It was possible for an invading Army to use tanks in the jungle; and in a short time the Japanese Army, made formidable by all the instruments of modern war, would be at its doors. This was the uncomfortable message which he preached, but virtually nobody attended to him.

It happens that one of the Japanese officers concerned with preparing the Japanese offensive has left a full account of the processes involved (*Singapore – the Japanese Version*, by Colonel Tsuji Masanobu). It was conceived as a rescue operation to free the inhabitants from British imperialism. It was not planned years ahead, and in great detail, as was wrongly supposed by the British Government. The expedition was improvised, and planned on a shoestring. The serious preparation and advance studies began only eleven months before the actual attack, in January 1941, at the same time as Admiral Yamamoto set to work on the plans to attack Pearl Harbor, and had started with a monthly budget of no more than 20,000 yen (or less than £2,000). The initial planning was carried out in Formosa, which was then a firm part of the Japanese Empire, and it was rehearsed on Hainan Island, which had been annexed to the Japanese Empire in February 1939. The Japanese forces were able to use a mass of photographs and other data which its enthusiastic agents had been busy gathering, partly as a matter of habit and by voluntary initiative. Every town and village had had its Japanese businessmen, Japanese doctors and Japanese dentists, and these were now revealed as the advance guard of the invasion that was being launched; but it is surprising how sketchy was much of the information. It was discovered that for their coastal operation the Japanese had to rely upon the data furnished by a single master mariner, who had collected the facts for years in case they should come in useful.

The invasion did not begin with a surprise massive Japanese attack from the air, similar to that on Pearl Harbor and the Philippines. The war started with the transport of two divisions of Japanese soldiers from Indo-China, and the overcoming of the weak coastal defences in northern Malaya. At first, the Japanese were too distant from Singapore to make effective use of the air; today it is overlooked how comparatively limited the range of massive air operations still was. The Japanese landing in the north did not take the British by surprise. It had clearly been a possibility ever since the Japanese took Indo-China, and plans had been worked out, which were in fact forestalled by the Japanese, for a possible seizure of a part of southern Thailand, as a defensive move. The British were, however, outmanoeuvred by the speed and resiliency of the Japanese in moving from their bridgeheads to a lightning drive on the south.

In the first two days of the war the British commanders at Singapore disposed of two major warships, the *Prince of Wales* and the *Repulse*, which the Government at home, as the skies blackened in the days before Pearl Harbor, had been persuaded to detach from other operations and to spare for the East. These were a powerful reinforcement: with them, Singapore appeared to be about to play the part intended for it by British planning. In theory, at least, they would restore mobility to British arms. They were meant to insure the safety of Malaya, in case the Japanese struck out during the negotiations at Washington. The battleship and battle-cruiser would enable Britain to strike at great distances. With sea power, Britain could exercise what Bacon had described as its natural advantage in all its wars: to take as much or as little of the war as it desired.

Yet the voyage of these two ships was a perilous excursion into the unknown, and filled those who ordered it with great alarm. They moved northward from Singapore with the intention of disrupting the landing of the Japanese forces and their supplies. It was a sound objective and it might have altered the course of the war. They were moving against forces which they could not compute. The Japanese had a history of waiting for, and dealing with, naval units sent out from European waters to alter the balance of force in the East. Admiral Rozhdestvensky had sailed a fleet half-way round the world in 1905 to be destroyed at the battle of the Japan Sea. In like manner, the *Prince of Wales* and the *Repulse* were to be the victims, not it is true of a waiting Japanese Navy, but of the new Japanese Fleet Air Arm which sank the two warships on the second day of the war. The commander of the two capital ships, Admiral Tom Phillips, had been confident of air support from local RAF units, but, disgracefully, that support never materialized and this was, perhaps, the main cause for the disaster that occurred.

With these warships swept from the chess board, the Japanese advance

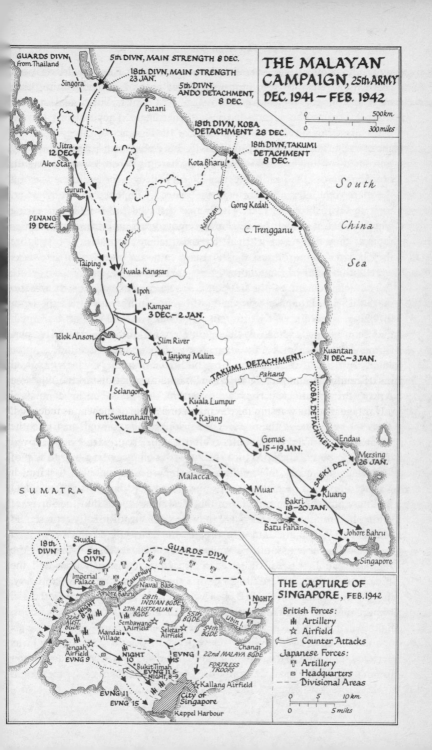

THE MALAYAN
CAMPAIGN, 25th ARMY
DEC. 1941 – FEB. 1942

0   500km
0   300 miles

GUARDS DIVN
from Thailand

5th DIVN, MAIN STRENGTH 8 DEC.

18th DIVN, MAIN STRENGTH
23 JAN.

5th DIVN,
ANDO DETACHMENT,
8 DEC.

18th DIVN, KOBA
DETACHMENT 28 DEC.

18th DIVN, TAKUMI
DETACHMENT
8 DEC.

Singora

Patani

Jitra
12 DEC.

Alor Star

Gurun

Kota Bharu

Gong Kedah

C. Trengganu

South

China

Sea

PENANG
19 DEC.

Taiping

Kuala Kangsar

Ipoh

Kampar
3 DEC. – 2 JAN.

Telok Anson

Slim River

Tanjong Malim

TAKUMI DETACHMENT

Kuantan
31 DEC. – 3 JAN.

Pahang

Selangor

Kuala Lumpur

Kajang

Port Swettenham

Gemas
15–19 JAN.

Endau

Mersing
26 JAN.

SUMATRA

Malacca

Muar

Bakri
18–20 JAN.

Batu Pahat

SAEKI DET.

Kluang

Johore Bahru

Singapore

19th
DIVN

Skudai

5th
DIVN

GUARDS DIVN

Imperial
Palace

Causeway

Naval Base

Johore Bahru

28th
INDIAN BGDE

27th AUSTRALIAN
BGDE

55th
BGDE

Ubin I.

NIGHT
7

22nd AUST.
BGDE

Sembawang
Airfield

Seletar
Airfield

SHIN
BGDE

Mandai
Village

Changi

EVNG
15

22nd MALAYA BGDE

Tengah
Airfield
EVNG 9

NIGHT
10

Bukit Timah
EVNG 11 &
NIGHT 8–9

FORTRESS
TROOPS

Kallang Airfield

EVNG 11

EVNG 15

City of
Singapore

Keppel Harbour

THE CAPTURE OF
SINGAPORE, FEB. 1942

British Forces:
♛ Artillery
☆ Airfield
⌒ Counter Attacks

Japanese Forces:
⚑ Artillery
▪ Headquarters
--- Divisional Areas

0   5   10 km
0   5 miles

down the peninsula to Singapore could go forward unimpeded. Troops came in by transport from Indo-China, and nothing availed to stop them; more alarmingly, they were accompanied by tanks, which against forecasts, overcame the natural barriers of the jungle. They advanced south with surprising speed. A clear picture of the Japanese strategy began to show itself. The British Army, heavily burdened with its impedimenta, untrained for jungle warfare, resisted as hard as it could by throwing up positions across the roads. Meeting their challenge, the Japanese forsook the main road, advanced through the allegedly impenetrable jungle, and took the British in the rear. The jungle betrayed the British; the jungle which had been in their possession for eighty years and whose possibilities for war they had never learned. By these means, repeated so often that they became monotonous, the Japanese came on, and within six weeks were within sight of Singapore.

The achievement of the Japanese has been glossed over. It was remarkable. The Japanese Army had until now acquired its battle experience in China, a terrain vastly different from Malaya: and its battle training had been almost exclusively the steppe country of Manchuria. Its performance in the tropics showed an adaptability and resourcefulness in the Japanese officers, and endurance by the Japanese soldiers, which had been insufficiently recognized. Though the imaginative qualities of the Japanese Army were not afterwards always apparent, they shone in this campaign.

The manner of fighting by the Japanese surprised their antagonists. They showed none of the preference for long-range combat, such as most of the other civilized combatants exhibited. They seemed to exult in struggle body to body. They produced gestures of defiance and glee and also of fear which, by most other soldiers, were regarded as childish. A skirmish was accompanied by grunts, gasps and blood-curdling yells. Later, when Japanese films became popular in the West, it was seen that the Japanese soldier had fought very much as Japanese actors traditionally represented him as doing. It made him a surprising and alarming adversary.

As the Japanese assault on Malaya intensified, it was noticed that the Japanese had a string of successes in air raids upon British aircraft. Time and again the British were caught on the ground. Japan's aircraft appeared in great force just when the British were getting ready to take to the air. Finally one reason for this striking good fortune of the Japanese came to light. An officer in the R A F, a citizen of southern Ireland, was pursuing his country's feud of twenty years back with the British Government, and was detected signalling to the Japanese. This affair was kept secret. It accounted for an unfortunate part of the air losses in the early stages of the campaign.

*

In the confused ill-temper of the retreat – and it was always retreat, without one solid success to restore self-respect – there was recrimination between the British commanders, and the commander of the large force of Australians which had been a part of the Allied garrison and who had shared in the defence. It was reflected in the lower ranks. Many of the Australians had been stationed in the Middle East before they fought the Japanese. As this was largely a time of defeat they had formed a disgruntled view of British competence. Their transfer back to the defence of the region where Australian interests were more vitally at stake had been agreed to with a rather ill grace by Churchill; this put the Australians in the mood to be touchy partners. By ill fortune they were under a general, Gordon Bennett, who, though a rather dashing soldier, had in addition qualities which hardly endeared him to the usual type of British officers. He was not of a modest nature, he did not minimize any affronts shown to him, he did not agree with those people who saw virtue in silence.

To the necessary disgraces which afflicted the beaten Army, there was thus added the scandal of a dangerous difference of opinion between England and one of the Dominions, which at bottom had always been loyal to it, and whose feelings were the more ruffled because they had been so warm. The quarrel threatened to widen out into a dispute which uncovered a diversity in war aims. Australia was left with the feeling that it had been betrayed. Its interests were treated as of slight concern. It seemed that England would unfeelingly sacrifice Australian soldiers for its own advantage. It was the type of ill-feeling which sooner or later was bound to cloud the cooperation of England and the Dominions. A considerable effort was needed to overcome the bitterness: Britain was too occupied for the diplomacy needed. Singapore, which was becoming a curse to the Empire which it had been called into being to serve, merely added to its demerits that, in the turmoil of this period, it caused London and Canberra to be for some weeks estranged.

In the long retreat through Malaya, the British had suffered much more than a great military reverse. For the first time their administrative system in oriental countries had been exposed, and was reduced to ridicule. They, the masters of political craft in conciliating the oriental, found that they had used up all their reserves of prestige, and had no comfort anywhere. In Penang, in Kuala Lumpur, in all the centres of administration, the events were disastrous. The institutions built up over decades, the loyalties so laboriously produced, the habits which the British had so complacently regarded as fixed and permanent – all were swept away. The British were not regarded with fear or hatred: had that been so, they would not have been so quickly written off. Their day was regarded as closed. The local Malay population (not the Chinese), giving a lead to other colonial communities of the Empire, regarded it as politic to transfer their loyalties as quickly as possible to the Japanese.

When the backward movement of the British began, it was supposed by home public opinion that, with the example of a scorched earth policy in Russia before them, arrangements would be made for the Japanese to meet with a similar bleak reception. But in almost all cases, the Government lacked the nerve to demand the sacrifice from the local people, or, more rarely, the demand was made, generally too late in the day, and the people refused to cooperate. The British efforts to build up a resistance behind the rear of the Japanese Army, and to create an adequate spying and Intelligence system were at first unsuccessful. Later on in the war, when the Japanese had made themselves detested, SOE and other similar organizations were to begin to function effectively: but this was to be in the future.

It must not be supposed that the psychological atmosphere changed abruptly to contempt or hostility towards the British. There were many warm and compassionate acts of loyalty and friendship by the Malays and the very mixed population of this cosmopolitan peninsula. The British, in defeat and disillusion, often found unexpected shelter.

How news of great and dramatic events transmits itself in Asia, by what means it travels to remote valleys and distant villages, is not clear. At this time there were very few radio sets outside the larger towns. But in these months a great sensation was felt throughout Asia. The British Empire was dying. It had been overturned in Malaya, and was found to have rotten roots. Soon it would be treated in the same way in the other countries, and in all parts of Asia where the union flag still flew, Britain never recovered from the deplorable events of these few weeks. The happenings in one small section of its Empire were enough to destroy its prestige everywhere: and the life and soul of the British Empire had consisted of prestige, which is almost indistinguishable from the oriental concept of 'Face'.

While Singapore was in its death throes, the British committed one more egregious mistake. Large reinforcements of British troops, complete with equipment, had been spared from the war in Europe and ordered to Malaya. These arrived off Singapore when the siege of the fortress was about to begin. With remarkable folly, and in the belief that there would be a final effort to redeem the fortress by undertaking a siege, they were disembarked instead of sailing away to India or Burma where they were urgently needed, as quickly as they could. These troops, with all their artillery and stores, were put ashore, never to fire a shot, and were to enter on the long martyrdom of Japanese imprisonment.

On 31 January 1942, the British and Commonwealth forces, defeated, bewildered and demoralized, re-entered Singapore. Their rear-guard was led across the causeway which connected Singapore with Johore by the remnants of the pipe band of the Argylls.

The final defence lasted fifteen days. Singapore surrendered on 15 February. It gave in because its defences crumbled; because its water supply passed out of its control; because the Japanese, again falsifying expectation, managed to infiltrate the island's defences at all points, and, within a week of crossing, were seen to be everywhere; because the troops were disorganized, and no pattern of defence established itself; because it was clear that the civilian population in the city had been paralysed and most of it, lacking training or proper organization, did not commit itself to self-defence; because the enemy, which had penned them up in the fortress, had swollen in their imagination to such a size by a unique series of triumphs that further resistance was not really thinkable. He had sunk two battleships which the English had naïvely supposed would have over-awed him; at Pearl Harbor he had struck away the Navy that would have made the Americans an effective ally; he had demonstrated that the jungle, that was feared by all other armies, could be treated as the home of the Japanese, from which Japan could draw strength. When this Japanese Army began to follow the British into Singapore, and to infiltrate over the island, the British recognized that the battle for South-East Asia had gone against them. By a local decision the fact was recognized: and Singapore was Japan's.

Yet it remained true that the Army in Singapore was twice as large as the besieging force, and, in theory at least, a prolonged resistance would have been possible. Even the fact of the non-existence of prepared defences did not cancel out the fact of the great British superiority in manpower. There have been famous sieges in history that have been carried on long enough to embarrass the besiegers and which have been begun in circumstances as disastrous as those in Singapore. Exactly a year later, Singapore was to be followed in the news interest of the world by Stalingrad, and its defenders were not moved by the civilized sentiments of those who had to make the decision at Singapore. It is true that the defenders, unlike those of Stalingrad, could not have cut their way out to safety: but, in theory at least, they could have put up a notable resistance. The defeat was not gilded by any valiant enterprise, such as the rescue of the British troops at Dunkirk, which in after days made Dunkirk a stirring myth, instead of one of the worst reverses to British arms on the continent. In fact it became known later that General Yamashita Tomoyuki, the rather eccentric commander of the Japanese, had outrun his supplies. He would have been in no position to support the troops which he had filtered through to the island; they must have fallen back if the garrison had made the determined counter-attack of which it was capable. Thus, to other humiliations, the British added that of being bluffed.

To one man, the decision was particularly unwelcome, to the British Prime Minister. It is a little hard to say how at any one moment the events of the war in the Far East affected him. On the whole they were always secondary to affairs in Europe. It would seem that throughout the brilliant first hundred days of Japan he never succeeded in getting a grip of what was happening. Before the Japanese attack, he had continually underrated the chances of Japanese intervention. He did not equal the grasp which he had on the war in the Middle East. His speeches and his writings about it have a faint note of unreality, of a theatre of war where his views are not translated into action. The impression is dreamlike, of playing with vast conceptions which are fatally unrelated to fact; there is the occasional tumble into an abyss, which he must have foreseen but could not be reconciled to. Lieutenant-General Arthur Percival's decision to surrender at Singapore had been approved by General Sir Archibald Wavell, who only two days before, had ordered the landing of the Eighteenth Australian Division at Singapore against the advice of Auchinleck. Percival, the man on the spot after all, evidently convinced Wavell, who paid him a flying visit on 10–11 February, that the battle was lost. Percival took the view that the soldiers had done all that could be expected of them, and that further resistance would have been a pointless waste of life. Wavell went off to Java after trying to salvage what he could from the disaster. In Churchill's distrust of Wavell, which was to become so painfully obvious, perhaps there was an element of resentment for his part in the capitulation.

Churchill's speeches at this juncture are very curious. They are the comment of a detached observer rather than of a committed politician who had to explain the disaster which had befallen one of his projects. The British had surrendered Singapore: that was the bare fact, which people in Britain must stomach, and which they could not be expected to dwell on with satisfaction.

There departed into Japanese captivity a large British force and most of the civilian staff who had passed their lifetime in the administration of Malaya. They had little further part to play in the war, though the suffering of the prisoners was very great and was periodically used by the

British Ministry of Information to stir up public effort, and to keep the people resolute on their liberation. Given the chance to resist, these same prisoners, many of whom died before they could be released, might have preferred to be sacrificed in making the end of Singapore a little more creditable than it was.

The Japanese rejoiced, and not without cause. They looked almost incredulously at the size of their forces, and what they had achieved against much larger British forces. Usually the attacking force has to be considerably greater than the defenders if it is to have any chance of success; in the Malaya campaign this was reversed. The Japanese losses had been extravagantly small. From the time of their first landing to their occupying the Johore causeway and beginning the assault on Singapore their casualties were, according to Japanese official information which need not in this case be disbelieved, 1,793 killed and 2,772 wounded. They had deployed a force at Singapore not greater than 35,000 men, leaving another 35,000 or so men up country in Malaya. From information afterwards obtained, they found that the defending force numbered 85,000 out of an original strength of 139,000 British, Australian, Indian and local volunteer forces. In the actual assault on Singapore they lost a further 1,714 men killed, and 3,378 wounded. The Japanese claim that not a single Japanese soldier was captured. Certainly it would appear that none of those who did, lived to tell the tale: at least five wounded Japanese prisoners were among those murdered by rampaging Japanese troops at the Alexandra Hospital in Singapore following the British surrender. The myth has grown up that the Japanese troops were helped by having a corps of men trained in Malayan affairs. This is quite false. The number of Malayan experts in Japanese service was less than ten.

During 1940 and 1941 Germany had discussed with the Japanese from time to time the possibility of an attack on Singapore. But the German estimate was that the initial campaign would last one and a half years and would need five and a half divisions. Actually Japan required fifty-five days and only two divisions. At the outset of the campaign, Yamashita had been offered a third division but had declined it. His employment of the forces he had, and their logistical support, was masterful.

Japanese publications since the war have shown a high, rather theatrical morale among Japanese troops. The telegrams are still extant which Japanese generals sent to one another; their style is extremely patriotic, conventionally moralistic, reasonably free of the rivalries between officers and between services which were so common later in the war. One of the ceremonial acts which the Japanese performed after their victory was to build a tower which was dedicated to holding Buddhist requiem masses for the British killed in the campaign.

The Japanese, perhaps because they had taken Singapore with such an inadequate force, established there an occupation régime which governed it with extreme strictness, and rather purposeless brutality. They felt uneasy. Soon reports began to circulate of extraordinary Japanese measures against any suspected organization. Singapore was principally inhabited by Chinese, and the Kuomintang had used its citizens to extract funds for the Chinese Government. They were determined to stop this. The Chinese, in general, were irreconcilable; some had the reputation of being extremely radical in politics, which Japan also feared. The existence, in a peculiarly ramifying form, of the Chinese secret society, was another thing which provoked them. So, from the earliest days of their triumph, ugly tales of police terror and torture were mingled with a great victory. In the first days of the occupation of the city, they compiled a list of hundreds of Chinese and arrested them *en masse*. The beaches near the centre of the city became execution grounds by night where the *Kenpeitai* – the Japanese military police – took their preventive action. Altogether more than 5,000 Chinese were massacred at Singapore by the Japanese as a matter of policy in those few days.

BORNEO

With the sinking of the *Prince of Wales* and *Repulse*, the last obstacle was removed from the advance of the Japanese into Borneo. This thinly inhabited island, the third largest in the world, at 260,000 square miles the size of Texas and two and a half times the area of the United Kingdom, holds a central position from which it is possible to dominate the sea lanes to Singapore and to threaten Java, Sumatra, the Celebes, Malaya, Indo-China and the southern Philippines. It was, indeed, the security of Borneo that led Britain to consider, however briefly, proposals that emanated from President Quezon of the American Commonwealth of the Philippines in the mid-thirties for Britain to take possession of the Philippines in order to guarantee its defence against Japan in the event of an American withdrawal. Now, as dawn broke on 13 December, three days after the extinction of British naval power in the East, an absurdly small force of three destroyers, a sub chaser and ten transport vessels set sail from Camranh Bay in French Indo-China and put out to sea, bound for Borneo. Shortly afterwards, it was reinforced by a more substantial force of three cruisers, a further pair of destroyers and a solitary seaplane tender. The operation was regarded as a necessary adjunct to the Malayan campaign. With British forces fully occupied in the defence of Malaya, the Japanese were quick to exploit their opportunities. It was, by all accounts, a relatively laid-back invasion. Thanks to the Dutch, two Japanese destroyers and two transports were sunk and a further three other transports were damaged. The Anglo-Dutch oil denial schemes in Miri and elsewhere operated relatively smoothly. Nevertheless, the outcome of the campaign was never in doubt: the bulk of the British defence forces fled across the border into the Netherlands East Indies and on 19 January the remaining British forces on Borneo surrendered.

BURMA

In Burma, the history of the Malayan campaign repeated itself. The Japanese Army invaded it on 11 December from Thailand.

Burma, one of the smaller countries of the British Empire, had had, in the half century of its membership, a comparatively uneventful history. Now it became lurid in the extreme. In the minds of most English people, Burma became known, no longer as an oriental paradise inhabited by a merry, picturesque people, but as a fated, evil country, the arena – from no fault of its own, it is true – for some of the most horrible fighting of the war. It was not simply to flare into prominence by the brief experience of being overrun. It was to remain a contested land until the end of the war.

Burma had formerly been attached to India. It had been annexed to it as the result of three wars in the nineteenth century. It was an act of convenience for Britain; by no shadow of claims could it be regarded as an Indian land. Its majority people, the Burmese, were one of the Asian peoples with the clearest national consciousness; their economy was not inevitably linked with the Indian; their language and script had only a distant connection with Sanskrit; their religion, to which they were peculiarly devoted, was the Hinayana form of Buddhism, which ultimately derived from India, but which had practically died out there. Hinduism, which Buddhism had once rivalled in India, had revived there powerfully, and had overtaken Buddhism in the sub-continent. But in neighbouring Burma, Buddhism had no competitors, and flourished mightily. This rendered Burmese culture different from Indian.

The unnatural union of Burma with India was resented by the Burmese. Their desire for freedom was two-fold, freedom from Britain and freedom from India. This second freedom they won at the time of the great political recasting inaugerated by the Government of India Act of 1935. It was perceived that to continue to enforce the unity of the two countries would impose an unnecessary strain on the problematical machinery of government devised for India. Burma was allowed to settle its own destiny, and the Burmese legislature voted to go its own way. It had a constitution which half met Burma's growing demand for complete freedom. Its Government had the same liberties as a provincial government in India under the Act of 1935. But what in India were to be the federal powers of government were in Burma controlled by the British.

In the days of the union between India and Burma, the British had neglected to build up communications between the two countries. A railway was planned, chiefly for military reasons, but was never made. Its absence was to have a powerful effect on the shape of the fighting now to break out. Shipping interests, powerful with the Government, saw in it a threat to their monopoly of traffic with Rangoon, and successfully opposed the scheme.

In the years just before the war, political life developed rapidly. The professional and commercial classes were organized in orthodox political parties, which were willing to pursue their national aims through non-revolutionary means and within the framework of the institutions already conceded. But the desire for independence was greater, perhaps, than it was in India, though it was not taken as seriously. Moreover there were revolutionary parties, notably the Thakins, which meant the party of the 'masters' or 'gentlemen', which were ready to seek any aid, and do anything, which would bring about the end of British rule. These parties, which stirred up political consciousness in Burma, had a growing clientèle among students, and among people who had no limiting restrictions placed on their political activity by economic considerations.

Japan found the political situation in Burma more suited to its intervention than in any other country. Moreover Burma, through the existence of the Burma Road, had become a major preoccupation of Japanese strategic plans.

Japan had prepared its action in Burma for several years, and more carefully than in most other centres. It had sent there a naval officer who, disguised as a trader, had made the first contact with Burmese politicians. The results were so promising that a Japanese consul was instructed to build up a pro-Japanese network. This, however, had brought the Japanese Ministry of Foreign Affairs into the picture. Fearful of angering the British unnecessarily, the Ministry demanded extreme caution.

Progress came, not from persons engaged in this part of the enterprise, but from the coming to Burma of a Japanese Army officer, Colonel Suzuki Keiji, who was a natural genius at all kinds of espionage and subversion. He modelled himself on Lawrence of Arabia. Until 1939 he had had a career as a regular combat officer; it ended with Suzuki under a somewhat mysterious cloud, brought about by an incident in 1939 in the war with China. Thenceforward he was a spy. He chose Burma as his field of activity, and he was as little subjected to control in what he did there as was Doihara, a much more celebrated agent and planner of subversive action in Manchuria and China. Officers like him were given much latitude by Japan. They might create a situation which the Japanese Army would be free, when the time came, to manipulate or to ignore, as circumstances decided.

Disguised as a mild-mannered newspaper reporter for the *Yomiuri Shinbun*, Suzuki explored Burma for a year and a half, concentrating upon gaining an understanding of its political and ethnic divisions. He decided that the Thakins offered promising material with which to work. He was a curious man; he was genuinely interested in promoting the movements of Asian peoples to be free; he took seriously the claims of Japanese propaganda that Japan supported all movements for independence; he was regarded with suspicion and as a nuisance by the more orthodox Japanese, who had no intention of conquering large parts of Asia, and simply transferring them to native hands. In Japanese service, he was advancing views and actions which were not at all favoured. He has been described as a rebel by temperament, a conformist by upbringing. His conversation fascinated the Burmese with whom he came into contact. He would tell them to insist on being independent. If, after the Japanese conquered their country, they refused to grant independence, the Burmese ought to shoot back.

Suzuki and his handful of associates set themselves to form the nucleus of a Burmese independent Army, which could be extended as soon as a Japanese Army crossed the borders. He calculated that a Burmese force would prove a valuable auxiliary for bringing about the discomfiture of the British, whether in harrying them politically, in forming a link with the Burmese population, or in straightforward military operations. In 1940 he began to select likely young revolutionaries from the class of political adventurers and arranged for thirty of them to be sent over to Formosa for military training in Japanese schools. The thirty Thakins received this education partly in Formosa, partly in Hainan Island; Suzuki had them well grounded, by strict Japanese discipline, in combat tactics, in methods of civilian cooperation with the Japanese Army, and in all ancillary methods. It is clear that he had some difficulty in getting these young men accepted in the various training camps, for he acted as a lone wolf, and had not fully emerged from the disaster which had temporarily blocked his military career. The Thakins, for their part, objected to the strenuous quality of their training, and contemplated desertion. They had actually got control of a small sailing ship with which they proposed to sail for home. On their fate depended much of the modern history of Burma. The accident of who was chosen among the thirty Thakins, the founder members of the Burma Independence Army, governed the course of Burmese politics down to the present day. Because of personality difficulties, the Thakins tended to fall into factional groups, which were reflected for long after, quite irrationally, in Burmese politics.

Suzuki, together with a staff of adventurous Japanese who were looked at rather askance by the Japanese Army, transported his thirty Thakins to join the two divisions of Japanese troops waiting to invade Burma. By a shrewd move to catch the Burmese imagination, he gave each of the Thakins a new name from Burmese folklore, which was peculiarly rich in such things. He devised ceremonial oaths to link them together. And he revived the old Burmese legend that they had discovered ancient charms which brought them invulnerability. This, which was traditionally affected by Burmese insurrectionists, and had been the sustaining weapon of the peasant leader, Saya Sen, in a rebellion in 1930, was obstinately believed by the Burmese populace. It was to support the Thakins handsomely. The atmosphere in their camp was that of a boy scout jamboree, the same vague high-mindedness, the same enjoyment in devising ruses, rather the same kind of humour. The Thakins, half in terrified awe of Suzuki, half in naïve enthusiasm for him, admired the way he genuinely fought for their interests with his orthodox Japanese colleagues.

This Japanese dealing with Burmese politicians was to have interesting consequences as the history of Burma unfolded. But, in the actual conquest, the principal agent was the Japanese Army. This fought the battles, and defeated the British. The British were embarrassed by the Burma Independence Army, but it only contributed marginally to their downfall. They complained of the treachery of the population, the clamour against them by the Pongyis (Burmese monks), the betrayal of their movements to the Japanese, and the false Intelligence often given to the Army by the villagers. For all these things, the Burma Independence Army, playing the part of aide to the Japanese, was partly responsible. Their experience permanently soured the British troops, and gave Burma a bad reputation as a country to fight in. Anything to do with Burma was thought to be unlucky, and the country filled the Army with great apprehension.

However, for their rout, the British had to blame the Japanese directly. They had invaded at the start with two divisions with which they overran the south and took Rangoon, the capital. As in Malaya, the British had placed their confidence in the natural obstacles to troop movements in the rugged, jungle country of the border. Again it had become axiomatic that tanks could not penetrate this, and again the fact had not been tested. They quickly found out that they had deceived themselves. Unlike Malaya, the country was held by too few troops, badly trained, with a defective Air Force. From the start, the British were too unevenly matched to have any chance of holding the Japanese advance. After Singapore fell, the Japanese were reinforced by another two divisions, which had been campaigning there, and they advanced to the north, pushing back the British before them.

The British accepted the offer of Chiang Kai-shek to send a Chinese Army to assist in the defence. They did so reluctantly because, through awareness of maps which were being published in Chungking, they had reason to suspect that Chiang had designs on the Burma frontier, and that, once they were in, the Chinese troops would be hard to evict. Japan, however, prevented this danger by driving them back into China. On the borderland some of the Chinese were broken up, and also suffered a great defeat.

By the end of April, the British were expelled from the country. They were pushed right out of Burma. Eventually the greater part of their forces escaped into India, marching out through the trackless jungle land which intervened between Burma and India. Only a part of the far north remained out of Japanese hands. It was inhabited by Chins and Kachins with whom British rule was unfamiliarly popular, being, like all British administration of the jungle fringes of their Empire, so light as hardly to be noticed. This territory was held by a body of irregular troops, recruited chiefly from the Chins, which was raised by British anthropologists. The exploits of this force, the intelligence and devotion of the Chin people, are one of the subjects which has escaped narration.

The same incidents marked the Japanese advance as had happened in Malaya. The civil government collapsed. It showed itself again and again to be extremely incompetent, its officers were lazy, its resolution was contemptible, its planning was certain to be based on faulty information, its complacency was unlimited. Its poor showing did not come altogether as a surprise. Before the war, the British administration in Burma had been notorious for delays and muddle. When it was put to the test, it perished with the same sense of scandal as the administration in Malaya. The machine of government had been allowed to rust, and its levers broke in the hand when pulled. It was unfortunate because the British could not rely upon any machine of popular government to provide a link with the people, or to rouse any enthusiasm on the Government

THE CHINA—BURMA—INDIA THEATRE 1942-5

DEVELOPING LINES OF COMMUNICATION TO NORTH-EAST FRONTIER OF INDIA AND BURMA 1944–5

- ■ Allweather RAF/USAAF airfields
- ○ Fairweather RAF/USAAF airfields
- +—+—+ Railways ·—·—· Narrow gauge
- —— Roads
- —— 4" pipeline ---- 6" pipeline

```
0        100       200       300 km
0              100            200 miles
```

Darjeeling
Siliguri
La
Mokameh Ghat
Parbatipur
Katihar
Santahar
Ra
Abdulpu
Dumri
Poradha
Asansol
Panagarh
Burdwan
Ranaghat
Jamshedpur
Kharagpur
Calcutta

LINES OF COMMUNICATION IN NORTHERN INDIA AND BURMA 1942

- +—+—+ Railways
- ——— Barge routes
- ===== Proposed Ledo road

```
0         500       1000      1500 km
0              500            1000 miles
```

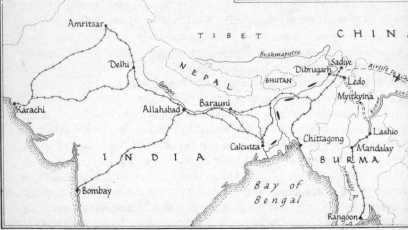

Amritsar
Delhi
TIBET
CHIN
Brahmaputra
NEPAL
Sadiya
Dibrugarh
Airlift to Ch
BHUTAN
Ledo
ROAD
Karachi
Ganges
Myitkyina
Allahabad
Barauni
Calcutta
Chittagong
Lashio
Mandalay
INDIA
BURMA
Bombay
Bay of
Bengal
Rangoon

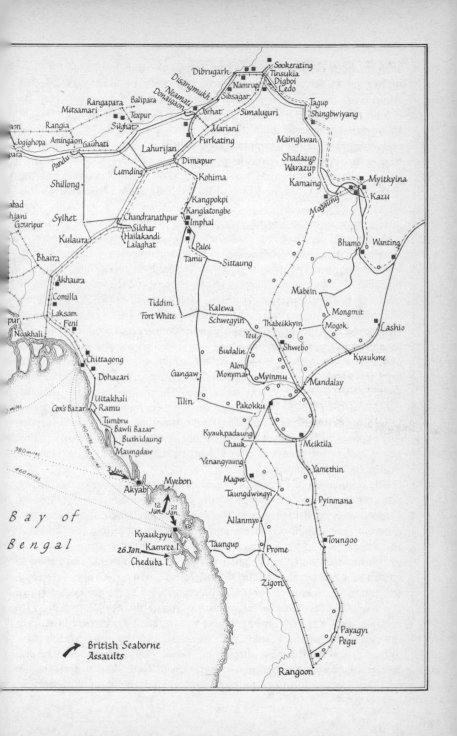

British Seaborne
Assaults

*Bay of
Bengal*

side for the war. Shortly before the start of the war, the Prime Minister of Burma, U Saw, who had been on a visit to London, was detected while returning home in making contacts with the Japanese. He was arrested and interned in the Seychelles, but although U Saw was made harmless, the episode did little good to the British sense of security, and brought little change among the politicians who replaced him. (U Saw, a turbulent figure, was the powerful opposition leader in post-war Burma. He came to world notoriety in 1947, when he organized the assassination of U Aung San and half the Burmese Cabinet. For this he was hanged.)

The growth of the Burma Independence Army took place as Suzuki had foreseen. By the time that they were able to parade in liberated Rangoon, they numbered 5,000 men, and claimed to number 10,000. Their appeal had been great. But their methods of recruitment were deplorable. The Burmese villages, partly because of the peculiarly rapid tendency of the Burmese to resort to violence, had always had a higher proportion of criminal types than was usual in the East. As the Burma Independence Army advanced through the country it proved to be irresistibly attractive to this sort of recruit. An armed force, with licence to rob and pillage, provided the ideal shelter behind which it was possible to hold the whole country to ransom. The Army spread a reign of terror behind the Japanese advance. Its original Thakin leaders found that the control of their troops was passing out of their hands. For seventy-five years Burma had experienced deep and unfamiliar peace in its rural life. The exploits of the Burma Independence Army abruptly destroyed this peace, and, to Burma's cost, it was to prove impossible to restore peace in this or the next generation.

The population of Burma consisted of a Burmese majority, and many non-Burmese people, organized with different customs and religions. Under the long British peace, these had relaxed their suspicions; the different peoples had mellowed, and their government had seemed easy. But the exploits of the Burma Independence Army stirred up the feeling of the Burmese that they ought by right to be dominant, and raised a consequent feeling among the minorities of great insecurity. In panic, the minorities organized for self-protection: where a minority possessed the remains of tribal life, its institutions were rapidly brought into play. In no time, civil war was provoked and was spreading, especially between the Burmese and the Karens, the Burmese and the very large Indian minority, and the Burmese and the hill people, the Kachins. As a result, there took place a terrified mass migration to India, and it is estimated that India, in the midst of war, had to receive half a million refugees. For every refugee to cross the Indian frontier, there were several others who starved and died on the way.

The Japanese became aware of the chaos which was being provoked. Having driven out the British from the whole country, except for a comparatively small corner which was inhabited by Chins, they were looked to by the law-abiding part of the population as the only power able to secure basic order in the country. They had been manoeuvred by Suzuki into giving countenance to Burmese revolution, but it had served its term, and they had really no sympathy with its explosive purposes. Japan, whatever its propaganda might declare, was never a revolutionary power, and generally was on the side of property and privilege. In the middle of June it applied itself to the problem of providing a Government for the country. It was not willing to proclaim Burma's independence, but established a provisional Government, made up of politicians of the orthodox parties. The Burmese Cabinet could only rule the country through the civil service structure of the British, and this the Japanese sought to preserve. Burmese civil servants were promoted to take the place of British officials.

Stability, however, could not be expected as long as the Burma Independence Army was allowed to roam the country, doing its will by sheer force. The decision was therefore arrived at to suppress the Army. Colonel Suzuki was to return home to Japan. He sought to stay, claiming that as he held a commission for what he had had done from Prince Kan'in Kotohiko, who had been Chief of the Imperial General Staff until 1940, his orders had therefore come directly from the imperial house, of which Prince Kan'in was a member. Suzuki asserted that this freed him from control by the Japanese Army. It was a variant of an old theme tune played by generations of swashbuckling Japanese military officers, who trumpeted the doctrine of their superior allegiance to the Emperor as a means of sidestepping restraints imposed on them by their military commanders. But Suzuki argued in vain. In place of the Burma Independence Army, a new force was raised, much more regular in its structure, more firmly under the control of the new Government.

This was a natural, merely prudent step of the Japanese Government. It was a decision which any responsible government was bound to take: the Burma Independence Army had stirred up so much feeling that any orderly administration was really impossible so long as it persisted. But the apparent repudiation of Burmese revolutionary nationalism by the Japanese was held by nationalists all over Asia to be difficult to square with Japanese propaganda claims; the more so since the Japanese were at first unwilling to satisfy the Burmese with any talk of independence. In Burma it caused the start of a long-drawn-out quarrel between the

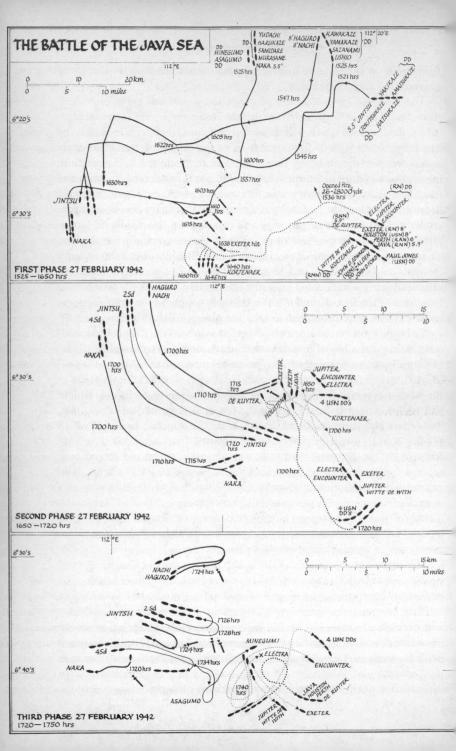

THE BATTLE OF THE JAVA SEA

FIRST PHASE 27 FEBRUARY 1942
1525 – 1650 hrs

DD MINEGUMO ASAGUMO DD
YUDACHI HARUKAZE SAMIDARE MURASAME
NAKA 5.5"
8" HAGURO 8" NACHI
KAWAKAZE YAMAKAZE SAZANAMI USHIO
112° 20'E
DD

1525 hrs
1525 hrs
1521 hrs

YAKIKAZE AMATSUKAZE DD

5.5" JINTSU (TOKITSUKAZE HATSUKAZE) DD

1547 hrs
1545 hrs

6°20'S

1605 hrs
1622 hrs
1600 hrs
1557 hrs
1603 hrs

Opened fire, 26-28000 yds 1536 hrs
(RN) DD

1650 hrs

6°30'S

JINTSU

NAKA

1610 hrs
1615 hrs
1638 EXETER hit
1640 hrs KORTENAER
1650 hrs 1645 hrs

ELECTRA JUPITER ENCOUNTER

(RNN) 5.9 DE RUYTER
EXETER (RN) 8"
HOUSTON (USN) 8"
PERTH (RAN) 6"
JAVA (RNN) 5.9"

(RNN) DD WITTE DE WITH KORTENAER
JOHN D EDWARDS (USN) ALDEN 600 JOHN D FORD
PAUL JONES (USN) DD

SECOND PHASE 27 FEBRUARY 1942
1650 – 1720 hrs

112°E

2 Sd
HAGURO NACHI

JINTSU
4 Sd
NAKA

1700 hrs
1700 hrs
1700 hrs
1710 hrs
1715 hrs
1720 hrs JINTSU
1710 hrs 1715 hrs
NAKA

6°30'S

EXETER PERTH JAVA
DE RUYTER
HOUSTON
1650 hrs
JUPITER ENCOUNTER ELECTRA
4 USN DD's
KORTENAER
1700 hrs
1700 hrs
ELECTRA ENCOUNTER EXETER
JUPITER WITTE DE WITH
4 USN DD's
1720 hrs

THIRD PHASE 27 FEBRUARY 1942
1720 – 1750 hrs

112°E
6°30'S

NACHI HAGURO 1724 hrs

JINTSU 2 Sd
4 Sd
NAKA

1726 hrs
1728 hrs
1724 hrs
1720 hrs 1734 hrs

ASAGUMO

MINEGUMI
X ELECTRA
4 USN DDs
ENCOUNTER
1740 hrs
JAVA HOUSTON PERTH DE RUYTER
JUPITER WITTE DE WITH
EXETER

6°40'S

Japanese and Burmese nationalism, which was to play a part in the Japanese downfall at the end of the war.

The fate of the Dutch Empire was the same. Because of oil, the territory was especially attractive to Japan. The first Japanese landing in Indonesia had taken place on 6 January. On 6 March, Batavia, its capital, fell. A large-scale naval battle had been fought between 27 and 29 February and resulted in the destruction of five Dutch cruisers, and of the few British cruisers which were still afloat in these waters. By April the fighting was at an end.

The experience of the Dutch was generally similar to that of the British. They had a considerable Army in Indonesia; 98,000 men surrendered, almost without fighting, and were interned. Apparently the Dutch could not rely sufficiently on their Indonesian troops to risk combat. A feature of Dutch colonialism was the far greater number of Dutch residents in their colonial territories. The number of civilian internees was therefore greater.

The impressions formed by the Dutch of the victorious Japanese Army were interesting, since they come from people who formerly had less to do with the Japanese than the British or Chinese. Their first feeling was one of unwilling admiration. The Japanese marched in, in perfect discipline. For whatever reasons, the disorders of the Japanese occupation, which had been reported in the Philippines, Malaya and Burma, were avoided. There was no deliberate relaxing of discipline while the troops ran wild. Plundering and unlawful high-handedness by the soldiers were prevented. Before long, these first impressions were found to have been much too favourable but in the early days were unquestionably widespread.

The Dutch noticed that the Japanese carried very little impedimenta, and went without demur wherever their officers ordered them. It is usually reckoned that, in modern armies of the West, for every fighting man there are eight supporting soldiers; among the Japanese the ratio was said to be as low as one to one. The Japanese continually demonstrated before the eyes of the Dutch that no obstacle could deter them. And there was no sign that the Japanese private soldier, or junior officer, murmured against the savage discipline which was used against them.

With these conquests, there came to an end the extraordinary hundred days of Japan. The Army and Navy had raced ahead, and, after a period of rattling and shaking down the Empires of Britain, the Netherlands and the United States, they needed time to rest, and to make new plans. The extent of the territory which had fallen into their hands bewildered, while

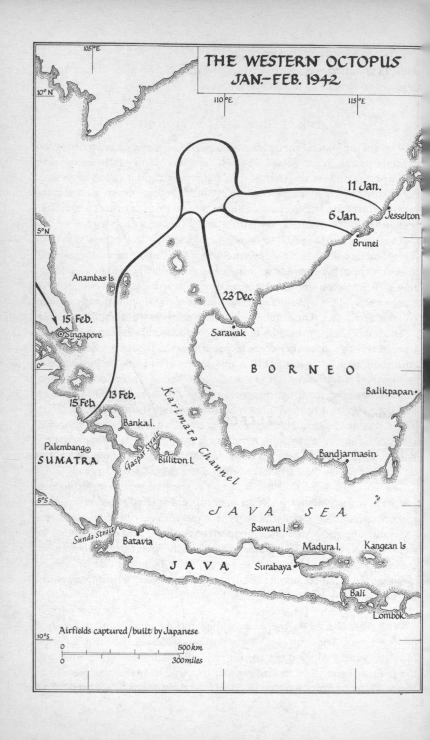

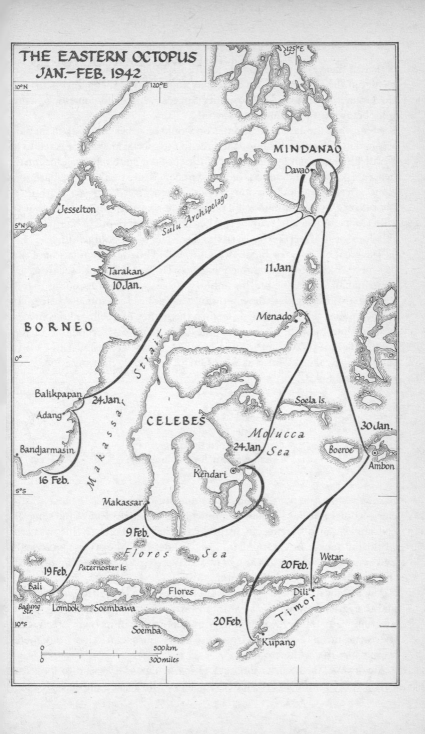

THE EASTERN OCTOPUS
JAN.–FEB. 1942

10°N

125°E

120°E

MINDANAO

Davao

Jesselton

5°N

Sulu Archipelago

Tarakan
10 Jan.

11 Jan.

Menado

BORNEO

0°

Makassar Strait

Soela Is.

Balikpapan

24 Jan.

30 Jan.

Adang

CELEBES

Molucca
Sea

Boeroe

Bandjarmasin

24 Jan.

Ambon

Kendari

16 Feb.

5°S

Makassar

9 Feb.

Flores Sea

19 Feb.

Paternoster Is.

20 Feb.

Wetar

Bali

Flores

Dili

Badung
Str.

Lombok   Soembawa

Timor

10°S

Soemba

20 Feb.

Kupang

0   500 km
0   300 miles

it excited them. They had to provide for its administration. They had also to fill out the contents of the extremely vague and propagandist plans for the Greater East Asia Co-Prosperity Sphere, which had come into being long before it was planned as a reality.

Meanwhile the Japanese population would have been more than human if it had not given itself up for the time to the spectacle which was fed to it by all the propaganda machines of the modern state and was meant to generate a profound mood of self-wonder. The streak of exhilaration came after a long and anxious period which preceded Pearl Harbor, a period of grave economic anxiety, of regrets over the interminable war with China, of fears that Japan was getting out of its depth in international relations, and of perplexity over the disorders in its political life.

The great outburst of Japanese victories had lifted the reputation of the Japanese soldier to unexampled heights. He was suddenly regarded as superhuman and invincible: his military virtues were so stupendous that it seemed astonishing that they had not been noticed adequately before. It seemed to be useless to struggle against them: they had eclipsed the virtues of the white man, until then incontestably the most formidable in the imagination of the Orient. As the Japanese Army went to war in 1941 it sang a song called 'Umi Yukaba'. One of its verses, in translation, goes as follows:

> Across the sea,
> Corpses in the water;
> Across the mountain,
> Corpses heaped upon the field;
> I shall die only for the Emperor,
> I shall never look back.

No British or American troops ever sang such lugubrious or unsophisticated words. But the Japanese sentiment was precisely that of the song. It epitomises the difference in attitude to the war between the western world and Japan; Japan found it hard to understand the cryptic, quizzical, and somewhat ambiguous songs of the Western Allies: the simplicity of the Japanese view gave them strength.

The downward turn in Japan's war fortunes set in in the autumn of 1942, and thereafter its way was steadily towards disaster. Day after day there was only bad and worsening news; nowhere, either in its own fortunes or by rescue through possible triumphs of its European Allies, did there appear any rift in the clouds.

Meanwhile, in the brief moment of joy in Japan, it is vain to look for any lasting monument of Japanese achievement in art, music or letters.

The Japanese spirit remained strangely barren. No works of poetry, philosophy, architecture or painting during this time have come to the notice of the international world of cognoscenti, or have won sympathy for the civilization which was about to endure such ravage and destruction. No sounds of natural gaiety appeared to come from Japan: it seemed a world now devoted to material advance: devoid of lightness, wit, romantic lyricism, the cultivated intelligence of women. In politics there was no originality: in science, having borrowed from abroad, Japan was ingeniously adaptive, but was without a creative impulse; in sociology, it was unimaginative. The Japanese pursued their war in a grey atmosphere of the human spirit.

CHAPTER 18

The Storm in India

WITH Singapore and Burma lost, the storm was breaking on the edge of India. There the consequence was not at first military action, but an intensification of the political crisis which had lasted thirty years and which was compendiously called the freedom struggle.

A great excitement swept India. The British in India had the mortification of being made to realize that the military crisis did not signify for most people there a time of mortal danger, but was a time of opportunity and interesting uncertainty. The news of the rout in South-East Asia had the inevitable effect. Britain imposed only a very slight censorship on news, and it was in consequence possible to form a clear idea of Japan's military prowess. Under the influence of this situation the Indian political situation changed rapidly. The war, and its consequences, was suddenly at its gates: India was no longer to be the distant spectator of events: they were at hand.

By the time of the outbreak of war, it had been obvious, to all who chose to look, that India was nearing a period of deep change. Delhi, its capital, at this time was a place of unusual interest. The last days of the old order were bathed in a rather unreal light. They were touched by a sunset. This revealed possibilities and beauties of the scene which had never been noticed before. The British, who were about to put up the shutters on their period in India, suddenly discovered, as they were on the edge of terminating their role, the enchantment of the country, which most of them had ignored as long as they were in secure occupation. India was in the condition typical of countries which are approaching revolution. Only the first rustling of the storm could be heard. It was not yet disturbing because the politics were still interesting and had not yet become lethal.

New Delhi, built chiefly by Lutyens, was then at the height of its brief but real beauty. It had matured and had been sufficiently lived in to have the atmosphere of a city rather than a camp, as it had been only a short time before; but it had not been sufficiently encroached upon by planless building to be spoilt as it is today. Unlike most capitals which have played a part in this chronicle, it had remained outwardly at peace. It was full of talk, and uniforms, and war; but it remained unravaged. The war had brought a flood of new men to the city for the first time, especially young Englishmen of the citizen army of the war years: these were often intelligently attentive to the qualities of Indian life, and they refused to be bound by the restrictions of the colour bar – that fatal barrier which had done so much harm to race relations in the past, and also cut across the natural enjoyment of the country by British visitors. Though there was more political controversy than ever, there was a distinct thaw in the relations of the British and Indians. The old barriers were falling one by one. Life in the capital, though not in the backwoods, became more normal, relations more relaxed. Even while they were engaged in hot dispute, Indians and British alike began insensibly to sun themselves in the climate of emotional debate, which they enjoyed as the most engaging pastime in the world.

In the political arena war speeded up the struggle of Indian Nationalism against the British. But the war had the effect of inflaming even more intensely the divisions within Indian Nationalism: between Hindu Nationalism, which stood for a united India, and Moslem Nationalism, which envisaged a British withdrawal from the continent leaving the predominantly Moslem part to become the independent state of Pakistan. The Hindu–Moslem crisis was the heart of political India. In the critical war years, politics turned chiefly on this, and it was the key to almost everything which happened.

The issue between Hindus and Moslems was relatively simple. Over a part of North India, the Moslems, chiefly as a result of past invasions, were in a majority. This was limited to certain regions: over the country as a whole, the Hindus were in a substantial majority. They were, moreover, the more advanced community in political activity.

When Hindus raised the cry of Indian independence, they had assumed that the Moslems would support them, as following the most advanced political leadership, and, at the start of the national movement, most Moslems had done so. At this period, those Moslems who were politically interested, had been attracted by the parties, which, though predominantly Hindu, claimed to be national, transcending both Hindu and Moslem. But, as politics set light to ever-widening circles of people, the Moslems began to draw apart, and to question whether they would have any benefit from independence, if it were won by Hindus.

The issues thus opened up were plain. Could Hindus and Moslems, by a compact between them, still agree on a common plan? Or, when independence came, should there not more properly be an independence for a Hindu India, and another independence, involving the creation of a new state, for a Moslem India? It took time for this conception to spread among the Moslems, but when it had taken root, it was plain that from the Moslems would come a fierce demand for secession. The Congress claims for independence, which the Moslems represented as a plan for transferring British sovereignty over India into Hindu sovereignty over Moslems, lost its shine and became a matter for controversy.

The Moslem community was at first widely regarded as more backward than the Hindus. At first the Moslems had not taken the same advantage as the Hindus of the opportunities of adopting modern-style institutions. This was partly because the collapse of the Moghul power at the time when the British first arrived in India was a psychological blow from which it took the Moslem upper classes a long time to recover. Initially they had stood stubbornly aside from innovations and educational opportunities offered by the new Raj which, they felt, had displaced them. There was also the fact that Islam half a century ago was opposed to modern education: Moslems were more shackled by their faith at this time than were Hindus. The simplicity of the Moslem outlook commended itself to some temperaments among the British, who were mystified and repelled by the more subtle and exotic Hindu character: but some people sensed in the Moslem mind a greater confusion in the response to the modern world than was to be found among Hindus. The Moslem who fell back on Moslem traditions for guidance in the maze of the modern world often found himself afraid. The Islamic institutions were inadequate; they could not be brought up to date. Moslems tended to live in a world of the past, and, being called on to live in the present, were left with ways uncharted and with reactions for which there was no precedent. The Moslem response to the new life was often unpredictable, unreasonable, and, too often, violent.

The question turned on whether the Moslems were right in declaring themselves to be a separate nation from the Hindus, or whether both were fundamentally Indian, divided only by religion. Both Hindus and Moslems had shared a common Indian state for many centuries: at times the Hindus were dominant, at times the Moslems. Was religion alone sufficient to turn them into irreconcilables?

The Moslems argued that it was emphatically so. No common life for the two peoples was really possible; to hold them together was too artificial. Each community, though they had been joined under foreign rule, lived in isolation from the other. Each had a separate law, its own customs, wore its own clothes, had its own literature, preserved its own way of eating. Sometimes, after prolonged periods of ordered government, they would somewhat unbend and lower their guard. The natural affinities of neighbourliness would prevail to a limited degree over the divisiveness of religion. The common language would inevitably bear some influence in mingling the two peoples. But of a genuine merger of the two societies, there was no sign. Cases of intermarriage between the two communities were very rare, and free intermarriage is the best sign of the fraternization of communities.

The Hindus replied that this was a gross misrepresentation of the position. They could argue that in previous generations the Hindus and the Moslems had felt no such separateness, and automatically regarded themselves as forming a single people. Most Hindus were willing to concede that in recent years the relationship of Hindus and Moslems had often been bad, but this they attributed to the deliberate attempt of the Government to play off one community against the other. To divide and rule was, they held, the first principle of the administration. They argued too that the difference between the communities was largely one of economics, and that, if the economic processes were given free play, these would be enough to break down the communal differences and mould the peoples into a single great society.

As the political situation became more fluid, with signs from the British that they would contemplate withdrawal, there was deadlock between the two sides. The arguments of both appeared to be conclusive. Attempts at mediation proved always in vain.

The coming of wartime tension gave a great impetus to the deterioration. The Moslems, in the fevered atmosphere of the times, set themselves, under the lead of their principal Nationalist Party, the Moslem League, to mobilize their forces. In all the provinces of North India they agitated formidably, concentrating on drawing back all the Moslems who still supported the Nationalist Congress Party. With an ever-increasing show of force, they intimated that they would resort to civil war if any attempt were made to surrender British power to Hindu hands.

The achievements of the Moslem League at this time are due chiefly to a single man, Muhammad Ali Jinnah. He had two distinct careers. Before 1930 he was an all-India leader of the Congress. The interest of Indian Nationalism possessed him and the interest of the Moslem community seemed to be reconcilable with the ascendancy of Congress. In other words, he, though personally a Moslem, was very much like Motilal Nehru, the father of Jawaharlal Nehru, who, though a Hindu, assumed that Hindu interests would always be subordinate to Indian nationalism. In the beginning of the thirties, he had retired to England for some years, where he had a flourishing legal practice. During this time he reflected, brooded, thought about his previous career and meditated on the ways that his willingness to subordinate specific Moslem interests to national interests had not been met by a similar disposition in Hindu leaders. He returned to India, broke entirely with the old all-India ideas, and ceased to be in any sense a co-worker with the Congress leaders. Instead he challenged them, and on the whole out-witted and out-manoeuvred them. He denied their right to speak at all for the Moslems; his first major enterprise was to dislodge the Hindus from the foothold they had obtained in the Moslem community. Next he built up the Moslems as a formidable striking force which demanded a state for its expression and existence.

His achievement was to inform it with something like the questing assertive feeling of the Poles when for more than a century they had been deprived of a state. Eventually, in 1919, the Poles succeeded in breaking through, and forced themselves onto the map of Europe. In the same way the Jews, deprived of a state for many centuries, at last completed its reconstitution. Similarly the Indian Moslems had the will, at the time still partly subconscious, to carve out for themselves an independent state in the Indian sub-continent. Jinnah's contribution to history was to recognize the will in advance of anyone else, and to place himself in its service.

All his successes Jinnah won by the force of his character, by his iron will, and by his clearly marked intellectual superiority. He came to his ascendancy late in life. He had been obscurely born – he was a dentist's son in Karachi – and had had the handicap that he was hardly a true Moslem at all, but, according to local gossip, was the grandson of a converted Hindu. Gradually he made his career, and owed very little to any help which he received from any quarter. The unemotional single-mindedness of his character did not go with any of the amiable qualities which make a man the darling of the crowd. Nevertheless, his way forward was made in full view of the world. There were no secrets in his career: it could be discussed, analysed, appraised, and judiciously respected.

It was characteristic of the Moslem community that his worldly success won him solid esteem; as much as did Gandhi's unworldly conduct prevail with the Hindus.

At the beginning of the second chapter of his life history, his phase as leader of the Moslems, he began by taking over the leadership of a weak party, with a very vague ideology, representing every section of a deeply riven society. He hammered it together into an exceedingly effective political instrument, to which he then, relying for persuasion on intellectual power, dictated policy. He was the new force of Islam incarnate.

As such he was indisputably one of the great actors of the time in the war years. He was one of the few individual architects of the great changes which were coming about.

With the Japanese at the gates of India the British Government felt that something must be done to rally the country to its own defence. The Labour Party had at this time increasing influence on the policy of the British Government towards India, and they succeeded in persuading the Cabinet that the wisest course was to renew its attempt at conciliating Congress. The principal author of this policy was Sir Stafford Cripps. In the high tide of 'Appeasement', this left-wing firebrand had toured armaments factories in England and implored workers to 'refuse to make armaments; refuse to make war'. Later, in 1940, he had meddled in Anglo-Chinese relations and created a certain amount of mischief through the compound of his appalling reductionism and erratic energies. He was a peculiarly able lawyer, a masterly advocate, and firmly convinced of the benefits of democracy, which, he believed, was a suitable government for any territory, whatever might be its circumstances. He had devoted himself to the study of Indian problems. He was convinced that, if Congress demands were satisfied, it would be ready to take its share in the conduct of the war, and that, by a kind of political miracle, the Indian scene would be transformed.

Cripps was a busybody, mistrusted by Whitehall mandarins as well as by British diplomats and officials overseas. The more conservative influences in London believed that, in spite of the evidently superior quality of his mind, his judgement of reality was less than shrewd. They were convinced that his appreciation of India was wrong. The situation in India could not be transformed by eloquent appeal to Congress leaders; Congress support, they knew, might be bought at a price, but at a price which would worsen the situation, since it would bring about a revolt by the Moslem population, and would cause such chaos in India that it would be useless for the prosecution of the war and would drain off large forces of troops from elsewhere for internal pacification. At the same time Congress, if it were won round, could make no difference to the military circumstances. If Congress were given a free hand in war administration, it would, argued these critics, mismanage it. By its participation it would alienate a large part of India which, as the result of various appeals, was showing wartime zeal. There was a strong likelihood that Congress, having made a deal, would take the first opportunity of leading India out of the war altogether.

In spite of these doubts, Cripps was personally entrusted with the mission to conciliate Congress. The situation for Britain was at the time so bleak, and the Cabinet was so preoccupied with other matters, that his confidence that he could reason with the Indian leaders was contagious, and his offer to go out to see what he could do was welcomed. On 11 March 1942 he arrived and spent three weeks in the country, as a kind of Ambassador from Britain.

Cripps, as the chief motive of his tour, carried with him a specific offer to Congress from the British Cabinet. It proposed as the long-term part of the scheme, that at the end of the war a constituent assembly should draft a constitution for India, and no limitation should be put upon its work. Though it was hoped that India would stay inside the Commonwealth, it would be free to secede from it.

To most people in London, it had seemed that Congress could scarcely have asked for anything more complete or more explicit. Next, as a short-term measure, as something on account, Congress was offered immediate admission to the Indian Central Government, but on terms. The Government would be a diarchy, partly British controlled, partly Indian Nationalist in composition. It would continue to be under the chairmanship of the Viceroy. On its side Congress was to approve the war effort.

Bargaining on these terms had been what Congress had had in mind, when, in advance of the Cripps mission, it let it be known that the Labour Party pressure for a new initiative was welcome to it. But politics had moved a long way since the world had been at peace in 1939. In India they had become purely communal: the conflict between Hindu and Moslem, Congress and the League, had put all else, even the conflict between Nationalist India and the British, in the shade. The Cripps offer, being drafted in part by civil servants in London, had included matter to conciliate the Moslem League as well as Congress. A sense of realism dictated this. It would have been folly to win over the Hindus at the cost of causing inflexible hostility from the Moslems. In the midst of war, the British Government could do nothing which would provoke a civil war in India. Nor could it overlook the fact that a high percentage of the Indian Army was Moslem, and, in event of a Moslem rebellion, would have dissolved in its hands.

This explains why Cripps was equipped with a fatal document that came to be known as the 'Cripps Offer'. In the eyes of the Hindus, the proposals had the mortal defect that they were conciliatory to the Moslem League demand for Pakistan. The Cripps Offer included a provision that, if the Moslem parts of India declared their firm intention to be separate – by a plebiscite in the areas concerned – they should be permitted to secede and to form their own constituent assembly. This was a permissive clause, not a definite award; what was to be decided in fact was to remain open until the war was over. But though the plan was hedged round with limitations, and was only to be looked on as one among several possibilities, its proposal was a bitter shock to the Indian Nationalists, who had not yet been taught by frustration, disappointed hopes, and blows of fate, to adjust themselves to reality.

This was the point of major controversy. It was the reason why the Hindus felt they had nothing to gain from the offer. They could not bring themselves to complicate negotiations with Britain over what they considered the national demands of India by introducing a solution, if only tentative, of the Moslem problem; the more so because of their suspicion that the problem had been distorted by the British as a device to counter the national movement.

This was the reason for the breakdown of negotiations for long-term settlement. No less completely did Congress reject the short-term offer by which this was accompanied; this was the invitation to join the Central Government at once. Congress could argue, with some reason, that its Ministers, if it had supplied them, would have been installed in a subordinate position in the Central Government, from which they might have been again ejected; and, for this, they were asked, for the first time in history, for a solemn undertaking that, if the Moslems persisted in their demands, Pakistan would be conceded to them. Congress was quite sure that the Moslems would persist if they were encouraged to do so by the attitude taken up by Britain.

The Congress decision was not as unreasonable as it appeared at the time in London. The negotiations were not entirely straightforward. For tactical reasons, Congress preferred that the break with Cripps should come about over the powers which were to be offered to Congress Ministers if India threw in its lot with the war effort. These were to be limited in the Army itself to various matters of administration and supply, which the Government felt it would be safe to delegate; and it was made woundingly clear that in matters of the higher direction of the war, allied strategy and the organization of Intelligence, the Indian leaders would continue to be excluded. Nehru, after an exploratory session with Cripps, said that the offer boiled down to Indian Ministers being given control of the Army stationery and of canteens. In spite of exaggeration, there was some truth in this.

An American attempt to mediate in the negotiations was unsuccessful. The United States had become deeply disturbed at the situation. It saw a real danger that nationalist India would secede from the war, and, for military reasons, greatly feared the loss of Indian territory as a base. It feared also the effects upon its ally, China. Most Americans regarded India as unfathomable, a mysterious land full of magic, strife, heat, filth and teeming multitudes. Paradoxically, few Americans had ever even seen an Indian – or wished any acquaintance with one. They understood neither the complexity of Indian problems, nor the reasons which prompted the policies of the British Government. However much the British Raj excited their imagination, it did so only at a distance. At any closer examination, India – and the British connection with it – seemed to the Americans distasteful in the extreme. The British were kith and kin. The Indians emphatically were not. For others the situation in India was viewed simply as a repetition of the American War of Independence, and naturally their sympathies were strongly on the Indian side. The United States was embarrassed that, in a war which it increasingly advertised as a war for democracy and freedom, it should be tied in alliance with Britain, whose past role in India ran so counter to the principles of the Atlantic Charter. It therefore regarded itself as vitally interested in the outcome of Cripps's negotiations. But its endeavours to help them on, and to ease out difficulty, did not achieve their purpose.

Yet it was Gandhi who was ultimately responsible for Congress rejecting the British offer. Gandhi was still in effective command of Congress when Cripps came to India. Nominally he had for a long while stood aside from holding office in Congress. But in fact, as Congress adviser, he had the overriding – though never quite uncontested – influence on Congress decisions.

This was understood by the British. Cripps knew that he must convince Gandhi before anyone else. He had long interviews with him. At the end of one of them, it happened that Sardar K. M. Panikkar, an extremely able politician of the Indian princely states, was seen to be going from the sweepers' colony, where Gandhi was staying, on his way to report to his masters, some of the Indian princes whom the excitement of the times had brought to Delhi. He was asked what view Gandhi took of the Cripps Offer. Actually, Panikkar did not know: his visit had not been directly to Gandhi. But from a knowledge of Gandhi's mind, he was certain, and he expressed the opinion in an epigram which has the accent of the Mahatma. It was, he said, a post-dated cheque on a failing bank.

Gandhi later repudiated the latter part of the epigram; he said that he in no wise wished to impute failure to Britain in the war, or success to Britain's enemies. On the other hand, it was clear that his attitude towards the waging of war differed from that of the belligerents. He proposed that resistance to the Japanese on Indian soil should be non-violent. In a letter written to one of his followers in 1942 (quoted by Shri B. R. Nanda in his book on Mahatma Gandhi) he said:

Remember that our attitude is that of complete non-cooperation with the Japanese Army . . . If the people have not the courage to resist (non-violently) the Japanese unto death and not the courage or the capacity to evacuate the portion invaded by the Japanese, they will do the best they can. One thing they should never do – to yield willing submission to the Japanese.*

However, Gandhi realized that the British in India, and a large element in Congress, had it been brought to cooperate with the British by ironing-out their political differences, would not employ non-violent tactics in resisting Japan. He had, therefore, no wish to see a compromise between Britain and the Congress which involved the issue of waging war. He was, furthermore, possessed by the idea that if the British left India, Japan would then leave India alone, and it would be spared the fate of Burma and Malaya. Accordingly, his influence was thrown against the Cripps Offer, and, in the circumstances of the time, was strong enough to kill it.

In April, soon after Cripps had failed, Gandhi, by one of the daring simplications of issues which were a part of his strength, began to use the slogan 'Quit India'. The precipitating cause of his decision was his fore-boding of a coming crisis, should the Government take steps to compel the peasantry to adopt a scorched earth policy in the case of an invasion. Gandhi said that it was one thing for the Russians to adopt this policy voluntarily; it was another for a Government to impose it on a confused people, too poor to endure it.

The British protested that, as politically responsible beings, they could not, in the middle of war, walk out of India, without making arrangements for the orderly transfer of British power. The suggestion that they should go seemed self-evidently absurd, and the fact that it was made seemed to the local administration either to reflect on the political sense of the opposition, or to suggest that the demand was made for the purpose of whipping up national feeling, and was not expected to be considered seriously. The British had been willing to promise, in a series of policy statements, which gradually eroded their position, that British power should eventually be wound up. Most of

* B. R. Nanda, op. cit.

these were sincere. They felt injured when Congress doubted their word. They argued that they must have time: essentially it was impossible to set about the hazardous political experiment in wartime. The British side, although under pressure of the social radicalism which was mounting at home – increasingly liberal in statements and assurances about long-term intentions – remained adamant against immediate radical changes until they judged that the war had been won. The day-to-day pressure of wartime events at home was too great to permit the liberal forces in the Westminster Parliament to give their undivided attention to events in India. It was upon the constant distraction of the British Government in London that British bureaucrats in India chiefly relied; it saved them from having their hands tied.

Congress, in facing a renewed rebellion, had the experience of its two major collisions with the British to work upon. It had learned much in these. In 1942 Congress was better organized than it had been ten years earlier.

The traditional Congress means of working against the Government was to use the method of 'open conspiracy'. That it conspired could not be doubted: but it avoided anything in the nature of a secret plot, since by doing so it strengthened its moral force. Politicians who plotted secretly drew on themselves some of the odium that terrorists are never entirely free from, even when the Government, as in India, was unpopular. Congress seldom made any secret of its plans; it carried them out in daylight.

Thus, when Gandhi turned from patient agitation and persuasion to direct action, he openly proclaimed it. Success in what he intended would depend on the willing cooperation of masses of the people. Therefore, after giving his ultimatum in late May, all through June and July he worked up the feeling of the country by explaining in every possible way what Congress, under Gandhi's direction, meant to do. He hoped, by summoning the people, to induce so many men at all levels to withdraw their support from the Government – while taking care to be non-violent – that the business of carrying on the Government would become impossible, and the British would evacuate. The Army would have a large number of deserters; so would the police; the workers in the towns, by going on strike, would halt the production of war materials; chaos would set in in the civil administration. And all would be done without violence. Gandhi, even at a great crisis, was enough of a lawyer to frame his own statements, and to persuade most of his colleagues to do the same, in such a way as to ensure that this point was clearly made.

Gandhi was waging a war of nerves. The British were bent on giving no provocation. Their interest was to prevent matters going to extremities. Though by the mid-summer, Japan had passed the peak of its war, though the battle of Midway Island was recognized by experts as having been a decisive test of strength, though Japan's *élan* was slightly drooping, the British Government had still only a very slight margin of safety to play with. The danger of invasion was still very real, and a Congress rebellion would be found to add to the emergency of the war; it would threaten the Allied use of India, which, geographically, seemed likely at this stage, before subsequent successes of the United States in the Pacific, to play a major part. To contain the outbreak of national feeling, which Gandhi knew he could command, required great coolness and discrimination on the part of the Government in deciding the precise moment for contending it.

The man who had to contend with Gandhi, and who at this stage flared into prominence, was Victor Alexander John Hope, Lord Linlithgow. He had been Viceroy for five years. On the whole he had not had an impressive term of office. He had arrived with the reputation of being an expert on agriculture, having been chairman of a commission which was expected to do something about this flagging but vital Indian industry; but he had totally disappointed the country by taking no initiative. By the time of the war he had shown that he entirely lacked the common touch, the ability to communicate with the masses, and, if he was sympathetic with anybody, it was with the bureaucrats. He may have been unlucky in this. His reports to London did little to inspire civil servants or Ministers, who regarded him as tiresome and a second-rate intellect. Although there were men who affected to find human feeling in him, few if any of the politicians ever established rapport with him. He had neither an evident enjoyment in the discharge of his great office nor a knack of handling the politicians of varying and often irreconcilable opinions who were his necessary acquaintances. He seemed totally to want imagination, and could not fire others with a vision of the importance of what he had to do. He had great industry without a capacity to turn this to account in ways which caught the imagination, considerable public spirit without it being able to gild any of his actions. Politically his main task had been to preside over the constitutional reforms which were meant to convert India into a Federation and to bring the Government of India Act of 1935 into operation; but in this also he failed to achieve anything. The Federation never got off the ground, and it was widely believed that its failure was partly due to Lord Linlithgow's willingness to let matters drift. He had allowed himself to be weighed down by the Indian realities and concluded, on seeing them at close quarters, that the proposed constitution was not really prudent.

There is no need to see Lord Linlithgow as an essentially fascist type, as was apt to be supposed by some Congressmen. In calmer times he would have been perfectly happy in presiding over a democratic and constitutional India; he was not a permanent adversary of liberalism. But in the conditions of war, he judged it clearly crazy to hand over political responsibility, even in part, to politicians who were untested, and whose statements had aroused a strong suspicion that they were opposed to the war. Lord Linlithgow's view was that of British common sense at the time. He had the strength of seeing India in the same nineteenth-century light as Churchill, whose stand against the 1935 Government of India Act had been recklessly anachronistic and ill-advised. The majority of Churchill's Cabinet during the war were not the kind of men to defy their master's voice on a matter so close to his heart. Linlithgow therefore was given their confidence in taking the steps which he proposed. One needed to be a man of exceptional political vision to see that Indian national feeling might still be enlisted for the war, and that political boldness might still achieve what it set out to do.

Lord Linlithgow's lack of imagination had allowed the initiative to pass to Gandhi. The Government only prevaricated and played for time; Gandhi promised action. Now Gandhi was about to use his opportunity, to take the steps which many men feared to tread but which their mood would support, and to commit Congress to the greatest gamble of its career. The expectation of action set in strongly among the people, so that Congress, though the organizers of the mood, found themselves finally swept along by it. Linlithgow had cool nerves. That which made him incapable of giving creative leadership and made him dull to the distressed conditions of all around him, served him well in this crisis.

In the first week of August, Gandhi summoned the Working Committee of Congress to Bombay. He made no secret of the fact that his intention was to speak the words which would set in motion a new civil disobedience movement on a grand scale.

Late at night the police pounced and arrested Gandhi and all the Congress leaders. They were transported to carefully arranged and not uncomfortable prisons. Gandhi himself was interned in a requisitioned palace of the Aga Khan. The operation had been carefully planned, and, unlike most actions of the Indian Government at that time, had been kept carefully secret. The success with which it was executed helped to restore the self-respect of the Government.

*

For the rest of the war, Congress was inactive. Most of its leaders continued to be in prison. The Government, which had been anxious about the extent of their popular support, discovered that this had been exaggerated; but exercised a perhaps understandable prudence in detaining the leaders until Hitler was defeated.

The continuing incarceration of the Congress leaders left the way clear for Moslem agitation. By the time that Congress orators were once again free, they found that the Moslem leaders had organized the Moslem community fairly solidly, and that Congress opposition counted for little. One of the unforeseen consequences of Gandhi's 'open revolt' had been to let in Pakistan.

The British authorities were relieved at the passing of a crisis. But, though they might have been expected to revise their general attitudes in the light of a proven weakness of Congress, they did not do so. Their policy followed very closely the official and unofficial statements of it. This was that time was nearly up for the British in India, and that at the end of the war Britain would do exactly what it had said it would do: make a sincere attempt to set up a Government, or Governments, in India and leave the sub-continent. Most of the politicians in England, even the less enlightened ones, and most civil servants in India, even the more elderly ones, were in agreement about this. For the present India's war-effort was still needed, and nothing would be done to rock the boat. But as the war went on, the Government gradually ceased to have the feel of certainty and stability, and took on the style and temper of a provisional Government. From London a strong breath of discouragement was blown at anyone who played with other concepts of the future.

Gandhi, the man of peace, who had been obliged by political circumstances to play such a large part in wartime politics, ceased to be a determining figure of the war. Indeed, never again was he to have the personal dictatorship which he had had of the opinion and actions of Congress. His decisions in 1942 marked his passage from supreme authority. After the war, though he had great influence, and though for a time a great deference was paid to him by all who sought to mould events in India, new forces had appeared, and he had to bend before these.

Gandhi's eclipse for the rest of the war, and the eclipse of Congress, removed from India the feature of its politics which had made India fascinating for so many. In a world given up to the contest for brute power, and, worse still, for military power, the claim of Congress that it was striving for higher things was refreshing. Congress politics were intensely histrionic; drama was the essence of them. They were also steeped in arguments over political and secular morality. It was breathtaking to find Congress, in the middle of the war, calmly demanding on moral grounds concessions which no Government could have made, least of all a Government which possessed a still unbeaten Army; yet it had the authority to compel the rational discussion of its demands. All this was now given up. The politics of India were deflated; they followed more practical, limited, lesser ends; greater vision had been dispersed by contact with reality. Yet never again were Indian affairs to be felt to touch the heart of humanity as they were when their arch prophet was moving around with his strange entourage which recalled, in manners and circumstances, that of St Francis of Assisi and the other compelling figures of the past.

Gandhi's adversary, Lord Linlithgow, also stalked out of the picture. Immensely tall, gaunt, awkward, he had been out of place in Hindu India, which liked to discuss with passion those ideas which seemed to mean little to Linlithgow. His final actions were not much to his credit. In the summer of 1943 there took place a frightful famine in Bengal. For the first time for thirty-five years this dreaded event had recurred in India. It was an ugly fact that this spectre, to exorcise which had been one of the claims made for British rule, had again appeared. This particular famine was man-made. Throughout the episode there was no actual shortage of food supplies in India. But these were allowed to remain hoarded because the railways, under pressure of wartime operations, had broken down, and because the civil servants, also under wartime pressure, realized too late what was happening. It did not adapt the famine code, which kept the country from starving in normal times, to the changed circumstances of war. It was too much harried by urgent and unfamiliar problems of administration.

In Bengal a great exodus took place from the countryside to the town, in the opposite direction to the population flow of the previous year when the panic set in that India was to be bombed. More and more frightful tales began to circulate of a population driven by hunger to roam until they fell dead from emaciation. The streets of the great modern city of Calcutta were strewn with corpses, and such sights began to appear there of the juxtaposition of extreme wealth and of stark hunger as had before the war been notorious of eastern metropolises such as Shanghai. Another blow had been dealt to the credit of the British Government in Asia.

As reports of what was happening began to come out of Bengal people expected that the Viceroy would tour the famine area, to bring what help was possible, to be seen communing with the people, and to inquire into

57 The Pearl Harbor attack,
7 December 1941 *Top*: The
battleship *West Virginia* sinks
alongside the *Tennessee*. A
survivor is pulled from the
water by a motor sailing
launch

58 *Bottom*: A scene of
general devastation

59 *Top*: US Army B25
aircraft fly off the USS
Hornet on the first American
air raid against the Japanese
mainland; they are led by
former test-pilot Colonel
'Jimmy' Doolittle

60 *Bottom*: Loss of the
aircraft carrier USS
Lexington, following the Battle
of the Coral Sea, 8 May 1942

61 *Top*: A Japanese propaganda photograph shows two exultant children cheering 'Banzai'. Note their civil defence gear

62 *Bottom*: A column of battleships steams in line: the most technologically sophisticated, complex and expensive machines of any description ever made by man before the Russo-American space race

63 *Top*: The Japanese heavy
cruiser *Mikuma* lies dead in
the water and sinking during
the Battle of Midway, June
1942. Over a thousand sailors
perished with her

64 *Bottom*: A US B25
medium bomber flies a sortie
over Wotje island in the
north-eastern Marshall Islands

65 *Top*: On Guadalcanal
four of the US Marines who
captured the island wade to
their tents through knee-deep
water

66 *Bottom*: Many Japanese
naval experts regard the loss
of Rabaul as the decisive
turning-point after which the
defeat of Japan was inevitable

67 *Top*: The Japanese
battleship *Yamato* undergoes
sea trials in October 1941. The
Yamato was the largest and
most powerful battleship ever
built

68 *Bottom*: The American
Resurrection. The Stars and
Stripes unfurls above the
parade ground at Topside,
Corregidor, on the return of
the Americans, 22 February
1945

69 *Top left*: This Pulitzer Prize-winning photograph shows the Stars and Stripes being raised above Mount Suribachi on Iwo Jima in February 1945 and had a powerful effect on the American public

70 *Top right*: A Japanese kamikaze aircraft attacks the *Missouri* on VE Day, the last day of the European war: months later the surrender of Japan was signed on the *Missouri*'s main deck

71 *Bottom*: US Marines wade ashore at Tinian Beach, August 1944

72   *Top*: Empty oildrums litter a beachhead established by US Marines on Okinawa in April 1945, evidence of the vehicles that have moved inland with the support of an armada of 1,300 ships

73   *Bottom*: The face of battle: three US Marines crouch under fire on Leyte Island in the Philippines in October 1944

what was evidently a failure of administration. To visit the scene of disaster was a tradition of the Viceroy. But, inexplicably, Linlithgow on this occasion departed from tradition. Week after week went by, and he spent the last days of his term of office in Delhi and Simla.

His successor, the new Viceroy, promptly reversed this behaviour. The solid benefit which by his immediate visit he was able to do the administration struck the country as a rebuke to his predecessor. It was evident that more could have been done by energy, imagination and improvisation. Field Marshal Lord Wavell called in the Army to relieve the miseries of the people, and for a period this enjoyed a very real and unusual popularity.

Yet Lord Linlithgow, reluctantly though he may be praised, played a great part in guiding Indian affairs so that events took one shape and not another. He was given much latitude by the Home Government. After the failure of Cripps, his judgement prevailed on most matters. He handled the open rebellion of Congress almost under the eyes of the would-be invader. That so few lives were lost, and that India continued belligerent, was due to his calm and to a sense of proper timing that actually belonged to his staff but has been credited to him.

CHAPTER 19

Four Loose Threads

FOR the dark months that followed Pearl Harbor, there were few military initiatives that America could take. In March 1942, at a time when the fall of the Philippines was imminent, President Roosevelt authorized a spectacular air raid upon Tokyo, primarily intended to lift morale in the United States. The raid, child of the fertile brain of Admiral Ernest J. King, Commander-in-Chief of the United States Fleet, and his senior operations officer, was not planned as more than a token gesture of defiance. Strictly speaking, it would serve no useful military purpose. Lieutenant-Colonel James H. Doolittle, a former stunt pilot, a qualified aeronautical engineer with a doctorate from MIT, and an outstanding aviator with a string of record-breaking aerial accomplishments to his credit, was selected to head a handpicked team of Army airmen whom he trained in less than a month to fly their specially adapted land-based aircraft off a tiny patch of runway intended to simulate a naval flight deck.

In April sixteen twin-engined B25s of the United States Army Air Force were loaded aboard the USS *Hornet* and, collecting an escort which included four cruisers, eight destroyers and an air umbrella provided by the USS *Enterprise*, they advanced into the Western Pacific. In the absence of radar, Yamamoto Isoruku had taken the precaution of stationing a line of picket-boats in a great arc, more than seven hundred miles out to sea east of the Japanese mainland, to provide early warning of any carrier-borne attack. The approaching task force spotted four of these boats, two of which flashed the news to Tokyo. The Japanese did not expect the Americans to launch long-range land-based aircraft from the decks of ships or at such a distance as to make their recovery aboard impossible. Having lost hope of nearing Japan undetected, however, Doolittle and Admiral 'Bull' Halsey, commander of the naval task force, decided that it would be too dangerous for the ships to venture closer or to linger within easy range of Japanese land-based aircraft. They agreed that the B25s should be launched without delay, correctly anticipating that Japanese misjudgement of the raiders' time of arrival would outweigh the risk that the aircraft were likely to run out of fuel before they could reach the safety of air bases in unoccupied China. It was a bold stroke and achieved effective surprise.

A solitary Japanese patrol aircraft six hundred miles out to sea had reported seeing one of the bombers heading westwards. Its warning was not heeded: the American carrier raid was expected to materialize on the morrow. Following the first signals from Yamamoto's picket ships, Japanese Naval Air Headquarters had ordered ninety fighters and 116 bombers to prepare for the contest at first light. Six heavy cruisers and ten destroyers set out at full steam to intercept the American warships. It was all in vain.

One of the American aircraft released a ton of incendiaries over Nagoya, while another hit Kobe and a third, originally scheduled for Osaka, bombed the Yokosuka Naval Yard and Yokohama instead. Twelve others headed straight for the heart of Tokyo, arriving from all points of the compass just as a full-scale mock air raid by Japanese aircraft was ending, throwing the Japanese air controllers into confusion. Tōjō himself, coming in to land at Tokyo in an Army transport aircraft following an inspection of troops outside the capital, was passed by one of the incoming B25s. The Americans encountered increasingly heavy anti-aircraft fire over Tokyo but released their bomb loads of incendiaries and high explosives unscathed. The sixteenth aircraft of the squadron, beset with fuel supply problems on its route to Japan, veered away from the Japanese mainland and headed alone for Vladivostok, where the Russians seized it and interned its crew. All of the other aircraft eluded pursuit and flew on to reach China, assisted by unexpectedly favourable tail winds. Their target landing fields were 1,500 miles beyond Tokyo. It had been hoped that any surviving aircraft would join Major-General Claire Chennault's hard-pressed air forces. None of them did so. Several flew directly over their intended landing field at Chuchow, but the Chinese, who had not been told that the Americans were heading there, mistook the planes for Japanese and switched off their field lights upon detecting the approaching aircraft. Four of the fifteen crash-landed when they ran out of fuel before reaching safety. The other eleven crews finally took to their parachutes, abandoning their aircraft in mid-air.

The raid shocked and mortified the Japanese nation and its leadership. There is no reason to doubt the genuine sense of moral outrage expressed by the Japanese, who had managed to suppress any twinges of conscience that some of them felt for the plight of the Chinese, Filipino and other civilian populations bombed so recklessly by Japanese aircraft earlier in this fifteen-year war. There is a great difference between those who give and those who receive the punishment of aerial bombardment.

The number of persons actually killed by Jimmy Doolittle's Raid was small, something like fifty people. Ninety buildings including a number of private homes were bombed and, in what appears to have been a tragic mistake, at least one of the aircraft attacked a school full of children, cutting down a number of teachers and their pupils by machine-gun fire. Tōjō and his Cabinet reacted strongly, issuing retroactive regulations condemning indiscriminate air attacks upon non-military objectives, private property or common civilians. These offences, as well as other serious infractions of the international laws of war, would now be treated as criminal acts punishable under Japanese military law. Captured enemy airmen convicted under these new regulations would be liable to a term of imprisonment of not less than ten years and could forfeit their lives.

The four-man crews from two of the Doolittle aircraft were taken captive by Japanese occupation forces in China and were paraded through the streets of Shanghai and Nanking respectively. They were subjected to torture in efforts to discover how they had made their way to Tokyo and where they had intended to land. The Japanese were briefly confused by the fact that the B25s and their crews belonged to the US Army Air Force, not the Navy. How had they reached Tokyo? The naval carriers, so it was believed, had sailed off as soon as their distance and bearing had become known. President Roosevelt's one-line jest that the aircraft had come from 'Shangrila' cut no ice. Bit by bit the Japanese soon pieced together more or less the whole story.

In due course exceptional pressure was imposed upon General Hata Shunroku, Supreme Commander of the Japanese Expeditionary Forces in China, to haul the captured fliers before a court-martial at which they were given no opportunity to defend themselves. The result was a foregone conclusion. Hata himself seems to have resisted the duties that he was required to perform, but in the end he had no choice but to carry out his instructions as directed. All eight airmen were condemned to death on 20 August 1942. Afterwards Tōjō commuted five of the sentences to life imprisonment as a practical demonstration of the Emperor's divine benevolence, but the remaining three prisoners were executed on 10 October 1942. All but one of the others miraculously survived the war and lived to tell their tale.

That the trial and punishment of the Doolittle fliers was a mockery of due process cannot be disputed, and it proved to be merely the beginning of what became the policy of the Japanese to execute Allied bomber crews taken captive by the Japanese. After the war Tōjō told the Tokyo War Crimes Tribunal that he had enacted the new Army regulations mainly to deter the Allied Powers from undertaking similar terrorist raids in future.

So far as the Japanese were concerned, these unfortunates were nothing less than war criminals, not entitled to protection as prisoners of war.

It is difficult to read the 1907 Rules of The Hague Convention (IV) on Land Warfare and the 1923 Hague Air Warfare Rules (although the latter document, commissioned by Britain, the United States, France, Italy and Japan in 1922, does not have the sanctity of a formal treaty) without feeling that the Japanese had a valid complaint. The declarations of statesmen, judgements of legal tribunals and unanimous resolutions of the League of Nations during the years before the war showed a well-nigh universal condemnation of aerial warfare directed against civilian population centres. Japan herself had declared as early as 1937 that in the conduct of the war in China she would abide by the 1923 Hague Air Warfare Rules. It was the common practice of all belligerents in the Second World War to ignore these provisions. Yet even though the experience of that conflagration confirmed in so many ways that nations tend to resort to the most fiendish means of war that they can devise except when deterred by their vulnerability to reprisals, most people on our planet today would still agree that any resort to indiscriminate attacks upon civilian targets is – or ought to be – in breach of the basic principles of international law. Indeed, the distinguished jurist Sir Hersch Lauterpacht, although cautiously sensing his way in the immediate aftermath of that war, goes much further:

These new problems raised by air warfare cannot be deemed to have affected the validity of the general principle of immunity of non-combatants from direct attack. They are not such as to provide a legal justification for offensive action which, although disguised under the cloak of attack upon a military objective or as a measure of reprisals, is directed in fact exclusively and deliberately against the civilian population. Non-combatants are not, under existing International Law, a legitimate military objective . . . International Law protects non-combatants from deliberate bombardment from the air directed primarily against them for the purpose of instilling terror or for similar reasons; recourse to such bombardment is unlawful.*

Nevertheless, the Japanese case was entirely vitiated by their own past violations of the same rules and by their callous disregard for just about every other international law of war on the books. Moreover, one of the other immediate consequences of the Doolittle Raid was that the Japanese launched a systematic counter-offensive of terror and punitive raids in the provinces of Chekiang and Kiangsi where all but one of the Doolittle aircraft had come down.

* L. Oppenheim, *International Law: A Treatise*, vol. II, *Disputes, War and Neutrality*, 7th edn, ed. by H. Lauterpacht, Longmans, Green & Co., London, 1952, pp. 516–30, especially p. 525.

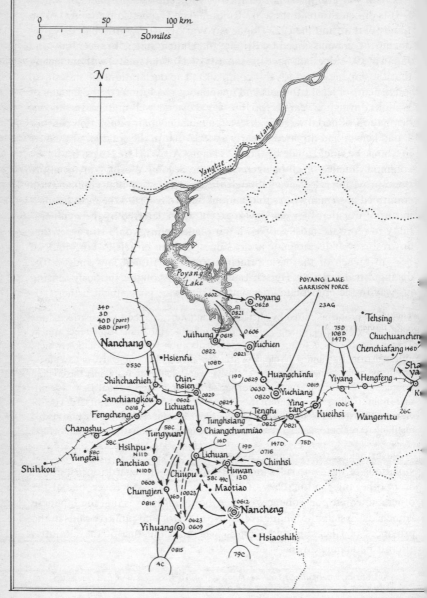

JAPAN'S CHEKIANG–KIANGSI OFFENSIVE
MAY–SEPTEMBER 1942

0   50   100 km

0   50 miles

N

Yangtze kiang

Poyang Lake

POYANG LAKE
GARRISON FORCE

0602

Poyang
0628

0821

0606

23AG

Tehsing

34 D
3 D
40 D (part)
68 D (part)

Nanchang

Juihung
0615

0822

0530

•Hsienfu

0821

Yuchien

108 D

75 D
108 D
147 D

Chuchuanchen
Chenchiafang 146 D

0829

19 D

0629

Huangchinfu

Yiyang

Hengfeng

Sha
ya

Shihchachieh

Chin-
hsien

0630

0820

Yuchiang

0819

0624

Sanchiangkou

0602

0824

Tengfu

Ying-
tan

Kueihsi

100 C

Wangerhtu

Fengcheng

0618

Lichuatu

0822

0821

Changshu

Tunghsiang
Chiangchunmiao

147 D

75 D

58 C

Tungyuan•

16 D

19 D

0716

Chinhsi

58 C

Hsihpu•
N 11 D

Lichuan

Shihkou

Yungtai

58 C

Panchiao
N 10 D

Chiupu

Huwan

58 C 49 C

13 D

Maotiao

0608

0623

Chungjen

16 D 0802

•

0612

Nancheng

0816

0609

• Hsiaoshih

Yihuang

0815

79 C

4 C

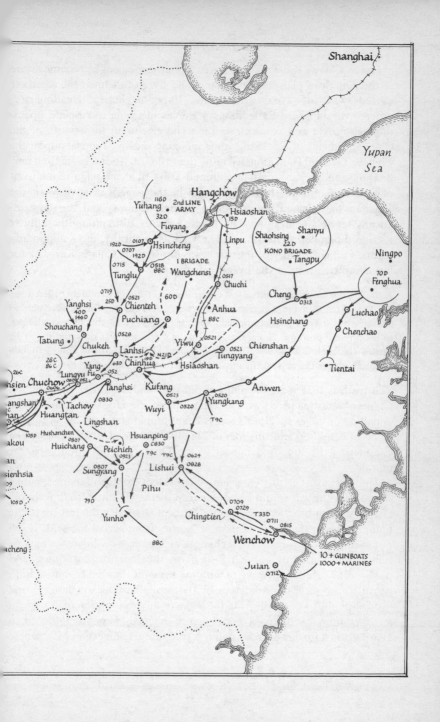

Just as Chiang Kai-shek had feared from the moment he became aware of the American plan to bomb Japan and fly on to China, the Japanese moved swiftly to avenge themselves. Imperial General Headquarters ordered the Japanese Expeditionary Forces in China to suspend operations elsewhere and concentrate their energies upon the seizure of the Chinese airfields in Chekiang while inflicting massive reprisals upon the Chinese. General Hata amassed more than 100,000 troops, more than nine divisions, and began to advance in mid-May. In a campaign reminiscent of Sherman's march through Georgia in the American Civil War, the Japanese first cleared the Chekiang–Kiangsi Railway and then systematically set about smashing the Chinese airfields, dismantling the railway itself and plundering the entire area. Characteristically, the Kuomintang régime's official history of the war heaps praise upon Chiang Kai-shek for his 'complete grasp of the overall situation':

Knowing the enemy and ourselves, Generalissimo Chiang resolutely ordered the 3rd War Area to avoid a decisive engagement . . . Thus our forces were able to conserve our strength and continued to harass the enemy, forcing him to fall back to his original position. Generalissimo Chiang's decision was outstanding, as he caused the enemy to waste strength and time and enabled our forces to tide themselves over the most difficult period.*

The truth is that it was a military disaster, and a quarter of a million Chinese were butchered as a direct result of the Doolittle Raid. These appalling outrages by Hata's forces bear comparison with the notorious Rape of Nanking, and this loss of life must be added to the scales when considering the supposed impact of the Doolittle Raid upon Japanese morale.

The Americans greatly exaggerated the extent to which Japanese public support for the war would be undermined by the Doolittle Raid: it simply had no discernible effect upon morale except to harden the resolve of the nation to resist the 'hairy barbarian' hordes from across the seas. It did not even produce fundamental changes in Japanese civil defence and air raid precautions. For another year or so the Japanese authorities and public alike deluded themselves with the thought that the Doolittle Raid provided an accurate indication of the probable scale of damage and disruption that would follow in the wake of any resumption of American air operations over Japan. Local fighter defences were strengthened to guard against further attacks, and it is true that this diversion of Japanese

---

* Hsu Long-hsuen, Chang Ming-kai *et al.*, *History of the Sino-Japanese War (1937–1945)*, Chung Wu, Taipei, 2nd edn, 1972, pp. 379–90, especially p. 390.

air strength seriously undermined the ability of the Japanese Army Air Force to send badly needed air reinforcements to support frontline troops elsewhere. In truth, however, the number of aircraft and crews recalled from the Chinese mainland to the home defence of Japan was of little consequence when measured against the ever-accelerating disparity between the air resources of the Allied Powers and Japanese. The Doolittle Raid did boost the morale of the American people which the President had wanted so badly after the string of defeats that American arms had sustained in the war thus far. More significantly still, it forced the Japanese Naval General Staff to abandon its opposition to Admiral Yamamoto's ill-fated plan for another great strategic riposte: the battle for Midway, which meant the ruination of Japan's best chances to secure the capture of Port Moresby and was the first great turning point of the Pacific War.

INDIAN OCEAN EXCURSIONS LIMITED

Though the attention of the Western Allies was fixed uneasily upon the territorial gains of the Japanese, that of the most influential Japanese strategists continued to concentrate upon the war at sea. It was to be the greatest naval war in history. The great prize of war would be the mastery of the Pacific Ocean, and this would go to whichever Navy proved to be the stronger. The Japanese war planners, in the months after Pearl Harbor, had kept a very flexible outlook. Some favoured a blow in the Indian Ocean, which would open the way to military operations in the region. There was even talk of a naval sweep of the Indian Ocean, which would end with the Japanese making contact at Suez with the victorious German armies. Others wanted an attack in the South Pacific which would isolate Australia; others a renewal of the attack on Hawaii which Pearl Harbor had begun.

Nearly all sections agreed that Japan must continue to be aggressive. Only by exploiting the impetus gained by Pearl Harbor could Japan even seem to prosper. The long-term odds against Japan were so desperate that the conversion of the war into a defensive one would have been half to admit defeat. The best course lay in a constant series of surprises, which would divert attention from the sombre reality of Japan's true position.

During all this period, the Japanese Army showed little willingness to embark on joint plans with the Navy. At this time the situation and prospects of Germany were very uncertain: it was in the middle of its great adventure against Russia, which, if successful, would have altered the complexion of the war; the Japanese Army was therefore anxious to keep its hands free, so that it could be ready to strike whenever this might, by the unfolding of events, become desirable. Although, by its southward move, Japan had turned its back upon Russia, and was genuinely anxious to make its Non-Aggression Pact with Russia a reality, it could not ignore the fact that Russia was reeling. If it were to be defeated, or to be in obvious danger of defeat, a new situation would come into being, and Japan would be driven to interfere in Siberia. Its divided attention during these months probably accounts for the salvation of India, and perhaps of Australia, from invasion.

The centre of initiative in the months between Pearl Harbor and June 1942 was the brain of Admiral Yamamoto Isoroku. It is true that, as Commander-in-Chief of the Combined Fleet, he remained technically subordinate to the Naval General Staff. But he was regarded by everyone as the author of the victory at Pearl Harbor, and he used the prestige which this gave him to impose his concepts upon more conservative Japanese admirals. In Yamamoto, Japan had produced one of its undisputed geniuses of the war: a man whose ideas gave a new turn to naval strategy, and who had the capacity to translate the ideas into action.

As a next move, Japan sent a fleet of five aircraft carriers and four battleships, one light and two heavy cruisers and eleven destroyers, into the Pacific Ocean in the direction of Ceylon. It was a superbly well-balanced fleet, incomparably stronger and more efficient than any other then afloat. It was under the command of Admiral Nagumo Chūichi, who had had the operational command at Pearl Harbor. It was a task force very similar to that which had raided Pearl Harbor, and its objective was to bomb Colombo and a naval base at Trincomalee in the same manner, though of course it could not hope for the same element of surprise. It was seeking out the Eastern Fleet of the British Royal Navy, and would try to put it out of action in the Far East by dealing it the same crippling blow that had been inflicted on the American Pacific Fleet. In support of Nagumo, and to throw the enemy into confusion, a Second Expeditionary Fleet, called Malay Force, raided shipping and attacked shore installations along the east coast of India. This Fleet was split into three divisions covered by a screening force. Altogether this meant that Nagumo's Striking Force effectively was augmented by the *Ryūjō* (a light carrier carrying forty-eight aircraft), three heavy cruisers, two light cruisers and fifteen destroyers. The Japanese operations in the Indian Ocean were destined to be short-lived, but their formidable nature is self-evident from the size of the forces which the Japanese devoted to the accomplishment of their objectives.

This was a foreshortened version of the plan first prepared by Yamamoto's Combined Fleet Staff. They had wanted the Army to contribute an expeditionary force of five divisions, far larger than the forces employed in Malaya or the Philippines, to occupy the entire island of Ceylon. This in turn was to be the precursor of a grand plan to link up with German forces advancing from the Caucasus through the Middle East. The Army, owing to its preoccupations with the magnetic north, refused to take part in the plan.

On 1 April 1942 the British Admiral, Sir James Somerville, was alerted to the presence of Nagumo's fleet, and concentrated his available force to meet him. Somerville had a fairly large fleet, five battleships, five light and two heavy cruisers, three aircraft-carriers and fourteen destroyers; but only one of his lumbering battleships, H M S *Warspite*, was modernized. All five of his capital ships were fatigued, having begun their active service in the midst of the First World War, a quarter century before. Somerville's two fleet carriers, H M S *Indomitable* and H M S *Formidable*, were of the latest British designs and carried thirty-five to forty aircraft. His only other carrier, tiny H M S *Hermes*, the British first ship ever designed and built as an aircraft carrier, normally carried a complement of only nine obsolete swordfish torpedo-bomber/reconnaissance aircraft but could squeeze in half a dozen extra aircraft at a cost of seriously reduced ship efficiency. All these vessels were thoroughly outclassed by the fighting ships of Nagumo's Carrier Strike Force, which deployed more than 360 aircraft. On the other hand, Somerville had the enormous advantage that he held the Japanese naval cipher; and the Japanese did not suspect this. No major shift took place in the Japanese disposition but he was aware of it as soon as it happened. The eyes which this gave him were probably decisive in the action which followed.

On 4 April the Japanese made what was intended to be a major air strike at Colombo. They found the British alert to the attack; no warship was in harbour; the British air forces were already in the air, and gave the Japanese a fair fight. The Japanese, denied the advantage of surprise, broke off the attack to bomb, and sink, two British heavy cruisers, which had approached dangerously near to the Japanese aircraft-carriers from which the bombing planes had come.

Somerville had in the meanwhile discovered that Nagumo's force was larger than he had at first supposed. He recognized that he was hopelessly outclassed; his old and very slow battleships were no match for the enemy. He was therefore forced to take evasive action by day, and attempt to engage the Japanese at night, although in fact no naval engagement took place. On 9 April Nagumo made an air strike at Trincomalee, the British

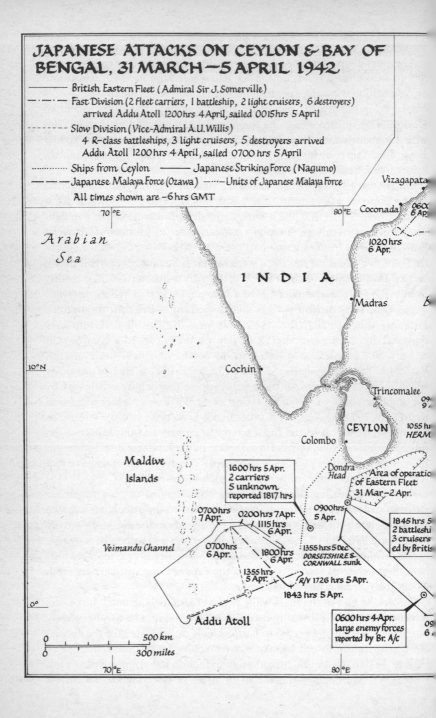

JAPANESE ATTACKS ON CEYLON & BAY OF BENGAL, 31 MARCH – 5 APRIL 1942

——— British Eastern Fleet (Admiral Sir J. Somerville)
—·—·— Fast Division (2 fleet carriers, 1 battleship, 2 light cruisers, 6 destroyers)
    arrived Addu Atoll 1200 hrs 4 April, sailed 0015 hrs 5 April
– – – – – Slow Division (Vice-Admiral A.U. Willis)
    4 R–class battleships, 3 light cruisers, 5 destroyers arrived
    Addu Atoll 1200 hrs 4 April, sailed 0700 hrs 5 April
··········· Ships from Ceylon ——— Japanese Striking Force (Nagumo)
— — — Japanese Malaya Force (Ozawa) —·····— Units of Japanese Malaya Force

  All times shown are –6 hrs GMT

Arabian Sea

70 °E

80 °E Coconada Vizagapata

0600
6 Ap.

1020 hrs
6 Apr.

I N D I A

Madras

b

10° N

Cochin

Trincomalee

09·
9·

CEYLON

1055 h·
HERM·

Colombo

Maldive Islands

Dondra
Head

Area of operatio
of Eastern Fleet
31 Mar–2 Apr.

1600 hrs 5 Apr.
2 carriers
5 unknown
reported 1817 hrs

0900hrs
5 Apr.

1845 hrs 5
2 battleshi
3 cruisers
ed by Britis

0700 hrs
7 Apr.

0200 hrs 7 Apr.
1115 hrs
6 Apr.

0700hrs
6 Apr.

1800 hrs
6 Apr.

1355 hrs 5 Dec
*DORSETSHIRE &
CORNWALL sunk*

Veimandu Channel

1355 hrs·
5 Apr.

R/V 1726 hrs 5 Apr.

1843 hrs 5 Apr.

0°

Addu Atoll

0600 hrs 4 Apr.
large enemy forces
reported by Br. A/c

09·
6 ·

| 0 | 500 km |
| 0 | 300 miles |

70°E

80°E

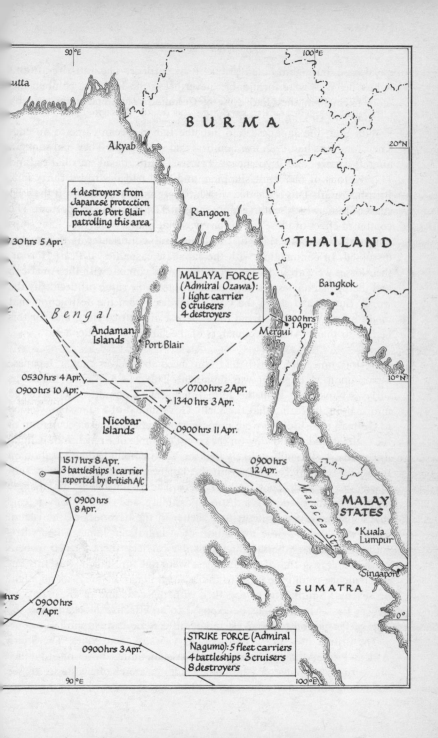

90°E   100°E

B U R M A

Akyab   20°N

4 destroyers from
Japanese protection
force at Port Blair
patrolling this area

Rangoon

730 hrs 5 Apr.

T H A I L A N D

MALAYA FORCE
(Admiral Ozawa):
1 light carrier
6 cruisers
4 destroyers

Bangkok

1300 hrs
1 Apr.

Mergui

Bengal

Andaman
Islands

Port Blair

0530 hrs 4 Apr.

0900 hrs 10 Apr.

0700 hrs 2 Apr.

10°N

1340 hrs 3 Apr.

Nicobar
Islands

0900 hrs 11 Apr.

1517 hrs 8 Apr.
3 battleships 1 carrier
reported by British A/c

0900 hrs
12 Apr.

0900 hrs
8 Apr.

M A L A Y
S T A T E S

•Kuala
Lumpur

Singapore

hrs

0900 hrs
7 Apr.

S U M A T R A

0°

0900 hrs 3 Apr.

STRIKE FORCE (Admiral
Nagumo): 5 fleet carriers
4 battleships 3 cruisers
8 destroyers

90°E   100°E

naval base, but again failed to take it by surprise. The anti-aircraft and fighter defences were formidable: nevertheless the Japanese bombers did more harm than they had done at Colombo. They ended the raid by locating and sinking the little *Hermes*.

With that, the Japanese raid into the Indian Ocean came to an end. Their total loss had been five bombers and six fighters. They had sunk an aircraft-carrier and two heavy cruisers, with naval auxiliaries and 112,312 tons of merchant shipping, and they had destroyed thirty-nine British aircraft. This coincided with Japanese submarine raids off the west coast of India which sent five more ships of 32,404 tons to the bottom. The combined effect of these operations was that military and merchant shipping traffic on both sides of the Indian sub-continent was thoroughly disrupted. In conjunction with the Japanese casualties at Pearl Harbor, their losses were absurdly low from this initial combat with the American and the British navies. In ships traded, Somerville came off decidedly the worse. But he had saved the bulk of his fleet from the destruction that might have overtaken it from the Japanese aircraft-carriers, and for this he had to thank Allied decipherers of the Japanese naval codes.

By this time, the British had convinced themselves that a Japanese attack upon Madagascar was imminent. This was a familiar theme: as early as November 1940 the Joint Intelligence Committee had received information indicating that the Vichy Government of France had yielded to German pressure and were prepared to accept Japanese occupation of the entire island. Following on the recent example of French Indo-China, it seemed exceptionally unlikely that the Vichy colonial administration on the island would refuse to permit the Japanese to establish at least submarine berths and depot facilities there. The establishment of Japanese air bases on the island was a distinct possibility, and there were even fears that Japanese cruisers might find shelter in the harbours of the island. Thus, even prior to the mutilation of Admiral Sir James Somerville's Eastern Fleet by Admiral Nagumo's five carriers, there seemed to be a considerable risk that if the Japanese were not forestalled, Britain's imperial lifeline round the Cape to India, Australia and New Zealand might be severed; South Africa, together with the coastline of the whole of British East Africa, might be exposed to an effective blockade and the flow of Persian oil to the West might suffer serious disruption.

The British also had to consider the views of their Allies. The South African Prime Minister, General Jan Christian Smuts, never one to mince his words with Winston Churchill, made no secret of his desire to see something done quickly: he regarded Madagascar as 'the key to the safety of the Indian Ocean'. The Americans were inclined to agree: they encouraged the British to take the matter in hand. General Charles de Gaulle, likewise, fancied his own chances at capturing the whole island for the Free French, provided that the British gave him the necessary air and naval cooperation. Neither the British nor the South Africans were willing to risk another joint venture with de Gaulle's forces after the débâcle at Dakar.

Churchill and his advisers mulled over these ideas for several months. Ultimately, the Prime Minister brushed aside doubts expressed by the Chief of the Imperial General Staff and the objections of his Director of Military Operations to 'Bonus', a plan to invade Madagascar. 'We are not setting out to subjugate Madagascar but rather to establish ourselves in key positions to deny it to a far-flung Japanese attack,' he reminded the Chiefs of Staff. The War Cabinet, as usual, gave the Prime Minister what he wanted. Smuts and Roosevelt were informed; de Gaulle was not.

The forces required for the operation, renamed 'Ironclad', interspersed themselves in the stream of reinforcements bound for India and Ceylon. They assembled in Cape Town at the end of April and then moved on to Durban a few days later before setting sail for the short voyage to Madagascar. The attack on 5 May was spearheaded by Force 121, a commando and three brigades of Royal Marines led by Major-General R. C. Sturges, RM, supported by air and naval gun protection afforded by a considerable task force comprising two British aircraft-carriers, the venerable dreadnought HMS *Ramillies*, two cruisers, eleven destroyers and thirty other vessels. It was the first large-scale amphibious operation conducted by British forces since Churchill's Dardanelles campaign of the First World War. Nevertheless, Madagascar is an island larger than metropolitan France and more than twice the size of the United Kingdom. The plan was predicated upon a hope that the French colonial governor would offer no more than token resistance. The French garrison was believed to number only 6,000 troops, mostly African, and a few ragtail aircraft. The two initial objectives therefore were confined to storming of the outstanding natural harbour at Diego Suarez on the northern tip of the island and seizure of an airfield five miles to the south. Against all odds, the French stoutly resisted, however, and Churchill finally ordered the overall commander of the task force, Vice-Admiral Sir Neville Syret, to break off the attack in order to give the French Governor-General of Madagascar, Armand Annet, time to reconsider his predicament.

Meanwhile, at the end of April, five fleet submarines of the Japanese Fourth Submarine Flotilla had proceeded from Penang across the Indian Ocean towards East Africa on the first of two special missions by such

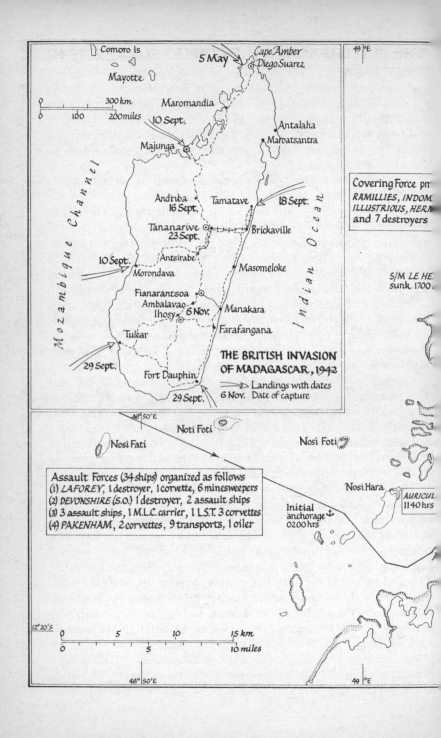

Comoro Is

Mayotte

5 May · Cape Amber · Diego Suarez

Maromandia

10 Sept.

Majunga

Antalaha
Maroatsantra

Mozambique Channel

Andriba
16 Sept.

Tamatave

18 Sept.

Tananarive
23 Sept.

Brickaville

Antsirabe

10 Sept.

Morondava

Masomeloke

Fianarantsoa

Ambalavao
Ihosy

6 Nov.

Manakara

Farafangana

Tulear

29 Sept.

Fort Dauphin

29 Sept.

Indian Ocean

**THE BRITISH INVASION
OF MADAGASCAR, 1942**

⟹ Landings with dates
6 Nov. Date of capture

0 ___ 300 km
0 ___ 100 ___ 200 miles

49°E

Covering Force pr—
RAMILLIES, INDOM—
ILLUSTRIOUS, HERM
and 7 destroyers

S/M *LE HE—*
sunk 1700

48° 50'E

Noti Foti

Nosi Fati

Nosi Foti

Nosi Hara

AURICUL—
1140 hrs

Initial
anchorage ⚓
0200 hrs

Assault Forces (34 ships) organized as follows
(1) *LAFOREY,* 1 destroyer, 1 corvette, 6 minesweepers
(2) *DEVONSHIRE* (S.O.) 1 destroyer, 2 assault ships
(3) 3 assault ships, 1 M.L.C. carrier, 1 L.S.T. 3 corvettes
(4) *PAKENHAM,* 2 corvettes, 9 transports, 1 oiler

12° 20'S

0 ___ 5 ___ 10 ___ 15 km
0 ___ 5 ___ 10 miles

48° 50'E

49°E

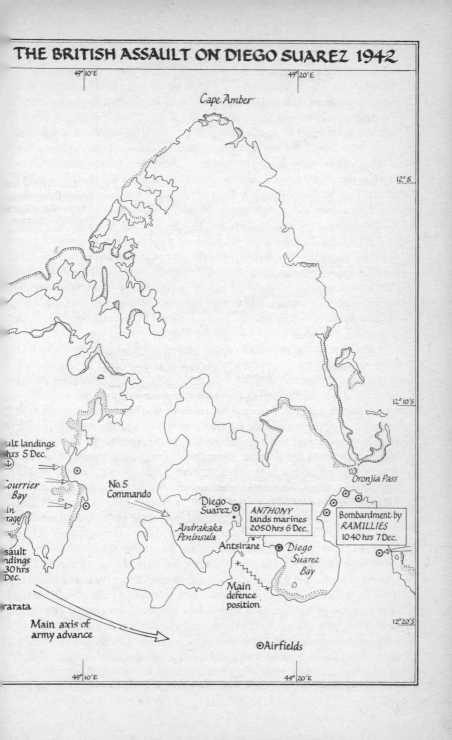

THE BRITISH ASSAULT ON DIEGO SUAREZ 1942

49° 10'E   49° 20'E

Cape Amber

12° S

12° 10'S

Oronjia Pass

ult landings
hrs 5 Dec.

ourrier
Bay

in
rage.

No. 5
Commando

Diego
Suarez

Andrakaka
Peninsula

Antsirane

ANTHONY
lands marines
2050 hrs 6 Dec.

Bombardment by
RAMILLIES
1040 hrs 7 Dec.

Diego
Suarez
Bay

sault
ndings
30 hrs
Dec.

Main
defence
position

rarata

Main axis of
army advance

12° 20'S

⊙Airfields

49° 10'E   49° 20'E

forces intended to distract Allied commanders from the forthcoming Midway and Aleutians campaign. Refuelled by two supply vessels which sailed with them, the little hunting pack soon reached its target zone. Floatplanes catapulted from the decks of the 2,400-ton headquarters submarine *I-10* and at least one scouting submarine searched in vain for enemy warships in the ports of East Africa from as early as the first week of May. They only narrowly missed finding the British task force at Durban by four days. The Japanese then headed north towards the commotion at Diego Suarez. During a reconnaissance flight over the British invasion force after nightfall on 29 May, one of the Japanese floatplanes was spotted by the British, who opened fire without result. The British forces were alerted but to no avail. On the next night, at a distance of about ten miles from the harbour entrance, two midget submarines of the same class as those launched prior to the Pearl Harbor attack were released from their mother ships, the *I-16* and *I-20* attack submarines. Penetrating the British defensive screen, they entered the harbour, sank a tanker and badly damaged HMS *Ramillies*. Only luck and efficient d. ..age control saved the battleship from total loss.

It was an effective reminder of that vulnerability which the British had every reason to fear in eastern waters, and it scuppered any remaining hopes that the desultory armistice negotiations then underway with Annet would lead to any early solution. As these negotiations dragged on without result, British patience waned. The Chiefs of Staff in London, concerned at recent reverses in the Middle East and worried at the possibility of a Japanese invasion of India, ruled out any resumption of the offensive on Madagascar until the broader strategic picture looked more favourable. As the summer drew to a close, a fresh East African brigade and a brigade of South African troops arrived in September to assist one of the brigades that had taken part in the initial landings and between them they mopped up what remained of the Vichy forces on the island. Two months later, the French governor finally surrendered in November after it had become abundantly clear that his position was untenable.

All but a remnant of the marines employed in the initial assault had re-embarked and sailed for India as soon as Diego Suarez itself was secured. Most of the naval support ships also quickly resumed their normal work. However the campaign as a whole was far more protracted than the British had anticipated. While the casualties sustained in the fighting had been light, malaria had cut a swath through the British troops during their cat and mouse game with the French after the initial struggle. Plans to reinforce frontline troops in India utilizing the forces engaged in this part of the Madagascan operation suffered setbacks and, according to the

British official history of the war against Japan, this in turn was to have a considerable effect upon Wavell's plans in the following months. This, like much of the Madagascan operation, remains a somewhat contentious point.

Ironically, the Japanese never had any intention of using Diego Suarez for themselves. Even Hitler recognized that the Vichy authorities would not have agreed to such a suggestion. The Japanese Navy regarded the Indian Ocean as a comparative backwater. They had missed a few opportunities yet they could look with satisfaction upon the whole Madagascan campaign as a fine short-term success.

Their next blow was another feint by submarines, this time delivered against Sydney Harbour in New South Wales. It was more or less intended as a carbon copy of the East African raid. Twenty-four hours after the attack on the British at Diego Suarez, a submarine-borne scout plane reconnoitred the harbour and escaped detection. On the following night four other submarines launched their midget submarines. The raiders sank one vessel of no military significance and failed to hit a nearby American heavy cruiser anchored in the harbour. The attack produced fright and pandemonium locally but had no greater result. Allied cryptanalysts had begun to unmask the true objectives of Yamamoto's main forces. Although it is tempting to compare the tip-and-run tactics of the Doolittle raiders and those of the Japanese submariners, their consequences were altogether dissimilar.

In May 1942 the United States became aware of the fact that the Japanese were concentrating massive land, sea and air forces in the Japanese Mandated Islands in preparation for another major offensive. At this point it was not clear where the Japanese intended to strike. For a time Admiral Nimitz, as Commander-in-Chief of the Pacific Fleet (CINCPAC), was advised by his cryptanalysts and radio traffic analysts that the next move of the enemy might well be to enlarge the Coral Sea operation into the maelstrom of a final main fleet action fought between the two sides. As early as 6 May, however, CINCPAC correctly revised this estimate and observed that the Japanese might move into the Central and North Pacific areas. The Navy Department's own cryptographic team in Washington, DC, Op20G, worked on similar material but still believed that the Japanese were intent on moving south. General MacArthur's people supplied him with information which supported his demands for 1,000 more aircraft, 100,000 fresh troops and two carriers of his own to add to his existing strength in the South-West Pacific: he anticipated that the Japanese intended to complete their conquest of New Guinea and

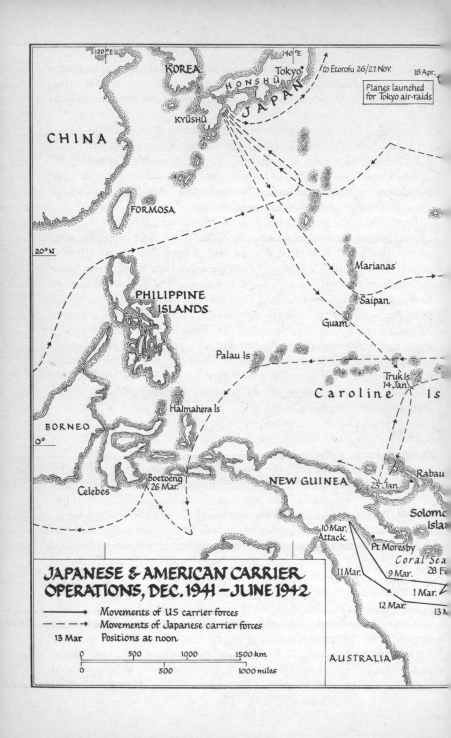

JAPANESE & AMERICAN CARRIER
OPERATIONS, DEC. 1941 – JUNE 1942

⟶ Movements of US carrier forces
⟶ Movements of Japanese carrier forces
13 Mar   Positions at noon

0 ___ 500 ___ 1000 ___ 1500 km
0 _____ 500 _____ 1000 miles

KOREA
Tokyo   to Etorofu 26/27 Nov.   18 Apr.

Planes launched
for Tokyo air-raids

HONSHŪ
JAPAN
KYŪSHŪ

CHINA

FORMOSA

20°N

PHILIPPINE
ISLANDS

Marianas
Saipan
Guam

Palau Is
Truk Is
14 Jan.

Caroline   Is

Halmahera Is

BORNEO

0°

Celebes

Boetoeng
26 Mar.

NEW GUINEA   23 Jan.   Rabau

Solomo
Isla

10 Mar.
Attack

Pt Moresby   Coral Sea

11 Mar.   9 Mar.   28 F

1 Mar.

12 Mar.   13 M

AUSTRALIA

120°E   140°E

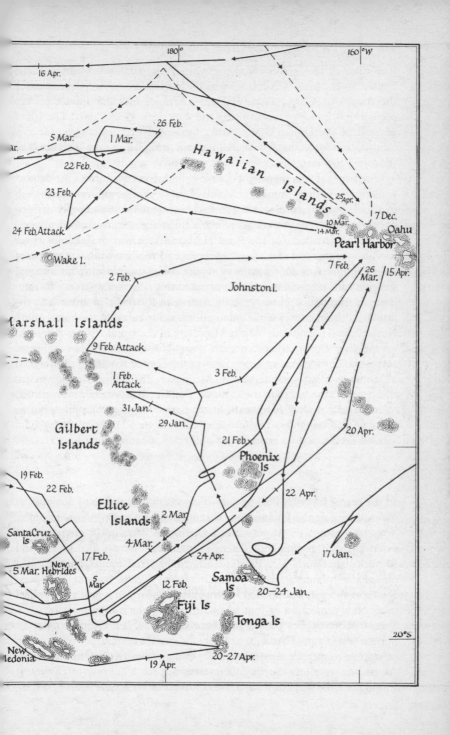

then catapult themselves on to the Australian mainland. Meanwhile the United States Army's Air Intelligence experts were advising the head of the Army Air Corps, General Henry Arnold, that the Japanese were preparing to mount an assault on the American West Coast. The Chief of Staff of the United States Army, however, withstood pleas for any massive reinforcement of the American position in the Pacific. The 'Europe First' strategy agreed with the British was in safe hands.

Whether that was the wisest course will always be a subject for debate. Franklin Roosevelt himself had his doubts. Public opinion, although unaware that any formal decision had been reached, was deeply divided over the issue. The American public's thirst for a campaign of revenge against the architects of the Pearl Harbor attack was unslakable. There was also the thought so bitterly expressed by President Mañuel Quezon of the Philippine Commonwealth as his life ebbed away during his unequal struggle with tuberculosis: 'I cannot stand this constant reference to England, to Europe . . . How typically American to writhe in anguish at the fate of a distant cousin while a daughter is being raped in the back room!' Nevertheless, the political centre of gravity in the United States remained on the East Coast, where concern about the spread of Nazi influence across the European continent and over the United Kingdom outweighed all countervailing considerations. Moreover, the Third Reich was incomparably stronger than the Japanese Empire. Most Americans regarded themselves as merely temporary foster parents of the Philippines but as the sons and daughters of European cultures that Hitler and Mussolini seemed determined to brutalize or obliterate. Europe came first.

THE CORAL SEA

In the spring of 1942, flushed with the success that they had achieved at the outbreak of the Pacific War, the Japanese embarked upon an ambitious new campaign. It was called Operation *Mo*, and it envisaged an extension of the Japanese defensive perimeter across the length and breadth of the South-West Pacific. It all stemmed from events that had taken place back in January, when the Japanese Navy seized Rabaul in the New Hebrides virtually unopposed and quickly transformed it into a major fleet base. Now protection of that base had to be given a high priority.

Port Moresby lies on the southern coast of New Guinea, near the northernmost tip of Australia. From its occupation Japan counted on being able to menace Australian ports and airfields (where they knew the Americans were busy sorting themselves out for a counter-offensive). It would open the way for a Japanese conquest of New Caledonia and that, in turn, might enable Japan to cut off the vital movement of military equipment and personnel already beginning to flow westwards from North America to Australia. Indeed the capture of Port Moresby, as some optimistic Japanese Army appreciation asserted, might even force Australia out of the war. The naval force needed for this operation appeared to be so small that, for once, the Army had the ready cooperation of the Navy, which, in a revival of a Japanese inter-service tradition going back hundreds of years, consented to convoy a Japanese Army landing-force. The Americans and the British agreed with the Japanese appreciation, and decided that, though still far from ready to offer serious opposition to the Japanese, the operation must be resisted.

It was several months after the Japanese took Rabaul when Imperial General Headquarters resolved to capture Port Moresby by a naval *coup de main*. This attack was scheduled for March. Then Japanese Intelligence reported that the Allied Powers were amassing forces to counter just such a move. Yamamoto ordered the operation to be delayed until early May. The Japanese then assembled a veritable armada of seventy ships, including two attack carriers detached from Admiral Nagumo's force on their way back to Japan after the Indian Ocean campaign. An additional light carrier, the little 12,000-ton converted submarine tender *Shōhō*, was ordered to join the force. The fleet also included a seaplane tender, half a dozen heavy cruisers, three light cruisers, fifteen destroyers and fourteen Army troop transports.

To meet this formidable threat, the Allied Powers hurriedly assembled a scratch fleet comparable in size, including two American attack carriers, the *Yorktown* and the *Lexington*, together with a British battleship, two American battleships, four heavy cruisers, four light cruisers and seventeen destroyers.

Yamamoto split his forces in the South-West Pacific Operation into seven parts under the operational command of Admiral Inoue Shigeyoshi at Rabaul. The Port Moresby Transport Force, led by Rear-Admiral Abe Kōsō and consisting of twelve Army and Marine troop transports, a mine-layer and a number of supply vessels, was earmarked for the occupation of Port Moresby. It would be escorted by Rear-Admiral Kajioka Sadamichi's small Port Moresby Attack Force of a light cruiser, five destroyers, a patrol boat and some other auxiliaries. Rear-Admiral Marumo Kuniori's Close Cover Force, comprising two light cruisers, a seaplane carrier and three gunboats, would help protect the landing operations where required. The more powerful elements of Inoue's fleet were divided into Vice-Admiral Takagi Takeo's Carrier Strike Force, comprising two heavy carriers, the *Zuikaku* and *Shōkaku*, escorted by two

heavy cruisers and six destroyers, and two support forces, both commanded by Rear-Admiral Gotō Aritomo, the first of which was designated
as a Close Support Force and consisted of a light carrier accompanied by
a single destroyer, and the Main Body Support Force, a powerful squadron of four heavy cruisers. The remaining section of the fleet was the
Tulagi Invasion Force under Rear-Admiral Shima Kiyohide, consisting
of two destroyers, two mine-layers, a troop transport and some auxiliary
craft. Each of these forces was given a separate mission to accomplish in
Yamamoto's complicated plan, which relied upon precision timing and
the convergence of sections from various points of the compass.

Knowing the main features of the Japanese plans – and that, of course,
made all the difference – the USS *Yorktown* and the *Lexington* hoped to
join forces in the New Hebrides, far to the south-east, and then to jump
the Japanese at Rabaul as soon as the enemy's attack developed. A mixed
cruiser squadron of two Australian cruisers and the USS *Chicago*, under
the command of Rear-Admiral J. G. Crace of the British Royal Navy,
would rendezvous with the two American carriers as they joined forces
to surprise the Japanese. The only other American carriers in the Pacific
were on their way home to Pearl Harbor after having taken part in
Jimmy Doolittle's Raid over the Japanese mainland: ordered to the South
Seas as soon as they refuelled, they arrived too late to take part in the
action which followed.

In April 1942 Japanese assault forces opened Operation *Mo* with the
subsidiary attack on Tulagi, an insignificant speck of land off the coast of
Florida Island in the mid-Solomons, just twenty miles off a far larger
island that was due to assume a greater significance in the months ahead:
Guadalcanal. Acting on information derived from 'Magic' intercepts and
augmented by the efficient 'Coastwatcher' bush-telegraph network organized by European and Australian planters and native islanders, the Australian garrison at Tulagi had been prudently withdrawn from the island
before it could be overwhelmed. The Japanese saw nothing suspicious in
this. They were intent upon their objective, which would soon be achieved,
of transforming the island into a major seaplane base to protect the
bastion which the Japanese were fast establishing at Rabaul, 600 miles to
the north-west, and the eastern flank of the Japanese forces then fighting
their way across New Guinea.

Confident of success, the Japanese anticipated that their next move
would be to utilize the Tulagi Invasion Force to block off the back alley
to their new property by taking Nauru Island and Ocean Island, 600 and
800 miles to the north-east. Then, secure in their new domains, the
Japanese would be well placed to dispose of any forces sent out to dislodge

them. Meanwhile, the assault on Port Moresby could be expected to entice the United States Pacific Fleet within range before it could recover from the losses it had sustained at Pearl Harbor. With good fortune, this might lead to the destruction of what remained of America's offensive capabilities at sea. It was just possible that the Midway Operation might prove to be unnecessary.

The Japanese believed that they could rely upon speed to achieve their objectives before the arrival of any Allied counterstroke. The Midway Operation was already scheduled to take place in June, and Admiral Yamamoto Isoruku, a master at poker as well as at other games of chance, anticipated that he would need to place nearly the whole resources of the Imperial Navy in the stakes at Midway if his gamble there were to succeed.

The Japanese plan began to unravel almost at once. On 4 May the Port Moresby Transport Force and the Close Cover Force were in the Louisades, expecting to rendezvous with the Port Moresby Attack Force before rounding the tip of New Guinea on their way to Port Moresby (which was already under attack by a naval air fleet operating out of Rabaul). To the north, off New Georgia Island, lurked the Distant Cover Force which would have to protect the Japanese flanks during both the Tulagi and Port Moresby invasions. Having approached the Solomons from the north, the Japanese Carrier Attack Force shortly moved south-easterly to skirt the islands on a course which was to take it round San Cristobal. At this moment aircraft from the USS *Yorktown* intercepted the Tulagi Invasion Force and broke its back. The *Yorktown*, acting completely independently, hared off alone to the doorstep of Tulagi when a reconnaissance aircraft from Australia reported that the Japanese were busy disembarking their forces there. This seemed too good an opportunity to be missed. On this occasion it might have been better to wait.

Swathed in a protective blanket of cloud and closing upon their enemy at 27 knots, the *Yorktown* and her destroyer escort neared the mid-Solomons and in a series of three strikes delivered by *Yorktown*'s aircraft in rapid succession, the Americans created havoc in the harbour area. But the light force of Rear-Admiral Shima's ships covering the Japanese landing were scarcely worth the effort. About half of that force was sunk, the seaplanes were cut to ribbons, and most of Shima's other vessels sustained heavy damage. But this sally by the *Yorktown* had deprived the Americans both of surprise and of the significant trophies that would have justified the effort. Up to this point, the Japanese had been completely ignorant of the fact that there were any American carriers in the vicinity. The Japanese landing force was evacuated, apart from a small

Kavieng

Bismarck Arch.

New
Ireland *Arch.*

Rabaul

Bismarck Sea

INVASION FOR[CE]
Transports & De[s-]
troyers from Rab[aul]
1800 hrs 4-Ma[y]

NEW GUINEA

PAPUA

Huon Gulf

Solomon

Joined b[y]
from Tula[gi]
force, mi[d]

Triobrand Is.

Woodlark I.

Gulf of
Papua

Port Moresby

Bombed by carrier
Force, 5 May

10°S

*Milne
Bay*

1030 h[rs]
Aust. ba[sed]
bomb *Sh[ōhō]*

0800 hrs 7 May.
Invasion Force
retires

SHŌHŌ b[ombed]
again an[d]
1135 hrs

Louisiade Arch.

0800 hrs 8 May

Under heavy air attack
from shore-based aircraft
1400-1445 hrs 7 May

1425 hrs
7 May

Attack groups
launched 1000[hrs?]

1358 hrs 7 May
air attack fails

2000hrs 7 May

2000hrs.
7 May

2000 hrs 8 May

2000 hrs 9 May

SUPPORT GROUP (Crace)
*AUSTRALIA HOBART
CHICAGO* 2 destroyers

Attack groups [?]
0900 hrs 8 Ma[y]
SHOKAKU and [?]

15°S

QUEENSLAND

AUSTRALIA

145°E

150°E

C O R A L

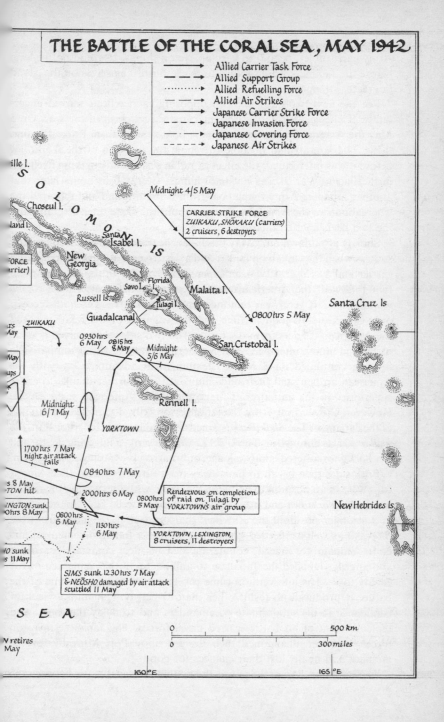

THE BATTLE OF THE CORAL SEA, MAY 1942

→ Allied Carrier Task Force
--→ Allied Support Group
······→ Allied Refuelling Force
—→ Allied Air Strikes
→ Japanese Carrier Strike Force
---→ Japanese Invasion Force
→ Japanese Covering Force
---→ Japanese Air Strikes

lle I.

S O L O M O N   I S

Choiseul I.

Midnight 4/5 May

land I.

Santa
Isabel I.

FORCE
arrier)

New
Georgia

CARRIER STRIKE FORCE
ZUIKAKU, SHOKAKU (carriers)
2 cruisers, 6 destroyers

Russell Is.

Florida I.
Savo I.
Tulagi I.

Malaita I.

Santa Cruz Is

Guadalcanal

0800 hrs 5 May

ZUIKAKU
ay

0930 hrs
6 May

0815 hrs
6 May

Midnight
5/6 May

San Cristobal I.

May

ups

Midnight
6/7 May

Rennell I.

YORKTOWN

1700 hrs 7 May
night air attack
fails

0840 hrs 7 May

8 May
TON hit

2000 hrs 6 May

0800 hrs
5 May

Rendezvous on completion
of raid on Tulagi by
YORKTOWN's air group

New Hebrides Is.

NGTON sunk
Ohrs 8 May

0800 hrs
6 May

1130 hrs
6 May

YORKTOWN, LEXINGTON,
8 cruisers, 11 destroyers

O sunk
s 11 May

X

SIMS sunk 12.30 hrs 7 May
& NEOSHO damaged by air attack
scuttled 11 May

S E A

0 ———————— 500 km
0 ———————— 300 miles

N retires
May

160° E

165° E

Army garrison left behind to keep an eye on things. It would not be long before the Japanese would return to re-establish themselves on the island in greater strength.

For the next two days, the two opposing carrier fleets moved uncertainly, if not nervously, towards their first direct clash of the war. On 5 May the Americans shot down a flying boat sent up from Rabaul to find them. The aircraft had no time to report the location of the *Yorktown* before it was intercepted: the effect of radar was already making itself felt in the Pacific War. It was not until almost twenty-four hours later that another Japanese Army flying boat from Rabaul found and reported the whereabouts of the American fleet. At about the same time, aircraft from the two fleets spotted their enemy's vessels.

Shortly after dawn on 7 May the Japanese were the first to achieve any success when they hit an oil tanker and a destroyer, initially mistaken for a carrier and a cruiser. It was an expensive error, for in the general mêlée that followed, the Americans sank the almost defenceless little *Shōhō* while its aircraft were away hunting the American carriers without success: only exceptionally good fortune and the vagaries of the weather saved the American carriers from discovery. The two sides then played a game of cat and mouse interspersed with sporadic bursts of aerial combat. The fighting continued on 8 May. The numerical advantage lay with the American airmen, and their odds improved still further thanks to a 2:1 superiority in the anti-aircraft firepower of the American surface fleet. However, this was offset by the far superior skill, discipline and aircraft of the Japanese. The *Shōkaku* sustained severe damage. Her sister ship, the *Zuikaku*, was untouched. The USS *Lexington* sank, a lingering death, and the *Yorktown* suffered bomb damage, only narrowly escaping serious harm.

Both sides then began to limp away from further trouble. The Americans were in no position to continue the battle without running the risk of losing the *Yorktown* and other valuable ships as well. The Japanese were in a stronger position: the *Zuikaku*, thanks to aircraft landed from the *Shōkaku* as well as its own squadrons, carried a full complement of aircraft. Yamamoto, indeed, countermanded his fleet commander's order and angrily signalled the Japanese to annihilate all that remained of the enemy force. His intervention came too late to alter the outcome of the battle. It produced no result other than to betray Yamamoto's lack of confidence in his subordinate commanders and to delay the repair and replenishment of his battle-scarred naval forces. The Japanese invasion forces, however, abandoned their designs upon Port Moresby for the moment and finally lost their chances for good.

The Battle of the Coral Sea was the first major naval battle between the two opposing sides to demonstrate the strengths and weaknesses which were to affect the future course of the war. It was a conflict entirely different in character from what had occurred before.

By standards of subsequent phases of the Pacific War, the Battle of the Coral Sea was amateurish and not particularly costly. The Americans and Crace's forces had lost sixty-six aircraft, 543 dead, the 42,000-ton USS *Lexington*, a single destroyer and a fleet oiler as well as the damage sustained by their only other carrier in the engagement, the USS *Yorktown*. The Japanese lost seventy-seven aircraft, 1,074 dead, the 12,000-ton carrier *Shōhō*, a destroyer and three auxiliary vessels. Strictly speaking, the Japanese had won the engagement but at a higher price than was immediately evident. Both of their other carriers in the engagement had been crippled. The two heavy aircraft-carriers returned safely to Japan, but in a condition which put them out of use for several months while undergoing repairs and the training of new flight crews. The absence of these two ships in the impending engagements was probably of decisive consequence.

There were lessons to absorb. The rival forces had never sailed within sight of one another, and the battle had resolved itself into a hunt for one another by their aircraft. It was the first naval battle in history to be decided by a struggle for air supremacy. The surface ships engaged in the action never exchanged fire.

The Japanese regarded the Battle of the Coral Sea as a success, although one costly enough to remind them of the possibilities of defeat. Tactically speaking, it was a Pyrrhic victory for the Japanese. In a wider context, the result was something of a draw. Japanese plotting officers and air controllers had proved themselves far superior to their enemy in the course of the battle, but Japanese combat communications and the coordination of their surface vessels had proved clumsy and unresponsive to the demands of a modern, highly mobile and rather confused mêlée. Beneath the unedifying and exaggerated claims and counter-claims made by the two sides, the *élan* of the Japanese naval command never recovered.

The Americans, though they were concerned about the eventual loss of the *Lexington*, were not entirely displeased at the result of the battle, which had brought to an end the run of easy and almost insolent successes by the Japanese. As a result of the air battles, the Americans drew various tactical conclusions and strengthened the force of fighter aircraft on their carriers. Yamamoto, it began to be whispered abroad, had allowed his methods of warfare to outstrip the personnel which would have made these decisive. Against this, the hit-rate of the Japanese aircraft against the enemy warships had achieved a remarkable 58 per cent, confounding pre-war estimates where figures as low as 3 per cent had been bandied about.

Although the Battle of the Coral Sea weakened both sides on what was to be the eve of the Battle of Midway, the really important fact that would become apparent only in retrospect was that the Battle of the Coral Sea thwarted the Japanese attack on Port Moresby and with it their advance towards the northern approaches of Australia. This was to prove of great significance for the future development of the war.

After the Coral Sea campaign, the Japanese Army wanted to mount another attack on Port Moresby, this time by an overland assault. Once that objective had fallen into Japanese hands, the Army hoped to cross the Coral Sea and invade northern Australia in order to counter the forces which MacArthur was building up for the re-conquest of the Southern Regions. The Naval General Staff, in their turn, was anxious to sever the long line of communications between North America and Australia by seizing New Caledonia, Samoa and the Fiji Islands. This scheme was abandoned when Admiral Yamamoto's Midway Island Campaign was adopted.

THE BATTLE OF MIDWAY

These two operations strengthened Yamamoto in his belief that the further acquisition of territory was not of consequence, and that any action which distracted Japanese power from its main preoccupations was dangerous. At his insistence, it was decided that Japan must concentrate its efforts on the destruction of what was left of the sea power of the Western Allies, especially of the American Pacific Fleet. He, who had inspired the raid on Pearl Harbor, was under no illusion about Japan's hopeless position if the war was prolonged, or until Japan had gained the full advantage which had been hoped for in that bombardment. At the moment when Japan at home was still exulting in the mastery of the lands in the South Seas, he saw only the danger preparing for it in the American dockyards. If the United States had the time to bring its economic strength into play, and to translate this into warships, the United States would be irresistible. Japan could find safety only by striking again, and at once.

Yamamoto had his mind set upon enticing the United States Pacific Fleet out to its destruction by his numerically superior forces. He had little option but to attempt this. His defensive line, 3,000 miles long, was in no sense a barrier impervious to enemy task forces advancing westwards across the Pacific. United States naval operations in the Atlantic and in the Caribbean had deprived the US Pacific Fleet of the superior numerical strength that had figured so largely in pre-war calculations. Nevertheless, United States task forces could be expected to penetrate the Japanese perimeter soon and at any point. Only a dynamic, not static, defence stood any chance of victory in the Pacific. Yamamoto perceived that the only hope of the Imperial Navy lay in luring those task forces into well-laid traps. To that end he formulated a masterful plan. It would incorporate features of Japan's traditional naval strategy, rehearsed a thousand times in Japanese blackboard and table-top exercises, a strategy based upon an attrition of the enemy by auxiliary forces prior to a main engagement from which there would be no escape. It would manifest all the intricacy and counterpoint that the Japanese had learnt from Chinese classical studies of the art of war. The rather simpler and more hidebound dogmas of Admiral Alfred Thayer Mahan and the strictures of Admiral Sir Herbert Richmond, although understood and appreciated by the Japanese, would be expected to limit the initiative of the Americans, who would find themselves mystified, befuddled and demoralized by the dazzling synchronization and complexity that the Japanese attack would display. It was to be an operation, then, well worthy of this historic occasion in the destiny of nations.

Yamamoto urged, and after strong dissent from the Naval General Staff had it accepted, that Japan's next move should be a conquest of Midway, a small coral outcrop composed of two tiny islands less than 1,200 acres in size, linked together to form a circular atoll located near the geographical centre of the North Pacific, where the prevailing oceanic currents sweep 1,100 miles west by north-west of Pearl Harbor along the arc of the Hawaiian Islands. The Doolittle Raid, quite apart from its other consequences, had convinced the Japanese Government and High Command that Yamamoto had been right all along in advocating the importance of depriving the United States of its commanding position in Hawaii.

Hawaii, then, as recent scholarship now shows, was the ultimate objective of the great strategical game that ended in disaster for Japan at Midway. In any event, there were other sufficiently compelling reasons for the Japanese to regard the capture of Midway as a major prize worthy of the risks and expense involved in the operation. If Midway fell into Japan's hands, it would be ideal for mounting Japanese raids against the Pacific coast of America. Yamamoto counted on the United States accepting that its defence was of vital interest, and that it would bring out what was left of the American Navy in its defence. In the battle which would result, he reckoned on sinking the American carriers; and this was the main objective of the expedition. The force which chance had put beyond Japan's reach at Pearl Harbor he would now succeed in driving into action.

Another motive which also weighed with him was to deprive America of the possible use of Midway Island as the airfield for the bombardment of Japan. Though Midway Island had played no part in the recent Doolittle air raid, Midway was only 2,500 miles from Tokyo. Yamamoto felt himself heavily burdened by the duty of protecting the capital of his lord the Emperor from the indignity of bombardment. Everything pointed to Midway Island as the next target at which he should strike. Yamamoto hoped that if the Combined Fleet decisively won the Battle of Midway, as he expected, he could ride the crest of his personal popularity to induce Prime Minister Tōjō to offer the United States a generous peace on terms that the United States could not afford to refuse. Yamamoto's plan involved the extension of Japan's defensive perimeter 2,000 miles into the Pacific through a balletic sequence of offensives executed by half a dozen task forces.

The United States had been in occupation of Midway Island since as long ago as 1867; but it was only in 1938, two years after the expiration of the Washington Treaty limitations, that it recognized its importance. It began to spend large sums of money in fortifying it as a kind of outpost of Pearl Harbor. It was to prove one of the chief theatres of the Pacific War. It was a small coral atoll; the colours, in the dazzling sunshine, were so bright and assertive that they wearied the eye. In the years just before the war, the Americans had built a small but very up-to-date hotel. Its public rooms had, uncannily, the feeling of mountain hotels in, say, Austria; it was strange because the nearest mountains were thousands of miles away; the illusion was heightened because the views from the hotel rooms might have been alpine. The vivid white of the ubiquitous coral might have been snow. The strangest phenomenon of the island was its prehistoric appearance. On all sides were small, gnarled, dried-up, gaunt trees, of stilted and incredible shape, looking like fossils. The whole place was unnaturally silent. There were noises of traffic and motor cars; but behind this a great hush prevailed. The impression was unreal and nightmarish. This was now to be the scenery for one of the greatest battles of the war.

The Japanese assembled a huge fleet. It included eight aircraft-carriers of which four were very large, eleven battleships, twenty-two cruisers, sixty-five destroyers and twenty-one submarines. It was the greatest fleet concentration which had been known in the history of the Pacific. The 145 ships in the fleet were divided into no less than sixteen divisions under four separate commands each assigned a role in Yamamoto's grand strategy to envelop the American fleet. Admiral Nagumo's First Carrier Striking Force, in which were four aircraft-carriers, two battleships, one heavy cruiser, one light cruiser and eleven destroyers, was to make for Midway. They would operate in close support of Vice-Admiral Kondō's Midway Invasion Force, consisting of two battleships, one light carrier, two seaplane carriers, eight heavy cruisers, two light cruisers, twenty-one destroyers and one patrol boat. Under the shadow of Kondō's formidable gunnery was a convoy of fifteen transports under Rear-Admiral Tanaka Raizō carrying an Army regimental force of 3,000 troops and two battalions of marines to form the necessary landing party. Following this, 300 miles in the rear, lurked an even more powerful surface fleet, designated Main Force. It comprised seven battleships, one light carrier, two seaplane carriers (one loaded with midget submarines), three light cruisers and twenty-one destroyers. Very oddly, Yamamoto, who this time did not confine himself to making the general plan of action and supervising it from his headquarters in Japan, placed himself aboard the 72,000-ton monster battleship *Yamato* in command of this section. It was held in reserve to take whatever action might be required after the invasion of Midway, but its intended role was to spring the trap when the United States main battlefleet emerged from its lair at Pearl Harbor to break up the landings. The fourth section of the Japanese fleet, Northern Force, commanded by Vice-Admiral Hosogaya and grouped round two carriers supported by three heavy cruisers, three light cruisers, an armed merchant cruiser, twelve destroyers and three troop transports, was to detach itself from the main body and to move up to the Aleutian Islands, attacking and landing on some selected places three days before the invasion of Midway. This was included in the general plan as the complication and the feint which nearly all Japanese plans contained. The concept was that the United States would divide whatever forces were available to it, and one force would sail for the North Pacific in search of this decoy.

The plan as a whole was a re-run of the Battle of Jutland, in which the stage encompassed the whole of the mid-Pacific rather than the confines of the North Sea. As in the classical, time-honoured battle plan upon which Japan had relied prior to 1941, an advance screen of Japanese submarines, spread across the line of the American advance, would weaken and demoralize the American main fleet as it sailed towards its obliteration in a final duel to the death. Any misjudgement of the American response on the part of Yamamoto and his commanders, however, would doom the Japanese fleet to the destruction of its widely dispersed divisions. It was a calculated risk which went contrary to Admiral Mahan's injunction against divisions into inferior fleets. It ignored Admiral Richmond's reminders that larger capital ships and carriers were not necessarily more capable of performing their mission than smaller ones. It was, however, a gamble worthy of the player, and it went wrong.

From the start there were grave doubts about the expedition among the Japanese Naval Staff, as indeed there were, privately, in the upper echelons of the Combined Fleet. There was anxiety about the deficient preparation of officers, about their inadequate briefing, about the speed with which the expedition was launched, about the lack of time for adequate digestion of the lessons of the Battle of the Coral Sea, about the wisdom of the tactics which had been used in that, about the security which had been observed, even about the morale of some of the fleet. The senior officers were despondent at the boasting and indiscipline of some of the younger men. The Navy pilots, whom Yamamoto had trained, were held in suspicion by the rest of the Navy, and this was not relieved by their tendency to regard themselves as a race apart. Especially by the more responsible officers, Yamamoto was criticized for the speed which he demanded. This meant that the two powerful aircraft-carriers which had been badly damaged in the Battle of the Coral Sea could not take part; they had to be in dock under repair for several months. Their absence was severely felt. So was the fact that the remaining carriers and their crews, worked to the limits of their endurance since 7 December, were sorely in need of extensive refurbishment and rest. But Yamamoto felt that the political situation required immediate action, and everything was subordinated to this.

The sailing of the fleet from Hashira through the Bungo Channel on 21 May for two days of fleet exercises was one of the most spectacular sights in any country during the war years. There were cheers and enthusiasm from the considerable crowd who witnessed it. The Japanese, though they lived with extreme frugality on all their expeditions, contrasting spectacularly in this with the standards of well-being required by British and American forces, observed ritual and ceremony for commemorating the start of a major operation. On their return to their anchorages on 25 May, Yamamoto gathered together his senior commanders to issue them with final instructions. On 27 May, Navy Day, celebrations were held in harbour to mark the anniversary of Admiral Tōgō's victory over the Russians at Tsushima. All present were conscious that the destiny of Japan now lay with them. The sailing of a fleet which was intended to complete the work of Pearl Harbor and to destroy the capacity of the American Navy to restrain Japan in Asia, was blessed by all the forms of Shinto, the Japanese state religion, and also, though less wholeheartedly, by Buddhism. Cups of sake were drunk which were a present from the

Japanese Emperor. Early on the morning of 28 May, the first elements of Yamamoto's forces weighed anchor, sailing away from Hashira and from other harbours for their appointed positions. For two days, other ships followed at pre-set intervals. The weather was fair, and along the shores, where people once more gathered to watch in awe as the ships departed, it was widely rumoured that the destination of the fleet was Midway. Yamamoto, however, hoped that the complexity of his plan would disguise his ultimate objective. He knew from intercepted radio transmissions that American submarines reported his departure. Western scholars, reading of these scenes, may remember the account by Thucydides of the sailing of another fleet on what was meant to be the culminating operation of a war 2,300 years before:

The ships being now manned, and everything with which they meant to sail being put on board, the trumpet commanded silence, and the prayers customary before putting out to sea were offered, not in each ship by itself, but by all together to the voice of the herald; and bowls of wine were mixed through all the armament, and libations made by the soldiers and their officers in gold and silver goblets. In their prayers joined also the crowds on shore, the citizens and all others that wished them well. The hymns sung and the libations finished, they put out to sea, and sang. The first ships then raced each other in columns as far as Aegina.

The battle came on 4 June 1942. The Americans had been better informed than Japanese Intelligence allowed for, and had again been admirably served by what they were able to learn from cracking the Japanese naval codes. On 1 April the Japanese Naval General Staff had taken the precaution of distributing new codes to the fleet, but the United States Navy had recovered a set of codebooks and cipher tables from a Japanese fleet submarine sunk in shallow waters off the coast of Australia in January. This, together with the activities of a United States Navy codebreaking team based in Hawaii, had enabled the Americans to unravel vital naval ciphers that had previously eluded them. Problems in distributing the new codebooks led the Japanese to delay their introduction until 1 June. By then it was too late. The broad outlines of the Japanese plans were known (although it would take the Americans months to adapt to the new codes afterwards).

We may pause to marvel at the fact that on the other side of the globe German naval Intelligence had come to believe that the Japanese naval ciphers were being read by the Allied Powers. Their long-standing suspicions had been confirmed by documentary evidence acquired after the German surface raider *Thor* intercepted the Australian steamer *Nankin* in the Indian Ocean on its way from Sydney to Colombo on 10 May 1942: mail bags found aboard the vessel included Intelligence summaries prepared by the Combined Operations Intelligence Centre at Wellington. In spite of this hard information, the Germans remained silent, doing nothing to alert the Japanese. It was a decision which speaks volumes about the contemptuous disregard of the Germans for their most powerful ally, and it was a disastrous misjudgement.

The Americans, then, and their British Allies were aware of what Japan had gone to ingenious lengths to hide: that Yamamoto's main objective was Midway, and that the assault on the Aleutians was a diversion. Yamamoto was right in supposing that the Americans would fight, even though their Navy had not yet recovered from Pearl Harbor, and was manifestly not ready; he was wrong in thinking that they would divide their inadequate fleet, and would send a part to hunt for the raiders in the Aleutians. The Americans could assemble on the spot three aircraft-carriers: in the whole American Navy at this time there were seven. One of these carriers was the *Yorktown*, which had been so heavily damaged in the Coral Sea that the Japanese believed it sunk, and had accredited themselves with a groundless victory. In fact it escaped to Hawaii, and, while the Japanese ships in a similar plight had entered the Japanese shipyards for thorough repairs, and were out of action for some months, the Hawaiian shipyards, under pressure of the news about Midway, made the *Yorktown* fit for fighting again in three days, though their first estimate had been that it would take three months: 1,400 men worked on her round the clock. The Americans also assembled eight cruisers and fifteen destroyers. The Japanese had therefore a more formidable resistance to overcome than they had thought it possible for the United States to assemble, especially as they also underestimated the American strength in aircraft and troops on Midway.

The poor state of Japanese naval Intelligence at Midway is illustrated by an expectation at the Imperial General Headquarters that the Invasion Force would have to overcome 750 American troops and 60 land-based enemy aircraft. It was anticipated that the 5,000 Japanese marines and close to 234 operational Japanese naval aircraft available to cover them would quickly overwhelm the defenders. In fact, however, Midway was protected by a battalion of more than 3,000 marines and 126 aircraft, and since the 230 aircraft in the combined task forces of Rear-Admiral Raymond Spruance and Rear Admiral Frank Jack Fletcher were lying in wait for the Japanese to strike, the odds were stacked heavily against the success of the invasion.

Bad preliminary Intelligence on the Japanese side was compounded by haphazard fleet reconnaissance during the operation. The over-confidence felt by the Japanese naval forces affected every aspect of the battle in its initial phases. Luck favoured the Americans as it had at the Battle of the Coral Sea. Ever since March, Kawanishi flying boats based in the Marshall Islands had flown periodic night-time reconnaissance missions over Pearl Harbor, hazardous undertakings made possible only by refuelling from big I-class submarines at an isolated anchorage known as French Frigate Shoals. Between 27–30 May, however, while the USS *Yorktown* was under repair at Pearl Harbor, the submarines signalled Tokyo that a tanker, two American destroyers and two flying boats were patrolling the reef where the rendezvous was expected to take place: the Americans, having discovered what the Japanese were doing, were determined to put a stop to it. On 30 May the Naval General Staff ordered the flights suspended. Unaccountably, the Japanese had failed to provide a fall-back plan and no attempt was made to divert the submarine to nearby Necker Island where refuelling could have taken place. Had a flight been possible on the following day, the Japanese would have found Pearl Harbor empty: the hunted had turned hunters. Meanwhile Yamamoto had sent out thirteen I-class submarines to form a picket line between Pearl Harbor and Midway. They were intended to detect the approach of the American fleet and then to attack it. They arrived too late: the Americans were already in the vicinity of Midway. Although Yamamoto had not expected to surprise the Americans at Midway, the Japanese Fleet continued to remain in the dark concerning the size and location of the US Pacific Fleet.

The Japanese Navy had no radar. That Japan, and that Admiral Yamamoto, who had espoused everything to do with the air, had neglected to acquaint himself with this invention, is astonishing. The fact must detract something from Yamamoto's reputation for alertness. Radar had already been widely used in Britain for more than two years, and a form of it was also known in Germany. The Germans sent the Japanese two radar sets by submarine, but either they did not send technicians with the apparatus, or these made no impression upon the Japanese. This incident, together with the Germans' failure to advise the Japanese about the insecurity of the Japanese ciphers, shows how slight and ineffective was much of the technical cooperation of the two Powers. In the present case the deficiencies of Intelligence, working without adequate equipment, was to exact a price.

As the two American task forces awaited the approaching Japanese, a US Navy Catalina PBY flying boat, only thirty miles within the extreme range of his aircraft, early on the morning of 3 June located Rear-Admiral

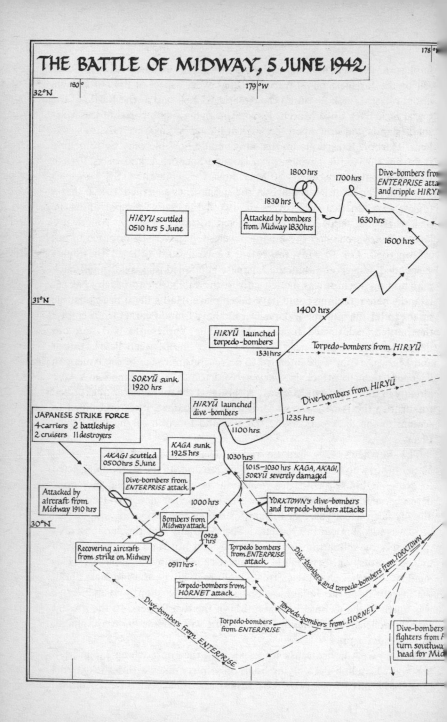

THE BATTLE OF MIDWAY, 5 JUNE 1942

178°

180° 179°W

32°N

31°N

30°N

1800 hrs 1700 hrs

Dive-bombers from ENTERPRISE atta... and cripple HIRY...

1830 hrs

HIRYŪ scuttled 0510 hrs 5 June

Attacked by bombers from Midway 1830 hrs

1630 hrs

1600 hrs

1400 hrs

HIRYŪ launched torpedo-bombers 1331 hrs

Torpedo-bombers from HIRYŪ

SORYŪ sunk 1920 hrs

HIRYŪ launched dive-bombers

Dive-bombers from HIRYŪ

1235 hrs

1100 hrs

JAPANESE STRIKE FORCE
4 carriers 2 battleships
2 cruisers 11 destroyers

KAGA sunk 1925 hrs

1030 hrs

1015-1030 hrs KAGA, AKAGI, SORYŪ severely damaged

AKAGI scuttled 0500 hrs 5 June

Dive-bombers from ENTERPRISE attack.

1000 hrs

YORKTOWN's dive-bombers and torpedo-bombers attacks

Attacked by aircraft from Midway 1910 hrs

Bombers from Midway attack

0928 hrs

Torpedo bombers from ENTERPRISE attack

Dive-bombers and torpedo-bombers from YORKTOWN

Recovering aircraft from strike on Midway

0917 hrs

Torpedo-bombers from HORNET attack

Torpedo-bombers from HORNET

Dive-bombers from ENTERPRISE

Torpedo-bombers from ENTERPRISE

Dive-bombers, fighters from ... turn southwa... head for Mid...

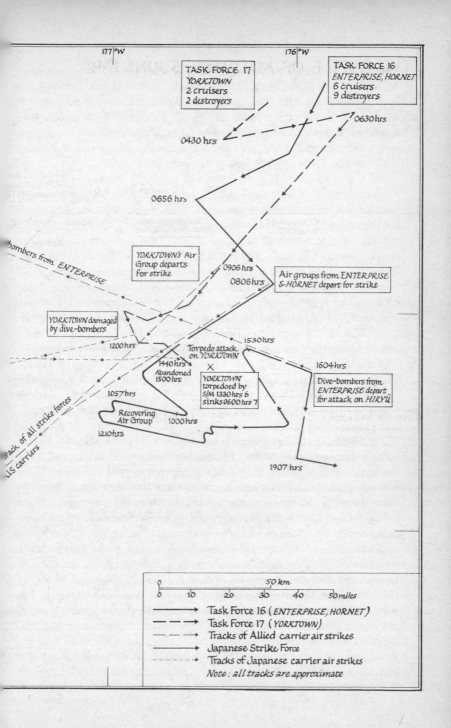

177°W   176°W

TASK FORCE 17
YORKTOWN
2 cruisers
2 destroyers

TASK FORCE 16
ENTERPRISE, HORNET
6 cruisers
9 destroyers

0630 hrs

0430 hrs

0656 hrs

bombers from *ENTERPRISE*

YORKTOWN's Air
Group departs
for strike

0906 hrs

0806 hrs

Air groups from *ENTERPRISE*
& *HORNET* depart for strike

YORKTOWN damaged
by dive-bombers

1200 hrs

1530 hrs

Torpedo attack
on *YORKTOWN*

X

1140 hrs
Abandoned
1500 hrs

YORKTOWN
torpedoed by
S/M 1330 hrs 6
sinks 0600 hrs 7

1604 hrs

Dive-bombers from
ENTERPRISE depart
for attack on *HIRYŪ*

1057 hrs

rack of all strike forces

Recovering
Air Group

1000 hrs

1210 hrs

US carriers

1907 hrs

0   50 km
0   10   20   30   40   50 miles

→ Task Force 16 (*ENTERPRISE, HORNET*)
→ Task Force 17 (*YORKTOWN*)
→ Tracks of Allied carrier air strikes
→ Japanese Strike Force
→ Tracks of Japanese carrier air strikes
Note: all tracks are approximate

Tanaka Raizō's Second Fleet Occupation Escort Force 670 miles west of Midway. A few hours later, nine land-based B17 bombers attacked this force, scoring no hits. Before the B17s returned, four Catalinas left Midway in search of the same targets. In a moonlit night attack, they torpedoed a tanker and raked one of Tanaka's fifteen troop transports with machine-gun fire. As the Catalina crews neared home, their radios reported that Midway itself was under enemy air attack.

At 4.30 a.m., 108 Japanese aircraft prepared for take-off aboard Admiral Nagumo's four carriers in fine weather and calm seas 220 miles west of Midway. Within a quarter of an hour, 36 Aichi high-level bombers and 36 Nakajima torpedo bombers accompanied by 36 Zero fighters were airborne. Half an hour later, a Catalina reconnaissance aircraft sighted the *Akagi* and flashed its location to Midway. The USS *Enterprise* overheard the exchange and passed the message to the USS *Yorktown*. Another Catalina reported sighting the incoming enemy aircraft heading for Midway at a distance of 150 miles from the atoll. Within minutes radar installations on Midway began tracking the Japanese aircraft. At 5.53 a.m. every American aircraft on Midway capable of flight was ordered into the air to meet the enemy.

A motley collection of 6 Navy Avenger torpedo bombers, 16 Marine Corps Dauntless dive bombers, 16 Army B17s and 4 strange torpedo-carrying B26s left Midway in a splendidly brave but vain effort to destroy Nagumo's Carrier Strike Force. They caused little direct damage. Few of them survived.

The air raid on Midway went ahead at 6.34 a.m. In the one-sided aerial combat that ensued, 17 of the 27 hopelessly outdated Buffaloes and Wildcat fighter aircraft flown by US Marine Corps airmen perished. Of the remaining 10, 7 sustained such severe damage that they would never fly again. None of the Japanese aircraft fell victim to the American fliers, a tribute to the skills of the Japanese and to the performance of the latest Japanese Zeke fighters (which were incomparably superior to the Zeros that had proved so successful in the opening days of the Pacific War). Nevertheless, exceptionally accurate anti-aircraft fire took a toll of 38 Japanese aircraft and disabled a further 29. That left Nagumo with only 167 aircraft to match against the 230 of the American carriers. The advantages of experience and better aircraft still lay with the Japanese, but it was apparent that Admiral Yamamoto had been unfortunate in frittering away a third of his total air combat forces by detaching the *Ryūjō* and *Junyō* to the Aleutian Campaign, the *Hōshō* to his Main Force battleships and the *Zuiho* to Admiral Kondō's Second Fleet.

The first that the Japanese admiral commanding the aircraft-carrier, who was again Nagumo, knew of the proximity of the Americans was when, about 9 a.m. on 4 June, he was surprised by an American raid when he had his aircraft assembled on deck for a raid on Midway, but when they had not yet taken off. As it appeared afterwards, the fate of the mighty armada, of the Midway expedition, and of the possibility of a future descent on the American coast, was decided in five minutes. Nagumo's carrier was torpedoed at this time, and three of the four carriers in his Strike Force were mortally struck. The battle continued all that day, very similar to the Coral Sea, with the two navies out of sight of each other; this time the Japanese pilots, in contrast to the Americans, proved definitely inferior. The action was a confused affair of aircraft from each side which savagely attacked the others, and then pounced on each other's carriers when they were inadequately guarded.

The Japanese had more than their share of misfortune. Radio messages were received five minutes too late; cloud movements happened in such a way as just to obscure the movements of the enemy. But in all the confusion, it is clear that on this occasion the high commanders, and the Japanese Navy as a whole, did not display the professionalism, the power of rapid adaptation, the coolness amid the horrors of air combat at sea, which were necessary to bring victory in this kind of action.

Apart from the deficiencies in their communications equipment, the defects in the Japanese Fleet were personal rather than mechanical. Japan did not lose the battle because of the engineering superiority of the United States. In the actual fighting, the Japanese aircraft, the Zeke fighter, which was first tried out at Midway, was the best plane on either side.

Skilful shiphandling by the Japanese, far superior skill by the Japanese pilots in their even more superior aircraft – all of this was set at nought by reconnaissance failures and errors in judgement of Admiral Yamamoto, Admiral Nagumo and their subordinate commanders. Yamamoto himself cannot escape blame for his failure to obtain reliable Intelligence confirming his assumptions that the *Yorktown* had perished in the Coral Sea and that the *Hornet* and *Enterprise* had remained in the South-West Pacific. Equally, he alone had the responsibility of determining the moment when the screen of submarines should take their appointed place in the line: it is difficult to fathom why he failed to dispatch them earlier. These errors were compounded by his inability to change the plan once it was set in motion. He and his subordinate commanders were handicapped by a completely inadequate radio communications system. Even after his forces were detected, Yamamoto imposed a radio silence throughout the battle; he was virtually a spectator of the action. Thus Yamamoto, his fleets widely and needlessly dispersed, condemned himself to impotence in the kind of battle which he had for so long preached as inevitable at the stage which naval strategy had reached at the time.

The American fleet, as it appeared later, did not realize for some time how complete and profound their victory had been. In the confusion of the conflict, they assumed for some time that two of the carriers, which had in fact been sunk, had escaped and were on their way back to Japan. Ultimately the facts were established and they were these. Within the space of twenty-four hours, Japan had lost all four of its largest aircraft-carriers (the fourth sank later in the day) and a heavy cruiser. Another heavy cruiser suffered serious damage, two destroyers were disabled, and three further vessels including a battleship were slightly damaged. The Japanese had lost a total of 332 aircraft, including 10 flying boats, 6 aircraft shot down by anti-aircraft fire during the Midway air strike, 12 fighters that failed to return from combat air patrol, 24 aircraft lost in attacking the American carriers, and another 280 (including 70 partially dismantled fighter aircraft which the carriers were ferrying to Midway) that went down when their carriers sank. A total of 3,500 Japanese sailors lost their lives.

By contrast, the American losses were the *Yorktown*, which was finally sunk, a destroyer, 38 shore-based aircraft, 109 carrier-based aircraft, and 307 lives. A number of ground installations on Midway were destroyed and others were temporarily put out of action.

The nature and source of the losses reveals the scale of the Japanese misfortune. The Imperial Navy lost a high percentage of its best pilots not in air combat (where they continued to excel) but aboard the carriers where the Americans caught them rearming their aircraft. Others dropped one by one into the sea when their fuel supplies were exhausted and there was nowhere else left to land. These airmen, many veterans of the China Incident and years of training, were irreplaceable. Midway marked a turning-point in the fortunes of the Pacific War, and the Japanese Navy never again fought from a position of strength.

Admiral Yamamoto, with the Main Force of battleships, made some effort at retrieving the disaster. He ordered Vice-Admiral Tanaka's Invasion Force back to Japan before it had even attempted to storm the Island of Midway. He recalled the aircraft-carriers which had been sent to the Aleutians, and resumed the hunt for the American carriers, which had destroyed his own fleet. But, in the end, he broke off the battle, partly, it seems, because he felt he could no longer rely on Japanese Intelligence, and because he wisely decided not to risk his battleships further. He brought the Combined Fleet home to Japan, reorganized it, and with an oddly disembodied sense of purpose, laid plans for what should be done next.

Only the Alaskan venture wént ahead to achieve a modest success before it petered out in aimless sailings. An American weather station, fuel dumps, a handful of vessels and a few aircraft were attacked at Dutch Harbor on the eastern end of the Aleutians. Japanese troops made unopposed landings on Attu and Kiska at the extreme western end of the island chain and thereby had the distinction of becoming the only enemy garrisons ever to establish themselves on the soil of the Western Hemisphere at any time during the Second World War. Without the strength of the Combined Fleet to give it support, it was to be only a question of time before it would wither on the vine. It was a thoroughly bad detachment. Eventually the Americans were sufficiently distracted by the bait to tie up tens of thousands of troops and considerable naval forces in what became a protracted effort to recapture the two islands. But from the Japanese point of view it became costly to maintain the garrisons, which anyway suffered excruciating hardships. Any small gains produced by their fortitude and endurance, however, were as nothing compared to the importance of the losses sustained by the Japanese at Midway.

The Japanese Government, very prudently, did not allow the shock of the defeat and the collapse of hopes to become public. Its first aim was to hush up the defeat. Admiral Kondō Nobutake, to whom Yamamoto had handed command of Admiral Nagumo's carriers after the latter's disgrace, said: 'Our forces suffered a reverse so decisive and so grave that details of it were kept as a secret to all but a limited circle, even within the Japanese Navy. Even after the war, few among high ranking officers were familiar with the details of the Midway operation.'* A Japanese naval captain complained of the way that the returning sailors were held incommunicado. The wounded were brought ashore after dark, and taken to hospital through the rear entrances. He was himself among those who suffered. The experience is described in *Midway: The Battle that Doomed Japan* by Fuchida and Okumiya.† 'My room was in complete isolation,' he says. 'No nurses or medical attendants were allowed in, and I could not communicate with the world outside. All the wounded from Midway were treated like this. It was like being a prisoner of war among your own people.' After the Japanese surrender in 1945, all the papers that the Japanese authorities could

* John Deane Potter, op. cit.

† Fuchida and Okumiya, *Midway: The Battle that Doomed Japan*, US Naval Institute, Hutchinson, London, 1957.

find about the defeat, classified as top secret, were burned. The extent and gravity of the disaster which Japan had suffered did not become plain to the Japanese public until publication of accounts of the battle by survivors in the course of the 1950s.

The long run of sensational Japanese victories, bought at such little cost, had come finally to an end. The crippling of the US Pacific Fleet at Pearl Harbor, and the blows at the Royal Navy, had all been made at the ridiculously small expense of the loss of four destroyers. This period was over. At Midway a technically smaller American fleet had challenged the passage of the Japanese Imperial Navy, had defeated it, had turned it back. It had lost prestige hopelessly, it had lost the *élan* of victory, and the margin of its losses turned decisively against it. It had forfeited its ability to strike where it chose, and to govern the course of the war. Having lost this initiative, it had condemned Japan to convert the war into a holding operation – this, as Admiral Yamamoto had warned, condemned Japan to defeat by the United States as soon as the American economic mobilization was complete.

CHAPTER 20

MacArthur in the Pacific

THE naval war between Japan and the United States was to be waged henceforward with the utmost ferocity in the crucial theatre of the South-West Pacific. Japan had not foreseen that its action there would become so critical for its fate: but it had lost the freedom of action at the Battle of Midway Island. The United States set itself to wrest the South-West Pacific from its hold, and Japan, which had committed itself heavily in the region, set itself doggedly to oppose it, first of all trying to enlarge its position, and later selling its territory inch by inch, and with such grimness that it hoped that the United States would become tired of the enterprise.

As the fighting grew in intensity, it gradually became plain that, in this Pacific theatre, the war against Japan could be won. The Pacific offered the path to Tokyo. Interest fell away from the other theatres and other activities, from India and from China, and was concentrated on two American commanders, General Douglas MacArthur and Admiral Chester Nimitz, who shared the direction of events in this region.

General MacArthur, in whom burned most clearly the determination to restore the United States' position, and whose skill, confidence and military genius were thought to have made him the most effective commander for the purpose, had in March 1942 been ordered to withdraw from the fighting in the Philippines. He began his duel with Japan under something of a cloud. His withdrawal from the Philippines, though it had been ordered by Roosevelt, and though it was common sense, had, in the hectic atmosphere of the time, been criticized by the American Army, especially by the troops he had left behind. MacArthur was a general whose behaviour often flouted the conventions of the day. In the Philippines he had won disapproval by insisting that his wife and family should remain with him: he was able to do so because he had been under Filipino regulations and was free of American Army discipline. This singular man was to impose himself on the American and Australian Armies, who were almost fanatical in their dislike of privilege, and to make himself respected by virtue of his cult of personality if not superiority.

On his escape from Manila in a speedboat, he had had an adventurous voyage to the southern tip of the Philippines. When he got there, he found difficulty in going further. Rivalry between the American services made the American admiral in command in the region unwilling to spare any aircraft for his rescue. Application had to be made over his head through Washington to transport MacArthur to Australia.

It had been agreed between President Roosevelt and Churchill that operations in Australia should be under an American command, and to this post MacArthur was designated. The Australian forces, many of them battle-trained in the Middle East, passed under his control. On taking over, MacArthur found the Australians thinking in terms of defence. Their morale had been shattered by the events in Singapore, which they had been accustomed to thinking of as a guarantee of Australian security, and they did not quickly adapt themselves to its overthrow. Psychologically they were in the position of France after the loss of the Maginot Line. The Japanese appeared to be unstoppable, and were heading for Sydney and Melbourne; and the Australians looked round in despondency for a remedy. They aimed at holding the southern part of the continent on a line which passed through Brisbane. That portion to the north of this they had virtually reconciled themselves to losing when the Japanese invasion, which was expected in a matter of weeks, should begin.

MacArthur's initial success was to change this attitude. He infused the Australians with confidence, and with the offensive spirit. His command was extremely short in manpower: it was poorly equipped, and its air power was deficient. But within three months the counter-offensive started.

The area which was the scene of the fighting was a chain of coral islands which lies to the north of Australia and curls around to the northeast. The pressure of the original Japanese offensive had nearly carried them to this region. But it had begun to flag before Japan had occupied the whole system. If Japan had overrun the islands, it would have been able to set up bases there from which it could have interrupted communications between Australian ports. The chain of islands was half-held by the Japanese, but their firm occupation came to an end in the Solomon Islands, and did not extend to the New Hebrides or New Caledonia. The objective of their next offensive, with a dangerously extended line of communication, was the Australian outpost of Port Moresby in the south of Papua, which was the Australian extension of New Guinea. This lay just to the south of the islands occupied by Japan and well within range of their new stronghold at Rabaul, a superb natural harbour in New Britain, easily captured from the Australians in January and then quickly transformed into an impressive fleet base surrounded by a cluster of airfields and military installations.

It was a matter of urgency to scatter the Japanese forces, which were preparing to take Port Moresby. The first engagement was the drawn naval battle between American and Japanese aircraft-carriers off the coast of Papua at the beginning of May 1942: the Battle of the Coral Sea. It was said to be drawn because losses on both sides had been roughly equal; but the Japanese had been convoying troops, which were intended for a *coup de main* against Port Moresby, and these were turned back and never came again. Thus the issue of the battle in truth favoured the Allies.

The Japanese were, however, favourably placed. From their bases they bombed Port Darwin, on the Australian coast, and severely damaged it. Having abandoned their hopes of taking Port Moresby by a frontal assault from the sea, the Japanese Army landed the first of 15,000 troops on the northern coast of Papua on 21 July 1942 with the intention of advancing overland across the Owen Stanley Range to take Port Moresby from the rear. MacArthur moved to counter the attack, inadequate though his force was. Three weeks after the Japanese landing, MacArthur sent reinforcements to New Guinea with orders to wrest Papua from the Japanese. At first the Japanese pushed the Australians southward until, suffering from severe malnutrition, dysentery and food poisoning – all of which affected both sides – the Japanese advance ground to a halt barely thirty miles from Port Moresby in mid-September. By that time MacArthur had assembled two Australian divisions (less one brigade) and leading elements of a United States Army division which was on its way. They could call on no effective naval support and their air support was supplied by a hodge-podge of aircraft of indeterminate vintage. On 23 September MacArthur handed over the counter-offensive to General Sir Thomas Blamey, the Australian Commander-in-Chief for Allied Land Forces in the South-West Pacific. In a painful struggle which took a further four months under appalling conditions, they prevailed. The struggle ended in January 1943 when the few surviving Japanese were no longer capable of organized resistance.

The backbone of the force was the Seventh Australian Division, veterans of the Middle East who had been among the Australian forces originally sent out as a rag-tag force, under-equipped and under-trained, to Palestine, then ordered to Greece, but diverted first to the Western Desert and back to Palestine whence it earned its spurs in a difficult but forgotten campaign in Lebanon and Syria against the Vichy French. With the collapse of British resistance in Malaya, the Seventh had been pulled out of the Middle East as part of the forces shifted to defend Australia.

Wavell, with Churchill's support, had wanted them in Burma and tried to hijack them when they reached Ceylon, but the Australian Prime Minister insisted they proceed to Java, which was how they came to be in Papua. Gripped by political and strategical forces beyond its ability to influence, the Division's history of irritating administrative confusion and muddle was perhaps no more than characteristic of army life. The fighting in Papua well suited the individual qualities of the men of the Seventh.

It was largely a series of savage hand-to-hand conflicts, and there was less skill in manoeuvre than was to be usual in the campaigns designed by MacArthur. It was, however, notable for the skilful use of aircraft, themselves largely improvised for supplying troops (as in Burma later). It was also remarkable for the endurance of the troops, and for their overcoming mountainous jungles in conditions of equatorial heat, humidity and mud that make the area one of the most unhealthy and exhausting climates in the world.

It was a battle on a scale smaller than many, yet the maniacal tenacity of the Japanese which was to be a feature of the entire campaign is summed up in the final tally of human lives: of 13,000 Japanese losses in action in the final stage, only thirty-eight men were taken prisoner. The Australians lost 5,700 men, the Americans a further 2,800.

This operation in eastern New Guinea was quite a small one, and, with so much happening in the rest of the world, not very much noticed. But in the record of the whole war, it was significant. It marked the end of the Japanese offensive. It was the start of expeditions, desperately hard-fought but in the end universally successful, to force Japan back across the sea which it had sailed out to dominate so spectacularly. But MacArthur, surveying the tasks which still lay before him, was painfully aware of the difficulties which lay ahead.

He was fighting over a vast area, large parts of which were still unmapped. This was a handicap which has been little recognized, but was very grave indeed. For an American general to plan a troop landing in Europe with maps and charts showing the tidal movements was one thing: to plan the same operation for coral islands, where all that was available was native guess-work, was quite another. He was short of ships; he was given only medium-range bomber aircraft when he needed essentially long-range bombers; everywhere he went, airfields had to be constructed, often hacked out of the jungle by indigenous labour. For his supplies he had to compete with seven or eight rival theatres of war, and, as it seemed to him, invariably came out worst. Disease, especially malaria, was a still more deadly enemy than the Japanese, and the means of overcoming it could only be found by experimenting – and by exposing his armies at first to its ravages.

Nevertheless, from Port Moresby and the operations which he conducted for its relief in the encircling Owen Stanley Mountains, he was led on to the steps which, laborious operation after perilous initiative, in the end resulted in the reconquest of all New Guinea from the Japanese. From this position, he prepared to leap ahead, to wreak havoc among the forces guarding the Japanese Empire.

As the campaign in Papua was coming to a close, in the first part of 1943 the Ninth Australian Division, which had displayed superb fighting qualities against Field Marshal Erwin Rommel's forces at the Battle of Alamein, was returned to Australia for a much-needed period of recovery. After training in jungle warfare in Australia, the Ninth was dispatched to help four other Australian divisions and several American regiments to expel the Japanese from the Huon Peninsula, the area of the New Guinea mandate nearest to New Britain (and therefore Rabaul). The Japanese had taken control of the whole of the Peninsula and its southern approaches in March 1942 and had utilized their year of grace to construct airstrips and well-prepared fixed defences. The whole operation took a year to complete between early 1943 and the first few months of 1944. The vast difficulties of nature took its toll as it had elsewhere in New Guinea and the lesser islands nearby, where American forces were also overwhelming the Japanese defenders. Lieutenant-General R. L. Eichelberger, Commander of the Thirty-second US Army Division in Papua, painted the scene:

It was about one part fighting to three parts sheer misery of physical environment. It was climbing up one hill and down another, and then, when breath was short, fording streams with weapons held aloft or wading through swamps. It was sweat and then chill; it was a weariness of body and spirit; and once again tropical illness was a greater foe than enemy bullets.[*]

The eventual victory of the Allied forces, costly though it was, had never been in doubt. MacArthur was not a sporting man, and he used his superior numerical strength to advantage. The Huon Peninsula campaign, however, is interesting from another point of view as well: in the event, it was to be the last major campaign involving Australian Army forces in the Second World War.

In retrospect, it is plain that the Japanese, from the point of view of their long-term interests, would have done well to limit their offensive; to avoid overlong lines of communication; to have declined combat when

[*] R. L. Eichelberger, *Jungle Road to Tokyo*, Odhams Press, London, 1951, p. 109.

this could be avoided; above all, not to have been lured into a contest for the possession of islands, which could only be of marginal use to them. This was the view of many of the Japanese generals, and if it had prevailed in shaping the strategy would have greatly increased the difficulty of the Americans in coming to grips with the Japanese Empire. But the Japanese Navy, still determined to conduct the Pacific War as a naval war, still over-confident in spite of the Battle of Midway, still with an abundance of battleships and cruisers which it could safely risk, overruled the Japanese Armies. Little by little the scope of the war enlarged, and eventually spread through all the intricate chain of coral islands in the Pacific. There was little rational planning behind the operations.

From the start the Americans had had a second headquarters command in the Pacific Ocean. In March 1942 the Pacific, by a decision of President Roosevelt, ratified perforce by the British, Australians and Dutch, was divided formally between General MacArthur and Admiral Nimitz. MacArthur's command included Australia, the Philippines, the Solomons, and most of the Dutch East Indies. The rest of the Pacific fell to Nimitz. But it was not a clear-cut geographical division of responsibility. Each of these officers was entrusted formally with the command of all armed forces in his area, whether on land, sea or in the air; but, by the instrument providing for the division between the commands, it was provided that Admiral Nimitz should have general control of all amphibious operations, whether these took place in his own zone or MacArthur's.

This rather peculiar division caused trouble about the demarcation. It was against logic, and ran counter to the teaching of experience in other theatres of war. MacArthur wrote:

Of all the faulty decisions of the war, perhaps the most inexpressible one was the failure to unify the command in the Pacific ... It resulted in divided effort, the waste of diffusion and duplication of force, and undue extension of war with added casualties and cost.*

The division was difficult to maintain. For example, MacArthur's operations in clearing the menacing Japanese from Port Moresby were on various occasions more amphibious than military, but he succeeded in keeping the campaign to himself. MacArthur wrote with a personal interest about the danger of divided aims. It galled him that it was freely suggested that he, though he was celebrated for his caution, could not be trusted with the safety of the Navy's precious ships. A further limitation

* C. Willoughby and J. Chamberlain: *MacArthur 1941–51*, McGraw-Hill, New York, 1954.

on him was that the charter setting up the respective commands laid down that Nimitz was from the start to be offensive in his operations; MacArthur, by contrast, was to fight defensively. This grudging attitude was to run, as a discordant thread, throughout the early years of the American counter-attack.

In this issue, MacArthur set himself, not for the only time in his career, to oppose the general political plan of Washington, on which the plan of campaign eventually depended. The Navy had for long looked forward to a war with Japan. War in the Pacific must essentially be a naval one; the principal interest with which it was fought must be the aircraft-carriers and battleships and the commander of these must be an admiral. The plans according to which it was fought had for two or three generations been the basic manuals for American naval training. This was the prevailing conception among the service chiefs in Washington; MacArthur was a general, and that was fatal to him. American naval officers form a curious, exclusive caste in American society; the war was an opportunity for this caste which it could not neglect. It is true that in the European War the Navy took second place; circumstances had taken charge and had directed a land strategy. It seemed only compensating justice that in the East Asian and Pacific Conflict, where geography restored primacy to the sea, the Navy and its traditional ancillary arm, the Marines, should be the main protagonists.

The arrangement of the two commands had further consequences. It had been agreed between Roosevelt and Churchill that the United States should have a large measure of independent initiative in the organization of military affairs in the Pacific. As Britain had the lion's share of the initiative in the Middle East and in the Indian Ocean, so did the United States rule the Pacific War. This was in contrast to the convention operating in Europe and the Atlantic, where the planning was a matter of joint British and American responsibility; in the Pacific, any British initiative came to be headed off. By this process, the United States to some extent evaded the general directive, laid down very soon after Pearl Harbor, that the war in the Pacific was to take second place to the war in Europe. In 1942 the Americans systematically built up their war-making capacity in the Pacific through the sympathetic connivance of the Chiefs of Staff in Washington. MacArthur might groan that he still had ridiculously inadequate supplies, but they were very much larger than had been envisaged by the directive. Twice as many supplies were sent across the Pacific in the first six months of March 1942 as were sent to the European theatre of war. By the end of 1942, the United States had reinforced its stations in the Pacific by a total of 15,000 troops more than had been originally intended.

In August 1942 the Navy had its first chance to take charge of amphibious operations on a large scale. These were in Guadalcanal, a tiny island
in the Solomons: it was in MacArthur's command area, but the campaign
there was directed by the Naval Chiefs of Staff and played little part in his
biography. Once more, the area of combat was in the disputed coral
islands which ringed Australia. Guadalcanal was very little known or
explored; before its conquest by Japan, it had been a British colony; the
local people were extremely primitive; a few traders were like characters
from a novel by Joseph Conrad. The colony, which is only ninety miles
long and twenty-five miles broad, is the epitome of a tropical island.
Along its sandy beaches are coconut palms; abruptly behind them there
rise jungly mountains and extinct volcanoes to a height of seven thousand
feet. The flat ground is dark, steamy, rotting jungle, the perfect terrain for
breeding the malaria mosquito.

The Japanese nearly beat the Americans to possession of it. They had
occupied it with a skeleton force, and American air reconnaissance showed
that they were building an airfield on it. They were interrupted by a
counter-invasion: the Americans landed a force of 11,000 men. At first,
both sides supposed that the fate of Guadalcanal would be settled within
a week. Actually a savage and terrible struggle developed there which
lasted until February 1943, when the Japanese decided to release their
grip. The Americans had discovered what war in the Pacific amounted to,
and had done so at horrendous cost. There had been no such gruelling
campaigns before in the history of the war. The victory won by the
Americans eliminated a threat to the Allied supply lines and provided the
United States forces with a valuable forward airbase.

The battle cost the Americans six major naval engagements, and a heavy
toll of shipping. Both sides lost an equal number of warships (twenty-four
of all classes), though Japanese losses in supporting ships, such as transports, were much heavier. The Japanese dead among the ground troops
numbered 24,000: American losses were lighter, but by a remarkable feint
the Japanese managed to rescue 12,000 of their soldiers. The Japanese
troop commander killed himself as the final troops were withdrawn.

This savage battle marked out the pattern of operations which was to
be repeated again and again in the Pacific during the next few years.
Careful and skilful preparation by the American staff had been the main
factor in the American victory; and so it was to be at Tarawa, in the
Gilbert Islands, at Kwajalein and Eniwetok and Bougainville Island. The
Navy concentrated upon the islands and pushed the Japanese relentlessly
back. This strategy was a head-on assault. It was effective, and remorseless; but it was not very imaginative.

As the Nimitz campaign developed, General MacArthur was simultaneously attacking in his corner of the Pacific and the strategy of the two campaigns inevitably invited comparisons. Both showed undoubted successes. From September 1942 down to the middle of 1944, MacArthur was employed in re-occupying New Guinea. It was not the extent of the land occupied which was significant; MacArthur had overcome the arts of the Japanese in defensive warfare, in territory very favourable to them, and he had inflicted enormous losses of manpower on them.

Nimitz's war machine had rolled over the Gilbert Islands and the Marshalls. Little by little the Japanese gave way at the edges of the vast Empire they had seized; but Nimitz gained his successes by weight of assault and as a result of the endurance of his troops. His casualties were usually considerable. The American troops who were flung into action were for the most part a civilian Army. Many of them had, however, been harshly prepared in the rather barbaric training grounds of the United States Marines in the Carolinas. Stories of these which seeped out during the war seem to have been well founded. Some troops had been less well prepared, and this accounted for some of the reverses which the Americans suffered in this campaign, which was the most sanguinary of any which were fought during the war. The American advance proceeded atoll by atoll. It was a war fought among tropical islands, with the same unreal beauty as a background, the same refusal to surrender among the Japanese, the same monotony of desperate attack and desperate defence. It became taken for granted that the Japanese did not surrender, but were killed. Often the sites which occasioned the worst slaughter were incredibly small. MacArthur, on the other hand, won his battles by sheer artistry. No other captain of the war based his strategy so consistently on principles. He commanded with style. He was conscious of history, and of the examples of other generals. The ghosts of all the battles of the world stalked the combats for which he was responsible. In the map rooms of his headquarters there was an atmosphere of erudition which was unfamiliar in the war. The bloody patterns of assault on these remote coral reefs were studiously compared with Napoleon's famous victories, and even on one occasion with the victory of Hannibal at Cannae in 204 B.C. He also had a self-conscious, narcissistic regard for his own place among the pantheon of American military giants.

MacArthur despised brute strength. He sought, in a way which was rather like the principle on which the Japanese system of judo is based, to bring his force to bear on the enemy in places and at times that would find his opponent off balance. In this way he could hope to succeed with weaker strength, which was usually the position in which he found himself,

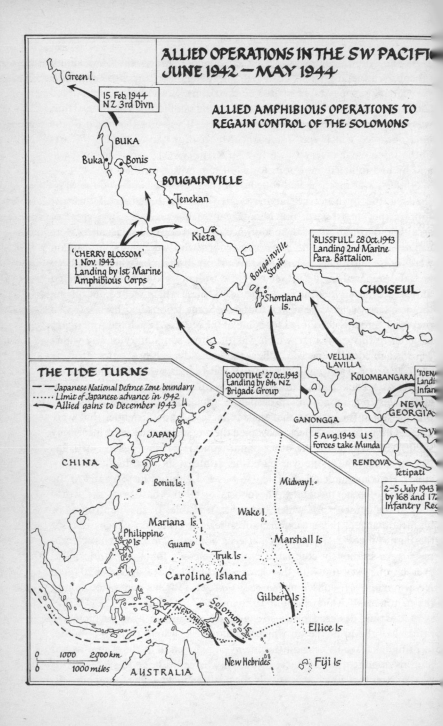

ALLIED OPERATIONS IN THE SW PACIFIC JUNE 1942 – MAY 1944

ALLIED AMPHIBIOUS OPERATIONS TO REGAIN CONTROL OF THE SOLOMONS

Green I.

15 Feb.1944
N.Z. 3rd Divn

BUKA
Buka • Bonis

BOUGAINVILLE

Tenekan

Kieta

'CHERRY BLOSSOM'
1 Nov. 1943
Landing by 1st Marine
Amphibious Corps

Bougainville Strait

'BLISSFULL' 28 Oct.1943
Landing 2nd Marine
Para Battalion

CHOISEUL

Shortland Is.

VELLIA
LAVILLA

KOLOMBANGARA

'TOEN
Landi
Infan

'GOODTIME' 27 Oct.1943
Landing by 8th N.Z.
Brigade Group

NEW
GEORGIA

GANONGGA

5 Aug.1943 U.S
forces take Munda

RENDOVA
Tetipati

2–5 July 1943
by 168 and 17
Infantry Reg

THE TIDE TURNS

— Japanese National Defence Zone boundary
···· Limit of Japanese advance in 1942
⟵ Allied gains to December 1943

JAPAN

CHINA

Bonin Is.

Midway I.

Wake I.

Mariana Is.

Marshall Is.

Philippine
Is

Guam

Truk Is.

Caroline Island

Gilbert Is

New Guinea

Solomon Is

Ellice Is

0   1000   2000 km
0   1000 miles

New Hebrides

Fiji Is

AUSTRALIA

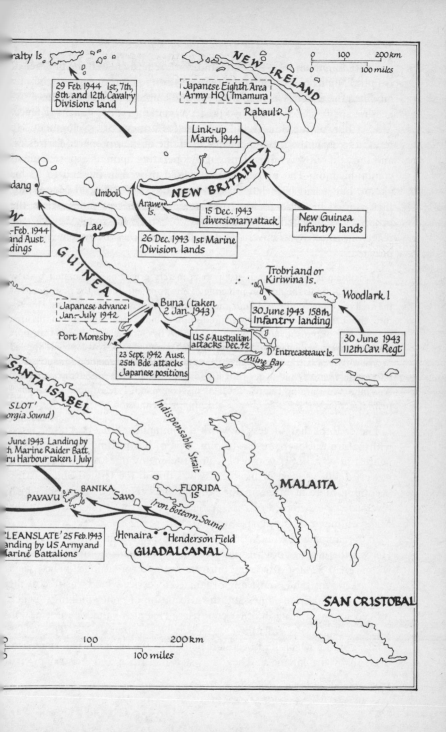

ralty Is.

NEW IRELAND

0 ____ 100 ____ 200 km
0 ____ 100 miles

29 Feb. 1944 1st, 7th,
8th and 12th Cavalry
Divisions land

Japanese Eighth Area
Army HQ (Imamura)

Rabaul

Link-up
March 1944

dang

Umboi

NEW BRITAIN

Arawe
Is.

15 Dec. 1943 diversionary attack

New Guinea
Infantry lands

-Feb. 1944
and Aust.
dings

Lae

GUINEA

26 Dec. 1943 1st Marine
Division lands

Trobriand or
Kiriwina Is.

Woodlark I

Japanese advance
Jan.–July 1942

Buna (taken
2 Jan. 1943)

30 June 1943 158th
Infantry landing

Port Moresby

US & Australian
attacks Dec.42

30 June 1943
112th Cav. Regt

D'Entrecasteaux Is.

23 Sept. 1942 Aust.
25th Bde attacks
Japanese positions

Milne Bay

SANTA ISABEL

SLOT'
orgia Sound)

Indispensable Strait

June 1943 Landing by
h Marine Raider Batt.
ru Harbour taken 1 July

BANIKA

FLORIDA
IS.

MALAITA

PAVAVU

Savo

Iron Bottom Sound

LEANSLATE' 25 Feb.1943
anding by US Army and
Marine Battalions

Honaira

Henderson Field

GUADALCANAL

SAN CRISTOBAL

0 ____ 100 ____ 200 km
5 ____ 100 miles

and with minimum loss. In this island warfare he eschewed the practice of Admiral Nimitz of reducing the Japanese strong-points one by one. Nimitz modified these tactics as time went on, and employed a limited plan of by-passing small islands which would have made an inconvenient defence. MacArthur, on the other hand, practised a strategy of envelopment. He refused to assail the Japanese head-on in one of their prepared fortresses, and thought out ways of isolating it by operating upon its exposed line of communication. The by-passed stronghold proved in the end to be his victim, but it had been left to 'die upon the vine'. General MacArthur then shifted his base forwards by some hundreds of miles, when the process was repeated with care never to expose his forces beyond the reach of protective air cover. He described as follows the system which he pursued:

The system is as old as war itself. It is merely a new name dictated by new conditions given to the ancient principle of envelopment. It was the first time that the area of combat embraced land and water in such relative proportions. Heretofore, either the one or the other was predominant in the campaign. But in this area the presence of transportation of ground troops by ships as well as land transport seemed to conceal the fact that the system was merely that of envelopment applied to a new type of battle area. It has always proved the ideal method for success by inferior in number but faster-moving forces. Immediately upon my arrival in Australia and learning the resources at my command, I determined that such a plan of action was the sole chance of fulfilling my mission.*

The concept that success lay with a commander who best cooperated with nature was ever-present to him. One of his maxims was: 'Nature is neutral in war, but if you beat it and the enemy does not, it becomes a powerful ally.' A part of his success was due to the United States Army becoming more at home in the coral islands than the Japanese: which reversed the experience of the Japanese and of the British Army in the Malayan jungle at the start of the war.

In his campaigns, MacArthur relied to an exceptional extent on spying. He was fortunate enough to discover an Australian, Commander Long, with a great gift for attracting information and for sifting it. This was a new art in Australia, and Long organized a service which was free of the traits – the elaborate games and the affectation of policy making – which proved so constricting in other countries. The most valuable information was given by a force called the 'coast watchers of the islands'. These were a fifth column which had been left behind in the islands when they were overrun by the Japanese. They consisted of British and Australian civil

* Willoughby and Chamberlain, op. cit.

servants, anthropologists, telegraph operators, traders: and they were admirably served by bands of local natives. They were able to communicate by wireless with MacArthur's headquarters. In war of unorthodox character, this kind information about Japanese strong-points and the distribution of Japanese manpower was often worth a whole division of troops. The exploits of these men are one of the most exciting chapters of war history; and it is very extraordinary that they have not become part of the folklore of the war.

To MacArthur's military tasks were added the military and diplomatic ones of welding Australia and the United States in a close alliance. The Australians, in spite of their many positive qualities, were at this period notoriously hard to deal with: they were touchy, quick to take offence where none was intended, hypercritical as a kind of self-defence. In spite of a grotesque side to his character – which was self-assertive and boastful and which went with genuine confidence and did not mask self-distrust – MacArthur actually made himself liked, and won the confidence of Australia. He esteemed and got along well with Curtin, the Australian Prime Minister, and the two of them often collaborated in opposing Washington or London. He took an interest in preparing the reorganization of the Australian supplies so that by re-orienting Australian industry his armies actually received from Australia itself a much larger proportion of its needs than had been supposed possible.

In playing this role, MacArthur was much helped by accidents in his previous career which had detached him from the ordinary life of an American soldier. In his service as military adviser to the Philippine Government, he had come to conduct himself with an unusual detachment from the American military machine. This, combined with a natural tendency to a certain Caesarism in politics, had brought it about that in his Pacific command he was often handled by the American Government as if he were an independent political power and not a subordinate officer. His relation to the American authorities was like that of a much-prized condottiere to an Italian city state. The legend of MacArthur as the great American pro-consul was enhanced by the fact that when the war began he had not been back in America for years, nor was he to return until 1951. Though MacArthur undoubtedly gained from this position, he had as a rule to forgo the ability to influence the military planners by personal knowledge of the officers concerned. A remoteness from understanding American politics complicated his career. Piercing political insight into fundamentals was combined with a pathetic political incompetence in day-to-day matters.

Throughout this fatal combat in which Americans were locked with

Japanese in a contest from which neither side could free itself, one single fact stood out. The war was waged with the utmost ferocity, but often under the eyes of relatively idle armies who were obliged to remain spectators of what was going on. Of the vast number of men mobilized for the war, the greater part were destined never to come into combat. Japan had an Army of fifty-one divisions: until the very end of the war, forty of these divisions were either occupied in China, which for most of this period had a totally inactive front, or were employed in guarding the frontier with Russia. And on the American side the number of troops employed in the actual offensive by MacArthur, and later in the reduction of the Pacific islands, was very small indeed in comparison with the vast army which the United States had concentrated for war in the Far East. (Similarly in this Far Eastern War the British troops who had actual combat experience were limited to the four or five divisions in Burma.) The Western Allies could not make use of a larger force. They had chosen to fight the Japanese on narrow fronts – in New Guinea and in the Pacific islands – and the circumstances of the war were such that there was no room for a great concourse of troops. Thus the war came to resemble the war at Troy. The serried ranks stood and watched the combat fought between the heroes. Their fate was decided in battles in which they had no part.

In this desperate fighting in the Pacific, Admiral Yamamoto, still the central figure and imaginative genius at war whom the Japanese, with their great military gifts, had contributed to that conflict, was taken out of the picture. His death was plotted in Washington. It was brought about by arranging an ambush by American fighter aircraft which fell on him in great strength as he was flying on a tour of inspection to one of the Pacific bases held by Japan. This was in April 1943, soon after the Japanese withdrawal from Guadalcanal. The details of his flight, the precise time of arrival, were all obtained by intercepting cipher messages which could be read. Yamamoto was always punctual to the moment: the surprise depended on the ambushing aircraft being able to count to the minute upon his presence at the destined place of encounter. Yamamoto went to his death with a punctuality that was a rare virtue among orientals, even among commanding officers. His end was like the death of Hector who was similarly taken at a disadvantage by a force of Achilles' myrmidons:

> Look Hector how the sun begins to set
> How ugly night comes breathing at his heels
> Even with the veil and darkling of the sun
> To close the day up, Hector's life is done.

The American Admiral, having plotted his overthrow, could find no more fitting words to announce it than the following telegram to the exterminators: 'Congratulations Major Mitchell and his hunters; sounds as though one of the ducks in their bag was a peacock.' Democracies have curious lapses of taste when they go to war. At the press conference to celebrate the success of the plan, the same Admiral observed: 'I had hoped to lead that scoundrel up Pennsylvania Avenue in chains with the rest of you kicking him where it would do the most good.' It is said that the audience whooped and applauded.

By July 1943 the American planners were already satisfied that they had chosen the right road. They lifted their sights, and began to consider what they should do when they drew near to Japan. Could intense air bombardment, from Chinese airfields and from their great aircraft-carriers, and unremitting submarine warfare, really reduce this proud people, or would the unemployed army of over a million be ready to dispute their way? Would an invasion be necessary; and, if so, would the history of the fanatical defence of small atolls be lived through once again, this time in the island centre of the terrible and warlike race?

MacArthur and Nimitz were the two American personalities who dominated the Pacific. They had taken up the initiative when it had been dashed from the Japanese by the Battle of Midway Island. They had begun to attack, and had succeeded in their campaigns ever since. To halt them began to appear as being beyond Japan's capacity: the only doubt was how long they would take to cross the Pacific, and to make war on Japan at its gateway.

Part IV

THE DEFEAT OF JAPAN

CHAPTER 22

Two Indian Armies

THE Japanese, after overrunning Burma, had been content for two years to remain on the defensive. They had repelled the attack organized by General Wavell from India in the autumn of 1942, against Arakan. The operation, which was encouraged from London in the hopes that it would repair British prestige, was premature and was made with inadequate force and troops insufficiently trained; the Japanese were never embarrassed by it – except that it restricted a move which they had been intending to make at the same time into North India – and, by outmanoeuvring and outflanking the British, they compelled the British to retreat.

The country between India and Burma was peculiarly difficult; communications almost did not exist; the disease-infestations required that armies, if they were to operate with any degree of efficiency, should be remarkably well organized with medical and sanitation services, which in many areas they were not until 1944. These facts, as much as any other, kept the British and Japanese apart, though great pressure was brought on British troops by Churchill to go on the offensive. In fact, the Japanese had acted on the principle that geography had contrived to give Burma the perfect scientific frontier, and calculated that they would do enough if they posted troops to guard the few practicable approaches from India.

In 1943 the adventure of General Orde Wingate in Burma took place. This strange, eccentric soldier, who had formed his ideas in Palestine and Abyssinia, and who took T. E. Lawrence and the Arab revolt in the First World War as his model, was confident that Burma would make an ideal field for guerrilla war. If it was hard for armies to make contact, he suggested that guerrillas should do their work for them; and that, once these had made a long-range penetration behind the Japanese lines, they could, by superior mobility and surprise, produce as much havoc as would be caused by a successful army invasion.

Wingate convinced the Indian Army with great difficulty, and made an expedition with just over three thousand men. The higher Japanese officers regarded him without anxiety, and said that he must starve in the jungle; the more junior officers were shocked by the boldness of his strategy, and by their inability to hunt him down. The advance of Wingate upon T. E. Lawrence was in the use of wireless and of aircraft. Wingate lost a thousand men, one third of his force, and put a Burmese railway temporarily out of action. Whether his guerrilla successes came near justifying his theory was an open question; a much larger operation, employing aircraft, was planned for the next year, but it met with disaster at the outset, Wingate being killed on taking off. He is a hard man to assess. England, for prestige reasons, urgently needed a success, and it possessed at this time a propaganda machine, which could create heroes overnight. Wingate's personality and achievement were written up and blazed across the world. It may be that Wingate demonstrated not the success of his own guerrilla strategy but the success of British propaganda. He supplied to the waiting and idle troops of the British Army, in the tedious interval of training and before they were offensively engaged, the spectacle of exciting warfare and of individual performance. Wingate believed himself to be a man of destiny and that the situation was also one of destiny.

A far more orthodox, and forceful, attack was intended by the British in the spring of 1944. The Fourth Army Corps was preparing it, using the small town of Imphal in North-East India as its base. The Japanese, who had two divisions in the region, had Intelligence that it was coming, and resolved to strike first.

The campaign inside the borders of India which resulted was interesting partly because, in it, Japan again put to the test its claim that it was fighting, not simply for itself, but for the freedom of the Asian peoples. It is true that the organized forces of allegedly 'free India', which it had among its troops, played only a minor part; the campaign was so interesting, so stubborn, so terrible, and the 'free Indians' played such a small role in it, that the history of it, and its narration by the Japanese, might well overlook their presence. Yet, symbolically, the event is important, and was certainly seen to be so by the people of India and South-East Asia. Japan had announced that it had opted out of the circle of imperial predatory powers, and that it could rightly claim to be the patron of free Asia. It had not, until this time, done anything very striking to show that it was living up to this claim. In Japan, all attention was given to the gallantry of the Japanese forces. The average Japanese subjects scarcely thought of their army as fighting Asian battles, or that their Asian Allies could be of much worth to them. The opportunity had come to show that this was a mistaken view.

Chance presented itself in the shape of the Indian leader Subhas Chandra Bose. He played at this stage an extraordinarily decisive part. By accident, and by seizing an exceptional opportunity, he was able to cut a figure which made him outstanding among the comparatively small number of men who influenced the course of the war by their individual qualities. He chanced to be available to the Japanese to lead a movement to free India, and, in retrospect, it appears that this was the last chance of saving itself with which Japan was presented.

Bose was a Bengali, the son of a comparatively high civil servant who became a judge. Bengal had a special place in the history of Indian nationalism. It stood by itself culturally, and bred a type which was peculiar in being the exponent of a classical strain of regional loyalty. Bengali patriotism was deeply devotional: it was less associated than in other parts of India with day-to-day economic interests: the Bengali really believed the singularly powerful oratory which surged over the province especially after 1905. The passionate quality of Bengali nationalism, monomaniac, hot, somnambulist, is rather like that of the Sinn Fein patriot who is heard, off-stage, as a repeated theme in Sean O'Casey's play, *Red Roses for You*, repeating his hypnotic oratory. This nationalism expressed itself, to a degree quite unknown in other parts of India, in a fascination with violence and in a cult of terrorism. The typical Bengali nationalist was quite carried away, renounced his home and the ties of ordinary business, and plunged into secret conspiratorial activity in a way which horrified the rest of India as being extravagant and an affront to domestic obligation.

Bengal differed so much in temperament from the other parts of India that political cooperation with it was not easy. Bose became a leader of Bengali nationalism, and was so powerful a personality that his shadow fell over the rest of India. He was in the recognizable succession to the Bengal leaders of his youth who used to be carried away by the poetical implications of 'mother India', Hinduism, and Indian uniqueness. Always, Bose saw himself, and conducted himself, as a man of destiny. He had a great appeal to youth, frustrated, very poor but very proud, liking rhetorical leadership, always responding enthusiastically to the idea of a solution through some act of violence. He sought to turn Indian nationalism into the kind of movement which grew in Bengal.

As a young man, Bose, who was born in 1897, had been sent by his family to England, where he studied so diligently at Cambridge that he passed the entrance examination into the Indian Civil Service. This still enjoyed so much prestige in India that a lifetime spent in it, or a resignation from it, produced equal *réclame*. Bose chose the latter course. By resigning even before he had been posted to any particular duty, he gained a flying start in the Bengal Congress Party. Two decades of serious attachment to Congress, and a spell of office as Mayor of Calcutta, brought him, after a term of imprisonment which he spent in Mandalay Fort in Burma, to the presidency of the All-India Congress in 1938. Though the inner springs of his being may have been poetical, he developed, during his time as Mayor, a businesslike aptitude, which won recognition from British officers.

This proved to be a parting of the ways with his non-Bengali Congress colleagues. In his struggle with them, and partly because of his temperament, he moved sharply to the left, though for him there was no special attraction in socialism, and he was not moved by the conflict between this and free enterprise. The left meant simply extremism, more determined personalities, a more congenial emotional atmosphere. He advocated ever more extreme Congress policies: and in particular he opposed Gandhi's stubbornly held advocacy of non-violence. In this contest, Gandhi faced the blind emotional forces of Bengali nationalism, which repudiated Gandhi's homespun philosophy of the spinning wheel and of the virtues of simple peasant life. A religious preoccupation such as Gandhi's – a religion which dwelt on the virtues of the Sermon on the Mount which Gandhi had taken over in his version of Hinduism – was alien to Bose. Bose's passion was summed up in his favourite slogan: 'Give me blood and I promise you freedom.'

The year of his final breach with Gandhi was also the year of the outbreak of the war in Europe. Bose was not inclined to sit still among such events. For the attitude of Gandhi and Vallabhai Patel, the men he was opposing, it is possible to feel much admiration. They were realists, as intransigently opposed to the British as he was himself. But they accepted that military action was not the way to strike at them. They were organizing a vast, poor, ignorant, apathetic nation in the only way it could be mobilized. A military adventure was just the kind of thing the British would expect and would know how to deal with. They were helpless against this unspeakable groundswell. Subhas Bose was simply too impatient for this Himalayan wisdom.

Bose thought otherwise. The world was being changed by armies, and he was impatient to have an Indian Army. His agitation grew unrestrained of bounds. He was arrested, rather oddly for a seditious speech in connection with the agitation for the removal of a memorial to the victims of the Black Hole of Calcutta, which was thought to be hurtful to national sentiment. In prison he meditated upon the progress of the war, on the might of Germany, on the great opportunities for Indian freedom which he felt that Gandhi, with a senile attachment to non-violence (as it appeared to Bose) was at this time allowing to pass by. He was distracted when he thought of what he might be able to effect if he was at liberty. He procured his temporary release by beginning a hunger strike, and ensured that he would not thereafter be restored to jail by absconding from his home in Calcutta early on a January morning of 1941, disguised as an elderly Moslem mullah.

By a daring journey he made his way across India, through Afghanistan and through the Soviet Union, into Germany. There he found his spiritual home, and probably would have done better if he had stayed there instead of answering the call of Japan. He had alway been attracted by Germany. His temperament was Wagnerian: the Nazi grandees proved attractive personally. The colourful side of Nazism appealed to him profoundly. The heroics, the mythology, the dangerous and insidious concepts, the affected contempt for weakness and pity, the invocation of history, all seemed congenial to him. Bengali culture is strongly patriarchal, and the Nazi concept of the place of women in the warrior's life appealed to one who, till he went to Germany and married a German, had apparently been indifferent to women. In the Siegfried cult and the heroic life, he saw a model which he found admirable. He was deficient in the sense of humour that was the best preservative against Nazi fantasy; and his Hindu education had given him a natural tendency towards a narrow concentration on whatever happened to appeal to him for intellectual reasons. Even the Nazi brutality he found brisk, salubrious and invigorating.

In politics he found the Nazi form of state entirely congenial. The rule by the Nazi Party, and the authoritarian rule of the party by a small caucus of leaders, seemed to him to provide India with a model form of government. Discipline, before all else, was what India seemed to need for overcoming its problems of the division into separate castes and communities, and for dealing with its great economic problem of poverty. The democratic type of government which it might imitate from Great Britain had the fatal weakness of permitting so much liberty that the state might fall in pieces. New vistas opened for an Indian Government which would be equipped with a Gestapo, concentration camps and an SS. On the precise details of the policy he would pursue if the war should bring him to power, he was vague. It was enough that he should proclaim the bracing virtues of authoritarianism.

Bose therefore found the situation promising. He was satisfied with his personal reception. The Germans invited him to take charge of organizing the rebellious Indians in their hands into a body which might be useful for war purposes. He was given access to the Indian prisoners captured by the Germans in North Africa. He broadcast to India over the German radio; and he took part in the controversy over the Cripps mission to India. Volunteers began to come forward to form an Indian Legion, and about two thousand men were enlisted for training. There was much ceremonial feasting and mutual compliment.

Spiritually this was probably the happiest part of Bose's somewhat neurotic life. But after some months Bose had to recognize that his German friends had not acknowledged him as the head of an Indian Government-in-Exile. Perhaps this was due, as was explained to him, to the fact that they could as yet, while Russia remained undefeated, have brought no effective aid to an Indian rebel government; perhaps it was because Hitler could not bring himself to recognize that Indians would be equal citizens in the post-war world which he was planning. Hitler, if Germany won the war, intended to dispose of India by a diplomacy in which Indians would play no part.

Whatever the reason, the Germans put no obstacles in Bose's way when an invitation reached him from the Indians in South-East Asia to transfer himself to this new sphere, and to take charge of the Free India movement which was being organized by the Japanese. His imagination, the dramatic part he might play, the appeal of the idea of Pan-Asianism, his calculation of how India, or at least Bengal, might respond to new situations, all impelled him to accept.

Bose sailed from Keil in a German U-boat in February 1943. He left behind some lieutenants to continue the work of organizing the available Indians, though he had failed to come to an agreement with the Nazis on precisely how they were to be used. The U-boat sailed to Madagascar, and there, off shore, it made a rendezvous with a Japanese submarine which carried him for the last half of his journey. He reached Tokyo on 13 June, after a voyage of thirteen weeks. That he was permitted to be so slow may suggest that the Japanese, at least at this time, did not found great hopes on the plan for which he had been imported.

Indeed they had been making half-hearted bids at raising the Indians in revolt against the British ever since the first days of the war; and they had suffered a series of disappointments. At first the project had been entrusted to a man named Major Fujiwara Iwaichi, of the Army General Staff, who appears to have been of some probity, with an understanding of what would appeal to Indians. He was fortunate in lighting, in the first days of the war, on a sick prisoner, Captain Mohan Singh. Singh was a man of character; he was a cousin of the Maharaja of Patiala, a great prince of the Punjab; he was a capable professional soldier, and he had become, apparently without the knowledge of the Indian Army, a convinced nationalist. With the backing of Fujiwara, and the financial aid of some of the leaders of the 800,000 Indians resident in Malaya, he undertook to raise from the Indian prisoners of war a force which might prove useful to the Japanese.

Of the total of 115,000 men who surrendered during the whole of the Malayan Campaign, Indians made up a very large number. Though at first a near-blind confidence was put in their loyalty by the Indian Government, this had an unenviable, if amiable, record, of being deceived. The inquiries which followed the Indian Mutiny of 1857, had shown that an almost insane trust had been placed in troops which had given every sign that they were preparing for rebellion.

Certainly the experience of some of the troops, in the months immediately before the surrender of Singapore, had not been such as to ensure their fidelity. Malaya was in many ways the weakest link in the British imperial chain. Among other disservices, it brought about the demoralization of many of those who served the Raj in the Indian Army. The culture and atmosphere of Malaya has been described very exactly in the stories of Somerset Maugham, and this society did not seem to most Indians as one worth dying for. Near Singapore there was a very luxurious country club with a much sought-after swimming pool. In the six months before the war, it became known in Singapore that the wives of the planters and of local white businessmen had objected to the swimming pool being used by Indian officers. British officers from the same regiments were eagerly invited, solicitously treated, and competed for assiduously. The Indians were dismayed when this action of the club was officially condoned: at least no protest against it was made from the Government or from the military command. This insult, casually offered by the Tanglin Club, did more than many other graver measures to undermine the British Empire in Asia. A dispassionate observer, surveying what was done, must have decided that the English, and especially their wives, were mad. It is not politic to insult a man mortally who is about to defend you.

The Japanese attempts at subverting the loyalty of the prisoners had as their background this resentment at the arrogance of the white society of Malaya. In spite of this preparation of the soil, the first attempts of Fujiwara and of Mohan Singh to set up the Indian National Army, which was inaugurated at Singapore on 12 February 1942, had only limited success. True, they had much to offer the Indian captives – immediate freedom, good wages, the resumption of their military careers, an apparently bright political prospect, exemption from the dreadful forced labour squads, for which Japanese prison camps soon became notorious. Yet the response was poor and Mohan Singh proved anything but an obedient tool. He laid down conditions that the Japanese were unwilling to accept; he stated plainly that if the Japanese aimed at replacing the British in India, they would, after a short time, have to face the aroused opposition of Indian nationalism. In December 1942 Mohan Singh resigned from his position and was arrested by the Japanese, and the first stage of the Japanese experiment at collaboration with Indian nationalism was over.

The Japanese had been handicapped in their efforts because of a deep-seated contempt which they had for prisoners of war, and, still more, for prisoners who were willing to be untrue to their oath of service. Nothing struck them as so contemptible as disloyalty, and they were unable to hide this. Simple-mindedly they judged their prisoners by the same exacting standards which they would have applied to their own people. This made them maladroit in the project of raising an army out of defaulters and deserters.

The decision was, however, taken to persevere in this venture. It was resolved to see whether better results could be obtained from enlisting a politician of standing to head the movement, instead of working exclusively through military men. Subhas Bose, whose mission in Germany had been favourably reported on by the Japanese Military Attaché there, seemed to be well qualified for this role.

Bose, on returning to Asia, threw himself energetically into organizing the Indian movement, and, in a short time, he gave it a life of its own, irrespective of the intentions of its Japanese sponsors. Bose was a different type from the sycophants and commercial adventurers who were usually available to support the Japanese enterprises. The qualities of action he had once displayed as Mayor of Calcutta were now directed to the preparation of a Government-in-Exile, which should be ready to replace the existing Government of India. On 23 October 1943 the Provisional Government of Free India (Azad Hind) was set up in Singapore with Bose at its head. He bled the Indian businessmen white for funds for his enterprise, being given by the Japanese the power to levy taxes on them, and having acquired in the service of Congress the right combination of contempt for millionaires and of businesslike respect for money. Bose worked under the great handicap that adequate human material for forming a provisional administration was absent. In spite of this, the sketchy organization of Azad Hind was set up.

Though Bose, between June and October, had transformed the position of the Indians in South-East Asia, and had built them into one of the forces which had to be taken account of, yet he had not succeeded in getting Japan to the point of recognizing a full-fledged Government-in-Exile. The most that he gained was an invitation to take part as an observer, along with the puppet Governments of the Japanese system, in the Greater East Asia Conference in November 1943, although his status was certainly inflated by the oratory of those present; Japan also declared its readiness to hand over the Andaman and Nicobar Islands in the

Indian Ocean to Bose's administration. But as his organization grew in effective power, the relation with local Japanese officials deteriorated. All the vexations which Ba Maw had had to endure, also faced Subhas Bose. The Japanese Army was aware of the nuisance which an opinionated exiled government could make, and, deeply suspicious, was anxious to thwart it. However, the Japanese commanders agreed to test out what effect the Indians could bring upon a battle; and Bose glowed at the opportunity.

In the meanwhile the Japanese had made their plans for an offensive from Burma which was to be directed against India. Their position was gradually growing dangerous. Large forces were being prepared against them – potentially fourteen divisions from China in the north, three or possibly six divisions from India in the west. In the spring the Japanese in Burma were reinforced, and the decision was made. Basically, the Japanese attack on India was intended to forestall an ultimate offensive against themselves by striking at once and dispersing the gathering British force. The conception was sound, if somewhat optimistic. The Japanese threw into disorder the aggressive plans on the British side.

First the Japanese hoped to overrun the British in Arakan, and then to advance into India, taking in the Assamese towns of Imphal and Kohima. From there they would move into Bengal, though probably they intended no larger action which would have taken them beyond that province. They affected, however, to fall in with Bose's plans for the general invasion of India, as they made stirring material for propaganda. In March 1944 they began their attack and crossed the Indian frontier. The Japanese Army employed three divisions.

Bose was determined that they should be accompanied by regiments of the Indian National Army. His Provisional Government had been transferred to Burma in January 1944. He is described by Ba Maw at the time as a 'bold, khaki-clad figure, carrying with him everywhere the aura of his vast, fabulous country'. In what followed, Bose's sense of reality, his strong point compared with the Indian leaders on the British side of the dividing line, deserted him. He proclaimed the slogan 'Chalo Delhi'. ('On to Delhi'). Its Red Fort, the ancient citadel built by Shah Jahan, hypnotized him, and its occupation became an obsession. In his elation, he foresaw himself sweeping on, made master of the country by a popular upsurge; able, with the strength which this would bring him, to dictate terms to the surrendering British, and to ensure that the Japanese did not misuse their victory, or ride roughshod over the country. He calculated that a Japanese invasion of India would create a very divided feeling among

Indians, and might even, the reputation of Japan being what it was, bring a mass of them to the side of the British; but the appearance on Indian soil of an Indian army of liberation would have the most rousing effect all over the country. The world would hear for the first time of the Indian National Army, and thousands of Indians would surge to it. It is strange to find a politician as practical as Bose nursing such illusions. The conversations at this time between Bose and his captains in the Indian National Army, the records of which have survived, are the proofs of his misconception.

The Japanese took a cooler view of his prospects. They wanted to divide the INA (Indian National Army) up into units of 250 men, who would act as liaison troops, guides and spies, and who would each be attached to a Japanese force. In the end a compromise was arrived at. The INA had three organized divisions in the expedition, each of two thousand men. The remainder moved as auxiliaries. It became known that the Japanese Army had reserved for itself the right of gaining the first victory on Indian soil, and looked forward to offering Imphal as a birthday present to the Emperor, which would be the more welcome because the war was going badly on other fronts.

The Army against which it moved, the Fourteenth Army, was, like the armies in the Middle East, a joint Anglo-Indian one. Battalions were either British, Indian or Gurkha, but the battalions were mixed up, and the brigade, and still more the division, were heterogeneous. Throughout the war, there was general good feeling and cooperation between the British and Indians. Whatever the grievances, they did not show themselves on the battlefield. This Army, by the reorganization of command which took place in 1943, had passed under the supreme direction of Lord Louis Mountbatten, Commander-in-Chief in South-East Asia, with the ultimate command post at Colombo.

The Army which was about to receive its first campaigning experience represented, at least in part, a new kind of India in arms. Its old pre-war armies had been drawn from a relatively few districts and, among Hindus, from a few chosen castes. Now, under wartime necessity, the Army had very much widened its intake of recruits: and with surprising results. For example, Madrasis, who had formed an important part of the armies of Lord Wellesley at the Battle of Assaye, had not been recruited for many years. Now they were offered employment, and the Madrasis celebrated their readmission by supplying the most decorated Air Force pilots that came from any region of India.

The Army undoubtedly gained from opening its ranks; and in so doing the Government met a long-standing grievance of the people. The conomic benefits of supplying troops were very considerable, and these ccounted in part for the prosperity of such regions as the Punjab. It ad seemed unjust to favour some parts of the country and to withhold enefits from the others. The lot was cast by a theory, largely arbitrary nd false, that some of the people were naturally martial, others not; a fact the distinction dated from the Indian Mutiny, and it operated hiefly on the principle of rewarding the classes which had not joined the Mutiny and of discriminating against those which had. At last the Army hook itself free from baleful memories, and thereafter it recruited itself on a more national basis.

This new Army began to reflect the new interests of India. Whereas the old Army had been entirely non-political, the new entries inevitably brought in with them something of their political interests. The attempt to debar contacts with political leaders had to be given up: the brightest of he recruits, especially for the officer corps, were the most political: the pride in being above politics had to give way. These new recruits thought it unnatural and absurd to volunteer their lives for use in a war in which hey had no say. The mess rooms became forums where every aspect of he world and of government action was under constant scrutiny. This was reflected in the concern of the Government in seeing that the reading ooms of the Army were well stocked with propaganda. The older genera- ion of thoroughly professional Army officers and of Indian NCOs ooked on disapprovingly, but they could do nothing to stem this constant debate. Increasingly the Government was compelled to open the barrack- oom gates, so the Army became less cloistered. In these months of the war, the old life of India was talked away in the heroic and mock bravura of undergraduate politics conducted by an Army of civilians in uniform.

In the campaign which was about to begin, many of the regular Indian officers, whose admission to the Army had been the great event in its history during the 1930s, were to be for the first time in action. Soldiers who afterwards became well-known, such as Ayub Khan, later to become President of Pakistan, were tested in this fighting.

About the British soldiers in this Army, the main fact was that they began the campaign by being war-weary. They had many of them been on duty for a long time, in an unhealthy climate. They were unsettled by the separation from their families. They were bored by inactivity. They, too, regarded themselves as true professional soldiers, but they complained – with some reason – that they were the 'forgotten Army': an Army which had lain in preparation too long and had not the bracing experience of coming into action. It did not take to the poisonous atmosphere of the country it was to fight in, to the jungles and the eerie silences, to the

leeches and snakes: its medical services were inadequate, and, before th
introduction of mepacrin, it was always decimated by malaria.

The Japanese advance became bogged down in the siege of Imphal. Fc
over eight weeks, beginning on 8 March 1944, a terrible contest, perhap
the most primitive of the war with the exception of the struggle for th
Pacific atolls, took place for the possession of the city: there was resolut
hand-to-hand fighting.

At the beginning of the siege, the Japanese, at the start of their offensive
looked very likely to succeed. But the expedition was doomed when th
Japanese found it impossible, because of the nature of the country and th
blockage of supply routes from the air, to reinforce it with men anc
materials to overcome the defence. For days the Japanese were convincec
that a final effort by them would deliver the city into their hands: bu
always they were disappointed. They beat off British and Indian sorties
but their own attacks were repulsed. There was great carnage, the mor
intense because the Japanese had to be killed at their posts, in th
bunkers and wherever they had found cover. A similar struggle took plac
a little to the north of Imphal for Kohima, where a gigantic battle wa:
waged over the possession of a tennis-court in the garden of the Com
missioner's house.

A tactical innovation which deprived the Japanese of one of thei
habitual means of securing advantage was made during the campaign
In their drive through Malaya and Burma two years before, they had
using their superior mobility, habitually surrounded British forces; and
when this took place, the British habitually withdrew. This time the
British did not retreat; and, though surrounded, relied on being suppliec
by air. An elaborate organization of the RAF flew in large amounts o
food and ammunition. Without this airlift Imphal would have fallen.
This change in tactics, which was due to the improved strength of the
RAF in the area, changed the situation. The Japanese plans went awry
when the troops, whom they thought they had trapped, stayed to fight
it out instead of retiring in disorder. They misjudged profoundly the
quality of the troops they opposed. They had formed so low an opinion
of the British in the Malayan fighting that this betrayed them; the extent
to which British troops under British command were underrated turned
out to be one of their principal assets.

Another important, significant, hopeful change was that, for the first
time in the war the Japanese began to surrender. Not in large numbers:
the majority were still faithful to the idea that defeated Japanese are killed
or commit suicide. But that some at least, when wounded, depressed, cut

74 *Top*: An American bulldozer scoops out a mass grave for some 2,000 Japanese killed in Saipan during a final 'Banzai' charge on 7 July 1945

75 *Bottom*: A prisoner-of-war stockade holds some 300 Japanese who surrendered to US Marines during the last twenty-four hours of fighting on Okinawa

9621 GENERAL VIEW OF POW STOCKADE FILLED WITH SOME OF 300 JAPANESE PRISONERS WHO CAME

76 *Top*: Air reconnaissance
of Tokyo, along the Sumida
river, shows the effect of
firestorms caused by a US
Army Air Force B29
incendiary-bomb attack on 13
September 1945

77 *Bottom*: After the first
firestorm in Tokyo, caused by
the Allies, Emperor Hirohito
walks through the same
district as the ruins smoulder

78 *Top*: The small-parts assembly line of the Mitsubishi aircraft works at Nagoya after air raids by B29 superfortresses based in the Marianas

79 *Bottom*: Central Hiroshima at the very moment of its destruction by an atomic bomb, 6 August 1945. The building on the right, an astronomical observatory, was one of the few buildings to survive. It became a memorial

80 *Top*: A panorama of
Hiroshima half a mile west of
ground zero, looking away
from ground zero. Everything
within a radius of 4.4 miles
has been burned out

81 *Centre and bottom*: After
a Japanese military arsenal at
Kokura was obscured by haze,
Nagasaki became the second
city to fall victim to an atomic
bomb on 9 August 1945

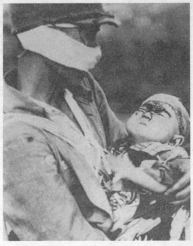

82 *Top*: The Kwantung Army's main bacteriological warfare complex at Pingfan, Manchuria

83 *Bottom left*: Japanese subjects bow in reverence on a bridge over the moat of the Imperial Palace in Tokyo as the Shōwa Emperor broadcasts the surrender of Japan on 15 August 1945

84 *Bottom right*: The Japanese regarded the Allied policy of mass destruction of enemy cities as criminal. Here a convicted Australian airman is beheaded at Fukuoka Prison immediately after the Emperor announced the surrender of Japan

85 *Top*: Scene of the
surrender of Japanese forces in
China at Tsingtao Race
Course

86 *Bottom*: US Marines in
post-war China: the First
Marine Division occupies
Tientsin, 1 October 1945

87   *Top*: The courtroom of
the International Military
Tribunal for the Far East

88   *Centre*: Lieutenant-
General Fukuei Shinpei,
formerly officer in command
of the Japanese prisoner-of-
war camps in Singapore and
Malaya, is executed by a
British firing squad in April
1946

89   *Bottom*: Japanese
prisoners of war stacking shell
casings after defusing and
removing their powder charges
following the surrender of
Japan

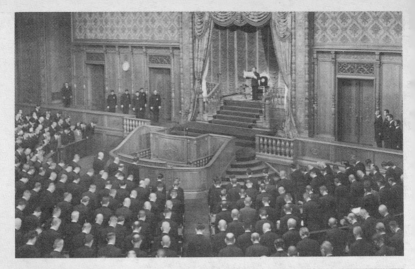

90   *Top*: The Emperor
promulgates the new post-war
Constitution of Japan in
ceremonies before the Imperial
Diet

91   *Bottom*: Part of the US
Navy's 'mothball' fleet
anchored at the Eleventh
Naval District, San Diego,
California

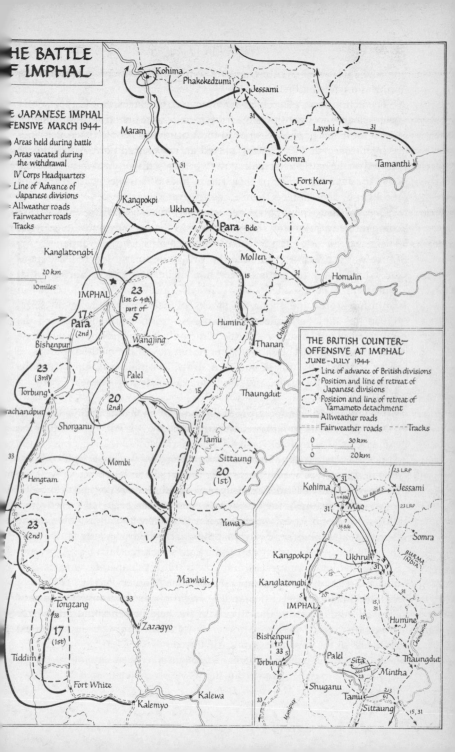

THE BATTLE OF IMPHAL

THE JAPANESE IMPHAL OFFENSIVE MARCH 1944

- Areas held during battle
- Areas vacated during the withdrawal
- IV Corps Headquarters
- Line of Advance of Japanese divisions
- Allweather roads
- Fairweather roads
- Tracks

20 km
10 miles

Kohima
Phakekedzumi
Jessami
Maram
Layshi
Somra
Tamanthi
Fort Keary
Kangpokpi
Ukhrul
Para Bde
Kanglatongbi
Mollen
IMPHAL
23 (1st & 4th) part of **5**
Humine
Homalin
17 & Para (2nd)
Wangjing
Bishenpur
Thanan
23 (3rd)
Palel
23 (3rd IV)
Torbung
20 (2nd)
Thaungdut
rachandpur
Shorganu
Tamu
Mombi
Sittaung
Hengtam
20 (1st)
Yuwa
23 (2nd)
Mawlaik
Tongzang
33
Zazagyo
17 (1st)
Tiddim
Fort White
Kalewa
Kalemyo

THE BRITISH COUNTER-OFFENSIVE AT IMPHAL
JUNE–JULY 1944
Line of advance of British divisions
Position and line of retreat of Japanese divisions
Position and line of retreat of Yamamoto detachment
Allweather roads
Fairweather roads
Tracks

30 km
20 km

Kohima
31
23 LRP
Mao
Jessami
23 LRP
Somra
Kangpokpi
Ukhrul
BURMA / INDIA
Kanglatongbi
IMPHAL
Humine
Bishenpur
33
Palel
Sita
Thaungdut
Torbung
Mintha
Shuganu
Tamu
Sittaung

off and cold, acted as other soldiers similarly placed were accustomed to do, was a cheering fact.

The action took place in the country of the Nagas. Some spectacular achievements brought the Naga tribesmen into the light of world publicity. Much more has happened since to these attractive people. Their activities in Intelligence, and as porters, played an unexpected part. A monument erected on the battlefield recalls how two Nagas, disguised as mess servants, stole the Japanese plans of their future lines of advance, passed these to the British, and enabled them to be frustrated.

One Japanese newspaper reporter wrote: 'These fierce battles are comparable with Verdun in the last war.' Finally, logistics were decisive. There was an utter failure of communications, and the Japanese Air Force was too weak to emulate the British in air transport. The Japanese could bring in neither rice, nor medical supplies, nor essential equipment. The Japanese, who always travelled light, had relied on capturing stores and living on stocks of rice which they might seize; but in this they had failed. The Japanese troop commander issued the following order: 'A decisive battle is the only battle known to a Japanese soldier, or fitting to the Japanese spirit, but now other methods may have to be adopted.' By this he meant a strategic withdrawal. On 4 July the Japanese lifted the siege, and, on their way back, their retreat became a disaster.

They began the campaign with an army of 85,000 men; in it they lost 53,000. British and Indian casualties amounted to 16,700. The result of the campaign was a terrible, wasteful, ignominious defeat. It was one of the worst disasters that the Japanese Army suffered in the whole war; comparable in disgrace, if not in magnitude, to that of the Japanese Navy at the Battle of Midway Island. Primarily, when all due allowance had been made for the performance of the Fourteenth Army, it had been due to ineffective staff work by an Army which was not familiar with campaigning in the tropics. It must be remembered that the war in Malaya had been before this the only large-scale operation of this kind which the Japanese Army had fought, and, on balance, its training was still for temperate climates. The higher officers would not cooperate with one another. Perhaps because of this, the Japanese GHQ demanded a rigid obedience to orders and thus checked initiative from the officers in the field, which could often have turned defeat into victory. Another cause of the rout was the numerical weakness of the Japanese Army Air Force.

But that the Japanese soldiers had fought like tigers cannot be denied. A quotation may be given from the book on the campaign by Colonel Barker entitled *The March on Delhi*:

Recruits in the Japanese Army were subjected to an intense three-month course of indoctrination which changed them into fanatics, ready to die for their Emperor, their country and the honour of their regiments. The slogan 'Our highest hope is to die for the Emperor' was chanted until it became a positive obsession. The indoctrination of their families was not forgotten either; soon after the new recruit was called up, his relatives received a letter from his commanding officer asking them to be careful not to block his road to an honourable death. The effectiveness of the propaganda may be judged from the fact that there were cases of wives killing their children and committing suicide so that their husbands would not be reluctant to die. Many officers and men even had their funeral rites performed before leaving for the front to show their intention of dying for their country . . .*

Yet, impressive as their military behaviour was, it was undoubtedly an aberration. There was madness in it, as well as remarkable self-discipline. For, as the war dragged on to its close, and as the Japanese position grew steadily worse, so did the Japanese military behaviour become more ferocious. Its extreme cult of death was a new thing of this century, as least in the form which it took at the time. Early in this century, the Russo-Japanese War had not been particularly savage. And the new sternness was only to be found in the Japanese overseas. As long as they were in the homeland, they did not seem to be possessed, as were the troops in Burma, in the Philippines and in China. It was as if the Japanese Army, once it had had battle experience, succeeded in passing its *furor Japonicus* to all the reinforcements which came to it from Japan. The madness came out in some of the battle orders which were captured:

You men have got to be fully in the picture as to what the present position is. Regarding death as something lighter than a feather you men must tackle the task of capturing Imphal. You must accept that the division will be almost annihilated. I have confidence in your courage but should any delinquency occur, I shall take the necessary action. In order to keep the honour of his unit bright, a commander may have to use his sword as a weapon of punishment, shameful though it is to have to shed one's own soldiers' blood on the battlefield.†

Some of the men who were the victims of this military discipline, some of the officers who enforced it, are now living quietly in Japan, and they must look back on their wartime experience with surprise and almost with disbelief.

The news of the defeat on 4 July arrived in Tokyo at the same time as the news of the loss of Paris by Germany. It was hard to say which of them

* A. J. Barker, *The March on Delhi*, Faber, London, 1963.
† ibid.

faced the blacker prospects, Germany or Japan. The disaster increased the bad relations between the Army and the Navy: this came, said the Navy, of the Army 'taking walks' in Asia, and entering on unnecessary adventures instead of concentrating on the problems of the defence of the homeland.

The adventures were nearly at an end. The Army would be needed in the Japanese islands. This campaign was nearly the finish of the Japanese in Burma. For a time they were saved from effective pursuit by the monsoon, which put an end to all war. But when the monsoon ended, the Fourteenth Army moved forward. The offensive had already been joined by a bitterly fought advance of Americans and American-trained Chinese troops (who had fallen back on India in 1942) led by General Stilwell; a thrust from Arakan for which the prelude was the taking of Akyab from the sea; and by four Chinese divisions reluctantly introduced by Chiang Kai-shek from Yunnan. This time the offensive progressed. The Allies had clear air supremacy, and this was decisive, particularly because it enabled them to keep their armies fully supplied. The Japanese had stirred up opposition from all corners of the world; they must however have felt somewhat surprised at finding among their pursuers divisions of West African and East African troops. They had been raised by the British, and the war in Burma in tropical conditions offered them appropriate employment. That the African people had no quarrel with Japan, that Japan had no significance to them except as the exporter of textiles which were prized by them, did not seem to cause any comment.

As the British slowly reoccupied Burma, they felt the imperial itch reviving. An Imperial Army in advance bred different sentiments from an Imperial Army in retreat. 'By English bones the English flag is stayed.' This old line of poetry took on a new meaning.

By April 1945 Rangoon had fallen. It fell actually to the advance from Akyab, which beat by a few hours the advance from the north. The Japanese soldiers continued to fight savagely, but they were the victims of the bad strategy of their generals. Soon all Burma was clear. The end was made more certain because most of the Burmese Army, which had been raised and trained by the Japanese, revolted and changed sides at a critical moment.

In the course of this campaign, there had taken place a sharp revision of the complacency of the Japanese about the demerits of the British soldier. Soon after the start of the war, the Japanese had met with such success, and the morale of the white troops they had encountered had been so low that they had supposed that the prestige the British had enjoyed during the previous century had been the result of a confidence trick. Caution towards the British was succeeded by extreme scorn. They could not have held them in lower esteem, and this probably accounted for their over-confidence in the Kohima operations, which otherwise appeared light-headed. They preferred to have British troops to deal with rather than Indian, since, in the new reckoning of the Japanese Army, white troops were less tenacious than Asian troops. In the vicissitudes of this campaign, however, they learnt, very expensively, that they had made a wrong assessment. The British troops put on their laurels again, and their recent campaign gave the Japanese new respect for their adversary.

In the battle, the Indian National Army had proved useless. In nearly all the fighting, it had disgraced itself. Its largest losses were from desertion. Its heart was not in combat with the Government to which it had formerly owed allegiance. Its performance had a depressing effect on the hopes of seeing the war turn into an Asian defensive operation against the western counter-attack. Subhas Chandra Bose sustained himself in his disappointment, and against the contempt which the Japanese military did not bother to hide, by putting out an account of near-treachery by the Japanese. Imphal, according to him, had been helpless before the Indo-Japanese force, but the Japanese had held back the Indian advance which would have taken it. They were unwilling that the Indians should have the great prize of the campaign; they wished to present Imphal as a Japanese conquest to the Emperor on his birthday. An Indian governor had been ready to take possession, but the Indian troops were forestalled from inducting him.

The tale was too inaccurate to be effective. Subhas Bose lost nearly all his magical appeal. In despair, he turned away from his concern with the Indian National Army to the political regimentation of the million Indians living in South-East Asia. But his fortunes sank with those of the Japanese. When these were finally overwhelmed, and had surrendered, he prevailed on a local officer to let him try to escape by air to Russia. It was a move consonant with his daring and his obstinate opportunism. He foresaw that relations between the West and Russia would be bad, and hoped that Moscow would see the opportunity of letting him set up in Russia his provisional Government of India. But the aeroplane in which he was flying crashed on the way to Formosa, on 18 August 1945, and Bose ended his melodramatic life. In spite of his failure, he had, by his daring, so much caught the imagination of the Indians who had been in touch with him, that they refused to believe that he had really been killed. The rumour spread that he had gone underground and had become a Sadhu (there is some evidence that some of the defeated rebels did this in 1858 after the failure of the Indian Mutiny), and that he would emerge again to lead a triumphant rising against the British. The legend was firmly believed in by his brother, Sarat Chandra Bose, a leading, and apparently hard-headed, Congressman of Bengal.

Bose's idea of corrupting the Indian Army, and of leading it back in triumph against the British in Delhi, though it turned out to be a fiasco could have been a formidable threat to Britain. Its concept was sound: it was fortunate for Britain that the morale of the INA was such as to make the plan unworkable. For months the news of the INA caused very deep anxiety among the Army Staff and the informed civilians in Delhi, and their failure in action was received with intense relief. The enterprise had been kept reasonably secret from the public in India. It was not entirely unknown, for the information about it was contained in the monitoring report which had a fairly wide circulation; moreover, Bose's radio was listened to fairly extensively. But the public was surprised when it learned later from the press how wide the conspiracy had been.

Of 70,000 Indians who had been captives, over half resisted all the lures to serve either Japan direct or else rebel India. They had nothing very much to induce them to remain loyal beyond their oath of service and their regimental pride. These ties held; and their strength was an important factor in determining the history of the war in Asia. For this the main credit goes to the regimental commanders of the previous two or three generations who, by and large, were trusted by their men to stand up for their interests, for fair treatment, and for an honourable status. These men built up the ties which between 1942 and 1945 bore the great strain.

This left the problem of what to do with the soldiers who had been less loyal. Most of those who had enlisted in the INA had passed into British hands, and for the second time had become prisoners of war. Technically they were all of them guilty of an internationally agreed crime of the darkest nature. For desertion, treason, rebellion and levying war against the King, a harsh penalty was likely to be exacted. Actually, no drumhead court-martials were held on any of the prisoners upon capture. They were kept in captivity, and what to do about them became a political case which was hotly debated.

It was not decided until the war ended. The Congress leaders, on coming out of their own wartime captivity, saw in it an ideal means of attacking the Government. The INA were presented as the true heroes of the Indian nation, and, if harshly dealt with, would become revered martyrs. The British were impressed by this danger. They were inclined to act in the spirit of Winston Churchill, who advising clemency on another occasion, had said: 'The grass grows quickly over the battlefield. Over the scaffold, never.' They decided to release the undistin-guished mass of the prisoners. But they hesitated at the ring-leaders, and those who, in the course of the campaign, had been guilty of war crimes, or had tortured their former comrades because these had stood firm against the allurements of the Japanese. They had to keep it in mind that those who felt most bitterly against the Indian National Army were the officers and men of the Indian Army who had remained loyal. For the sake of the morale of this Army, it was scarcely possible to release without some punishment at least the more spectacular of the prisoners. Therefore, after much indecision, and much discussion which became involved with the renewed negotiations between the Government and Congress, the decision was made to limit prosecution to a few cases, ultimately restricted to three.

The trials were held in the Red Fort of Delhi in 1946. A more peculiarly inept setting could not have been chosen. The Red Fort had become, in Indian national mythology, the shrine of Indian national hopes. It had been built as a citadel and palace by the Moghul Emperors, and sym-bolized the time before the British conquest, when all that Britain meant had been individual merchants coming to beg for patronage from the great ones of India. The trials gave so much publicity to the Congress lawyers, who were able to defend the prisoners, and to Jawaharhal Nehru who, having once been a barrister, could appear before the courts, that the Government was glad to call them off quickly. It was content with the simple dismissal from further service of the great majority of officers and men. Such dismissal was punishment in itself, since service in the Army brought with it economic privilege; and, by confiscating this advantage from the disaffected, it was thought that the loyal part of the Indian Army would be at ease.

Burma had been freed as the result of a sustained thrust of the British and the Americans against the Japanese Army, which had worn itself out by the offensive at Imphal and Kohima. From recovered Burma, the victors prepared to move afresh. Singapore and Malaya were the next targets: and Japan had there, and elsewhere in South-East Asia, a very large Army, as yet unscathed, its morale untouched by Allied propaganda, with vast supplies of arms and ammunition. The prospect which this opened up, and the length of time which would be taken in ejecting Japan from one well-defended post to another, caused a great upsurge of cri-ticism of British strategy. Had the drive on Burma, even though it was ultimately successful, really been justified? Were there not better ways of using British power than in following the withdrawal of Japan? Could

Britain, using its recovered naval supremacy, not strike at some vital ports, less protected?

There is a notable passage in Tolstoy's *War and Peace* describing men's behaviour on the battlefield. When he is stricken on the field of Austerlitz, Prince Andrei sees two opposing men, French and Russian, both seizing hold of a ramrod, and struggling for its possession. Each would have done better to release his hold of it, and to free himself to use his musket. But they were too much hypnotized by the struggle to let go. So they continued to tussle. In the circumstances of the war in Asia, it was asked whether the British and Japanese really did any good for themselves, or brought the war nearer to an end, by remaining locked in conflict.

In fact, the decisive fighting was going on in the Pacific. Britain was denied a role in this: it could supply no adequate force, and the American commanders were under pressure to distance themselves from allies who put their cause in such an imperialist colour. Keeping the British at arm's length was held to improve the American image with the national parties of South Asia. The future of that part of the world was held to lie with them.

CHAPTER 23

China 1942-4

BEFORE describing the end of Japan, and the breakthrough of the American ships from the Pacific, it is necessary to review the fate of China up to this point. After all, China had been one of the principal causes of the war in the Far East. This conflict, which had spread so widely, had begun as the result of the refusal by Chiang Kai-shek to come to terms with Japan. China had not ceased to count. But, after the intervention of the United States, it had taken a relatively minor part in the military affairs of the nations.

Before the conflict was enlarged, Chiang had calculated that, if he held out, sooner or later Japan would come into collision with other Powers. He had resolved, and it was more or less public knowledge, that, when this time came, China, which for four years had borne the fury of the Japanese offensive, would retire from the actual fighting, and would leave it to the fresher forces which should become engaged to complete the wearing down of Japan, of which China felt that it had done enough. Without fighting further, Chiang Kai-shek counted on being able to join in the eventual share-out of territory, and in the other benefits, when the world was rearranged at the general peace. In this, events had gone more or less as Chiang expected. Chiang, the simple and, in the eyes of the sophisticated statesmen of the West, rather primitive soldier, seemed at the time to have his judgement vindicated, his diplomacy confirmed.

It appeared to the Americans that China, poor in resources for making war, now held the best cards. The United States had chosen to take up the challenge of Japan. But it had handicapped itself by the decision to concentrate on fighting Germany first, Japan afterwards. In the interval before it could concentrate its whole attention on Japan, allies in the East seemed likely to be of greater moment to the United States than the United States was to them. It became a major preoccupation with it to keep China in the war, at the cost of offering it all possible inducement to stay. China could have all that it asked, in exchange for its willingness that the total commitment of American force in the Far East should be delayed. In the long run, the United States believed that the use of Chinese territory was indispensable for making it geographically possible for the

Allies to defeat Japan; it had no confidence that Russia, which also had a land army able to get to grips with Japan, would ever, in the way that events were shaping themselves, break its neutrality with Japan. For the United States, China represented the corridor along which their armies might eventually proceed, and get at Japan on level terms. In the meanwhile, China was to be the subject of a holding operation: to be kept in the war at all costs. For this the Americans were prepared to pay a great deal, and they had insufficient regard for the fact that the Chinese were accustomed to considering long-term as well as the short-term interests of their country. Chiang Kai-shek and his supporters could read their balance sheets and were masters at calculating profit and loss.

The impediment lay chiefly in geography. With the fall of Burma, the precarious link with Chungking along the Burma Road was interrupted. China was cut off. Between it and the Americans there was the enormous barrier of the Himalayas. To keep China in the war, the Americans, with ingenuity, tried by every means to circumvent the obstacle. They organized an airlift to China over the mountain ranges from India; they sent American officers to re-train the Chinese Army; they put continual pressure upon India to demonstrate that China might eventually find aid there. In immediate aid, China was given a large Anglo-American loan: America subscribed $500 million and Britain £50 million: this relieved its immediate financial problems.

This aid the Allies intended for China as a whole. It was directed to whoever in China would fight Japan. Chiang Kai-shek's aim was to engross it all for himself. It was to ensure that his hold over the country was continuously and decisively strengthened; it was to deny aid to those who might threaten it. In his thinking at that time dollars counted for more than morale in the upkeep of government. He saw danger principally in one fact – that the communists, the party of revolution, might obtain the economic backing which would transform the situation, and put them on equal terms with the Government. In a China in which the ferment of revolution was working ever more actively, in which communism had already mastered the circumstances of the war, it was essential that the communists should be denied their share of foreign aid, even at the cost of their military efficiency as allies against Japan. Technically, the Kuomintang and the communists were still allies; they were pledged together to fight Japan; the American aid, on a reading of the military situation, should have been divided between them. That it should not became the governing aim of Chiang's policy. He was still the embodiment of Chinese nationalism, but he was first and always a warlord.

At first, the prospects appeared bright for Chiang. His more distant ambitions, of being the supreme force in Asia at the end of the war, buoyed him up when his Government, as the result of the intensification of the blockade, suffered blow upon blow. Chiang was sanguine: this perhaps explains why he took phlegmatically even the worst of news. Both his enemies, Japan and Chinese Communism, were being trampled into ruin by the United States. His long-term prospects were heady. His standing in Washington mattered more to him than military realities in the Far East. In this he was served zealously, alike by plausible Chinese and by foreigners over whom China had cast its spell.

Chiang, in order apparently to gratify his sense of importance, struck out in directions which caused surprise, and ways which were unwelcome to his allies. He had insisted on visiting India, in February 1942, and seeing Indian affairs for himself. He could urge that India had suddenly become vitally important for China, both as a base, and as transit territory for American supplies. The bad relations between the Government of India and Indian nationalists were a menace to China, because they could result in a situation which interrupted communication. Chiang insisted on studying matters for himself, and tried, by personal diplomacy with the Viceroy and Indian leaders, to bridge the gap between them.

The British were annoyed. They found Chiang extremely ill-informed, and privately judged that, in the guise of a mediator, he was prospecting the ground for Chinese intervention in case the military necessity in Europe should compel a British withdrawal from India. They objected to the need for providing Chiang and his wife with banquets at the moment when, too late in the judgement of many observers, they had become conscious of their desperate state. Especially, though, they demurred at the increased prestige which his interest brought to the Indian Congress in its duel with the Viceroy.

Chiang Kai-shek could not blame the Indian Administration for a failure to back him. This somewhat lethargic Government went out of its way to provide, with energy and great speed, the institutions which were needed to bind the two Governments together in their war effort. On the Indian side, a China Relations Department was brought into being, to whose good offices a thousand things were owing: the Department did everything, from supply to strengthening military cooperation. It was efficient, it was prompt, it cut through delays. It was so much out of character for the Government of India that it quite astonished the Chinese.

In spite of these inducements to be up and doing, China remained more or less militarily inactive. The performance of Chinese troops, in the rare

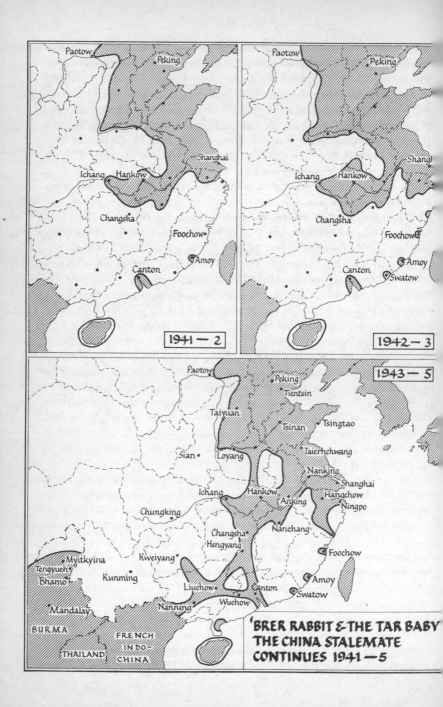

1941—2

1942—3

1943—5

'BRER RABBIT & THE TAR BABY
THE CHINA STALEMATE
CONTINUES 1941—5

actions in which they were engaged, was unmemorable. Nor was this surprising. Their armies were shockingly organized; relations between officers and men were deplorable. The officers were increasingly arrogant and corrupt; they embezzled the wages of the soldiers; they were often brutal and ignorant. The soldiers either were separated for many years from their families, or, if they had news of them, were rightly disturbed at the news of worsened conditions in the countryside. The rank and file had nothing to fight for.

Chiang Kai-shek chose, in March 1943, to publish under his name a highly controversial book. It was written in Chinese. The book was called *China's Destiny*. It contained the familiar story of the unjust dealings with China by the Great Powers, the unequal treaties, the shearing away from China of her dependencies. Thus it revealed that China still nursed her grievances when it might have seemed better policy to have concealed them. The Powers which had done China its past wrongs had now shown a willingness to repair the damage, and the exposure of China's wound could only damage their cooperation. The effect of its publication was to cause mistrust, rouse suspicion, and generate bad blood. Madame Chiang Kai-shek shrewdly advised against an English translation: this did not appear therefore until 1947. The book, however, had come to the attention of the West's China hands when it first appeared in Chinese, and therefore it had precisely the effect which Chiang wanted to produce.

Chiang, in his relations with his Allies, followed the tactics of 'threatening to fall'. He advertised that his position was calamitous. The weaker he was, the more anxious the Americans were for him, and the greater the efforts which they were willing to make on his behalf. Naturally he led them on; and he was helped by the chance that President Roosevelt revealed, from the United States' entry into the war until his death in 1945, an extraordinary partiality for China. The accidents of personality played here a fateful part. Roosevelt, active in Washington, had an even greater influence on events by the climate of opinion which he germinated, than by the measures he took as head of the American Government. He was himself endowed with no special perspicacity, but he did surround himself with able men who dwelt much on the shape which the world must take as a result of the war; and he became convinced that, round a firm Sino-American axis, the Asian countries were destined to revolve. American aid would supply strength to China; China would revert to its traditional art of radiating its great civilizing influence out across its borders.

Roosevelt saw rightly that the crisis in East Asia was due ultimately to the collapse of the political power of China. The United States would restore it. This time there would be no imperialists to undermine it again; President Roosevelt was satisfied that the eastern role of Britain and other colonial Powers was coming to an end and he had a curious blind spot in relation to the Soviet Union's inheritance of Imperial Russian pretensions in world politics. Asia would be safe again, except from its own dissension, and what power would thrive better in this atmosphere than China. He gained comfort from the signs that China's appetite for its historic greatness was beginning to recover. He became convinced that he was serving alike the interests of the United States and also all the world by throwing his mantle over China.

Roosevelt had an extraordinary power of communicating his vision to the public. In this case, however, he preached mostly to the converted. The United States' attitude towards China in the later stages of the war was rather unbalanced. If one nation can be said to adopt another, the United States adopted China. The United States has been liable to periodical phases of extreme partiality to certain foreign countries; in its fervent feeling towards China at this time, it outdid itself. The United States was hallucinated; like Titania by Bottom the Weaver. The reality was that the United States became enthusiastic for the tyranny of the Kuomintang, which was passing increasingly into the most reactionary hands; the Americans saw it, not as it was, but as a democratic party full of vigour and promise. In place of a military rabble, the United States saw in the Chinese Army an inspiring force, which was a mixture of a romanticized version of the American armies of the Revolution and the Civil War. Where there was evident and apparently irreparable economic ruin, it saw lively economic promise. China's intellectual and artistic life, which, to the trained eye, was in the ruins of a great cultural past, appeared to the USA to be full of a fresh, imaginative view of the world. China appeared as nearly a new Utopia. The United States of course produced its realists, who protested against its romantic illusions, but they could scarcely make themselves heard against the newspapers and radio, which almost all of them followed the fashion.

Roosevelt's policies, the American hallucination, the realities of geography and of logistics in the East, produced, between them, a mood of accommodation to China which bewildered the rest of the world. China was pitied, but the United States postponed coming to its aid with immediate and effective military succour. It was encouraged by the United States to pass its time in discussing its growing ambition. American patronage ensured that China's claims were not regarded as simply ludicrous. Men like Winston Churchill took a sceptical view, but it was ardly worth their while to oppose the United States over this. In war, aked strength is in the last resort the thing which counts; but prestige nay be manufactured by handfuls of dedicated officials and the few tatesmen who matter, and may, in the short run, pass for strength. China vas in this condition, and advanced by several degrees in the world's steem.

All the while that this was happening, the Chinese press, which was of course under strong Government influence, had, as was natural in the relations between states, been biting the hand which fed it. The newspapers were full of articles which attacked the United States very bitterly. They made use of the stale propaganda methods of the Nazis early in the war in Europe. They claimed that the United States would fight until the ast Chinaman; they envisaged that China, having made great sacrifices 'or democracy, would be a certain loser at the peace, and would itself be sacrificed. They painted a picture of the riotous life lived by Americans in uxurious camps in the midst of the poverty of China. This mood, when it became known in the United States, took a little of the glow out of the American feeling for China. But the work of the China lobby had been very far-reaching, and the suspicion that the Chinese were ungrateful was lightly borne by American philanthropy.

Although there was much criticism of Chiang Kai-shek by some Americans with a clearer vision, too much can be made of occasional Sino-American friction. In particular, the incompetence and bad morale of the Chinese were probably overrated by some American experts. There was no real likelihood of China making a separate peace. Chiang Kai-shek had steered China's policy since the earliest years of the conflict, but, by the latest years, China had probably steered itself. The muddle, constant criticism, and apathy misled the United States. China, though it detested war, was averse to surrender. It would have opposed Chiang if he had wished to make a dishonourable peace with nearly as much compulsive force as it had done when it suspected him in 1937. China's mood was frightening. It had not the least enthusiasm for the war; it was profoundly weary of it; but it was determined to continue to resist. If ever a war had in fact been a 'people's war', this was one, even though there were large and respectable elements of the population who were cooperating with the Japanese. The Government was forbidden by the nation to make peace: by a nation which, by all reasonable arguments, yearned for peace. The war seemed likely to continue indefinitely.

It was the Americans who had to serve in China who were naturally less affected by the pronounced American enthusiasm for all things

Chinese. Their position was extremely difficult; they suffered much les
from the delusions which were making American policy, but they wer
expected to act as if they did so. The attitude of the much-tried America
General Joseph Stilwell deserves study. His mishaps are part of the mis
understandings of the time.

He was a naturally bilious man aptly nicknamed 'Vinegar Joe': he wa
extraordinarily suspicious of everyone, especially of Americans wh
fawned on Chinese; of all British, with whom he had to be in alliance bu
whom he suspected of outwitting the United States, and of the Chinese
above all of Chiang Kai-shek, whom he saw playing a gigantic confidenc
trick on the United States. The irony was that he, who had few illusions
was inclined to be grimly friendly towards China, and, in a professiona
manner, to defend its interests.

After Pearl Harbor, when American aid began to pour into China, i
was clearly desirable to appoint someone to be responsible on the spot fo
its distribution. A commander was needed for the American personne
who were militarily active in or near China. A military expert was als
necessary to work out joint military plans with the Chinese. Stilwell, as a
person of unquestionable experience, and available immediately, was
appointed. He had spent most of his career in China, with some dedication
had studied the Chinese language since 1919 (when he had been appointed
the first Chinese language officer in the history of the US Army), and had
served for many years in a quasi-diplomatic status in the American
Embassy. At Roosevelt's insistence, in his instinct to mix up America's
affairs with those of its Allies, Stilwell was given by Chiang Kai-shek the
Chinese rank of his Chief-of-Staff.

When, as described earlier, the British formed their South-East Asia
Command in 1943, Stilwell was appointed as the deputy of Mountbatten.
From a comparatively minor position, he had accumulated appointments,
all of which gave him authority. Few men in the war were in a position of
such power.

The multitude of functions was a mistake. With such divergent pressures
upon him, no man could have made a success of being a loyal servant of
the United States and China. For a joint post to be workable, there must
be coincidence of interests between the countries to which a man is jointly
responsible. Stilwell, in serving Roosevelt and Chiang, had an impossible
task. Much as Roosevelt respected the role that China was destined to
play, the interests of the United States and China were different. Stilwell
had decided that he would be through and through American: he would
serve the United States and would correct Roosevelt's rather eccentric
judgement.

The difficulty was increased because Stilwell's own judgement was defective. He did not see that, for the issue of the war, it really was unnecessary for Chiang to fight much more. Roosevelt himself had probably glimpsed this truth. But Roosevelt erred because he supposed that it was necessary for the United States to make strenuous efforts to keep China in the war. China would have remained belligerent in any circumstances, and its real interests, which Chiang saw very clearly, were all against making a separate peace. Having won credit with the Western Allies, China would have been suicidal to fling it away by becoming a renegade towards the end of the war, in which the difficult part had been the beginning. Nor would it have gained any advantage by doing so. The United States and Britain were satisfied as long as China remained formally at war, and turned a blind eye to the reality of much of China's wartime record.

Stilwell, however, did not perceive this. He had a mania to drive China back to war: both its bureaucrats living in comfort in Chungking, and its wretched conscripts herded to war by force. Chinese guile, Chinese pretence that it was doing much more than it was, he exposed with relish. Stilwell obtained Chinese agreement that thirty Chinese divisions should be allotted for cooperation with the British from India for the operations in Burma and to reconquer South-East Asia. To facilitate these operations, the Ledo Road was constructed across the southern slopes of the Himalayan mountains through dense jungles.

It linked the Calcutta-Dimapur-Ledo rail line up the North-East Frontier of India (in Assam) with a south-easterly cross-country track right across North Burma via Myitkyina and Bhamo until it joined the route of the original Sino-British Burma Road, north of Lashio, to Kunming and Chungking. The Ledo Road was one of the major engineering enterprises of the war.

Stilwell, and the toadies who clustered round him on his American staff, made no secret of the fact that they greatly desired that American and Chinese forces should get into many of these regions in advance of the British, and they wished to eradicate British influence where it still survived. They considered the British Empire obsolete and effete, and they had no desire to see it re-established. They counted on a peace settlement which would create an Asia of self-determining nation-states, always the American ideal, as 1919 had shown in Europe. For this, they considered it of first-class importance that they should end the war in military possession of disputed territory. But the thirty Chinese divisions proved to be a paper force. Only a fraction was ever available. For Stilwell's aim, there was to be no Chinese manpower.

Stilwell, in his vigour for the war, could get little response from the Kuomintang officials, and from Chiang Kai-shek personally. He became increasingly obsessed with the fact that Chiang was employing 200,000 of his best troops for cordoning off the area that was occupied by the Red Army; and that this Army, alone of China's military forces, had proved that it was anxious to fight, and had shown the value of its guerrilla strategy against the Japanese. But it was prevented by the Kuomintang from playing its part in the war. Chiang, in his fear that substantial economic aid would reach the communists, and would make them dangerous to him, blockaded them shamelessly.

Stilwell denounced him to the Americans as a bad ally: Chiang complained that he could have no confidence in such a Chief-of-Staff. To do him justice, he could say that Stilwell had not grasped the fact that the civil war in China was continuing. The merger of the armies, which was to have taken place by the pact which Chiang made with the communists and the Young Marshal of Manchuria at the time of the Sian kidnapping, had never been carried out. The communists had laid down their own strategy in their war with Japan, and, as by their guerrilla methods of war they penned Japan more and more to the towns, they continually occupied a larger and larger area of the country. All the while the communists were consolidating their hold. Was Chiang to assist them by removing his forces which kept them under surveillance?

The problem was difficult; Chiang was notable for his obstinacy, which had established him where he was; Stilwell was notorious for pertinacity and for courting disfavour. With Stilwell's agreement, a whitewashing of the communists took place in America. The news about them was surprising, and cheered an America which was hungry for hopeful news. It was said that they were not real communists at all; they were Jeffersonian democrats, simple rural reformers, who desired only to fight for their country, and they were held back by Chiang Kai-shek, the real nature of whose Government had by this time become plain. They were a brandnew and unexpected ally, waiting to be used against the Japanese if the United States would sanction it. Chiang Kai-shek, treating this as a threat of American repudiation of him, fulminated, and put the blame on Stilwell. He supposed him responsible for the agitation in the press.

By the autumn of 1944 the breach between Chiang and Stilwell had become wider, beyond reconciliation. Chiang officially demanded that Roosevelt should dismiss Stilwell. Roosevelt, though his confidence in Chiang had been half-changed by Stilwell – but not his confidence in China – consented.

With the fall of Stilwell there vanished a plan which had been dear both to him and to Roosevelt. This was for the re-training and modernization by American officers of the entire Chinese Army. The United States was characteristically ready to take responsibility for this gigantic task; but it required Chinese consent to the appointment of Stilwell as Chief-of-Staff, and Chiang would not trust such authority to any foreigner.

Admittedly it would have been difficult; there would have been storms, and, whilst Stilwell's attitude to the communists was at best ambiguous in the view of Chiang Kai-shek, it was clear that there were many fundamental principles on which the two men were divided in any reform. Stilwell would certainly have wanted to incorporate part of the Red Army, and much of its system of command and administration. Neither of them would compromise. But Chiang, in winning his point that there should be no foreign command in his Army, sacrificed the possibility of ending the war with a re-born, reliable, modernized force.

The war was very depressing when seen in these years from Chungking. Air raids, which had been plentiful, had died down, and had become rare. But with this there had come hunger and a dreadful boredom with nothing to distract people from being conscious of their extreme discomfort. The city was overcrowded: it was full of refugees. The lives of most people had become a nightmare because of inflation; it was still under a semblance of control; it was to reach fantastic proportions, as in Germany during the period at the end of the First World War, only when the war was over; but already inflation in China cast very deep shadows, and it had become the main impediment in life.

The extent of the inflation was a novelty in human history. In Chungking, prices rose by two hundred and fifty times in the two years 1942–4. The price index of goods, quoted at 100 in 1937, was 125,000 by 1945. How to cope, how to find money, became the overriding concern of everyone, including all the Army officers, and the events of the war sank a long way behind. Another stunning blow had been dealt at human society, seen from a Chinese perspective, and strong suspicions grew up as to whether life could ever be normal again, even if peace was restored. It was the classical effect of an uncontrolled inflation. 'If you wish to make a revolution,' Lenin had said, 'first debauch the currency.'

In spite of this, many people were growing very rich out of wartime enterprises and profiteering, but they hid themselves, and no bright plumage lit up the drab scene. Only gossip and scandal circulated wildly. The inflation had the usual effects in disintegrating the society. The corruption became impudent. One day, when a general of the Indian Army was paying a visit to the city, a cousin of the Chinese Finance Minister called on him by night, and outlined a plan of partnership by which the two could make a fortune. All that was necessary was the use of the general's means of transport, and of his prestige to keep official interference at arm's length.

To keep their armies in the field, the Chinese had to make more and more use of conscription. It was an ordinary sight to see in the country-side, even close to Chungking, squads of soldiers being deported to fighting areas; the soldiers were all chained together. Across the length of the huge country, there was constant, small-scale, sporadic action, which, though of little military consequence, did much material damage. The Japanese occupying the cities were harried, and in many parts of the country could not venture, except in great force, into the countryside; they raided and massacred sporadically. Insecurity was constant; the war had apparently ceased to have a reason and the possibility of an end.

In parts of the country, however, the war seemed to have run its course, to be exhausted, and to have fought itself out. It was succeeded by the armed forces on both sides following the age-old instincts for trade. The armies became trading organizations. Trading is a passion with the Chinese; with the Japanese it is familiar. As soon as the armies stood still, the Chinese put out their feelers, and the Japanese, who were not paid very highly and welcomed some supplement to their wages, responded. The metamorphosis of the barbaric Japanese conquerors into the scheming Japanese traders was curious to watch. The attempts by high Japanese officers to restrict the trade were in vain. The Japanese generals, even at the highest level of direction of the Japanese Armies, were too deeply engaged. China, by the action not of its Government or of its soldiers but by the private enterprise of its merchants, had woven a web of commerce. Within a month or so of conquest it snared the Japanese as well as their opposite numbers and bound them in all sorts of ways to courses of action which aimed at the satisfaction of private wants rather than the advancement of Japan's public enterprise of subjugation. And so it was to continue until the end of the war. The spectacle is of exuberant trade springing up and flourishing wherever the two belligerents came in contact. Patrolling warships operated most. The Japanese Navy was particularly notorious for doing traffic with the Chinese. This was very well attested by watchers in Hong Kong in the months before the island was invaded.

Stilwell's fall in 1944 coincided with the last great military effort in China by the Japanese. During 1943 and the first part of 1944, the Americans had built up a new war machine on Chinese soil with which they had at last succeeded in reaching the heart of the Japanese war effort, and which held out hopes of being deadly. This they did by expanding greatly the activities of General Claire Lee Chennault. This man had begun by recruiting a private air force, mercenaries, drawn from the staff of American airlines and college youths. They were known as Chennault's Flying Tigers. In the summer of 1941, while the United States was still neutral, this force, put at the service of the Kuomintang, proved itself indispensable for the air defence of Chungking. Later, when the United States entered the war, it was incorporated in the United States Army, and Chennault also returned to it. In the course of time he established airfields in South-East China, and from there B29 bombers began the first systematic bombardments that the Japanese had had to endure. By prodigious efforts, huge stockpiles of munitions, fuel and other supplies were flown over the 'hump' of the Himalayas to the new forward airfields which 300,000 Chinese coolies had built under American direction. It was exceptionally costly in terms of time, manpower, airlifting capacity and expense, and it proved to be an almost entirely unproductive diversion from more useful enterprises.

The Japanese were not inclined to wait while America surmounted the technical challenges involved in carrying out very long-range strategic bombing raids over the Japanese home islands. Spurred on by the early bombing runs, Japan decided that it was necessary to renew their military effort against China. They had halted large-scale military campaigning at the end of 1938, and, during the years since then, it had seemed that they were best served by letting time work for them. They hoped that the discomfort, and the upset from the perpetual strain of trying to appease the communists, would in the end induce Chiang Kai-shek to submit his stubborn neck to peace negotiations. They could place their trust in Chinese racial dislike of the country's Western Allies. During this period, the Japanese were satisfied with the steady stream of defections from the Kuomintang to the side of the Wang Ching-sei Government and its Japanese guardians of law and order. It occurred as a natural by-product of fraternization, propaganda, a desire for greater material comfort and an interest in self-preservation. By 1942, the communists estimated, and published with some smugness, that twenty-seven Kuomintang generals had gone over.

Times had changed. In 1944 the Japanese Army in China gathered itself together and commenced an offensive which they named *Ichi-Gō* (literally, 'Operation Number One'). It was an exceptionally ambitious plan designed to extend Japanese control deep into the interior of China and possibly to open the way for yet another attempt to seek a negotiated peace with Chiang Kai-shek or his forces. The campaign was in part prompted by the need to establish secure overland communications extending from Manchuria and North China right the way through to

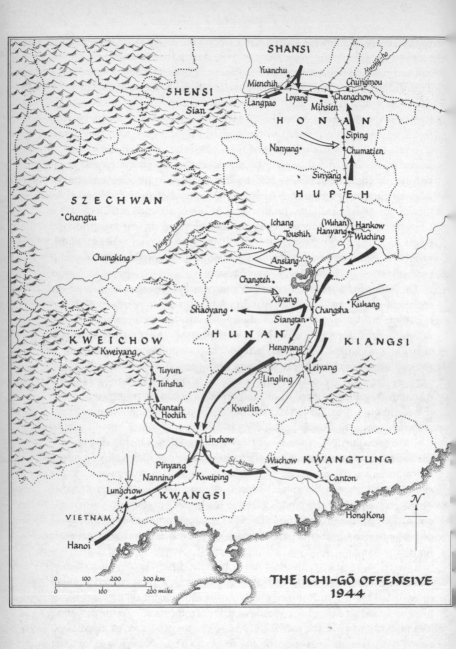

THE ICHI-GŌ OFFENSIVE
1944

Japan's forces in Occupied South-East Asia. This need sprang from the fact that Allied attacks had decimated Japanese merchant shipping. One of the main purposes of the whole campaign, however, was to capture and dismantle the American air bases on Chinese soil.

The first phase of *Ichi-Gō* opened with an onslaught to clear out the Chinese nationalist forces from northern Honan which had concentrated on the plains of central Honan. For some time these had remained undisturbed along the Japanese flanks south of the Yellow River and north of the Yangtze, where thus far the southernmost sector of the Peking–Hankow Railway had lain beyond the limits of the Japanese occupation zone. If any of the Chinese armies were to stand fast, they were simply to be minced. And so the Japanese plan was put into effect.

The new Japanese offensive burst upon China like a thunderclap. Lieutenant-General Okamura Yasuji (Neiji), who had distinguished himself in the Japanese campaign against Hankow in 1938 but who had languished since then as the Japanese Army Commander-in-Chief within the comparative backwater of North China, was given his big chance. At the head of 150,000 troops drawn from his forces in North China and from far-off Manchuria (where they had passed the war in idleness, watching Russia), his powerful forces swarmed across central Honan. There was far more devastation than had occurred in the bad old days of Chiang Kai-shek's bandit-suppression campaigns. The Japanese Army found in its renewal of the Chinese war an opportunity to work out its feeling of frustration. The new divisions roared through the seaboard of Central China and cut a broad swath further inland, not meeting any Chinese Army able to stand up to them in pitched battles. Where there was a struggle, as in Hunan, the Chinese, when they were eventually broken, were set on by an enraged population, who blamed them for having disturbed the unofficial armistice. To such a squalid end had the Chinese Army's defence of the country been reduced.

Thirty-four Chinese divisions simply evaporated into thin air. As the Chinese nationalist armies melted away, the Japanese winkled out scattered pockets of resistance. In the next phase of the campaign, however, the Japanese planned to adopt even more extreme measures. The pressure upon the Chinese air bases became too perilous for the Americans to endure. They had to abandon one airfield after another across the whole of South-East China. Priceless equipment and supplies had to be destroyed in the path of the Japanese offensive.

The loss of General Chennault's airfields drew the world's attention once more to China's weakness. It settled a controversy which had been going on among strategists. One side had taken the view that Chennault had proved that land operations were unnecessary: it was enough to build airfields in distant places, lightly protected by guerrilla operations, and leave the air forces to carry on the war. The other side had argued that, without a properly equipped and efficient army, airfields were entirely vulnerable. The latter view proved correct; and it was found that the Chinese armies were inadequate to safeguard them.

The American advance across the Pacific, however, now provided the long-range bombers with safer havens. By mid-September 1944 orders were given to withdraw the last of the B29 bombers from China to the relative safety of the Mariana Islands. Two months later, they began to operate in earnest. But the usefulness and importance of China to the Western Allies had changed sharply.

The beginning of 1943 had seen the last great western incentive offered to the Chinese. In that year, the West (following the diplomatic precedent already set by Japan) had made the gesture of terminating their right to maintain Treaty Ports in China. The largest tool of imperialism was renounced. The Japanese renunciation of extra-territorial rights had been hemmed in by restricitive conditions. The Allies led by the United States were now far more ready to sacrifice commercial interests to suit their broader political objectives. The negotiations, which the Western Powers had pursued desultorily since the 1920s, were accelerated, and agreement was reached. If the war had ultimately grown out of China's endeavour to extirpate these foreign footholds in China, it had, by this decision of the Allies, been won. Later in the year, Roosevelt had secured an Allied statement of the intention to associate China as an equal Power with themselves in remoulding the pattern of the world at the peace conferences. Other countries may have had their tongue in the cheek at this, but Roosevelt had his way.

Nevertheless the period of excessive complacency towards Chiang Kai-shek was immediately after this brought to an end, or was very much qualified, by the events of the Teheran Conference in November 1943. Just before had come the high point of Chiang Kai-shek's apotheosis. At the conference at Cairo of Roosevelt and Churchill, which Chiang Kai-shek had attended – but Stalin, because of his neutrality towards Japan, did not – Chiang had reached the peak of his fortunes. He received a pledge from the Allies that Manchuria, Formosa and the Pescadores would be returned to China at the peace.

On leaving Cairo, Churchill and Roosevelt went to Teheran for a meeting with Stalin. They were told for the first time that Russia had begun to make troop dispositions to enter the war against Japan as soon as Germany was defeated.

This changed the picture of the war. China would no longer be indispensable to the Allies. Japan could be reached in other ways; all attention was now focused on obtaining Russia's eventual permission to operate from Russian bases in the Maritime Provinces. The huge new factor of the Red Army operating against the Japanese in Manchukuo had to be digested. From that time on, China was no longer treated with such careful solicitude as it had been hitherto, though it was not solely the reason for the change of attitude. China still enjoyed the delusive grandeur which had been built up in President Roosevelt's time, and communicated by him to the public, but this was a wasting asset.

China, as an object of strategic concern, became of secondary importance. Chiang Kai-shek, his suspicions and ambitions, no longer held the centre of the picture. The war, which had originated in the crisis in China, was to come to an end with the fate of China of apparently small concern to the Great Powers, which now pressed on towards the final kill.

In the course of the war, a profound change had, however, come over the prestige of the Kuomintang and of the communists. They had both of them engaged in warfare, which they had fought by different means using different arms. They had been in competition with each other. The upshot, though it was not yet definite, was that, in the judgement of the various important groups of Chinese society, the communists had shown themselves more durable than the Kuomintang. True, the Kuomintang was, technically, to be one of the victorious powers. But the Kuomintang had lost face irrevocably.

It was not so much that the communists had shining victories to their credit. They had latterly fought very little. But their Government survived the war with an infinitely better morale than the Kuomintang.

Soon after the war, the two Governments would come into open conflict. Support would vanish away from the Kuomintang. It would transfer itself to the communists.

The Kuomintang had plenty of opportunity to see how unpopular its régime was becoming, and plenty of opportunity to take up some more popular course. But it kept obstinately on its disastrous career. As it became manifest that China, thanks to its Allies, was to be on the winning side in the war, there grew up naturally a discussion about the form that post-war politics was to take. Similarly the Kuomintang could have met the public half way, and announced the approaching end of its party dictatorship. But its reply, as the demand for this grew, was to increase the size of the secret police. Its activities became intolerable. The Kuomintang gave every indication that it would continue unreformed.

CHAPTER 24

Twilight

THE attention now turns to the American offensive, far across the Pacific, and it turns away from all the other theatres of the Asian War. Fighting still continued in these, but it became obvious that it was irrelevant. The turmoil in the Pacific dwarfed all other, and this became increasingly so until the end.

In the middle of June 1944, the Americans invaded Saipan in the Mariana Islands. This island, 1,350 miles from Tokyo, was the most vital point in the outer defences of Japan. It had become strongly fortified, so strongly that even the naval experts believed it to be impregnable. Its strategic importance was appreciated; from Saipan, the Americans would be able to bomb Tokyo; they could also disrupt the communications of the remaining forward posts in the Pacific with Japan. Its loss would breach what was called in Japanese 'the absolute zone of national defences'.

The Americans had assembled huge forces. They had an escort fleet, for the troop transports for the invasion, of 7 battleships, 12 escort carriers, 11 cruisers and 91 destroyers. It took only half an hour for the assault forces to get ashore at Saipan, but it still remained to be captured. At once the Japanese assembled their still very formidable fleet, and sought a decisive battle. They had foreseen the American moves and were not taken by surprise; they had ample strength in Guam and in the islands of the Philippines. The battle which resulted was the fourth large-scale naval combat of the war. The sense of occasion was in the message of the Japanese admiral to the fleet before the action began: 'The fate of the Empire rests on this one battle.'

The result was entirely disastrous to Japan. The successive strikes by Japanese aircraft were beaten off, and in the whole battle Japan lost nearly four hundred aircraft. The destruction of these, and the repelling of the Japanese attacks, were more spectacular than the loss of ships, though the operation cost the Japanese two battleships and an aircraft-carrier; two other carriers were disabled. This was far beyond the capacity of the Japanese shipyards, at this stage of the war, to make good. The American damage was very slight.

As was usual, the Japanese Navy silenced the news of the defeat. Even high officials of the Foreign Office remained without knowledge of what had been happening. They were especially confused because, after the defeat, they were invited by naval officers to banquets to celebrate a great Japanese triumph.

Admiral Toyoda Soemu, die-hard Commander-in-Chief of the Combined Fleet from May 1944 to May 1945 and Chief of the Naval General Staff during the last five months of the war, told investigators of the United States Strategic Bombing Survey that retrospectively he believed at the beginning of the Pacific Conflict that American submarines had posed a greater danger to Japan than any other enemy weapon system. Nevertheless, he stressed, the principal threat to Japan throughout virtually the whole Greater East Asia War had come from the depredations of US Navy surface forces. The other forces of the United States and their Allies were of far less importance. The critical factor was oil. Japanese fuel shortages had become serious as early as Midway, when fleet oil usage had far exceeded expectation. This had a knock-on effect felt in all subsequent operations. The real turning-point, however, was the loss of Japanese control in the Philippines, for thereafter American air and naval control over South China was secure and Japanese shipping lanes to the south were completely cut off: 'By the time of the Saipan operations, the greatest hindrance to the drafting of the operations plans was the fact that we did not have sufficient tankers to support it.'

The fall of Saipan could not, however, be hidden. The news began to circulate in the middle of July 1944. To most people it came as an entire shock, and for the first time the average Japanese, without any such information as had been weighing on the experts, began to surmise that Japan was in fact losing the war. Saipan had fallen with such ease; the Americans were ahead of their timetable. An evident *frisson* went through the nation, well disciplined though it continued to be.

A result was the resignation of General Tōjō, who had remained not only the Prime Minister but Minister of War, Minister of Munitions and Chief of the Army General Staff. He fell, now, after a complicated intrigue of the politicians. This was the first sign of serious political malaise which had come from Japan during the war; and it was received with relief by those watching among its enemies. The actual procedures by which government changes were brought about in Japan were as a rule more convoluted and dynamic than the dry official processes engraved on the marble cornerstone of the Japanese Constitution. In this instance, a group of high civilian and Army officers, especially those who had formerly held official positions, began to agitate more strongly for what they had long wanted in their hearts: that General Tōjō's Cabinet should resign. Saipan had caused them to open their eyes, and to press their arguments as a matter of life or death. Their dissensions were heard at high level, and they arranged that they should be transmitted to the throne.

A great agitation was set afoot among a large circle of those holding the various offices of importance. Tōjō, who, a week earlier had apparently been completely safe, suddenly found the ground trembling under his feet. He sought to appease his critics by yielding to one of their demands, and proposed that he should no longer combine the posts of Prime Minister, War Minister and Chief of the Army Staff. The arrangements were made for General Umezu Yoshijirō to become Minister of War. But by this time, the opinion of the inner circle had moved on, and it could be satisfied with nothing less than the resignation of Tōjō as Prime Minister. He demurred, and argued in vain. On the day of the announcement of the loss of Saipan, on 18 July 1944, his resignation from all his duties was in the hands of the Emperor.

The choice of a successor to the premiership fell to a formal group of seven elder statesmen, the *Jūshin*, all former prime ministers themselves. This body was unknown to the written constitution; it had in consequence no rights, such as access to government papers; it came, however, to exercise great power. It had an influence like that of the Genrō, or elder statesmen, though the power of the Genrō had been openly recognized. The re-entry to Japanese politics of such an influence was important. It was the more so at this period because the Jūshin had tended, with some exceptions, to work for peace. Most of them thought that the war was irrevocably lost, that the leaders knew this well, but that, floundering and indecisive, they saw no means of terminating it.

Their deliberations about Tōjō's replacement appear to have been unsubtle. All they could do was to agree on the nomination of General Koiso Kuniaki, an Army officer who had a bad reputation from the days of terrorism in the thirties when the Army was promoting a series of crises with the civilian Ministers in order to advance its claims of controlling the Government.

At the outbreak of the Manchurian Incident, Koiso had been Chief of the powerful Military Affairs Bureau in the War Ministry, one of the big 'Three Chiefs'. When the Japanese Army's conquest of Manchuria was secure, he was promoted to Vice-Minister of War. Shortly after the establishment of Manchukuo, he was then sent to serve as Chief of Staff of the Kwantung Army and as head of the Japanese Army's secret service there in the critical period between August 1932 and March 1934. A year and a half later, he became Commander-in-Chief of the Korean Army and held that position until he temporarily fell from grace at the outbreak of the Changkufeng Incident in July 1938. From then on, he was to make his mark as a reliable manager in Japan's exploitation of its occupied territories: he served two terms as Minister of Overseas (Colonial) Affairs, firstly in the six months which led up to the outbreak of the European War, and then during the first six months of 1940. When the China War spilled out into the Pacific, Koiso was on the sidelines. So long as General Tōjō was in power, Koiso was kept well away from duties which might undermine Tōjō's influence. At the time of General Koiso's recall to Tokyo to take up the premiership of Japan, He had been Governor-General of Korea since the middle of 1942. He had a track record as a competent administrator, someone who could make sense of civil/military relations. The Emperor, however, appointed him as Prime Minister simply beause he had been recommended by the Jūshin: it was the established way. The thing was done properly.

It was a choice which was apparently made under the compulsion of avoiding events such as those which had happened a year earlier in Italy. The elder statesmen judged it necessary to avoid nominating a man who might play in Japan the same part as General Badoglio. The extent to which Badoglio had captured the mind of Japan is curious. It showed perhaps how much the Japanese desired a Badoglio, and for how long they found it imperative not to disclose this.

Kase Toshikazu, a senior Foreign Ministry official, has described these confused and rather dark transactions. He himself belonged to the 'pro-British, pro-American' circles. His book, *Eclipse of the Rising Sun*, is useful in showing how many of these men had continued thoughout the war to hold high position in the Foreign Office, in certain Ministries, at the imperial court. They had been inactive from prudence: from the fall of Saipan, however, they began to work for peace. They had still to be very cautious, for they would have been rendered helpless if it had become known how specific, and actively specific, were their intentions. By their sympathies becoming known they would at best have made themselves ineffective: at the worst they would have been assassinated. And there were of course many who, when the war was over, claimed to have been pro-Ally, but whose memory may have exaggerated its degree.

At the end of 1944, Kase Toshikazu wrote in his diary the following:

Defeat now stares us stark in the face. There is only one question left: how can we avert the chaos attendant upon a disastrous defeat? The preservation of my fatherland, that is a paramount task assigned to me by fate. The hostile attack is developing so surprisingly swiftly that it may be that diplomacy cannot intervene before it is too late. I must redouble my efforts to expedite the restoration of peace. For that purpose I shall secure friends in the army who will collaborate with me secretly, and enlighten public opinion through wider exchanges of view with politicians, publicists and press representatives. The chances are that the re-orientation of our policy is yet feasible. If so the nation will escape annihilation. Even so, it will probably be accompanied by civil disturbances. Much blood will flow – and who knows that mine, too, will not be spilt? . . . This, in short, is my New Year's Day prayer.*

This sums up very well the feeling of the small class of clear-sighted, non-fanatical men. But a difficult task lay ahead for them. Kase Toshikazu and his friends had to convert a sufficient number of patriotic Japanese to enable them to shift the vital balance against the fanatical, the deluded and the ignorant. They had to do this with the certain knowledge that charges of treason might well be brought against them, and would be paid for either with execution or else by the familiar old Japanese resort to private violence.

The American drive from the Pacific continued. After Saipan, the strongly fortified positions of Tinian and Guam were captured in August 1944. These were also considerable victories, made possible only by mobilization of resources, and their concentration upon tiny islands, which were possibly unique in military history. A feature of all these operations was the disparity of the losses. The Americans should in theory, being attackers, have suffered at least three to one more heavily than the Japanese. But, in all three operations, the American dead numbered just over 5,000, while the Japanese lost 42,000. On Guam, for the first time, there had been a dent in Japanese morale: over 12,000 prisoners were taken. Usually these island defences ended in a great *banzai* charge of the remaining garrison, who plunged to death, rather like the death charge of the chivalry among the Rajputs of medieval India, who vowed themselves thus to self-destruction. The generals on both Saipan and Guam committed ceremonial seppaku.

In October, General MacArthur, in the South-West Pacific, made his expected attack on the Philippines. He was still under the disadvantage of the somewhat complicated command arrangements which shared between him and Admiral Nimitz the control of operations in his area. He could count upon a powerful fleet detached from the Central Pacific. Japan chose to regard his attack as a crisis of the war. Its generals recognized that, if the Philippines were occupied by the Americans, the supply lines of the Japanese Empire would be fatally obstructed. Therefore Japan stated that, on its ability to defend the Philippines, the issue of the war would depend.

* K. Toshikazu, *Eclipse of the Rising Sun*, Jonathan Cape, London, 1951.

Such repeated pronouncements were foolish, and, in making them, the Japanese generals should have had in mind their grave embarrassment if their defence proved ineffective. They would be in the position of carrying on the war even while admitting that the war was a lost cause. That they permitted themselves so talk so rashly was the best proof that the morale of the Japanese General Staff was beginning to fail even though the Japanese soldiers fought as tenaciously as before.

The Japanese lived up to the words of their military leaders. They gathered their Navy, which was still very powerful in surface ships – only in the loss of the aircraft-carriers had it been gravely weakened – and sought, by putting all their effort into a single decisive blow, to turn their great danger into a decisive victory. And circumstances played into their hands. It had been calculated that the local airfields would be operational for the landings, but the rainy season broke, and they were flooded. The Japanese had a period of air superiority, flying in from Samar. For a few days it was touch and go whether the American advance would be disastrously defeated.

MacArthur's invasion force, which landed on 20 October 1944 on the shores of the Gulf of Leyte which is a central island of the Philippines, had the protection of very powerful warships. The Japanese sought to lure this naval force away by sending a decoy fleet, and then, with a much larger fleet, aimed to sink the American transports, and to destroy MacArthur's Army, which was to be taken at a disadvantage while they were still engaged in disembarkation. The Japanese placed their confidence in the battle upon the greater fire power of the Japanese Navy; the days of attacking by waves of aircraft from carriers was over, since the Japanese naval air force had been virtually eliminated. The Navy was back to reliance upon its battleship fleet, and among this it included the battleship, *Yamato*, which had been built free of the former limitations on the size of battleships. It was the most formidable ship in the world, well-protected and mounting eighteen-inch guns which fired 3,220 lb (1460 kg) projectiles to a range of up to twenty-six miles (41.4 km).

If they had succeeded in their plan, the Japanese would have achieved a second Pearl Harbor, this time destroying the American Army in Asia as formerly they had annihilated the American Pacific Fleet. Even so, the United States, with its economic might only just beginning to operate at its full strength, could, in all reasonable probability, have regarded a defeat as a temporary setback, and the inevitable conclusion of the war would have been merely postponed by a year or so. But, though this possibility must have been clear to the Japanese admirals, an interruption of the continuous American advance would have been dear to them. They rejoiced in the likelihood of a pause in the war: Japanese optimism would have taken on new life: victory would have set alive again Japanese hopes that their staying power might outlast America's. Nobody can foresee all the unexpected circumstances which might happen in war. Given time, Japan could begin to hope that the germs of a negotiated peace might sprout.

MacArthur's moves had therefore created a situation more fraught with consequence than even he, with his flair for reading the Japanese mind, at first realized. His landing had created a profound stir, alike in America and throughout Asia. He had chosen the elements of drama. He was not far from the point from which he had made his take-off in his direct contact with the Japanese in 1942, and, as he had promised to do, he had returned. But at once the Japanese Navy pounced, and dreamed of plucking from this nettle, danger, the flower, which might be the checking of the American guillotine as it was about to fall, the dismantling of the instrument, and the creation of the necessity to rebuild it if the war were to continue. Its ships, some from Borneo, some from Formosa and Japan itself, converged upon the Gulf of Leyte.

The officer in command of the Japanese fleet was Admiral Toyoda Soemu. There is no doubt of the merit of his overall plan, which he directed at long range from Tokyo. The ships from Japan he formed into a decoy force, with which he aimed at dividing the Americans from their protective force of battleships and aircraft-carriers, which were commanded by Admiral W. F. Halsey. This force included what remained of Japan's once formidable fleet of aircraft-carriers; it was less strong than it seemed for, as was discovered afterwards, the Japanese carriers sailed empty of planes. Japan had used up its planes and pilots, many of the last batch of these at the futile battle of Guam, and oil was running desperately short. Nevertheless, the manoeuvre was successful. Admiral Halsey went in pursuit, and left MacArthur dangerously exposed.

With two forces of battleships which were held in readiness in Borneo, Toyoda planned to attack the American transport fleet as soon as it was deprived of much of its protective escort. The first of these forces was exceptionally powerful; it contained five battleships, all of them larger and faster than any which they were still liable to meet. Toyoda gambled on these making unimpeded contact with the enemy, free from the diversion of air attack – which was reasonably certain, as the American transport fleet was beyond the range of land-based aeroplanes – and, by superior fire power, sinking it.

Against reasonable expectation, however, both the Japanese fleets failed in their objects. The lesser of the two was ambushed by what had been left behind of the American fleet, which was rather larger than was foreseen by Japanese Intelligence, and was completely annihilated except for one destroyer. The Japanese had the mortification of seeing their ships sunk by ships which were technically inferior to their own. Ironically, in this action, the Americans employed battleships which were obsolete, had already been once sunk by the Japanese – at Pearl Harbor – and which had been dredged up from the mud of the sea bed. The larger Japanese fleet, though it was engaged and disorganized earlier on, got through the American defences, and for a time, if it had but known this, had the American transports at its mercy, but because of muddle, of being let down by other ships, and because of deep misunderstanding of what was being done by the American ships, the Japanese Admiral did not bombard but sailed away inexplicably. His losses had been heavy; his actual gains were very slight; his potential gains, those which he had unaccountably let slip through his fingers, made this, their final battle of the war, very poignant to the Japanese Navy.

Among the warships employed, the Japanese decoy force from the north alone avoided heavy losses. It retired in good order. Similarly Admiral Halsey's powerful battleships, which had been the main concern of the Japanese, were never in serious action throughout. They steamed 300 miles to the north, and when, as was afterwards discovered, they were within forty miles of the decoy force, they steamed 300 miles south. Upon their arrival, they found that the battle of Leyte was over. Admiral Halsey was much criticized for having made so powerful a fleet ineffective in the action, but, given the system of communication prevailing among warships, he could hardly have done other than he did.

For the Japanese defeat, the same forces seemed to operate as before in the melancholy history of this Navy. Bad Intelligence work, bad coordination between commanders, the scarcely trained generation of naval fliers, and an inability of the Japanese commanders to retrieve disaster and to provide a new plan: these, which had dogged the Navy since the battle of Midway, continued to do so until the death of the Navy at Leyte.

The principal defect was in the quality of the command. The Japanese admirals and captains had been too old for their work. They were too fearful of risking their ships; they were certainly brave, and reasonably competent, but they creaked in manoeuvring a modern fleet, which was beyond their capacity. No common doctrine of strategy or tactics united them, and they were handicapped by the failure of Japanese engineers to provide for the Navy some of the devices which had become common among other belligerents. Above all, it had turned out that, where the Japanese had been forced to make an innovation in the arts of naval

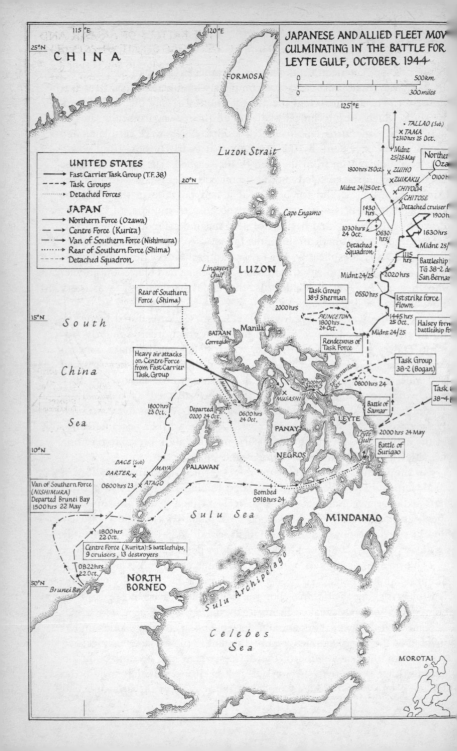

JAPANESE AND ALLIED FLEET MOV[E]
CULMINATING IN THE BATTLE FOR
LEYTE GULF, OCTOBER 1944

| 0 | | 500km |
| 0 | | 300 miles |

CHINA

FORMOSA

Luzon Strait

· *TALLAO (Sub)*
✕ *TAMA*
2310 hrs 25 Oct.

Midnt
25/26 May

Norther[n]
(Oza[wa])

0100 h[rs]

1800 hrs 25 Oct.   ✕ *ZUIHO*
                   ✕ *ZUIKAKU*
Midnt 24/25 Oct.   ✕ *CHIYODA*
                   · *CHITOSE*

Cape Engaño

Detached cruiser f[orce]
1900 h[rs]

1430
hrs

1630 hrs

1030 hrs
24 Oct.

0630/
hrs

Midnt 25[/26]

Detached
Squadron

1115
hrs

Battleship
TG 38-2 de[tached]
San Bernar[dino]

UNITED STATES
→ Fast Carrier Task Group (T.F. 38)
→ Task Groups
···> Detached Forces

JAPAN
→ Northern Force (Ozawa)
--→ Centre Force (Kurita)
-·-→ Van of Southern Force (Nishimura)
····> Rear of Southern Force (Shima)
-··-→ Detached Squadron

Midnt 24/25   2020 hrs

LUZON

*Lingayen
Gulf*

Rear of Southern
Force (Shima)

2000 hrs

Task Group
38-3 Sherman

PRINCETON
1800 hrs
24 Oct.

Midnt 24/25

0550 hrs

1st strike force
flown

1445 hrs
25 Oct.

Halsey for[ms]
battleship for[ce]

South

BATAAN
Corregidor

Manila

Rendezvous of
Task Force

San Bernardino

Task Group
38-2 (Bogan)

Heavy air attacks
on Centre Force
from Fast-Carrier
Task Group

China

1800 hrs
23 Oct.

Departed
0200 24 Oct.

0600 hrs
24 Oct.

Mindoro Str.

1100 hrs
24 Oct.

0800 hrs 24

Task [Group]
38-4 [Da]

Battle of
Samar

Sea

✕ *MUSASHI*

PANAY

LEYTE

Departed

*Leyte
Gulf*

2000 hrs 24 May

Battle of
Surigao

DACE (Sub)
DARTER ✕

✕ *MAYA*

PALAWAN

NEGROS

Van of Southern Force
(NISHIMURA)
Departed Brunei Bay
1500 hrs 22 May

0600 hrs 23   ✕ *ATAGO*

Sulu Sea

Bombed
0918 hrs 24

MINDANAO

1800 hrs
22 Oct.

Centre Force (Kurita): 5 battleships,
9 cruisers, 13 destroyers

Sulu Archipelago

0822 hrs
22 Oct.

**NORTH
BORNEO**

Brunei Bay

*Celebes
Sea*

MOROTAI

115°E   120°E

25°N

20°N

15°N

10°N

5[0]°N

125°E

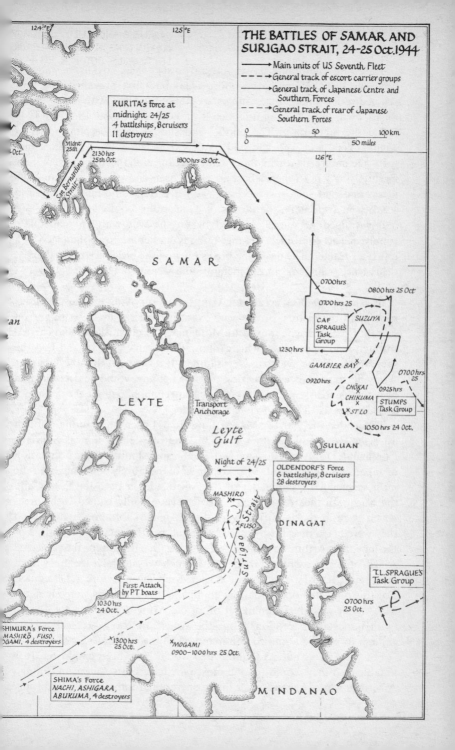

THE BATTLES OF SAMAR AND SURIGAO STRAIT, 24-25 Oct.1944

→ Main units of US Seventh Fleet
--→ General track of escort carrier groups
→ General track of Japanese Centre and Southern Forces
--→ General track of rear of Japanese Southern Forces

0   50   100 km.
0   50 miles

124°E   125°E   126°E

KURITA's force at
midnight 24/25
4 battleships, 8 cruisers
11 destroyers

Midnt
25th

2130 hrs
25th Oct.

1800 hrs 25 Oct.

San Bernardino Strait

S A M A R

0700hrs

0700 hrs 25

0800 hrs 25 Oct

CAF
SPRAGUE'S
Task
Group

SUZUYA

1230 hrs

GAMBIER BAY ×

0920 hrs

0925 hrs

0700 hrs
25

CHŌKAI
CHIKUMA ×
× ST LO

STUMPS
Task Group

1050 hrs 24 Oct.

L E Y T E

Transport
Anchorage

Leyte
Gulf

SULUAN

Night of 24/25

OLDENDORF'S Force
6 battleships, 8 cruisers
28 destroyers

MASHIRO
×

× FUSO

DINAGAT

Surigao Strait

First Attack
by PT boats

1030 hrs
24 Oct.

SHIMURA's Force
MASHIRŌ, FUSO,
OGAMI, 4 destroyers

1300 hrs
25 Oct.

× MOGAMI
0900-1000 hrs 25 Oct.

SHIMA's Force
NACHI, ASHIGARA,
ABUKUMA, 4 destroyers

T.L.SPRAGUE'S
Task Group

0700 hrs
25 Oct.

M I N D A N A O

warfare – in combining naval and air power – this advantage had not been sustained. Yamamoto, whose ideas had first prevailed, had not succeeded in training up a younger section of the Navy with ideas similar to his own, and Yamamoto's death at Bougainville on 18 April 1943 ended the innovation. The pilots, who should have become principal commanders, and who had had battle experience, had all of them met their premature death in the Pacific Ocean, and the direction of new recruits was left to men who had never been converts to Yamamoto's ideas, and had seen his successes with a certain amount of envy and scepticism. Especially, the tactics of Yamamoto required an expert and highly trained personnel; he had begun the war with an inadequate supply; it had continued lacking; nobody had come to prominence as a gifted air trainer. The dash, the precision, and the brilliance of his fliers at Pearl Harbor lingered in the memory and were gone.

In January 1945 General MacArthur, thus surviving his most perilous passage in the history of the war, overcame the Japanese resistance on Luzon. From there he moved to Mindanao, the main island, and carried through land operations, which followed the same pattern and had the same results as the events in New Guinea. It turned out that the Japanese Army, in spite of its emphasizing that the fighting would be decisive, had been unable to assemble a land force strong enough to make the resistance as tenacious as that of the Pacific Islands.

This ended the war for MacArthur. He did no more fighting, though after the war's end, another great historic role fell to him as Supreme Commander for Allied Powers, with chief responsibility for the occupation of Japan. For the present, MacArthur wore the laurels of having been the most spectacular commander of the Allied side, in both the Pacific and the European theatres of war. His victories, usually gained with forces which were in the minority, were due to remarkable imagination; and they were made possible by an extreme cult of efficiency by his staff. For the time, MacArthur busied himself with the preparation for the projected Allied offensive against Japan itself, which was to have begun with a landing on Kyushu Island; not expected, however, before 1 December. For this projected operation, the command arrangements were changed. MacArthur was given command of all the Army throughout the Pacific (with important exceptions); but the American Navy was still strong enough to oppose a unified command of all the sea forces.

For the first assault, 5 million men would have been employed. It is notable that they would for the most part have been American; though American Allies begged a place in the operation, room was found for only a token force of three divisions from the Commonwealth. The war was coming to an end in a very different way from the war in Europe. The invasion of Normandy and the campaigns in France and Germany had been genuinely joint enterprises: there was not even the pretence of such in Japan.

As the end of the European War approached, the British Chiefs of Staff were keen to restore Britain to a position of genuine partnership alongside the United States in the Pacific. The difficulty was in finding a credible way to do that. Somewhat diffidently Prime Minister Churchill approached President Roosevelt with an offer of help in the summer of 1944. By the end of that year, a new British Pacific Fleet was more or less in being, although it was not pitted against serious opposition at the time. As a prelude, elements of the new force sailed away under Rear Admiral Sir Philip Vian to attack the oilfields of Sumatra. They struck at Belawan Deli and Palembang and overcame intense ground-based defences. At Palembang the Japanese had the two largest oil refineries in South-East Asia: it was estimated that together they could meet three-quarters of the aviation fuel requirements of the Japanese Empire. The raids succeeded beyond the hopes of the Royal Navy. One of the refineries was all but destroyed and the other one was so seriously damaged that three months afterwards the combined facilities were producing no more than a third of their previous output. Vian's force retired without much loss and linked up with other units to complete the formation of the new fleet. The command of the British Pacific Fleet was placed in the hands of Admiral Sir Bruce Fraser, who previously had been engaged in shepherding arctic convoys that carried supplies to the Soviet Union. He now had the delicate task of reconciling his responsibilities to the British Admiralty for the safety and handling of his fleet and its supplies, not only with the demands pressed upon him by the Australian and New Zealand authorities (although they were difficult to appease) but also with the subordination of his force to operational orders given to him by the Americans.

At first General MacArthur and Admiral Nimitz argued over who should be placed in overall operational command of the British Pacific Fleet. MacArthur wanted to use it in the reconquest of the Philippines which was still underway, and Nimitz wanted to use it in support of the planned invasion of Okinawa. Nimitz won and, in the closing months of the war, first he and then Admiral 'Bull' Halsey, the two successive Commanders-in-Chief of the United States Pacific Fleet, employed the British as a flexible, self-contained reserve. It was from the British Pacific Fleet's subordination to CINCPAC that its fleet train became known as Task Force 112 and its main force of 4 aircraft carriers, 2 battleships, 5 cruisers and 14 destroyers was named Task Force 113. Together they soon became known as Task Force 57. In fact, when the BPF sailed off to fight the Japanese, under the tactical comand of Vice-Admiral Sir Bernard Rawlings, his force consisted of nearly the whole of the frontline strength of the Royal Navy. It was more powerful and larger than any other assemblage of British and Commonwealth fighting ships brought together in the Second World War. However, the expansion of the United States Navy after the Pearl Harbor attack had been so huge that the British Pacific Fleet was only equivalent in strength to a 'task force' within the United States Fifth Fleet. The Americans cordially welcomed 'the British Carrier Task Force and attached units', respected its efficiency and gave it considerable tactical independence. But naturally from fleet admirals down to swabbies, the men of the United States Navy made it their business to put the sailors of the Royal Navy in their proper place. The days of naval parity were long since over. In the war in the Pacific in the later stages America had become very conscious that the United States was first, the Allies nowhere. In the conquest of Japan the fact was to be rubbed in. The United States welcomed this sign that European imperialism had little part to play in the new Asia.

The way to final assault had been opened by the success of the United States' other campaign which advanced from the Central Pacific to the entrances of Tokyo Bay. The fall of Saipan had been an important stage in this advance; it marked a change in Japanese defensive tactics. Hitherto the Japanese had sought to repel American invaders by making mass charges on them as they landed. But at Iwojima, the next island to be attacked after Saipan, the Japanese fought in prepared positions, inflicting great damage on the Americans before they were overwhelmed in March 1945. The island had to be wrenched from them, trench by trench. The Japanese losses were 20,000: the American Marines lost 26,000 killed, and the US Navy nearly 900 killed or missing and about 2,000 wounded.

From Iwojima, Nimitz had first intended to make his main target Formosa. He changed his plan, and launched his attack on Okinawa, a heavily fortified island, forty miles long, in the Ryukyu Islands, 500 miles from Japan Proper. On 1 April 1945 the Americans landed, and at first met with almost no opposition. But they were in an enormous ambush: they realized suddenly that the northern part of the island was alive with troops, all of them skilfully hidden. A feature of the resistance was their use of light artillery, among the most effective of the war. While the Americans were meeting deadly resistance from the north, their plans were disordered by the Japanese use of Kamikaze aircraft. These were manned by volunteer

quads of suicide pilots, who flew their planes to crash on the decks of ships
and there explode. The Kamikaze, who were first used by the Japanese
in the Battle of Leyte, had by now been incorporated in the general plan
for the defence of Japan. The Kamikaze were genuinely volunteers; the
Americans were unwilling to believe that such a corps could be formed on
a free-will basis, but their efforts to find that they had been conscripted
were in vain. By the ferocity of their action, by the unreason of their
suicidal intentions, they struck the Americans with peculiar horror. The
Kamikaze fought with a peculiar exaltation, they appeared insanely exhilarated, and they went to their death as though to a fascinating ceremony. It was the eschatology of war. In the battle for Iwojima they did
very great damage. On one day they sank twenty-four ships. But they
could not alter the fact that the number of aeroplanes, as also the number
of pilots, was shrinking fast, and would presently be used up.

The battle for Okinawa changed rapidly into nightmare. It progressed
like a surrealist film. On the sixth day, 6 April, the Japanese dispatched
from the Inland Sea their huge battleship, the *Yamato*. It was a huge
Kamikaze. Its mission was to wreak as much havoc as possible: it carried
only enough oil for a one-way trip, and was meant for destruction. In fact
it was engaged by American aircraft, and was sunk before it could do
much damage. But the madness of the sacrifice in such a way of the
world's largest battleship convinced Japan's antagonist that the Japanese
staff was near the end of its judgement.

The battle lasted until 21 June. It ended in scenes of horror. The
Japanese commander and his deputy both committed ceremonial seppaku.
Over a hundred thousand Japanese were dead. A very small number
survived as prisoners.

The Americans were satisfied that a weighty section of the Japanese
command, both in the Navy and the Army, now saw no chance of success
in war, and no opportunity of gaining even a temporary respite, and
would be glad to make peace. The war might have ended then. But how
were these high officers to terminate it? They were afraid of being assassinated if they made any move: the mass of the Army and Navy was still
able to fight, and there was still a minority of the more senior officers who
were willing to fight on to the end. No mutinies or outbreaks of any kind
took place among the forces.

The difficulty for the United States was that it lacked the means of
making contact with the politically reasonable sections in Japanese life.
The attempt to signal to the East that the United States would respond
favourably to any bid for surrender was made again and again, usually by
cryptic speech on the American broadcasting stations; but they met with

no reply from any who could speak responsibly in Japan. Still the wa
went on, and no peace was yet possible, though the majority of all classe
of Japan desired it greatly. The civil servants, the industrialists an
bankers, the trade union leaders, the considerable classes of the intel
ligentsia – all despaired of war, and regarded with frenzy the piece b
piece destruction worked on them by the American aircraft. But th
intransigent section of the military, who had gained control of th
direction of Japan ten years before, could not be set aside. The American
persuaded themselves and the British that a dramatic and novel develop
ment in the art of war was necessary for this.

A picture of the Japanese Empire in twilight, and approaching dis
solution, is given by the puppet Prime Minister, Ba Maw. Ba Maw, as ha
been seen, had had his quarrels with the Japanese, and, though he had
made his position tolerable, he had hardly cause to love them. The more
remarkable is his sober account of the way in which they faced defeat and
international disgrace. He was invited to Japan in November 1944, just as
the systematic bombing of Japan's home islands was beginning, in an
endeavour to organize Asian support for the tottering Japanese imperial
structure. Ba Maw owed his eminence to the Japanese, and knew that he
must fall with them. This is the general impression which he describes:

Tokyo and its people had changed since I had seen them a year ago, visibly
subdued and disillusioned by events, but most of them as determined and defiant
as ever. They were now a people in the grip of the biggest crisis in all their history
and grimly waiting for the worst. But they were facing the situation wonderfully
and revealing their latent racial qualities, their almost inexhaustible capacity to
take whatever should come, to endure and survive and wait and even hope. They
were more or less the same outwardly, but in the course of a long quiet talk they
could not help but betray their true thoughts and fears. Unlike before, they now
spoke mainly of the Kamikazes, thus showing that they were placing most of their
hopes on something which was really an act of desperation. The people were
living with a new terror, the threat of American mass air bombing; they knew that
they had no real way to protect their millions of paper and bamboo houses; not
even, as it turned out, the Imperial Palace.*

The topic of chief concern was the air bombardment, and the damage
which that was able to do, especially on the morale of the population.
This is what Ba Maw says of this:

One of the worst incendiary bombings of Tokyo occurred when I was there
near the end of November 1944. The result was quite literally a holocaust, a mass

* Ba Maw, *Breakthrough in Burma*, op. cit., p. 374.

burning of one of the densest areas of the city. I saw the ghastly devastation the next morning. But there was no panic or self-pity or even audible complaint among the huge mass of victims. In fact some of them were able to express their happiness that the Imperial Palace had escaped. It was a heart-breaking sight but it also lifted one's heart immensely to see so much human endurance and strength of character displayed in so dark an hour.*

Ba Maw was taken round the headquarters of the Japanese Army. The Kamikaze were exhibited to him as a kind of Japanese secret weapon. He met Koiso, the Japanese Prime Minister, and General Sugiyama, the War Minister, who was soon to play a decisive part. He took every opportunity of discussing with the Japanese commanders their defence tactics, and represented that a scorched earth policy would be intolerable to the Burmese as was also the plan of using the Burmese forces to fight the rear-guard action against the British. Ba Maw had the satisfaction of saving the Shwe Dagon Pagoda from being incorporated in the Japanese defence perimeter. At least he gives himself the credit of having achieved it by the negotiations of his visit.

* ibid.

CHAPTER 25

The End

THE war had entered its final stage. Japan still battled on, but its position was hopeless. The United States, still arming, poured out its fleet and aircraft across the Pacific, and was preparing the great offensive against the sacred Japanese homeland. The expectation was that the American war machine, which had swallowed up so many Pacific islands, would in the long run devour Japan Proper. The economic might of the United States must finally prevail. The war machine moved on, and the only uncertainty was the length of time it would take to complete the process. Japan, as Germany before it, was given no time to summon up its resources and to organize them for the optimum defence of its own country.

Japan, in its final phase, was like Macbeth cooped up in Dunsinane, without any rational hope of a happy issue from his adversities, mechanically wound up to continue to shout defiance at the armies investing him.

> Some say he's mad: others that lesser hate him
> Do call it valiant fury: but, for certain,
> He cannot buckle his distemper'd cause
> Within the belt of rule.
> ANGUS: Now does he feel
> His secret murders sticking on his hands; . . .
> Those he commands move only in command,
> Nothing in love; now does he feel his title
> Hang loose about him, like a giant's robe
> Upon a dwarfish thief.

One hope alone sustained Japan. The Soviet Union had not renounced the Non-Aggression Treaty which Matsuoka Yōsuke, Japan's Foreign Minister, had been able to negotiate with it in 1941. In spite of the bad blood between them five years earlier, this treaty, to the surprise of onlookers, had kept the peace between the apparently predestined enemies, though war had raged universally elsewhere. Japan could reckon that peace in Europe would bring to a head the issues between Russia and the United States. Was it too much to expect that Russia, threatened and hwarted by the United States, might see that its true interest lay in accepting the partnership of Japan? Japan could claim that it had already shown, by refraining from striking at Russia when Hitler was at the doors of Moscow in 1941, that no insuperable cause of conflict lay between it and the Soviet Union. It could represent that, in spite of the severe destruction which it had suffered, it still possessed an army which was one of the key pieces on the board internationally. The Japanese Army still had fighting spirit, still had ammunition, and could hope to take an immense toll from a threatened invasion. It boasted that to overrun Japan, when all its natural advantages of defence were taken into review, the United States would need a force of 10 million men, a force which it could not hope to transport. If the United States came to be at loggerheads with Russia, it was unlikely that it would willingly force through the attack on Japan to its conclusion, which would be frightful carnage.

In 1945, as the Japanese position grew evidently more desperate, Russia began to unmask its intentions. At the Yalta Conference in February, Roosevelt offered Russia a larger bait to enter the war against Japan. He unilaterally raised the stakes. Confident of Churchill's support, he promised their recognition of the Russian protectorate in Outer Mongolia and, much more importantly, their support for the reversion to the Soviet Union of 'the former rights of Russia violated by the treacherous attack of Japan in 1904'. By this formula the Treaty of Portsmouth, a treaty for which another American President had been happy to accept responsibility, would be set aside. Southern Sakhalin (Karafuto) would be returned to the Soviet Union, the 'pre-eminent interests of the Soviet Union' in the commercial port of Dairen would be 'safeguarded', the Russian leasehold over ice-free Port Arthur would be restored, Russia's claims to the Kurile Island chain would be upheld, and the Russians would once again assume the same rights and interests over the South Manchurian Railway and the Chinese Eastern Railway that Japan had enjoyed at the height of its power. In exchange Stalin promised Churchill and Roosevelt that he would enter the war against Japan within two or three months after the surrender of Germany. It was an ominous, although secret, bargain, one which was scarcely affected by the agreement between the three leaders that Chinese concurrence would be sought in matters affecting their historic suzerainty over the whole of Manchuria and Mongolia. Roosevelt, by negotiating on these lines, had taken upon himself to re-make history. With Churchill's acquiescence, he had behaved in a very cavalier fashion in disposing of huge 'Chinese' assets and settling vast issues in disregard of wholly legitimate Chinese claims. To be perfectly plain, the Yalta trade-off was no more legitimate and no less aggressive than the offensive behaviour of the Japanese against which the world had complained for half a century.

In April, at the time of the attack on Okinawa, the Soviet Government announced that it would not renew the Russo-Japanese Non-Aggression Pact, which was due to expire one year hence. When the Japanese made proposals about the possibility of a new agreement (and offered terms that were very much like those conceded by Britain and America at Yalta), the Russian Ambassador was ominously evasive. Russia gave every sign that it was preparing for war with Japan. Thus its final hope was nearly extinguished. 'Despair thy charm' seemed to cry out the omens for Japan.

In the light of what is now known, it seems probable that Japanese Intelligence had heard of Stalin's information to Churchill and Roosevelt at the Teheran Conference: Russia was preparing for war with Japan as soon as Germany was defeated. Confirmation of this should have come easily to Japanese spies, although there seem to have been no figures in Japan's employment comparable to Richard Sorge, the Russian agent, who, in the critical phase before Pearl Harbor, had spied on Japan for the USSR. He had been able to reassure Russia that Japan had decided not to hasten to the aid of Germany, and refused to attack Russia as Germany wished.

It is a canard that there is no record of Japan having been well-served by Intelligence. On the contrary, the Japanese networks learned a great deal. Unfortunately for Japan, there was no effective mechanism for ensuring that information acquired by the Intelligence apparatus would affect the Government's basic strategy or perceptions. Throughout these years of Total War, the Japanese were handicapped by having by far the most cumbersome policy-making and policy-review machinery of any belligerent in the conflict, worse even than that of Germany and not a patch on the brilliant system for strategical coordination that the British pioneered and which the Americans copied.

Japan was of course under the handicap that, if it employed men of its own nation as agents, they were more conspicuous than others. Japanese could hardly wear the appearance of blank anonymity which is essential to espionage. The same is broadly true of western spies in an eastern country. They may succeed, by exceptional audacity, in exceptional circumstances, as Sorge was able to do, or as the West's and China's Korean agents did at lower levels in Japanese-occupied territories. But in a war between East and West, where racialism and jingoism are harnessed together, espionage is likely to play less part than in a war in which the contestants share a similar racial background. As it happens, the Japanese did cultivate White Russian émigrés and European Jewish refugees with an eye on their utility in espionage: the results of this collaboration remain obscure, although the size of the networks involved tens of thousands of people directly or indirectly. In any event, the Japanese Government's Russian experts warned that the Soviet Union was girding itself for war, and they were mocked for their pains by the same adventurers whose singularly misconceived optimism had carried havoc into every other corner of East Asia.

Espionage, likewise, paid the British and Americans only very mean dividends. British SOE operations in South-East Asia do not appear to have affected the outcome of the war in any significant way, but the quality of Intelligence produced at great personal risks and sacrifices by the agents involved deserves our respect and appreciation. In Japan Proper, however, the situation was otherwise, and it would appear that little information of value was gained by the use of secret agents. In pre-war days, British and American language officers were seconded on a regular basis to Japanese regiments, training establishments and man-oeuvres. The military, naval and air attachés of the western democracies were restricted in their freedom of movement, but they nevertheless displayed a marvellous capacity to mislead their Governments about the quality of Japanese weaponry and technological sophistication. It is worthwhile recollecting that the Japanese Zero, which made its first appearance in the China theatre on April Fool's Day 1939, made no significant impression upon those whose job it was to keep up to date on the capabilities of potential enemies. In a word, the quality of Allied military Intelligence about Japan prior to Pearl Harbor was abysmal. It was a commonplace assumption almost everywhere in the West during the years leading up to the Pacific War that the Japanese were master copycats who possessed little native ingenuity. There was, for instance, a British air attaché who reported that the Japanese held 2:1 reserves of spare engines for their frontline aircraft, from which he deduced that the Japanese, with their well-known mechanical incompetence, were obliged to throw away faulty or damaged engines rather than repair them! This is about on a par with the other hoary chestnut that most Japanese made poor pilots because they nearly all wore glasses and suffered from vertigo. The patent absurdity of such things is self-evident, but the magnitude of the miscalculations was not. Even to this day, many people who lived through the war still believe that the Japanese never displayed any orig-inality in their weapons development. In fact, as we now know, the

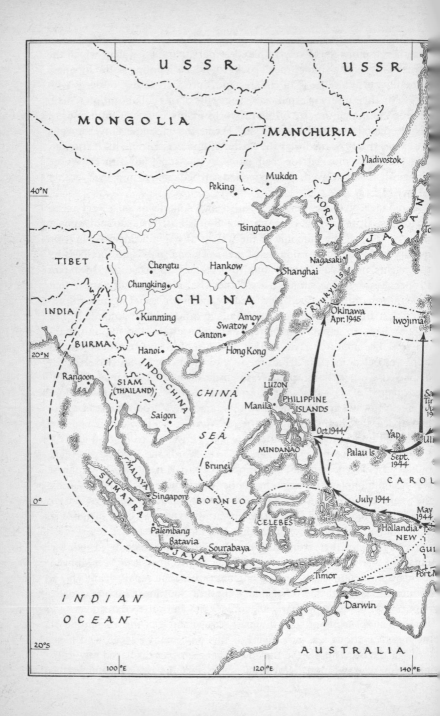

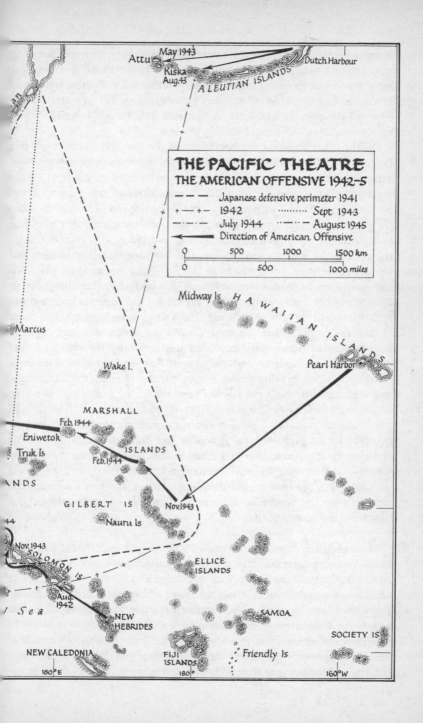

THE PACIFIC THEATRE
THE AMERICAN OFFENSIVE 1942–5

- - - Japanese defensive perimeter 1941
- + - + - 1942   ·········· Sept 1943
- · - · - July 1944   - ·· - ·· - August 1945
→ Direction of American Offensive

0   500   1000   1500 km
0   500   1000 miles

May 1943
Attu
Kiska
Aug.43
Dutch Harbour
ALEUTIAN ISLANDS

Midway Is
HAWAIIAN ISLANDS

Marcus

Wake I.

Pearl Harbor

MARSHALL
Feb. 1944
Eniwetok
Truk Is
Feb. 1944
ISLANDS

ANDS

GILBERT IS
Nauru Is
Nov. 1943

Nov. 1943
SOLOMON Is
ELLICE
ISLANDS

Aug.
1942
SAMOA

Sea
NEW
HEBRIDES
SOCIETY IS

NEW CALEDONIA
FIJI
ISLANDS
Friendly Is

160°E   180°   160°W

Japanese were technologically superior to the western armed forces in most classes of weaponry. Contrary to all expectation, the Japanese were masters of technical improvisation. What defeated them in the end of course was the scale of America's mobilization, her industrial capacity and the pace at which the Allies were able to evolve and produce new generations of weapons during the war.

On the other hand, at the beginning of the war and during the years beforehand, the perceptiveness of British political Intelligence about Japan was exceptionally high, and it stood in marked contrast to the inadequacy of the information that filtered through the political Intelligence about Japan gathered by the United States. During the war, there was a dramatic improvement in the quantity and quality of Allied and especially of American Intelligence, and this had a crucial role in the conduct of military operations. But the misperceptions which had led to the outbreak of hostilities in the first place stemmed largely from the ignorance of American policy-makers and their unwillingness to understand the limits within which Japanese Governments had to operate. It is remarkable how little was the knowledge which reached them in this way from Tokyo. Japanese counter-espionage was very capable, but the United States had succeeded in developing the eyes and ears which pried on Japanese moves, though this tended to be done at a distance by code-breaking, and not by means of spies. Its advantages and limitations in this have already been noted, for example at the time of the negotiations before Pearl Harbor, and in naval battles; it had continued to read the Japanese codes throughout the war, and never betrayed to the Japanese that it was in fact doing so. It required great restraint by the Americans and their British Allies to take no step by which it should become obvious to the Japanese that they possessed the secret. It is, in fact, recorded in Japan that a few men doubted from time to time the degree of security of Japanese communications, but they were not attended to.

Meanwhile the American air raids on Japan went on relentlessly. Until 1944 American aircraft, except those in Lieutenant-Colonel Doolittle's adventure in 1942, had not been over Japan. Thereafter the Japanese homeland was subjected to a bombardment which was utterly destructive. Even before the Japanese attack on Pearl Harbor, the United States had begun the long process of developing an aircraft known as the B29 Superfortress which from the beginning was conceived as a weapon of mass destruction for use against Japan in time of war. In peacetime it was not unusual for bomber aircraft to take ten years to advance from draw-

ing-board to full production, and the B29 was perhaps the most complicated and sophisticated bomber aircraft of its generation. Not surprisingly, it experienced teething problems. Gradually, however, everything
moved into place. To utilize this special weapon, General 'Hap' Arnold,
Commanding General of the United States Army Air Force, took over
executive control of a unique B29 bomber command, responsible only to
the Joint Chiefs of Staff and the President. President Roosevelt, after
considering the advantages of deploying the B29s from bases in Ceylon,
India and Australia, chose to use them in support of China.

Before leaving India to establish themselves at the new Chinese air
bases, the B29 crews carried out the first of a series of raids on relatively
soft targets to gain experience. On 5 June 1944 ninety-eight B29s set
off to bomb Bangkok. The raid was thoroughly bungled. Ten days later,
ninety-two of the aircraft left for Chengtu, in Szechuan, on their way
to attack the Imperial Iron and Steel Works at Yawata on Kyushu,
their first attack against a Japanese city. Only one bomb hit the plant,
but the Japanese, as we have seen, received the message. In the months
that followed, four other raids on Kyushu and others against targets in
Manchuria and Sumatra were scarcely more successful. The Japanese,
in their Ichi-Go campaign, fared rather better.

Driven out of China, the B29s gradually established themselves in the
Marianas. Progress, if it is right to use such a word, was slow. On 12
October 1944 the first B29 raid on Tokyo took off from Tinian. It achieved
nothing. A raid by a hundred massed aircraft attacked the Okayama
aircraft assembly plant on Taiwan in November 1944. It, too, was ineffective. The US Army Air Force found its exalted expectations regarding
the performance of the Superfortresses plunging as rapidly as their payloads towards the ground. No less than eight attempts were made between
late November 1944 and early March 1945 in an extended effort to destroy
the Nakajima factory on the outskirts of Tokyo by high-level bombing
runs. All of these raids were unavailing, even humiliating. The failure of
the strategic bombing campaign stood out in marked contrast to the
successes which rival services were clocking up against the Japanese at sea
and in the Philippines.

Thirty-eight-year-old General Curtis H. Le May was brought in to
direct the United States strategic bombing operations against Japan. He
was a skilled technician, with experience of the air war against Germany.
Fresh from his 'successful' destruction of Hamburg, he soon chafed with
frustration. His superiors wanted results, certainly, but many felt qualms
of conscience about resorting to the indiscriminate use of fire bombs. In
December 1944, however, a number of B29s had attacked Japanese-

occupied Hankow with incendiaries, reducing much of that city to ashes. On 23 February 1945 Le May ordered a daylight attack upon Tokyo by 130 aircraft loaded with incendiaries. It produced only 640 casualties but destroyed 25,000 buildings. This whetted the appetite of the Americans. Arnold authorized Le May to conduct a series of large-scale fire-bomb attacks upon Tokyo, Nagoya, Osaka and Kobe, targeted upon selected blocks of twelve square miles in which there was a population density calculated at the time as in excess of 128,000 per square mile.

What followed was sheer, unadulterated murder. It was also the greatest air offensive in history. No one believed that the horrors about to be inflicted upon Japanese civilians would suddenly melt Japanese resistance or produce a wave of popular rebellion against the Japanese Government. But it was nonetheless an effort designed to undermine Japanese morale and came as the Japanese were emerging from a particularly hard winter exacerbated by acute food and fuel shortages. The United States Army Air Force generals hoped to inflict such great punishment that the Japanese would learn respect for the power and relentless determination of the United States in a manner reminiscent of the determination of Kaiser Wilhelm's men to 'educate' the Chinese by inflicting upon them punitive demonstrations of German savagery after the Boxer Rebellion: as the creatures of the observant American humorist Finley Peter Dunne had commented then:

' 'Twill civilize th' Chinnymen,' said Mr Hennessy,
' 'Twill civilize thim stiff,' said Mr Dooley.*

On the night of 9–10 March 1945 General Le May launched his first full-scale incendiary attack against Tokyo. A huge force of 334 big four-engined B29 Superfortresses rose up from the new American runways on Guam, Tinian and Saipan in a strike at the heart of the Japanese Empire. It took two and a half hours for the planes to assemble in their formations. Desirous of increasing their bomb payloads, and confident of encountering little resistance, the American aircraft had been stripped of all their ammunition and defensive armament except what they carried in their tail-turrets. Le May's bombers flew abnormally low that night: this was a protection against anti-aircraft guns, which were abundant in Tokyo. The Japanese, even as late as this, did not have their guns adjusted to radar: they were operated manually, and they were made largely ineffective by Le May's strategy. There was no attempt to single out military

* 'The Future of China (On German Intervention in China)', in *Mr Dooley's Philosophy*, R. H. Russell, New York, 1900.

argets, nor was this raid in reprisal for any specific Japanese breaches
f international law. It was deliberate, indiscriminate mass murder,
entred upon the *shitamachi* (downtown) district of southern Tokyo, the
most heavily populated urban quarter on earth, where actually upwards
f a million people were packed in an area four miles by three to a density
f 103,000 per square mile. The Japanese in their flimsy wooden buildings
nd narrow back streets had no advance warning before the bombs began
o fall at a quarter past midnight. The raid lasted two and a half hours.
here was very little flak and negligible fighter opposition. The fires
pread well beyond the target zone. Somewhere between 70,000 and
140,000 people died. The injuries suffered by many of the survivors were
nightmarish. Nearly a million people were left homeless: 267,000 buildings
were destroyed. All of this cost the United States Army Air Force a mere
?,000 tons of incendiaries and the loss of fifteen B29 aircraft. It was to be
only the first of such raids, but its effects were by far the most catastrophic
of all the Allied 'conventional' air stikes against the Japanese in terms of
human mortality.

Individual instances of courage or resourcefulness counted for very
little in the firestorm that began fifteen minutes after the first bombs fell.
The intensity of the flames within the conflagration exceeded 1800°F. They
generated a holocaust which surpassed even the horrors of Dresden and
Hamburg: much more damage could be done to Japanese cities by fire
bombs because of the light structure of most buildings; the same weight
of explosives led to much more destruction. It was the most destructive
man-made fire in recorded history, and the loss in terms of human lives
was of a similar order of magnitude to the toll which was to be exacted
by the atomic bomb blasts at Hiroshima or Nagasaki. Japanese not
immediately caught by the flames are said to have stood musing at the
terrible hypnotic beauty of the spectacle. This was Total War at its most
awful. With unspeakable grief, the Emperor, accompanied by his
Lord Privy Seal and Grand Chamberlain, went on foot to tour the
smoking remains of the worst-hit areas of the *shitamachi*. The ordeal
cannot fail to have made a huge impression upon them. It would take
twenty days to bury the dead, many of whom were committed to mass
graves.

Meanwhile, less than thirty hours after the first great Tokyo firestorm,
three square miles of Nagoya were subjected to a concentrated attack by
317 B29s. Eight square miles of the industrial heartland of Osaka were
laid waste in a three-hour raid on 13 March. Kobe suffered the same fate
on 16 March. Then Nagoya was hit again. Assessing the results at the end
of this ten-day experiment, the United States Army Air Force examined

its balance sheet. It had expended 10,000 tons of bombs in a total of 1,60
sorties and sustained a loss of less than 1 per cent of its striking force. I
the months that followed, the campaign of destruction spread out in al
directions. Le May's strike force grew until it reached nearly 600 aircraf
Nearly every conurbation in Japan came under brutal attack. At the pea
of the bombing campaign, Le May's B29s dropped 40,000 tons of bomb
on Japan in a single month.

In the B29 campaign, Total War nurtured one of the most revoltin;
monsters ever conceived by modern technology. These grim tactics
operated with the thoroughness of General Le May, were new, and
marked a change in air warfare. In the aftermath of such a development
it is appropiate to feel an abiding revulsion. Yet it must be said that ther
is no evidence to suggest that the Japanese would have shirked from
utilizing such fearful weaponry had they themselves been able to do so
The overwhelming consensus among Americans was that the mass
murders being carried out in their name were justified. They felt that the
havoc wrought by the B29s would bring a rapid end to the war. After the
war, Prince Konoye recalled that the B29 raids were responsible for
hardening the determination of the Japanese Government to make peace
More than that, however, the American people regarded the bombings as
a fitting punishment to inflict upon the Japanese people. Here was no fine
distinction between an enemy Government and its people. Both were
to be execrated. Americans reminded each other that in the aerial
bombardment of Chinese cities, beginning in August 1937, Japan had
been the first nation since the First World War to adopt a programme of
systematic terror and mass destruction against densely populated
conurbations. And so the Americans rededicated themselves to their grim
task and felt little remorse. Indeed, few foreigners at the time were inclined
to share in the grief of the Emperor for the wretched sufferings of his
subjects.

The Japanese authorities tried to rise to the occasion, and ambitious
schemes were put forward to counter or at least to mitigate any repetition
of such horrors. Japanese schools had already closed throughout the
capital. By March 1945 1.7 million people had been evacuated from
Tokyo, but 6 million still remained huddled in the city. Now the mass
evacuation of Tokyo became uncontrollable. Like much of the Japanese
civil defence effort, chaos and confusion prevailed. The air-raid shelters,
fire precautions, provisions for medical services and preparations for the
maintenance of public order were hopelessly inadequate, primitive and
anyway came far too late to cope with dangers for which the Japanese
authorities had ample forewarning. The evacuation had always lacked

hat systematic planning and administrative coordination which had characterized the precautions taken by the British in the early days of the war and during the perils of the Blitz. Now as many Japanese fled their great cities in blind panic and descended upon ill-prepared and starving surrounding country districts like locusts, many of those left behind went into an almost catatonic state of shock. The uncharacteristic despair of the Japanese people was nowhere more clearly exemplified than by the fact that after the raids Japanese civil defence training was all but abandoned. Japanese medical and fire services for a time simply disintegrated. These terrible months had their counterparts in the European War, but running throughout the whole of the Second World War was a curious inability of either hemisphere to learn from what was happening on the opposite side of the globe.

The economic consequences were devastating. At first the destruction, as was the case in Germany, had less effect on industrial production than might have been supposed, but, as it became more wholesale, and surpassed the war damage in Europe, so its effects became harder to circumvent. The Japanese Government took more sweeping powers to direct the economy of the country; but where was the economy left to direct? The food supplies began to fall dangerously, and could not be distributed because of the destruction of the railways and the breakdown of commercial organization. The description of the life of the Japanese worker at this stage of the war, underfed, harried to inhuman extremes by the Government, lacking the elementary comforts of a safe home, must touch even the reader who knows something of the terrors endured by the German population. A great flight began from the towns to the countryside.

For the first time the civilian part of the nation began to turn against the military. In parts of the country it became positively dangerous to wear uniform. Such aberrant behaviour shook deeply the Army General Staff.

Japanese experts at the time said that the Japanese standard of nutrition in the towns in the last year was below that of Germans in the fateful winter of hunger after the end of the first European War. Even the Army, which was the last to be affected, was put on short supplies. The soldiers were found to be bartering military equipment for the scanty food supplies which filtered through to private hands. In spite of all this, both the civilian and military morale remained astonishingly high. There were no food riots in the Japanese towns, such as were already causing great concern in Germany in the First World War as early as 1916. It may be that the Japanese were less shocked by this adversity than were European populations, because they had been inured to it. Twenty years before, the people of Tokyo had experienced similar devastation in their capital city that time from the horrors of the Tokyo earthquake.

In April 1945 the Prime Minister, Koiso Kuniaki, fell from office. He had engaged in negotiations with questionable Chinese emissaries, by which he had intended to split the Chinese and the Western Allies. They were of course secret, but when they failed, they leaked out and he was dismissed. His years of intrigue and adventurism had come full circle Mistrusting the services and skills of diplomats, he held himself out as an astute judge of men, expert in negotiations. Koiso believed the assurances of his Chinese contacts that he could detach China from the war by signing a truce agreeing to the abandonment of the puppet régime of Wang Ching-wei and the withdrawal of all Japanese forces from China. In exchange, or so Koiso believed, Chiang Kai-shek would guarantee to prevent American forces from landing in China. The Supreme War Council regarded the whole idea as fatuous. There were, however, other factors, equally important. Koiso had shown himself unable to hold himself apart from the myopic propaganda issued for public consumption by the Army. He took so little trouble to establish the truth that he succeeded in embarrassing the Supreme Command as well as appalling those who knew that the time had come to seek peace on whatever terms the Allied Powers would accept. The Palace and Government bureaucrats had expected Koiso to work closely with Admiral Yonai Mitsumasa, a perceptive and highly personable former Prime Minister, a man known to be committed to the search for peace, who was entrusted by the Emperor to act as Koiso's Deputy Premier and served concurrently as Navy Minister. Yonai did not lack bravery, and his personal views were unequivocal: in May 1945, indeed, he went as far as declaring, 'If we can just protect the Imperial family, that will be sufficient. Even if it means the Empire is reduced to the four home islands, we'll have to do it.'* Unfortunately, as a Japanese diplomat with some knowledge of the facts wrote afterwards with uncharacteristic bluntness:

Koiso was utterly ignorant of the realities of the military situation. It was thus impossible to get him to work for a termination of the war. Yonai told me he was

---

* Quoted by I. Saburō in *Japan's Last War*, Blackwell, Oxford, 1979, pp. 230–31, citing the private records of Rear-Admiral Takagi Sōkichi, one of Yonai's closest confidants, a brilliant man who had been deeply involved in a secret conspiracy to find a suitable formula for the surrender of Japan ever since heading a Navy research team that had investigated America's productive capacity at the beginning of the war.

surprised to discover that Koiso had come from Korea with a ready-made list of cabinet members, mostly names of his old henchmen and cronies in Korea. These men were entirely unacquainted with the difficulties then confronting the country. They were popularly dubbed the 'Korean Cabinet' in contrast with Tōjō's 'Manchurian Cabinet'. Yonai gave what advice he decently could under the circumstances but it remained for the most part unheeded. The Koiso Cabinet was clearly a severe disillusionment to him and his friends. There was little opportunity left for Yonai to work for peace.

While the Emperor desired to see the new Cabinet operated on the basis of a close working partnership of Koiso and Yonai, actually Yonai thought, or preferred to think, that his responsibility as Koiso's partner ended with the formation of the Cabinet. After that, he was a mere Navy Minister and, as such, he did not like to interfere with what Koiso did as Prime Minister.*

Long before the failure of the Chinese negotiations, therefore, the Jūshin had come to recognize the country's urgent need for a change of premier. Within the Daihon'ei he was regarded with derision as 'a snobbish, senile general on the reserve list without any influence whatever in the Army'.† The public, dismayed by what news filtered through to them about the disasters in the field, also seemed to appreciate that the Prime Minister was out of touch with reality. As American forces stormed ashore on Okinawa, Koiso conceived the fantastic idea that he might ride out the crisis and consolidate his authority by returning to active military service and taking on additional responsibilities as Minister for War in addition to his responsibilities as Premier. The Army refused. Only then did Koiso accept his humiliation, bow to the inevitable and resign.

Baron Suzuki Kantarō, a retired admiral, succeeded him. It was remarked that he was sworn in on the day after the loss of Japan's prize battleship, the *Yamato*: it seemed as though Japan had turned to the Navy for its Prime Minister just at the time that it had lost its fleet. He had a good record, having been a target of the military conspirators of February 1936, by whom he was badly wounded. He was an aged hero of the Russo-Japanese War. He had a likeable, rather enigmatic, personality, and was almost universally popular – a rare thing in Japan. From experience, he believed that the scope for personal intervention in public affairs was limited, and he was apt to preside benignly over them, and, like many Japanese, to acquiesce philosophically in what came to pass. In fact there was, in Suzuki, a touch of Tolstoy's Kutuzov: the much respected figure, clothed with glory from the past, who is wise enough to collaborate with events, rather than to withstand them – or even to attempt to understand them.

* K. Toshikazu, *Eclipse of the Rising Sun*, Jonathan Cape, London, 1951, pp. 86–7.
† ibid., p. 106.

But he was eighty years old: too venerable to be effective, even by roundabout means. Having the virtue of open-mindedness, he lacked the decisiveness, the singlemindedness, which were essential qualities in a Prime Minister in such a crisis. The choice of Suzuki, however, was a sign that the peace party was gradually prevailing. He was not a born leader, did not aspire to the office thrust upon him, and did not incarnate the fabled Japanese desire to go down fighting. Intellectually, he needed no convincing that Japan had lost the war; he was himself more than ready for peace. But he moved too slowly to be able to save Japan. The peace party, backed by the Imperial Court and by responsible members of that solid corps of professional bureaucrats that is the repository of common sense in most countries, was looking for a totem, was ready to be rallied, and to assert itself, but it was beyond Suzuki to provide this.

In the next month, May, Japan lost its ally, Germany. The Supreme War Council met and approved the decision to carry on the war notwithstanding. It declared, however, that Japan was released from the provisions of the Tripartite Pact (which was somewhat overdue and rather went without saying). Japan had now to face the switch of the Allied forces engaged in the European War, and their addition to the force already employed against Japan in the East; it had also to meet the possible use against it of the Russian Army, now disengaged.

In the summer of 1945, Prime Minister Suzuki, his Foreign Minister and the two Service Ministers decided to send Prince Konoye Fumimaro to Moscow as head of a peace delegation, provided he proved acceptable to the Soviets. This decision may have reached the Moscow Embassy only after Molotov had departed for the Potsdam Conference. Konoye, thrice Prime Minister, remained in favour as a man behind whom the whole country could feel a sense of unity in adversity. In any event, the Soviet Union made no reply. Then came news of the Potsdam Declaration, which fell upon the Japanese leadership like a thunderclap. Obviously something had to be done. Several Cabinet meetings were held to decide how to proceed: these broke up in confusion and despair.

An outside chance for Japan lay in the complications set up by the death of Roosevelt on 12 April, and his succession by Vice-President Harry Truman. But to have used these to advantage, to have extricated Japan from the net which was closing in, would have required a very flexible diplomacy. Flexibility was never a strong point with the Japanese and the number of neutral centres where Japan could operate, and from which it could obtain its Intelligence, had, to the advantage of the United States, become very small.

In spite of their Yalta agreement with the Russians, which had been so dearly purchased, the Americans, and to a large extent the British, continued to be profoundly distressed by the memory of the savage Japanese defence of the Coral Islands. The ferocity of their resistance in the homeland was expected to be as formidable. Nothing like the same internal collapse was foreseen as followed the death of Hitler in Germany. The war might continue for as much as a year, and with what was foreseen as the mounting strain of tension with Russia, in spite of the glitter of the terms of Yalta, the upshot was not clear.

In the meanwhile it became known that the Japanese General Staff was pressing on with plans for a fanatical defence of the Japanese islands. Rightly it was supposed that the principal American blow would be directed at Honshu. To deal with this it could assemble two and a half million troops in the home islands. Tales arrived to the effect that a vast underground headquarters was being dug out at Tokyo. The Japanese Army was said to be gambling on the blind determination which would halt the Americans on landing. Clearly the Americans had still much effort before them.

But very shortly after, a great change came over the situation. It was brought about by the completion of the atom bomb. Partly this was the result of German-Jewish genius, which, barred from Germany by racial madness, had been mobilized in the invention of this device of war, which had been meant in the first place for the overthow of the Nazi system. Part of the early work was done in England: and, when it was concentrated in the United States, British scientists participated. The war against Germany had come to an end in May 1945, with the bomb still a project, and not realized in fact: but by June it was clear that it was about to become operational. The news that it was to be so, and would be available for use against Japan, had already been grasped by the very small circle in which, at this stage of the war, had been concentrated the making of American policy. Its immense, hardly credible, destructive power could quench the continuing flame of Japanese fanaticism. With its finality there could be no discussion.

By this trick of fate, the need to cajole and coax Russia, the need for Russian complicity and Russian power, were all removed.

By the summer of 1945 it was stated that American policy would be revised: Russian aid was now no longer so necessary for bringing to an end the war with Japan. The United States had initially perceived that through the possible intervention of Russia it could go ahead without perpetually needing to keep China contented, and now it saw that it would be able to discard Russia in its turn.

In fact America was by this time as zealous to deter Russia from entering the war as before it had been to bring Russia in. Truman had succeeded Roosevelt; his period was from the start different from the period of Roosevelt. Other considerations apart, Truman was less inclined to exert himself to maintain good relations with Russia. He was less of a historian. He was less inclined, especially at this point of his career, to look into the future, and to adjust his actions accordingly. Instinctively, Truman was thinking in terms of the containment of Russia, and he was anxious that in East Asia as elsewhere, Russia should make as little headway as possible. If Russia once went to war and invaded Manchuria, there would be little chance of keeping it out of Port Arthur and Dairen (which it had already been promised at Yalta). Even though Truman, who was new to these issues of foreign policy, did not himself stress all these points, he was more available than Roosevelt had been to advisers who suggested a frankly anti-Russian policy. None of the advisers knew, but Truman did, that the atom bomb would be available for putting Japan out of the war. For the time being he was satisfied that Russian demands would not be extravagant. If the effects of the bomb were to be as he was advised, a Power without the bomb could not argue aggressively with the Power which possessed it.

The condition of Japan continued to deteriorate. It was uncertain that the bomb would ever be required. General Le May was claiming that his air bombardment had totally paralysed life in sixty major cities. He claimed that Japan was being driven back to the stone age. The Joint Chiefs of Staff reported at the beginning of July: 'Japan will become a nation without cities, with her transportation disrupted, and will have tremendous difficulty in holding her people together for continued resistance.' By March 1945 Japan had lost 88 per cent of the merchant fleet tonnage with which it had begun the war, and it had become almost impossible to import any goods, even the most essential. The Service departments of the Government cried out for the punishment of those engaged in the economic administration; but this could do no good. American Intelligence was, however, rather less optimistic. It gave due allowance to the putting out of action of much of Japanese heavy industry by the blockade and through air bombardment. But it reported that the Japanese output of combat aircraft was still between 1,200 and 1,500 a month (as compared with a peak production of 2,300 reached late in

1944). The greatest shortage was of fuel oil, which was bringing orthodox air operations to a standstill. On the other hand Japan had little to worry about in its stock of ammunition. The Intelligence Committee still thought that the highly trained Japanese Army, the greater part of which had as yet never been in action, was a formidable fighting force. It reckoned that it would probably take another twelve months to subdue it. It made its report, it must be noticed, without knowledge of the bomb.

At the Potsdam Conference in July, when the three masters of the world met face to face, Truman, with careful premeditation and calculated misdirection, told Stalin, apparently in passing, that the Allies had in their hands a more powerful bomb than any previously used. No word was said about the bomb being nuclear, or about the transformation of the war by its invention. Churchill, who knew the true facts, and who watched Stalin carefully, agreed that he had not suspected the truth behind Truman's apparently routine information. He took it as an announcement that the United States had been able to charge its bomb with a heavier load of dynamite. There is drama in the spectacle of these two men, the pillars of the western world, systematically observing the demeanour of a man whom they both regarded as their potential enemy, while in public they played on him something which resembled a confidence trick. The drama is heightened because Stalin had in his pocket, in the communist offensive which he knew he could release in Europe, something like an atom bomb in politics.

A race, in which one of the partners, Stalin, was in darkness about the true facts and about their urgency, then took place between the Americans, who were about to explode the bomb, and the Russians, who were in the last stages of the preparation to attack in Manchuria. Russia had become aware of the change of attitude by the United States, of the desire that it should not participate, though it may have been partly puzzled about the reason. The United States rushed the preparations. At one time the bomb was to have been used on 1 August. Last-minute delays in completing its manufacture put this back a few days. Further delay came because the weather made it almost impossible to raid Japan accurately.

During the Potsdam Conference it was learnt that Japan had requested Swedish mediation in working out surrender terms. It was plain that peace could not be far off. The United States, however, showed surprisingly little zeal in developing this initiative.

The United States made at this time the decision to exclude Russians as members of an occupation force in Japan. The plans for occupying Japan were made surprisingly late. Their details were all improvised. For example, the decision to divide the occupation of Korea and to fix the boundary between the American zone and the Russian zone at the thirty-eighth parallel, was made between an American captain and a Russian major. Thus, casually, there came into being a frontier problem which subsequently divided the world. The Americans and the British were informed by Molotov about the repeated, almost frenzied, attempts by Japan to enlist the support of Russia as a mediator. They were being rebuffed by Russia. It was clear that Russia was not going to back Japan as a move in the war that had already begun between it and its Allies.

At Potsdam, on 26 July 1945, the Allies had issued a final and solemn summons to Japan to surrender. Its terms were broadcast over the wireless. They were that those Japanese who had been responsible for the policies which had led to war were to be forever eliminated; that Japan must renounce all its overseas empire; that war criminals must be punished; that Japan should be occupied. As had become the habit of the United States with beaten adversaries, Japan was required to surrender unconditionally. These demands, though exceedingly radical, were not entirely rejected by Japan, so desperate had its position become.

An answer was understood to have been given in a press conference on 30 July by the Japanese Prime Minister, Admiral Suzuki, at which he spoke in Japanese. It was, as might have been expected from an old man, doubtful, temporizing and ambiguous. Apparently he had meant to say that he withheld comment. The Allies interpreted the Japanese word he used as meaning that Japan not only would not comment, but would treat the summons with contempt. This was taken by the handful of Americans who knew what was intended as the signal for dropping the bomb. Actually it has been suggested since that a word was mistranslated, and meant much less than was supposed, signifying merely that Japan's first reaction to the summons was not being published. The subsequent controversy about what really happened has been inconclusive. That the confusion in fact occurred, is typical of the Japanese language, one of the most involved and ambiguous languages of the world, and the reader must not be astonished that it should have betrayed Japan towards its disaster.

The bomb was dropped on Hiroshima, the chosen target, on 6 August 1945. The attack was made from Tinian, not far from Guam, which had been taken in the previous year. The plane, a B29 bomber, had been blessed for its mission by a Roman Catholic priest. The havoc made was as great as was forecast. It was clear that the war could not be pursued when America could drop bombs of this kind. Within three days a second bomb, of a different and even more deadly type, was dropped on the civilian port of Nagasaki. It did slightly less damage, because Nagasaki had better air-raid precautions and because the bomb did not set off a fire-storm; but its blast was greater than that at Hiroshima. This time, to signalize the joint responsibility of the United States and Britain, the death plane was accompanied by a plane carrying British observers, Dr W. Penney, the physicist, and Wing Commander L. Cheshire, who, by one of the ironies of these events, was later to win celebrity in Britain as the leader of one of the most inspired missions of the day, that of bringing comfort and the opportunity of decent existence to the incurably disabled. With the bomb at Nagasaki, there was released a manifesto to a top Japanese physicist, addressed to him by his American colleagues and explaining some of the details of the bomb. It urged him to enlighten the Japanese Government.

Ironically, Nagasaki was one of the parts of Japan which had the connections of longest duration with the West. It was founded in the sixteenth century by a feudal lord who was a Christian, and who wanted the trade between Japan and the Christian world to be based on it. For a time the port was actually ceded to the Jesuit missionaries, who organized its administration. It was subsequently the centre of persecution of Japanese Christians when the Japanese Government become alarmed by their number.

The dropping of the atom bomb was so dramatic, the awed shock it provoked throughout the world was so final, and the sense that it was, in President Truman's phrase, 'the greatest thing in history', seemed so incontestable that there was a general instinct to think that it had brought to an end one phase of human affairs. From then onwards everything would be dwarfed by events. But the appalling news of the disaster produced by atomic radiation, the vaporizing and burning of human beings, the whole vast panorama of unutterable suffering, somehow failed to register with most people who lived through those days. Even the horrible details, published some months afterwards and set out with all the technical skill of American publicity, were too terrible for belief. The mind set up impediments to taking in such information. There was born at that time an uneasiness which has affected a whole age.

The Americans had thus won the race. They had set themselves against Russia; but it was virtually a dead heat because on the next day, before Japan had had time to surrender, the Russians crossed the frontier of Manchuria. By a four-pronged offensive, Russia overran the country as neatly as Germany had picked off countries earlier in the war. Though the fate of Hiroshima has stuck in the world's memory and though it has been regarded as the final cause of Japan's capitulation, the Russian invasion shares in the distinction of having tilted the Japanese over to put an end to the war.

The effects of the atom bomb and the grim finality of its consequences were not immediately clear. Among most people outside Hiroshima itself, even among those in Tokyo, there was doubt about what had really happened. A great bomb had fallen; terrible destruction had been wrought; but Japan had become thoroughly used to such calamities. Actually the loss of life in the atomic phase, though it was rendered peculiarly horrible by atomic radiation, was less than that in the great B29 raids, to which Japan had been subjected since March 1945. Prince Konoye afterwards told American investigators that Japan's greatest fear of the Soviet Union in the closing stages of the war had been this psychological fear, especially after the Soviet Union's renunciation of the Russo–Japanese Non-Aggression Pact. But all Japan knew the significance of the dreaded invasion of Manchuria, the advent of the Russian hordes, the coming into reality of that threat which had, as long as man could remember, been the governing fact in Japan's foreign policy. Japan could not face war with another Great Power. It was this which made it 'despair its charm', and accept the facts.

The history of the way Japan surrendered is dramatic, and even today, has probably been only partly told. At least, new accounts are constantly appearing in Japan with new details, which, true or false, require the narrative of events to be considered afresh.

A new personality in Japan played a large part at the conclusion. This was the most august person in the land. Hitherto he had been content to be a spectator of the great events, but now he entered the arena. This was the Japanese Emperor.

He was a virtuous prince. The irony is that such dark proceedings had been allowed to happen under his aegis. In the whole range of personalities who held positions of distinction in the war, whether of actual power or of decorativeness, he, and the English monarch, George VI, were the only ones without serious blemish. Like George VI he had a stammer; like him, he held in reality very little political power. It must have been discouraging for this young man, entering on his life's career, that he succeeded his father, who had been deranged during almost the whole of his reign. Yet that fact had not compromised the monarchy, and this speaks highly of the reserves of credit which the institution enjoyed. In one respect the Emperor was ahead of George VI. He had strong intellectual interests, though these were concentrated on a single subject, marine biology. The corollary of the secure eminence of the Japanese Emperor was that ordiarily public opinion severely restricted the range of his activities; he was expected to do almost nothing because his role was almost deified. And Hirohito could not be said to have contributed anything remarkable to the political debates of his time. From the day he ascended his throne in 1926, to the day when he nearly lost it at the time of Japan's defeat, he did what was expected of him. He was reliable; he was thoroughly constitutional; he gave no trouble to the politicians by threatening to use the stored-up prestige of the Japanese monarchy to embarrass them. The inner circle of Japanese with knowledge of what went on behind the façade of public life knew that the course of Japan's affairs – the autonomy of the military, and a foreign policy which brought it into collision with the United States and Britain – was profoundly antipathetic to him. But beyond asking the occasional awkward question at imperial conferences, or confiding his anxieties to those few who had audiences with him on rare occasions, he gave no sign of his continual vexation.

However, at the crisis of Japan, he acted with much common sense. He borrowed from the Confucian philosophy of China the maxim by which he governed his actions. The Confucian wisdom was not to stand up like an oak tree before a raging tempest: in a storm, the oak tree is uprooted and perishes. The willow tree has the better chance of survival; it bends before the wind, but, when the hurricane is over, its root is unsnapped, and it stands up once again by its own resilience. Thus, before the storm of the Japanese military, which was to blow away many persons in its time, the Emperor bowed, and was inconspicuous. Now the storm was nearly blown out, and the opportunity came for the reassertion of the powers of the monarchy, which were real and legitimate even if they had been so long unused. He was guided, in the crucial days when he felt that his personal intervention was timely, that in fact the spirit of the Japanese constitution called for it, by a suave and subtle sense of correct timing. He was capable of choosing the right men to collaborate with – or he was very lucky in these being available, and in offering their services. His conduct at the time suggests that this marine biologist had developed a political instinct during the years of inoffensive constitutional practice.

Throughout July the conviction of defeat had been gripping one person after another and one institution after another. In the past year the fortunes of the civilian elements of government in their control of the military had begun to revive. In the complex balance of forces which made up Japanese politics, the centre of authority began to pass a little away from the soldiers and towards the civilians.

But the services, both the Army and Navy, were obdurate for continuing war: and the senior officers, even if compelled by reason to admit the hopelessness of their case, could point out that they were powerless to assent to peace. They would have been assassinated. The spirit of the nation had passed into the custody of the patriotic societies which would have employed the sanction of murder against anyone who dared to speak of surrender. Both the Jūshin, and the more reasonable service officers, had to mask their intention, to carry on their intrigue behind walls of extreme secrecy, and had to say one thing while in fact strenuously doing another. As a result, Japan's resolution to fight on appeared undented. It had become as good as impossible for it to capitulate. Japan, having made a cult of the principle that no Japanese ever surrendered to the enemy, now found it impossible to accept the findings of common sense.

Behind the scenes, however, and with every secrecy, Japan had been sounding the possibilities of an honourable peace; and peace, with honour that would satisfy Japan meant, in effect, a peace on the simple condition that Japan was allowed to keep its Emperor. In every other respect Japan was ready, except for the irreconcilables in the Army, to surrender unconditionally; with the Emperor's position guaranteed, the Japanese would sigh with relief and cease their hopeless resistance. There is undeniable pathos about these last days of Japanese agony. Japan was willing to trade the entire substance of capitulation for this one concession to a principle which, to its western conquerors, appeared perverted and of no worth. To the West, attachment to an Emperor was sentimental; a defeated Japan must eventually have a chief executive, and the title he would use of himself was no matter. But to the Japanese it was beyond price. Even so, some of the Jūshin were frankly disposed to sacrifice the Emperor, if peace could be gained by this.

President Truman had to take account of the fact that feeling against the monarchy was strong in the United States. Those in favour of tolerating it were accused of being appeasers. Truman himself, backed by Henry L. Stimson, the Secretary for War, was in favour of accepting the Japanese terms on this point. They were influenced by the argument that the American occupying force would find it much simpler to do its work if it had the Japanese Emperor on its side. His prestige was so immense that he would, as it were, legitimize the occupation in Japan's eyes. Also, an American commander, able to speak through him, would be able to gain control of the surrendering Japanese armies; which, otherwise, would have presented a problem. Truman did not directly meet the Japanese condition. But he drafted the American reply in terms that, while avoiding all mention of the Emperor problem, conveyed the general sense that the Emperor would be kept.

These exchanges came between two vital meetings in Tokyo, the first on 13 August, between the Japanese Emperor and the Supreme Command, the committee of which directed the war; the second on the next day, a conference of the Emperor with the Japanese Cabinet. The meetings were held in a dug-out in the imperial palace. In spite of the belligerent circumstances, a certain formality was observed. All those taking part wore full dress uniform, or morning dress; the long table at which they sat was covered with a precious gold brocade. But the Emperor himself, appearing unshaven, increased the general sense of gloom. At the first meeting, no decision was reached: the case for further resistance, the case for immediate capitulation, were fully argued. But the Prime Minister, Admiral Suzuki, succeeded in getting agreement that the Emperor should be asked to decide personally what should be done. To follow such a procedure was revolutionary in Japan: the convention was that he should never be embarrassed by having to give instructions to his Ministers. At the second meeting, after those present had again expressed their views, and the American attitude towards the Emperor had been weighed up, the decision was taken by the Emperor. 'The unendurable must be endured', was the imperial pronouncement which terminated the war. It was a conscious echo of Hirohito's grandfather's remarks at the end of another great humiliation of Japan, and it therefore was understood to contain elements of continuity and regeneration as well as of despair and resolution.

With the last military hope gone, with the Red Army pouring into Manchuria, and with further air attacks expected, which nobody had the remotest idea of how to resist, the Japanese Emperor, in form using the procedure with which he had committed Japan to the calamity of Pearl Harbor, but in fact having taken on himself the personal responsibility for what was now done, gave instructions that hostilities were to cease and, on 14 August Japan replied, accepting the Potsdam declaration.

Until the last moment, it continued to be uncertain if even the intervention of the Emperor would succeed. The military, which had made the war, would not lightly abdicate. It was one thing for the Emperor to forbid further war; it was another for him, great though the Imperial prestige was, to be obeyed. Moreover the United States, in refusing all bargaining, had not satisfied the Army that it stood to gain nothing by forcing American troops to fight their way ashore in Japan. Action was precipitated because a fairly accurate account of the peace negotiations had leaked to the Army. On the night after the decision to end the war was taken, a melodrama took place in Tokyo which was equal to any of the sensational passages in the history of conspiracy. It recalls Hitler's night of the long knives, in which there culminated the feud between him and the SA leaders; St Bartholomew's Eve in Paris four centuries earlier; the fight, again at Paris, on the night of Robespierre's fall, between the moderate politicians and those who wanted the Terror to continue. A group of young, well-connected, passionately unappeasable officers tried to halt the negotiations, make a coup, and seize the sacred person of the Emperor.

To succeed, they needed the support of three or four generals, who were in key positions in Tokyo. Their plot began in the office of the general commanding the First Imperial Guards Division, which was garrisoning the imperial palace. For hours they pleaded with him: then, their tempers breaking, and pressed for time, they abruptly murdered him. In these bloody proceedings, there is an odd atmosphere of a family quarrel which had passed out of control and become terribly serious. Many of the officers were related to the generals with whom they were pleading. One of them was the son-in-law of General Tōjō Hideki, the former Prime Minister. Another was the brother-in-law of General Anami Korechika, the War Minister.

The officers went to the part of the palace where the Emperor was. Comedy then took over. On the evening before, the Emperor was known to have recorded a wireless address, which would be broadcast to the people of Japan on the next morning, 15 August, and in which he had declared the Japanese decision to surrender. When it was once played on the air, the act would be irrevocable; it was therefore vital to the officers to seize the record and destroy it. It was known to be present in the palace until it was needed for broadcasting, and the soldiers in the plot spent some hours searching for it in vain. Some of those taking part, with the curious detached Japanese aestheticism, remarked on the great beauty of the night, the uncanny and eerie moonlight which provided a backcloth of deep peace for these disordered events. The Emperor, the occasion of this wild conspiracy, was sleeping peacefully, a few yards away, and when it came to the point nobody would commit the impiety of waking him. In a cellar, directly underneath, the Lord Keeper of the Privy Seal, Marquis Kido Kōichi, who was deeply committed to the peace negotiations, was quaking for his life, for, if the officers had discovered him, they would certainly have slaughtered him. Some radio officials, who had played a part in manufacturing the record, were rounded up and kept prisoner for a while. Their lives were also in danger.

The conspiracy ended because, with the passage of time, the officers began to ask themselves whether they were not going too far. Sake flowed; but this did not avail to stifle doubt. The failure to find the gramophone record put a lesion on the unfolding of the plot. Resolution drained away, and the band dispersed. Fake orders, which they had issued to the Guards division to rise and seize the place, were intercepted. They did not dispose of a sufficient body of rank and file troops.

As a result of this sacrilege of Army officers in seizing the imperial palace, the War Minister committed seppaku. He had been on the verge of this supreme act as a gesture of atonement for the behaviour of the Japanese Army in losing the war; the night's doings probably overcame his natural hesitancy, and made death the way out of a situation which had become unbearable to him. In the ministerial debates of the previous days he was one of those whose opinion was most consulted, and had been the most vacillating. He had readily agreed that the military situation was hopeless; but he had been withheld from advising surrender as the only rational course by doubts over what the Americans intended to do about the Emperor. Now he was for capitulation, now he veered towards those who suggested that Japan should try again to save itself by force. His attitude, even towards those who attempted the military coup, was ambiguous. He was not taken by surprise; for days he had known that something was afoot. He had said to those around him that a coup would be impious and impossible; but, at the same time, he had shown marked favour to the more irresponsible officers. He summed up in himself the weakness that was general in the higher ranks of Japanese officer considered from the point of view of their reliability to the state. He took it as axiomatic that a general need not in all cases obey instructions which reached him, but should be free to connive at gangsterism when the situation required. It was clear that his heart yearned for a coup: and his head only partially restrained him from siding with the young officers. Very distressingly, and rather characteristically, he bungled his suicide, and lived in great agony until the following day.

In the anti-climax which followed these exciting events, the rumours of which began to get about, Hirohito's speech was played over to the Japanese people. It was still touch and go how the speech would be received. In fact, the speech was not generally or at least clearly understood, and that for a very curious reason. The Japanese Emperor spoke the language of the court, very flowery, with a strange lilt, which it was hard for modern Japanese to grasp, at least auditorily. This, and the uncharacteristically high pitch of his voice which came from his nervousness on this occasion, combined with sentiments so unexpected – to the uninformed – coming from such a source, produced at first a general bewilderment.

Meetings of colonels and majors were taking place the whole time in all parts of Japan. The plan for a final national effort by Air Force pilots who had sworn themselves to act as suicide squads was nearly put into effect. The proposal was to bomb the United States warship, the *Missouri*, which was steaming into Tokyo Bay, to accept the Japanese surrender. This was narrowly averted. Hirohito's speech contained a notable sentence, probably inserted on the Emperor's own responsibility, which may have irritated American and British listeners, but which represented the Emperor's own, perhaps naïve, views. He said:

We declared war on America and Britain out of our sincere desire to ensure Japan's self-preservation and the stabilization of South-East Asia, it being far from our thought either to infringe upon the sovereignty of other nations or to embark upon territorial aggrandizement.

He continued with a statement of the incontrovertible fact of Japan's utter helplessness, and the lunacy of continuing the war. He was aware of the danger of seeming to break faith with those who had been killed, but the plight of those still alive required peace absolutely.

The Japanese people wept tears of disbelief and shame, but also of relief, when the imperial message at last sank home. The long nightmare of hypnosis under which they had been held by the military at last was shaken off. With the disciplined self-control of their race, which usually succeeded in clamping down upon their very volcanic emotion – which always so surprised the onlookers – they switched their behaviour over-night, and became the welcoming hosts to the advancing wave of American occupiers. By one of the psychological swings, irrational and extra-ordinary, which are evident among people under severe strain, the Japanese passed abruptly from regarding the Americans as barbarians, who were contemptible and to be treated with unappeasable hostility, to accepting them as a people who had incontestably proved their superiority by victory, and who had earned their consequent respect. Peace had come partly because of the effort, at the risk of their lives, of the peace party, and, when they had succeeded, it was plain that it had the support of the majority of the people. But this mass had, to the very end, remained completely unorganized. Peace was brought about with the Japanese public still as spectators of the event. They contributed nothing to it.

Everywhere the Japanese Empire surrendered, or crashed. In Burma it was already a memory, and the Japanese were gone. In Indonesia they had delayed too long to proclaim independence under Japanese auspices. This move, which was calculated to earn them plaudits in defeat, had been sabotaged by the Japanese Army, which had no confidence in the return which could be gained by apparently serving the Asian cause. On 17 August 1945, the impatient leaders of the Indonesian National Party declared independence for themselves, thus forestalling the return of the Dutch. They persuaded Sukarno, the apparently fiery but in reality circumspect principal leader of the revolution, to read out the document which, in Indonesia ever since, has been famous. Sukarno's courage had failed him at the last moment, but his confederates held him to his task, and induced him, at pistol point, to go through with his broadcast statement. Thus a national leader was compelled to go through a historic act for which he must have been very grateful ever afterwards. Soon British troops would arrive to supervise the Japanese surrender, and soon their relation with the Indonesian nationalists would deteriorate. Within a matter of days an action would take place between the Indonesians and the Japanese, who were fighting under the command of British officers. To such a topsy-turvy condition had affairs been brought in that country.

In Manchukuo the Russians streamed in. Under the direction of Marshal Vassilievsky, the Russians attacked in a four-pronged offensive. One huge Army of Soviet troops commanded by General Meretskov had assembled in the region of Vladivostok. On 9 August it advanced swiftly across the Ussuri River into northern Korea and eastern Manchukuo, crushing all opposition in its path. At the same time, a second Army under General Purkayev rolled forward, crossed the Amur River and spread across northern Manchukuo. A third Russian Army, largest of the three and led by Marshal Malinovsky, struck the north-west sector of Manchukuo. On his southern flank, the Army of the (Outer) Mongolian People's Republic sliced through Chahar and Jehol. Stalin afterwards boasted that the combined strength of these forces amounted to seventy divisions. The Japanese, who may have had forty, stood no chance. It was an awful invasion, one of terrible massacre, incredible speed, confusion and panic. The way in which the Soviets sacked Manchuria, their revenge upon the White Russians and small colonies of East European refugees, the plight of defenceless Japanese, Korean and Manchurian non-combatants and local militia caught up in the destruction, the disintegration of the Kwantung and Korean Armies (shells of their former selves, long ago stripped of seasoned warriors to stiffen the far-flung Japanese forces where mettle might prevail), the fate of those taken as prisoners of war – slave labour – by the Red Army and its political commissars, all of these things should be remembered and unforgiven, but here the details must be left to the imagination.

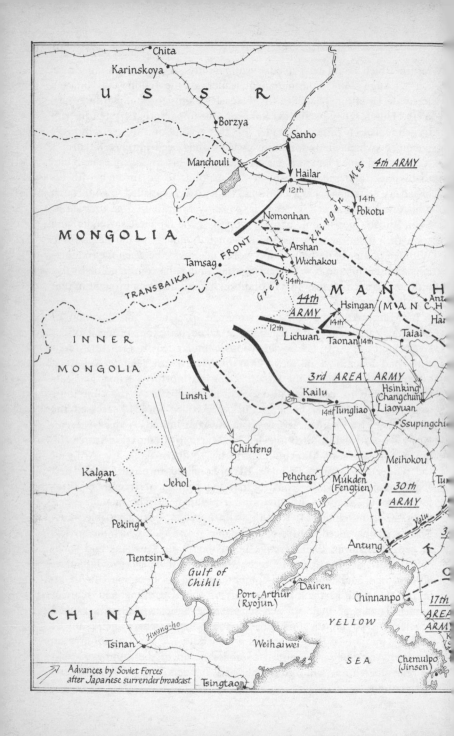

Chita
Karinskoya
U S S R
Borzya
Sanho
Manchouli
Hailar
12th
4th ARMY
14th
Pokotu
Nomonhan
M O N G O L I A
Khingan Mts
Arshan
Tamsag
FRONT
Wuchakou
TRANSBAIKAL
14th
Great Khingan
M A N C H
44th
ARMY
Hsingan (MANCH
Ant
Har
12th
Lichuan
14th
Taonan 14th
Taiai
I N N E R
M O N G O L I A
3rd AREA ARMY
Hsinking
(Changchun)
Linshi
12th
Kailu
14th Tungliao
Liaoyuan
Ssupingchi
Chihfeng
Meihokou
Tu
Kalgan
Pehchen
Mukden
(Fengtien)
30th
ARMY
Jehol
Liao
Yalu
3
Peking
Antung
Tientsin
Gulf of
Chihli
Port Arthur
(Ryojun)
Dairen
Chinnanpo
17th
AREA
ARM
K
C H I N A
Hwang-ho
Weihaiwei
YELLOW
Chemulpo
(Jinsen)
Tsinan
SEA
Advances by Soviet Forces
after Japanese surrender broadcast
Tsingtao

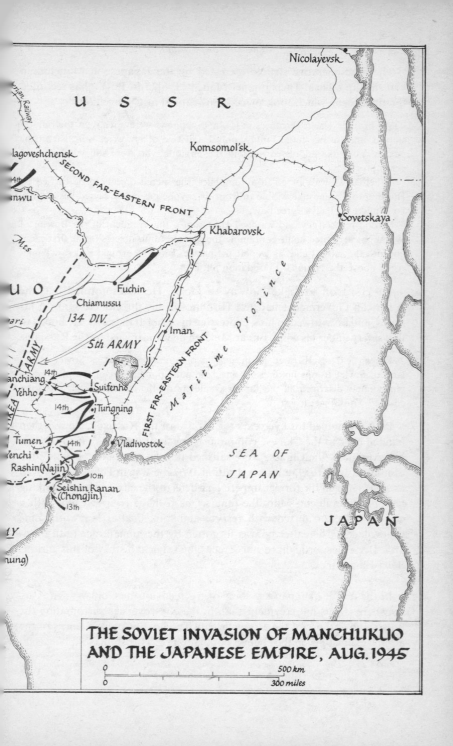

THE SOVIET INVASION OF MANCHUKUO
AND THE JAPANESE EMPIRE, AUG. 1945

0   500 km
0   300 miles

The administrative structure erected by the Japanese in Manchukuo vanished in a flash. Their puppet Manchu Emperor, Pu-Yi, has recorded the final scene which took place in his capital at Changchun:

My brother, sisters, brothers-in-law and nephews were already at the railway station, and, of my entire family, only I and two of my wives were left in the palace. Yoshioka addressed me and the servants who were still with me in a peremptory tone:

'Whether we walk or go in automobiles, the sacred objects to be carried by Hashimoto Toranosuke will go in front. If anyone passes the sacred vessels they must make a ninety-degree bow.'

I stood respectfully and watched Hashimoto, the President of the Bureau of Worship, carry the bundle containing the sacred Shinto objects to the first car. I got into the second and, as we left the palace, I looked around and saw flames rising above the National Foundation Shrine.*

Pu-Yi set off to make his way to Japan. He was informed that the American Government had left Hirohito on his throne. He sank to his knees, and kow-towed to him, expressing his relief at the news. He hoped to find safety under his wing. But at Mukden he was arrested by the Russians.

The airfield reverberated to the sound of aircraft engines as Soviet planes landed. Soviet troops holding sub-machine guns poured out of the planes and immediately disarmed all the Japanese soldiers on the airfield, which was soon covered with Soviet troops.†

Pu-Yi remained for five years the captive of the Russians. He was then handed over to the Chinese communists for 'brainwashing'. It took time, but eventually the Chinese were satisfied that he was in a desirable state of mind. From 1959, until his death in 1967, he was in Peking, employed as a gardener in the former imperial gardens of the city and was a striking national monument. Mao Tse-tung seems to have regarded him with a curious affection mixed with respect and looked after him with some benevolence. Thereafter he was forgotten by the human race until Bernardo Bertolucci brought to our screens the tragical history of this curious 'Last Emperor'.

In the defeat of Japan lay some of the seeds of the Cold War in Asia. Nowhere is this more evident than in the controversies surrounding the possession and use of the atomic bomb. The horrific consequences of the atomic explosions on the civilian populations of Hiroshima and Nagasaki

* Pu-Yi, *From Emperor to Citizen: the Autobiography of Aisin-Gioro Pu-Yi,* Foreign Language Press, Peking, 1965 (OUP, 1987).
† ibid.

may have killed fewer people than conventional bombs had done but nevertheless created an entirely new arms race and balance of terror. At the same time, but covertly, the efforts made by the United States, Britain, China and the Soviet Union to acquire what the Japanese had learned from its practice of biological warfare and human experimentation undoubtedly contributed to the poisoning of relations between the 'Great Powers' (a phrase rather out of fashion after 1945) in the post-war era. There were other ways, too, in which the very collapse of Japan hastened the breakdown of the wartime Alliance.

It is abundantly clear that the Japanese themselves often took a more important part in this than is generally appreciated. Late in the war, Japanese administrators in Indonesia, Indo-China, Burma and elsewhere helped to nurture militant nationalist movements which often had a communist taint. With the defeat of Japan in prospect, the Japanese hoped that they could produce conditions which would poison the European imperial administrations about to return. At some time in the future, so these Japanese dreamt, their actions might create favourable opportunities for Japan to rise again and lead independent Asian nations in a crusade for a second Greater East Asia Co-Prosperity Sphere. These were not merely spoiling operations. They were consistent with the sense of guardianship that so many Japanese truly believed they would exercise towards their Asian brethren. In the end, Pan-Asianism failed to have the impact its adherents devoutly wished. It was vitiated not by the efforts of the Allied Powers but rather by the nationalist passions unloosed during the war within each of the countries occupied by the Japanese. This is scarcely to be wondered at: European, South American and more recently African and Arabic regional solidarity have foundered upon the same rock.

Individual Japanese took other employment which had a subsequent bearing on the development of the Cold War in Asia. Many took positions as valued military advisers to the contending forces in the Chinese Civil War, chiefly on the side of the Kuomintang. Others, particularly former Intelligence officers, helped General MacArthur and his Occupationaires to fathom the complex military and political conditions of areas such as Manchuria and Korea which had lain under the exclusive control of Japan, or adjacent areas under communist control which had been more closely and systematically observed for many years by the Japanese than by the Western Powers. The Japanese Research Division, established under the wing of Military Intelligence within MacArthur's Far East Command, commissioned former Japanese military and naval officers to prepare nearly two hundred monographs on their observations and experiences for information and guidance. With time, it was discovered that many of these monographs were unreliable. Intensive research was conducted to make them more accurate and comprehensive: the unit, having accomplished its work, was disbanded only in 1960. Meanwhile, as late as the early fifties, Japanese airmen were flying covert reconnaissance missions over North Korea, North China, Manchuria and as far away as the Soviet Union. Japanese minesweepers secretly helped to clear the way for United Nations landings on the North Korean coasts: their availability and undoubted familiarity with these waters outweighed the risk of political repercussions. Japanese factories were used to repair damaged American tanks sent back into action in Korea. All of these instances suggest that at least some Japanese know-how was used with effect by the Americans and Japanese preconceptions gained during the years of Total War slowly percolated into the American military establishment in Japan during the years which followed the termination of hostilities. Although there are indications that the Soviets were no less eager to make use of their former enemies, it would appear that the exclusion of the Soviet Union from the occupation of Hokkaido, or indeed from the administration of any Japanese territory not overrun by Red Army troops, was of more consequence in the refrigeration of politics in East Asia (and in the national salvation of post-war Japan).

Power was everywhere passing away from those who had held it, and a new world was being created. It was the same in those parts of Asia which were, at least formally, on the victors' side. In India the negotiations were beginning which resulted in its complete emancipation within two years.

The war was at an end, and no further attempt will be made to trace the history of the countries, or to examine the effects of the rewards and penalties which they incurred. It is arbitrary to mark a divide anywhere in history, and the new age in Asia which began in 1945 is really the pendant of Asia at war, and is inseparably connected with that. It would take decades to work out the consequences of the great struggle. But the history of the world must be chopped into comprehensible lengths. For the purpose of this book the dropping of the bomb is the terminus.

By dropping the atom bomb the British and Americans had done much more than put an end to the war with Japan. They had put an end to a chapter of human history, and had transformed the nature of war. In the future neither governments nor people would enter on a war as lightly as the Japanese had done. The interest of the historian lies in the question of what induced the British and Americans to take the responsibility of dropping it.

Why did the two great Allies, who had it in their power to terminate the war by simply notifying Japan of the terrible effectiveness of the new weapon which had come into their hands, go to the lengths of actually dropping it? Why did they not content themselves with one bomb, but in a matter of hours, and without waiting to see the consequences of Hiroshima, drop the second bomb on Nagasaki?

The answer to these questions is, and is likely to remain, the greatest single matter of controversy of the war. The documents do not clarify the reasons. Churchill, for instance, is hardly enlightening. In his memoirs, he says, quite simply:

> The historic fact remained, and must be judged in the after time, that the decision whether or not to use the atomic bomb to compel the surrender of Japan was never even an issue. There was unanimous, automatic, unquestioning agreement around our [Council] table.

The Allies were nearly as well aware as Japan of the desperation of the Japanese.

American cryptographers had continued to listen in on exchanges of information between the Japanese Government, its outposts, and its agents and diplomats abroad. The Americans, who had been quick to appreciate the fact that they were overwhelmed by the sheer quantity of Intelligence they had been receiving from deciphered Japanese Purple code transmissions since 1940, had taken steps to put this information into an appropriate context shortly after the lessons of Pearl Harbor had been studied. Thereafter, daily summaries were prepared from these exchanges, known as Magic. These were remarkable in their clarity of analysis and were valued by those privileged enough to receive them.

Magic circulated among the highest echelons of Allied policymakers and field commanders. In contrast with the British Ultra code-breaking operation, the Magic Summaries, prepared by the Special Branch of the U S Army's Military Intelligence Branch, were circulated with background notes and a sophisticated commentary on the strategical implications of the information contained within the intercepted Japanese code transmissions. As time passed, other agencies, British as well as American, had fed Special Branch with additional information that became interwoven into the summaries. Now, as the war was drawing to a close, Magic took on a new significance. The horror of the B29 raids was unmistakable. The upheaval in Europe made its mark, and the disintegration of Germany took place in full view of the Japanese. Soviet interference with Japanese diplomatic pouches now seemed dangerous, not simply irksome. The Japanese said farewell to Germany and stood alone against the might of the western democracies. Soviet reinforcements sped to the East: the Japanese watched them go. Reports came through from Berne on talks with Allen Dulles of the prospects for peace negotiations. Other transmissions between Stockholm and Tokyo expressed the same desire for peace. The evacuation of Japanese families from China began in earnest. Food shortages grew worse. Fuel was unobtainable. There were strikes at currency printing plants in Shanghai. Civil unrest grew in North China and Inner Mongolia. The despondency of Tokyo and of Japanese diplomats and espionage agents abroad became increasingly clear and rapidly translated into straightforward defeatism. The reports filed from Tokyo left the recipients in no doubt about the frantic efforts of the Japanese to seek an early peace. There was no determination to fight the war to the last Japanese. On the contrary, the importance which the Japanese attached to the good offices of the Soviet Union was unmistakable. As the summer of 1945 drew on, the Japanese missions in foreign countries gradually closed down, and their agents, one by one, twinkled out like little stars. Reading the Magic Summaries today is a strangely moving experience, for together with our relief at the imminent termination of hostilities, it involves us in a strong sense of tragedy as well. The Summaries continued throughout the days and the weeks that followed Hiroshima, the Soviet invasion of Manchuria and Korea, Nagasaki, the death of Bose, the disintegration of Ba Maw's Government, the end of the Nanking Government, the possible abdication of Hirohito, exchanges on the treatment of Wainwright, and on to the end of radio communications in early November 1945, a full two months after the Japanese surrender. The Summaries, trusted by those fortunate few who read them day by day, must have given their readers much pause for thought. And through it all the question persists: Why the Bomb? Why twice?

In Japanese prisoner-of-war and civilian internment camps they had answers to those questions. So did those who worked in the secret chambers of Anglo-American technical Intelligence. There were reports of a Japanese atomic bomb, and there was an abundance of information about the mad, super-scientific world of Japanese chemical and biological warfare.

Orders had already been issued instructing the prison camp commanders to annihilate all prisoners in certain eventualities. Many of the prisoners had seen the elaborate preparations that had been made. Some were told by horror-struck guards or outside Intelligence agents. The orders themselves survived and were introduced in evidence at post-war trials of Japanese war criminals. The Allied Powers prepared plans to take the camps by storm. The Bomb, it is said, saved the lives of these prisoners. But it is more accurate to suggest that luck, the Emperor's broadcast, and the arrival of Allied relief teams at a time when prison camp guards were still in a state of shock at the end of the war, all played contributory parts. The peaceful liberation of the camps, in scenes repeated all over East Asia, resulted from the fact that The War Had Ended. It is quite illogical to suppose that the lives of these hostages to fortune were saved through any fine appreciation by the Japanese authorities that, a fortnight ago, their barbarous enemies had compounded the offences perpetrated by the B29 incendiary raids and had rejoiced in two further massacres of hundreds of thousands of innocent Japanese non-combatants in contravention of every recognized conventional law of war or principle of humanity.

The Japanese also possessed their own weapons of mass destruction, and they were not averse to using them where it seemed profitable to do so. Japanese employment of chemical and biological warfare (and Japanese research involving the vivisection of thousands of prisoners of war in CBW experiments) has become a matter of great public concern in Japan today. Western text-books have been mute on the issue, doubtless accepting British and American official denials of accusations dismissed as blatant and groundless communist propaganda in the late 1940s and early 1950s. More than forty years after the end of hostilities, however, fresh documentary evidence from British and American official sources, amounting to thousands of pages concerning this highly sensitive area, has come to light. Disclosure of this information has been somewhat piecemeal until recently, but those examining the totality of what is now known on the subject are bound to question the probity and integrity of their wartime Governments to a degree matched only by the controversy surrounding the use of the atomic bomb on Hiroshima and Nagasaki.

Briefly, the story of Japanese biological warfare implicates more than half the persons tried by the International Military Tribunal for the Far East, and more than 5,000 others who worked on the BW programme in some capacity. It involved a genuine conspiracy of silence that began soon after the Japanese occupation of Manchuria and spread its tentacles throughout all Japanese occupied territories during the Greater East Asian War. Thousands of people were butchered in the name of science and for the sake of war technology in experiments conducted by a secret network of research establishments. The first of these was established in 1932 in Manchuria, where others followed. A detachment spirited off victims for experimentation on the outskirts of Nanking in 1937. That detachment became a major research institute in its own right. University medical faculties on the Japanese mainland were headhunted for the brightest and

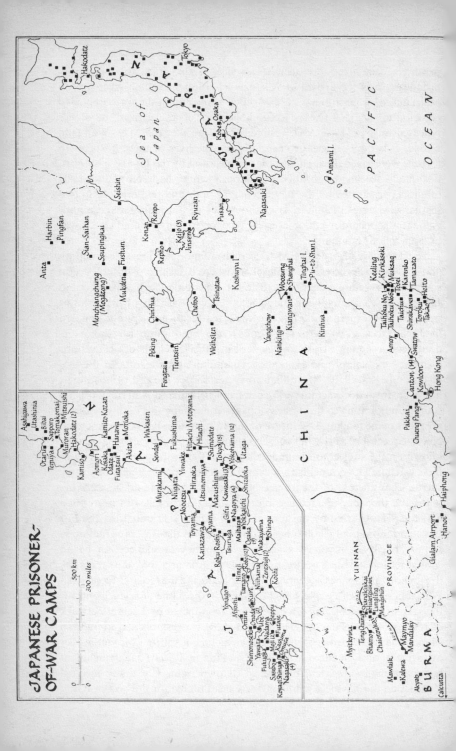

JAPANESE PRISONER-OF-WAR CAMPS

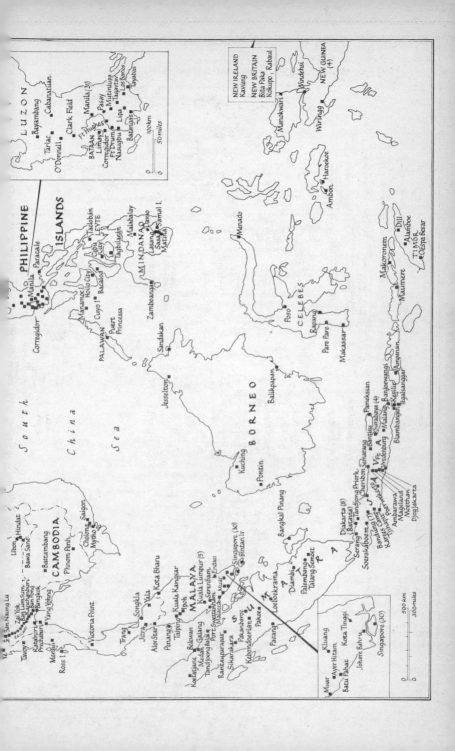

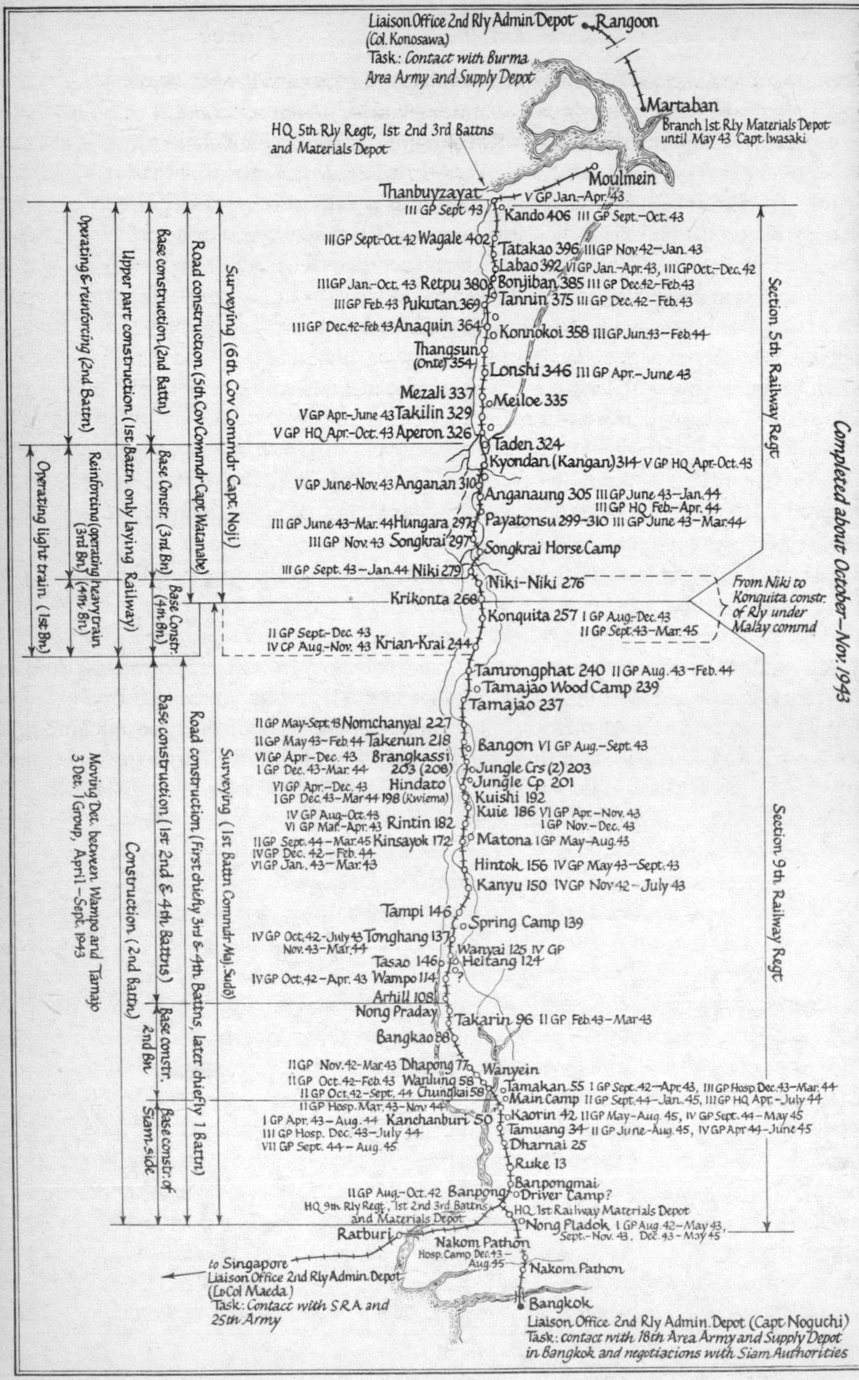
Completed about October–Nov. 1943
Liaison Office 2nd Rly Admin Depot
(Col. Konosawa)
Task: Contact with Burma Area Army and Supply Depot
Rangoon
Martaban
Branch 1st Rly Materials Depot until May 43 Capt Iwasaki
HQ 5th Rly Regt, 1st 2nd 3rd Battns and Materials Depot
Moulmein
Thanbuyzayat
V GP Jan.–Apr. 43
III GP Sept 43
Kando 406 III GP Sept.–Oct. 43
III GP Sept.–Oct. 42 Wagale 402
Tatakao 396 III GP Nov. 42–Jan. 43
Labao 392 VI GP Jan.–Apr. 43, III GP Oct.–Dec. 42
III GP Jan.–Oct. 43 Retpu 380
Bonjiban 385 III GP Dec. 42–Feb. 43
III GP Feb. 43 Pukutan 369
Tannin 375 III GP Dec. 42–Feb. 43
III GP Dec. 42–Feb. 43 Anaquin 364
Konnokoi 358 III GP Jun. 43–Feb. 44
Thangsun (Onte) 354
Lonshi 346 III GP Apr.–June 43
Mezali 337
Meiloe 335
V GP Apr.–June 43 Takilin 329
V GP HQ Apr.–Oct. 43 Aperon 326
Taden 324
Kyondan (Kangan) 314 V GP HQ Apr.–Oct. 43
V GP June–Nov. 43 Anganan 310
Anganaung 305 III GP June 43–Jan. 44
III GP HQ Feb.–Apr. 44
III GP June 43–Mar. 44 Hungara 297
Payatonsu 299–310 III GP June 43–Mar. 44
III GP Nov. 43 Songkrai 297
Songkrai Horse Camp
III GP Sept. 43–Jan. 44 Niki 279
Niki-Niki 276
Krikonta 268
Konquita 257 I GP Aug.–Dec. 43
II GP Sept. 43–Mar. 45
From Niki to Konquita constr. of Rly under Malay commd
II GP Sept.–Dec. 43
IV GP Aug.–Nov. 43 Krian-Krai 244
Tamrongphat 240 II GP Aug. 43–Feb. 44
Tamajão Wood Camp 239
Tamajão 237
II GP May–Sept. 43 Nomchanyal 227
II GP May 43–Feb. 44 Takenun 218
VI GP Apr.–Dec. 43
I GP Dec. 43–Mar. 44 Brangkassi 203 (208)
Bangon VI GP Aug.–Sept. 43
Jungle Crs (2) 203
VI GP Apr.–Dec. 43
I GP Dec. 43–Mar 44 Hindato 198 (Kwiema)
Jungle Cp 201
Kuishi 192
IV GP Aug.–Oct. 43
VI GP Mar.–Apr. 43 Rintin 182
Kuie 186 VI GP Apr.–Nov. 43
I GP Nov.–Dec. 43
II GP Sept. 44–Mar. 45 Kinsayok 172
IV GP Dec. 42–Feb. 44
VI GP Jan. 43–Mar. 43
Matona I GP May–Aug. 43
Hintok 156 IV GP May 43–Sept. 43
Kanyu 150 IV GP Nov 42–July 43
Tampi 146
Spring Camp 139
IV GP Oct. 42–July 43 Tonghang 137
Nov. 43–Mar. 44
Wanyai 125 IV GP
Tasao 146
Heitang 124
IV GP Oct. 42–Apr. 43 Wampo 114
Arhill 108
Nong Praday
Takarin 96 II GP Feb. 43–Mar 43
Bangkao 88
II GP Nov. 42–Mar. 43 Dhapong 77
Wanyein
II GP Oct. 42–Feb. 43 Wanlung 58
II GP Oct. 42–Sept. 44 Chungkai 58
Tamakan 55 I GP Sept. 42–Apr. 43, III GP Hosp. Dec. 43–Mar. 44
Main Camp II GP Sept. 44–Jan. 45, III GP HQ Apr.–July 44
II GP Hosp. Mar. 43–Nov 44
I GP Apr. 43–Aug. 44 Kanchanburi 50
III GP Hosp. Dec. 43–July 44
VII GP Sept. 44–Aug. 45
Kaorin 42 II GP May–Aug. 45, IV GP Sept. 44–May 45
Tamuang 34 II GP June–Aug. 45, IV GP Apr 44–June 45
Dharnai 25
Ruke 13
Banpongmai
II GP Aug.–Oct. 42 Banpong
Driver Camp?
HQ 9th Rly Regt, 1st 2nd 3rd Battns and Materials Depot
HQ 1st Railway Materials Depot
Nong Pladok I GP Aug. 42–May 43, Sept.–Nov. 43, Dec. 43–May 45
Ratburi
Nakom Pathon
Hosp. Camp Dec. 43–Aug. 45
Nakom Pathon
to Singapore
Liaison Office 2nd Rly Admin. Depot
(LtCol Maeda)
Task: Contact with SRA and 25th Army
Bangkok
Liaison Office 2nd Rly Admin. Depot (Capt Noguchi)
Task: contact with 18th Area Army and Supply Depot in Bangkok and negotiations with Siam Authorities
Section 5th Railway Regt
Section 9th Railway Regt
Surveying (6th Cov Commdr Capt. Noji)
Road construction (5th Cov Commdr Capt Watanabe)
Base construction (2nd Battn)
Upper part construction (1st Battn only laying Railway)
Operating & reinforcing (2nd Battn)
Base Constr. (3rd Bn)
Base Constr. (4th Bn)
Reinforcing (operating heavy train (3rd Bn) (4th Bn)
Operating light train (1st Bn)
Surveying (1st Battn Commdr Maj. Suda)
Road construction (First chiefly 3rd & 4th Battns, later chiefly 1 Battn)
Base construction (1st 2nd & 4th Battns)
Construction (2nd Battn)
Moving Det. between Wampo and Tamajo 3 Det. 1 Group, April–Sept. 1943
Base constr. 2nd Bn
Base constr. of Siam side

…SITION AND STRENGTH OF POW CONTINGENTS DURING CONSTRUCTION OF THE BURMA–SIAM RAILWAY

best biochemists and physiologists the Japanese Army could buy or conscript, and university medical laboratories in Tokyo, Osaka, Kyoto and a number of other places were utilized in the research and experimentation. Delivery systems were refined, vast quantities of bacteria were produced. Thousands of cultivators grew so much bacteria that at full capacity the monthly output of germ-laden froth could be measured in tonnes.

Field trials of Army biological munitions were conducted, first in Manchuria and then in China Proper. Attacks were made at Ningpo in 1940, at Changteh in 1941, in the Chekiang offensive of 1942 (in the revenge attacks that followed the Doolittle raid), and elsewhere. Early (and as it happens exceptionally accurate) Chinese medical and Intelligence reports were brought to the personal attention of President Roosevelt and Prime Minister Churchill: their experts found them unconvincing. Later the mad Japanese medical scientists operated in Burma, Malaya, French Indo-China, Thailand, the Netherlands East Indies and New Guinea. They applied their skills at Nomonhan against the Russians and sent saboteurs across the Soviet Union itself in a succession of secret missions carried out over a number of years, allegedly in response to Russian biological warfare attacks carried out against the Japanese in China and Manchuria. A ship carrying a biological warfare assault team was dispatched to Saipan to slow down the American advance: it was sunk *en route* by an American submarine. Funds amounting to a ten million yen annual budget were allocated for offensive BW research as the B29 raids on Japan intensified. The money, as always, was channelled through the Kwantung Army. Production facilities increased more or less continuously: three million rats were to be ready for use by September 1945; storage of the food to sustain them required a four-storey building. A proposal to employ BW following the defeat of Japanese forces on Iwojima was only turned down on the grounds that it would have no effect on the outcome of the Pacific War. *

Allied prosecutors from half a dozen countries affected by the issue remained silent at the Tokyo War Crimes Trial about what they knew. The scientists and technicians who were involved in these, the most ghastly atrocities of the Eastern War, were granted immunity from prosecution by General MacArthur with the blessing of the United States Government, with at least the tacit consent if not complicity of the British Government and the acquiescence of the Chinese. The British and Americans pooled what they knew. This was a standing measure of their technical collaboration, but there were practical benefits to both sides. Porton

* D. Wallace and P. Williams, *Unit 731: Secret of Secrets*, Hodder & Stoughton, London, 1989.

Down's scientists were regarded as a cut above their American counter-parts; the Americans had systematically assembled a vast amount of in-formation from their Intelligence during the latter stages of the war and during their early days in Japan. Meanwhile, in Singapore, the Central Pathology Laboratory of Lord Mountbatten's forces had occupied the only Japanese BW laboratory now known to have remained operational following the surrender of Japan: records concerning what happened next are unavailable. The Chinese, whose own knowledge about the Japanese use of BW was quite extensive (as appears not only from the quality of their wartime reports but also from information which they shared with Allied prosecutors on the eve of the Tokyo Trial), must have lived in hope of gaining some kind of a quid pro quo for their silence during the Court proceedings. The Russian authorities, who sought to raise the matter at Tokyo, allowed themselves to be silenced. The French and the Dutch Governments, on whose territories in Indo-China and the East Indies human experimentation also took place, were kept in the dark by the British and Americans but may have learned of what had happened by other means.

What seems quite incredible is that the cover-up conspiracy – for it is by no means a demonological exaggeration to speak of it as a conspiracy – was maintained throughout the three years which elapsed between the Japanese defeat and the conclusion of the Tokyo Trial and that, apart from mischief-making communist mudslinging, this conspiracy was sustained for so long afterwards. The conspiracy extended into the post-war period of Anglo-American weapons research, surfaced again during the Korean War, and is rumoured to have carried on beyond. Much more research needs to be done to complete our understanding of this astonish-ing story, but what is already known makes chilling reading.

The decision to use the atomic bomb to terminate the war involved no fine calculations, however, and it seems to have been taken without any special regard for the dangers of a last-minute BW offensive. Japan virtually had conceded defeat at the end of July, and had put out peace feelers, first asking the Russians to act as mediators, and, on finding them unobliging, had approached the Swedish Government. Anyone with ex-perience of diplomacy could perceive that the upshot, after a few days' natural hesitation, must be the surrender so much desired. In the days of decision during the Potsdam Conference anything like a sustained Japanese defence, from strong defensive positions, had clearly become impossible. By ending the war in a ghastly and fearful massacre, the British and Americans cast over their triumph a dark shadow, and one which may, as is the way in great historical transactions, return to haunt the doers in the future.

After the bomb had been exploded, Russian policy became, for the time being, very conciliatory. It was in this period that Truman announced his recent decision that the Occupation of Japan should fall exclusively to the Americans. The details of the Occupation of Germany had been discussed inexhaustibly, and continued to be a major issue among the Allies: by contrast, the Occupation of Japan seemed to have been arranged at very short notice, and by the United States alone. Great Britain made no demur at the American decision. Russia limited its protests to a proposal that the surrender on the battleship, the *Missouri*, should have its counterpart on Hokkaido with a ceremony of the surrender of the Kwantung Army to Russia. This was rejected. Probably the existence of the bomb frustrated Russian plans for insisting on a joint occupation of Japan, and the consequences of this were incalculable. It avoided endless intrigue, and conflict of puppet parties: probably it saved Japan from a great deal of hardship and made the return to normal life in Japan much quicker. By taking out Japan as a major question of dispute, it probably made the relations of Russia and the United States by that much easier to handle. It may even have kept them from war. It was perhaps the only good thing which came out of the dropping of the bomb.

The fateful decision to drop the bomb was made within a matter of days. Most of the men who were responsible for Japan's policy had not known a fortnight before that the atom bomb was in existence. Even General MacArthur, who, more than any other man, was responsible for the overthrow of Japan, was given the information only a very brief time before the bomb was due. He had said that he deplored it, but he had no time to make his protest effective. Admiral William D. Leahy, the Chief of Staff of the President, was consulted in advance and said, bluntly, that he thought that the use of the bomb was brutal, and served no rational end. It is possible that President Truman, whose subsequent decisions about the bomb were on the whole sober and responsible as, for example, during the later Korean War, may have acted in these days very much in the dark; and it is at least charitable to suppose that he did so. Churchill remarked that, as soon as the news of successful tests arrived, the President seemed to be determined to use it. Churchill judged it useless to press for discussion. All these statesmen suddenly found the bomb at their disposal, and they had no reasonable opportunity to think out the implications of atomic warfare, nor, it seemed, was the phenomenon of fall-out clear in their minds. The real essential difference between an atom bomb and a larger conventional weapon had not been grasped. Most Americans supposed, like Stalin, that it was simply a bigger and more lethal weapon. The discovery of atomic power required that men of exceptional vision and judgement should have been in power, who could see the consequences of the action they took then upon the politics of the next half century or longer. Those men were hardly likely to have been thrown up by the circumstances of directing the war.

There is a misperception, finally, that commonly surrounds Japan's 'unconditional surrender', and it serves no purpose today to ignore it. The fact is that the Japanese surrender was *not* unconditional (although at the time it was regarded as such by most Japanese themselves). Under the terms of the Potsdam Declaration, the Imperial Rescript ending the war, the Instrument of Surrender, etc., the Japanese *armed forces* surrendered unconditionally. But the Japanese Government retained its *civil* powers. Indeed, under the terms of the surrender, the Japanese Government was obliged to exert those powers in order to ensure compliance with the terms of the Potsdam Declaration. Accordingly, many of the steps taken by General Douglas MacArthur and his forces to impose their will upon the civil Government of Japan amounted to a usurpation of authority which breached the terms of the surrender. In no places were this more evident than in the establishment of the International Military Tribunal for the Far East and in the great purges and blacklists imposed upon the Japanese by MacArthurian *Diktat*. In short, the differences between 210,288 individual Allied Occupation of Germany and that of Japan deserve attention: the former occurred as a result of the Allied conquest of German territory and its sub-division by the occupying Powers. But the war against Japan ended as a result of a contract between the two sides, and while the Japanese civil power was clearly in no position to contest the issue, the fact remains that the Occupationaires grossly exceeded the terms of that contract. American defence attorneys challenged the International Military Tribunal on this basis (and on other grounds), and they were ruled out of order. Nevertheless, the truth of the matter is perfectly clear and is a subject of some controversy in Japan in our own day. Unfortunately, it has the effect of diminishing still further the gulf which was once believed to exist between the capricious and arrogant abuse of power by the Japanese armed forces in Occupied East Asia and the self-righteous morality of the Allied Powers who brought them down.

Epilogue

IT may have been useful to tell the facts of this conflict. There can seldom have been fought a war which engaged so much of the attention of so many Powers, the details of which have so rapidly been allowed to become vague. Within a generation the dramatic events of Japan's surrender, the particulars of the relations between Japan and China, the great struggle at Imphal, the island-hopping across the Pacific by the United States, the great naval battles, have all begun to be touched by the waters of Lethe. Even Pearl Harbor, which has naturally entered into the folklore of the USA, today appears far-off, and what happened there is only vaguely understood.

The Eastern War was inevitably overshadowed by Hitler's War in Europe. It was interdependent with it, and its events criss-crossed with those of the western conflict. But, in retrospect, they have seemed to some to assume a subordinate part. The events of the European War stand out clearly; they are remembered sharply; the events of the war in the East are, by contrast, hazy in the public memory, and are heaped together in a certain confusion. Ask any young man born at or after the dropping of the bomb at Hiroshima, be he of Asian or European origin, to outline the events which led up to the fearsome drama, and you will be surprised to find what lacunae lie in his narrative.

And yet the events which had to be settled by arms, and by the atom bomb, were as great as the issues in Europe, the suffering was as widespread, the events spread over as many continents, involved more civilizations, and left as large a dent in the history of world culture. For this reason, it has seemed to be worthwhile seeking to protest a little at the progress of the waters sweeping away the recollection of those years – even if the waters are fundamentally healthful, doing the saving work of washing away the memories of brutality and the hatred of nations for one another, and other things which are best forgotten. The famous feats of endurance of the peoples, the daring projects of the national leaders, may, with justice, be offered up as alms to oblivion; yet no people can afford to neglect the history which has made them what they are.

The war, for all the damage it had done, was not, by the standards of past wars, a particularly long one. Three series of wars, which were needed to settle the opposition of deeply conflicting forces, and which turned upside down the affairs of all the participants, took somewhat longer. One was the Thirty Years War between Protestant and Catholic Europe: its historians are quick to point out that its protagonists and allegiances changed as it progressed through a succession of phases linked only by opportunism, cause and effect, rather than by a single national will. Another, the Peloponnesian Wars, which checked finally the Athenian attempt at imperialism, lasted nineteen years: it had the same elements of fundamentalist irrationality, hysteria and total commitment that we have traced throughout the conflict that subsumed East Asia and the Pacific. The wars which rose out of the French Revolution ran a course which ended at the Battle of Waterloo, and covered twenty-three years: like the Japanese war(s) of the twentieth century, they brought together unlikely coalitions of Allies, all with different aims and mutual mistrust, linked only in their abiding determination to rid the world of a peculiarly bloodthirsty Empire. The present war, from the time that the fighting commenced in earnest on the Asiatic mainland in 1931, and excluding the opening skirmishes between China, Korea and Japan, was over in fifteen years.

The War in the East can be addressed by many names. The Japanese wartime censor regarded it as 'The Greater East Asia War'. His successors in the (mainly American) Allied Occupation Forces banned that phrase and substituted 'The Pacific War'. Can it really be regarded as 'The Second World War in the Pacific', bearing in mind that the China Incident preceded the outbreak of the European War by two years and only ended with the Japanese surrender to the Allied Powers in 1945? Surely the Japanese experience of Total War really began with the Manchurian Incident in 1931, and what of the mental and physical resources expended on the inevitable clash over the preceding decades? The trend in Japan today is to call it 'The Fifteen-Year War', a somewhat unsatisfying and curiously anonymous sobriquet if ever there was one: it does not seem likely to find favour in the United States or in British countries. 'The Far East War' offends some people not only because it is Eurocentric in its geographical conception but because that conception involves an ineluctable sense of isolation and irrelevance. 'The War against Japan' is revealing but one-sided: the war also involved the positive aspirations of dozens of racial and national groups. In the end, we have to come to terms with the war's ambivalence, its complexity and, above all, its size. If it must be known and remembered in a single evocative phrase, let us simply call it 'The East Asian and Pacific Conflict'.

The great modern wars have reflected the deadly nature of modern armaments, and international efforts to control their spread and influence. The causes nevertheless have been weighty and complex. Economic issues contributed to the struggle but did not, perhaps, outweigh the conceits and misperceptions of individual men acting collectively. The issue of the strife in Asia settled a number of conflicts which, but for the war, might have dragged on for years, causing constant unrest, and keeping the region in continual uncertainty. It settled which of various trends were to continue, and which, among those which had seemed strong and flourishing a few years before, were either to stop abruptly or else to fade away.

The decision was sharpest for Japan. The attempt to maintain Japan's unnatural pre-eminence in East Asia, and to spread it over the lands to the south and west, had failed. Japan's Empire was dissolved. A relatively small country in relation to its dependencies and enemies (although larger than Britain, metropolitan France or Germany), its principal assets were the ardent will of its citizens and their regimentation. It had had the temerity to challenge three quarters of the world to come against it in arms; and had shaken the established order of the earth more than many had thought possible. Yet the war did not spring from a foolish intent by the Japanese to conquer the globe, to bring, as the ancient Japanese phrase has it, 'all the eight corners of the world under one roof'. The American Ambassador to Japan, Joseph Grew, distinguished Bostonian though he was, found illumination in comparing Japan to the Uncle Remus story of Brer Rabbit, who attacked a tar baby for spite, and other fatuous reasons, and then found himself stuck to it ever more thoroughly as he struggled to break free from his ill-advised entanglement. The image works well, and is worth remembering.

It is also important to bear in mind that the history of the 'East Asian and Pacific Conflict' is not a sequence of events between the Japanese attack on Pearl Harbor and the surrender aboard the battleship *Missouri* which can properly be isolated from the previous half-century of conflict on the Asiatic continent. The titanic and enduring contest between Russia and Japan for domination of North-East Asia changed the political map of the world early in the twentieth century as it did again in August 1945: the latter-day changes were not merely echoes but the extension of the former. The tug-of-war between the Japanese, local upstart bullies as they were, and the imperialists of faraway Europe, took place over the recumbent body of China. Japan emerged from that a monster, conscious of its feats of strength and daring, aware of past humiliations and foreign contempt, determined to establish an area of peace and security, governing by means of what it chose to name 'cooperation', hoping for what it called 'co-prosperity' in regions and markets that suited it. The

Manchurian Incident and the transformation of Manchukuo into a dependency of the Japanese Empire form an inseparable part of the Greater East Asian War and therefore of the 'East Asian and Pacific Conflict' as a whole: it was a hinge, a fulcrum around which turned the histories of China, Japan and the West.

The Japanese of that generation had passed through a strange phase of their national history. In the past, there had been little to single them out for particular reprobation. They were always very vigorous, usually artistic, often somewhat muddled intellectually, which was apparently due to the imprecision of their language. They were also perhaps outstanding for an exaggerated conformism, though they expressed this in an unusual manner by extending the pale of conformism to include those whose vision of the national future was grander, and who dared to call for radical change. Traditionally also the Japanese relaxed the tyranny of society over the older members of the community, and gave them a licence to do and say what they pleased. All of this gave colour to a land where the vigilance of thought police was well developed. And always, as with any generalization about an entire people, one is conscious at once of many eccentric members of the community for whom the general rule did not apply.

The main fact in the twentieth century is the acute military phase that the Japanese lived through. It was an aberration. It was not really traditional. It may be that Japanese society has a Samurai streak, and a prolonged feudal period had left it too ready to respond to the call of arms. Many of its ways of thought were military in origin. But, if one looks back on Japanese history, the Japanese do not appear to have been an unduly military people. At one period they were predominantly artists, and would not allow matters of soldierly concern to interfere with the artistic life. In the great Heian period, which is perhaps the outstanding example in history of a leisured class giving up all its time to artistic living, there was once a complaint that the imperial bodyguard could not be properly maintained. The soldiers could not ride horses: they constantly fell off them. The detailed history of the society of this time is full of anecdotes of the extreme lengths to which Japanese aestheticism would go. The men of the Heian period are strange ancestors of the Japanese who took Singapore.

The Japanese of recent generations were conditioned by the institutions of their society to offer themselves in the bid to establish a Japanese imperialism. These institutions, most of them borrowed from the West though given a peculiar slant in their development, are the monument of the Meiji Restoration. Gradually they induced in the mass of the people the willingness to support a more and more aggressive national policy. The institutions took on a life of their own. In the end, they carried the Japanese people into a great war, and brought down half a continent.

The prime evil of Japan was certainly the ascendancy of the military. This led, in time of war, to the Supreme Command conducting the war as a state secret from the civilian parts of the Japanese administration. Whatever else may be said of such a system, it proved to be most incompetent militarily. Thus Japanese militarism held within it the seeds of its own defeat. It was unable to organize Japanese society so that in modern warfare it could compete with the Powers which were organized to be more flexible.

The same militarism, as far as it was able to prevail in making Japanese foreign policy, was responsible for the basic error which brought about Japan's downfall. This was to found Japan's policy on fear of the outside world, and to meet this by seeking to spread a counter-fear of Japan. Because Japan was in a difficult position internationally, because it was vulnerable, because its economic position required that it should have unimpeded access to imports and a constantly growing market overseas for its exports, and because it feared that these might be interrupted by force by an unfriendly Power, it counted that prudence required it to be ever on its guard, to arm and show its teeth in a way that would fend off dangerous intentions in its rivals. There were Japanese voices which protested at such a policy, and pointed, rightly, to the inevitable end; but they were not attended to. The result was a long period of tension, culminating in a war in which Japan lost everything, a war which could not possibly have safeguarded the things which Japan had armed itself to save.

The contradictions of Japan's foreign policy are stated compendiously by the Foreign Ministry official, Kase Toshikazu, who played such a useful part as intermediary of the court circles in bringing the war to an end. 'For a poor country like Japan,' he said,

the construction of costly warships meant a crushing burden upon the national treasury. And yet we built a good number of them. We also maintained a vast Army and an ever expanding Air Force. In the end we became like the mammoth whose tusk, growing ever bigger, finally unbalanced its bodily structure. As everything went to support the huge tusks, very little was left to sustain the rest of the body. The mammoth finally became extinct.

Why did the mammoth arm itself with weapons such as ultimately to bring about its own destruction? Because it was apprehensive. In its desire to defend itself against external enemies the poor creature forgot the very fact that its tusks were its own mortal enemy! Why did Japan arm herself to the teeth? Because she was apprehensive. Why was she apprehensive? Because she had enemies. Why were there enemies? Because her aggressive policy excited suspicion in others. Rather than abandon the objectionable policy she augmented her armaments. But armaments are a relative affair. There is no end to an armament race.*

The men who served ruthless, imperialist Japan were not by nature particularly ruthless or imperialist. They bore no signs of predestination, and there was nothing about them which marked them as enemies of the human race. The Japanese generals, though superficially they might seem to conform to a rather brutal and disgusting pattern, were often men of singular eccentricity. In other circumstances, they might have appeared as rather engaging. Many of them had a vivid and vigorous interior life, and the most varied traits of personality. Some of them practised Japanese archery and fencing each day, not for athletic reasons but for the self-control which these disciplines induced, and for greater proficiency in the art of meditation. They were an interesting contrast to the British Army, much more emotional, much more given to adjusting their philosophy and their actions. The contrast between them and the commanders of the Anglo-Saxon forces was often richly comical. Rigid behaviour patterns in their native environment made them what they were and, uprooted from this environment, their behaviour was unpredictable. It could, of course, be terrible; occasionally, however, it was the reverse.

The behaviour of the Japanese soldiers, and their cult of non-surrender, may have seemed to those fighting them to mark them out as an especially desperate, unreformable species of military man. This, too, is only an example of the lengths to which institutions may go in marking their victims. Biologically similar young men, transported to another society and brought up under other institutions, turned out to be enthusiastic liberals or democrats, and found reprehensible the Japanese cult of military national aggrandizement and the pursuit of death.

The Japanese, in the last war, were shocked at finding a most rigid refusal to respond to the call of their country and race on the part of the *Nisei*, the children of the Japanese emigrants to America, who had most of them continued to marry with Japanese. In this they were much disappointed: they had counted on being able to convert this class, and if they had succeeded, would have disposed a valuable ally for their war-making. The Nisei had some reason to attend to their call, for the United States was less than generous in its treatment of them, and did not hide its suspicion. The deportation or preventive confinement of the large masses of Americans of Japanese origin, who had given no reason for doubting their loyalty, was one of the blots on wartime American government. But

* K. Toshikazu, *Eclipse of the Rising Sun,* op. cit.

he Nisei almost without exception, refused the appeal of their blood
elations, and were almost fanatical in their devotion to the new institu-
ions among which they had been brought up.

The Nisei show that there is no such thing as a militarist through and
hrough, made such by his physical make-up, and a stranger to civilization
ecause of the military activities of his ancestors.

Most significant of all, the Japanese, since their surrender, have under-
one a thorough change of heart. In no country in the world is militarism
o thoroughly reprobated. All Japan's energies are now concentrated on
emaining a friendly civilian state. Possibly the very completeness of the
motional swing is suspicious. What is today so violently renounced may
omorrow be once more violently espoused. But all the signs are that the
vorld has, as the result of the war, gained a new Japan.

At the end of the war an international tribunal was set up by the Allies
n order to put on trial a representative group of those who had allegedly
een responsible for crimes against peace and other war crimes. The
apanese had wished to reserve a trial of war prisoners to themselves as a
ondition of Japanese surrender, but that had been denied to them by the
llied Powers. At the major War Crimes Tribunal in Tokyo, twenty-five
apanese leaders were sentenced, seven of them to death, others to life
mprisonment: among these were General Tōjō Hideki, the Prime Minis-
er; General Koiso Kuniaki, his successor; the wily court chamberlain,
Marquis Kido Kōichi, who played so large a part in bringing about
Japan's surrender; Tōgō Shigenori, the Foreign Minister who had showed
a most un-Japanese independence of judgement; and Hirota Kōki, another
former Prime Minister. The conveners even proposed trying Prince
Konoye Fumimaro, but he evaded arrest by poisoning himself. These
doubtful proceedings went like a swath through all those who had been in
any way prominent in Japanese politics of the period. The biographical
footnotes of a book on Japanese history at this time make heavy reading
because of the end of many of the characters. The major good that came
out of these proceedings at Tokyo was that they are the most complete,
exhaustive account of Japanese politics in the militarist period.

Other war crimes trials were held in Hong Kong, Singapore, Borneo
and elsewhere in the recent Japanese Empire. Detainees were arraigned
for cruelty towards local populations and prisoners of war, and over 900
were executed. Thoughts of these melancholy figures, and the deeds
which in many cases preceded this toll of life, lead to the reflection that
had the war had a different result, the subsequent years might have been
the age of Japanese Imperialism. Asia has been spared that. The war, with
all its horrors, had achieved this positive good. A reluctant admiration for

Japan's military feats must not block out the consciousness of the sinister shadow which for a time hung over the eastern world.

Search the record how one will, it is almost impossible to find anything good to say of the Japanese Empire. Its liquidation was an unqualified benefit to the world. In the years before the conflict, Japan had had it opportunity to develop its Empire in miniature – in Korea, in Formosa and in the parts of China which it came to dominate – and in this exhibition of the Japanese spirit it failed to show many virtues. An empire which by its definition is a political structure housing peoples of different cultures and languages, is different from the nation-state, which is the most approved political form in the twentieth century. Nations object to being included in an empire. Empires are out-of-fashion. But some empires are more tolerable than others. They may have qualities which actively catch the imagination of their people. In the case of a very few, their peoples will actually be willing to die in their defence, though instances of this have become increasingly rare. The classic case, in comparison with which other empires may be judged, was the Rome of antiquity. That Empire seems to have offered a wider life, richer opportunities, a larger destiny, than could be looked for within the confines of small states.

The Japanese Empire, if it is judged from its beginnings, was not at all likely to develop into one of these rarer structures. In its origin it was essentially primitive and of petty conception. It was put together by conquest, and its prime aim was to plunder the subjected peoples for the benefit of the Japanese. The Empire offered hardly anything to its citizens which led them to take pride in membership of it beyond a pride in being Asian. This should not be neglected. The Japanese made considerable play of Pan-Asianism. The contemporary writing is all about the joy of being Asian. It was the outstanding fact of the time. But it was not long before the contrast between Japanese idealism and Japanese practice took away this enthusiasm.

The Japanese system was founded on no great code of law. In its organization it embodied no exhilarating concepts such as have led men elsewhere into giving their loyalty, even if divided – concepts such as liberty, equality and fraternity; the career open to talents; the greatest good of the greatest number or restraint of the evil of exploitation. The Japanese Empire signified no large cult of reason, a defective vision, few distinctive habits of thought or behaviour, a strange corpus of books by which to set the tone of people's thought, a pattern of individual behaviour which gave few people a liberating vision. It was the starting place of no system of philosophy which was likely to appeal to men of all races and different cultures: in other words, it lacked the universalist appeal. The most to which it invited its citizens was to the enjoyment of Japanese culture, and there the difficulty was that, though this culture is not inferior, it is one which most Asians find uncongenial and it is at best provincial and not a universal civilization. In particular, the Japanese language was unsuited as a medium of communication for holding the political machinery together. It seemed scarcely imaginable that anyone talked Japanese as a form of intellectual pleasure, as the subjects of the French Empire often spoke French: the language was thought to be muzzy and imprecise.

Japanese culture is especially strong in the inculcation of the correct attitudes for aesthetic appreciation: but aesthetics has never been strong enough to hold an empire together. Besides, this quality of mind was often considered out-of-date or parochial in Japan itself.

Calling on the people of its Empire to share Japanese culture was summoning them to a Barmecide feast. Responding to the call, the Chinese felt themselves (not for the first or last time) sitting with more primitive people than themselves. They found that Japanese culture was a tiresome and constricting limitation on their minds.

A peculiarly evil feature of the system was that it would endure only as long as Japanese military power lasted: it was sustained by that and by that alone. It invited head-on collision with all the emerging forces of Asia, and if it had not been destroyed in war, it would sooner or later have led to bloody wars of liberation.

When the war was over, when Japan had given up the pretence at founding a new political order, and gave free play to its natural talents, the Japanese surprised the world, and themselves, by solving their problems by simple hard work, and without any use of force or creation of grandiose political structures. With western help (and spared most of the expense of defence), they recovered economically in the minimum of time; they rapidly became a beacon-light in Asia; they proved – as to be fair they had always promised – that an Asian people could save itself by its own exertions. And all this without even the dream of empire. Energy, skill in planning, imagination in enterprise, ability in the application of techniques to the economic processes proved enough to get Japan over all its obstacles; and Japan has discovered the political advantages in having a foreign policy which is audacious by reason of its modesty. Socially, too, the war and its aftermath helped to emancipate many underprivileged elements in Japanese society. One thinks of the story of a young naval officer – now a distinguished professor of economics but then a Kamikaze pilot awaiting his turn to die – who sat in his bath, facing the setting sun, when news was brought to him of the surrender of Japan. As he arose, his batman reached forward to dry his back. The young officer, his eyes blazing with intensity turned on him and said, 'The war is over: don't you ever wash another man's back again.' It was the end of an era.

The war – or more precisely Japan – also precipitated everywhere the demise of western power in Asia. The Western Powers withdrew from China. The Treaty Port system was at an end: also the rights of extra-territoriality. Within two years Britain withdrew from India. This was a change which plainly doomed the French Empire in Indo-China, and the Dutch in Indonesia. Within ten years, they had each of them passed away. They did not go voluntarily, or reluctantly, as did the British Empire in India; they attempted to stay, and they were willing to go to war against the national parties which rose up to extrude them. But they were too weak to prevail. Moreover they were too much concerned with their problems in Europe to be able to give the war their whole-hearted attention.

The Japanese Empire having been destroyed and the Western empires put down, a power vacuum existed which only the nationalist organizations could fill. These were left to organize most of Asia in the pattern they desired. The West, including the United States, tried to influence them in one way or another, using their economic power to make their will effective, and in the case of Britain and the United States their armaments when the situation did not respond to economic manipulation. By indirect means they hoped to prevail as effectively as in the days when they sat with political power in Delhi and in the eastern capitals. This was the phase of neo-colonialism, and the emancipated countries of Asia have been on their guard against it and have sought to render themselves really free even at the expense of neighbouring territories.

China, released from the incubus of an Imperial Japan, has been free to develop as the inward forces in the country directed. Within four years of the ending of the war China became communist. The excessive corruption, the paralysis of will and venal incompetence of the later years of the Kuomintang were increased by its unnatural isolation from the rest of the country. Once this was removed its downfall was inevitable.

The prolonged agony which had been suffered by the Chinese people as the twentieth century wore on, opened the way to a violent remedy. The chief leaders of the Kuomintang escaped the vengeance of the opposing party by retiring, with vast fortunes, to the island of Formosa whence they kept up, under an American umbrella, a somewhat ludicrous show of still exercising an influence in world affairs. In the first flood of revenge, many of the landlords, who had lived for so long in the sun of prosperity in China, were violently put down, with sufferings as cruel as any which they had, by past insensibility and negligence, occasioned among the poor. Later, 're-education' was the term used to describe the method by which the bourgeoisie were broken in. The mass of the people were liberated into a new life of undreamed-of sufficiency in living standards and educational opportunity: as against this, freedom for the individual – of thought or self-direction – was largely absent. In foreign relations, communist China's extreme isolationism, and the mutual suspicions between it and the United States, have kept the world on edge, but from time to time have shown signs of relaxing. There is no doubt of the greatly recovered prestige of China since the war or its eventual re-emergence as a major Power in Asia.

What had been the effects in India? Great though the upheaval had been in India's domestic life, the war affected the pace of the development of its history, and accelerated the divorce of India and Britain: it did not necessarily give events an essentially new turn. Many who looked with the eye of history on India from 1930 onwards foresaw that the end of the British Raj was approaching. Others looked forward to India's elevation to full status as a self-governing Dominion at some faraway, indeterminate time. Even perceptive young revolutionaries elsewhere in the British Empire, like Jomo Kenyatta in East Africa, scarcely dreamt that they would ever see the independence of India within their lifetimes, much less the decolonization of Africa and beyond. They, at least, credit Japan with having shown the fragility of far-flung imperial bonds – and with having been the direct cause of the disintegration of the British, Dutch, French and Portuguese Empires east of Suez.

Yet in one fateful respect the war gave an unexpected twist to the long process of the freedom struggle by the Indian Congress. In the circumstances of wartime politics, a sudden and accelerated growth took place in the Moslem League. It had been provoked by the Congress success; it was already apparent before the war; but the war acted like a hot-house in compressing into a few years the development which might otherwise have been spread over decades. The Moslem League, which increased in strength so radically, was emboldened to press for the creation of the Moslem state of Pakistan.

After the Greater East Asia War, that state came into being and eventually led to the creation of a second independent nation, Bangladesh. These were, when still united, an exceptional creation which reminds us of the continuing force of religion in politics. Religion was the driving force in making for the existence of this state. As such, the creation of Pakistan seems to be a digression from the ideas of the Enlightenment and a return to the Middle Ages. Its establishment was accompanied by forebodings and very great reluctance on the part of the British Government. If independence had come in 1937, instead of 1947, it would undoubtedly have been given to a united India. The intensity of the great religious divide between Hindu and Moslem did not appear until later: they only manifested themselves in their full significance during the war years. But an undivided India would not have held together. The Hindu–Moslem cleavage would have declared itself under the strain of self-government. Sooner or later, unified government would have been made impossible: communal tension, and eventually communal civil war, would have brought it to a standstill.

It is easy to forget how at the end of the war the decision to partition the sub-continent was on a knife edge. Without the war, the British would hardly have considered the creation of Pakistan as a necessary act. The state of Pakistan is therefore one of the monuments to the war with Japan. It is an unlikely one: few today see any special connection between its history and that of Japan, yet the two are causally linked as is the enventual emergence of Bangladesh, and the vituperation that continues to exist between all three nations of the Indian sub-continent.

For the United States the war was an incident in its rise to be one of the two greatest Powers in the world. It received its baptism of fire. For many years before 1941, America had distorted the natural play of international affairs by utterly refusing to act the part of a Great Power. Its people, in general and except at certain conjunctures, appeared to be without the political instincts of the citizens of a major state. Because of their unique behaviour, and of the influence of this upon the official conduct of the American Government, the United States, at a time when fate and its economic power called upon it to exert tremendous influence, limited its voice in world affairs to be hardly of more account than that of a third-class European state. Doubtless the reasons for this lay far back in American history, and touch on George Washington, the fear of 'entangling Alliances' and the belief that foreign governments were very wily and would inevitably bamboozle an American Government which was rash enough to negotiate with them. But the United States had been in the First World War; its reaction to this experience and withdrawal into isolation had been a setback to normal growth. When Pearl Harbor happened, the United States, in a world at war, still had an army of about the same size as Sweden's; it still made the gestures, to which it had accustomed itself before its entry in 1917 into the First World War, of being 'too proud to fight'. It is true that American ideas and American business influence were very prevalent, as also was the uncontrollable propulsive power of American culture. But the American state did not set itself to propagate them.

In the course of the war, the United States developed amazingly. It grew with the alarming speed of Alice when she ate a small cake marked 'Eat me'. It began the war with organs and ministries for taking part in foreign affairs which seem like toys. But, with the creative wind of improvisation which swept through America, the institutions developed rapidly. Simultaneously its public opinion, and the institutions by which this was made effective, grew in self-confidence. By the end of the war, the United States was moving in international affairs with professionalism and boldness.

American democracy was to show that while it was surprisingly persevering as long as the war lasted, it was, once peace was restored, capable of a rapid, revolutionary change of mood. The fires died as swiftly as they had blazed fiercely. Within seven years America had come to feel towards Japan as towards its protégé: and had transferred to Japan some of the abnormally cordial feeling which it had held towards China, until China became communist.

Finally, this was probably the last major war which Great Britain took part in as a world Power, certainly an Asian Power. For the last time Britain manoeuvred as a government with interest and concern in every part of the world, especially in Asia. It ended its Asian history with panache. It was nevertheless an end, and the speed with which it was accomplished left men to ponder whether Britain's departure represented a policy of grace or scuttle. Either way, it was certainly an inevitable consequence of the economic exhaustion brought about by Total War and by the failure of Appeasement. Within two years of the dropping of the bomb on Hiroshima, Britain ended its responsibility for India. Although it took some time to work out the details, by this one act it terminated its Empire everywhere in Asia; for a British Empire in Asia which excluded India was not really a possibility.

Great Britain, at that time, was more than a small country, with a restricted part to play, as seemed to befit one of a cluster of West European islands. By the accident of history, by the energy of its peoples it had, for the previous two centuries, been shot out of its natural sphere. It had risen to a height of power and prestige which obviously it could not retain but to which people in Britain had become accustomed. The leaders of institutional life had risen to their opportunity, and for some decades this had been reflected in politics. These seemed to have an influence totally out of the proportion which would naturally be expected of such a numerically small people. Living in Britain at this time had a magnifying effect, so that what was done seemed to be done with a deep sense of responsibility. The proceedings of the Parliament at Westminster were gazed at by so many people that those who took part in it had the uneasy sense of acting on a great stage of the world, and being the cynosure of the world's eyes. This sense was often embarrassing. It often invested relatively trivial affairs with a false glamour. It would have been healthier if they had been dealt with without these overtones. Even so, thought in Britian was still apt to be large; small conceptions were still at a discount. It was this quality which perhaps most separates the Britain of those days from what it has become.

Within ten years of Indian Independence, Britain had liquidated practically all that was left of its Asian Empire. Ceylon, Malaya, Burma: it let them all go. It was not a matter of no longer discouraging their instinct to break away from the Empire which had once been thought of as a supra-national organization, a house where all the rising nationalisms of the Empire might, of their own free will, find asylum. They were positively conducted to the door. They were given a golden handshake – financially a rather mean one – and were sped into independence with expressions of goodwill.

Britain, which had enjoyed in Asia the great romantic period of its history, turned back, as a result of the war, and after an interval for readjustment, to the more sober task of discovering the contrast between being a world Power and being a small country off the north-west corner coast of continental Europe. It became preoccupied with the total revolution which should adapt Britain for its new role; with anxious debate as to whether it should think once more to become a European Power as it had been under its Angevin monarchs, or whether it could exist as a small island alone.

It is irony that, at the end, Britain finds itself in very similar circumstances to those which worried Japan at the start of this history. Transpose the islands off the north coast of Asia to the islands off the north-west of Europe, and the parallel, often remarked, is strangely apt. Its history, as Dean Acheson rightly diagnosed – only to be the object of bitter vituperation by people in Britain – was that it had lost an empire and not found a new part to play. The British may count themselves fortunate that the public opinion of the world has moved on, and it is unlikely that Britain will be tempted to try and solve its problems in a similar way to Japan.

*

And the human side? What of the war of the Little Peterkins of Asia? The conflict had a recognizable pattern, though there were so many confusing cross-currents. One purpose of this book has been to trace it out. It settled the influences which were to be dominant in the lives of people for the next generation or so – until new pressures meet new obstacles, and all is again in the melting pot, the issue having again to be settled by conflict. For this last great cataclysm, the price paid in human life and suffering was truly prodigious. The numbers of those killed in the war on all fronts have been analysed. Of two of the great Asian families of people engaged, the Chinese casualties, difficult to estimate, have been given by Chiang Kai-shek in his book, *A Summing-Up at Seventy*, as over 3 million. 'These figures,' he says, 'do not include the heavy losses in life and property sustained by the people in general.'* Japanese losses in battle and air-attack have been estimated at around 2.3 million. Of the people elsewhere in Asia, by far the largest proportion had no wish to take part in the quarrel. They neither understood, nor cared for, nor were consulted about, the objects of conflict. From first to last they viewed the war as a fact of destructive nature, which everyone in his senses sought to evade, but which was fated to make enormous waves. Those who voluntarily went to war, or felt passionately about the issues to the extent of being genuinely willing to die for them, were very few. Submitting to the economic inducements because of poverty and destitution was the nearest that most combatants came to acting by a reasonable decision. The only Asian people of whom this was not really true were the fatally indoctrinated Japanese.

It is, however, economic pressure alone which interests nine tenths of the population of Asia. It is idle to think that people living in conditions of Asian poverty, and with so much mass illiteracy, can be capable of acting in any other way. Any system of government which offers them the prospects of seeing a barely tolerable life, barely tolerable though it be, for six months ahead, will be more than welcome. Frills of government, freedom, choice, are suspect to them. Those combatants who came from a society in which the compulsion of hunger was less present were swept together by conscription, and had even less say in their destiny.

The war was probably the last major conflict which will be fought in Asia in which all the Asian antagonists except Japan were predominantly agrarian. This gave the war its peculiar, and rather antiquarian flavour. Time will ensure that, before another great contest can happen, larger segments of society will have become heavily industrialized, and, with

---

* Chiang Kai-shek, *A Summing-Up at Seventy*, Harrap, London, 1957.

industrialization, will have come the special type of social organization which renders society so different in behaviour from that which was traditional.

Even the very few of the educated classes – the Chinese university professors, the Japanese, the Indian leisured upper classes – who had the inclination and the ability to trace out the pattern of events behind the confusion, to understand the whys and wherefores, derived little consolation, when they were compelled to live among a collapsing economy and the dangers of loot and arson, from the fact that to them was vouchsafed some understanding of what the war was all about.

It is clear that, to the many millions who fought and suffered unvocally, to the ignorant armies clashing by night, unselfconsciously, those who survived owe an inexpiable debt. It seems at some points in history, that only through a convulsion involving millions is understanding painfully acquired. 'The cut worm forgives the plough', said the poet Blake. By invoking this kind of charity, there can perhaps be forgiveness for the ungovernable fury of the instruments by which history is made.

Afterword

We are left, as we began, lingering over thoughts collected by Sun Tzu twenty-three and a half centuries ago:

While an angered man may again be happy, and a resentful man again be pleased, a state that has perished cannot be restored, nor can the dead be brought back to life. Therefore, the enlightened ruler is prudent and the good general is warned against rash action. Thus the state is kept secure and the army preserved.

Chronological Skeleton

1937

July	7	Japanese attack Chinese at Marco Polo Bridge
Dec.	14	Fall of Nanking to the Japanese

1938

July	11	Japanese-Soviet battle of Chang-kufeng
Oct.		Chiang Kai-shek's Government withdraws to Chungking
Oct.	21	Fall of Canton to the Japanese
Oct.	25	Fall of Hankow to the Japanese
Nov.	5	Prince Konoye declares 'New Order' in Asia

1939

Sept.	1	Germans invade Poland
Sept.	3	Great Britain and France declare war
Sept.	17	USSR invades Poland
May–Sept		Battle of Nomonhan between Japan and USSR

1939

Oct.   USSR exacts mutual assistance treaties from Estonia, Latvia and Lithuania

Nov. 30 USSR invades Finland

Dec. 17 *Graf Spee* scuttled

1940

Mar. 12 Finland capitulates

Mar. 30 Setting up of Wang Ching-wei's puppet Government at Nanking

Apr. 9 Germans invade Denmark and Norway

May   British occupy Iceland

May 10 Germans invade Low Countries and France. Churchill Prime Minister

May 15 Dutch lay down arms

May 20 Germans reach English Channel

May 28 Belgium capitulates		
May 27– Dunkirk		
June 4		
June 10 Italy declares war		
June 14 Germans enter Paris		
June 22 France signs armistice		
July 3 British action against French fleet at Mers-el-Kebir		July– Closing of the Burma Oct. Road
July 10– Battle of Britain	Aug. 4 Italians invade British and French Somaliland	
Sept. 15		
Sept. 3 Anglo-US bases destroyers deal	Sept. 14 Italians invade Egypt	Sept. 27 Tripartite Pact between Japan, Germany and Italy
	Oct. Hitler confers with Mussolini (4), Franco (23), Pétain (24)	
	Oct. 28 Italians invade Greece	
Nov. 5 Roosevelt re-elected President	Nov. 11 British attack Italian fleet at Taranto	Nov. Hungary, Rumania and Slovakia brought into Tripartite Pact

1940	Dec. British offensive in North Africa captures Tobruk (Jan. 22) and Benghazi (Feb. 7) 1941	Dec. American embargo on sales of scrap iron and war material to Japan

1941		Mar. 1 Bulgaria joins Tripartite Pact	
Mar. 11 Lend-Lease Act signed			
	Mar. 27 Simovic coup: Yugoslavia refuses to join Tripartite Pact		
	Mar. 28 Battle of Cape Matapan		
	Mar. 31 First German offensive in North Africa: takes Benghazi and invests Tobruk		
Apr. US occupies Greenland	Apr. 6 Germans invade Yugoslavia and Greece		Apr. 13 Non-Aggression Pact signed between Japan and Russia
	May 2 British invade Iraq		
	May 20– Germans take Crete		
	June 2		
May 27 *Bismarck* sunk			

June 8   British defeat Vichy French in Syria and Lebanon

June 22   Germans invade USSR

July   US joins occupation of Iceland

July 2   Japan decides on extensive moves into Indo-China

July 12   Anglo-Soviet Treaty of Mutual Assistance

July 28 and 29   US, British and Dutch East Indies impose embargoes on the sale of oil and steel to Japan

Aug. 14   Roosevelt–Churchill conference, Placentia Bay: Atlantic Charter

Aug. 17   Fall of Kiev

Aug. 25   Anglo-Russian occupation of Iran

Sept. 8   Leningrad invested

Sept.   US 'shoot at sight' order

1941

Oct. 17		General Tōjō replaces Konoye as Prime Minister of Japan
Oct. 30		Sebastopol invested. German thrust for Moscow
Dec. 1		Russian counter-attack
	Dec. 7	Japan sends a declaration of war to the US
	Dec. 7	Japan attacks Pearl Harbor, the Philippines, Hong Kong and Malaya
	Dec. 8	US and Great Britain declare war on Japan
	Dec. 9	China officially declares war on Japan and Germany
	Dec. 10	Japanese sink the *Prince of Wales* and the *Repulse*
	Dec. 10	Japan captures Guam
	Dec. 11	Japan attacks Burma
Dec. 11		Germany and Italy declare war on US
	Dec. 23	Fall of Wake Island
Dec. 24		British re-capture Benghazi

1942

<table>
<tr><td>Jan. 28</td><td>Germans re-capture Benghazi</td><td></td><td>Jan. 11</td><td>Japan attacks the Dutch East Indies</td></tr>
<tr><td></td><td></td><td></td><td>Feb. 8</td><td>Fall of Rangoon</td></tr>
<tr><td></td><td></td><td></td><td>Feb. 15</td><td>Fall of Singapore</td></tr>
<tr><td></td><td></td><td></td><td>Feb. 19</td><td>Japanese bomb Port Darwin in Australia</td></tr>
<tr><td></td><td></td><td></td><td>Feb. 27–29</td><td>Battle of the Java Sea</td></tr>
<tr><td>Mar.</td><td>Bomber Command raids Baltic towns</td><td></td><td>Mar. 2</td><td>Fall of Batavia</td></tr>
<tr><td></td><td></td><td></td><td>Mar. 11</td><td>Cripps mission to India</td></tr>
<tr><td>Apr.</td><td>German 'Baedeker' raids</td><td></td><td>Apr. 4–9</td><td>Japanese raid into the Indian Ocean, bombing Ceylon</td></tr>
<tr><td></td><td></td><td></td><td>Apr. 9</td><td>US surrender of Bataan</td></tr>
<tr><td></td><td></td><td></td><td>Apr. 18</td><td>US air raid on Tokyo</td></tr>
<tr><td></td><td></td><td></td><td>May 1</td><td>Surrender of Mandalay</td></tr>
<tr><td></td><td></td><td></td><td>May 6</td><td>Surrender of Corregidor</td></tr>
<tr><td></td><td></td><td></td><td>May 6–8</td><td>Battle of the Coral Sea</td></tr>
<tr><td>May 30</td><td>'1,000-bomber' raid on Cologne</td><td></td><td></td><td></td></tr>
</table>

1942			
June	Destruction of PQ 17		June 4 Battle of Midway Island
			June 4 Japanese attack on the Aleutian Islands
July	Regular raids on Ruhr and Hamburg begin	July 3 Fall of Sebastopol	Aug. 7 US landings on the Solomon Islands
			Aug. 9 Civil disobedience campaign announced in India
Aug. 12– 15	Stalin–Churchill meeting in Moscow	Aug. 12– 15 Stalin–Churchill meeting in Moscow	
Aug. 17	First US raid on Germany		
Aug. 19	Dieppe raid		
	Aug. 31 Battle of Alam el Halfa: German–Italian advance stayed	Sept. 13 Battles for Stalingrad begin	Sept. 21 Opening of the Arakan offensive under Wavell
			Sept. 21 Opening of US offensive in New Guinea

Nov. Record months for sinking by U-boats

Nov. Regular raids on Berlin begin

Oct. 23 Battle of Alamein

Nov. 8 Allied landings in Morocco and Algeria

Nov. 11 Germans occupy southern France and Tunisia

1943

Jan. 14–24 Casablanca Conference

Jan. German retreat from Caucasus

Jan. 11 Treaty relinquishing extra-territorial rights between the US, Britain and China

Feb. 2 German surrender at Stalingrad. Russians recover Kursk (8) and Rostov (14)

Feb. 8 Wingate's expedition into Burma

Mar. 2 Battle of the Bismarck Sea

Mar. 29 Battle of the Mareth

Apr. 18 Death of Admiral Yamamoto, at Bougainville

Apr. 19–May 16 Rising and extinction of Warsaw Ghetto

1943

May 11	US begin to liberate Aleutian Islands
May 12	German-Italian surrender in Tunisia
May 17	Attack on Ruhr dams
May 26	Discovery of Katyn massacre and severance of Russo-Polish relations
June 29	US landings in New Guinea
July 5–Aug. 6	Battles in the Kursk salient and Russian recovery of Orel and Belgorod
July 10	Invasion of Sicily
July 25	Dismissal of Mussolini
Aug. 17	US daylight raids on Regensburg and Schweinfurt
Aug. 17	Quebec Conference: setting up of South-East Asia Command, under Mountbatten
Aug. 23	Russians recover Kharkov
Sept.	Russians recover Novorossisk and Smolensk (25)
Sept. 3	Invasion of Calabria and signing of Italian surrender
Sept. 9	Landings at Salerno
Sept. 12	Rescue of Mussolini

1943		
Oct. 13 Italy declares war on Germany	Oct. Russians recover Zaporozhe (14) and Dnepropetrovsk (25)	
	Nov. 6 Russians recover Kiev	Nov. 5–6 Greater East Asia Conference held in Tokyo
		Nov. US landings in the Gilbert Islands
		Nov. 22–26 Cairo Conference: unconditional surrender demanded of Japan
Nov. 28–Dec. 1 Teheran Conference		Dec. Opening of the assault on the Marshall Islands

1944		
Jan. 12 Landings at Anzio	Jan. 27 Leningrad relieved	
Feb. 15 Bombing of Monte Cassino		Feb.–Mar. Beginning of Japanese offensive on borders of India, siege of Imphal and Kohima
	Apr. 2 Russians enter Rumania	Apr. 17 Renewed Japanese offensive in China
		Apr.–July US advances through Dutch New Guinea

1944

	May 17 Germans evacuate Monte Cassino	May Russians recover Sebastopol and Crimea	June 15 Americans invade Saipan
June 6 Invasion of Normandy	June 4 Americans enter Rome		June 15 First B29 raid on Japan
June 12 First V1s hit London		June 23– Russians recover July 3 Byelorussia	July 4 Japanese defeated at Imphal
			July 9 Fall of Saipan
			July 18 Resignation of General Tōjō
July 20 Attempt on Hitler's life	July 23 Russians take Lublin and establish Polish Committee of National Liberation		

Aug. 15 Allied landings in southern France	**Aug.** Kesselring mans the Gothic Line	**Aug. 1– Oct. 2** Warsaw rising against the Germans	**Aug.** US recovery of Tinian and Guam
Aug. 17 Final victories in Normandy. Paris rises			
Aug. 24 Leclerc enters Paris			
Sept. 3 Brussels liberated		**Sept. 5** USSR declares war on Bulgaria	**Sept.** Allied counter-offensive in Burma, under Mountbatten
Sept. 8 First V2s hit London		**Sept. 12** Rumania signs armistice	
Sept. 17– 30 Arnhem operations fail		**Sept. 19** Finland signs armistice	
		Oct. 20 Partisans and Russians enter Belgrade	**Oct. 20** US landings in the Philippines
			Oct. 25 Battle of Leyte Gulf
			Nov. Beginning of systematic US bombing of Japan
Dec. 16 German offensive in the Ardennes			

1945

Jan. 9	US landings on Luzon
Jan. 12	General Russian offensive begins
Jan. 17	Russians enter Warsaw
Feb. 4–12	Yalta Conference
Feb. 13	Surrender of Budapest
Feb. 13–14	Dresden raids
Mar. 7	Americans cross the Rhine at Remagen
Apr. 1	US landings on Okinawa
Apr. 4	Japanese Prime Minister Koiso resigns and is replaced by Suzuki
Apr. 12	Death of Roosevelt
Apr. 13	Russians enter Vienna
Apr. 16	Last Russian offensive begins
Apr.	Russia refuses to renew her non-aggression pact with Japan
Apr. 28	Death of Mussolini
Apr. 30	Death of Hitler
May 2	Berlin in Russian hands. Germans in Italy capitulate
May 3	Japanese surrender Rangoon

May 7 Germans surrender at Rheims

July 17 Potsdam Conference

May 5 Prague rises

May 9 Russians enter Prague

July 26 Allies at Potsdam call on Japan to surrender

Aug. 6 Hiroshima

Aug. 8 Russia declares war on Japan

Aug. 9 Nagasaki

Aug. 14 Japan capitulates

Sept. 2 Japanese surrender signed

Bibliographies

The Second World War was the first truly global conflict in the history of mankind. The notion that it began with the German invasion of Poland in September 1939 is widely believed but is, in fact, absurdly parochial and unhistorical. It is always difficult to draw arbitrary distinctions between events, their causes and the causes of the causes. Any such attempt is bound to introduce subjective elements, distortions, illusions. Obviously, we gain a measure of understanding from making the attempt. When we look closely at the Thirty Years War that occurred between 1618 and 1648, we find a cluster of small wars, each of which lasted a few years and involved separate sets of belligerents. Together they changed the political geography and social fabric of the European continent. It is no use isolating one or other of those small wars without bearing in mind their relationship to each other; it is no less nonsensical to believe that the concatenation of these events produces a comprehensible, single, seamless progression of cause and effect: each of those small wars had special features which can be appreciated only when looked at individually, others which stand out only when looked at as part of a collective experience. And so it was with the Second World War. From a half-century of more remote events sprang a succession of wars that began in East Asia with the outbreak of the Manchurian Incident in September 1931 and continued with little interruption until the surrender of Japan in September 1945. As that succession of wars intertwined with the history of the European War of 1939–45, the combined conflict came to justify its epic description as a 'World War'. Those readers who wish to explore in greater detail some of the subjects this book has opened up may find useful the following suggestions for further reading.

PART I: ASIAN CONFLICT

General

A. P. Adamthwaite, *The Making of the Second World War* (London, 1977); G. C. Allen, *Western Enterprise in Far Eastern Economic Development: China and Japan* (London, 1954); W. G. Beasley, *Japanese Imperialism, 1894–1945* (Oxford, 1987), *The Modern History of Japan* (New York, 1963); C. Beaton, *Far East* (London, 1945); G. Bienstock, *The Struggle for the Pacific* (Port

Washington, NY, 1937); C. Browne, *Tōjō: The Last Banzai* (London, 1967); R. D. Burns and E. M. Bennett, *Diplomats in Crisis: United States-Chinese-Japanese Relations, 1919–1941* (Santa Barbara, 1974); C. A. Buss, *The Far East: A History of Recent and Contemporary International Relations in East Asia* (New York, 1955); W. H. Chamberlin, *Japan over Asia* (London, 1938); A. S. Cochran (ed.), *Magic: Diplomatic Summary*, 8 vols. (New York, 1980); B. Collier, *The Second World War: A Military History from Munich to Hiroshima* (Gloucester, Mass., 1967); W. F. Craven and J. L. Cates, *The Army Airforces in World War Two*, 7 vols. (Chicago, 1948–58); P. Darby, *Three Faces of Imperialism: British and American Approaches to Asia and Africa, 1870–1970* (New Haven, 1987); J. P. Davies, *Dragon by the Tail: American, British, Japanese, and Russian Encounters with China and One Another* (London, 1974); R. A. Dayer, *Bankers and Diplomats in China, 1917–1925: The Anglo-American Relationship* (Totowa, New Jersey, 1981); J. M. Dorwart, *Conflict of Duty: The US Navy's Intelligence Dilemma, 1919–1945* (Annapolis, 1983); J. W. Dower, *Empire and Aftermath: Yoshida Shigeru and the Japanese Experience, 1878–1954* (Cambridge, Mass., 1979); P. Einzig, *The Japanese 'New Order' in East Asia* (London, 1943); J. K. Fairbank *et al.*, *East Asia: The Modern Transformation* (Boston, 1965), and S. Y. Teng, *China's Response to the West* (Cambridge, 1954); J. Gunther, *Inside Asia* (New York, 1939); S. Henny and J.-P. Lehmann (eds.), *Themes and Theories in Modern Japanese History: Essays in Memory of Richard Storry* (London, 1988); E. P. Hoyt, *Japan's War: The Great Pacific Conflict, 1853–1952* (London, 1987); E. R. Hughes, *The Invasion of China by the Western World* (London, 1937); R. Hughes, *Foreign Devil: Thirty Years of Reporting in the Far East* (London, 1972); S. Ienaga, *Japan's Last War: World War II and the Japanese, 1931–1945* (New York, 1978); T. Ishimaru, *The Next World War* (London, 1937); D. Kahn, *The Codebreakers* (New York, 1968); M. Kennedy, *A History of Japan* (London, 1963); R. Lewin, *The American Magic: Codes, Ciphers and the Defeat of Japan* (New York, 1982); Sir B. H. Liddell Hart, *History of the Second World War* (London, 1970); H. Michel, *The Second World War* (London, 1975); H. B. Morse, *The International Relations of the Chinese Empire*, 3 vols. (London, 1910–18), and F. H. McNair, *Far Eastern International Relations* (Boston, 1931); I. H. Nish, *The Story of Japan* (London, 1968); Sir J. T. Pratt, *Before Pearl Harbour: A Study of the Historical Background to the War in the Pacific* (London, 1944); C. R. Shepherd, *The Case against Japan* (London, 1939); B. Smith, *The War's Long Shadow: The Second World War and its Aftermath: China, Russia, Britain, America* (London, 1986); R. H. Spector, *Eagle Against the Sun: The American War with Japan* (New York, 1985); G. R. Storry, *A History of Modern Japan* (London, 1960); J. Toland, *The Rising Sun: The Decline and Fall of the Japanese Empire, 1936–1945* (New York, 1970); T. Troy, *Donovan and the CIA: A History of the Establishment of the Central Intelligence Agency* (Frederick, Maryland, 1983); United States Army: Headquarters, Far East Command, Military History Section, Japanese Research Division, *Japanese Monographs*, 185 vols. (Tokyo and

Washington, DC, 1945–60); W. W. Willoughby, *Japan's Case Examined* (Baltimore, 1940).

The Sino-Japanese Conflict, 1894–1927

R. F. Hackett, *Yamagata Aritomo and the Rise of Modern Japan* (Cambridge, Mass., 1971); S. R. MacKinnon, *Power and Politics in Late Imperial China: Yuan Shi-kai in Beijing and Tianjin, 1905–1908* (Berkeley, 1980); H. B. Morse, *The International Relations of the Chinese Empire*, 3 vols. (London, 1910–18); M. Mutsu, *Kenkenroku: A Diplomatic Record of the Sino-Japanese War, 1894–95* (Tokyo, 1982).

The Russo-Japanese War, 1904–5, and its Aftermath

K. Asakawa, *The Russo-Japanese Conflict: Its Causes and Issues* (London, 1904); M. Baring, *With the Russians in Manchuria* (London, 1905); R. V. C. Bodley, *Admiral Togo* (London, 1935); W. C. Braisted, *Report on the Japanese Naval, Medical and Sanitary Features of the Russo-Japanese War to the Surgeon General* (Washington, DC, 1906); Lord Brooke, *An Eye Witness in Manchuria* (London, 1905); R. Charques, *The Twilight of Imperial Russia* (London, 1958); E. L. V. Cordonnier, *The Japanese in Manchuria*, vols. I–II (London, 1912, 1914); R. Dua, *The Impact of the Russo-Japanese War on Indian Politics* (Delhi, 1966); T. E. Ewing, *Between the Hammer and the Anvil? Chinese and Russian Policies in Outer Mongolia, 1911–1921* (Bloomington, Indiana, 1980); E. A. Falk, *Togo and the Rise of Japanese Sea-Power* (London, 1936); Great Britain, Committee of Imperial Defence, *Official History (Naval and Military) of the Russo-Japanese War*, 3 vols (London, 1910, 1912, 1920); R. F. Hackett, *Yamagata Aritomo and the Rise of Modern Japan* (Cambridge, Mass., 1971); Sir I. Hamilton, *A Staff Officer's Scrap Book during the Russo-Japanese War*, 2 vols. (London, 1905, 1907); H. Hayashi, *The Secret Memoirs* (New York, 1915); R. Hough, *The Fleet that Had to Die* (London, 1958); D. James, *The Siege of Port Arthur* (London, 1905); A. Lloyd, *Admiral Togo* (Tokyo, 1905); A. Malazemoff, *Russian Far Eastern Policy, 1881–1904* (Berkeley, 1958); N. A. McCully, *The McCully Report: The Russo-Japanese War, 1904–05* (Annapolis, 1977); I. H. Nish, *The Anglo-Japanese Alliance: The Diplomacy of the Two Island Empires, 1894–1907* (London, 1966); B. W. Norregaard, *The Great Siege: The Investment and Fall of Port Arthur* (London, 1906); S. Okamoto, *The Japanese Oligarchy and the Russo-Japanese War* (New York, 1970); D. Walder, *The Short Victorious War: The Russo-Japanese Conflict, 1904–5* (London, 1973); J. M. Westwood, *Witnesses of Tsushima* (Tokyo, 1970); J. A. White, *The Diplomacy of the Russo-Japanese War* (Princeton, 1966).

Korea

G. A. Lenson, *Balance of Intrigue: International Rivalry in Korea and Manchuria,*

1884–1899, 2 vols. (Tallahassee, 1982); R. R. Swartout, *Mandarins, Gunboats, and Power Politics: Owen Nickerson Denny and the International Rivalries in Korea* (Honolulu, 1980).

The Post-War Settlement, Arms Limitation and Collective Security

R. L. Buell, *The Washington Conference* (New York, 1922); H. Bywater, *Sea-Power in the Pacific: A Study of the American-Japanese Naval Problem* (London, 1921); P. T. Etherton and H. H. Tiltman, *Japan: Mistress of the Pacific?* (London, 1933); A. Iriye, *After Imperialism: The Search for a New Order in the Far East, 1921–1931* (Cambridge, Mass., 1965); T. Ishimaru, *Japan Must Fight Britain* (London, 1936); T. F. Mayer-Oakes, *Fragile Victory: Prince Saionji and the 1930 London Treaty Issue from the Memoirs of Baron Harada Kumao* (Detroit, 1968); F. Moore, *America's Naval Challenge* (New York, 1929); S. E. Pelz, *Race to Pearl Harbor: The Failure of the Second London Naval Conference and the Onset of World War II* (Cambridge, Mass., 1974); E. S. Rubinow, *Sino-Japanese Warfare and the League of Nations* (Geneva, 1938); H. L. Stimson, *The Far Eastern Crisis: Recollections and Observations* (New York, 1936); G. E. Wheeler, *Prelude to Pearl Harbor: The United States Navy and the Far East, 1921–1931* (Columbia, Missouri, 1963); G. Woodcock, *The British in the Far East* (London, 1969).

Japan and Manchuria

R. Bassett, *Democracy and Foreign Policy: A Case History: The Sino-Japanese Dispute, 1931–1933* (London, 1952); J. D. Doenecke (ed.), *The Diplomacy of Frustration: The Manchurian Crisis of 1931–1933 as Revealed in the Papers of Stanley K. Hornbeck* (Stanford, 1981); F. C. Jones, *Manchuria since 1939* (London, 1949); League of Nations, *The Report of the Commission of Enquiry into the Sino-Japanese Dispute* (Tokyo, n.d.), *The Verdict of the League: China and Japan in Manchuria* (Boston, 1933); G. A. Lenson, *Balance of Intrigue: International Rivalry in Korea and Manchuria, 1884–1899*, 2 vols. (Tallahassee, 1982), *The Damned Inheritance: The Soviet Union and the Manchurian Crises, 1924–1935* (Tallahassee, 1974); G. McCormack, *Chang Tso-lin in Northeast China, 1911–1928: China, Japan and the Manchurian Idea* (Stanford, 1927); J. W. Morley ed., *Japan Erupts: The London Naval Conference and the Manchurian Incident, 1928–1932* (New York, 1984); S. N. Ogata, *Defiance in Manchuria: The Making of Japanese Foreign Policy, 1931–1932* (Berkeley, 1964); Y. P. Pickering, *Japan's Place in the Modern World* (London, 1936); H. Pu-Yi, *From Emperor to Citizen: The Autobiography of Aisin-Gioro Pu-Yi* (Peking, 1965; OUP, 1987); G. B. Rea, *The Case for Manchukuo* (New York, 1935); J. A. B. Scherer, *Manchukuo: A Bird's-Eye View* (Tokyo, 1933); E. B. Schumpeter *et al.*, *The Industrialization of Japan and Manchukuo, 1930–1940* (New York, 1940); P. S. Tang, *Russia and Soviet Policy in Manchuria and Outer Mongolia, 1911–1931* (Durham,

North Carolina, 1959); C. Thorne, *The Limits of Foreign Policy: The West, the League and the Far Eastern Crisis of 1931–1933* (London, 1972); United States Army: Headquarters, Far East Command, Military History Section, Japanese Research Division, *Japanese Studies on Manchuria*, 13 vols. (Tokyo and Washington, DC, 1945–56); W. W. Willoughby, *The Sino-Japanese Controversy and the League of Nations* (Baltimore, 1935); T. Yoshihashi, *Conspiracy at Mukden: The Rise of the Japanese Military* (New Haven, 1963); C. W. Young, *Japan's Special Position in Manchuria: Its Assertion, Legal Interpretation and Present Meaning* (Baltimore, 1931).

Japanese Expansion in North China, 1934–7

China: Delegation to the League of Nations, *Japanese Aggression and World Opinion, July 7 to October 7, 1937* (Geneva, 1938); China: Delegation to the Nine-Power Conference, *Development of the Crisis in the Far East in the Last Six Years Brought About by Continuous Japanese Aggression against China* (Brussels, 1938); Foreign Affairs Association of Japan, *How the North China Affair Arose* (Tokyo, 1937); J. W. Morley, ed., *The China Quagmire: Japan's Expansion on the Asian Continent, 1933–1941* (New York, 1983).

Chinese Internal Revolutions and Foreign Policy

R. W. Barnett, *Economic Shanghai: Hostage to Politics, 1937–1941* (New York, 1941); S. de Beauvoir, *The Long March* (London, 1958); R. E. Bedeski, *State-Building in Modern China: The Kuomintang in the Prewar Period* (Berkeley, 1981); L. Bianco, *The Origins of the Chinese Revolution, 1915–1949* (London, 1971); C. Brandt, *Stalin's Failure in China, 1924–1927* (London, 1958); E. F. Carlson, *The Chinese Army: Its Organization and Military Efficiency* (New York, 1940); A. B. Chan, *Arming the Chinese: The Western Armaments Trade in Warlord China, 1920–1928* (Vancouver, 1982); K.-S. Chiang, *A Summing Up at Seventy* (London, 1957), *China's Destiny* (London, 1947); O. E. Chubb, *Twentieth Century China* (New York, 1966); L. E. Eastman, *Seeds of Destruction: Nationalist China in War and Revolution, 1937–1949* (Stanford, 1984); J. K. Fairbank (ed.), *The Cambridge History of China:* vol. XII, *Republican China, 1912–1949*, pt 1 (Cambridge, 1983), and A. Feuerwerker (eds.), *The Cambridge History of China:* vol. XIII, *Republican China, 1912–1949*, pt 2 (Cambridge, 1986); Great Britain: Admiralty, Naval Intelligence Division, *China Proper:* vol. II: *Modern History and Administration* (London, 1945); A. Isaac, *The Tragedy of the Chinese Revolution* (Stanford, 1938, 1951); F. C. Jones, *Shanghai and Tientsin: With Special Reference to Foreign Interests* (London, 1940); T. Kataoka, *Resistance and Revolution in China: The Communists and the Second United Front* (Berkeley, 1974); G. N. Kates, *The Years that were Fat: Peking, 1933–40* (New York, 1952); D. Lary, *Warlord Soldiers: Chinese Common Soldiers, 1911–1937* (Cambridge, 1985); 'G. E. Miller' [M. Fresco], *Shanghai:*

Paradise of Adventurers (New York, 1937); R. Pelissier, *Awakening of China, 1783–1949* (New York, 1967); M. N. Roy, *Revolution in China* (Calcutta, 1951); F. Schurmann and O. Schell (eds.), *Republican China: Nationalism, War and the Rise of Communism, 1911–1949* (New York, 1967); B. Schwarz, *Chinese Communism and the Rise of Mao* (Cambridge, Mass., 1952); E. Snow, *Red Star over China* (London, 1937); L. W. Snow, *Edgar Snow's China: A Personal Account of the Chinese Revolution, compiled from the Writings of Edgar Snow* (New York, 1981); A. N. Young, *China and the Helping Hand, 1937–1945* (Cambridge, Mass., 1963), *China's Wartime Finance and Inflation, 1937–1945* (Cambridge, Mass., 1965).

Japanese Internal Revolutions and Foreign Policy

G. C. Allen, *Japanese Industry: Its Recent Development and Present Condition* (New York, 1940); M. A. Barnhart, *Japan Prepares for Total War: The Search for Economic Security, 1919–1941* (Ithaca, 1987); W. G. Beasley, *Modern Japan: Aspects of History, Literature and Society* (London, 1975); G. M. Berger, *Parties out of Power in Japan, 1931–1941* (Princeton, 1977); H. Byas, *Government by Assassination* (New York, 1943); E. E. N. Causton, *Militarism and Foreign Policy in Japan* (London, 1936); K. W. Colegrove, *Militarism in Japan* (Boston, 1936); L. Connors, *The Emperor's Adviser: Saionji Kinmochi and Pre-war Japanese Politics* (London, 1987); J. B. Crowley, *Japan's Quest for Autonomy: National Security and Foreign Policy, 1930–1938* (Princeton, 1966); M. S. Farley, *The Problem of Japanese Trade Expansion in the Post-war Situation* (New York, 1940); W. Fleisher, *Volcanic Isle* (London, 1942); M. Hane, *Emperor Hirohito and his Chief Aide-de-Camp: The Honjo Diary, 1933–36* (Tokyo, 1982); K. Harada, *Saionji-Harada Memoirs* (Tokyo, 1945–6); J. A. Harrison, *Japan's Northern Frontier: A Preliminary Study in Colonization and Expansion with Special Reference to the Relation of Japan and Russia* (Gainsville, 1953); K. Haushofer, *Japan bout sein Rich* (Berlin, 1941); J. Herbert, *Shinto: The Fountainhead of Japan* (London, 1967); A. E. Hindmarsh, *The Basis of Japanese Foreign Policy* (Cambridge, Mass., 1930); S.-H. Hsu, *Japan and the Third Powers*, 4 vols. (Shanghai, 1941); T. Kase, *Journey to the Missouri* (New Haven, 1950); T. Kawai, *The Goal of Japanese Expansion* (London, 1938); K. K. Kawakami, *Japan in China: Her Motives and Aims* (London, 1938); Y. S. Kuno, *Japanese Expansion in the Asiatic Continent* (Berkeley, 1937); L. N. Kutakov, *Japanese Foreign Policy on the Eve of the Pacific War: A Soviet View* (Tallahassee, 1972); J. C. Lebra, *Japan's Greater East Asia Co-Prosperity Sphere in World War II: Selected Readings and Documents* (Kuala Lumpur, 1975); D. J. Lu, *From the Marco Polo Bridge to Pearl Harbor: Japan's Entry into World War II* (Washington, DC, 1961); J. M. Maki, *Government and Politics in Japan: The Road to Democracy* (London, 1962), *Japanese Militarism: Its Cause and Cure* (New York, 1945); M. Maruyama, *Thought and Behaviour in Modern Japanese Politics* (London, 1963); Y. C. Maxon, *Control of Japanese Foreign*

Policy: A Study in Civil-Military Rivalry, 1930–1945 (Berkeley, 1957); M. J. Mayo (ed.), *The Emergence of Imperial Japan: Self Defence or Calculated Aggression?* (New York, 1970); R. H. Mitchell, *Censorship in Imperial Japan* (Princeton, 1983), *Thought Control in Pre-war Japan* (Ithaca, 1976); J. W. Morley, *Dilemmas of Growth in Pre-war Japan* (Princeton, 1971), *The Fateful Choice: Japan's Advance into Southeast Asia, 1939–1941* (New York, 1980); W. F. Morton, *Tanaka Giichi and Japan's China Policy* (New York, 1980); T. Nakano, *The Ordinance Power of the Japanese Emperor* (Baltimore, 1923); I. H. Nish, *The Story of Japan* (London, 1968); I. Nitobe, *Bushido: The Soul of Japan* (Tokyo, 1969); R. A. Scalapino, *Democracy and the Party Movement in Pre-war Japan: The Failure of the First Attempt* (Berkeley, 1953); B.-A. Shillony, *Revolt in Japan: The Young Officers and the February 26, 1936, Incident* (Princeton, 1973); G. R. Storry, *The Double Patriots: A Study of Japanese Nationalism* (London, 1957), *A History of Modern Japan* (London, 1960); M. Shigemitsu, *Japan and her Destiny* (London, 1958); Takeuchi, *War and Diplomacy in the Japanese Empire* (Chicago, 1935); C. Thorne, *Allies of a Kind: the United States, Britain and the War against Japan, 1914–1945* (London, 1978); H. H. Tiltman, *The Far East Comes Nearer* (London, 1936); D. A. Titus, *Balance and Politics in Pre-war Japan* (New York, 1974); S. Togo, *The Cause of Japan* (New York, 1956); M. Tokayer and M. Swartz, *The Fugu Plan: The Untold Story of the Japanese and the Jews during World War II* (London, 1979); O. D. Tolischus, *Tokyo Record* (London, 1943); G. O. Totten, *The Social Democratic Movement in Pre-war Japan* (New Haven, 1966); T. Uyeda, *The Recent Development of Japanese Foreign Trade with Special Reference to Restriction Policies of Other Countries and Attempts at Trade Agreements* (Tokyo, 1936); W. W. Willoughby, *Japan's Case Examined* (Baltimore, 1940); A. M. Young, *Imperial Japan, 1926–1938* (New York, 1938).

The China Incident, 1937–45

H. Abend, *Chaos in Asia* (London, 1940); C. Boyd, *The Extraordinary Envoy: General Hiroshi Oshima and Diplomacy in the Third Reich, 1934–1939* (Washington, DC, 1980); J. H. Boyle, *China and Japan at War, 1937–1945: The Politics of Collaboration* (Stanford, 1972); G. E. Bunker, *The Peace Conspiracy: Wang Ching-wei and the China War, 1937–1941* (Cambridge, Mass., 1972); H.-S. Ch'i, *Nationalist China at War: Military Defeats and Political Collapse, 1937–1945* (Ann Arbor, 1982); China: Delegation to the League of Nations, *Japanese Aggression and World Opinion, July 7 to October 7, 1937* (Geneva, 1938); China: Delegation to the Nine-Power Conference, *Japanese Aggression and the Nine-Power Conference of Brussels*, 2 pts (Brussels, 1937); China Information Committee, *Organized Pillaging by Japanese* (Hankow, 1938), *Sino-Japanese Hostilities in North China: A Survey of the First Five Months of Armed Conflict North of the Yellow River* (Hankow, 1937); A. D. Coox, *Year of the Tiger* (Tokyo, 1964); D. S. Detwiler and C. B. Burdick, *War in Asia and the*

Pacific, 1937–1939: Japanese and Chinese Studies and Documents, 15 vols. (New York, 1980); E. M. Gunn, *Unwelcome Muse: Chinese Literature in Shanghai and Peking, 1937–1945* (New York, 1980); L.-h. Hsu *et al.*, *History of the Sino-Japanese War, 1937–1945* (Taipei, 1971); F. C. Jones, *Japan's New Order in East Asia: Its Rise and Fall, 1937–1945* (London, 1954), *Shanghai and Tientsin, with Special Reference to Foreign Interests* (London, 1940); L. Li, *The Japanese Army in North China, 1937–1941* (London, 1975); M. Lindsay, *The Unknown War: North China, 1937–1945* (London, 1975); K. Miki and K. Hosokawa, *Introductory Studies on the Sino-Japanese Conflict* (Tokyo, 1941); J. W. Morley ed., *The China Quagmire: Japan's Expansion on the Asian Continent, 1933–1941* (New York, 1983); K. Nichi, *Introductory Studies on the Sino-Japanese Conflict* (Tokyo, 1941); R. Payne, *Chungking Diary* (London, 1945); H. S. Quigley, *Far Eastern War, 1937–1941* (Boston, 1942); H. J. Timperley, *Japanese Terror in China* (Freeport, New York, 1938); F. Utley, *Japan's Gamble in China* (London, 1938); J. G. Utley, *Going to War with Japan, 1937–1941* (Knoxville, 1985); D. Wilson, *When Tigers Fight: The Story of the Sino-Japanese War, 1937–1945* (Viking, 1982).

British Commonwealth Interests and Policies in East Asia

H. T. V. Baker, *The New Zealand People at War* (Wellington, 1965); J. Bertram, *The Shadow of a War* (London, 1947); B. Bond (ed.), *Chief of Staff: The Diaries of Lt.-General Sir Henry Pownall*, 2 vols. (London, 1972, 1974); M. H. Brice, *The Royal Navy and the Sino-Japanese Incident, 1937–41* (London, 1973); H. Burton and B. R. Pearn, *The Far East, 1942–46* (London, 1955); R. A. Butler, *The Art of the Possible* (London, 1971); S. J. Butlin, *The War Economy, 1939–1942* (Canberra, 1955); Lord Casey, *Personal Experience, 1939–1946* (London, 1962); Lord Chatfield, *It Might Happen Again* (London, 1947); W. S. Churchill, *The Second World War*, 6 vols. (London, 1948–54); C. Clifford, *Retreat from China: British Policy in the Far East, 1937–1941* (London, 1967); C. Cooke, *The Life of Richard Stafford Cripps* (London, 1957); Sir R. L. Craigie, *Behind the Japanese Mask* (London, 1946); Lord Cunningham, *A Sailor's Odyssey* (London, 1951); H. Dalton, *Memoirs, 1931–1945: The Fateful Years* (London, 1957); A. L. P. Dennis, *The Anglo-Japanese Alliance* (Berkeley, 1923); D. Dilks (ed.), *The Diaries of Sir Alexander Cadogan, 1938–1945* (London, 1971); L. G. Elliott, *A Role of Honour: The Story of the Indian Army* (London, 1965); S. L. Endicott, *Diplomacy and Enterprise: British China Policy, 1933–1937* (Manchester, 1975); E. Estorick, *Stafford Cripps: A Biography* (London, 1949); H. V. Evatt, *Australia in World Affairs* (Sydney, 1946); K. Feiling, *The Life of Neville Chamberlain* (London, 1977); I. S. Friedman, *British Relations with China, 1931–1939* (New York, 1940); H. G. Gelber, *Problems of Australian Defence* (London, 1970); N. H. Gibbs *et al.*, *Grand Strategy*, 6 vols. (London, 1957–76); M. Gilbert, *The Roots of Appeasement* (London, 1966); A. Gilchrist, *Bangkok Top Secret* (London, 1970); P. Gore-Booth, *With Great Truth and Respect*

(London, 1974); E. M. Gull, *British Economic Interests in the Far East* (London, 1943); P. Haggie, *Britannia at Bay: The Defence of the British Empire against Japan, 1931–1941* (Oxford, 1981); J. Harvey (ed.), *The Diplomatic Diaries of Oliver Harvey, 1937–1940* (London, 1970); F. H. Hinsley et al., *British Intelligence in the Second World War: Its Influence on Strategy and Operations*, 3 vols. (London, 1981–8); M. Howard, *The Continental Commitment* (London, 1972); Lord Ismay, *Memoirs* (London, 1960); M. D. Kennedy, *The Estrangement of Great Britain and Japan, 1917–1935* (Manchester, 1969); Sir H. Knatchbull-Hugessen, *Diplomat in Peace and War* (London, 1949); R. and N. Lapwood, *Through the Chinese Revolution* (London, 1954); B. A. Lee, *Britain and the Sino-Japanese War, 1937–1939* (London, 1973); R. Lewin, *The Other Ultra* (London, 1982); W. R. Louis, *British Strategy in the Far East, 1919–1939* (Oxford, 1971); P. Lowe, *Great Britain and the Origins of the Pacific War: A Study of British Policy in East Asia, 1937–1941* (Oxford, 1977); H. Macmillan, *The Blast of War, 1939–1945* (London, 1967), *Winds of Change, 1914–1939* (London, 1966); N. B. Mansergh, *Documents and Speeches on British Commonwealth Affairs, 1931–1952* (London, 1953), *Survey of British Commonwealth Affairs: Problems of External Policy, 1931–1939* (London, 1952), *Survey of British Commonwealth Affairs: Problems of Wartime Co-operation and Postwar Change, 1931–1952* (London, 1958); A. J. Marder, *Old Friends, New Enemies: The Royal Navy and the Imperial Japanese Navy: Strategic Illusions, 1936–1941* (Oxford, 1981); W. N. Medlicott, *The Economic Blockade*, 2 vols. (London, 1952, 1959); R. G. Menzies, *Afternoon Light* (London, 1967); P. Moon (ed.), *Wavell: The Viceroy's Journal* (London, 1973); I. Morrison, *Malayan Postscript* (London, 1942); I. H. Nish, *The Anglo-Japanese Alliance: The Diplomacy of the Two Island Empires, 1894–1907* (London, 1966), *Alliance in Decline* (London, 1972), (ed.) *Anglo-Japanese Alienation, 1919–1952: Papers of the Anglo-Japanese Conference on the History of the Second World War* (Cambridge, 1982); R. Ovendale, '*Appeasement' and the English-Speaking World* (Cardiff, 1975); G. C. Peden, *British Rearmament and the Treasury, 1932–1939* (Edinburgh, 1979); F. S. G. Piggott, *Broken Thread* (Aldershot, 1950); Sir J. Pratt, *War and Politics in China* (London, 1943); L. R. Pratt, *East of Malta, West of Suez: Britain's Mediterranean Crisis, 1936–1939* (Cambridge, 1975); R. J. Pritchard, *Far Eastern Influences upon British Strategy towards the Great Powers, 1937–1939* (New York, 1987); R. Roskill, *Hankey: Man of Secrets*, vol. III, *1931–1963* (London, 1974), *Naval Policy between the Wars*, 2 vols. (London, 1968, 1976); B. E. V. Sabine, *British Budgets in Peace and War, 1932–1945* (London, 1970); K. Sansom, *Sir George Sansom and Japan: A Memoir* (Tallahassee, 1972); A. Shai, *Origins of the War in the East: Britain, China and Japan, 1937–39* (London, 1976); R. P. Shay, *British Rearmament in the Thirties: Politics and Profits* (Princeton, 1977); Lord Strang, *At Home and Abroad* (London, 1956); C. Thorne, *Allies of a Kind: The United States, Britain and the War against Japan, 1914–1945* (London, 1978); A. Trotter, *Britain and East Asia, 1933–1937* (Cambridge, 1977); A. Watt, *Australian Diplomat* (Sydney, 1972), *The Evolution of Australian Foreign Policy* (Cambridge, 1967); D. C. Watt, *Personalities and Policies: Studies in the Formulation of British Policy in the Twentieth Century* (London, 1965), *Too Serious a Business* (London, 1975); G. Wint, *The British in Asia* (New York, 1954); A. Wolfers, *Britain and France between the Two Wars* (New York, 1966); S. Woodburn Kerby *et al.*, *The War Against Japan*, 5 vols. (London, 1957–69); Sir L. Woodward, *British Foreign Policy in the Second World War* (London, 1970–76).

German Interests and Policies in East Asia

K. Bloch, *German Interests and Policies in the Far East* (New York, 1940); H. von Dirksen, *Moscow, Tokyo, London* (London, 1951); J. P. Fox, *Germany and the Far Eastern Crisis, 1931–1938: A Study in Diplomacy and Ideology* (Oxford, 1982); F. W. Iklé, *German-Japanese Relations, 1936–1940* (New York, 1956); V. Issraeljan and L. Kutakov, *Diplomacy of Aggression: Berlin, Rome, Tokyo Axis: Its Rise and Fall* (Moscow, 1970); H.-h. Liang, *The Sino-German Connection: Alexander von Falkenhausen between China and Germany, 1900–1941* (Assen and Amsterdam, 1978); B. Martin, *Die Deutsche Beraterschaft in China, 1927–1938: Militär-Wirtschaft-Aussenpolitik* (Düsseldorf, 1981); J. M. M. Meskill, *Hitler and Japan: The Hollow Alliance* (New York, 1966); J. W. Morley *et al.*, *Deterrent Diplomacy: Japan, Germany, and the U.S.S.R., 1935–1940* (New York, 1976); E. L. Presseisen, *Germany and Japan: A Study in Totalitarian Democracy, 1933–1941* (The Hague, 1958); T. Sommer, *Deutschland und Japan zwischen den Machten, 1935–1940: von Anti-Kominternpakt zum Dreimächtepakt* (Tübingen, 1962).

French and Italian Interests and Policies in East Asia

J. Decoux, *A la barre de l'Indochine* (Paris, 1949); A. Hytier, *Two Years of French Foreign Policy: Vichy, 1940–1942* (Geneva, 1958); J. Legrand, *L'Indochine à l'heure japonaise* (Cannes, 1963); R. Levy *et al.*, *French Interests and Policies in the Far East* (New York, 1941); Marchand and Rollet, *L'Indochine en guerre* (Paris, 1954); Mordant, *Au service de la France en Indochine* (Saigon, 1950); G. Sabatier, *Le destin de l'Indochine* (Paris, 1952); F. Tamagna, *Italy's Interests and Policies in the Far East* (New York, 1941).

American Interests and Policies in East Asia

G. Alperovitz, *Atomic Diplomacy: Hiroshima and Potsdam* (London, 1966); C. A. Beard, *President Roosevelt and the Coming of the War, 1941: A Study of Appearances and Realities* (New Haven, 1945); T. A. Bisson, *American Policy in the Far East, 1931–1941* (New York, 1941); J. M. Blum, *From the Morgenthau Diaries*, 2 vols. (Boston, 1958, 1965); D. Borg, *Historians and American Far Eastern Policy* (New York, 1966), *The United States and the Far Eastern Crisis of 1933–1938: From the Manchurian Incident through the Initial Stage of the Undeclared*

Sino-Japanese War (Cambridge, Mass., 1964), and S. Okamoto (eds.), *Pearl Harbor as History: Japanese-American Relations* (New York, 1973); R. J. C. Butow, *Tōjō and the Coming of the War* (Stanford, 1961), *The John Doe Associates: Backdoor Diplomacy for Peace, 1941* (Stanford, 1974); J. F. Byrnes, *Speaking Frankly* (London, 1948); T. Campbell and G. Herring (eds.), *The Diaries of Edward R. Stettinius, Jr., 1943–1946* (New York, 1975); C. L. Chennault, *Way of a Fighter* (New York, 1949); J. W. Christopher, *Conflict in the Far East: American Diplomacy of China, 1928–33* (Leiden, 1950); S. Conn and B. Fairchild, *The Framework of Hemisphere Defence* (Washington, DC, 1960); R. Dallek, *Franklin Roosevelt and American Foreign Policy, 1932–1945* (London, 1979); R. A. Divine, *Roosevelt and World War II* (Baltimore, 1969); E. R. Drachman, *United States Policy toward Vietnam, 1940–1945* (Rutherford, New York, 1970); J. K. Emmerson, *The Japanese Thread: A Life in the US Foreign Service* (New York, 1978); M. S. Farley, *American Far Eastern Policy and the Sino-Japanese War* (New York, 1938); H. Feis, *The China Tangle: The American Effort in China from Pearl Harbor to the Marshall Mission* (Princeton, 1953), *The Road to Pearl Harbor: The Coming of the War between the United States and Japan* (Princeton, 1950); R. H. Fifield, *Southeast Asia in United States Policy* (New York, 1963); J. Forrestal, *The Forrestal Diaries* (New York, 1951); J. C. Grew, *Report from Tokyo: A Message to the American People* (New York, 1942), *Ten Years in Japan* (New York, 1944), *Turbulent Era: A Diplomatic Record of Forty Years, 1904–1945*, 2 vols. (Boston, 1952); A. W. Griswold, *The Far Eastern Policy of the United States* (New York, 1938); J. H. Herzog, *Closing the Open Door: American-Japanese Diplomatic Negotiations, 1936–1941* (Annapolis, 1973); S. K. Hornbeck, *The United States in the Far East* (Boston, 1942); C. Hull, *Memoirs*, 2 vols. (London, 1948); M. H. Hunt, *The Making of a Special Relationship: The United States and China to 1914* (New York, 1983); H. L. Ickes, *The Secret War Diary of Harold L. Ickes*, vol. III (London, 1955); A. Iriye, *Across the Pacific: An Inner History of American-East Asian Relations* (New York, 1967), *Mutual Images: Essays in American-Japanese Relations* (Cambridge, Mass., 1975), *Power and Culture* (Cambridge, Mass., 1981); E. J. King and W. Whitehill, *Fleet Admiral King* (London, 1953); R. Y. Koen, *The China Lobby in American Politics* (New York, 1974); W. Langer and S. E. Gleason, *The Challenge to Isolation, 1937–1940* (New York, 1952), *The Undeclared War, 1940–1941* (New York, 1953); D. W. Leahy, *I Was There: A Personal Story of the Chief of Staff to Presidents Roosevelt and Truman* (New York, 1950); J. Leutze (ed.), *The London Observer: The Journal of General Raymond E. Lee* (London, 1972); D. J. Lu, *From the Marco Polo Bridge to Pearl Harbor: Japan's Entry into World War II* (Washington, DC, 1961); D. MacArthur, *Reminiscences* (New York, 1964); M. Matloff, *Strategic Planning for Coalition Warfare, 1943–1944* (Washington, DC, 1959), and E. Snell, *Strategic Planning for Coalition Warfare, 1941–1942* (Washington, DC, 1953); H. Morgenthau, Jr, *Diary: China*, 2 vols. (Washington, DC, 1965); S. E. Morison, *American Contributions to the Strategy of World War Two* (London, 1958);

J. W. Morley (ed.), *The Final Confrontation: Japan's Negotiations with the United States, 1941* (New York, forthcoming, 1989); L. Morton, *Command Decisions: United States Army in World War Two* (Washington, DC, 1962), *Strategy and Command: The First Two Years* (Washington, DC, 1962); Y. Nagai and A. Iriye (eds.), *The Origins of the Cold War in Asia* (Tokyo, 1977); A. Offner, *American Appeasement* (Cambridge, Mass., 1969); R. Ovendale, *'Appeasement' and the English-Speaking World* (Cardiff, 1975); H. Perry, *The Panay Affair: Prelude to Pearl Harbor*, 8 vols. (New York, 1969); F. C. Pogue, *George C. Marshall*, 3 vols. (New York, 1964–73); W. D. Puleston, *The Armed Forces of the Pacific: A Comparison of the Military and Naval Power of the United States and Japan* (New Haven, 1941); A. Saxton, *The Indispensable Enemy: Labor and the Anti-Chinese Movement in California* (Berkeley, 1971); P. W. Schroeder, *The Axis Alliance and Japanese-American Relations, 1941* (Ithaca, 1958); J. S. Service, *The Amerasia Papers* (Berkeley, 1971); R. E. Sherwood, *Roosevelt and Hopkins: An Intimate History* (New York, 1948); K. E. Shewmaker, *Americans and Chinese Communists, 1927–1945* (Ithaca, 1971); D. M. Shoup, *The Marines in China, 1927–1928: A Contemporaneous Journal* (Hamden, Conn., 1987); G. Smith, *American Diplomacy during the Second World War* (New York, 1965); R. H. Spector, *Eagle against the Sun: The American War with Japan* (New York, 1985); H. L. Stimson, *Far Eastern Crisis: Recollections and Observations* (New York, 1936), and M. Bundy, *On Active Service in Peace and War* (New York, 1948); T. Tang, *America's Failure in China, 1941–50* (Chicago, 1962); J. C. Thomson et al., *Sentimental Imperialists: The American Experience in East Asia* (New York, 1981); C. Thorne, *Allies of a Kind: The United States, Britain and the War against Japan, 1941–1945* (London, 1978); H. S. Truman, *Memoirs:* vol. 1, *Year of Decisions, 1945* (London, 1955); B. Tuchman, *Sand Against the Wind: Stilwell and the American Experience in China, 1911–45* (New York, 1970); T. V. Tuleja, *Statesmen and Admirals: Quest for a Far Eastern Naval Policy* (New York, 1963); United States: Department of State, *Foreign Relations of the United States: The Far East* [annual vols.] (Washington, DC), *Foreign Relations of the United States: Japan, 1931–1941*, 2 vols. (Washington, DC, 1943); P. Varg, *The Making of a Myth: The United States and China, 1897–1912* (East Lansing, 1968); M. S. Watson, *Chief of Staff: Prewar Plans and Preparations* (Washington, DC, 1950); S. Welles, *A Time for Decision* (London, 1944); R. D. Weston, *Racism in U.S. Imperialism* (Columbia, South Carolina, 1972); T. H. White (ed.), *The Stilwell Papers* (New York, 1948), and A. Jacoby, *Thunder out of China* (London, 1947); C. A. Willoughby and J. Chamberlain, *MacArthur, 1941–51* (New York, 1954); J. E. Wiltz, *From Isolation to War, 1931–1941* (London, 1969); R. Wohlstetter, *Pearl Harbor: Warning and Decision* (Stanford, 1962); E. M. Zacharias, *Secret Missions: The Story of an Intelligence Officer* (New York, 1946).

Soviet Interests and Policies in East Asia

M. Beloff, *Soviet Policy in the Far East*, 2 vols. (London, 1953); O. Braun, *A Comintern Agent in China, 1932–1939* (Stanford, 1982); O. E. Clubb, *China and Russia: The Great Game* (New York, 1971); A. D. Coox, *The Anatomy of a Small War: The Soviet-Japanese Struggle for Changkufeng/Khasan* (Westport, Conn., 1977), *Nomonhan: Japan against Russia, 1939*, 2 vols. (Stanford, 1985); J. Degras, *Soviet Documents on Foreign Policy*, 3 vols. (London, 1953); H. Feis, *Churchill, Roosevelt, Stalin* (Princeton, 1957); G. A. Lenson, *The Strange Neutrality: Soviet-Japanese Relations during the Second World War, 1941–1945* (Tallahassee, 1972); H. Lupke, *Japans Russlandpolitik von 1939 bis 1941* (Frankfurt, 1962); H. L. Moore, *Soviet Far Eastern Policy, 1931–1945* (Princeton, 1945); J. W. Morley, *The Japanese Thrust into Siberia, 1918* (New York, 1957), (ed.) *Deterrent Diplomacy: Japan, Germany, and the U.S.S.R., 1935–1940* (New York, 1976); G. D. R. Phillips, *Russia, Japan and Mongolia* (London, 1942); R. Swearington, *The Soviet Union and Japan* (Stanford, 1978); P. S. Tang, *Russia and Soviet Policy in Manchuria and Outer Mongolia, 1911–1931* (Durham, North Carolina, 1959).

Indian Nationalism

J. G. Elliott, *A Roll of Honour: The Story of the Indian Army, 1939–1945* (London, 1965); N. Mansergh *et al.*, *The Transfer of Power, 1942–1947*, 12 vols. (London, 1970–83); P. Morn, *Gandhi and Modern India* (London, 1968); B. R. Nanda, *Mahatma Gandhi* (London, 1958); B. N. Pandey, *The Break-Up of British India* (London, 1969); B. R. Tomlinson, *The Political Economy of the Raj, 1914–1947: The Economics of Decolonization in India* (London, 1979).

PART II: OCEAN CLASH

The Outbreak of the Pacific War

L. Allen, *Singapore, 1941–1942* (London, 1977); C. A. Beard, *President Roosevelt and the Coming of the War* (New Haven, 1948); T. Carew, *The Fall of Hong Kong* (London, 1960); S. Chapman, *The Jungle is Neutral* (London, 1949); D. Crisp, *Why We Lost Singapore* (Bombay, 1945); L. Falk, *Seventy Days to Singapore: The Malayan Campaign, 1941–1942* (London, 1975); S. Falk, *The March of Death* (New York, 1962); R. Grenfell, *Main Fleet to Singapore* (London, 1951); P. Herde, *Pearl Harbor, 7. Dezember 1941: Der Ausbruch des Krieges zwischen Japan und den Vereinigten Staaten und die Ausweitung des Europäischen Krieges zum Zweiten Weltkrieg* (Darmstadt, 1980); R. Hough, *The Hunting of Force Z* (London, 1963); N. Ike, *Japan's Decision for War: Records of the 1941 Policy Conferences* (Stanford, 1967); J. Leasor, *Singapore: The Battle that Changed the World* (London, 1968); W. Lord, *Day of Infamy* (London, 1957); G. Morgenstern, *Pearl Harbor: The Story of the Secret War*

(New York, 1947); I. Morrison, *Malayan Postscript* (London, 1942); L. Morton, *The Fall of the Philippines* (Washington, DC, 1952); A. E. Percival, *The War in Malaya* (London, 1949); G. W. Prange, *At Dawn We Slept* (New York, 1981); B. Rauch, *Roosevelt from Munich to Pearl Harbor* (New York, 1950); C. P. Romulo, *I Saw the Fall of the Philippines* (London, 1943); D. Russell-Roberts, *Spotlight on Singapore* (London, 1965); I. Simson, *Too Little, Too Late* (London, 1970); Sir J. Smith, *Percival and the Tragedy of Singapore* (London, 1971); J. Toland, *Infamy: Pearl Harbor and its Aftermath* (London, 1982); H. L. Trefousse, *What Happened at Pearl Harbor* (New York, 1958); M. Tsuji, *Singapore: The Japanese Version* (London, 1962); United States Congress: Joint Committee on the Investigation of the Pearl Harbor Attack, *Hearings* and *Report* (Washington, DC, 1946); H. Wallin, *Pearl Harbor: Why, How: Fleet Salvage and Final Appraisal* (Washington, DC, 1968); R. Wohlstetter, *Pearl Harbor: Warning and Decision* (New York, 1963); S. Woodburn Kirby, *Singapore: The Chain of Disaster* (London, 1971).

PARTS III–IV: THE GREATER EAST ASIA AND PACIFIC WAR

War Crimes and the Misconduct of War

J. and C. Blair, *Return from the River Kwai* (London, 1979); T. Bowden, *Changi Photographer: George Aspinall's Record of Captivity* (Sydney, 1984); R. Braddon, *The Naked Island* (London, 1952); Committee for the Compilation of Materials on Damage Caused by the Atomic Bombs in Hiroshima and Nagasaki, *Hiroshima and Nagasaki: The Physical, Medical and Social Effects of the Atomic Bombings* (London, 1981); H. Feis, *The Atom Bomb and the End of the War in the Pacific* (Princeton, 1961); J. Fletcher-Cooke, *The Emperor's Guest, 1942–45* (London, 1971); A. Girdner and A. Loftis, *The Great Betrayal: The Evacuation of the Japanese-Americans during World War II* (Toronto, 1969); C. V. Glines, *Doolittle's Tokyo Raiders* (Princeton, 1964); E. Gordon, *Miracle on the River Kwai* (London, 1963); L. Groves, *Now It Can Be Told* (New York, 1962); M. Hachiya, *Hiroshima Diary* (Chapel Hill, 1955); R. Hammond, *The Flame of Freedom* (London, 1988); Lord Hankey, *Politics, Trials and Errors* (Oxford, 1950); J. Hersey, *Hiroshima* (New York, 1946); B. Jeffrey, *White Coolies* (Sydney, 1954); J. Lane, *Summer Will Come Again: The Story of Australian POWS' Fight for Survival in Japan* (Fremantle, 1987); T. Lawson, *Thirty Seconds over Tokyo* (London, 1943); H. L. Leffelaar, *Through a Harsh Dawn: A Boy Grows Up in a Japanese Prison Camp* (Barre, Mass., 1963); C. Lemay, *Mission with Lemay* (Garden City, New York, 1966); C. Lucas, *Prisoners of Santo Tomas* (London, 1975); C. McCormac, *You'll Die in Singapore* (London, 1956); J. Miller, *Guadalcanal: The First Offensive* (Washington, DC, 1949); R. H. Minear, *Victors' Justice: The Tokyo War Crimes Trial* (Princeton, 1971); P. R. Piccigallo, *The Japanese on Trial: Allied War Crimes Operations in the East, 1945–1951* (Austin, 1979); Laurens van der Post, *The Night of the New Moon* (London, 1970); R. Prising, *Manila, Goodbye* (London, 1976); R. J.

Pritchard and S. M. Zaide (eds.), *The Tokyo War Crimes Trial: Index and Guide*, 5 vols. (New York, 1981–7), *The Tokyo War Crimes Trial: The Complete Proceedings of the International Military Tribunal for the Far East*, 22 vols. (New York, 1981); L. Rawlings and B. Duncan, *And the Dawn Came Up Like Thunder* (n.p., 1972); A. F. Reel, *The Trial of Yamashita* (Chicago, 1949); R. D. Rivett, *Behind Bamboo: An Inside Story of the Japanese Prison Camps* (Sydney, 1947); Lord Russell of Liverpool, *The Knights of Bushido* (London, 1958); C. Sleeman, *Trial of Gozawa Sadaiichi and Nine Others* (London, 1948), and S. C. Silkin, *The 'Double Tenth' Trial* (London, 1951); A. P. Staufer, *The Quartermaster Corps: Operations in the War against Japan* (Washington, DC, 1956); D. S. Thomas and R. S. Nishimoto, *The Spoilage: Japanese-American Evacuation and Resettlement during World War II* (Berkeley, 1946); J. Thomas, *Exile Within: The Schooling of Japanese Americans, 1942–1945* (Cambridge, Mass., 1987); Y. Uchida, *Desert Exile: The Uprooting of a Japanese American Family* (Seattle, 1982); USSR, *Materials on the Trial of Former Servicemen of the Japanese Army charged with Manufacturing and Employing Bacteriological Weapons* (Moscow, 1950); F. J. P. Veale, *Advance to Barbarism: The Development of Total Warfare from Sarajevo to Hiroshima* (New York, 1959); L. Warner and J. Sandilands, *Women Beyond the Wire* (London, 1982); P. Williams and D. Wallace, *Unit 731: The Japanese Army's Secret of Secrets* (London, 1989).

The War in the Pacific

H. Agawa, *The Reluctant Admiral: Yamamoto and the Imperial Navy* (Tokyo, 1979); R. Appleman *et al.*, *Okinawa: The Last Battle* (Washington, DC, 1948); H. H. Arnold, *Global Mission* (New York, 1949); D. E. Barbey, *MacArthur's Amphibious Navy* (Annapolis, 1969); J. H. and W. M. Belote, *Titans of the Seas: The Development and Operations of American Carrier Task Forces during World War II* (New York, 1975), *Typhoon of Steel: The Battle for Okinawa* (New York, 1969); C. Blair, *Silent Victory: The US Submarine War against Japan* (Philadelphia, 1975); T. E. Buell, *The Quiet Warrior: A Biography of Admiral Raymond Spruance* (Boston, 1974), *Master of Seapower: A Biography of Admiral Ernest J. King* (Boston, 1980); H. Cannon, *Leyte: The Return to the Philippines* (Washington, DC, 1954); R. W. Coakley and R. M. Leighton, *Global Logistics and Strategy*, 2 vols. (Washington, DC, 1955); R. H. Connery, *The Navy and the Industrial Mobilization in World War II* (Princeton, 1951); P. Crowl, *Campaign in the Marianas* (Washington, DC, 1960), and E. G. Lowe, *Seizure of the Gilberts and Marshalls* (Washington, DC, 1955); M. Dexter, *The New Guinea Offensives* (Canberra, 1961); P. S. Dull, *A Battle History of the Imperial Japanese Navy, 1941–1945* (Annapolis, 1978); G. C. Dyer, *The Amphibians Came to Conquer: The Story of Admiral Richmond Kelly Turner*, 2 vols. (Washington, DC, 1969); S. Falk, *Decision at Leyte* (New York, 1966); M. Fuchida and M. Okumiya, *Midway: The Battle that Doomed Japan* (Annapolis, 1955);

K. R. Greenfield (ed.), *Command Decisions* (Washington, DC, 1960); B. Greenhill *et al.*, *The Second World War in the Pacific: Plans and Reality* (London, 1974); S. Griffith, *The Battle for Guadalcanal* (New York, 1963); W. F. Halsey and J. Bryan, *Admiral Halsey's Story* (New York, 1947); M. Hashimoto, *Sunk: The Story of the Japanese Submarine Fleet* (New York, 1954); P. Hasluck, *The Government and the People, 1939–1941* (Canberra, 1956); S. Hayashi, with A. D. Coox, *Kōgun: The Japanese Army in the Pacific War* (Quantico, 1959); G. P. Hayes, *The Joint Chiefs of Staff and the War against Japan* (Annapolis, 1982); R. D. Heinl, *The Defense of Wake* (Washington, DC, 1947); W. Hoffman, *The Seizure of Tinian* (Washington, DC, 1950); C. W. Hoffmann, *Saipan: The Beginning of the End* (Washington, DC, 1950); W. J. Holmes, *Double-Edged Secrets* (Annapolis, 1979); A. Iriye, *Power and Culture: The Japanese-American War, 1941–1945* (Cambridge, Mass., 1981); J. A. Isely and P. A. Crowl, *The US Marines and Amphibious War* (Princeton, 1951); M. Ito, *The End of the Imperial Japanese Navy* (London, 1962); D. C. James, *The Years of MacArthur*, 2 vols. (New York, 1972, 1975); E. J. King and W. Whitehill, *Fleet Admiral King: A Naval Record* (New York, 1952); R. Leckie, *Strong Men Armed: The US Marines Against Japan* (New York, 1962); D. Lockwood, *Australia's Pearl Harbour: Darwin, 1942* (Sydney, 1967); W. Lord, *Incredible Victory* (London, 1968); J. B. Lundstrom, *The First South Pacific Campaign: Pacific Fleet Strategy, December 1941–June 1942* (Annapolis, 1976); W. Manchester, *American Caesar: Douglas MacArthur, 1880–1964* (Boston, 1978); S. Milner, *The War in the Pacific: Victory in Papua* (Washington, DC, 1957); S. E. Morison, [Official] *History of United States Naval Operations in World War II*, 15 vols. (Boston, 1947–62); R. Newcomb, *Iwojima* (New York, 1965); M. Nichols and H. Shaw, *Okinawa: Victory in the Pacific* (Washington, DC, 1948); G. Odgers, *The Air War against Japan, 1943–1945* (Canberra, 1957); M. Okumiya and J. Horikoshi, *Zero* (New York, 1956); C. M. Petillo, *Douglas MacArthur: The Philippine Years* (Bloomington, Indiana, 1981); F. C. Pogue, *George C. Marshall: Ordeal and Hope, 1939–1942* (London, 1968), *George C. Marshall: Organizer of Victory, 1943–1945* (New York, 1973); J. D. Potter, *Admiral of the Pacific: The Life of Yamamoto* (London, 1965), *Nimitz* (Annapolis, 1976); C. G. Reynolds, *The Fast Carriers: The Forging of an Air Navy* (New York, 1968); H. M. Smith and P. Finch, *Coral and Brass* (New York, 1949); R. R. Smith, *The Approach to the Philippines* (Washington, DC, 1953), *Triumph on the Philippines* (Washington, DC, 1963); S. Smith, *The Battle of Sawa* (New York, 1962); J. J. Stephen, *Hawaii under the Rising Sun: Japan's Plan for Conquest after Pearl Harbor* (Honolulu, 1984); R. W. Tregaskis, *Guadalcanal Diary* (New York, 1962); A. J. Watts and B. G. Gordon, *The Imperial Japanese Navy* (London, 1971); A. C. Wedemeyer, *Wedemeyer Reports!* (New York, 1958); L. Wigmore, *The Japanese Thrust: Australia in the War of 1939–1945* (Canberra, 1957); F. L. W. Wood, *The New Zealand People at War: Political and External Affairs* (Wellington, 1958); W. T. Y'Blood, *Red Sun Setting: The Battle of the Philippine Sea* (Annapolis, 1980); M. Yoshida, *Requiem for Battleship Yamato* (Seattle, 1985).

The War in South-East Asia

L. Allen, *Burma: The Longest War, 1941–45* (London, 1984); M. A. Aziz, *Japan's Colonialism and Indonesia* (The Hague, 1955); Ba Maw, *Breakthrough in Burma* (New Haven, 1968); A. J. Barker, *The March on Delhi* (London, 1963); H. Benda, *The Crescent and the Rising Sun: Indonesian Islam under Japanese Occupation* (New Haven, 1958); M. Collis, *First and Last in Burma, 1941–48* (London, 1956); E. R. Drachman, *United States Policy toward Vietnam, 1940–1945* (Rutherford, New York, 1970); R. L. Eichelberger, *Our Jungle Road to Tokyo* (New York, 1950); F. Eldridge, *Wrath in Burma* (New York, 1946); W. H. Elsbree, *Japan's Role in Southeast Asian Nationalist Movements, 1940–1945* (Cambridge, Mass., 1953); T. Friend, *Between Two Empires: The Ordeal of the Philippines* (New Haven, 1965); A. Gilchrist, *Bangkok, Top Secret* (London, 1970); L. E. Gleek, *General History of the Philippines: V, vol. 1: The American Half-Century, 1898–1946* (Manila, 1984); A. W. H. Harterdorp, *Japanese Occupation of the Philippines* (Manila, 1967); D. Jajanama, *Thailand im Zweiten Weltkrieg* (Hamburg, 1970); J. Keats, *They Fought Alone* (London, 1964); J. Legrand, *L'Indochine à l'heure japonaise* (Cannes, 1963); Marchand and Rollet, *L'Indochine en guerre* (Paris, 1954); J. Masters, *The Road Past Mandalay* (New York, 1961); H. J. van Mook, *The Netherlands Indies and Japan: Battle on Paper, 1940–41* (New York, 1944), *The Stakes of Democracy in South-East Asia* (London, 1950); Mordant, *Au service de la France en Indochine* (Saigon, 1950); Sir L. Mountbatten, *Report to the Combined Chiefs of Staff* (London, 1951); A. W. McCoy (ed.), *Southeast Asia under Japanese Occupation* (New Heaven, 1980); M. Murray, *Escape a Thousand Miles to Freedom* (Sydney, 1965); T. Nu, *Burma Under the Japanese* (London, 1954); T. O'Brien, *The Moonlight War: The Story of Clandestine Operations in South-East Asia, 1944–5* (London, 1987); C. Ogburn, *The Marauders* (London, 1960); W. Peers and D. Brelis, *Behind the Burma Road: The Story of America's Most Successful Guerrilla Force* (Boston, 1963); J. D. Potter, *A Soldier Must Hang: The Biography of an Oriental General* (London, 1963); B. Prasad (ed.), *Official History of the Indian Armed Forces in World War II: Defence of India: Policy and Plans* (n.p., 1963), *Indian War Economy: Supply, Industry and Finance* (n.p., 1962); G. Sabattier, *Le destin de l'Indochine* (Paris, 1952); W. Slim, *Defeat into Victory* (London, 1956); S. Woodburn Kirby, *The Reconquest of Burma*, 2 vols. (London, 1958, 1961).

The War in China

A. Chennault, *Chennault and the Flying Tigers* (New York, 1963); C. L. Chennault, *Way of a Fighter* (New York, 1949); J. W. Esherwick (ed.), *Lost Chance in China: The World War II Despatches of John S. Service* (New York, 1974); H. Feis, *The China Tangle: The American Effort in China from Pearl Harbor to the Marshall Mission* (Princeton, 1953); L. L. Liu, *A Military History of Modern*

China (Princeton, 1956); M. E. Miles, *A Different Kind of War: The Little Known Story of the Combined Guerilla Forces Created in China by the US Navy and the Chinese during World War II* (Garden City, New York, 1967); C. F. Romanus and R. Sunderland, *Stilwell's Mission to China, Stilwell's Command Problems* and *Time Runs Out in CBI* (Washington, DC, 1953, 1956, 1959); L. K. Rosinger, *China's Wartime Politics, 1937–1944* (Princeton, 1944); L. van Slyke (ed.), *The Chinese Communist Movement: A Report of the United States War Department, July 1945* (Stanford, 1968); J. W. Stilwell, *The Stilwell Papers* (London, 1949); G. Stuart and A. Levy, *Kind-Hearted Tiger* (London, 1965).

The War in Japan

E. J. Drea, *The 1942 Japanese General Election: Political Mobilization in Wartime Japan* (Lawrence, Kansas, 1979); G. K. Goodman (ed.), L. de Asis, *From Bataan to Tokyo: Diary of a Filipino Student in Wartime Japan, 1943–1944* (Lawrence, Kansas, 1979); B.-A. Shillony, *Politics and Culture in Wartime Japan* (Oxford, 1981); G. Terasaki, *Bridge to the Sun* (London, 1958).

Russo-Japanese Relations During the Second World War

J. W. M. Chapman, *The Sorge Cover-Up* (Brighton, 1980); F. W. Deakin and G. R. Storry, *The Case of Richard Sorge* (London, 1966); C. Johnson, *An Instance of Treason: The Story of the Tokyo Spy Ring* (Stanford, 1964); G. A. Lenson, *The Strange Neutrality: Soviet-Japanese Relations during the Second World War, 1941–1945* (Tallahassee, 1972); C. A. Willoughby, *Sorge: Soviet Master Spy* (London, 1952).

The Surrender of Japan

L. Allen, *The End of the War in Asia* (London, 1976); L. Brooks, *Behind Japan's Surrender: The Secret Struggle that Ended an Empire* (New York 1967); J. F. C. Butow, *Japan's Decision to Surrender* (Stanford, 1954); W. Craig, *The Fall of Japan* (New York, 1967); H. Feis, *Japan Subdued: The Atomic Bomb and the End of the War in the Pacific* (Princeton, 1961); T. Kase, *Journey to the Missouri* (New Haven, 1950).

The Aftermath of the War

E. A. Ackerman *et al.*, *Japan's Prospect* (Cambridge, Mass., 1946); J. E. Auer, *The Postwar Rearmament of Japanese Maritime Forces* (New York, 1973); H. Baerwald, *The Purge of Japanese Leaders under the Occupation* (Berkeley, 1959); T. A. Bisson, *Zaibatsu Dissolution in Japan* (Berkeley, 1954); R. Buckley, *Occupation Diplomacy: Britain, the United States and Japan, 1945–1952* (Cambridge, 1982); T. W. Burkman (ed.), *The Occupation of Japan: Education and Social Reform* (Norfolk, 1982), *The Occupation of Japan: The International Context* (Norfolk, 1982); J. F. Cady, P. G. Barnett and S. Jenkins, *The Development of Self-Rule in Burma, Malaya and the Philippines*, 3 vols. (New York, 1948); W. J. Coughlin, *Conquered Press: The MacArthur Era in Japanese Journalism* (1952); W. H. M. Creemers, *Shrine Shinto after World War II* (Leiden, 1968); R. Dingman, *Documents on New Zealand External Relations:* vol. II, *The Surrender and Occupation of Japan* (Wellington, 1982); F. S. V. Donnison, *British Military Administration in the Far East, 1943–46* (London, 1956); R. Drifte, *The Security Factor in Japan's Foreign Policy, 1945–52* (London, 1983); R. Fifield, *The Diplomacy of South-East Asia, 1945–1958* (New York, 1958); J. W. Gaddis, *Public Information in Japan under American Occupation* (Geneva, 1950); G. Goodman (ed.), *The American Occupation of Japan: A Retrospective View* (Lawrence, Kansas, 1968); E. M. Hadley, *Anti-Trust in Japan* (Princeton, 1970); R. K. Hall, *Shushin: The Ethics of a Defeated Nation* (New York, 1949); N. Ito, *New Japan: Six Years of Democratisation* (Tokyo, 1952); K. Kawai, *Japan's American Interlude* (Chicago, 1960); D. MacIsaac, *Strategic Bombing in World War II* (New York, 1976), *The United States Strategic Bombing Survey*, 10 vols. (New York, 1976); E. Martin, *The Allied Occupation of Japan* (Stanford, 1948); J. D. Montgomery, *Forced to be Free: The Artificial Revolution in Germany and Japan* (Chicago, 1957); Y. Nagai and A. Iriye (eds.), *The Origins of the Cold War in Asia* (Tokyo, 1977); I. Nish (ed.), *The British Commonwealth and the Occupation of Japan* (London, 1983), and C. Dunn (eds.), *European Studies on Japan* (Tenterden, Kent, 1979); T. Nishi, *Unconditional Democracy: Education and Politics in Occupied Japan, 1945–1952* (Stanford, 1982); E. W. Pauley, *Report on Japanese Reparations to the President of the US, November 1945 to April 1946* (Washington, DC, 1948); J. C. Perry, *Beneath the Eagle's Wings: Americans in Occupied Japan* (New York, 1980); L. H. Redford, *The Occupation and its Legacy to the Post-war World* (Norfolk, 1976); M. Schaller, *The American Occupation of Japan: The Origins of the Cold War in Asia* (London, 1985); W. Sebald with R. Brines, *With MacArthur in Japan: A Personal History of the Occupation* (New York, 1965); K. Tsurumi, *Social Change and the Individual: Japan Before and After Defeat in World War II* (Princeton, 1970); J. Williams, *Japan's Political Revolution under MacArthur: A Participant's Account* (Georgia, 1979); R. Wolfe (ed.), *Americans as Proconsuls: United States Military Government in Germany and Japan* (Carbondale, Illinois, 1984); W. P. Woodard, *The Allied Occupation of Japan, 1945–52 and Japanese Religions* (Leiden, 1972); S. Yoshida, *The Yoshida Memoirs: The Story of Japan in Crisis* (London, 1961); M. M. Yoshitsu, *Japan and the San Francisco Peace Settlement* (New York, 1982).

LIMITS OF GERMAN, JAPANESE AND ITALIAN
DOMINANCE 1934 - 1944

GREENLAND

ICELAND

Murmansk

SWEDEN

Leningrad

Moscow

USSR

UNITED
KINGDOM

Stalingrad

Montreal

New York
Washington

Casablanca

Atlantic

IRAN
Basra

Cairo

WEST
INDIES

FRENCH
W. AFRICA

NIG.

FR. EQ. AFRIC.

SUDAN

VEN.
COL.

GUIANAS

Accra

ECUADOR

PERU

BRAZIL

Natal

BEL.
CONG.

KENYA
TANGANYIKA

BOL.

Ocean

ANGOLA

Rio de Janeiro

S.W.
AFRICA

Madagascar

CHILE

ARGENTINA

Buenos
Aires

Cape
Town

SOUTH
AFRICA

~ARTHUR BANKS~

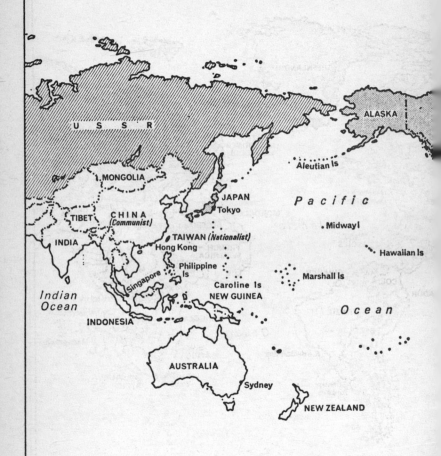

WORLD POWER 1949

U S S R

ALASKA

Aleutian Is

MONGOLIA

JAPAN
Tokyo

Pacific

TIBET

CHINA
(Communist)

TAIWAN *(Nationalist)*

Midway I

INDIA

Hong Kong

Hawaiian Is

Philippine
Is

Singapore

Caroline Is

Marshall Is

*Indian
Ocean*

NEW GUINEA

Ocean

INDONESIA

AUSTRALIA

Sydney

NEW ZEALAND

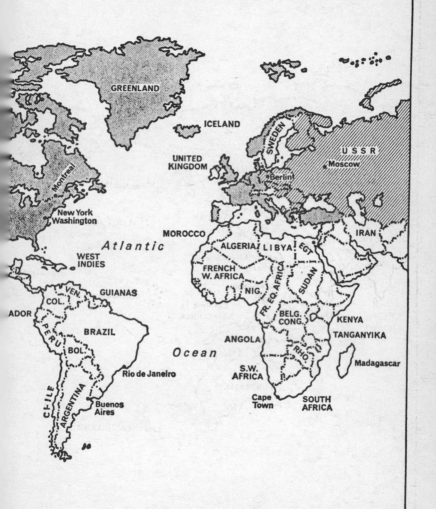

GREENLAND

ICELAND

SWEDEN

U S S R
Moscow

UNITED
KINGDOM

Berlin

IRAN

Montreal

New York
Washington

MOROCCO

Atlantic

ALGERIA LIBYA

EGY.

WEST
INDIES

FRENCH
W. AFRICA

FR. EQ. AFRICA

SUDAN

VEN.

GUIANAS

COL.

NIG.

ADOR

BELG.
CONG.

KENYA

PERU

BRAZIL

Ocean

ANGOLA

TANGANYIKA

BOL.

RHO.

Madagascar

Rio de Janeiro

CHILE

S.W.
AFRICA

ARGENTINA

Cape
Town

SOUTH
AFRICA

Buenos
Aires

USA and allies (NATO and Japan).

USSR and dependencies.

~ARTHUR BANKS~

INDEX

FOR THE BEST IN PAPERBACKS, LOOK FOR THE

In every corner of the world, on every subject under the sun, Penguin represents quality and variety – the very best in publishing today.

For complete information about books available from Penguin – including Pelicans, Puffins, Peregrines and Penguin Classics – and how to order them, write to us at the appropriate address below. Please note that for copyright reasons the selection of books varies from country to country.

A CHOICE OF PENGUINS

Trail of Havoc Patrick Marnham

In this brilliant piece of detective work, Patrick Marnham has traced the steps of Lord Lucan from the fateful night of 7th November 1974 when he murdered his children's nanny and attempted to kill his ex-wife. As well as being a fascinating investigation, the book is also a brilliant portrayal of a privileged section of society living under great stress.

Light Years Gary Kinder

Eduard Meier, an uneducated Swiss farmer, claims since 1975 to have had over 100 UFO sightings and encounters with 'beamships' from the Pleiades. His evidence is such that even the most die-hard sceptics have been unable to explain away the phenomenon.

And the Band Played On Randy Shilts
Politics, people and the AIDS epidemic

Written after years of extensive research by the only American journalist to cover the epidemic full-time, the book is a masterpiece of reportage and a tragic record of mismanaged institutions and scientific vendettas, of sexual politics and personal suffering.

The Return of a Native Reporter Robert Chesshyre

Robert Chesshyre returned to Britain from the United States in 1985 where he had spent four years as the *Observer*'s correspondent. This is his devastating account of the country he came home to: intolerant, brutal, grasping and politically and economically divided. It is a nation, he asserts, struggling to find a role.

Women and Love Shere Hite

In this culmination of *The Hite Report* trilogy, 4,500 women provide an eloquent testimony of the disturbingly unsatisfying nature of their emotional relationships and point to what they see as the causes. *Women and Love* reveals a new cultural perspective in formation: as women change the emotional structure of their lives, they are defining a fundamental debate over the future of our society.

A CHOICE OF PENGUINS

Adieux: A Farewell to Sartre   Simone de Beauvoir

A devastatingly frank account of the last years of Sartre's life, and his death, by the woman who for more than half a century shared that life. 'A true labour of love, there is about it a touching sadness, a mingling of the personal with the impersonal and timeless which Sartre himself would surely have liked and understood' – *Listener*

Business Wargames   James Barrie

How did BMW overtake Mercedes? Why did Laker crash? How did MacDonalds grab the hamburger market? Drawing on the tragic mistakes and brilliant victories of military history, this remarkable book draws countless fascinating parallels with case histories from industry worldwide.

Metamagical Themas   Douglas R. Hofstadter

This astonishing sequel to the bestselling, Pulitzer Prize-winning *Gödel, Escher, Bach* swarms with 'extraordinary ideas, brilliant fables, deep philosophical questions and Carrollian word play' – Martin Gardner

Into the Heart of Borneo   Redmond O'Hanlon

'Perceptive, hilarious and at the same time a serious natural-history journey into one of the last remaining unspoilt paradises' – *New Statesman* 'Consistently exciting, often funny and erudite without ever being overwhelming' – *Punch*

The Assassination of Federico García Lorca   Ian Gibson

Lorca's 'crime' was his antipathy to pomposity, conformity and intolerance. His punishment was murder. Ian Gibson reveals the truth about Lorca's death and the atmosphere in Spain that allowed it to happen.

The Secrets of a Woman's Heart   Hilary Spurling

The later life of Ivy Compton-Burnett 1920–69. 'A biographical triumph . . . elegant, stylish, witty tender, immensely acute – dazzles and exhilarates . . . a great achievement' – Kay Dick in the *Literary Review*. 'One of the most important literary biographies of the century' – *New Statesman*

A CHOICE OF PENGUINS

Fantastic Invasion   Patrick Marnham

Explored and exploited, Africa has carried a different meaning for each wave of foreign invaders – from ivory traders to aid workers. Now, in the crisis that has followed Independence, which way should Africa turn? 'A courageous and brilliant effort' – Paul Theroux

Jean Rhys: Letters 1931–66
Edited by Francis Wyndham and Diana Melly

'Eloquent and invaluable . . . her life emerges, and with it a portrait of an unexpectedly indomitable figure' – Marina Warner in the *Sunday Times*

Among the Russians   Colin Thubron

One man's solitary journey by car across Russia provides an enthralling and revealing account of the habits and idiosyncrasies of a fascinating people. 'He sees things with the freshness of an innocent and the erudition of a scholar' – *Daily Telegraph*

The Amateur Naturalist   Gerald Durrell with Lee Durrell

'Delight . . . on every page . . . packed with authoritative writing, learning without pomposity . . . it represents a real bargain' – *The Times Educational Supplement*. 'What treats are in store for the average British household' – *Books and Bookmen*

The Democratic Economy   Geoff Hodgson

Today, the political arena is divided as seldom before. In this exciting and original study, Geoff Hodgson carefully examines the claims of the rival doctrines and exposes some crucial flaws.

They Went to Portugal   Rose Macaulay

An exotic and entertaining account of travellers to Portugal from the pirate-crusaders, through poets, aesthetes and ambassadors, to the new wave of romantic travellers. A wonderful mixture of literature, history and adventure, by one of our most stylish and seductive writers.

FOR THE BEST IN PAPERBACKS, LOOK FOR THE

A CHOICE OF PENGUINS

The Diary of Virginia Woolf
Five volumes edited by Quentin Bell and Anne Olivier Bell

'As an account of intellectual and cultural life of our century, Virginia Woolf's diaries are invaluable; as the record of one bruised and unquiet mind, they are unique' – Peter Ackroyd in the *Sunday Times*

Voices of the Old Sea Norman Lewis

'I will wager that *Voices of the Old Sea* will be a classic in the literature about Spain' – *Mail on Sunday* 'Limpidly and lovingly Norman Lewis has caught the helpless, unwitting, often foolish, but always hopeful village in its dying summers, and saved the tragedy with sublime comedy' – *Observer*

The First World War A J P Taylor

In this superb illustrated history, A J P Taylor 'manages to say almost everything that is important for an understanding and, indeed, intellectual digestion of that vast event . . . A special text . . . a remarkable collection of photographs' – *Observer*

Ninety-Two Days Evelyn Waugh

With characteristic honesty Evelyn Waugh here debunks the romantic notions attached to rough travelling; his journey in Guiana and Brazil is difficult, dangerous and extremely uncomfortable, and his account of it is witty and unquestionably compelling.

When the Mind Hears Harlan Lane
A History of the Deaf

'Reads like a suspense novel . . . what emerges is evidence of a great wrong done to a minority group, the deaf' – *The New York Times Book Review* 'Impassioned, polemical, at times even virulent . . . (he shows) immense scholarship, powers of historical reconstruction, and deep empathy for the world of the deaf' – Oliver Sacks in *The New York Review of Books*

A CHOICE OF PENGUINS

The Uses of Enchantment Bruno Bettelheim

Dr Bettelheim has written this book to help adults become aware of the irreplaceable importance of fairy tales. Taking the best-known stories in turn, he demonstrates how they work, consciously or unconsciously, to support and free the child.

The City in History Lewis Mumford

Often prophetic in tone and containing a wealth of photographs, *The City in History* is among the most deeply learned and warmly human studies of man as a social creature.

Orientalism Edward W. Said

In *Orientalism*, his acclaimed and now famous challenge to established Western attitudes towards the East, Edward Said has given us one of the most brilliant cultural studies of the decade. 'A stimulating, elegant yet pugnacious essay which is going to set the cat among the pigeons' – *Observer*

The Selected Melanie Klein

This major collection of Melanie Klein's writings, brilliantly edited by Juliet Mitchell, shows how much Melanie Klein has to offer in understanding and treating psychotics, in revising Freud's ideas about female sexuality, and in showing how phantasy operates in everyday life.

The Raw and the Cooked Claude Lévi-Strauss

Deliberately, brilliantly and inimitably challenging, *The Raw and the Cooked* is a seminal work of structural anthropology that cuts wide and deep into the mind of mankind. Examining the myths of the South American Indians it demonstrates, with dazzling insight, how these can be reduced to a comprehensible psychological pattern.

FOR THE BEST IN PAPERBACKS, LOOK FOR THE

A CHOICE OF PENGUINS

The Second World War (6 volumes)   Winston S. Churchill

The definitive history of the cataclysm which swept the world for the second time in thirty years.

1917: The Russian Revolutions and the Origins of Present-Day Communism
Leonard Schapiro

A superb narrative history of one of the greatest episodes in modern history by one of our greatest historians.

Imperial Spain 1496–1716   J. H. Elliot

A brilliant modern study of the sudden rise of a barren and isolated country to be the greatest power on earth, and of its equally sudden decline. 'Outstandingly good' – *Daily Telegraph*

Joan of Arc: The Image of Female Heroism   Marina Warner

'A profound book, about human history in general and the place of women in it' – Christopher Hill

Man and the Natural World: Changing Attitudes in England 1500–1800
Keith Thomas

'A delight to read and a pleasure to own' – Auberon Waugh in the *Sunday Telegraph*

The Making of the English Working Class   E. P. Thompson

Probably the most imaginative – and the most famous – post-war work of English social history.

FOR THE BEST IN PAPERBACKS, LOOK FOR THE

A CHOICE OF PENGUINS

The French Revolution Christopher Hibbert

'One of the best accounts of the Revolution that I know . . . Mr Hibbert is outstanding' – J. H. Plumb in the *Sunday Telegraph*

The Germans Gordon A. Craig

An intimate study of a complex and fascinating nation by 'one of the ablest and most distinguished American historians of modern Germany' – Hugh Trevor-Roper

Ireland: A Positive Proposal Kevin Boyle and Tom Hadden

A timely and realistic book on Northern Ireland which explains the historical context – and offers a practical and coherent set of proposals which could actually work.

A History of Venice John Julius Norwich

'Lord Norwich has loved and understood Venice as well as any other Englishman has ever done' – Peter Levi in the *Sunday Times*

Montaillou: Cathars and Catholics in a French Village 1294–1324
Emmanuel Le Roy Ladurie

'A classic adventure in eavesdropping across time' – Michael Ratcliffe in *The Times*

The Defeat of the Spanish Armada Garrett Mattingly

Published to coincide with the 400th anniversary of the Armada. 'A faultless book; and one which most historians would have given half their working lives to have written' – J. H. Plumb

FOR THE BEST IN PAPERBACKS, LOOK FOR THE

A CHOICE OF PENGUINS

The Apartheid Handbook Roger Omond

This book provides the essential hard information about how apartheid actually works from day to day and fills in the details behind the headlines.

The World Turned Upside Down Christopher Hill

This classic study of radical ideas during the English Revolution 'will stand as a notable monument to . . . one of the finest historians of the present age' – *The Times Literary Supplement*

Islam in the World Malise Ruthven

'His exposition of "the Qurenic world view" is the most convincing, and the most appealing, that I have read' – Edward Mortimer in *The Times*

The Knight, the Lady and the Priest Georges Duby

'A very fine book' (Philippe Aries) that traces back to its medieval origin one of our most important institutions, marriage.

A Social History of England New Edition Asa Briggs

'A treasure house of scholarly knowledge . . . beautifully written and full of the author's love of his country, its people and its landscape' – John Keegan in the *Sunday Times*, Books of the Year

The Second World War A J P Taylor

A brilliant and detailed illustrated history, enlivened by all Professor Taylor's customary iconoclasm and wit.

A CHOICE OF PENGUINS

Adieux Simone de Beauvoir

This 'farewell to Sartre' by his life-long companion is a 'true labour of love' (the *Listener*) and 'an extraordinary achievement' (*New Statesman*).

British Society 1914–45 John Stevenson

A major contribution to the Pelican Social History of Britain, which 'will undoubtedly be the standard work for students of modern Britain for many years to come' – *The Times Educational Supplement*

The Pelican History of Greek Literature Peter Levi

A remarkable survey covering all the major writers from Homer to Plutarch, with brilliant translations by the author, one of the leading poets of today.

Art and Literature Sigmund Freud

Volume 14 of the Pelican Freud Library contains Freud's major essays on Leonardo, Michelangelo and Dostoyevsky, plus shorter pieces on Shakespeare, the nature of creativity and much more.

A History of the Crusades Sir Steven Runciman

This three-volume history of the events which transferred world power to Western Europe – and founded Modern History – has been universally acclaimed as a masterpiece.

A Night to Remember Walter Lord

The classic account of the sinking of the *Titanic*. 'A stunning book, incomparably the best on its subject and one of the most exciting books of this or any year' – *The New York Times*

A CHOICE OF PENGUINS

The Literature of the United States   Marcus Cunliffe

The fourth edition of a masterly one-volume survey, described by D. W. Brogan in the *Guardian* as 'a very good book indeed'.

The Sceptical Feminist   Janet Radcliffe Richards

A rigorously argued but sympathetic consideration of feminist claims. 'A triumph' – *Sunday Times*

The Enlightenment   Norman Hampson

A classic survey of the age of Diderot and Voltaire, Goethe and Hume, which forms part of the Pelican History of European Thought.

Defoe to the Victorians   David Skilton

'Learned and stimulating' (*The Times Educational Supplement*). A fascinating survey of two centuries of the English novel.

Reformation to Industrial Revolution   Christopher Hill

This 'formidable little book' (Peter Laslett in the *Guardian*) by one of our leading historians is Volume 2 of the Pelican Economic History of Britain.

The New Pelican Guide to English Literature   Boris Ford (ed.)
Volume 8: The Present

This book brings a major series up to date with important essays on Ted Hughes and Nadine Gordimer, Philip Larkin and V. S. Naipaul, and all the other leading writers of today.